HEAVENLY BODIES

HEAVENLY BODIES

Incarnation, the Gaze, and Embodiment
in Christian Theology

Ola Sigurdson

Translated by Carl Olsen

WILLIAM B. EERDMANS PUBLISHING COMPANY
GRAND RAPIDS, MICHIGAN

Wm. B. Eerdmans Publishing Co.

2140 Oak Industrial Drive N.E., Grand Rapids, Michigan 49505

22 21 20 19 18 17 16   1 2 3 4 5 6 7

Library of Congress Cataloging-in-Publication Data

Names: Sigurdson, Ola, 1966- author. | Olsen, Carl, translator.

Title: Heavenly bodies : incarnation, the gaze, and embodiment in Christian theology /
   Ola Sigurdson ; translated by Carl Olsen.

Other titles: Himmelska kroppar. English

Description: Grand Rapids, Michigan : Wm. B. Eerdmans Publishing Co., [2016] |
   Includes bibliographical references.

Identifiers: LCCN 2016011344 | ISBN 9780802871664 (cloth : alk. paper)

Subjects: LCSH: Human body—Religious aspects—Christianity. | Incarnation.

Classification: LCC BT741.3 .S5413 2016 | DDC 233/.5—dc23

   LC record available at https://lccn.loc.gov/2016011344

www.eerdmans.com

Contents

Acknowledgments

A number of years ago a friend and former teacher leaned towards my ear and whispered: "Write a book on the body." Since I listen to my friends, I have now, as I type the last period of the book, done as he suggested. The unavoidable material conditions for a project of this size have, however, been provided from a different direction. In Fall 1999 Professor—now also Vice Chancellor—Göran Bexell nominated me as a candidate for the faculty of the humanities and theology at Lund University for a four-year national research fellowship in memory of Torgny Segerstedt. Accustomed to the harsh conditions for scholars in the humanities and theology in Sweden, I didn't think much more about this until Dan Brändström, CEO of the Swedish Foundation for Humanities and Social Sciences (Riksbankens Jubileumsfond), called me in early December and congratulated me on the position, which would begin the first of January 2000.

The conditions for research that the Swedish Foundation for Humanities and Social Sciences (Riksbankens Jubileumsfond), along with the Swedish Collegium for Advanced Study in the Social Sciences (SCASSS) and the Swedish Foundation for Cooperation in Research and Higher Education (STINT), have created through these Pro Futura positions—as they are also called—must be among the very best imaginable. I think not only of the warm welcome and the intellectual vitality that I met as a fellow with SCASSS in the semester of Spring 2000, or the international components of this program, but at least as much of the faith shown in the scholars themselves, with the opportunity to design one's research project within the framework of the position itself. The semester at SCASSS continues to affect my thinking, and along with all colleagues and personnel I want to thank directors Björn Wittrock, Barbro Klein, and Göran Therborn. Björn in particular has been an inexhaustible source of renewed inspiration. His intellectual breadth combined with his humble attitude sets an international standard for the scholar as a person, and I am happy that this project has been designed in conversation with him.

Within the framework of my research position there was, as said, also space for international cooperation. I spent the academic year 2001–2002 at Cambridge University, England, as a Visiting Fellow at the Centre for Advanced Religious and Theological Studies (CARTS), Faculty of Divinity, and as a Visiting Scholar at Wolfson College. This stay was made possible by a stipend from STINT. The academic year in Cambridge offered good opportunities for discussing my project with people of very different disciplinary perspectives. I want to especially mention Janet Martin Soskice, Oliver Soskice, Graham Ward, and Andrew Wernick, who over many and long conversations have given me numerous ideas, some of which have ended up in the resulting book. Big thanks as well to Gavin D'Costa, David Ford, Susan Frank Parsons, Catherine Pickstock, Ben Quash, and Denys Turner. I want to also mention Chad C. Pecknold, who, with great generosity, saw to it that I could stay at Clare Hall College in the Spring, and who introduced me to numerous people.

An additional source of inspiration has been the seminar that Mats Rosengren and I have run at Göteborg University since Fall 2000. Inspired by the seminars we had participated in during our shared stay at SCASSS in Spring 2000, we wanted to create a forum for an advanced theoretical discussion within philosophy and theology, as well as connect to other scholarly communities by inviting prominent international scholars. The seminar Logos/Pathos, which has now been going for six years, has also become an opportunity for me to both directly and indirectly test my thoughts on this project on embodiment. Big thanks to Maria Johansen, Ola Nilsson, Nils Olsson, Cecilia Rosengren, Mathias Söderlund, Orla Vigsø, and many others.

I have also had the opportunity to present portions of my material at various seminars and conferences. The Higher Seminar in Religious Studies at Uppsala University welcomed me as early as my Uppsala stay in Spring 2000. In Fall 2000 I presented an additional angle at the Higher Seminar in Systematic Theology at Lund University. Other portions were given at the Higher Seminar in Comparative Literature in Fall 2004 and the TAP seminar in Spring 2006, both at the University of Gothenburg. In Spring 2004 I presented a paper at Senior Seminars in Systematics at the Faculty of Divinity, Cambridge University, and the same year another paper as well at the conference "The Body and Embodiment: Intersection of Literature,

Imagery, and Science," at the University of Gothenburg. Thanks to Anna-Karin Hammar, Ninna Edgardh Beckman, Oloph Bexell, Sven-Erik Brodd, Håkan Gunnarsson, Gösta Hallonsten, Mark D. Jordan, Mats Malm, Jesper Svartvik, and Lennart Thörn. My colleague at the Department for Religious Studies and Theology, Bo Claesson, has been invaluable with his breadth of knowledge and his willingness to help out. Big thanks as well to additional colleagues at the institution.

Some of what makes up this book has been previously published in more or less different form: "Kristus och människan: Om inkarnationen och kärleksbegreppet," *Svensk Teologisk Kvartalskrift* 76, no. 2 (2000): 66–76; "Den erotiska blicken," *Teologi[er].* Aiolos 220–21 (2003): 127–42; "Herdemakten och biktens hemlighet," *Res Publica: Hemligheter* 59 (2003): 56–65; "Kärleken till det samma? Om teologi och sexualitet," *Svensk Teologisk Kvartalskrift* 80, no. 2 (2004): 84–91; "Kristna kroppar? Om kristologi, kroppslighet och kön," *Kvinnovetenskaplig tidskrift* 1 (2006): 29–44. Thanks to these journals for allowing their articles to be reused.

I have had three exceptional readers aiding me in making my thoughts clearer, who are also my friends and my principal philosophical and theological conversation partners: Jayne Svenungsson, Werner G. Jeanrond, and Mats Rosengren. Together these three have, aside from the fact that they have discussed my project with me over the course of this journey, read the manuscript in all but final form, and helped me understand that some work still remained. Having three such well-read friends with such good insights into the subject is a source of joy and continual frustration; there are always additional aspects to take into account that Jayne, Werner, and Mats remind me of. To Mats I want to direct a special thanks: a quick review shows that we must have spoken of what has now become a book several hundred times since our shared stay in Uppsala. Both his philosophical insight and his editorial eye have touched every single page of this book and made it better than what its author could have managed on his own.

Other sharp eyes have examined my manuscript: Erna Roos has gently but firmly tightened up its language and has additionally proofread it along with Sverker Lundahl. A contribution from Tore G. Wärenstam's foundation has made it possible to repay them to some degree for this thankless work, whose goal is of course to be invisible.

The publication of this book would not have been possible without the fact that I was able to enjoy the generosity of the Riksbankens Jubileumsfond for a second time in the form of a generous subvention. At the publishing house Glänta I want to thank Göran Dahlberg, Richard Lindmark, Malin

Lundh, Ulf Karl Olov Nilsson, and Anders Johansson for their work with my book, as well as Jens Andersson, Bok & Form, for his tasteful cover.

Finally I want to thank Monica, Linus, and Johannes. To express what they have meant for me during the work on this book—and before, and after—is of course impossible. If Monica is "the god of my idolatry," my sons are no less important in the role they play in my life.

Ola Sigurdson
Ascension Day, 2006

An additional phase in the work on this book was initiated in Fall 2010 when I was a Fellow at the Center for Theological Inquiry in Princeton, USA. CTI's director William Storrar introduced me to Jon Pott, editor-in-chief at Eerdmans, with the aim of arousing his interest in an entirely different book. The meeting resulted, however, in Jon's attention being directed toward *Heavenly Bodies,* the Swedish edition of which I had with me. Both Will and Jon have played critical roles in bringing about the English translation of my book, and I am very grateful for the unceasing support and encouragement of both. Riksbankens Jubileumsfond has once more supported this book by paying for its translation, and I want to yet again express my thanks, this time especially to its current CEO Göran Blomqvist. Last, but not least, I want to also give a big thank-you to my translator Carl Olsen. The fact that my book has been translated in sunny California during even the darkest seasons in Sweden has been a pleasant thought, and I have had great pleasure in the exchange with Carl, who has taken on this very considerable task with drive as well as style.

Ola Sigurdson
Septuagesima, 2015

1. Introduction

In his posthumously published work *The Anti-Christ,* Friedrich Nietzsche argues that Christianity is nihilistic.[1] Its nihilism consists in its denial of this world in favor of another and better world. With this, things such as desire, embodiment, even life itself come to be denied, become nothing in the eyes of the Christian church. We often hear echoes of Nietzsche's critique in our time as well, if in a less sophisticated form. The Christian church is, at times, hostile to the body. This hostility is often linked to alleged "Platonic" influences. Paul has, as it were, entered into an alliance with Plato in the struggle against the body. In this context "Christianity," "Platonism," and "Gnosticism" are more often than not lumped together without accounting for the rather different conceptions of the body that characterize these different traditions. They are then dismissed without any real argument.

If one looks a bit more closely at the matter, there is something odd in both Nietzsche's criticism and its more superficial and popularized variants. To begin with, one may wonder (especially in the latter case) what lies behind the criticism of the Christian church's contempt for the body when it is presented in an age that so clearly sees itself as body-affirming. Could this "the best defense is a good offense" strategy stem from a suspicion of the hollowness of our era's own affirmation of the body? Perhaps it is only

---

1. Friedrich Nietzsche, *The Anti-Christ,* in *The Anti-Christ, Ecce Homo, Twilight of the Idols,* Cambridge Texts in the History of Philosophy, trans. Judith Norman (Cambridge: Cambridge University Press, 2005). Cf. also Friedrich Nietzsche, *On the Genealogy of Morals,* Oxford World's Classics, trans. Douglas Smith (Oxford: Oxford University Press, 1998). I am thereby not, however, claiming that this is *all* that Nietzsche has to say about either Christianity or nihilism. For a summary of the most recent research on Nietzsche and Christianity, see Jayne Svenungsson, *Guds återkomst: En studie av gudsbegreppet inom postmodern filosofi,* Logos/Pathos 3 (Göteborg: Glänta, 2004), pp. 53–71.

against the background of a contempt for the body in ancient times that our own era's regimentation of manageable bodies can appear to be an improvement in the body's worth. Furthermore, one may ask how it happens that the Christian tradition, which, according to John 1:1, began when God took on flesh in Jesus Christ, could become so body-denying. One would expect that the church's doctrine of incarnation, i.e., God's becoming human in Jesus Christ, would have kept it from the worst anti-corporeal excesses. How could it go so wrong?

What is missing, especially in the more vulgar variants of the assertion of the hostility of the Christian church towards the body, is a critical somatology, i.e., a theological understanding of the body that does not take its own time-bound understanding of embodiment as an unproblematic horizon for the historical understanding of the body. What Nietzsche, among others, has taught us is that the body actually has a history, both the representation of the body in text and picture, and embodiment itself as such. An understanding of the history of corporeality or the historicity of the body, which makes possible a more differentiated view of the body, is thus needed in order to understand the body as a philosophical, theological, or history of ideas problem. Such a critical somatology would be able to relate skeptically to the understandings of the body in earlier periods, and simultaneously make possible, not least through its historical work, a critical distance from current understandings of the body. Historical embodiment and contemporary embodiment may each constitute their own horizon, and yet allow for a mutually critical posture between horizons.

Nietzsche's own critique of the Christian view of the body is not as naïve. He understands the historicity of the body. The critique of Christianity's nihilism, and implicitly its ethereality, is a part of his more extensive critique of metaphysics. However, we may object that even Nietzsche's critical somatology is not sufficiently critical, as it reduces the extremely varied history of theological somatology to a general proposition in a rather sweeping manner. Nietzsche's critique presumably applies more aptly to the view of the body in his own contemporary Protestant, puritanical Christianity. The challenge for this book is therefore to present a more nuanced reading of theological history—in line with Nietzsche's intention, if not with his (in this case) all-too-generalized proposition—that would offer resources for a new, non-nihilistic theological somatology for our time. In certain respects I can therefore also *agree* with Nietzsche's criticism of certain elements of nihilism in theological somatology, both historically and in the present.

The fact that I intend to carry out a critical and self-critical theology of the body does not mean that I am bound by either the historical or the contemporary horizon, but that I intend to present my own (hopefully) constructive contributions to somatology in relation to both historical and contemporary conceptions of the body. It is therefore important for my task in this book not only to critique historical attitudes towards the body within theology, but also to gain some distance from my own period and its views. If, in my investigations of the understanding of the body in Plato, Paul, Plotinus, or Augustine, I come to the conclusion that they were not as grossly hostile to the body as is sometimes claimed, my theological somatology does not accordingly need to assert that everything they wrote on the body was right and correct, nor would this fact constitute an absolute standard for my theological somatology. An important lesson that theology takes from a historical investigation like this is the necessity of maintaining a distance from a contemporary view of the body that might otherwise appear self-evident. It may be the case that theological somatology has Nietzsche to thank for the historical possibility of returning to a more fruitful and constructive somatology following modern Christianity's dismissal of the corporeality of the Christian faith. Perhaps theology after Nietzsche can once more allow itself to be inspired by the conceptions of the body in ancient theology.

In this study of incarnation, the gaze, and embodiment, I will examine the relationship between Christian theology and embodiment against this historical background via three questions:

1. Does the idea of incarnation, God's becoming human in Christ, involve a denial, or at least a reduction, of the human, in that the deity of Christ, doctrinally or functionally, is permitted to dominate in a way that does not let the humanity of the human being come into its own?
2. With what kind of gaze may humanity be said to behold the divine, and how does this gaze relate to the relationship between the visible and the invisible? If the gaze is a constitutive aspect of a person's being-in-the-world, through which she can express her relationality as such, how can a theology of the gaze, a theological "optics," be formulated such that it will manage to preserve humanity's relationship to the presence of God in a way that neither denies that it concerns *God's* presence nor denies *humanity's* relationship to this presence? The problem of incarnation returns here as the question of the finite managing to behold the eternal within finite conditions, without in turn reducing the eternal to something finite, i.e., to behold the eternal as eternal.

3. How has the Christian tradition imagined human embodiment in light of God's incarnation in Jesus Christ? Has God come as *logos* and taken human form in order to do away with human embodiment? Or can one imagine that the incarnation means an affirmation of embodiment as such, as the fundamental way through which we humans relate to other humans and to God? And what does one mean by embodiment in that case?

Another way to formulate my aim, as well as hold these three questions together, would be the following: to examine some of the anthropological implications of the doctrine of incarnation for the human mode of being-in-the-world from the perspective of Christian theology. Such an investigation does not intend only to feature different Christian conceptions of embodiment for a general audience—although this is in itself an important task—but also, more constructively, to contribute to changing the Christian conception of the body within contemporary theology.

No proper somatology has been included in the *loci communes* of classical dogma, and so this study represents an investigation of what could be designated a doctrine on the margins of theology. For reasons that I will clarify in this chapter, my study will not limit itself to interpreting explicitly theological texts. It is equally concerned with interpreting the understanding of the body that is expressed in various Christian practices. "Doctrine" and "life" are intimately intertwined in the Christian tradition, not least when it comes to the body. It can therefore be productive not only to interpret the doctrines as they would be made concrete in a life, which would hardly be startling, but also to interpret life as though it implied a doctrine.

My study will accordingly treat not only embodiment in the Christian tradition, but also incarnation and the gaze. These three concepts or notions are associated with each other, and a parallel study of them can therefore allow them to mutually elucidate each other—and at the same time allow the overarching question of the body to emerge even more clearly. In order to better circumscribe the theme for this study, I will here give a short explanation of these three concepts. Then I will give some methodological considerations, both philosophical and theological, regarding procedure and central ideas. Finally, I will briefly describe the plan of the study.

Incarnation, the Gaze, and Embodiment

Incarnation

The theological starting point for my study is the Christian doctrine of God's becoming human, God's incarnation in Jesus Christ.[2] The word incarnation itself comes from the late Latin *incarnatio,* from the verb *incarnere,* "to change to flesh," i.e., in a figurative sense, to become human. In a more general sense the word can designate the embodiment of an abstract idea, but in a theological context it is used for God's incarnation in Jesus Christ. Without anticipating our discussion about which Christology appears in the prologue of the Gospel of John, we can find a central biblical understanding of incarnation in 1:14: "And the Word became flesh and dwelt among us" *(kai ho logos sarx egeneto kai eskēnōsen en hēmin).*[3] This verse from the prologue emphasizes the fundamental meaning of the doctrine of the incarnation, namely that God actively and concretely takes human form through the Word—Jesus Christ—and thereby becomes actively present with us human beings.

The doctrine of incarnation is a part of Christology, i.e., "the doctrine of Christ," which is the area of Christian theology that systematically studies Jesus of Nazareth, who came to be called Christ. We might say that Christology is a reflection on the question that Jesus posed to the disciples by the villages around Caesarea Philippi (Mark 8:27–30): "Who do people say that I am?" According to the disciples, there was a range of opinions about who Jesus was: "John the Baptist; and others say, Elijah, others, one of the prophets." But according to the Gospel of Mark, Peter gave a very different answer to the follow-up question regarding who the disciples thought he was: "You are Christ." The discussion of who Jesus was thus got started very early.

Traditionally, Christological reflections are usually divided into two areas: reflections on the person and existence of Jesus (who is/was he and what is/was he?) and reflections on the deeds of Jesus (what does he do/has he done?). If the first area concerns the doctrine of incarnation in the sense given above, the other area is usually called soteriology—the doctrine of salvation. One sometimes differentiates between ontological and functional

2. For a traditional but good introduction to the problem of incarnation, see Gerald O'Collins, *Incarnation,* New Century Theology (London/New York: Continuum, 2002).

3. My ambition in this book is that even those who do not have any particular knowledge of Greek (or, in some cases, Hebrew) will be able to distinguish some significant technical terms.

christologies, in which case it is this division between the doctrine of incarnation and soteriology—between "who he is" and "what he does"—that is intended.[4]

If Christology covers both the doctrine of incarnation and soteriology, how do these relate to each other? One common opinion, both historically and in the present, has been that "what he does" is more important than "who he is," but that these questions are of course interdependent. Although there are good arguments on behalf of such a hierarchy, in this study I want to examine the doctrine of incarnation relatively marked off from soteriology. Such a change in perspective opens, in my opinion, the possibility of a new perspective on soteriology, or at least on its conditions. In relation to the modern theological distinction between function and ontology, the following study of the doctrine of incarnation in a sense involves the study of the ontological conditions of possibility for Christology, and thereby an indirect criticism of the reduction of Christology to soteriology. Such a reduction is anticipated in what Martin Luther's colleague Philipp Melanchthon already writes in 1521: "For through these topics Christ is properly known, if it is true that to know Christ is to know his benefits, and not, as [the scholastics] teach, to contemplate his natures and the modes of his incarnation."[5] Another way to formulate this is to say that I want to discuss the doctrine of incarnation for the same reason as the theologians of the early church, namely, in order to better preserve soteriology. Without a doctrine of incarnation it is entirely possible that soteriology would evaporate into a generally held, philosophical doctrine of atonement, which could justifiably be accused of idealism, since one thereby, consciously or unconsciously, avoids thematizing the material basis for theology, and so also for atonement. Alternatively, one can imagine that a lot of the modern theological discussion of atonement and soteriology unconsciously implicates a particular ontology (at least in a Christological sense); the task should in that case involve making oneself reflexively conscious of the implicit ontological conditions, in order to be able to relate to them critically, rather than naïvely assuming the ontology presupposed by a particular culture. One might say that the Greek-French philosopher Cornelius Castoriadis's assertion that "the idea of a science of facts which would not imply an ontology has never amounted to more than

4. Walter Kasper, *Jesus the Christ,* New Edition (London/New York: T. & T. Clark, 2011), pp. 3–13.

5. Philipp Melanchthon, *Commonplaces/Loci communes 1521,* translated with introduction and notes by Christian Preus (Saint Louis: Concordia Publishing House, 2014), p. 24.

an incoherent phantasy of certain scientists," also applies, *mutatis mutandis,* to attempts to design a soteriology without any ontological counterpart.[6] However, my focus on the doctrine of incarnation, and thereby on the ontological aspect of Christology, should not be taken as evidence that I represent a speculative interest in ontological questions independent of salvation, such as the modern emphasis on function within that Christology has reacted against. In this study I want to bring embodiment into focus as a theological problem, and so a treatment of the problem of incarnation becomes necessary. There is thus no pretension of a complete investigation of all classic *loci* on behalf of systematic theology; we are concerned with a partial study.

In general terms, one might say that the problem of incarnation in Christian theology concerns how one imagines God's difference in a way that makes it consistent with God's presence in our world. Can the absolute be present in the concrete without coming too near or being too far away? On the one hand, an emphasis on the presence of God risks identifying the Creator with creation, and so making God a prisoner of creation, as in Hegel's slogan: "Without the world, God is not God."[7] On the other hand, an emphasis on God's difference risks making God something sublime, something radically absent—and thereby keeping us in a demystified world, if still one with negative attributes. Nietzsche is in this case in agreement with Christianity regarding the value of this world. A divine alterity that never manages to be incarnated in a radical way in a certain sense gives up the body, the gaze, and all of earthly human life for the benefit of a sublime intervention. The emphasis on God's difference is hardly suitable as a warning against confusing the Creator with the creation if it is not combined with a positive understanding of the historical, the social, and the embodied as open to the transcendent, without, because of this, reducing the transcendent to something immanent. The doctrine of the incarnation in Christian theology thus treats the question of how transcendence and immanence may be related to each other in a way that respects both their integrity and their affinity.

Apart from such a rather general definition of incarnation, there is no agreement on how incarnation ought to be understood. The prologue

6. Cornelius Castoriadis, *The Imaginary Institution of Society,* trans. Kathleen Blamey (Cambridge: Polity Press, 1987), p. 335.

7. Georg Wilhelm Friedrich Hegel, *Vorlesungen über die Philosophie der Religion I.* Werke 16 (Frankfurt am Main: Suhrkamp, 1990), p. 192. We find such a tendency in, for example, Sallie McFague, *Models of God: Theology for an Ecological, Nuclear Age* (London: SCM Press, 1987).

to the Gospel of John is one of the late fruits of a many-faceted historical development of christologies that have been collected in the New Testament. But even by the conclusion of the development of the canon more than a hundred years after the death of Christ the church and its theologians had not managed to establish the implications of the notion of incarnation to any definitive degree. In a sense, the theological discussion of the notion of incarnation has never been completed, although there have been more or less intensive periods. The first five hundred years of the history of the Christian church must be characterized as an intensive period. In the post-biblical Christological debates there are some milestones in the creeds that were formulated by the Council of Nicea in AD 325 and Chalcedon in AD 451, but neither of these meant that the debates ceased. Although contemporary Christological discussions have often taken a critical distance from the formulations of the councils, they have in certain respects nevertheless reproduced this pattern by starting from, if only in order to distance themselves from, the Christological definitions of these creeds in order to formulate a modern Christology.

The typology established by the English theologian Sarah Coakley in her study of Ernst Troeltsch's Christology offers an overview of the Christian doctrine of incarnation's different possibilities.[8] Coakley lists six different types of incarnational christologies. The first type she calls incarnational *theology,* in opposition to incarnational *Christology*. With this more general category she wants to emphasize a theology that asserts the active presence of God in human history independent of, if not necessarily exclusive of, Jesus Christ. According to Coakley such a general category is typically not the common usage of the term incarnation, at least not in Christian theology. A second type of incarnational Christology maintains that God takes "a special initiative in Jesus for the sake of humankind."[9] In opposition to the first type, the link to Jesus Christ is explicit in this case, since it is precisely in Christ that God acts in a special way. The third type, which, according to Coakley, is even more common, focuses the question on the preexistence of Christ, i.e., the belief that Christ in some sense personally existed in a divine or quasi-divine form (as *logos,* i.e., "the Word") before his earthly and human mode of existence. Incarnation then means—as is actually closer to the literal meaning of the word—that Christ becomes human. All three types

---

8. Sarah Coakley, *Christ without Absolutes: A Study of the Christology of Ernst Troeltsch* (Oxford: Clarendon Press, 1988), pp. 104–6.

9. Coakley, *Christ without Absolutes,* p. 104. Original in italics.

deal with the presence of God in the human world, but where the first type speaks about a more general presence of God, it becomes more intimately linked to Christ in the second and third types.

A fourth type of incarnational Christology asserts a "total interaction of the divine and the human in Christ."[10] Here the presence of God in Jesus Christ becomes a quantitatively superior divine revelation, since God gives God's own self in Jesus Christ. Christ is "entirely divine" just as he is "entirely human." A fifth type adds that the divine revelation in Christ is qualitatively superior. Christ is unique, since God's revelation in him can never be surpassed, but is exclusive and final. Finally, Coakley suggests a sixth type where incarnational Christology is used synonymously with Chalcedonian Christology, and where belief in the incarnation is identified with the use of the technical terminology of the above-mentioned Chalcedonian Creed (above all, the concepts *physis, hypostasis,* and *ousia*).

According to Coakley these six types are not mutually exclusive. It is moreover easy, despite Coakley's explicit intention, to understand the typology as an increasing intensification of the degree of incarnation. The risk in such a (mis)understanding is that the discussion of incarnation would revolve around the establishment of any given theologian's degree of orthodoxy. Such a discussion is not especially fruitful. Apart from the fact that it is not self-evident that a reiteration of, for example, the Chalcedonian Creed in our period automatically vouches for a continuity with that which the church fathers wanted to profess at the Council in 451, such a repetition hides the point in asking after a specific doctrine of incarnation. Here as elsewhere in theology there is no continuity other than that which proceeds via change. If both critics and proponents are able to see the Chalcedonian confession not as a conclusive definition, but rather as one context-specific attempt to articulate the significance of Christ's becoming human, it becomes interesting to look at how Chalcedon was used in its own time, respective to its use in later ages. What was the problem when Chalcedon was formulated, what was assumed without being questioned, and what was not interesting at all? How has Chalcedon come to be used in the theologies of later times? Questions like these will be guiding for my survey of doctrines of incarnation and incarnational theologies in chapters 2 and 3 (with regard for their thematizing of the humanity of the human being). The thesis I will pursue in these chapters is that an incarnational Christology that treats the question of God's relationship to the human risks becoming abstract if it does not also

---

10. Coakley, *Christ without Absolutes,* p. 105. Original in italics.

take up the question of the person's relationship to God, i.e., what I called in my formulation of objectives above the anthropological implications of the doctrine of incarnation for the human mode of being-in-the-world. I want to do this by means of observing gaze and embodiment as two ways to thematize human relationality.

The Gaze

The human gaze can be understood as a manifestation of relationality and meaning-creation. This applies within the Christian tradition as well. For the medieval person, for example, meaning was something that was shaped visually as much as it was verbally.[11] The image was accordingly important for that period's models of thought and action. The space of the church and its images constituted a symbolic universe, and a person's manner of being-in-the-world was constructed by her experiencing this symbolic universe not only with her eyes, but with her entire body. A person discovered her identity in collaboration with the pictures in the church in prayer, hymns, and liturgy, as well as through the social interactions that related to the church as Christ's body.

Sight has always been one of the most important ways that we humans orient ourselves in our existence. Not only during the Middle Ages, but in every period, even if in diverse ways (see chapter 4), sight has played a major role in people's manner of being-in-the-world, in what is often called our "identity." Since the days of ancient Greek philosophy, sight has often been described as the most noble of the five senses—Aristotle claimed in the introduction to *The Metaphysics* that we prefer sight over almost all else.[12] Sight has not only gotten to function as a metaphor for a person's intellectual capabilities, but has also constituted the standard for the other senses. In contrast to the primacy of the sense of sight within Western philosophy, with its Greek roots, modern biblical exegesis has instead wanted

11. Lena Liepe, *Den medeltida kroppen: Kroppens och könets ikonografi i nordisk medeltid* (Lund: Nordic Academic Press, 2003), p. 81. Liepe refers here to the work of English art historian Michael Camille.

12. Aristotle, *Metaphysics. The Complete Works of Aristotle,* Revised Oxford Translation, vol. 2, ed. Jonathan Barnes (Princeton: Princeton University Press, 1984), p. 1552 (A, 1, 980 a. 25). Cf. Hans Jonas, "Der Adel des Sehens: Eine Untersuchung zur Phänomenologie der Sinne," in *Das Prinzip Leben: Ansätze zu einer philosophischen Biologie* (Frankfurt am Main: Suhrkamp, 1997), pp. 235–64.

to assert the primacy of hearing in a Judeo-Christian biblical tradition.[13] In contrast with sight's distancing gaze, looking on something that appears before the sight as an object available to be mastered, hearing preserves the dynamic nature of a meeting that cannot be surveyed externally, but can only be lived through. Not least within the Lutheran tradition, the primary passivity of the sense of hearing has been contrasted with the more active role of the sense of sight; the eyes can wander over a group of items, and can even be closed, but hearing has no other choice than to hear that which sounds.[14] Thus the hearing human is constituted as a fundamentally receptive person, which fits well with a Lutheran emphasis on justification by grace alone.

Through the senses a person perceives her world in different ways, as well as expresses herself in it and relates to it through her impressions and expressions. The senses are constitutive for a person's being-in-the-world, through which she can discover and express her relationality as such. Her embodiment is thus in a fundamental way mediated through the senses. In this study I will concentrate on one of these senses, namely sight. This may appear to be an odd choice, especially in view of the contrast between a Greek philosophical tradition and a Judeo-Christian biblical tradition. Is not hearing a more obvious choice? There are several reasons to choose sight specifically. To begin with, I believe that it is important to realize that sight as a sense is important even for a tradition that may want to privilege the sense of hearing. Sight plays a big role for how human identity is constituted, and if there is any truth in the assertions of certain cultural philosophers that the West is becoming an increasingly visual culture, in opposition to the older, textual culture, there is every reason to examine the role of sight in the constitution of the person—even within theology.[15]

Another reason to examine the role of sight is that I suspect that my initial polemical contrast of sight as an active sense and hearing as a passive one is excessive. Such a thesis can certainly be presented in more sophisticated ways by its advocates, but I nevertheless want to indicate the possibility of several different gazes, and to argue that the relationship between activity and passivity in the sense of sight is considerably more complex than the

13. See, for example, Rudolf Bultmann, *Das Urchristentum im Rahmen der antiken Religionen,* 2nd edition (Zürich: Artemis-Verlag, 1954), p. 20.

14. See Wilfried Joest, *Ontologie der Person bei Luther* (Göttingen: Vandenhoeck & Ruprecht, 1967), pp. 291–94.

15. See, for example, Nicholas Mirzoeff, *An Introduction to Visual Culture* (London/New York: Routledge, 1999).

picture that a simple either-or argument can give.[16] I contend that just such a complex gaze is hidden in the Christian tradition, and I will attempt to demonstrate this by examining the understanding of sight in some significant contributions from the Christian tradition—in part the New Testament's understanding of sight (chapter 5), in part the gaze that is implicated by the icon (chapter 6). If one takes a closer look at the Christian tradition, one finds that it is not at all self-evident that there are good reasons for contrasting sight and hearing in the way that is sometimes done from a theological perspective. On the contrary, it is possible to find material that testifies to their intimate entanglement.[17] The understanding of sight in Christian theology has just as much to do with confessional bases as with theological arguments, and I will therefore attempt to take different confessions into consideration in my account of sight.

Yet another reason for examining the role of sight, and that which may be most interesting for this study, is the polarization that is sometimes painted between the understanding of the sense of sight and the understanding of embodiment. That the eye is a part of the body is certainly not news, but, not least thanks to the fact that the sense of sight has been associated with human intellectual capabilities, sight has at times been described as aloof and nearly disembodied—which in turn has led to a reduction of the body to a lifeless object.[18] The French phenomenologist Jean-Louis Chrétien has made some objections to such a position, among other things by pointing out how the entire body is engaged when we look at a work of art: When we look at a picture, we do not suddenly become one big eye, for we have two eyes that make a single gaze, which the whole body brings to bear upon that which presents itself, and upon that in front of which the gaze, too, presents itself.[19]

In order to really look at a work of art, we move ourselves closer to it, then draw ourselves back a step, then forward and back again. We stop and fall silent in order to take in as many aspects of the work as possible. The gaze becomes a vehicle for the whole body: "It is not with one's eyes but rather with all one's being that one looks upon a picture."[20] Our body is in

16. For more literature on the subject, see the references for chapter 4.

17. See Jean-Louis Chrétien, *The Call and the Response,* trans. Anne E. Davenport (New York: Fordham University Press, 2004), pp. 33–43.

18. On the latter, see Hans Jonas, "Das Problem des Lebens und des Leibes in der Lehre vom Sein," in *Das Prinzip Leben,* pp. 25–49.

19. Jean-Louis Chrétien, *Hand to Hand: Listening to the Work of Art,* trans. Stephen E. Lewis (New York: Fordham University Press, 2003), p. 18.

20. Chrétien, *Hand to Hand,* p. 18.

other words intimately involved in our gaze, and certainly the fact that we do not, like the cyclops, have a single large eye, serves to underline the fact that our sight is radically incarnated in our body, at the same time that the embodiment of this sight presents a range of different possibilities to the gaze (chapters 4 and 7).

Something may be additionally said about why I have chosen to focus on sight rather than touch. Even if Aristotle claimed that sight was the sense that most prefer, in *On the Soul* he nevertheless ascribed to the tactile sense the quality of being the sense where human perception surpasses that of the animals in precision, which makes the human the most judicious of all living beings. In addition, Aristotle suggests that without the sense of touch, living creatures cannot have any other perceptions either. Touch is thus the most fundamental sense, the sense that living creatures have, not primarily for the sake of their well-being, but simply in order to exist.[21] Touch appears as well to be the most intimate, the least aloof sense, and is in addition impossible to detach from the body even in the imagination, since touch is perception by direct contact.

The latter is, however, a truth with a qualification. As Aristotle himself points out, direct contact is not synonymous with immediacy of sense, but there instead always remains an interval of water or air between touch and its subject.[22] All perception occurs through a medium, even if the distance between the sense and that which is perceived can be of different degrees for different senses. The crucial contrast between the senses is not constituted by whether a sense touches the object that it perceives or not, but by whether this object is near or remote. Since the distance is minuscule with touch, we do not notice it. The vicinity of touch thus simultaneously involves a distancing from the touched object, but this distance is hidden by the medium of touch: the body.[23] The difference between the sense of touch and the sense of sight should therefore not be exaggerated. To a certain degree this entire study will treat the question of the tactile sense, since its overall theme is the body. That I have chosen to focus more directly on the sense of sight is, however, tied up with the well-known difficulties in describing touch, which means that material is sparse, if not nonexistent.[24]

21. Aristotle, *On the Soul*, in *The Complete Works of Aristotle*, vol. 1, ed. Jonathan Barnes, revised Oxford translation (Princeton: Princeton University Press, 1995), pp. 670, 691–92 (421a20 f., 435a11–435b25).

22. Aristotle, *On the Soul*, pp. 673–74 (423a1–423b16).

23. Chrétien, *The Call and the Response*, pp. 87–88. Cf. 83–131.

24. See, for example, Jacques Derrida, *On Touching: Jean-Luc Nancy*, Meridian: Crossing Aesthetics, trans. Christine Irizarry (Stanford: Stanford University Press, 2005), together

The sense of sight is in certain respects a more explicit sense as regards its trace in various distinct experiences, which makes my investigation easier— and in the end, it is also a challenge to show how the sense of sight is tied up in a fundamental way with human embodiment, and in many different conceptions of the same.

The question of human sight is thus associated with the question of human embodiment, and thereby—as we shall see—with questions of power as well.[25] A study that focuses on the gaze in the way that I do here means, of course, that a seeing person's perspective will be privileged. Although I will argue that the eye of faith does not imply the sort of survey and control that is sometimes associated with sight, but is instead a situated and embodied way to be-in-the-world that thereby approaches the blind person's necessary understanding of the deficiency of perspective, my point of view is still undeniably that of the seeing person. If an investigation similar to this one were to be carried out from the perspective of a blind person, not only would the visual metaphor in theological, philosophical, and everyday parlance presumably be more clearly noted, but also the ways in which "sight" and "blindness" are often constructed, especially in the biblical texts, as binary oppositions that tend to connect a physical difference with a moral difference.[26] Although I distance myself here from such a moral privileging of an "ocularcentrism" in the Western tradition, it is de facto difficult to guard against. At the same time, it is hardly the case that such positions in relation to "gaze" and "blindness" are determined forever. The possibility always remains to read the ocularcentrism of the tradition in a different way than that offered in the dominant perspective.[27] I therefore see it as both legitimate and fruitful, in a study of this kind from the perspective of a seeing person, to study various gazes and thereby, hopefully, open the way to some small degree for such an alternative reading. Insight into the ocularcentrism of the Western theological and philosophical tradition and the different shapes it has taken can potentially contribute to making it less self-evident. At the same time, it is not a given that "gaze" and "blindness" actually constitute

---

with Graham Ward, *Christ and Culture,* Challenges in Contemporary Theology (Malden, MA/ Oxford: Blackwell, 2005), pp. 67–77.

25. Jonathan Crary, *Techniques of the Observer: On Vision and Modernity in the Nineteenth Century* (Cambridge, MA/London: MIT Press, 1990), p. 3.

26. At the same time, blindness is sometimes presented as a "cure" for too self-confident a gaze. Cf. Tob, Apg 9:10–25.

27. Cf., for example, John M. Hull, *In the Beginning There Was Darkness: A Blind Person's Conversations with the Bible* (London: SCM Press, 2001).

the opposites that they are sometimes depicted as.[28] Each concrete gaze may be thought to require a specific, partial blindness, and it is likely conceivable that each concrete blindness is blind in relation to a concrete gaze. The demarcation between the senses is itself both historically and physically so far from self-evident that it becomes a simplification—to the advantage or disadvantage of the gaze—to contrast it with the other human senses.[29] Given this, even from a seeing perspective we might, hypothetically, imagine that the visual metaphor would not be entirely useless from the perspective of a blind person, if, at least, the dependence on human embodiment is shown more clearly than is typical.

Embodiment

So what are body and embodiment? A general definition ought to be simple enough. In *Nationalencyklopedin,* the most comprehensive contemporary Swedish-language encyclopedia, one finds the following definition for "body": "a person's outer, physical being, in opposition to her internal, spiritual being."[30] Apart from the fact that this explanation seems to enact a particular philosophical tradition's understanding of the body in contrast with the soul or the spirit, this leaves several unanswered questions: Is the body a machine steered by the nerve impulses that the consciousness sends out, or should we say that the body itself is alive and aware? Is the body a medium for human communication with and relationship to the surrounding world, and in that case, how? Is the body a private or a social phenomenon? It is understandable that *Nationalencyklopedin* confines itself to just one point, given the philosophical, theological, and biological controversies over the embodiment of the body that arise as soon as one attempts a more detailed definition.

Of the three fundamental concepts that structure this study, embodiment is perhaps the most difficult to give even a preliminary, heuristic

---

28. See Astrid Söderbergh Widding's essay *Blick och blindhet,* Bonnier Alba essä (Stockholm: Bonnier Alba, 1997), as well as Jacques Derrida, *Memoirs of the Blind: The Self-Portrait and Other Ruins,* trans. Pascale-Anne Brault and Michael Naas (Chicago: University of Chicago Press, 1993), together with James Elkins, *The Object Stares Back: On the Nature of Seeing,* A Harvest Book (San Diego/New York/London: Harcourt, 1997), pp. 86–124, 201–35.

29. Crary, *Techniques,* p. 59.

30. "kropp" (body), *Nationalencyklopedin,* vol. 11 (Höganäs, Sweden: Bra Böcker, 1994), p. 471.

introduction to. To begin with, this has to do with the fact that the two other concepts, incarnation and the gaze, in a certain sense fall under this concept. A more crucial reason, however, is that, from the perspective of the body as having a history, a clear-cut definition of the body is impossible. As Nietzsche writes in *On the Genealogy of Morals:* "all concepts in which a whole process is summarized in signs escape definition; only that which is without history can be defined."[31] In a certain sense, the body is just one prime example of that which withdraws from language at the same time that its only possibility of expressing itself is in fact through language.

The difficulty of finding a self-evident starting point for a thematization of the body has been affirmed by many who have attacked the body as a theoretical problem. The philosopher Stephen Crites believes that discourse about the body is in a certain sense an abstraction, since the body itself is a reification of one particular function of the person herself, which cannot be divided from her consciousness: "Neither disembodied minds nor mindless bodies can appear in stories. There the self is given whole, as an activity in time."[32] The difficulty of getting a hold of the body in a theoretical discussion has also been indirectly affirmed by medieval historian Caroline Bynum when she writes that "despite the enthusiasm for the topic, discussions of the body are almost completely incommensurable—and often mutually incomprehensible—across the disciplines."[33] The reason for this incommensurability and mutual unintelligibility between different disciplines is precisely the difficulty of agreeing on a straightforward definition of the body, a difficulty that is a condition of both the fundamental conceptual intangibility of the body and the angle of approach in the different disciplines that study the body.

But it would be unfortunate for my project of interpreting the body to already go aground here, on these different reasons for the impossibility of thematizing the body in a theoretical discussion: its historical nature, the abstraction that is associated with each formulation of the body, and the incommensurability of the theoretical disciplines. Is it possible, then, to pursue a theoretical argument without doing violence to that which is studied, or reducing it to a concept that keeps its meaning locked up tight?

31. Nietzsche, *On the Genealogy of Morals,* p. 149.

32. Stephen Crites, "The Narrative Quality of Experience," in *Why Narrative? Readings in Narrative Theology,* ed. Stanley Hauerwas and L. Gregory Jones (Grand Rapids: Eerdmans, 1989), p. 85.

33. Caroline Bynum, "Why All the Fuss about the Body? A Medievalist's Perspective," *Critical Inquiry* 22 (1995): 5.

If we want to avoid the violence involved in forcing someone to play a role in which he or she does not recognize him or herself, we must realize that this is a risk in the conceptualization of the body as well.[34] In order to avoid being forced into silence, our strategy must therefore deal with how the body can be affirmed without establishing an unambiguous definition of the same (and here we realize as well the significance of the question of whether or not sight involves a necessary objectification of the seen).[35] In this study, such a strategy will consist in offering an interpretation of the body from several philosophical and theological angles, in the hope that a trace of the body, rather than the body itself, will thus come forth. It is my hope that hermeneutic phenomenology will offer a method that allows me to interpret the body without objectifying it. Phenomenology involves a thematization of the experience of the body prior to the division between subject and object. Such a thematization does not involve an abstract definition of the body, philosophically or theologically, but attempts instead to show how conceptions of the body have consequences for the human life-world and vice versa.

In his book *Incarnation: Une philosophie de la chair* the French philosopher Michel Henry has made a fundamental distinction between the body *(le corps)* on the one hand and the flesh *(la chair)* on the other, and has pointed out that while the body can be divided up into different parts or reduced to atoms, it is impossible to do the same with the flesh. The flesh consists instead of "pleasures and pains, hunger and thirst, desire and fatigue, strength and joy."[36] I will not follow Henry's terminology, but he points out something essential: the experience of the body is not primarily

---

34. Cf. Emmanuel Levinas, *Totality and Infinity: An Essay on Exteriority*, trans. Alphonso Lingis (Pittsburgh: Duquesne University Press, 1969), p. 21.

35. This is a problem that discourse about the body shares with other discourses about linguistically transcendent phenomena. Cf. James K. A. Smith, *Speech and Theology: Language and the Logic of Incarnation*, Radical Orthodoxy (London/New York: Routledge, 2002), pp. 3–15.

36. Michel Henry, *Incarnation: Une philosophie de la chair* (Paris: Éditions de Seuil, 2000), p. 27. Original in italics. Henry is one of several phenomenologists with an express interest in embodiment as well as theology. I will however not discuss Henry's phenomenology of the body in this study, primarily for two reasons: 1) the fact that the sort of transcendental embodiment that Henry calls the flesh risks reducing embodiment to an ideality; 2) the fact that my interest is oriented towards the concrete practices where embodiment is perceived, which calls for a hermeneutic phenomenology rather than a transcendental theology. For a theological critique of Henry that in part concerns these reasons, see Antonio Calcagno, "The Incarnation, Michel Henry, and the Possibility of an Husserlian-Inspired Transcendental Life," *Heythrop Journal* 45, no. 3 (2004): 290–304.

an experience of a swarm of atoms, or of an arm that cooperates with a torso, in throwing a spear for example, but of different states that determine all of the person's existence. I can, of course, experience how my head and my arms are tired after a workday, but at the same time, it is my whole self that is tired, rather than certain parts of my body. Henry's phenomenological distinction between the body and the flesh gives a more fruitful explanation than *Nationalencyklopedin* of the angle from which I will study human embodiment, and simultaneously avoids objectifying the body. The perspective of phenomenology, not only Henry's, but more generally, will accordingly be of great significance for my theological interpretation of the body. This does not mean that the biological body is uninteresting, but the more I have studied embodiment, the more certain I have become that it is an abstraction to separate anatomy from history and discourse.

Before I move on, in a more methodological section, to presenting phenomenology and the theological use of the same, I will briefly mention some reasons that human embodiment has been and is important for the Christian tradition. One of these reasons may be called the sacramental quality of the Christian faith. According to the British theologian Tina Beattie, "Sacramentality refers to the Christian belief that the material world is suffused by grace, so that it can become the medium of God's presence among us."[37] Although sacramentality is not always thematized within theology via human embodiment, there are, at the very least, implicit theological grounds for thematizing the body as a "means of grace," i.e., as a medium through which God's mercy is provided to humanity. This sacramental quality of the Christian faith is a consequence of the belief in incarnation, i.e., the active presence of God among humans in Jesus Christ. Representations of the relationship between words and world, between language and the body, between the symbolic and the material, have thus continuously permeated the Christian tradition, in both thought and deed. The body is, so to speak, not given as a naked fact or phenomenon, but is always intertwined with different theological interests and ideas. In order to be able to pose the question of the body in the Christian tradition, an investigation is therefore needed that not only thematizes incarnation and the gaze, but also the different doctrines, theologies, and practices in which the body has come to expression. My investigation of the Christian body in chapters 9, 10, and 11 will therefore thematize human embodiment from several different angles: as

---

37. Tina Beattie, *Woman*, New Century Theology (London/New York: Continuum, 2003), p. 163.

the liturgical, the erotic, and the grotesque body. Although it is consequently not possible—or even desirable—to establish an unequivocal definition of the body right from the start, my argument above shows that there is no less rich a material for a theological somatology to build on.

It would be a mistake to believe that the Christian tradition is homogeneous, even as regards its more or less implicit conception of the body. Another reason why human embodiment has been and is important for the Christian tradition is that the body is, for this as well as other traditions, a crucial arena for conflictual and competing conceptions of, for example, the relationship between materiality and spirituality.[38] The conception of the body of Christ as a social body inclusive of the entirety of Christian humanity was considerably more alive in the Middle Ages than in our time. But it is clear that the body is an arena for negotiations between personal and cultural identity in our time as well, including in religious contexts. With the study of the body in Christian tradition it is therefore important that the analysis of the different embodiments that are taken up is also carried out from the perspective of power. Feminist theory and theology in particular have in various ways observed the body as an arena where different power relationships become visible. There are perspectives here on the Christian body that are important to take into account, as will also be the case in various ways in the other chapters. With that, I will now go over to the more methodological arguments.

Phenomenology, Life-World, Interpretation

Phenomenology

Taken generally, the philosophical dimension of the method that I make use of in this study may be said to be phenomenological, or at least inspired by phenomenology. People usually point to the German philosopher Edmund Husserl as the founder of modern phenomenology, who in large portions of his philosophical authorship attempted to explain the significance of phenomenology. Husserl was teacher to several of phenomenology's later interpreters, including Martin Heidegger, and has inspired a philosophical current that is still very active. Among those who have chosen to work within

---

38. Sarah Beckwith, *Christ's Body: Identity, Culture and Society in Late Medieval Writings* (London/New York: Routledge, 1993), p. 38.

the phenomenological tradition, or at least those inspired by it, are such varied philosophers as Simone de Beauvoir, Jean-Louis Chrétien, Jacques Derrida, Hans-Georg Gadamer, Emmanuel Levinas, Jean-Luc Marion, Maurice Merleau-Ponty, Paul Ricoeur, and Jean-Paul Sartre, to name only a few of the philosophers I will make use of here.

According to a very short definition (which I take from the philosopher Robert Sokolowski), one can say that phenomenology is "the study of human experience and of the way things present themselves to us in and through such experience."[39] Phenomenology is thus concerned with how things appear to a person, but also with how our human consciousness makes it possible for things to appear in the way that they appear. Husserl speaks of "clarifying the essence of knowledge and known objectivity" as the first and fundamental task of phenomenology.[40] In this sense phenomenology realizes modern philosophy's focus on epistemology ever since Kant; it deviates from modern philosophy in other respects, however, as we will see.

With Husserl as the starting point, phenomenology has developed in various ways. There is the existential or hermeneutic phenomenology of Heidegger, Gadamer, and Ricoeur, which I present in more detail below. To a degree one can discern a school of thought that may be called radical phenomenology, which we find in Levinas, Marion, Chrétien, and even partially in Derrida.[41] These philosophers are critical of Husserl's treatment of the problem of intersubjectivity, and attempt to show how, on the basis of the conditions of phenomenology, it is possible to describe phenomena that exceed the horizon of the human subject—the trace, the face of the other, divine revelation—and that thereby cannot be conceptualized, but instead call into question the primacy of human subjectivity. For example, in his central work *Ideas Pertaining to a Pure Phenomenology and*

---

39. Robert Sokolowski, *Introduction to Phenomenology* (Cambridge: Cambridge University Press, 2000), p. 2. For additional introductory perspectives, see Dermot Moran, *Introduction to Phenomenology* (London/New York: Routledge, 2000), and, short and concise, Dan Zahavi, *Fænomenologi* (Frederiksberg, Denmark: Roskilde Universitetsforlag, 2003).

40. Edmund Husserl, *Die Idee der Phänomenologie: Fünf Vorlesungen*, Philosophische Bibliothek vol. 392, ed. Paul Janssen (Hamburg: Felix Meiner Verlag, 1986), p. 23; English translation: Edmund Husserl, *The Idea of Phenomenology*, Collected Works vol. 8, trans. Lee Hardy (Dordrecht/Boston/London: Kluwer Academic Publishers, 1999), p. 19.

41. Cf., for example, the account in Jean-Luc Marion, *Reduction and Givenness: Investigations of Husserl, Heidegger, and Phenomenology*, Northwestern University Studies in Phenomenology & Existential Philosophy, trans. Thomas A. Carlson (Evanston, IL: Northwestern University Press, 1998).

to a Phenomenological Philosophy from 1913 Husserl had denied that the transcendence of God could be the subject of a phenomenological investigation, since all earthly as well as unearthly transcendence falls outside the phenomenological reduction to immanence, i.e., to "a field of pure consciousness."[42] For radical phenomenology, however, human subjectivity is understood as a response to being addressed, rather than a fundamental act of self-reflection.[43]

As will become clear below, I believe that there are certain insights within hermeneutic phenomenology that are necessary for my investigation of incarnation, the gaze, and embodiment. However, this does not mean that I forgo those insights that can be gained from phenomenologists outside the hermeneutic tradition, or, for that matter, insights gotten from philosophers more or less critical of phenomenology, such as Michel Foucault and Judith Butler. Before I turn to the question of the relationship between hermeneutics and phenomenology, I will first look a bit closer at a central concept within contemporary philosophy, namely the "life-world." Finally, I will also say something in this section about how I see the relationship between phenomenology and theology, and why this study does not lay claim to being phenomenological in a strict sense.

Phenomenology and Life-World

One of the concepts that Husserl introduced and has since been widely disseminated is the concept of the "life-world" *(Lebenswelt)*. It was introduced by Husserl in a work from his later production, more precisely, the last work that was published in his lifetime, *The Crisis of European Sciences and Transcendental Phenomenology,* first published in the Yugoslav journal *Philosophia* in 1936.[44] For Husserl, the concept is meant to show that the ideal world

---

42. Edmund Husserl, *Ideas Pertaining to a Pure Phenomenology and to a Phenomenological Philosophy: First Book: Introduction to a Pure Phenomenology,* Edmund Husserl Collected Works vol. 2, trans. F. Kersten (The Hague/Boston/Lancaster: Martinus Nijhoff, 1983), p. 134 (§58). Cf. pp. 133–34 and pp. 114–16 (§51). Why "a worldly God is evidently impossible" is not clear, however. Is this not, in a certain sense, precisely what Christian theology speaks of as incarnation? Cf. James K. A. Smith, *Speech,* p. 55.

43. Cf. the already-mentioned work of Jean-Louis Chrétien, *The Call and the Response,* as one of the best examples of this.

44. Edmund Husserl, *The Crisis of European Sciences and Transcendental Phenomenology: An Introduction to Phenomenology,* trans. David Carr (Evanston, IL: Northwestern University

that natural scientists presuppose is not the primary or most fundamental world as regards human knowledge. Philosophy must therefore regain the lived world as a subject for philosophical investigation.

What does Husserl mean then with the concept of the life-world? It is in the life-world that we live with all of our being. But in this world we find "nothing of geometrical idealities, no geometrical space or mathematical time with all their shape."[45] The life-world is "the world constantly given to us as actual in our concrete world-life."[46] The life-world is therefore the world that we live in and that we take for granted. It is thus more than the sum of the things that surround us, and is better understood as a world prior to the division between consciousness and its object. Rather than an objectifiable world, it is a practical field open to the actions and schemes of the person. The life-world is pre-scientific and pre-philosophical, but is presupposed by all scientific and philosophical arguments. The life-world is permanent, but not static, the horizon for the person's thinking and acting. To borrow a quotation from Merleau-Ponty, one of the philosophers who follow Husserl, and whose phenomenology I will return to in more detail in chapter 8, the world is thus "not what I think, but what I live through. I am open to the world, I have no doubt that I am in communication with it, but I do not possess it; it is inexhaustible."[47] The life-world is not a world that we are capable of exhaustively explaining or thematizing, but both the "environment" in which our entire being is located, and the condition for all pragmatic actions and theoretical arguments. The "crisis" for the "European sciences" that constitutes the theme for Husserl's *Crisis* deals precisely with

---

Press, 1970). There is a longstanding debate whether Husserl modified his transcendental phenomenology in a radical way through his concept of the life-world—possibly induced by Heidegger's *Sein und Zeit,* which was published for the first time in 1927 in Husserl's *Jahrbuch für Philosophie und phänomenologische Forschung* with a dedication from his former student. I, however, tend towards the opinion that Husserl's phenomenology of the life-world is instead a way to take up the task of transcendental phenomenology in new territory, rather than a radical break with the ideal of "philosophy as a strict science." See Hans-Georg Gadamer, "Die Wissenschaft von der Lebenswelt," *Neuere Philosophie: I. Hegel, Husserl, Heidegger.* Gesammelte Werke vol. 3 (Tübingen: J. C. B. Mohr [Paul Siebeck], 1987), pp. 147–59. Already in 1913 Husserl had suggested the possibility of just such a phenomenology of the life-world in *Ideen* (see Husserl, *Ideas,* p. 111 [§30]).

45. Husserl, *The Crisis,* p. 50.

46. Husserl, *The Crisis,* p. 51.

47. Maurice Merleau-Ponty, *Phénoménologie de la perception* (Paris: Gallimard, 1945), pp. xiff.; English translation: Maurice Merleau-Ponty, *Phenomenology of Perception,* trans. Colin Smith (London: Routledge, 1992), pp. xvi-xvii.

the loss of the life-world within philosophy and, paradoxically enough, with the crisis of legitimacy that the natural sciences end up in if the life-world is reduced to an objectifiable world. The life-world is thus important for Husserl's transcendental phenomenology because phenomenology's task, in Husserl's opinion, was to give the sciences a solid foundation. Thus, the "Cartesian" thread in Husserl's phenomenology is not, as a more superficial reflection might lead one to believe, about taking over Descartes's conception of the world and its mathematizing of existence, but with a more radical reduction than Descartes, a reduction that also sets the mathematical sciences and geometry in question.[48]

The concept of the life-world has, however, meant a number of new questions for phenomenology. If the life-world is the condition for human thinking and acting, then how does it relate to the relativity of the different life-worlds that we as concrete persons find ourselves in and that vary with time and space? Even if Husserl could analyze universal structures that apply for all life-worlds in accordance with his phenomenological reduction, the question arises whether he has not thereby reduced the concrete life-world to an ideal. It would thus once more be philosophy, rather than the life-world itself, that would constitute the horizon for human thinking and acting. But then, as Gadamer asks himself, is not the life-world the condition for transcendental reflection as well?[49] Given his continual effort to repulse every threat of relativism, it is not unthinkable that Husserl's ultimate conclusion would be the primacy of transcendental phenomenology over every concrete life-world. Even in *Crisis* Husserl holds on to his fundamental conception of a transcendental ego and a scientific reason that is able to comprehend every pre-scientific action or thought. But with that we can also see that the concept of the life-world is philosophically mined, and has blasted the framework of transcendental phenomenology. In my study I will not proceed specifically from Husserl's own transcendental conception of the life-world, but from a more existential-hermeneutic understanding of the life-world.[50]

48. Cf. Edmund Husserl, *Cartesian Meditations: An Introduction to Phenomenology,* trans. Dorion Cairns (The Hague/Dordrecht: Nijhoff/Kluwer, 1973), §3, p. 10.

49. Hans-Georg Gadamer, *Truth and Method,* 2nd, revised edition, translation revised by Joel Weinsheimer and Donald G. Marshall (London/New York: Continuum, 2004), pp. 239–41.

50. For a concise summary of the differences between different phenomenological conceptions of the life-world, see Tania Eden, "Lebenswelt," in *Wörterbuch der phänomenologischen Begriffe,* Philosophische Bibliothek vol. 555, published by Helmuth Vetter (Hamburg: Felix Meiner Verlag, 2004), pp. 328–30.

Phenomenology and Hermeneutics

With regard to Husserl's phenomenology, the eternal suspicion has lain in ambush that the relationship between the transcendental and the everyday life-world experience is ultimately dualistic, and that Husserl's phenomenology thereby, in spite of everything, remains caught within the framework of a philosophy of consciousness. Within hermeneutic phenomenology, however, as it is found in the tradition of Heidegger, Gadamer, and Ricoeur, the primacy of consciousness has come to be questioned. The subject is not so much something that relates to the life-world, as something that finds itself through an interpretation of its experiences in the life-world. As Ricoeur writes: "[T]he subject that interprets himself while interpreting signs is no longer the cogito: rather, he is a being who discovers, by the exegesis of his own life, that he is placed in being before he places and possesses himself."[51] Ricoeur's subject and the hermeneutic subject are no longer a transcendentally understood subject, but a situated subject that thereby does not have any possibility of surveying existence in an absolute way, nor is transparent to itself. Self-understanding is only possible—and this is an insight that, in principle, is prevalent in hermeneutic phenomenology—via a "detour" through the life-world in which the being finds itself, and so via an interpretation of the life-world itself.[52]

The condition for human knowledge is thus not the subject's noetic relationship to an object, but human existence as a primary belonging, or what Heidegger calls a "being-in-the-world," that precedes and is presupposed by each relationship between a subject and an object. The person relates to her world horizontally rather than vertically. The person as an interpreting being thus finds herself thrown *in medias res,* neither at the beginning nor the end of the conversation. But since interpretation is an open process, a final and absolute ground for human knowledge in some transcendental subjectivity is impossible. All understanding is mediated through interpretation, by, as Heidegger suggests, understanding something *as* something.[53] Thus there is always an anticipatory aspect to the interpretation of something as

---

51. Paul Ricoeur, "Existence and Hermeneutics," in *The Conflict of Interpretations: Essays in Hermeneutics,* ed. Don Ihde, trans. Kathleen McLaughlin (London: Continuum, 2004), p. 11.

52. For a solid introduction to and discussion of Ricoeur with reference to the questions that are taken up here, see Bengt Kristensson Uggla, *Kommunikation på bristningsgränsen: En studie i Paul Ricoeurs projekt* (Stockholm/Stehag: Brutus Östlings Bokförlag Symposion), 1994.

53. Martin Heidegger, *Being and Time,* trans. John Macquarrie and Edward Robinson (Oxford/Cambridge, MA: Blackwell, 1962), p. 189. Cf. pp. 188–95.

something, where the understanding of the parts is always anticipated by an understanding of the whole. Heidegger speaks of understanding as a circle, writing: "What is decisive is not to get out of the circle but to come into it in the right way. This circle of understanding is not an orbit in which any random kind of knowledge may move; it is the expression of the existential *fore-structure* of Dasein itself."[54] In contrast to the transcendental foundation that situates the transcendental subject outside the circle, hermeneutic phenomenology thus implies that the circle of understanding precedes the subject. A person's understanding happens in a deployment of the life-world, and this deployment is always an act of interpretation that understands a thing, a phenomenon, or an act, *as* something.

One of the critical questions usually posed to hermeneutic phenomenology is whether its emphasis on the belonging of the person means that she can never escape from the hermeneutic circle, but is doomed simply to reinforce her own life-world.[55] But the point, as Heidegger writes in the above quotation, is not to take oneself out of the circle, but to take oneself into it in the right way. Situating the person within her life-world does indeed imply that she does not have any objective or neutral position from which she can describe this life-world. In other words, the life-world precedes the division between subject and object that such an ideal presupposes. But the possibility of a critical stance is not given by such absolute distancing—it lies instead in the dynamic character of language and understanding themselves. Because it is, in principle, not possible to complete the process of interpretation, and because phenomena carry a semantic potential that makes possible various ways of articulating them, the ideal for hermeneutic phenomenology is not one absolute and unambiguous body of knowledge. Ricoeur speaks of a "surplus of meaning" that comprises the semantic inexhaustibility of being.[56] Outside of a given context our words can always have more than one meaning, and a concrete act of interpretation thus occurs as a negotiation between the horizon of the interpreter on the one hand, and the horizon of the interpreted on the other.[57] This distance between the horizons of the interpreter and the interpreted means that the hermeneutic act of interpretation is not merely an interpretation of the life-world that the interpreter

54. Heidegger, *Being and Time*, p. 195.

55. Cf. Jürgen Habermas, "Der Universalitätsanspruch der Hermeneutik," in *Hermeneutik und Ideologikritik,* ed. Karl-Otto Apel (Frankfurt am Main: Suhrkamp, 1971), pp. 120–59.

56. Paul Ricoeur, *Interpretation Theory: Discourse and the Surplus of Meaning* (Fort Worth: Texas Christian University Press), 1976.

57. Gadamer, *Truth and Method,* pp. 301–6.

belongs to by birth, habit, or choice. The possibility of both a critical and a self-critical posture is given in the gap between these two horizons. At any rate, the critical hermeneutic of, for example, Ricoeur implies an element of distancing from the given tradition as the hermeneutic interrupts belonging via a reflexive act, namely the interpretive act itself, and so even in Ricoeur we find a correspondence to Husserl's differentiation between the natural and the philosophical posture.

This distancing is not a consequence of one or another scientific method, but rather it is language itself that bears such a distancing, as Ricoeur claims: "The linguistic sign can *stand for* something only if it *is not* the thing."[58] Likewise, we find a paradigmatic example of distancing in the text, which, thanks to its materiality, manages to communicate something over great distances in both time and space.[59] Rather than suggesting the immediate presence of "face to face" verbal communication, the text is instead communication at a distance. There is thus an element of distancing within the framework of belonging itself that both is productive for understanding, and makes possible a critical distance: "*Verfremdung* is not only what understanding must overcome, but also what conditions it."[60] Thus for Ricoeur interpretation never has to do with a romantic immediacy, a fusion between two consciousnesses (or horizons), but is a critical act where, for example, one who attempts to interpret an ancient text is ineluctably set before the questions of the text, just as the text is set before the questions of the interpreter. The act of interpretation thereby becomes possible, as both a critical and a self-critical judgment, without requiring an absolute distancing from the life-world. Ideological criticism becomes an element within the bounds of the hermeneutic process, rather than a criticism of hermeneutics as such.[61] Ricoeur is, in other words, critical of portions of Gadamer's hermeneutics, which sets belonging and distance in opposition

58. Paul Ricoeur, "Phenomenology and Hermeneutics," in *From Text to Action: Essays in Hermeneutics II,* trans. Kathleen Blamey and John B. Thompson (Evanston, IL: Northwestern University Press, 1991), p. 40. On the problematic relationship between the sign and ideal meaning in Husserl, see Jacques Derrida, *Voice and Phenomenon: Introduction to the Problem of the Sign in Husserl's Phenomenology,* Northwestern University Studies in Phenomenology & Existential Philosophy, trans. Leonard Lawlor (Evanston, IL: Northwestern University Press, 2011).

59. Paul Ricoeur, "The Hermeneutical Function of Distanciation," in *From Text to Action,* p. 75. Cf. pp. 84–86.

60. Ricoeur, "The Hermeneutical Function," p. 84.

61. Ricoeur, "Hermeneutics and the Critique of Ideology," in *From Text to Action,* pp. 270–307.

to each other.[62] But in light of the above, and even in light of what Gadamer himself says about the productive significance of the spacing of time for understanding, and the polarity between familiarity and alienation as the ground of hermeneutics, this antinomy is only apparent.[63]

Phenomenology and Theology

In this discussion of just what sort of hermeneutic phenomenology will guide this study, let me finally mention something about how I see the relationship between phenomenology and theology. As I mentioned above, criticism has been aimed at the radical phenomenology of Levinas, Henry, Marion, and Chrétien to the effect that they have created a phenomenology which, like a Trojan horse, has secretly smuggled theological suppositions into phenomenology and thereby crippled the character of phenomenology as a pure and rigorous science. The French philosopher Dominique Janicaud believes that phenomenology has been taken hostage by a theology that will not say its name, and that the theological turn within French phenomenology has meant a break with phenomenology's immanent method, i.e., with its reduction of the question of existence in favor of an investigation of intentionality as such.[64] I am on the one hand skeptical that the idea of a pure phenomenology—in particular in the sense of Husserlian orthodoxy—would be especially fruitful for phenomenology as such, but on the other hand I believe that there is something to the criticism insofar as, for example, Marion's phenomenology is hardly wholly independent of his theology (whatever he may think of this himself).[65] Despite this, such a critique does not directly concern my use of phenomenology in this project. What I aim for in this study is not a phenomenology of the body, but rather a theology

62. Ricoeur, "The Task of Hermeneutics," in *From Text to Action,* pp. 70–74.

63. Ricoeur, "The Hermeneutical Function," pp. 83f. Cf. Gadamer, *Truth and Method,* pp. 291–99.

64. Dominique Janicaud, *The Theological Turn of French Phenomenology,* in *Phenomenology and the "Theological Turn": The French Debate,* Dominique Janicaud et al. (New York: Fordham University Press, 2000), pp. 42–43. Cf. pp. 35–49.

65. See Jean-Luc Marion, *Being Given: Toward a Phenomenology of Givenness,* Cultural Memory in the Present, trans. Jeffrey L. Kosky (Stanford: Stanford University Press, 2002), pp. 3–4, 71–74. For a critical reading of Marion's self-description of differentiating between phenomenology and theology, see Thomas A. Carlson, *Indiscretion: Finitude and the Naming of God* (Chicago: University of Chicago Press, 1999), pp. 193–214.

of the body, and so I am not primarily interested in the possibility of sharply differentiating between a purely phenomenological approach and a theological approach.

However, the critique of radical phenomenology indicates the direction for a critique of the pretension of universality that hermeneutic phenomenology carries within itself: Is it not the case that even the analyses of phenomena in phenomenology are mediated by a concrete, particular interpretation of the human life-world, an interpretation that cannot claim to have radically distanced itself from the socially, linguistically, historically, and religiously contingent context of this specific interpretation? The experiences and dispositions that phenomenology examines are never visible in a "naked immediacy," but are given form in accordance with a given life-world's schemata and regularities.[66] This prevents neither a phenomenology nor a theology from bringing up certain claims of universality for its interpretations of phenomena, but these claims of universality do not stem from some insight into the true nature of the phenomena or thing apart from any concrete embodiment, but remain simply candidates for universality and truth, and do not therefore constitute in themselves some apodictic, obvious evidence for every person, time, and place. My decision to call this study theological rather than phenomenological therefore does not stem from a false humility regarding its claims, or a lack of interest in the phenomenological tradition as such, but rather from the desire to be able to identify the horizon against which I raise my claims about knowledge, and on the basis of which I argue. The restriction to the Christian tradition thus does not have to do with a lack of interest for the other, but with the fact that I am here, as Ricoeur writes, "content . . . with tracing the ample hermeneutic lines of only one religion" as an admission of the peculiar limitations of the requirements of knowledge.[67]

The above discussion also has consequences for the perspective on the relationship between phenomenology and theology that I work with in this study. Heidegger argues in his article "Phenomenology and Theology" from 1927 that phenomenology relates to theology as a fundamental ontology to a specialized science.[68] This means that phenomenology provides the structural conditions, of which theology then examines a concrete realization.

---

66. Paul Ricoeur, "Experience and Language in Religious Discourse," in *Phenomenology and the "Theological Turn,"* p. 130.

67. Ricoeur, "Experience and Language," p. 131.

68. Martin Heidegger, "Phenomenology and Theology," in *Pathmarks,* trans. James G. Hart and John C. Maraldo (Cambridge: Cambridge University Press, 1998), pp. 39–62.

So sin, for example, is a concrete realization of the qualification of human existence as guilt.[69] Guilt is the transcendental condition of possibility for sin, which does not mean that it is possible to deduce sin from guilt. But such an argument assumes that the universal always precedes and is required by the concrete. In a lecture on the relationship between faith and knowledge and the return of religion ("Belief and Knowledge"), Derrida has shown that the concrete and the abstract are always dependent on each other, as well as how the meaning of the most general concepts, such as, for example, "religion," is dependent on both their original and their contemporary context.[70] To think "religion" is thus to think both the Roman and the Christian. Even Heidegger's phenomenology is not as removed from a Christian theology as he would sometimes like to have us think, but in certain respects it can instead, at least in *Being and Time,* be understood as a reiteration of Christian theology with an ontological-existential language and without the name.[71] Guilt as a human qualification is at most quasi-transcendental, or rather, a concept imported from Christian theology and stripped of its more explicit theological features. As Derrida has pointed out in a critique that also concerns Marion's phenomenology, is it therefore not so self-evident what comes first: the concrete, historical religion, or the ontological structures, the manifestation or the ability to manifest?[72] Phenomenology is instead quasi-transcendental, and thus has no obvious epistemological or ontological advantages over theology. Phenomenology and theology, one might say, interpret the life-world on the same level—but not necessarily with the same aim—and neither of these discourses can therefore make claim to being more fundamental than the other. Even the ontological claims are based on an interpretation of the life-world, and therefore cannot claim to represent more than what Ricoeur calls a "truncated ontology" *(une ontologie brisée).*[73]

69. Heidegger, "Phenomenology and Theology," pp. 51–52. Cf. Heidegger, *Being and Time,* pp. 325–35.

70. Jacques Derrida, "Foi et savoir: Les deux sources de la 'religion' aux limites de la simple raison," in *La religion,* ed. Jacques Derrida and Gianni Vattimo (Paris: Éditions du Seuil, 1996), pp. 9–86; English translation: Jacques Derrida, "Faith and Knowledge: The Two Sources of 'Religion' at the Limits of Reason Alone," in *Religion,* ed. Jacques Derrida and Gianni Vattimo, trans. Samuel Weber (Cambridge: Polity Press, 1998), pp. 1–78.

71. Cf. Svenungsson, *Guds återkomst,* pp. 84–92.

72. Cf. Jacques Derrida, "On the Gift: A Discussion between Jacques Derrida and Jean-Luc Marion," in *God, the Gift and Postmodernism,* ed. John D. Caputo and Michael J. Scanlon (Bloomington/Indianapolis: Indiana University Press, 1999), p. 73.

73. Ricoeur, "Existence and Hermeneutics," p. 19.

But now, after a general presentation of the methodological possibilities of phenomenology, have I not retreated back to a theology that does not need to listen to philosophy? Hopefully not. The aim in mentioning the critique of the theological conditions in radical phenomenology was not to make theology immune to a philosophical critique, but rather to point out the difficulty of implying that one works completely without presuppositions, in theology as well as philosophy. This also means that any strict policing of domains between phenomenology and theology is not possible, nor am I interested in establishing any such division. More interesting to me are the resources for a self-critical, reflexive posture that philosophy in the shape of phenomenology, especially hermeneutic phenomenology, offers to theology. My use of phenomenology is thus not conditioned by a hope of finding a fundamental ontology that offers theology scientific legitimation. Instead, I want to achieve the science of theology by letting it be a part of academic, critical reflection. One way to achieve this is to incorporate phenomenology into the perspective of theology. Such a perspective implies neither that theology becomes immune to criticism "from without"—as I have said, I do not mean this "from without" in any absolute sense—nor that it is itself prevented from directing criticism toward phenomenology. Such a perspective could be called dialogical or mutually critical.[74] This does not mean that the usefulness that my theological study can find in phenomenology is confined to its critical function alone, but value may also be found in its constructive contributions. It can hardly be forbidden for theology to eavesdrop on phenomenology's deliberations in order to see which perspectives these present for theology in one context or another. This is not about managing one or another philosophical or theological tradition in a satisfactory way, but about how I will be able, in a critical, self-critical, and constructive way, to reflect theologically on incarnation, the gaze, and the body.

74. David Tracy, in *The Analogical Imagination: Christian Theology and the Culture of Pluralism* (London: SCM Press, 1981), has laid forth an ambitious and nuanced program for a "mutually critical correlation." Even if I have largely been inspired by Tracy's theological method, I still hesitate to adopt any of its, as I perceive it, tendencies towards a free-standing epistemological legitimation of the theological project. See my chapter "Teologi efter Babel," in *Karl Barth som den andre: En studie av den scenska teologins Barth-reception* (Stockholm/Stehag: Brutus Östlings Bokförlag Symposion, 1996), pp. 293–332, together as well with David Tracy's later article "The Return of God in Contemporary Theology," *On Naming the Present: Reflections on God, Hermeneutics, and Church* (Maryknoll, NY/London: Orbis/SCM, 1994), pp. 36–46.

Theology, Church, Doctrine

Theology, Critique, and Interpretation

My primary concern in this study is not historical, but systematic. The crucial aim of the individual investigations I will implement is to present a constructive theology of the body. It is thus important to say something here about what conception of theology I work with, and how this relates to hermeneutic phenomenology.

This study stems from an understanding of theology as a critical, self-critical, and constructive reflection on the Christian faith.[75] Accordingly, its starting point is in a concrete life-world—which may vaguely be defined as the Christian church—which can be understood as a kind of cultural and/or linguistic space or medium that shapes a person's life and thought. The North American theologian George A. Lindbeck, a prominent representative of the so-called Yale school, writes of religion as such a life-world:

> [I]t is similar to an idiom that makes possible the description of realities, the formulation of beliefs, and the experiencing of inner attitudes, feelings, and sentiments. Like a culture or language, it is a communal phenomenon that shapes the subjectivities of individuals rather than being primarily a manifestation of those subjectivities.[76]

The life-world precedes the self and its expression, and shapes the background against which the self interprets and acts in her world. Thus far, Lindbeck's conception of the life-world seems to resemble the phenomenological. But he also believes that in the case of Christian theology this life-world shows itself in the church, and thus the emphasis comes to be on the life-world in more of a sociology of knowledge than a transcendental-philosophical or hermeneutic sense.[77] However, my main points here do not

---

75. See Werner G. Jeanrond, "Att reflektera över Gud idag," *Svensk Teologisk Kvartalskrift* 71, no. 4 (1995): 171–76.

76. George A. Lindbeck, *The Nature of Doctrine: Religion and Theology in a Postliberal Age* (Philadelphia: Westminster Press, 1984), p. 33. For a presentation and critique of Lindbeck's model that nevertheless stands in its effect history, see Reinhard Hütter, *Theologie als kirchliche Praktik: Zur Verhältnisbestimmung von Kirche, Lehre und Theologie,* Beiträge zur evangelischen Theologie vol. 117 (Gütersloh: Chr. Kaiser/Gütersloher Verlagshaus, 1997), pp. 64–97.

77. Even within phenomenology there is, however, a development of the concept of the life-world towards a more pragmatic and so eventually a sociology of epistemology direc-

concern the conception of the life-world, but the starting point for theology, namely that this starting point is not God's self-revelation in some unmediated form (a problematic idea in itself), but that the object of theology is instead the human response to God's address, in words and deeds within the Christian church or within a Christian cultural sphere.

By relating to the Christian church as the life-world in which God's revelation in Jesus Christ has primarily made itself known, theology therefore presupposes, in a certain sense, what is called a *verbum externum* in the Lutheran Church, as a kind of horizon for the theological task. Theology is not self-shaping activity *(autopoiēsis)*, but a reflection on, and on the basis of, a life-world that is already given.[78] Theology could therefore be called a reflexive self-description within the framework of a religious tradition, and so would differentiate itself from the perspective of comparative religion, which occupies a detached position relative to its object of investigation.[79] On the basis of such an understanding of theology, however, one may ask whether theology itself is a religious practice, i.e., if it is a part of the life-world that it also describes. The scholar of comparative religion Gavin Flood takes up an often-used distinction between theology as a first-order discourse—i.e., the self-reflection of the Christian church *(fides quarens intellectum)*—and theology as a second-order discourse—i.e., academic reflection on the Christian church's self-reflection—which lies nearer comparative religion. This would mean that my own theological interpretation of incarnation, the gaze, and embodiment ought to belong to second-order discourse, in view of its academic context, its phenomenologically inspired method, and its critical posture. But while I do not want to equate church-based and academic theology, the distinction between first- and second-order discourse is too simple. As Flood himself points out, it would be a mistake not to realize how even comparative religion and second-order theology are anchored in

---

tion. See, for example, Alfred Schütz, *The Phenomenology of the Social World,* Northwestern University Studies in Phenomenology & Existential Philosophy, trans. George Walsh and Frederick Lehnert (Evanston, IL: Northwestern University Press, 1967).

78. My understanding of theology thus differs from the "constructive theology" that one finds with, for example, the American theologian Gordon Kaufman, which, I believe, proceeds unproblematically from the life-world of Western modernity. See Kenneth Nordgren, *God as a Problem and Possibility: A Critical Study of Gordon Kaufman's Thought toward a Spacious Theology* (Uppsala: Acta Universitatis Upsaliensis, 2003).

79. See Gavin Flood, *Beyond Phenomenology: Rethinking the Study of Religion* (London: Cassell, 1999), pp. 18–28, 225–26. I agree with much of what Flood argues with regard to the perspective on religious studies methodology, but am somewhat skeptical towards his interpretation of Husserl and phenomenology.

a particular life-world that has above all been characterized by the growth of critical methods and of the public repudiation of religion in and with the Enlightenment—but also, I would like to add, by a deep religious and Christian imprint.[80] Second-order discourse is thus not so much a metaperspective, as a perspective from a different life-world, or perhaps instead, from other parts or dimensions of the same life-world.

If theology, including academic theology, is assumed to have a mission that has to do with offering constructive proposals for how the relationship between God and humanity can be understood, and does not only have a critical-interpretive mission, then it indirectly becomes a part of, for example, the self-reflection of the Christian church. I would therefore argue that what is typical for the modus operandi of academic theology is that it consciously works at the intersection between two communities or (epistemological and sociological) life-worlds, that of the church and that of the academy, and thereby systematically presents itself for the critical examination that other disciplines offer—as it, in turn, examines those other sciences. Such an "intertextual" rather than "intratextual" theology additionally safeguards the insight that meaning, even theological and other scientific meaning, is produced "between" different texts and subject positions, rather than "within" them.[81] Meaning is irreducibly intertextual, and not even the historical church shaped its theology independently of the challenges entailed by its own period.[82]

This understanding of theology recalls the model that Flood argues for within the framework of comparative religion, namely, a reflexive, dialogical model that is conscious of its own limitations and attempts to relate critically to them.[83] That which is critical to the study of religion, according to Flood, and which concerns both comparative religion and theology, is therefore no longer so much the distinction between "insider" and "outsider"—between an "emic" and an "etic" perspective—but the distinction between

---

80. Flood, *Beyond Phenomenology*, p. 24. For a theological critique of the distinction between first- and second-order discourse, see Kathryn Tanner, *Theories of Culture: A New Agenda for Theology*, Guides to Theological Inquiry (Minneapolis: Fortress Press, 1997), pp. 72–79.

81. See Mary McClintock Fulkerson, *Changing the Subject: Women's Discourses and Feminist Theology* (Minneapolis: Fortress Press, 1994), p. 165.

82. See Nicholas Lash, *Change in Focus: A Study of Doctrinal Change and Continuity* (London: Sheed & Ward, 1981), p. 64. Cf. my critique of Lindbeck's intratextual theology in "Från intratextualitet till intertextualitet: Bortom Lindbecks postliberala teologi," *Svensk Teologisk Kvartalskrift* 72, no. 3 (1996): 126–35.

83. Flood, *Beyond Phenomenology*, pp. 39, 226.

critical and noncritical. The challenge for a theology that wants to be both critical and constructive is to show how a certain doctrine or idea may be interpreted anew in light of a critical understanding of its significance, and at the same time be understood as a creative development of the theological tradition (which is not nor ever has been unambiguous). In such an understanding, there is room for theology to be free both to come with proposals in a constructive way to further develop, for example, the understanding of God, and also to be a part of the critical self-examination of the Christian church vis-à-vis the *content* in this discourse about God. Academic theology, as I understand it, is not identical with church-based theology, but instead conducts what one might call a conjectural argument, i.e., its modus is the suggestion or the hypothesis, rather than the imperative assertion.

What does this understanding of theology mean for the phenomenological inspiration that I outlined in the previous section? To start with, this study of incarnation, the gaze, and embodiment will progress through the interpretation of texts. Many of the texts belong to what might be called the source material of theology: biblical texts, confessional texts, liturgies, texts written by theologians of the early church, Middle Ages, and modernity. Hermeneutic phenomenology introduces an angle of approach in the interpretation of such texts that makes it possible to relate to them in a way that both lets them be sources for the world of theological construction, i.e., the work of trying to produce a theology of the body for our time, and at the same time makes possible a critical attitude regarding the assumptions they make and the different ideological asymmetries they may carry. These texts, along with the secondary literature that has helped me in the interpretive work, will become dialogue partners on the way to a contemporary theological somatology, but will not because of that be granted an unequivocal authority.[84] In these texts, which thus constitute the primary source material for theology, we find different configurations of human experiences of the presence of God in Jesus Christ.[85] Conceived of as the study of human

---

84. My perspective here is close to that which Werner G. Jeanrond presents in *Text and Interpretation as Categories of Theological Thinking*, trans. Thomas J. Wilson (New York: Crossroad, 1988), and now most recently in "Teologen som tolk," in *Penelopes väv: För en filosofisk och teologisk patologi*, ed. Mats Rosengren and Ola Sigurdson, Logos/Pathos I (Göteborg: Glänta, 2003), pp. 59-82.

85. Which does not mean that it is possible to separate out the experiences from the configurations like a seed from its shell. *Fides qua creditur* and *fides quae creditur* go intimately together. I thus believe that there are merits to Lindbeck's critique of the "experiential-expressive" paradigm within theology. See George A. Lindbeck, *Nature of Doctrine*, p. 16. At the same time,

experience, phenomenology is therefore appropriate for examining how these texts express human relationality in all the dimensions that I study here—incarnation, the gaze, and embodiment.

But phenomenology is of assistance in other ways as well. I want to avoid hawking an objectified version of any of these three categories, as though they were objects that can be laid out for a person's critical gaze. If we take the incarnation as an example, i.e., the doctrine of God's becoming human in Jesus Christ, or more generally of God's relationship to the human world, we can ask ourselves which relationship the theologian can restore to this idea without his or her already deciding the question, so to speak, about the understanding of the incarnation through his or her theoretical position. In this study I am not thinking so much of the different expressions that this doctrine has been given throughout history, but more of the thing itself. Now if God has become human in Christ—and what this might mean remains to be seen—and if this is an event or action that is of unique importance for the whole of humanity, it is a question of the greatest weight how the theologian positions him or herself in relation to this course of events. It would for theological reasons hardly be possible to take an observer position apart from the course of events with the intention of objectifying them; the attitude that the Gospels enjoin is instead that of the witness (cf. Luke 1:1–4). The (from a religious perspective) meaningful relationship to the incarnation is, in other words, concurrently both affective and cognitive, and it thus becomes important for the theologian who wants to study the incarnation as a phenomenon to respect this order, and to avoid reducing the relationship between God and humanity to a more theoretically convenient cognitive relationship. But at the same time, the task of the academic theologian and the evangelical witness is hardly the same—for the theologian, as for his colleagues in philosophy and comparative religion, it is, as noted, important to be able to relate critically to the topic.

As with the incarnation, our experience of the body is more fundamental than our ability to represent it in an objectifying act. A theology of the body therefore cannot begin from some unmediated, obvious conception of the body, either through self-evident, authoritative, divinely inspired texts, or through a transcendental phenomenological investigation. Rather, such

---

this does not mean that the philosophical treatment of the concept of experience would thereby be unproductive for theology. Cf., for example, Hans Joas, "On the Articulation of Experience," in *Do We Need Religion? On the Experience of Self-Transcendence,* The Yale Cultural Sociology Series, trans. Alex Skinner (Boulder, CO: Paradigm Publishers, 2008), pp. 37–48.

a pursuit of a theology of the body must take a long detour via a critical interpretation of different historical religious texts and practices in order to thereby acquire material for a constructive theology of the body. These Christian texts and practices indicate different ways of being-in-the-world, and therefore entail, implicitly or explicitly, a particular way of imagining the Christian body. Neither theology nor philosophy gets at the body as theme and phenomenon in the human life-world other than through an interpretation of the pre-theoretical—if not pre-linguistic!—conceptions and experiences of the body that find expression in these texts and practices. The task for a theological interpretation of the body is neither to defend nor to destroy the conceptions that it examines, but instead, in a critical dialogue with them, to contribute to a reflective and constructive theology of the body.[86]

What phenomenology offers me in this study is the possibility of an approach that goes beyond that of both instrumental rationality and pure testimony. In opposition to a totalizing theoretical approach, whose consequence is that it deprives "the object" of its alterity, we may, with Levinas, strive for an ethically defensible form of knowledge, which respects the alterity of that which the knowledge deals with, and thereby relates self-critically to the pretensions and possibilities of (theological as well as philosophical) knowledge.[87] For this reason, the possibility of a critical attitude is not something that has unambiguously been imported into theology from without; among the biblical texts, the stories of the exodus from Egypt in the book of Exodus and the resurrection narratives in the Gospels appear as prototypes for an ideology-critical attitude.[88] In post-biblical times theology has been continually reminded that this God-discourse risks, if understood overly literally, lapsing into an objectification of God, and thus into idolatry.[89] But phenomenology, not least in its hermeneutic variant, attempts to establish this critical attitude at the same time that, as much as possible, it attempts to let the phenomenon itself speak. In the section on the gaze (chapters 4 to 7) it will hopefully become clear how our relationship to that which we behold also determines how it is able to appear for us. This is then illustrated in chapter 8 through a discussion of the philosophical body, and

---

86. Cf. Paul Ricoeur, "The Question of the Subject: The Challenge of Semiology," in *The Conflict of Interpretations*, pp. 262–66.

87. Levinas, *Totality and Infinity*, pp. 12f.

88. Ricoeur, "Hermeneutics and the Critique of Ideology," p. 306.

89. On phenomenology, theology, and idolatry, see Bruce Ellis Benson, *Graven Ideologies: Nietzsche, Derrida & Marion on Modern Idolatry* (Downers Grove, IL: InterVarsity Press, 2002).

how different philosophies have implied different possibilities for presenting and representing the body: as corpse or as alive. Incarnation, the gaze, and embodiment are three categories that all attempt to point to dimensions of human relationality (relationships to God, to the world, to other people, and to oneself). As such they require a method that attempts to thematize these relationalities, without reducing them to objects and thereby hiding the life-world that constitutes the basis for all critical methods.[90] I find such a method in phenomenology.

There is yet another reason, which I want to mention in conclusion here, that in this book I have chosen to work throughout with historical examples and expressions for that which I want to say on a more systematic and constructive level. As I have already pointed out in the introduction to this chapter, the body has a history, and this is also the case with the theological reflection surrounding embodiment. By taking a detour through history I want to avoid, to some degree, the illusion that systematic-theological work happens without context and regardless of the history of effect that precedes it as its intellectual horizon. One welcome side effect of this historical work would be succeeding, to some degree, in dispelling the view that the theological tradition constitutes a single monolithic history, which is then either the standard of theology or its opposite. "The Tradition" as such does not exist, at least not in any uniform sense. What we have are different traditions, and so we choose, to a certain extent, which parts of the tradition we want to set against other parts. We do not think independently of history or tradition, but we find ourselves, as my colleague philosopher Mats Rosengren puts it, "always and inevitably downstream in relation to the practices, formulations, thinking, and traditions of earlier generations."[91] These historical examples and expressions thus serve to clarify the logic that characterizes earlier ways of thinking, so that we can become more aware of both how our own thinking is shaped by history, and how it is *not* shaped by history.[92] So they are here for a reason, and I thus consider them an important part of my argumentation, even though—it is conceded—it thereby becomes more strenuous.

---

90. One might, like the German theologian Eberhard Jüngel, speak of a positive concept of mystery, to which belongs "that it does not cease being mystery when it has been grasped." Eberhard Jüngel, *God as the Mystery of the World: On the Foundation of the Theology of the Crucified One in the Dispute between Theism and Atheism,* trans. Darrell L. Guder (Edinburgh: T. & T. Clark, 1983), p. 250.

91. Mats Rosengren, "Den ohörda tanken, den slumpartade formuleringen och den ny-tänkta idén: Skäl att bry sig om filosofins historia," in *Penelopes väv,* p. 11.

92. Rosengren, "Den ohörda tanken," p. 24.

Theology, Doctrine, and Life

Phenomenology's concept of the life-world indicates an understanding that will be guiding for this study: that Christian theology does not—either in its classical shape or in its more contemporary form—aim to establish truths about God in a merely theoretical sense. "Doctrines," "dogmas"—which we will deal with to a large extent in the section on the incarnation (chapters 2 and 3)—and "theology" carry, in our time, an intellectualist ring that has not always been self-evident. For the sake of clarity, I will here plunge into a slightly longer digression, whose primary aims are to show how theology relates to its life-world basis, but also to show which understanding of doctrines and dogmas will be operational in the following chapters.

As a starting point that connects to the theme of this study, we can take what the medieval historian Sarah Beckwith writes regarding the medieval conception of the body of Christ, i.e., the medieval church's conception of itself as the body of Christ: "Christ's body was the arena where social identity was negotiated, where the relationship of self and society, subjectivity and social process found a point of contact and conflict."[93] For the medieval church, the body of Christ was central for the identity of individual people, as well as for the social order. The body of Christ became an organizing symbol for the Christian person's particular being-in-the-world. It constituted the point of intersection between personal subjectivity and the social system—in other words, the life-world of medieval existence. The body of Christ was quite simply a way for the medieval church to create and find meaning through the fact that this symbol implicated "a *social perspective or vision*," on the basis of which social relationships could be understood and organized.[94] As a symbol, the body of Christ is a part of a concrete culture. According to Beckwith, this gives a perspective on the conception of the body of Christ that is not found in the more idealistic history of theology, which deals with questions of, for example, the medieval theology of incarnation. Beckwith's own perspective is thus more a study of religious practices than a history of theology or spirituality.[95]

93. Beckwith, *Christ's Body*, p. 23.

94. Beckwith, *Christ's Body*, p. 2.

95. For a definition of concept of practice see Alasdair MacIntyre, *After Virtue: A Study in Moral Theory*, 2nd edition (London: Duckworth, 1985), p. 187. Cf. as well Charles Taylor, *Sources of the Self: The Making of Modern Identity* (Cambridge: Cambridge University Press, 1989), p. 204.

How this relates to the idealism of the history of theology I will leave unsaid, but what I want to argue in this study is that the reception of the doctrine of incarnation in concrete, social practices and symbols is a part of the history of effect of the incarnation, and that the reflection on these practices and symbols is thereby (seldom thematized as theology in our time) a part of the theological reflection surrounding the incarnation. If for a moment I refer to the early Christian idea of *lex orandi, lex credendi,* i.e., that the rule of prayer is the norm of faith, it clarifies that the contents of faith have their origin and their coherence in the liturgical context. Accordingly, the doctrine of incarnation has its origin, so to speak, in the liturgical vision of the body of Christ. The doctrine of incarnation considered as doctrine would thereby be a function of the worship of Christ as the Son of God in the mass, rather than the other way around. Purely concretely, however, it comes down to a reciprocal process: the rule of prayer does not only affect what one believes, but the norm of faith also sets a boundary for how one may pray.[96]

Another example that, in principle, involves the same thing is found in Martin Luther's text *On the Councils and the Church* from 1539, where Luther argues that the work of the Holy Spirit is tied to six specific church practices, through which the Christian person is made holy in the church: the holy word of God, the sacrament of baptism, the sacrament of the Eucharist, the office of keys (i.e., the discipline of the congregation), the offices of the church, and the possession of the holy cross (i.e., enduring misfortune and persecution following Christ).[97] These practices should not only be seen as a person's response to God's address, but are primarily constituted through the Holy Spirit, and accordingly precede a person's receiving of sanctification. The German theologian Reinhard Hütter comments on Luther's view in the following way: "The Holy Spirit creates the ecclesial body of Christ through certain forms that are outwardly comprehensible, and with the aid of this fulfills its salvific-economic mission."[98] The Spirit's making-present of Christ thus takes place, according to Luther, in definite, concrete, instituted contexts of action, and the Spirit should accordingly not be understood as a disembodied ghost. On the contrary, the work of the Spirit is embodied in these concrete practices where the reception of the person is combined with

---

96. Cf. Graham Hughes, *Worship as Meaning: A Liturgical Theology for Late Modernity,* Cambridge Studies in Christian Doctrine (Cambridge: Cambridge University Press, 2003), pp. 181, 226–27.

97. Martin Luther, *On the Councils and the Church,* in *Luther's Works,* vol. 41: *Church and Ministry III,* ed. Eric W. Gritsch (Philadelphia: Fortress Press, 1966), pp. 148–67.

98. Cf. Reinhard Hütter, *Theologie als kirchliche Praktik,* pp. 175–79. Here p. 178.

the initiative of the Spirit. Through these spiritual practices social identity is negotiated for the Christian who participates in them.

Although many critics have pointed out the risk of idealism in both historical and contemporary systematic theology, theology is not idealistic in this sense out of any inherent necessity. A large part of modern theology assumes a division between theory and experience, which appears in neither ancient and medieval theology, nor in contemporary feminist theology, liberation theology, or postmodern theology. According to theologian Mark A. McIntosh, who does not believe that such a division is universal, "the goal of theoretical reflection must be not only to articulate people's encounter with reality but also to assist people in 'living according' to that reality."[99] Beckwith also notes this particular trait, not in her own literary-critical reflection, but in ancient and medieval theology: "An incarnational aesthetic and practice was implicit in the very earliest stages of Christianity and Christian theology."[100] As I will discuss further below, "doctrine" and "life" were not separate, and it is thus an abstraction to separate the explicit doctrinal formulations from the practices in which they are embodied.

To extend this argument, we therefore also find in our own day the need for a theology that more clearly calls for the making concrete, or even the embodiment of those doctrines that can so easily be reduced to or understood as theoretical assertions. Such a theology does not only allow itself to be challenged by a critique of its idealism, but also allows itself to be reformulated in relation to different investigations of the concrete reception or social contextualization of different theological doctrines in our human life-world. In my attempt here to present a theological somatology, a part of the work will thus be an attempt to interpret the conception of the body that implicitly lies in some of the concrete practices that are or have been central for the Christian church, and that we saw illustrated above in Luther's enumeration.

The above is also essential in order that we may understand early Christian doctrinal culture, which will play a big role in my account. It did not take place against the background of our modern distinction between "theory" and "practice" or "doctrine" and "life." "Theology"—or the practice that corresponds to it—was not only a theoretical pursuit, but was a reflection that aimed to cultivate the spiritual as well as the moral and intellectual sides of the person. For the early church, "doctrine" was coaching in a way to live in

99. Mark A. McIntosh, *Mystical Theology: The Integrity of Spirituality and Theology*, Challenges in Contemporary Theology (Oxford: Blackwell, 1998), p. 26.
100. Beckwith, *Christ's Body*, p. 47.

a form of discipleship that covered both the active and the contemplative life, what one in Antiquity called *paideia*.[101] Heterodoxy was thus not seen as simply an intellectual, but a moral and spiritual problem. The doctrines were formulated as a guide so that believers would not deviate from what was considered the correct path. The intention was never to offer an exhaustive truth or to depict the divine as some static object that captured the truth. This applies to Origen as much as to Gregory of Nyssa, Eusebius of Caesarea, and Theodore of Mopsuestia. The symbol for the Christian faith was a spiritual journey or maturation, seldom a permanent and timeless anchorage.[102] Not even the classical Trinitarian and Christological doctrines should be seen as static phenomena, according to the British theologian and historian of dogma Frances M. Young:

> In the Trinitarian and Christological controversies the issue of identity, and therefore of substantial reality, became the subject of debate, and it was inevitable that ontological terminology should dominate the discussion. This may give a static 'feel' to much of patristic thinking, but this terminology was employed to identify the living subject(s) of God's *oikonomia*.[103]

The basis for the Christian doctrines was thus a course of events, or rather an action, namely the *oikonomia* of God. *Oikonomia* is a Greek word that has come to typically denote the art of housekeeping (cf. our term "economy"), but which in theological contexts comes to stand for God's action of creation and salvation, which are understood as a dynamic and historical activity. In a sense, the truth may be considered static, namely in that it actually precedes the person's own movement towards the divine. It is God that reveals God's own self, not the person who intellectually aspires to God.

---

101. See Frances M. Young, "*Paideia* and the Myth of Static Dogma," in *The Making and Remaking of Christian Doctrine: Essays in Honour of Maurice Wiles*, ed. Sarah Coakley and David A. Pailin (Oxford: Clarendon Press, 1993), p. 266. Such a meaning of *paideia* fits well with the use of the term that is given by *A Greek-English Lexicon*, ed. Henry George Liddell and Robert Scott, 9th edition, revised and expanded by Roderick McKenzie et al. (Oxford: Clarendon Press, 1976). Cf. as well Pierre Hadot, "Ancient Spiritual Exercises and 'Christian Philosophy,'" in *Philosophy as a Way of Life: Spiritual Exercises from Socrates to Foucault*, trans. Michael Chase (Oxford/Cambridge, MA: Blackwell, 1995), pp. 126–44, together with Basil Studer, *Schola Christiana: Die Theologie zwischen Nizäa und Chalcedon* (Paderborn/Munich/Vienna/Zürich: Ferdinand Schöningh, 1998).

102. Young, "*Paideia*," p. 278.

103. Young, "*Paideia*," p. 280.

God simultaneously adapts his *paideia* to the level that the human recipient is able to receive. So the aspect of dynamic growth is still left, since *paideia* is a process between God and person, and in this sense not something statically given. Theology was for the church fathers what philosophy was for the ancient philosophers, namely, a means of achieving wisdom, which did not simply mean the acquisition of knowledge, but also an existential engagement. The French philologist and philosopher Pierre Hadot writes of the philosophers of Antiquity: "Philosophy was a method of spiritual progress which demanded a radical conversion and transformation of the individual's way of being."[104] Classical philosophy also distinguishes itself from what we often call philosophy today, which is of significance for our understanding of the Christological debates and disputes that I will reproduce in the following chapters.

The fact that the patristic authors did not distinguish between doctrine and life also means that it would be wrong to generalize their reflection as a speculative interest with no significance for the Christian "spiritual journey." Just as with the biblical texts, there is no interest in detached speculation, but ontology and soteriology are instead tied together. Even the ancient Hellenistic philosophies would be better understood as "therapies," i.e., methods for teaching oneself to live in a way that leads to human flourishing.[105] When, for example, the theologians discussed the question of Christ's human and divine nature, it was thus not simply an expression of a theoretical interest, but was concerned with the question of salvation. The church father Irenaeus of Lyons's formulation from the second century is classic:

> For unless man had overcome the enemy of man, the enemy would not have been legitimately vanquished. And again: unless it had been God who had freely given salvation, we could never have possessed it securely. And unless man had been joined to God, he could never have become a partaker of incorruptibility. For it was incumbent upon the Mediator between God and men, by His relationship to both, to bring both to friendship and concord, and present man to God, while He revealed God to man.[106]

104. Pierre Hadot, "Philosophy as a Way of Life," in *Philosophy as a Way of Life,* p. 265.

105. See Martha C. Nussbaum, *The Therapy of Desire: Theory and Practice in Hellenistic Ethics* (Princeton: Princeton University Press, 1994).

106. Irenaeus, *Against Heresies,* in *Ante-Nicene Fathers,* vol. 1: *The Apostolic Fathers, Justin Martyr, Irenaeus,* ed. Alexander Roberts and James Donaldson, revised by A. Cleveland Coxe (Grand Rapids: Eerdmans, 1979), p. 448 (3, 18, 7).

This formulation is followed up by Gregory of Nazianzus two hundred years later, when he argues that "what has not been assumed has not been healed."[107] The church fathers do not differ here from the authors of the biblical texts: there is no interest in a "speculative theology" cut loose from the question of salvation. The debate over the doctrine of incarnation in patristic theology is, as I pointed out above apropos the impossible distinction between functional and ontological Christology, a way to deal with the soteriological errand.

That which sets the early Christian church's theological reflections apart from the theology one can find in the biblical texts has its basis in the fact that the Christian authors ever more pointedly had to interpret the revelation in Christ and his person for non-Christian philosophers and authorities, which could only happen against the background and with the help of Greek philosophy, and led to an active acquisition of a Hellenistic and Greek conceptual and representational world. One might say that an exchange of linguistic idiom gradually occurred. Although the church fathers—including the most philosophically inclined, like Origen—often presented their theology as biblical exegesis, and thereby maintained a link to the biblical terminology, the understanding of the terms used by the biblical authors was changed.[108] One example is the word *hypostasis,* which is found in Hebrews 1:3, but which would come to have a more technical meaning in later Trinitarian debates, debates that the author of Hebrews hardly meant to contribute to.

Another part of the activity of the earliest Christian theologians is what one might call a "process of dogmatization." "Dogma" is a word that has fallen into disrepute in modern times, since it has instead come to stand for a statement that bases itself on a groundless authority, which is impossible to bear out empirically, and which moreover suggests associations with a static metaphysics. The word occurs already in Acts 16:4, and is translated there in the English Standard Version as "decision" (*föreskrift,* "prescription," in the 2000 Edition of the Swedish Bible Society). The "decisions" to be followed primarily had to do with the question of whether circumcision was necessary for the non-Jewish members of the Christian congregation. However, in the ancient church "dogma" stands for more of a spiritual teaching about God

107. Gregory of Nazianzus, "Epistle 101," in *Nicene and Post-Nicene Fathers,* ser. 2, vol. 7: *S. Cyril of Jerusalem, S. Gregory Nazianzen* (Grand Rapids: Eerdmans, 1978), p. 440.

108. Even a medieval theologian like Thomas Aquinas in the 1200s, whom we now happily call a "philosopher," primarily worked as an expositor of the Bible, *magister in sacra pagina,* and let the philosophical task be subordinated to the theological. See Per-Erik Persson, *Sacra Doctrina: Reason and Revelation in Aquinas,* trans. Ross Mackenzie (Oxford: Blackwell, 1970).

with a life-oriented aim, grounded on a formal resolution.[109] The concept can also mean the entirety of Christian doctrine. It is usually articulated as though the first ecumenical councils—for example, Nicea in 325 and Chalcedon in 451, which will be discussed in the next chapter—have laid down what "correct doctrine" is. From the late 1700s on, however, a view of dogma as "authoritatively prescribed, revealed truths" made itself current within the Roman Catholic Church, according to German theologian Hans-Joachim Schulz. This view is influenced by a secularized rationalism, but has been projected back onto these early councils.[110] These councils did not have to do so much with "deciding" something about the Christian faith, or "defining" it, but rather with professing, making present, or actualizing the apostolic faith. For that reason Schulz believes that the formulations of the councils ought to be denoted as *kērygma* rather than *dogma*, i.e., testimony rather than decision. The concept *dogma* was used regarding decisions in questions of church discipline, but also in order to describe doctrinal opinions in those who deviated from the apostolic faith.

Even the doctrines as they were professed by the councils thus have to do with the mass-celebrating congregation, and aim at "pedagogy" rather than "speculation." Again, this does not mean that doctrine should replace liturgical, narrative, or argumentative language, or take precedence over them in any straightforward way. The confessions that were formulated by the councils wanted to be transparent for scripture and liturgy. Thus it was rather a question of regulating the more chaotic diversity in these expressions with the aid of principles that would try to find what one might call the "grammar" in these linguistic expressions.[111] Speaking of theological doctrines as regulative principles does not mean denying them ontological pretensions. These pretensions belong, however, to the Christian faith's substance as a whole, rather than as separate doctrines. With the aid of the

---

109. See Eilert Herms, "Dogma," *Religion in Geschichte und Gegenwart: Handwörterbuch für Theologie und Religionswissenschaft,* vol. 2, 4th edition, ed. Hans Dieter Betz, Don S. Browning, et al. (Tübingen: Mohr Siebeck, 1999), pp. 895–89.

110. Hans-Joachim Schulz, *Bekenntnis statt Dogma: Kriterien der Verbindlichkeit kirchlicher Lehre,* Quaestiones Disputatae 163 (Freiburg/Basel/Vienna: Herder, 1996), pp. 110–79.

111. See Rowan Williams, "Doctrinal Criticism: Some Questions," in *The Making and Remaking of Christian Doctrine,* p. 250, together as well with Ingolf U. Dalferth, *Jenseits von Mythos und Logos: Die christologische Transformation der Theologie,* Quaestiones Disputatae 142 (Freiburg/Basel/Vienna: Herder, 1993). According to Dalferth, through Christology Christian theology has attempted to maneuver between *mythos* and *logos*. With philosophy it has been critical of *mythos* and with religion critical of *logos*.

doctrines one attempted to define oneself vis-à-vis what were considered deviations from the apostolic testimony of the presence of God in Christ. When, for example, the Alexandrian priest Arius (see the next chapter) argued that Christ belonged to creation, this was understood as a questioning of the genuine character of salvation, because the question thereby arose whether the salvation Christ provided actually was the true salvation, anchored in the true God. Arius's position was rejected by the Council of Nicea as an expression of Christian faith that contravened what was considered to be apostolic teaching. The terms that were used at the dismissal of Arius—for example, the controversial term *homoousios,* "same essence"—were therefore intended to regulate the "parlance" and to avoid deviations, rather than to directly replace the diversity. One could say that Arius— whose theology was condemned at the Nicean Council—committed a "grammatical" error (if this concept is permitted to implicate consequences of moral as well as spiritual kinds), since his way of speaking about Christ was thought to compromise salvation and the understanding of the relationship between Creator and creation.

The doctrines through which the councils attempt to express the "grammar" in the Christian faith gradually come to be themselves included as a part of the expression of this faith, for example through assimilation into the mass as the baptismal confession. In addition, a doctrine such as, for example, *homoousios* will come to change how the biblical and liturgical testimony is understood after the doctrine has been formulated, and becomes an unavoidable—in the sense that one is afterwards forced to take a position regarding such doctrines—part of the Christian tradition. One might say that the regulative doctrines, in accordance with the logic of the supplement, carry a "speculative excess," which not only articulates that which is implicit in the primary expressions, but also regulates their future interpretation (interpretation not only as *explicatio* and *meditatio,* but also necessarily as *applicatio;* the act of interpretation here does not only cover understanding and exposition, but also use).[112] The dismissal of Arius thus did not only have to do with reading out even more clearly what has always implicitly existed in the biblical texts, but also with, in a creative and constructive understanding, "inventing" (in a weak sense) the genuine Christian tradition.

112. Cf. Jacques Derrida, *Of Grammatology,* corrected edition, trans. Gayatri Chakravorty Spivak (Baltimore/London: Johns Hopkins University Press, 1997), pp. 144ff., together with Hans-Georg Gadamer, *Truth and Method,* pp. 306f., and John Milbank, *Theology and Social Theory: Beyond Secular Reason* (Oxford: Blackwell, 1990), pp. 382–88.

The interpreting anew of Christian theology that I would like to see as a task for the academic theologian is thus nothing that in principle has not existed in traditional confessional theology, even if it is implemented in different intellectual, social, and cultural circumstances in our time than in the fourth century.[113] A part of my contribution to the interpreting anew of the Christian tradition, for example as regards the perspective on sexuality in chapter 10, is rather radical in relation to what is considered an accepted approach—other schemes typically attempt to further develop the potential in a particular doctrine, for example, the significance of the church for human embodiment in chapter 9, which has been lost in modern times. The Christian tradition is a tradition in motion, and thus always carries with it the potential to be changed. The theologian, even the critically working academic theologian, is *one* part of such a process of change, even if it will not be identified as church teaching in the above sense. The academic theologian, in the sense used here, does not, however, hesitate to assume that there are applicable tools to retrieve even outside the traditional domains of theology. In this theological interpretation of incarnation, the gaze, and embodiment, the course of which I will soon begin, I will accordingly make use, consciously and without constraints, of different theological and non-theological traditions in order to elucidate the question of current and potential statuses of the Christian body. First, however, a short presentation of the plan of the study.

The Plan of the Study

In one regard, the plan of my study is quite simple. I will present each of my three themes sequentially. First chapters 2 and 3 on incarnation, where, besides offering a deepening of the problem of incarnation as a prerequisite for later discussing embodiment, I also investigate the meaning in different doctrines of incarnation in a critical and constructive way, with the aim of contributing to a doctrine of incarnation for our time. Since it is neither practically possible nor especially worthwhile in this sort of theological study to examine all the variants of doctrines of incarnation that have occurred in the history of Christian theology, I will limit myself to discussing doctrines of incarnation and theologies of incarnation during three periods:

113. See Rowan Williams, "Postscript (Theological)," in *Arius: Heresy and Tradition*, 2nd edition (London: SCM Press, 2001), pp. 233–45.

the New Testament, the patristic (both in chapter 2), and the modern (in chapter 3). The focus for my investigation of the problem of incarnation will be how different conceptions of the incarnation thematize the humanity of Christ, and in which respect they attempt to preserve the genuine humanity of Christ. My conclusion will be that a doctrine of incarnation that does not take into consideration the anthropological implications of the human mode of being-in-the-world will remain abstract. One can thus say that these two chapters on the incarnation both prepare for and require the chapters on gaze and embodiment.

Then in chapters 4 through 7 I will discuss the gaze from various perspectives. To begin with, in chapter 4 I investigate how cultural and historical factors influence our way of seeing by presenting three different "scopic regimes" or "epochs of sight." Chapter 4 also attempts to offer a brief suggestion regarding how the relationship between the gaze and the surrounding world can be understood on the basis of the understanding of the human as an embodied being. After the more general discussion of sight and gaze, in chapter 5 I examine what the New Testament has to say about the gaze in connection with its understanding of Jesus of Nazareth, and in chapter 6 what sort of gaze different representations of Christ in visual pictures, especially within the theology of the icon, implicate. Chapter 7 then draws these different aspects of the gaze together in a theological formulation of the specific gaze of the Christian faith with respect to the question of God's incarnation in Jesus Christ. What does this "gaze of faith" mean for the understanding of the human embodied relationship to God?

Chapters 8 through 11 constitute the third and largest part of this investigation: here, the problem of human embodiment and the possibility of a theological somatology are treated. The first chapter of these four, chapter 8, aims both to present how the body as theme has returned in contemporary philosophical discussion in a distinct way and to give different perspectives on human embodiment, which then contribute to structuring the following three chapters on the Christian body. The aim is not to create a formal philosophical framework for the subsequent theological discussion, but, more humbly, to find some grounds for our theological discussion of the body. Chapter 9 is the most general of the three theological chapters on the body. Here, I attempt to show that even the Christian tradition's views of the body vary depending on a number of different social, economic, spiritual, and theological factors. But the aim of chapter 9 is not historical, but systematic-theological. The historical investigation brings to the fore questions that appertain to the dualism between body and soul and the Christian contempt for the body, the representation of the body, the constitution and structure of the body in liturgy, the relationship between the individual body and the social body, along with the continuity between the earthly body and the heavenly body, problems that I bring up in chapter 9 and deepen in chapters 10 and 11. These two chapters treat two different aspects of Christian embodiment: if chapter 10 focuses on the experience of the body as present through a critical survey of sexuality and embodiment, the theme for chapter 11 is instead the experience of the body as absent through an investigation of sacrament, suffering, and resurrection.

In chapter 12 I build further on insights from the previous chapter on Christian embodiment as the experience of a body that is characterized by both intimacy and alienation. However, for a more complete Christian somatology it is necessary to also say something about the eschatological *telos* of the body. We find the purpose of the individual body in Christian sociality. The final chapter thus not only recapitulates that said earlier, but also more clearly places Christian somatology within its eschatological horizon, and thereby shows how a theology of embodiment in a certain sense emphasizes the inaccessibility of the body.

Although the plan for this investigation is consequently simple, several of the themes that are taken up at certain points over the course of the study will also return at later occasions. This is clearest with regard to an erotic theology that is treated both on the basis of the gaze in chapter 7, and on the basis of the body in chapter 9, and above all in chapter 10, but this is also the case in chapters 7 and 9 with regard to the liturgical understanding of the gaze with respect to the body, as well as the grotesque body that becomes a theme in both chapters 9 and 11. In addition, the section on the theology of the icon in chapter 6 may also be understood as a continuation of the presentation on patristic Christology in chapter 2. Even if I have not been able (or wanted) to avoid these overlaps and cross-references, I have tried to avoid repeating myself too much. This means that an investigation of a theme, for example, the erotic body in chapter 10, requires that which is said in earlier chapters. Now that which is said later can cast more light on what is said earlier as well, and this dilemma may be said to characterize this whole study; what is said about the body could precede what is said about the incarnation, just as well as what is said about the gaze. Without claiming that a more elegant solution than what I have achieved here is impossible, I nevertheless want to suggest that such are the conditions of written presentations: something must come first, something in the middle, and something at the end. My possibly somewhat utopian hope—in view of the length of the book—is that the reader will find time to read it several times, and thereby see how the different parts relate reciprocally to, and perhaps also enrich, each other.

PART I

INCARNATION

2. Incarnation and Humanity

In this chapter I will examine the biblical and patristic conceptions of incarnation with respect to how they understand the humanity of Christ, as well as the sense in which they attempt to preserve the genuine humanity of Christ, i.e., the concrete, historical existence of humanity, inclusive of embodiment, as a constitutive feature of the human being. In other words, I will make use of a historical material that has been foundational for the traditional formulations of the doctrine of the incarnation. In both historical and contemporary Christological thought, Christology is about how one may understand the relationship between God and us humans in a way that neither makes it unfathomable how God can be present in the person Jesus, nor transforms Jesus into something other than a person. Even if the historical Christology that I will examine here emphasizes the divine pole of the relationship while modern Christology emphasizes the human pole, so long as the relationship itself does not disappear from sight it still falls within the same context of inquiry. I presume, therefore, that this more historically oriented chapter can be of constructive value for this study's primary aim of examining the anthropological implications of the doctrine of the incarnation for the human mode of being-in-the-world.

A retrospective reflection might easily convince us that historical theology provides clear definitions, while all our own period has to offer is a fragmented diversity. It is therefore important to establish that early Christian history also offers a diversity of different christologies. In the New Testament's twenty-seven different texts, which were, of course, compiled within the space of just over a hundred years, one finds no isolated, clearly defined Christology, or, for that matter, Christian theology.[1] Even

---

1. James D. G. Dunn, *Unity and Diversity in the New Testament: An Inquiry into the Character of Earliest Christianity* (London: SCM, 1977), pp. 216-31, 372-74. Cf. also James D. G. Dunn,

the patristic period, i.e., the early theological thought that was set in writing by the church fathers during the centuries that followed the writing of the biblical texts up until about the eighth century, proves to have a number of different context-dependent Christological formulations. At the same time, both of these periods have had a history of effect that broadly exceeds their contexts of origin. Here the Christological doctrines were developed in a way that has been normative for the Christian church up until our time, even if during the nineteenth century it was questioned whether these formulations can actually satisfy the needs of a theology relevant to the present day.

Apart from the fact that a basic knowledge of historical Christology is necessary in order to understand our contemporary christologies, including their critical repudiation of traditional Christology, one of the reasons that I choose to devote an entire chapter to the interpretation of the biblical and patristic christologies is that I want to avoid taking these as static and ahistorical formulations intended to offer rigid definitions of God's nature. An uncritical complacency sometimes lurks behind overly simple contrasts between history and our time. I additionally believe, as will become clearer in the next chapter, that these historical Christological formulations can be made theologically fruitful even in our time—provided we avoid turning them into something more or something other than what they were intended to be. This means, among other things, that it becomes impossible to attribute an absolute distinction or contrast between "representations" and "doctrine" to the biblical vis-à-vis the patristic material. The biblical texts are written about concrete problems in the early Christian church, and the same goes for patristic theology—including, in the case of Christology, the historically normative councils in Nicea in 325 and Chalcedon in 451.[2] The task

---

Christology in the Making: An Inquiry into the Origins of the Doctrine of the Incarnation, 2nd edition (London: SCM, 1989). A good and concise summary of the New Testament's Christology with a broader perspective than my study is given by René Kieffer, "Den mångfacetterade kristologin i Nya testamentet," in *Jesustolkningar i dag: Tio teologer om kristologi* (Stockholm: Verbum, 1995), pp. 55–87. The question of the historical Jesus is discussed by Bengt Holmberg, "Den historiske Jesus—nutida diskussionsläge och bedömning," in the same book, pp. 23–54, and the question of the continuity between the preaching Jesus and the preached Christ is discussed by Edvin Larsson, "Jesu uppståndelse och kristologins framväxt" in the same book, pp. 88–118. Here there are also references to additional literature within the areas that I do not bring into the discussion here, for example, the question of the "historical Jesus."

2. Aloys Grillmeier, *Jesus der Christus im Glauben der Kirche,* vol. I: *Von der apostolischen Zeit bis zum Konzil von Chalcedon (451),* 3rd improved and expanded edition (Freiburg: Herder, 1990), p. 131. Martin Luther's disciple Philipp Melanchthon certainly thought that Romans was

in this chapter is thus to interpret the biblical and patristic conceptions of incarnation in order to see to what extent their formulations offer resources or create problems for a contemporary Christology, and I will proceed more or less chronologically: from the Old Testament to the New Testament, and from the council in Nicea in 325 to the council in Chalcedon in 451. I end with a short conclusion concerning the result of the investigation's question thus far: What do the biblical and the patristic conceptions of incarnation tell us about the humanity of Christ?

God's Personified Wisdom: The Old Testament

In a general sense, an incarnational theology deals with the active presence of God in human history, and a discussion of Christian conceptions of incarnation thus begins appropriately in that part of the Bible that Christians call the Old Testament. That the New Testament authors appropriated interpretive keys from the Hebrew Bible for their interpretation of the figure of Jesus is undeniable, but does this cover the representation of the incarnation as well?[3] In general there are a number of ideas about how God is present with God's own people Israel in the Hebrew Bible. Through the Spirit God is already present in creation in its infancy (Gen. 1:2), and God continues to renew creation through the Spirit as well (Ps. 104:30). God's presence is not thematized here, however, via an abstract doctrine of the being of God, but is given form through more or less historical narratives, poetry, proverbs, prophecies—in other words, through texts written in reaction to concrete situations. This applies as well to other candidate concepts for incarnational theology, such as the conviction that God's presence is linked to the name of God (*yhwh;*

"a compendium in the Christian religion," but even Romans is now understood by biblical scholars as an "occasional text," not as a theological treatise. See Karl P. Donfried, "Introduction: The Nature and Scope of the Romans Debate," in *The Romans Debate,* ed. Karl P. Donfried (Minneapolis: Augsburg, 1977), pp. ix-xvii. This does not, however, exclude there being additional possibilities for interpreting New Testament writings apart from their use as historical documents.

3. On Jewish conceptions of incarnation, see Elliot R. Wolfson, "Judaism and Incarnation: The Imaginal Body of God," in *Christianity in Jewish Terms,* ed. Tikva Frymer-Kensky, David Novak, Peter Ochs, et al. (Boulder, CO/Oxford: Westview Press, 2000), pp. 239-54. Cf. also Jesper Svartvik, "Teologi på andra sidan Hippos stadsmurar," *Svensk Exegetisk Årsbok* 69 (2004): 51-70.

cf. Exod. 3:14), and is manifested in God's active and compassionate presence in the affairs of the world.[4]

More personified Old Testament representations of the presence of God that later Christian incarnational christologists have been able to connect to are on the one hand the idea of Wisdom as the ultimate ground of Creation, on the other the idea of Messiah as the ultimate design for history.[5] Regarding the representation of Wisdom as the ultimate ground of Creation, we must note that according to the Hebrew Bible's understanding, it is only God who is "from everlasting" (Ps. 93:2). At the same time, there is a conception of a Wisdom that is beside God and that in some sense exists in addition to God. Such a conception comes forth most clearly in Proverbs 8:22–31 (I quote vv. 22–26):

> The LORD possessed me [Wisdom] at the beginning of his work,
>   the first of his acts of old.
> Ages ago I was set up,
>   at the first, before the beginning of the earth.
> When there were no depths I was brought forth,
>   when there were no springs abounding with water.
> Before the mountains had been shaped,
>   before the hills, I was brought forth,
> before he had made the earth with its fields,
>   or the first of the dust of the world.

Here we find a representation of Wisdom as a personal, female figure who is separate from both God and the rest of Creation. There does not seem to be any doubt, however, that Wisdom is created by God, and thus not herself divine. We find a similar representation of a personified Wisdom in Job 28:24–28 as well, and a more far-reaching one in Sirach 24:1–22 (from the Apocrypha). The point of these representations is not to question monotheism, but rather to give a dynamic picture of God. Representations of preexistence were a way to cultivate confidence that creation really was of God, and therefore good, despite the afflictions that befell God's faithful. Given these tribulations, what in fact was the origin of creation? The answer

---

4. Cf. Tryggve N. D. Mettinger, *Namnet och närvaron: Gudsnamn och gudsbild i böckernas bok* (Örebro, Sweden: Libris, 1987), pp. 47, 192, as well as Abraham J. Heschel, *The Prophets: An Introduction*, vol. 1 (New York/Cambridge: Harper Torchbooks, 1969), p. 24.

5. Karl-Josef Kuschel, *Born before All Time? The Dispute over Christ's Origin*, trans. John Bowden (London: SCM, 1992), pp. 181–221.

in the theology of Wisdom was that Wisdom was created by God, and that in the end it was therefore possible to have hope in existence.

The other representation, Messiah as the ultimate design of history, had an existential origin as well, and involved a more clearly personal figure. The increasingly hopeless struggle for Jewish independence from Hellenistic influence during the second century BC posed the question of the significance of history. This situation was developed into a theology that focused precisely on the significance and end of history and time. It was imagined that God would intervene in order to turn the situation to the better through the arrival of a "Son of Man" from heaven—an idea that has been of great importance for the later Christian interpretation of Jesus. The Son of Man in the Hebrew Bible was thus no normal earthly Messiah of David's family, but a heavenly being. In the dream vision in Daniel (7:13ff.) we are told that "one who resembled a human came with the clouds of heaven" and was led forth before the throne of God and was given power over all of Creation. The psychological function of the idea of the preexistence of the Son of Man is a confidence that God has history under control, with the aim of enabling perseverance in the prevailing circumstances.[6]

There are of course no representations of incarnation in a Christological sense in the Hebrew Bible, as is self-evident, nor in the more general sense of God taking form in a concrete, embodied way in human history. One may possibly speak of an incarnational theology in the sense that I describe in the typology in the previous chapter, namely a theology of God's active presence in history independent of Christ. The interesting thing to note for my purpose, however, is that the origin of the representations I present above is existential rather than speculative. The German theologian Karl-Josef Kuschel writes:

[C]oncepts of pre-existence in Jewish thought are clearly of a quite unmetaphysical kind. They are not abstract reflections on the ontological being of pre-existent entities; rather, they are the expression of practical efforts to cope with existential questions about the primal ground of creation.[7]

Admittedly, these existential questions eventually come to require more ontological reflection as well, but in the biblical writings the rhetorical mode

---

6. Kuschel, *Born,* pp. 212–14.

7. Kuschel, *Born,* p. 198. Partial italics in the original.

itself does not focus on taking a position in a theoretical discussion. In the same way, after a time, the primary matter in the New Testament is to be able to speak about the active presence of God in human history in a way that gives ground for hope.

Christ as the Active Presence of God: The New Testament

Even when we come to the representations of incarnation in the New Testament, it is important to construct a picture of what sort of material we are dealing with and what we can expect to find.[8] The New Testament is not made up of systematic theological treatises any more than the Old. Instead, we find narratives, hymns, and exhortations where the formulas of significance for incarnational ideas may be found in a subordinate clause without any further explanation. A number of different Christological themes and titles occur in the New Testament without any attempt to analyze how they relate to each other—so in the New Testament as well we can instead expect to find attempts to pragmatically master existential questions. In this section I will focus on two passages that have been crucial for the incarnational-Christological discussion, one early (the hymn in Phil. 2:6-11) and one late (the prologue to the Gospel of John). After that I will discuss the incarnational-Christological point of the narrative character of the Gospels. Then I will end by drawing some general conclusions based on the New Testament Christology.

Christ as Adam and the Word

When the different texts of the New Testament formulate their understanding of Christ, they do it, among other ways, through a number of different titles: "Son of David," "Servant of God," "Prophet," "Messiah," "Son of God," "Son of Man," "the last Adam," "Spirit of God," "Angel of God," "Wisdom of God," or "Word of God." The difficulty for the modern reader is that she or he

8. For varying approaches, in addition to the books of James D. G. Dunn mentioned above, see also Oscar Cullmann, *The Christology of the New Testament,* trans. Shirley C. Guthrie and Charles A. M. Hall (London: SCM, 1963); I. Howard Marshall, *The Origins of New Testament Christology* (Downers Grove, IL: InterVarsity Press, 1976); Eduard Schweizer, *Jesus Christus im vielfältigen Zeugnis des Neuen Testaments* (Munich/Hamburg: Siebenstern Taschenbuch Verlag, 1968).

does not have the same theological, religious, or historical associations that were expected in the original addressees of the different texts. In addition, several of these titles have had a long history of effect over the course of theological history, so that they have gradually assumed new and expanded meanings. In this section I will focus on two biblical texts where two different titles become current, with the aim of, to some degree, shaking loose our understanding of these texts from our immediate horizon of expectation within the history of theology.

One of the earliest Christological testimonies, and a candidate for an incarnational Christology, is the hymn in Paul's letter to Philippi (2:6–11):

> ... who [Christ], though he was in the form of God, did not count equality with God a thing to be grasped, but made himself nothing, taking the form of a servant, being born in the likeness of men. And being found in human form, he humbled himself by becoming obedient to the point of death, even death on a cross. Therefore God has highly exalted him and bestowed on him the name that is above every name, so that at the name of Jesus every knee should bow, in heaven and on earth and under the earth, and every tongue confess that Jesus Christ is Lord, to the glory of God the Father.

This hymn is generally considered to be pre-Pauline in origin, and also to constitute an independent literary unit that Paul inserted into his letter. There are some Christologically interesting statements here, such as that Christ "possessed the form of God" and was "equal with God," that seem to indicate a rather "high" Christology. According to a traditional Christian interpretation, the hymn is about how Christ comes from God (step 1) to the human world (step 2) in order to then return to God (step 3). This is usually called a three-step Christology. In modern times it has been objected that this is a mystical understanding of the incarnation. For example, in an opinion that developed into a school within twentieth-century exegetics, the German exegete Rudolf Bultmann suggested that in the Philippians hymn we find an example of a Hellenistic-Gnostic representation of a preexisting cosmic savior-figure, who comes down from heaven and assumes human form, a representation far from the earthly Jesus and from the Jewish conceptual world.[9] Bultmann suggests that the Gnostic concept is used to clarify the

---

9. Rudolf Bultmann, *Theology of the New Testament,* vol. 1, trans. Kendrick Grobel (London: SCM, 1988), p. 175.

Christian history of salvation, but at the same time involves a mythological exposition of the existential testimony, which must therefore be demythologized in order to be understandable in our time.

Bultmann's understanding of Gnosticism, as well as his interpretation of this text, has been strongly questioned.[10] The issue is whether the Philippians hymn has anything to do with a preexistent heavenly being. One alternative is that it is an example of an understanding of Christ as the "last Adam" (Hebrew *'ādām* means "human").[11] The Philippians hymn would thus have its origin in a more Jewish context than what Bultmann believed. The central emphasis in the Adam-Christology is eschatological: Christ as the last Adam is the eschatological human. A classic text for the interpretation of Christ as the last Adam is Romans 5:12–21. When the first Adam ate of the fruit in Genesis 3 and thereby defied the will of God, he lost his status as the image of God, which the Christian interpretation of the text attributes to him. The last Adam, on the other hand, obeys the will of God, according to Paul in Romans, and voluntarily chooses the road that the first Adam received as a punishment. Because the last Adam chooses that which the first Adam did not choose, he can also be given the dignity, the elevation that was God's original intention for humanity. The last Adam is the one that undoes Adam's sin. Unlike the more traditional three-step interpretation of the Philippians hymn (preexistence, earthly life, elevation), we have here, with the aid of Romans, an interpretation of the Philippians hymn as a two-step Christology, going from Christ's human existence (step 1) to the elevation (step 2). The formulations that have been interpreted as indications of an incarnational Christology are not actually about preexistence or the like, but are instead about an archetypal human choice. The text is thus not immediately relevant for a traditional conception of the incarnation, as that is not what it is about.

This interpretation has been questioned as well, but even those in our time who find a more far-reaching representation of incarnation in the hymn have stressed that this cannot be taken as a justification for projecting the incarnational representations of later times onto the text.[12] In other words, one cannot infer any detailed descriptions of the essence of the incarnation. The purpose of the hymn is not speculative, but rather existential.[13] It is the path, not the condition, that the hymn focuses on. The point is that

10. Cf. Kuschel, *Born,* pp. 245–50.

11. Dunn, *Christology in the Making,* pp. 114–21.

12. Cf. Kuschel, *Born,* pp. 252–53; John Macquarrie, *Jesus Christ in Modern Thought* (London/Philadelphia: SCM/Trinity Press International, 1990), pp. 58–59.

13. Grillmeier, *Jesus der Christus,* p. 87.

humanity would be given this elevation by God, not that we would grab it for ourselves. Through Christ, the human can once more become that which was her original role, and so understand God's purpose in Creation. Going from Paul's use of the Philippians hymn—and also from the representations of the cosmic Christ in the hymn in Colossians 1:15–20[14]—it is possible to describe God's presence in Christ as unique, since God has taken a special initiative in him for the salvation of humanity. But on the other hand there are no accounts of how Paul imagines the relationship between God and Christ at an ontological level. Paul's letters and the other Pauline writings thus keep themselves to a Christology that must be characterized as primarily existential. Irrespective of whether the exegetes tarry for an interpretation of Philippians in terms of the last Adam or not, such an exegesis nevertheless reminds us of the existential concern of the hymn.

We find a later candidate for an incarnational Christology, as well as the clearest and most high-Christological representation of incarnation in the New Testament, in the prologue to the Gospel of John. This (most likely) youngest of the New Testament writings thus offers, unsurprisingly, the most developed Christology. The prologue also constitutes a sort of hymn.[15] I quote verses 1–5, 9–14, 16–18 in sequence:

> [1]In the beginning was the Word *[logos]*, and the Word was with God, and the Word was God.
> [2]He was in the beginning with God.
> [3]All things were made through him, and without him was not any thing made that was made.
> [4]In him was life, and the life was the light of men.
> [5]The light shines in the darkness, and the darkness has not overcome it.
>
> [9]The true light, which enlightens everyone, was coming into the world *[ton kosmon]*.
> [10]He was in the world, and the world was made through him, yet the world did not know him.
> [11]He came to his own, and his own people did not receive him.

---

14. Colossians is possibly not written by Paul himself. See Eduard Schweizer, *Der Briefe an de Kolosser und an Philemon*, Kritisch-Exegetischer Kommentar über das Neue Testament vol. IX/2, 2nd edition (Göttingen: Vandenhoeck & Ruprecht, 1977), pp. 249ff.

15. See Raymond E. Brown, *The Gospel according to John: I–XII*, vol. 1 (London: Geoffrey Chapman, 1971), pp. 20–21.

¹²But to all who did receive him, who believed in his name, he gave the
   right to become children of God,
¹³who were born, not of blood nor of the will of the flesh nor of the will
   of man, but of God.
¹⁴And the Word became flesh [sarx] and dwelt among us, and we have
   seen his glory, glory as of the only Son [monogenous] from the
   Father, full of grace and truth.

¹⁶For from his fullness we have all received, grace upon grace.
¹⁷For the law was given through Moses; grace and truth came through
   Jesus Christ.
¹⁸No one has ever seen God; the only God [monogenēs theos], who is at
   the Father's side, he has made him known.

Here it seems to be clear that Christ is identified with God. Before the creation of the world, the Word existed (v. 2), the Word took its abode among
the people (vv. 9–11), and the Word, the only Son, showed the Father to the
people by virtue of being God (vv. 1, 14, and 18). With this *logos*-Christology
as well there is a relevant background in the representation of Wisdom in the
Hebrew Bible and in the apocryphal writings.[16] But representations of the
Word of God in the Hebrew Bible also constitute a significant background
to the prologue. The Word of God is understood there as God's action, a
personification of God's acting in Creation, and therefore not as something
that is separate from God. We find an example of this in Psalm 33:6: "By the
word of the LORD the heavens were made,/and by the breath of his mouth
all their host."

There are at least two things that seem to be beyond discussion. Firstly,
that this involves a *logos* that exists before the Creation in the prologue. The
Word, *logos,* existed in the beginning; it did not come to be—and "was" in
verse 2 is a translation of the verb *ēn,* which is in the imperfect, indicating
an event in the past with lasting significance. Thus the Word does not belong to the created, but everything created came to be through it. Secondly,
the Word became flesh (translated literally, but meaning "became human").
"Became" in verse 14 is a translation of *egeneto,* which is an aorist, indicating
a completed event in the past. This means that the prologue does not claim

16. Rather than Gnostic savior myths. See Bultmann, *Theology,* vol. 1, pp. 166–67; Bultmann, *Theology of the New Testament,* vol. 2, trans. Kendrick Grobel (London: SCM, 1983),
pp. 12–14.

that the Word took form in just some phantom body.[17] So it is not simply that God is present in a special way in Christ, but that Christ, in the sense of the Word, existed before everything, and that the preexistent and divine Word become human.[18] Verse 14 marks the transition from preexistence to incarnation, but also the transition from an impersonal personification to an actual person.[19] When the Word becomes human it is no longer a matter of the personification of the Word, but of the Word becoming an actual person.[20] In verse 18—which probably belongs to the Gospel of John's redaction of the prologue rather than to the original—it appears that this concrete person is the one who constitutes the connecting link between human and God, in that he "shows" *(exēgēsato)* God to us humans. This concrete person is none other than Jesus of Nazareth. John combines the idea of *logos* with the idea of the Son of God, sent by God in a way that combines the more impersonal representations of the Wisdom of God with the more personal representations of the Son of God. While this was scarcely acceptable for the Jews of the time, it would have consequences for later Christian representations of God.[21] The Word is not presented as *ho theos,* but as *theos,* and among other things it is through this distinction that the later Trinitarian distinction between the Father and the Son would be developed, since the Son could not be understood as a manifestation of an only God, but must be comprehended according to some form of intra-divine distinction.[22]

It is significant that the Gospel of John, despite its emphasis on the preexistence of the Word and its manifestation of the glory of God through human form, without a doubt retains a focus on Jesus of Nazareth as a concrete, historical, and embodied person.[23] Bultmann writes: "[J]esus' life on earth does not become an item of the historical past, but constantly remains present reality."[24] John's prologue and the Gospel of John can therefore hardly be identified with Gnostic or Docetic ideas, even if it makes use of such

17. Brown, *Gospel,* p. 31.

18. Dunn, *Christology in the Making,* p. 241.

19. Dunn, *Christology in the Making,* p. 243.

20. According to Dunn (*Christology in the Making,* p. 244) this concerns the prologue's original hypothetical wording (about as I have quoted it). From its place in the Gospel of John it appears that even in the earlier verses it was a matter of the incarnate and concretely personal Word, as well as through those verses that I have left out (vv. 6–8, 15). See also Raymond E. Brown's appendix on "the word" in *Gospel,* pp. 519–24.

21. See Kuschel, *Born,* pp. 372–74.

22. Cf. Brown, *Gospel,* p. 5.

23. Kuschel, *Born,* pp. 379–80.

24. Bultmann, *Theology,* vol. 2, p. 49.

representations, as for example in the dualism between darkness and light in verse 5. In 1 John 4:2–3 we find a clear polemic against Gnostic or Docetic tendencies: "every spirit that confesses that Jesus Christ has come in the flesh *[en sarki]* is from God, and every spirit that does not confess Jesus is not from God." Even if it is not necessarily the same author for both the epistle and the Gospel, the parallels are sufficient to illustrate that the Gospel does not abandon the concrete or the embodied.

Now this does not have to mean that we identify the historical person with the preexistent Word, as though the human Jesus had existed for all eternity. It is not until verse 10 that we may meaningfully speak of an incarnation.[25] In verse 14 the Word is identified with a concrete person, and this person's name is first mentioned in verse 17, namely Jesus Christ. In other words, it does not seem as though John's prologue claims that the preexistent Word *is* Jesus of Nazareth throughout eternity, but that the preexistent Word *becomes* Jesus.[26] The difference between the preexistent Word and the earthly Jesus emphasizes that the Gospel of John is not interested in abstract speculation over the relationship between *theos* and *logos* either.[27] The point of the prologue's discourse on the Word's becoming human in Jesus Christ is the affirmation and perfection of creation and creature.[28] One might say that John's prologue wants to speak about something nonmythological with moderately mythological means. It is not preexistence that is interesting for the Gospel of John, but God's initiative in the sending of the Son, who will reveal God to the people.[29] With this explanation of the eternal significance of Jesus of Nazareth, the Gospel of John wants to say that the salvation that the Christian experiences in her present is a salvation from the God who created everything. Jesus Christ is God's presence in the world.[30] In this way John's prologue keeps creation and salvation together. But in order to be able to speak about something that is indescribable—cf. verse 18—John's prologue must make use of those means that are available. John's prologue

25. Kuschel, *Born,* pp. 381–82.

26. Leonhard Goppelt, *Theology of the New Testament,* vol. 2: *The Variety and Unity of the Apostolic Witness to Christ,* trans. John Alsup (Grand Rapids: Eerdmans, 1982), p. 297; Karl-Josef Kuschel, *Born,* p. 382.

27. Kuschel polemicizes exegetically here against Karl Barth's dismissal of all talk of *logos asarkos,* i.e., the discussion of a not (yet) become human word, which Kuschel perceives as speculation and as a threat to the emphasis on Christ's true humanity.

28. Kuschel, *Born,* pp. 388–89.

29. Brown, *Gospel,* p. 24.

30. Cf. Brown, *Gospel,* p. 33.

and the rest of the Gospel of John thus make use of earlier representations of the Wisdom of God, the Word of God, and the Son of God in order to say that that which these representations had spoken of has become reality in Jesus of Nazareth.

In both the Philippians hymn and the prologue to the Gospel of John we find that these more or less clear representations of incarnation stand in the service of the existential problem. This does not mean that every form of ontological discussion based on these texts ought to be prohibited, or that later Christological doctrinal education must thereby be considered a corruption of the original message. Instead, I want to suggest that this can be taken as a common effort in the otherwise manifold New Testament material to hold theology and anthropology together in Christology. God and human, human and God, are not thematized individually, but—in Christology—together. There is thus no "abstract" doctrine of God or human in the New Testament, so far as I have investigated.

Incarnation and Narration

In order to approach the New Testament's representations of incarnation, however, it is not enough to give a few examples of hymns and the Christological titles they present. A major portion of the New Testament is made up of narratives about Jesus, namely the four Gospels. The three Synoptic Gospels Matthew, Mark, and Luke—synoptic because they have such a thoroughly common vision—differ from the epistles, and even partially from the Gospel of John, not because they are eyewitness accounts, but because they are structured as narrative.[31] This potentially complicates things if one is interested in representations of the incarnation in the New Testament: How does one talk about the incarnation? Could it be that an incarnational Christology presumes a level of reflection that is not seen in the narrative foundation of the Synoptic Gospels, without which it acquires a crudely mystical appearance? Whatever the incarnation may be imagined to be, it is not a question of one event among others in the life of Jesus. Only that which is lucid and which may be experienced concretely

---

31. A bit about the prehistory of the Gospels may be found in Birger Gerhardsson, *The Origins of the Gospel Traditions* (London: SCM, 1979), together with Rainer Riesner, *Jesus als Lehrer: Eine Untersuchung zum Ursprung der Evangelien-überlieferung*, 3rd expanded edition (Tübingen: J. C. B. Mohr [Paul Siebeck], 1988).

can be directly reproduced in a narrative—other things must be hinted at through various indirect rhetorical means. "Incarnation" is a reflection on the significance of a particular, unique narrative, rather than an element within this narrative.

These Christological titles become more concrete as they are presented in relation to the life history of Jesus. In the Gospel of Mark, generally considered to be the earliest written Gospel, Jesus is already designated in the preamble as the "Son of God" (1:1): "The beginning of the gospel of Jesus Christ, the Son of God." This title occurs often in the Gospel of Mark. At the baptism in the river Jordan (1:11) God calls Jesus "my beloved Son," and at the metamorphoses on the mount of Transfiguration God's voice is heard from the cloud (9:7): "This is my beloved Son; listen to him." The first time the name is used by Jesus about himself is when, imprisoned, he is interrogated by the high priest before the council (14:61ff.). The title is even put in the mouth of a pagan officer when he beholds the dying Jesus on the cross (15:39). Altogether Mark uses the title eight times (cf. 3:11; 5:7; and 12:6 as well), and in the central points of his narrative, which implies that it is a central title in Mark's Christology. One might say that for Mark, Christ is the suffering Son of God, the one who is recognized precisely in the death on the cross as the Son of God.[32] Rather than using the expression "Son of God" to guide our thoughts to a preexisting heavenly being, Mark wants us to think of the concrete passion narrative of Jesus. In the Synoptic Gospels, we can thus note an effort to tell about Jesus as a physical and historical person.

It may be the case that the narrative structure actually functions as a guard against excessively timeless speculations on the incarnation. The Gospels would have reminded the Christian church that God's dealings (with us humans) must in some sense be thought of as a story, rather than as a condition that can be caught in a doctrinal definition. So there is, for example, no generally accepted or defined doctrine of atonement within the churches, as with the definitions of the doctrine of the Trinity or the incarnation that different councils have suggested.[33] The exegete Ulrich Luz writes the following on the Gospel of Matthew, which can apply to all three of the Synoptic Gospels:

32. See Joachim Gnilka, *Das Evangelium nach Markus: Mk 1–8,26,* vol. 1, Evangelisch-Katolischer Kommentar zum Neuen Testament vol. II/1, ed. Josef Blank, Rudolf Schnackenburg, et al., 3rd revised edition (Zürich/Braunschweig/Neukirchen-Vluyn: Benziger Verlag/Neukirchener Verlag, 1989), pp. 60–64, together with Dunn, *Unity and Diversity,* pp. 46–48.

33. Gösta Hallonsten, "Är Jesus frälsare? Skiftande frälsningsuppfattningar och Jesus som konstant i teologin," *Svensk Teologisk Kvartalskrift* 77 (2001): 107–17.

It has fundamental significance that Christological statements are *narrated* as history. The reader learns that the deed of God who acts in the history of Jesus and whose actions the narrative of Matthew pursues is the foundation of any explicative Christianity.[34]

A common feature in the Synoptic Gospels is thus that they very clearly tell of an actual and concrete earthly life. It is not a question of a mystical heavenly figure visiting the earth. The passion narrative of Jesus' suffering on the cross constitutes a major portion of the scope of these three Gospels. In the Gospel of Luke Jesus is born in a stable (2:1–21), and in all three Gospels he dies on a cross. On the whole it is the narrative of a concrete, physically existing person that characterizes all three Gospels. The philosopher Luce Irigaray counts up the moments in the bodily history of Jesus as described by the Gospels:

> conception, birth, growth, fasting in the desert, immersion in the River Jordan, treks to the mountain or walks along the water's edge, meals, festivals, the laying-on of hands, the draining of physical strength after a healing, transfiguration, trials, suffering, death, resurrection, ascension . . .[35]

The emphasis on concrete embodiment in the Synoptic Gospels may be seen as a reaction against a Christology that tended to overemphasize the heavenly Christ at the expense of the earthly.[36] Even the resurrection in the three synoptics and the ascension to heaven as it is told in the Gospel of Luke (24:51) are described as bodily events. So the concrete character of, first and foremost, the Synoptic Gospels has also been used in modern times as an argument against an overemphasis on the doctrinal definitions, as, for example, with the Swiss theologian Karl Barth, which I will address in the next chapter.

The New Testament and the Incarnation

As I summarize the results of this investigation of the New Testament's conceptions of incarnation, I want to begin by stressing that there is a continuity

34. Ulrich Luz, *Matthew 1–7: A Commentary,* trans. Wilhelm C. Linss (Minneapolis: Augsburg, 1989), p. 100.

35. Luce Irigaray, "Equal to Whom?," in *The Postmodern God: A Theological Reader,* ed. Graham Ward (Oxford: Blackwell, 1997), p. 203.

36. Kuschel, *Born,* pp. 323–26.

with earlier Jewish conceptions of the active presence of God. In part, this continuity has to do with the connection to the Jewish conceptions of Wisdom, where Christians found a parallel to conceptions of Christ's unique presence with God. It also has to do with the fact that the purpose of these conceptions of incarnation was existential rather than speculative, a feature that pertains as well to the rhetorical mode itself of hymns and narratives. This is not to say that the more speculative-sounding expositions on the incarnation in later periods are improper, but only to point out the risk in reading these into the New Testament texts and so making them less dynamic and ambiguous than they actually are. An interest in ontology ought to be obvious for a theology that desires to keep creation and salvation together. Even if the focus is on the question of what the salvation that God has accomplished in Christ means for humanity, this does not mean that we cannot ask who Christ must be in order to do what he does. That said, the point I want to make on the basis of the biblical texts is that the absence of an independent speculative interest in these texts should tell us something about what is primary for even a more ontologically focused philosophy or theology.

Yet another common feature in the New Testament conceptions of incarnation is that the biblical texts, however willing they may be to attribute a cosmic significance to Christ, do not lose their connection to the earthly Jesus from Nazareth and the cross. All the texts I have discussed here seem to want to emphasize the human Jesus as the person where God makes God's own self present in a unique way for the sake of humanity. Even if Gnostic or Docetic features have found their way into the New Testament texts, and Christ is sometimes represented in a way that makes his genuine humanity less clear, the texts never leave the ground, so to speak, and lose contact with the earthly Jesus. Not even in the Gospel of John, which represents the most high-Christological expression in the New Testament writings, is Jesus of Nazareth, despite being understood as identical with the divine Word, anything other than a genuine human being. In summary, I would like to suggest that the language of incarnation in the New Testament is not about how Christ is or becomes something other than human, but is instead about a special intensifying of the humanity that Christ shares with all other people.[37]

These two features, the existential concern and the emphasis on the humanity of Jesus, will serve as guides for my continued investigation of the

37. Thanks to Jesper Svartvik for help with formulating this insight.

incarnation in the oldest theology of the church after the New Testament writings. Does this mean that, on being incorporated into a more unambiguously Hellenistic cultural sphere, the existential concern and the emphasis on Jesus' humanity are left to their doom, or is there a continued interest in keeping together that which the New Testament keeps together? In other words, what did the doctrinal formulations and the extra-biblical conceptual language mean for the understanding of the incarnation?

The Incarnation and Christian Monotheism: Nicea 325

In order to understand Christian doctrinal formation, it is extremely critical that we realize that this also has a history with a variety of conceptions. There was no cut-and-dried incarnational Christology to take from the biblical writings, but the different formulations of the incarnational doctrines constantly occur—and still occur—in relationship to the concrete existential and intellectual problems that arise in different cultural and historical situations. Although it could be said that the church councils, especially Nicea and Chalcedon, constitute a sort of crystallization point for doctrinal development, where certain effective formulations of the doctrine of incarnation were made normative for major portions of the Christian church, this does not mean either that the reception of these decisions was instantaneous and universal, or that the import of these decisions was self-evident. This last is shown in particular by the history of the council decisions, which in fact exhibits an intensive debate over what was meant by the formulations that the councils offered.

In this discussion of the early church's doctrinal reflections on the presence of God in Christ I am guided above all by two questions. Firstly, whether the Hellenization of the early Christian message meant that the existential concern was displaced by a more speculative interest. As I pointed out in the introduction to this chapter, a gradual change of genre and idiom takes place when it comes to the formulations of the incarnation, from a more poetic and narrative language to a doctrinal one—though we should not refine or exaggerate this distinction. In my introductory chapter I argued that there is *not* any necessary opposition between life and doctrine, but that there is in fact a connection between the two. But the question is whether it is possible to clarify whether or not early Christological thought involved an interest in Christ's divine nature as abstracted from a concrete human life-world. In light of this overall question, it becomes interesting as well to reflect on the relationship between the biblical testimony and the Christological doctrinal formation—does the latter replace the former, or should it instead be understood as a supplement of the former?

Secondly, I also want to pose the question of how the different theologians and theologies represented themselves in the relationship between the divine and the human. How did ancient Christological thought want to preserve the human, the concrete, and the embodied? Does the emphasis by the different christologies on the divinity of Christ mean that the human succumbs in the divine (the risk that the reverse would happen is more of a modern problem), or did they find a way to speak of God's presence in Christ that managed to also take the genuine humanity of Christ seriously? There are two church councils that have been of the greatest importance for the continued theological reflection on the incarnation, namely Nicea in 325 and Chalcedon in 451. In this section I will outline the developments that led to the council in Nicea, starting from my two guiding questions, and then in the next section I will do the same with a focus on theological thought up to and including the council in Chalcedon.[38]

Historical or Cosmological Salvation?

From the very start we find writings that formulate Christological thoughts in dialogue and in conflict with Judaism. Examples of this are the canonical Gospel of John, as well as *Didache, The Odes of Solomon, The Epistle of Barnabas,* and *The Shepherd of Hermas.* These Jewish-Christian writings agree with a rather functional Christology (the ontological question became more acute in dialogue with Hellenism). The difference between the early, Jewish-influenced, Christian understanding of salvation and the later Hellenistically influenced understanding was that, relatively speaking, salvation was considered ever less historically and ever more cosmologically, morally, and indi-

---

38. My account in this and the next section is based, apart from individual monographs and foundational texts, on the following handbooks: Aloys Grillmeier, *Jesus der Christus im Glauben der Kirche,* vol. 1: *Von der apostolischen Zeit bis zum Konzil von Chalcedon (451),* 3rd improved and expanded edition (Freiburg: Herder, 1990); Jaroslav Pelikan, *The Christian Tradition,* vol. 1: *The Emergence of the Catholic Tradition (100–600)* (Chicago/London: University of Chicago Press, 1971); Adolf Martin Ritter, "Dogma und Lehre in der alten Kirche," in *Handbuch der Dogmen- und Theologiegeschichte,* vol. 1: *Die Lehrentwicklung im Rahmen der Katholizität,* ed. Carl Andresen, Ungekürzte Studienausg. UTB Grosse Reihe (Göttingen: Vandenhoeck & Ruprecht, 1989 [1982]), pp. 99–283; Basil Studer, *Gott und unsere Erlösung im Glauben der alten Kirche* (Düsseldorf: Patmos Verlag, 1985).

vidually.[39] The Hellenistic worldview attempted to reduce all diversity to an underlying unity, and thereby came to understand the relationship between God and the world as a hierarchy where everything strove against unity. In contrast to a historical understanding of salvation, where the emphasis was on God's merciful action, a Hellenistically influenced view of salvation tended to exchange history for cosmology, and Christ's death on the cross for *logos'* mediation of the infinite and the finite. The problem with this Hellenization was that it changed a unique historical event into an eternal cosmic truth—from life to doctrine. At the same time, Hellenization contributed to the Christian message's universality being articulated more clearly. So there were both risks and advantages in articulating Christology with the aid of a different idiom than the biblical—clutching to a biblical mode of expression was not always any surety of the authenticity of the message.

Among the pioneers in confronting the Christian message with philosophical categories are the apologetes, who attempted to evangelize in this way. As an example we have Justin "the Martyr" or "the Philosopher" (died ca. 165). Justin suggested that the divine *logos* that the philosophers had long spoken of had become human in Jesus Christ. Even in the writings of the Greek philosophers one could find traces of *logos,* but now the fullness of *logos* had been revealed in Christ. Of greater significance for Christology itself, however, was another of the earliest theologians, Irenaeus of Lyons (died ca. 202). Irenaeus's best-known work is his combative writings against the Gnostics, *Adversus haereses.* Against the Gnostics Irenaeus wanted to maintain both that God actually revealed God's own self in the flesh in Christ, and that the redemption of the person was also a redemption of her flesh. The incarnation was required because the person had lost her status as God's image via the Fall, and because Christ as *logos* restored it:

> For I have shown that the Son of God did not then begin to exist, being with the Father from the beginning; but when He became incarnate, and was made man, He commenced afresh the long line of human beings, and furnished us, in a brief, comprehensive manner, with salvation; so that what we had lost in Adam—namely, to be according to the image and likeness of God—that we might recover in Christ Jesus.[40]

39. Studer, *Gott und unsere Erlösung,* pp. 34–37.

40. Irenaeus, *Against Heresies,* in *Ante-Nicene Fathers,* vol. 1: *The Apostolic Fathers, Justin Martyr, Irenaeus,* ed. Alexander Roberts and James Donaldson, revised by A. Cleveland Coxe (Grand Rapids: Eerdmans, 1979), p. 446 (3, 18, 1).

"Commenced afresh" is a translation of a perfect form of the verb *recapitulare* in the original Latin text. In Greek this corresponds to *anakephalaiōsis,* and a verb of the same stem is used in connection with Christ in Ephesians 1:10, and is translated there as "unite" in the ESV. According to Irenaeus, the objective of the "commencing afresh" was not only that the human would return to her lost nature as divine image, but also that she would be made divine, i.e., become like God. This means that the incarnation was a part of God's plan from the beginning, independent of the Fall of humanity. The polemic against the Gnostics we find above all in the emphasis that *logos* became human *(sarx)* in Christ. The whole person would be saved, i.e., made divine, and this included even human corporeality.[41] *Logos* took on a bodily as well as historical form, and so became a part of human history. Accordingly, the whole person could also be made divine. Salvation is thus not simply about a person's soul or spirit returning to its divine origins.

In Irenaeus the story of redemption had not yet been replaced by a cosmology, which would instead be the case in Origen (ca. 185–254). In a further development of Irenaeus's thought, and under the influence of Middle Platonic philosophy (Origen had studied with Ammonias Sakkas, the teacher of the philosopher Plotinus, not primarily to become a Platonist, but in order to acquire tools for apologetics), he had worked the Christian story of redemption into the framework of a cosmology whose fundamental problem is the relationship between the One and the Many. In Origen's theology the Father comes to be identified with the One, the absolute transcendent, while Christ becomes the mediator between the Father and the world of diversity, in order that this world will be able to return to the original unity. Christ belongs to both of the worlds, that of unity and that of diversity. According to Origen, the fact that *logos* had become human was a condition for humanity's path to God, since by becoming human God adapted God's own self to the human condition. But while the humanity of Christ was increasingly diminished in relation to the deity in the ascension of the human, his humanity was not entirely denied. It is instead like a transparent filter through which God acts as an intermediary for each person according to spiritual ability.[42] Origen was already suspected early on of having Hellenized the Christian message into unrecognizability, but at the same time his theology influenced the continued Trinitarian and Christological thought

41. Grillmeier, *Jesus der Christus,* p. 219.
42. Grillmeier, *Jesus der Christus,* p. 273.

in a pervasive way, among other things by pointing out the inevitable need to go beyond a salvation history formulation of theology in order to be able to take its contemporary intellectual challenges seriously.

Subordinationism and Monotheism

One particular theological problem that Irenaeus and Origen shared with their own period was how God's revelation in Christ could be prevented from corrupting the axiomatic monotheism of Christianity. Irenaeus imagined Christ and the Spirit as the hands of God the Father, and at the level of salvation history that picture is feasible, but it does not help clarify in which sense, for example, the Father and the Son are one with respect to God's being. Origen, with his Middle Platonic cosmological understanding of salvation, instead ended up thinking hierarchically. The Christological problem that plagued these early formulations was what is usually called "subordinationism," which means that Christ—as *logos* or the Son—is subordinated to the Father. In this more or less Hellenistically inspired theology Christ came to be thought of as a mediator between humanity and God—the meaning of *logos* shifted from the biblical sense of God's active, effective Word to a more Hellenistic sense of Reason. During the second century Christian doctrine also evolved with respect to creation *ex nihilo,* which in turn changed the conditions for *logos*-Christology.[43] This meant that *logos* could no longer simply be placed between God and the world. The doctrine of creation *ex nihilo* involved a critique of this sort of hierarchical thinking, and theologians were thus forced to make up their minds whether *logos* would be said to belong to the Creator or the created. This eventually led to the Arian crisis and the Nicene Creed.

The Arian crisis and the Nicene Creed both have to do with a problem that neither Irenaeus nor Origen managed to resolve in any satisfactory way, namely the problem of Christian monotheism. The complicating factor was that Christ was worshiped as divine in the liturgy. How could the divinity of Christ be reconciled with Christianity's obvious monotheism? The question of divinity in itself implicated several Christological questions: How should one understand the relationship between the Father and the Son? Does the Son belong to the Creator or the created, assuming that there is a difference

---

43. Cf. Gerhard May, *Schöpfung aus dem Nichts: Die Entstehung der Lehre von der Creation ex nihilo* (Berlin/New York: Walter de Gruyter, 1978).

between them? How should one understand the relationship between divine and human in Christ? The questions that the theologians discussed were brought up by the liturgy and scriptural readings that were considered normative, and even united the different theological parties, rather than by an independent interest in one or another sort of Greek philosophy. Thus it was seldom or never a matter of discussing questions that were conditioned by a speculative interest, disengaged from the soteriological problem, but it was instead a matter of clarifying which conclusions necessarily followed on the basis of the liturgical and biblical life-world that the different parties shared. Who must Christ be in order to do what he does? There was no obvious answer to this question either. It is thus improper to speak of a "pre-Nicene orthodoxy," since "correct doctrine" had not yet been defined.

On the side that would eventually leave the conflict defeated, we find theologians who had radicalized subordinationism more than either Irenaeus or Origen. One example is Eusebius of Caesarea (ca. 263–340), who is usually considered to be "the father of church history," primarily thanks to his book *Church History*.[44] Eusebius was a proponent of a subordinationist form of Origen-inspired theology with an interest in cosmology rather than soteriology. He maintained that *logos* was an independent hypostasis that had received its existence and its being from the Father, and was therefore a "second God." God the Father is the transcendent God, *ho theos,* and unequivocally superior to the Son. It is *logos* or the Son that acts as an intermediary between the Father and the created. In other words, we find in Eusebius a clear cosmic order of precedence, where the Son becomes a kind of liminal being that belongs neither to God nor to the created. That *logos* becomes human—*sarx*—in Jesus Christ seems to be motivated by a simple adaptation to the human capacity to receive God, not out of any internal necessity with respect to human redemption. The value of the human in Eusebius's understanding is strongly inhibited by fear of the doctrine that Christ is "merely human." Human flesh is radically subordinate and passive in relation to the divine *logos*.

We find—perhaps—an even more radical subordinationism in Arius (ca. 260–336), presbyter in Alexandria.[45] Because of the rejection of his theology by the council in Nicea, Arius has become almost the archetype for a

---

44. Eusebius of Caesarea, *Church History*, in *The Nicene and Post-Nicene Fathers*, ser. 2, vol. 2: *Eusebius,* ed. Philip Schaff and Henry Wace (Grand Rapids: Eerdmans, 1952).

45. See Rowan Williams, *Arius: Heresy and Tradition,* 2nd edition (London: SCM Press, 2001).

heretic in the history of theology. In the Middle Ages he was represented in church art side by side with Judas. It has thus been difficult for researchers to find a fairly balanced estimation of what Arius actually stood for, and the negative view of Arius has continued into modern time. An example is the great German historian of dogma Adolf von Harnack, who believed that Arius stood for a complete Hellenization of Christianity, and who thought that in his doctrine one finds that "all is hollow and formal, a boyish enthusiasm for playing with husks and shells, and a childish self-satisfaction in the working out of empty syllogisms."[46] Several contemporary researchers have attempted to give a more multifaceted presentation of Arius's theology, and point out that the debate between Arius and the victorious Niceans was pursued within the framework of a number of shared convictions, where they borrowed from each other as well as argued with each other.[47] Arius probably never intended to offer a philosophical, speculative system, but instead wanted as much as any other theologian of his time to articulate a biblically based theology that was also philosophically consistent. He had inherited theological problems from his precursors, which he attempted to solve via a new way of reconciling the elements that he found in earlier theologians.

Compared to Eusebius's subordinationism—which he was probably not dependent on—Arius goes a step further, and it is this step above all that led to the rejection of his theology. Arius maintained that God the Father was not eternally Father, since the Son was not eternal. The Father and the Son were—and here Arius stands in the tradition of Origen—distinct hypostases. But the Son belonged to the created, and like all else was created from nothing but God's will alone. There was therefore a time when the Son did not exist. For Arius the point of the Son was that he served as an intermediary between the radically transcendent God and the created world, as well as being a unifying link between the One and the Many. The transcendent God allowed for no differentiation, and thus arose the problem of how God the Father could be communicated to creation. Arius could indeed call the Son God as well—but the Son was not God of God's own being, but only by grace. That which first and foremost differentiates the Son from human beings is that the Son has a primary participation in God, and so is the one who acts as intermediary between God and humanity. Regarding the relationship

46. Adolf von Harnack, *History of Dogma*, vols. 4 and 5, trans. Neil Buchanan (New York: Dover Publications, 1961), pp. 41–42.

47. Williams, *Arius*, pp. 23–25. Cf. also R. P. C. Hanson, *The Search for the Christian Doctrine of God: The Arian Controversy 318–381* (Edinburgh: T. & T. Clark, 1988), p. xvii.

between the divine and human in Christ, Arius and his followers made use of a *logos-sarx*-scheme where *logos* becomes the all-overshadowing principle at the expense of humanity.

What was the problem with such a radical subordinationism? One way to formulate the problem was, as Athanasius of Alexandria would later present it, that this threatens the authenticity of redemption.[48] If there is no continuity between creation, the mediating Son, and the transcendent Father, God's nature appears to be impossible to communicate, and so we may ask ourselves what the function of the Son actually is. Or we may imagine that some kind of continuity does exist, since the Son must in some way stand in conformity with the nature of the Father in order to be able to communicate it to humanity, but then we have taken an initial step away from Arius and radical subordinationism. Another way to express the problem with Arius's position is that it transforms Christ into a mythological being, practically a superhero.[49] In its effort to defend Christian monotheism, subordinationism led to a dead-end. Its clear problems with conceiving of Christ as a genuine human forced it to conceive of Christ as a sort of liminal being, who, rather than being both divine and human, became neither. But such an idea was hardly theologically acceptable, and it was this problem that the council in Nicea attempted to solve.

The Council in Nicea 325

Before Nicea Christianity had to a large extent been a persecuted sect in the Roman Empire.[50] Now it suddenly found itself in a different situation, thanks to Emperor Constantine's policy of tolerance and his open support of the Christian church. The Arian crisis led to the council in Nicea

48. Cf. Athanasius of Alexandria, *Against the Arians*, in *The Nicene and Post-Nicene Fathers*, ser. 2, vol. 4: *Athanasius: Select Works and Letters*, ed. Philip Schaff and Henry Wace (Grand Rapids: Eerdmans, 1957).

49. Grillmeier, *Jesus der Christus*, pp. 278ff.

50. On the historical circumstances before, during, and after Nicea, see, besides the literature cited in note 38 above, Charles Pietri and Christoph Markschies, "Theologische Diskussionen zur Zeit Konstantins: Arius, der 'arianische Streit' und das Konzil von Nizäa, die nachnizänischen Auseinandersetzungen bis 337," in *Die Geschichte des Christentums: Religion—Politik—Kultur.* Vol. 2: *Das Entstehen der einen Christenheit (250–430)*, ed. Charles and Luce Pietri (Freiburg/Basel/Vienna: Herder, 1996), pp. 271–344. Cf. also Basil Studer, *Schola Christiana: Die Theologie zwischen Nizäa (325) und Chalzedon (451)* (Paderborn: Schöningh, 1998), pp. 66–73.

(present-day Iznik in Turkey), summoned by Constantine.[51] His purpose with this council was to consolidate the church as the spiritual dimension of his empire through the widest possible doctrinal unity. Earlier in the same year a local council in Antioch had condemned Arianism, but this had failed, and Constantine himself compelled to convene a new council where he could monitor the negotiations himself. The council of "318 fathers" that assembled in 325 consisted almost exclusively of bishops from the east.[52] Its task went far beyond putting an end to the Arian conflict, as it also attempted to overcome disputes within the Oriental church. With Christianity as the official religion in Constantine's empire, there were for the first time both the prerequisite and the need for a more uniform doctrinal formation.

The goal of the council was to follow biblical terminology as far as possible in the creed. In two philosophical, or rather, technical formulations, the council was nevertheless forced to deviate from this rule. One confessed that Christ was born "of the being of the Father *[ousia]*" and that Christ was also "of the same substance *[homoousion]* as the Father."[53] The crucial technical term here is *homoousios*. Scholarship is still divided over its origin and definition before the council. It was understood in different ways by different groups. That it was nevertheless put in the confession is due to the fact that they understood that it was impossible to express the biblical faith through exclusively biblical concepts and terms. *Homoousios* was a term that Arius had already rejected prior to the council, which in the eyes of the council participants made it all the more suitable to use in the rejection of Arian theology.

Even if the origin of the term *homoousios* is unclear, and even though it retains a certain ambiguity at the council in Nicea, this does not mean that this point in the confession is itself completely unclear. By establishing that Christ was "of the same substance" as the Father they wanted to profess that Christ really was divine in the same sense as the Father, and not a liminal being. By this they also implicitly rejected the subordinationism that several of the successors to Origen had articulated, and that had been

---

51. On the Council of Nicea see J. N. D. Kelly, *Early Christian Creeds,* 3rd edition (Harlow, UK: Longman, 1972), pp. 205–367.

52. Ritter, "Dogma und Lehre," p. 166.

53. Heinrich Denzinger, *Enchiridion symbolorum definitionum et declarationum de rebus fidei et morum,* improved and expanded edition with German translation, published by Peter Hünermann in cooperation with Helmut Hoping, 37th edition (Freiburg/Basel/Rome/Vienna: Herder, 1991), no. 125.

an endemic problem through the whole of the early doctrinal formation. There is a continuity between the Father and the Son that Nicea articulates via the term *homoousios*. The Son's birth "of the same substance as the Father" meant that the Son was a participant in the eternity of the Father. For the Nicene Creed, the term "birth" had no material connotations, as it had for Arius, but was instead a term that was used in contrast to "creation." In another formulation from the creed, the Son was "born, not created *[gennēthenta, ou poiēthenta]*." This was a way to emphasize the continuity between the Father and the Son, and thereby the reality of God's presence in Christ.[54] By extension, the Nicene Creed also made it possible to speak of the relationship between the Father and the Son in purely theological, i.e., intra-Trinitarian terms, in opposition to the economic, i.e., salvation history. This relationship was not dependent on the Son's role as mediator in creation and redemption, even if it was articulated in this salvation history. The distinction between theology and economy did not stem from speculative interest—even if such an interest could be an expected consequence of an excessive separation between theology and economy—but was instead an endeavor to articulate the freedom of God, and thus the character of grace of both creation and salvation.

Nicea was therefore a contribution to the discussion of Christian monotheism. The aim was not, however, to come up with some simple solution regarding the relationship between the Father, the Son, and the Spirit. As the British theologian Rowan Williams has pointed out, Athanasius and the consistent Niceans took up the challenge and the requirement of conceptual innovations. He writes:

> The doctrinal debate of the fourth century is thus in considerable measure about how the Church is to become intellectually self-aware and to move from a 'theology of repetition' to something more exploratory and constructive. Athanasius' task is to show how the break in continuity generally felt to be involved in the creedal *homoousios* is a necessary moment in the deeper understanding and securing of tradition; more yet, it is to

54. In *Gott und unsere Erlösung* Basil Studer summarizes Nicene theology in the following way (p. 136): "Nach dem nizänischen Glauben ist also Christus wahrer Gott, weil er der wahre Sohn Gottes ist. Technisch gesprochen: Er ist der *monogenes,* weil seine *usia* vom Vater stammt; und weil er aus dem Vater geboren und nicht geschaffen ist, ist seine *usia* derjenigen des Vaters gleich. Folglich ist er auch dem Vater gleichewig und nimmt als der aus dem Vater (*per naturam,* nicht *per voluntatem*) geborene Sohn so an der Natur des Vaters teil, daß er selbst auch Schöpfer ist."

persuade Christians that strict adherence to archaic and 'neutral' terms alone is in fact a potential betrayal of the historic faith.[55]

In a sense Nicea and its subsequent history is the Christian church's discovery that theological thought is not only legitimate, but also necessary, and it is here that doctrinal formation in the strict sense begins. Simply repeating a formula is not sufficient to maintain a continuity with earlier phases in the history of theology, if this continuity is going to be more than formal. Biblical terms were in need of being supplemented with extra-biblical terminology, since the meaning of the biblical terminology was itself at stake.

Continued discussions after Nicea were inevitable. There were several problems with the Nicene Creed. One was that the terms "substance" *(ousia)* and "of the same substance" *(homoousios)* had no unambiguous definition, and that the difference between *ousia* and *hypostasis* was not clear, such that these two terms could be understood as synonyms. There was thus the possibility of interpreting Nicea as a defense of modalism, which entailed denying that the difference between the Father, the Son, and the Spirit was a real difference. In other words, Nicea had not succeeded in investigating the doctrine of the Trinity satisfactorily, although it had given an important stimulus to what would become the "orthodox" solution to this problem. Another problem was how the relationship between *logos* and the world would be understood, or more concretely, between *logos* and the flesh in Christ. The emphasis on the continuity in the relationship between the Father and the Son eventually meant that the humanity of Christ would once more become a burning question, a question that lies woven into the larger question of the relationship between the Father and the Son, and God's presence with or in the human. Before I come to a more general conclusion regarding the degree to which this doctrinal development was able to do justice to the humanity of Christ, or whether it transformed Christ into a more mythological figure, I will thus first go a bit further ahead in history.

One Person and Two Natures: Chalcedon 451

The Nicene Creed had thus established that the Son was "of the same substance" as the Father, and thereby conceived of a formula that would be guiding for Christian monotheism after the council. But if the Son was now of the

55. Williams, *Arius,* p. 235.

same being as the Father, the question remained (and was in fact intensified) of how one should understand the Son's incarnation in the person Jesus of Nazareth without representing Jesus as an Arian "superhero," or denying his genuine humanity. Was this at all possible? This became the question that guided Christological thought up until the Christological council *par excellence,* the council in Chalcedon in 451. In this section, the path to Chalcedon goes via Arius's opponent Athanasius of Alexandria, but also through Apollinaris of Laodicea, whose *logos-sarx*-christologies had Monophysite tendencies, and so threatened to turn the genuine humanity of Christ into nothing. In response, different proposed christologies came from Antioch, which emphasized the difference between human and divine in Christ, and from Alexandria, which emphasized the unity between human and divine, and from Rome, which wanted to emphasize both the humanity and the divinity of Christ. Chalcedon 451 may be seen as a compromise between these three traditions, but its creed gave rise in turn to a number of discussions about how it should be understood. Although Chalcedon 451 had become normative for the Christian church (excepting the non-Chalcedonian churches), this did not mean an end to the Christological reflections and conflicts as such. I am guided here as well by the two questions I formulated in the previous section: whether the Hellenization of the message meant that the existential concern was displaced by a more speculative interest, and how the different theologians and theologies imagined the relationship between divine and human in Christ.

Monophysitism

One of the tone-setting theologians at the Nicean council, as well as one of Arius's chief opponents, was Athanasius of Alexandria (ca. 295–373).[56] Against Arius, Athanasius maintained that Christ was actually God in truth, and not a liminal being. *Logos* became flesh for the sake of the divinization of humanity, which meant victory over death and the restoration of the nature of the human as God's image, via her divinization. If this divinization is going to be true, Christ must be of the same substance as the Father, but also of the

---

56. See, besides the literature already mentioned, Alvyn Pettersen, *Athanasius,* Outstanding Christian Thinkers (London: Geoffrey Chapman, 1995). See Athanasius, *Against the Arians,* together with *Contra gentes/De incarnatione,* Oxford Early Christian Texts, trans. Robert W. Thomason (Oxford: Clarendon Press, 1971).

same substance as the human. Athanasius maintained that one who denies that *logos* is *homoousion tō patri* ("of the same substance as the Father") demotes *logos* to a demigod, and denies our salvation—in contradiction to Arius and his party.

But if Athanasius had thus avoided turning Christ into a demigod or a "superhero," he simultaneously risked diminishing the importance of Christ's humanity. Even Athanasius made use of the traditional *logos-sarx*-scheme in his understanding of the unity of Christ, in spite of the fact that it had been discredited by its association with the Arians. According to Athanasius's understanding of the incarnation, the divine *logos* was the active and life-giving principle in Christ, while the human flesh *(sarx)* was passive. All spiritual and moral deeds were credited to *logos,* and Athanasius thus saw no need to attribute a human soul to Christ. So even for Athanasius, the human body of Christ becomes a bearer of the divine *logos,* and so at most an instrument for the agency of *logos.* In this way Athanasius wants to preserve the unity within Christ, and to defend John 1:14, where *logos* became human, which he considered the foundational Christological statement. Of course, Athanasius could maintain that Christ's human body was the subject of Christ's suffering on the cross, and thus ascribe to the body those passions that were usually denoted as spiritual, but this was at most a strained attempt to resolve the problem without attributing these sufferings to the divine *logos,* which would compromise the axiomatic unchangeability and transcendence of God.

The problem with Athanasius's way of understanding the unity of Christ with the aid of the *logos-sarx*-schema is first and foremost what is usually called the Monophysite tendency—i.e., the reduction of the human to the divine—in his approach. This tendency becomes even clearer with Apollinaris of Laodicea (ca. 315–dead by 392), who took the *logos-sarx* Christology to its logical conclusion. Apollinaris supposed that the humanity of Christ was grounded in the combination of divine Spirit and human flesh. Through this combination a human creature was constituted, i.e., one being comprised of body and soul. Apollinaris thus refers to the one become human as a heavenly person. The salvation of the human comes about by means of an infallible divine reason *(nous)* operating in Christ's flesh and animating it. Because the whole animating principle proceeds from *logos* in the body, and ties both together into a unity in life and agency, Apollinaris believes that the body of Christ does not constitute an independent *physis* (a term that Apollinaris uses synonymously with *ousia* and should be understood as a dynamic principle, rather than as a static "nature"). Neither is there an independent human will in Christ. The God-person therefore consists not of two, but of one *physis,* one *ousia.* The problem with Apollinaris's position is that the entirety of Christ's humanity and human psyche is devalued and tends to disappear in the divine. The unity of Christ is a "coming together" of divinity with flesh, a substantial union, and in this union the role of the flesh is entirely instrumental, dependent, and without a will of its own. The divine, on the other hand, is the dynamic principle, and absolutely dominant. Unlike Athanasius's more contradictory solution, Apollinaris is thus forced to maintain that *logos* itself must have suffered on the cross, since there was no independent human nature in Christ.

As is so often the case with Christological thought during the patristic era, a more or less extreme position calls on its antithesis. The strength of the *logos-sarx*-scheme—even with Apollinaris—was that it preserved the concrete unity of Christ's person and being. The weakness was that it devalued the human integrity of Christ, and by this time the scheme seemed to have exhausted its potential for constructive solutions. Partially as a polemical reaction against the Alexandrian *logos-sarx*-scheme, other theologians with roots in Antioch and Constantinople will advance a *logos-anthrōpos*-scheme (where *anthrōpos* stands for "human"), where the difference between divine and human is more clearly stressed, and where the integrity of Christ's humanity is consequently taken with greater seriousness. The continued Christological controversies up until Chalcedon can, put simply, be said to have been between the theologians in Antioch, who emphasized the differences between the divine and the human natures in Christ, and those in Alexandria, who emphasized their unity, and eventually those in Rome, who would come to occupy an intermediary position.

Antioch, Alexandria, and Rome

The task in Antioch was to achieve a Christology where the indwelling of *logos* in Christ was understood in such a way that both the divinity of the Word and the integrity of the humanity of Christ were preserved. If the integrity of the humanity of Christ was not preserved, they believed, salvation itself would also be threatened. It is not only a body that is at stake, but a soul as well. Since the soul is the source of sin, it must also be assumed by *logos* in order for it to be saved. If Christ's human nature, inclusive of freedom, is to be taken seriously and respected as such, it cannot be thought of as simply an instrument for the divine. The school of Antioch thus sought a different scheme for understanding the unity of Christ.

One of the predecessors of the school, in fact one of Apollinaris's chief opponents, Diodorus of Tarsus (died by 394), still began from the traditional scheme *logos-sarx,* which meant that it was primarily his disciple Theodore of Mopsuestia (died 428) who would pursue his teacher's task in a more productive way. Theodore imagined the unity of Christ with the help of the scheme *logos-anthrōpos,* and maintained, moreover—in opposition to Apollinaris (but similar to Origen)—that Christ had a human soul. It was precisely this emphasis on the soul of Christ that was an important step in upholding the integrity of the human nature of Christ. Without this, patristic Christology would hardly have been able to maintain that Christ was a historical person who acted independently in the same way as other people. If Theodore's Christology and the Antioch Christology of difference succeeded in preserving the integrity of Christ's human nature, thereby averting the Monophysite threat, there nevertheless arose another problem: How shall one understand the unity of the divine and the human in Christ in a way that makes it clear that we are not speaking of two Christs who, so to speak, jointly decide how to act? One solution would be to situate the unity in the fact that they desire the same thing, but such a purely moral union is hardly a satisfactory solution. Although Theodore strove to articulate a unity of subject by maintaining that *logos* gives its character to the "assumed human," he never really succeeded in reaching an adequate formulation.

The Antiochene Christology was instead developed further by Nestorius (born after 381, died ca. 451), patriarch of Constantinople between 428 and 431. Nestorius has fallen into disrepute because he was understood by his opponents to advocate a duality in Christ, a duality that was not only a linguistic, but also an ontological distinction between human and divine—not just a difference, but a division. Nestorius wanted to protect the two natures in Christ from being blended together, and so maintained that both natures had their own *prosōpon* ("face"), which for Nestorius was a collective term for all that characterized a concrete reality. Nestorius also understood the unity between the two natures with the aid of the concept *prosōpon,* taking the *prosōpon* of the humanity of Christ as an instrument, as an *organon,* for the *prosōpon* of *logos.* Nestorius strives to articulate a substantial unity that allows the initiative to be God's, and thus not based on the merit of the human Jesus.

Nestorius came to be understood by his opponents, however, especially those from Alexandria, to be advocating a Christological difference with no true unity. The conflict reached its point of crystallization in Nestorius's concept *christotokos*, i.e., Bearer of Christ. Against the church's deeply rooted profession of Mary, mother of Jesus, as *theotokos*, i.e., Bearer of God, Nestorius maintained that Mary should instead be denoted as *christotokos*, since she only gave birth to the human nature of Christ. The foremost representative of the Alexandrian tradition, Cyril of Alexandria (died 444, bishop from probably 412), reacted against this. He understood Nestorius's Christology as a division, not simply a differentiation between the two natures.[57] Cyril believed that Nestorius stood for an "ecumenical scandal," and he worked to get Nestorius condemned. This succeeded at the council in Ephesus 431, which was summoned by Emperor Theodosius II. Nestorius was dismissed as patriarch, and in 436 he was forced into exile in Egypt.

If Antioch's emphasis was the difference between divine and human in Christ, Alexandria's focus was the unity between the two natures, and in accordance with this Cyril upheld a doctrine of incarnation in which Christ was ascribed a *hypostasis* or *physis*, terms that were nearly synonymous for Cyril. Although this could be understood as a Monophysite feature in Cyril's Christology, in opposition to Apollinaris he assumed the existence of a human soul in Christ. This means that the human nature of Christ becomes, despite everything, its own dynamic principle. The distance to the later Chalcedonian compromise between Antioch and Alexandria was thus not especially great, even if they came to abandon Alexandria's formula *mia physis* (i.e., "one nature") in favor of the formula *dyo physeis* (i.e., "two natures"). Alexandria's contribution to the Christology of the ancient church was to emphasize that the Gospels do not speak of an image of God with two histories, but of a single Jesus Christ in the paradoxical unity of divine and human. Even here the driving motive behind the emphasis on this unity was soteriology. Both Antioch and Alexandria represented legitimate concerns—the emphasis on the integrity of Christ's human nature vis-à-vis the emphasis on unity—but none of the involved parties commanded sufficient conceptual resources to be able to adhere to both of these concerns at the same time.

It was not until after the council at Ephesus 431 that Western theology came to play an especially prominent role, and this through Pope Leo I (died 461, pope from 440). At yet another synod in Ephesus in 449, Leo delivered a text, *Dogmatic Letter to Flavian,* later known as *To-*

---

57. See Cyril of Alexandria's second letter to Nestorius in Denzinger, *Enchiridion,* no. 250–51.

mus Leonis.[58] Content-wise, this text is a Christological account where Leo distances himself from Eutyches from Constantinople, who maintained that "before the combination" Christ comprised two natures, but after the incarnation only one.[59] Leo emphasizes the genuine humanity of Christ, and maintains as well that the different natures retained their respective individualities after the combination of the divine and human in the incarnation. Both natures are active in that which is appropriate to their nature, and the communion arises through the unity of person. Leo had probably been influenced by Augustine, who maintained that Christ was *"una persona in utraque natura,"* i.e., "one person in both natures." In terms of history of effect, the most important feature in Leo's letter is the emphasis on the remaining difference. Thus Leo and the Western tradition took a middle way between Alexandria and Antioch: with Antioch they wanted to emphasize the difference between the two natures, and with Alexandria the unity between the two natures.

The conflict between Cyril, Nestorius, and Leo can seem to be a conflict over insubstantial matters or speculative hypotheses. We should also remember that these Christological conflicts were not strictly intra-theological, but were also due to political and cultural differences. Yet when we try to understand these christologies, we must keep in mind the fact that all of these different perspectives struggled with problems that had a genuinely existential nature. They also began from certain common assumptions. The problem lay partially in that it was difficult for a solitary theology to do justice to every dimension of the Christological complex. All perspectives accepted that *logos* had become human, but how could they understand this in a way that did not deviate to one side or the other? They knew, so to speak, what they wanted, namely to confess the Christ that the Bible spoke of, but not how they would do it. Faced with different intellectual challenges, they were thus forced to go outside the biblical formulations. Antioch and Alexandria strove jointly, despite all their differences, towards one and the same goal, namely to articulate Christ as *one* in the distinction between divinity and humanity. The necessary effort to find adequate Christological formulas was an effort to avoid one-sidedness, which was not an easy task. It is thus not especially surprising that the emphases fell out so differently within the different Christological groupings. If Alexandria wanted to emphasize Christ's unity as

---

58. *Tomus Leonis* may be found in Denzinger, *Enchiridion*, no. 290–95.

59. Cf. Lionel R. Wickham, "Eutyches/Eutychianischer Streit," *Theologische Realenzyklopädie* vol. X (Berlin/New York: Walter de Gruyter, 1982), pp. 558–65.

subject, Antioch strove to emphasize the person Jesus as a complete human, and Rome to behave loyally with regard to both God and human.[60] Common to all three was that they desired to protect the fundamental soteriological concern. A compromise that could unite the different groupings was needed.

The Chalcedonian Compromise

Leo's letter was not read at the council in Ephesus in 449, and Leo described the meeting as a "synod of thieves." He and others requested a new "catholic" council. With the death of Emperor Theodosius II, the religio-political situation changed, and it became possible to win support for the opposition against a purely Alexandrian Christology. The emperor's successor, Empress Pulcheria, supported Leo's group, and she and her husband Marcian, who became the new emperor, convened the council at Chalcedon in 451, which focused almost entirely on the Christological question. Unlike, for example, the council in Nicea, the technical formulas they reached were strictly dogmatic, and were not situated in the confessional framework of a salvation history. The Chalcedonian Creed was a compromise between, above all, the Alexandrian, Antiochian, and Roman christologies. However, it did not succeed in quenching the Christological conflicts, which blazed up once more after the council. Despite this, the Chalcedonian Christological decision has had crucial importance for the Orthodox church, as well as the Roman Catholic and Protestant churches. It was, however, never accepted by the so-called Monophysite, or, perhaps more correctly, the non-Chalcedonian or Oriental churches.[61]

The Chalcedonian Creed intended to partake in the earlier creeds from Nicea and Constantinople (381; a refinement of the Nicene Creed), and saw itself as a clarification of these. In the preface to the definition, the council Fathers disassociate themselves from, on the one hand, those who do not teach that Mary is *theotokos,* so in other words, Nestorius and his sympathizers, but on the other hand, also from those who teach that the deity and the flesh are one nature *(mia physis),* i.e., Cyril and his followers.[62] They also

60. Studer, *Gott und unsere Erlösung,* p. 251.

61. On a non-Chalcedonian Christology, see Jan-Eric Steppa, *John Rufus and the World Vision of Anti-Chalcedonian Culture* (Diss. Lund, 2001).

62. See the council text in *Decrees of the Ecumenical Councils,* volume one: *Nicaea I to Lateran V,* ed. Norman P. Tanner (London/Washington, DC: Sheed & Ward/Georgetown University Press, 1990), pp. 84–85.

disassociated themselves from those who "tore up" salvation into a "duality of Sons," from those who believed that the deity could suffer, and from those who blended Christ's two natures, as well as from those who advanced the myth that Christ had been two natures before the union and one after (i.e., against Eutyches).

The definition itself, which is relatively short and technical, emphasizes that Christ is one person with two natures—a formula that came to be epoch-making.[63] The emphasis that Christ is a subject is clear in the formula "one and the same," which is repeated three times. Christ is perfect in his divinity as in his humanity; he is "truly God and truly man, of rational soul and body *[theon alēthōs, kai anthrōpon alēthōs, ton auton ek psychēs logikēs kai sōmatos]*." Further, Christ is "consubstantial *[homoousion]*" with the Father, but also "consubstantial with us as regards his humanity; like us in all respects except for sin." We come to know Christ's person in "two natures *[dyo physesin]*." These two natures "undergo no confusion, no change, no division, no separation *[asynchytōs, atreptōs, adiairetōs, achōristōs gnōrizomenon]*," and each nature's properties persist after the union, but they are simultaneously united in one person *(prosōpon)* and one hypostasis *(hypostasis)*. Unity and difference are kept together without being intermixed, and Christ is confessed not as two persons, but as "one and the same," which has been taught by the prophets and Christ himself, and attested by the Fathers. Through Chalcedon, the person-concept thus came into general use, a concept that was already highlighted by Tertullian (ca. 160–220), but which had not been noticed since.[64]

In view of the fact that the formulations from Chalcedon have had such an epoch-making theological influence, but also because these have at times been identified with an orthodox confession of Christ, it is important to get a handle on Chalcedon's real concern. I want to argue that the aim in Chalcedon was never to solve all Christological problems once and for all—it was, after all, a compromise-formula—nor was it meant to replace the Christological ideas that are articulated in biblical writings, liturgy, and preaching. The aim was much milder. In the words of the British philosopher Donald M. MacKinnon, Chalcedon's formulas were not "about Christ,

---

63. Tanner, ed., *Decrees*, p. 86.

64. On the concept of the person in the doctrine of incarnation, see Grillmeier, *Jesus der Christus,* pp. 250–57. Tertullian's terminology is found in Tertullian, *Against Praxeas,* in *Ante-Nicene Fathers,* vol. 3: *Latin Christianity: Its Founder, Tertullian,* ed. Alexander Roberts and James Donaldson, revised by A. Cleveland Coxe (Grand Rapids: Eerdmans, 1957).

but about statements about Christ."[65] In other words, Chalcedon does not constitute a substitute for the first-order statements about Christ in more ordinary preaching, but these formulas are rather the second-order rules for how these assertions should be understood and what they are about. The point in professing with Chalcedon that Christ is "of the same being" as the Father is not to say something more ontologically profound than "Christ crucified and risen," but is rather a way to say that it is God in person who meets us in Christ. One might say that Chalcedon's function is "grammatical" rather than "kerygmatic." The dogmas that were established at the different councils should, in accordance with the ancient church's apophatic understanding of theology, not be understood as exact definitions of divine things, but instead as providing a framework for how one could speak about God.[66] This applies to Chalcedon as well, which is thus not concerned so much with saying something about Christ, but instead saying something about the *significance* of Christ.

I will have reason to return to these perspectives on Chalcedon in the next chapter, but in conclusion here I want to note that the council's formulations did not become an endpoint for Christological thought.[67] After Chalcedon the ascetic movement in Egypt feared that the doctrine of two natures jeopardized the union with God. The debate eventually came to be about whether Christ had one or two wills, and the Eastern theologian Maximus the Confessor (580–662) argued that the authentic humanity of Christ was compromised if this humanity was not considered to have a

65. Donald M. MacKinnon, "'Substance' in Christology—a Cross-Bench View," in *Christ, Faith and History,* Cambridge Studies in Christology, ed. Stephen W. Sykes and John P. Clayton (Cambridge: Cambridge University Press, 1972), p. 291. Cf. Kenneth Surin, "Some Aspects of the 'Grammar' of 'Incarnation' and 'Kenosis': Reflections prompted by the writings of Donald MacKinnon," in *Christ, Ethics and Tragedy: Essays in Honour of Donald MacKinnon,* ed. Kenneth Surin (Cambridge: Cambridge University Press, 1989), pp. 93–116.

66. Cf. Studer, *Gott und unsere Erlösung,* pp. 289–90. This also concerns the question of the "Hellenization" of ancient church theology, a thesis that is pursued by Adolf von Harnack. We find one of von Harnack's most cited expressions in Adolf von Harnack, *History of Dogma,* vol. 1, trans. Neil Buchanan (New York: Dover Publications, 1961), p. 17: "Dogma in its conception and development is a work of the Greek spirit on the soil of the Gospel." For a balanced evaluation of von Harnack's thesis, see Gösta Hallonsten, "Harnack, helleniseringen och frågan om trons inkulturation—några synpunkter," in *Med hjärtats öga: Studier och essayer tillägnade Lars Cavallin på sextioårsdagen 15 augusti 2000,* ed. Ann Blückert and Kjell Blückert (Vejbystrand, Sweden: Catholica, 2000), pp. 239–52.

67. Cf. Karl Rahner, "Current Problems in Christology," in *Theological Investigations,* vol. 1: *God, Christ, Mary and Grace,* trans. Cornelius Ernst (New York: Crossroad, 1982), pp. 149–200.

will.[68] As I will discuss more closely in chapter 6, the Eastern church's icon-oclasm through the seventh and eighth centuries was an extension of the Christological debate as well. During the Middle Ages the Western church fought, among other things, over the doctrine of reconciliation (Anselm of Canterbury and Abelard) and about whether the incarnation would have taken place even if humanity had not fallen into sin (Thomas Aquinas and John Duns Scotus).[69] This short reckoning shows that, although Chalcedon had come to play a big role within both the Western and the Eastern Christian church, it did so not least by becoming a starting point for new discussions. Each period—not just the modern period—has been forced to think through these formulations anew. As the theologians at the council of Nicea had already learned, theological refinement is necessary in order to maintain continuity with earlier phases in the history of theology.

The Apophatic Character of Theological Language

Before I close this chapter and shift to discussing theologies of incarnation more contemporary to us, I want to return to those questions I posed at the start of this section, namely, whether these patristic formulations actually succeeded in safeguarding the existential concern of the New Testament Christology, such as the genuine humanity of Christ, including embodiment as a constitutive feature. I believe that the answer to these questions is dependent on what one looks for in these ancient church formulations. If it is an adequate Christology and anthropology for our own time, a repetition of the formulations and formulas that we find in these early writings will hardly do. The conceptual language alone, not least in the Chalcedonian Creed, can seem alien, and the anthropology they worked with rudimentary, and it is clear that our contemporary intellectual horizon has been displaced appreciably in relation to that of the early Christian church. But one may not therefore forget that the early Christian church also wrestled with theological problems that find their analogies in our time. One question that all

68. On Maximus, see Hans Urs von Balthasar, *Cosmic Liturgy: The Universe according to Maximus the Confessor*, Communio Books, trans. Brian E. Daley (San Francisco: Ignatius Press, 2003), together with Lars Thunberg, *Man and the Cosmos: The Vision of St. Maximus the Confessor* (Crestwood, NY: St. Vladimir's Seminary Press, 1985).

69. A good account of medieval Christology may be found in Rowan Williams, "Jesus Christus III Mittelalter," in *Theologische Realenzyklopädie* vol. XVI (Berlin/New York: Walter de Gruyter, 1987), pp. 745-59.

these Christological formulations and disputes dealt with, and even our own time cannot escape posing for itself, is how the relationship of God to the human may be understood in such a way that the genuine presence of God is emphasized without either the Otherness of God or the genuine humanity of the human being threatened.

So rather than being the result of theological hubris, the more doctrinal Christological reflections of the ancient church are an experiment in finding conceptual categories that correspond to an existential concern. This concern is to adequately articulate the genuine nature of salvation by clarifying the relationship between God and human, and at the same time respecting the apophatic character of theological language. Even if the more doctrinal Christological formulations make use of a more conceptual language than the New Testament's storytelling and hymn singing, the aim is still existential rather than speculative. The aim was to clarify and deepen the New Testament testimony, not to replace it. Where successful in this, not even a creed like Chalcedon's ought to result in an abstract doctrine of God or humanity. So the fact that the Chalcedonian Creed was technical and formula-like and not situated within the concepts of a salvation history confessional framework does not in itself have to mean that it was speculative and abstract, or, for example, that it understood God's presence with humanity as a state rather than an action. Whether or not this would have been the case would have had more to do with which context it would have been raised in, and these contexts could have varied considerably, then as now.

As regards the genuine humanity of Christ, at first sight there seems to be a greater clarity in the New Testament authors than in the patristic. When the theologians of the ancient church want to emphasize the human integrity of Christ, and thus a human agent, they do this by ascribing to him a human soul—the body remains, in most accounts, a passive instrument, and for certain theologians this passivity pertains to the entirety of human nature. At the same time, the prominence of Christ's soul is a defense of the integrity of the human against the background of a Hellenistically colored anthropology, and not primarily a contribution to the debate about the relationship between body and soul. Much of what we find in the Christological formulations of the patristic authors should thus be understood as a principled defense of the integrity of the human and our human embodiment, even if the formulations themselves can seem unsatisfactory from our contemporary perspective. Even the technical concepts of Chalcedon may thus function as a defense of the integrity of human nature.

My conclusion with respect to the doctrinal formation of the ancient church is thus that it constitutes a necessary (in the sense of historically inevitable) component even in contemporary Christology, but that it is in itself hardly sufficient to satisfy the demands we ought to set to a contemporary theological anthropology. Such an anthropology ought to be able to more comprehensively account for the relationship between the subjectivity of the human, embodiment, and sociality. At the same time, one result of the investigation in this chapter—and also of what I additionally have to say about human embodiment and sociality in the theology of the ancient church in chapter 9—is that even the Christology of the ancient church was open to these sorts of issues. The fact that I, in this study on incarnation, the gaze, and embodiment, will pose these questions in a different way than the Christology of the ancient church has to do with the fact that intellectual horizons constantly change, changes that occur within modern Christology as well. Before I specifically focus on the human gaze and embodiment from the theological perspective, I will therefore devote a chapter to how the incarnation has been understood within modern Christology, above all with regard for changed conceptions of human subjectivity.

3. Incarnation and Subjectivity

In the modern period various understandings and doctrines of incarnation have come to be criticized as irrevocably bound to past ways of formulating the doctrinal content of the Christian faith. It is primarily the doctrine of two natures that has taken the blame in the modern critique of the Christology of incarnation. The doctrine of two natures has been criticized as speculation with no ground in the New Testament testimony, and additionally as unintelligible, or, alternatively, meaningless according to the sensibilities of the modern person. The return to the New Testament has at times gone hand in hand with an appeal to leave the past and proceed into our own time. The motives behind the emergence of this critique are many, and the critique has been formulated in many different ways. In particular we can mention the relative secularization of Western culture, as well as the emergence of a historical awareness in the interpretation of the Bible and the commonly articulated critique of "metaphysics" in favor of empiricism.[1] A decisive break occurs here compared to the thousand years of Christological reflection that preceded the Enlightenment, and, despite significant differences in formulation as well as content, more or less moved within the framework of a traditional doctrine of two natures. The difference between the Chalcedonian definition, Thomas Aquinas in the thirteenth century, and Martin Luther in the sixteenth century, is less than the difference between, for example, Luther and Immanuel Kant in the eighteenth century. It was not the Reformation, but the Enlightenment

---

1. Cf., for example, Werner G. Kümmel, *The New Testament: The History of the Investigations of Its Problems,* trans. S. McLean Gilmour and Howard C. Kee (London: SCM Press, 1973), and Hans W. Frei, *The Eclipse of Biblical Narrative: A Study in Eighteenth and Nineteenth Century Hermeneutics* (New Haven/London: Yale University Press, 1974).

that challenged classical Christology, and its crucial objection has to do with the autonomous subjectivity of the human being, i.e., her quality of being a self-determining subject.[2]

Modern Christology has questioned how well the traditional Christological creeds actually manage to capture the true humanity of Christ. Can classical Christology really answer to the idea of human autonomy, or does it involve an explaining away of human agency? As we saw in the previous chapter, this issue was not unknown in the patristic period, but in modern times the question has been posed with greater emphasis. The question of the humanity of Christ is now *in spite* of the traditional creed, rather than *with its aid,* and it is moreover posed as a question *to* the creed. It is an oft-repeated truth that the modern epoch entails a turn from a theocentric to an anthropocentric worldview. For the Christological question, this means that the humanity of Christ becomes a matter of course and his divinity a problem. Even where the aim is not to question the divine nature of Christ *per se,* the result is often a reformulation of the traditional doctrines, or rather, of the way in which the traditional doctrines have come to be received, since they were thought to fail to express what is now considered primary, namely that Jesus is human just as we are. For modern Christology, it is the human, not God, that is the more or less self-evident starting point.

It would, however, be all too simplistic to imagine the difference between patristic and modern christologies as though it were simply a matter of a clear contrast. In the midst of all this difference, one possibility is to see how the modern christologies attempt to follow up the same tasks as are found in the historical christologies—the integrity of the human being and history and salvation—in different intellectual, cultural, and social circumstances. Certain of the critical questions that are posed by modern christologies to the historical formulations can be said to isolate problematic aspects of these that have been latent through the centuries. I therefore want to argue that even these modern christologies appear within the history of effect of the historical christologies. On the other hand, I believe as well that the mission of the historical christologies may have difficulty being heard within the contemporary situation precisely because of their history of effect. One

2. Cf. what Immanuel Kant writes in *Groundwork of the Metaphysics of Morals,* Cambridge Texts in the History of Philosophy, ed. and trans. Mary Gregor (Cambridge: Cambridge University Press, 1998), p. 47: "Autonomy of the will is the property of the will by which it is a law to itself (independently of any property of the objects of volition)." See also John Macquarrie, *Jesus Christ in Modern Thought* (London/Philadelphia: SCM/Trinity Press International, 1990), pp. 175-91, on Kant's Christology.

element of feminist Christology is, as we will see below, especially critical towards the Chalcedonian creed because of its androcentrism, but it is also possible to argue that feminist Christology in fact shares a Christological problem with Chalcedon. This apparent paradox is best explained as Chalcedon's history of effect having led to a particular reception of Chalcedon, which led thence to the Christology that feminist Christology opposes itself to. My point here is not that feminist Christology—or any other "revisionist" Christology—would not have grounds or capacity to criticize Chalcedon or any other Christological creed, but rather that it is difficult to know what it is one criticizes when one criticizes a creed like Chalcedon, since the understanding of the creed is so entangled with its history of effect.

The big difference between historical and modern Christology thus lies, I believe, in the modern emphasis on human subjectivity. We especially see the critical role of human subjectivity in the fact that even a theology or philosophy that is more or less critical towards the modern ideal of autonomy must nevertheless take a position regarding it. In this chapter I will present four different aspects of the turn to the subject within modern Christology with respect to their relationship to the classical creeds, above all to Chalcedon. I place these four aspects under the rubrics "subjectivity," "history," "language," and "sex," and they constitute a representative selection as regards those Christological tasks that the modern emphasis on human subjectivity has found urgent within the framework of the critical self-reflection of the Christian faith. They do not, however, exhaust in any way the themes that contemporary Christology has found urgent. Had I chosen to go outside the Christian church's own tradition, the question of the incarnation and religious pluralism would have become a primary question as well.[3] Another issue that touches mine, but which I will not treat either, is the question of the relationship between Christology and contemporary culture.[4] My survey limits itself to discussing four modern christologies with respect to their anthropology. I begin with Friedrich D. E. Schleiermacher, sometimes

3. For a constructive discussion of the relationship between Judaism and the Christian doctrine of incarnation, see Elliot R. Wolfson, "Judaism and Incarnation: The Imaginal Body of God," Randi Raschkover, "The Christian Doctrine of the Incarnation," together with Susan A. Ross, "Embodiment and Incarnation: A Response to Elliot Wolfson," together in *Christianity in Jewish Terms,* ed. Tikva Frymer-Kensky, David Novak, Peter Ochs, et al. (Boulder, CO/Oxford: Westview Press, 2000), pp. 239–54, 254–61, 262–68. On interreligious dialogue as a context for Christology, see Roger Haight, *Jesus Symbol of God* (Maryknoll, NY: Orbis, 1999), pp. 395–423.

4. See H. Richard Niebuhr's classic book (from 1951) *Christ and Culture,* Challenges in Contemporary Theology (Malden, MA/Oxford: Blackwell, 2005).

called the church father of modern Christology, as an introduction to the very question of incarnation and subjectivity, in order to go further with a theologian who has often been portrayed as Schleiermacher's antithesis, Karl Barth. With Barth we find a reflection on the historical concreteness of the person Jesus in relation to the classic Christological creeds. I then view the problematic issues surrounding incarnation and language with the aid of a famous Christological debate from 1970, which poses the question of whether the incarnation ought to be understood as a literal truth or as a myth, and I finally turn to feminist theology's questioning of whether a male savior can actually save women. History, language, and sex are all aspects of the question of subjectivity, and therefore can come to have great significance in different ways for how the incarnation may be understood within contemporary Christology. The critical question I want to pose to these different forms of modern Christological thought, and which will be the common denominator in this chapter, is in principle the same question as in the previous chapter, namely the question of the human being: Does the modern emphasis on human subjectivity actually succeed in recognizing the human being in her concrete, historical existence, or does modern Christology risk becoming abstract as well? I return to this question in a summary of sorts after having examined these four aspects.

Incarnation and Subjectivity

The German reformed theologian and philosopher Friedrich D. E. Schleiermacher (1768–1834) is probably the theologian of the nineteenth century who has meant most for later theology and philosophy in their adjustment to the ways that both Protestant orthodoxy and the Enlightenment present Christianity in intellectual or ethical categories. Schleiermacher's Christology has been called a "humanistic Christology," meaning a Christology that wants to emphasize the humanity of Christ, and that tries to avoid an understanding of Christ that in particular sacrifices his genuine humanity.[5] The modern understanding of human subjectivity is articulated in Schleiermacher in the very program for his theology. The criterion for the creed is "Christian consciousness," and on the basis of this measure Schleiermacher claims in *The Christian Faith* that one can assess which clauses in the creeds really belong to the Christian faith, and which are dispensable

---

5. Macquarrie, *Jesus Christ,* p. 203.

speculations.[6] The religious formulations that tradition has provided must therefore be critically scrutinized on the basis of their scientific legitimacy and their religious fecundity. The fact that something is included in a tradition does not in itself mean that it is either scientifically or religiously legitimate—it is the content of the formulations that must be treated critically. Doctrine is an expression of inner experiences of salvation that the Christian engages in within the Christian community.

Christ and Christian Self-Awareness

A central endeavor in Schleiermacher's Christology is to represent Christ's solidarity with the rest of humanity by avoiding differentiating between "natural" and "supernatural." Schleiermacher emphasizes in *The Christian Faith* that for Christians, Christ is a divine revelation. But he continues:

> But notwithstanding, it must be asserted that even the most rigorous view of the difference between Him and all other men does not hinder us from saying that His appearing, even regarded as the incarnation of the Son of God, is a natural fact. For in the first place: as certainly as Christ was a man, there must reside in human nature the possibility of taking up the divine into itself, just as did happen in Christ.[7]

The becoming human of the Son of God must be something "natural," since what is meant must link to the possibilities in human nature for solidarity with humanity, and it is by this that salvation will be genuine. The point of connection lies in the human nature's potential for "taking up the divine in itself." The fact that this becoming human is natural and is tied to human potential does not, however, mean for Schleiermacher that it may be reduced to an immanent process. On the contrary, it is in the natural that God makes God's more than natural initiative effective. Schleiermacher thus wants to argue that God works in a special way in Christ, but wants to avoid having this be understood as something that is happening apart from other, natural processes.

6. Friedrich D. E. Schleiermacher, *The Christian Faith,* ed. H. R. Mackintosh and J. S. Stewart (London/New York: T. & T. Clark, 1999), pp. 389-90 (§95). Cf. pp. 78-81, 125-27 (§§16, 30).

7. Schleiermacher, *The Christian Faith,* p. 64 (§13).

Who then is Christ, according to Schleiermacher? In what we might call Schleiermacher's version of the doctrine of two natures, he argues that Christ is on the one hand identical in his human nature to other humans.[8] On the other hand, Christ is different from all other humans through his God consciousness. The quantitative power of the God consciousness in Christ is what sets him apart from other humans, and it is this that is God's existence in him as well. Schleiermacher means that Christ must be understood as free of sin thanks to precisely this intensity of the God consciousness in him. Sin is, according to Schleiermacher, a consequence of the dimming of the person's "feeling of absolute dependency" *(schlechthinnige Abhängigkeitsgefühl)*—what he called earlier in *On Religion* her "sense and taste for the Infinite" *(Sinn und Geschmack für das Unendliche)*, which is a more active formulation of the understanding of the person's longing for and dependence on God.[9] The fact that her feeling of absolute dependency is dimmed also does damage to her God consciousness, since this is a correlate to this feeling. The feeling of absolute dependence is namely "in and of itself" coexistent with the presence of God in human self-awareness.[10] The difference between Christ and other humans is that the feeling of absolute dependency is not dimmed in Christ, and so neither is his God consciousness. Thus he can exist without sin. This freedom from sin means no sacrifice of his solidarity with other humans, since Schleiermacher's sin is regarded as a "disturbance," and thus not a constitutive part of a person's being.[11]

Schleiermacher's Interpretation of the Doctrine of Two Natures

Can one call this a doctrine of two natures in the classical sense? Strictly speaking, the answer is no. Schleiermacher is critical of the classical doctrine of two natures. One of his main objections is that the concept "nature" is used about both God and human in the Chalcedonian formula and its

---

8. Schleiermacher, *The Christian Faith*, pp. 385–86 (§94).

9. Friedrich D. E. Schleiermacher, *On Religion: Speeches to Its Cultured Despisers*, trans. John Oman (London: K. Paul, Trench, Trubner & Co, 1893), p. 39.

10. Schleiermacher, *The Christian Faith*, p. 126 (§30): "a co-existence of God in the self-consciousness." On the understanding of Schleiermacher's "feeling of absolute dependence," see Nicholas Lash, *Easter in Ordinary: Reflections on Human Experience and the Knowledge of God* (London: SCM, 1988), pp. 120–30.

11. Schleiermacher, *The Christian Faith*, p. 385 (§94).

reiterations. His problems with this concept are several.[12] To begin with, Schleiermacher believes that it is impossible to use a concept like nature to denote both divine and human without falling prey to ambiguity. The concept nature as we understand it cannot be used about God, since by nature we mean a finite existence, or an embodied existence in opposition to a historical existence. These categories cannot be used about God, since God is unbound and simple. Even if one pursues the concept of nature back to its Greek origins in *physis,* it carries with it traces of an unconscious influence from "heathen ideas" (i.e., polytheism). Second, Schleiermacher believes that it is impossible to assert that a person would have two natures. Nature is a universal concept that tends to be used to encompass several particular entities, but here a concrete person is said to encompass two natures, and in addition, two natures so radically separated as divine and human. Schleiermacher believes that the formula "one person in two natures" is quite simply incomprehensible, as shown by its history. Either divine and human have been blended together, against Chalcedon's explicit formulation, or they have been separated, which has the consequence that the unity has been lost, or that the one or the other pole has dominated. The unproductive nature of this discourse shows itself in the post-Chalcedonian debate whether Christ had one or two wills.

Third, Schleiermacher believes that the parlance of dogma becomes confused when a concept is used in different ways. He says that this is the case when it comes to the doctrine of the hypostatic union and the doctrine of the Trinity. Christology teaches "one person with two natures," while the doctrine of the Trinity speaks of "three persons with the same substance." While Schleiermacher clearly believes that "substance" is a more suitable term to apply to God than "nature," we still must ask ourselves whether these terms stand for approximately the same thing. What else would the relationship be between Christ's divine nature and the divine substance that the three persons share in? Moreover, the concept "person" seems to be used in different ways. Finally, Schleiermacher believes that the value for the church of this classic formulation of the doctrine of incarnation cannot be particularly great. A lot of effort has been devoted to attempting to give meaning to such an untenable articulation, and thus the true knowledge of Christ has been dimmed. Since even the reformers retained the doctrine, it is high time for a change.

Even if, expressed thus, Schleiermacher does not present a classical

---

12. Schleiermacher, *The Christian Faith,* pp. 391–96 (§96).

doctrine of two natures, he does not want to deny what he believes was the intention of the formulation,

> namely, to describe Christ in such a way *(frater, consubstantialis nobis)* that in the new corporate life a vital fellowship between us and Him shall be possible, and, at the same time, that the existence of God in Him shall be expressed in the clearest possible way; from which follows at once that the most unconditional adoration and brotherly comradeship are united in our relation to Him.[13]

But the account of the doctrine of two natures leaves a lot to be desired, both as regards its scientific legitimacy and its religious usefulness, Schleiermacher claims. A formulation that expresses Schleiermacher's conception of Christ is the following: Christ is the one "in Whom the creation of human nature, which up to this point had existed only in a provisional state, was perfected."[14] We might rephrase Schleiermacher's formulation thus: in Christ, we meet the true human, a person who is more authentic than anyone else, and because of exactly this we can understand how God is present in him in an especially complete way. We can thus also say that in him God has become human.[15]

In principle, this incarnation should presumably be understood as a quantitatively rather than qualitatively superior divine revelation. In a sense, in Christ God makes use of a potential that exists in all human beings. God's becoming human can be understood here as something "natural." But Schleiermacher does not have a narrow-minded evolutionary view of the incarnation, as though it were exclusively a consequence of immanent processes. In another sense it is precisely in Christ that God takes this special initiative that means the fulfillment of the human. Schleiermacher speaks of Christ as "the second Adam" and believes that God carried out a new Creation as a primordial act at the beginning of Christ's life.[16] The original creation and

---

13. Schleiermacher, *The Christian Faith*, p. 391 (§96).

14. Schleiermacher, *The Christian Faith*, p. 374 (§92).

15. Schleiermacher, *The Christian Faith*, pp. 396-98 (§96).

16. Schleiermacher, *The Christian Faith*, pp. 385-86 (§94). John Macquarrie *(Jesus Christ,* pp. 207-8) criticizes Schleiermacher for being theologically inconsistent when he criticizes the virgin birth but draws up a theological equivalence in God's special initiative in Christ. This may suggest a more fundamental ambivalence with Schleiermacher in his desire to on the one hand affirm the fundamental solidarity between Christ and all other people and on the other hand to emphasize the unique divine initiative in Christ.

the new spiritual creation are, however, two aspects that both go back to one and the same eternal divine predetermination.

The above may give the impression that Schleiermacher unilaterally advocates Christ as the absolute role-model, but not as the savior of the human in a more active sense. That is not the case. Although Schleiermacher is critical of the ways in which the representations of reconciliation have been presented by tradition, he does not want to reduce salvation to the possibility of following the example of Christ. A summary of how he understands Christ's salvation may be found in the following sentence: "The Redeemer assumes believers into the power of His God-consciousness, and this is His redemptive activity."[17] This salvation, which consists in believers getting to participate in the God consciousness of Christ, is experienced in the fellowship of believers. This mediating of the God consciousness has nothing to do with any ideas of a resurrection from the dead or an ascension into heaven—which is otherwise unexceptional—since these ideas do not express any connection with Christian salvation.[18] This does not mean that Schleiermacher denies everything that these doctrines entail, but rather that he denies that they would have an outer as opposed to an internal meaning, i.e., that the resurrection would be seen as (in some sense) a physical occurrence. Christ's activity in the Christian congregation is "the continuation of the divine activity out of which the Person of Christ arose."[19] God calls the congregation and the individual through Christ, and inspires them as well. Schleiermacher compares the presence of God in the Christian congregation to the relationship between body and soul: Christ is the soul, the congregation or the individual the body. In other words, the presence of God is an internal experience that is dependent on the social community, but that is shared by each individual in the community. It is this experience that is mediated by Christ for the congregation, and this mediation happens neither as a supernatural mediation with no basis in the natural, nor as a purely natural mediation by certain doctrines and examples—Christianity is neither magic nor philosophy, one might say.[20]

For Schleiermacher it was a fundamental part of his theology and philosophy that reality consisted in a network of relationships. A person who wants to have knowledge about a certain object cannot abstract it from the network in which it exists, without the object itself disintegrating. "Knowledge of an ob-

---

17. Schleiermacher, *The Christian Faith,* p. 425 (§100).

18. Schleiermacher, *The Christian Faith,* pp. 417–18 (§99). Cf. Rowan Williams, *Resurrection: Interpreting the Easter Gospel* (Harrisburg, PA: Morehouse Publishing, 1994).

19. Schleiermacher, *The Christian Faith,* p. 427 (§100). Cf. pp. 398–413.

20. Schleiermacher, *The Christian Faith,* pp. 428–31 (§100).

ject," writes theologian Richard R. Niebuhr apropos Schleiermacher, "means an exhaustive knowledge of all the relationships in which it stands, and hence true knowledge is only an eschatological possibility."[21] This means, among other things, that not even the theologian seeking to understand Christology can be abstracted from her or his historical position or relationship to Christ. Thus she or he must take her or his starting point in the relationship to Christ, namely in the humanity that Christ has redeemed and the relationship to God as the Christian consciousness understands it. What Schleiermacher wants to avoid when it comes to the formulation of a Christology are assertions that give the impression of speaking about God or the world abstracted from the relationship between God and the world. The crucial thing for the legitimacy of a theological doctrine is the doctrine's relationship to piety, not to abstract speculations. As I have pointed out in previous chapters, this is something that also characterizes historical Christology (whose mission was existential rather than speculative), nor is Schleiermacher out to deny the intention of the historical christologies, but rather to critically evaluate the result.

The Christian Consciousness and the Other

The criticism directed against Schleiermacher's Christology has, among other things, consisted in the fact that it does not seem to leave sufficient space between Christ and the Christian consciousness, such that Christ would be able to have a critical function with regard to this consciousness. Does Schleiermacher forget that Christ is more than the apotheosis of human nature—namely its judge? With his emphasis on the Christian congregation and its self-awareness, and on the continuity with Christ, a Christology of Schleiermacher's type risks falling prey to the sort of criticism that Karl Barth later directed against Schleiermacher, namely that his theology led to a kind of "cultural Protestantism." This critique is too extensive to discuss in detail here, but its core point can be described with the aid of Barth's own words, taken from a presentation from 1917, "The Strange New World within the Bible," where he argues that the Bible does not contain "the right human thoughts about God," but "the right divine thoughts about men."[22]

---

21. Richard R. Niebuhr, *Schleiermacher on Christ and Religion: A New Introduction* (New York: Charles Scribner's Sons, 1964), p. 70.

22. Karl Barth, "The Strange New World within the Bible," in *The Word of God and the Word of Man*, trans. Douglas Horton (Gloucester, MA: Peter Smith, 1978), p. 43.

Barth's criticism of Schleiermacher was more nuanced than this, but here we see at least one clichéd formulation of the problem with starting from the consciousness of the human being. Especially after the philosophical critique that has been directed against the idea of a self-reflexive subject since the end of the nineteenth century—among others by the "masters of suspicion" Marx, Nietzsche, and Freud—it becomes difficult for a Christology that starts from the subjectivity of the person to make claims of self-evidence. The problem with Schleiermacher is not that he criticizes a Christology that gives the impression of speaking about God and the world apart from the relationship between God and the world—on the contrary, I contend that that is the strength of Schleiermacher's Christology—or that he argues that a Christology must be made understandable in relation to the subjectivity of the contemporary human being. It has to do instead with the fact that Schleiermacher, in spite of everything, sets up contemporary human subjectivity as a superordinate norm and starting point for his Christological thought. A Christology of Schleiermacher's type thus risks becoming a legitimizing ideology both for the God consciousness of the time and for the science and church of the time. In Schleiermacher the human being is certainly a creature that exists in a network of relationships, but if her subjectivity becomes the horizon against which all theologically legitimate relationships to God must show up, Schleiermacher's understanding of the incarnation tends to become an affirmation of only those of the person's relationships that can be made understandable by her consciousness. Such an understanding of subjectivity means that the person is never confronted with anything alien; she remains alone with herself. For Barth, who had seen Schleiermacher's theological heritage developed into a kind of cultural Protestantism during the period up until the First World War, it was therefore important to emphasize the other pole in the relationship between the person and God. A Christology where Christ himself became the person's other, the horizon against which her subjectivity could show up, became Barth's mission following the First World War.

Incarnation and History

The Swiss theologian Karl Barth (1886–1968) is likely the theologian who has presented the most comprehensive Christological work in the twentieth century, which he often does in both indirect and direct polemic against Schleiermacher and liberal theology. He is one of the twentieth century's foremost proponents of a theology of incarnation, shown not least in that which is the center of his Christology, namely a Bible verse, John 1:14: "And the Word became flesh *[sarx]*."[23] The formula that he uses in order to speak about the incarnation throughout the entire *Church Dogmatics,* "truly God and truly human," is, according to himself, simply a rewriting of this central New Testament statement. Barth has often been set forth as one of the great renewers of the patristic heritage within Christology, and a cursory reading of his books easily gives the impression that they have to do with a positive attachment to traditional Christology, even if with certain minor shifts in emphasis.[24]

A Christological Grammar

Given modern Christology's suspicion of a traditional Christology, the question arises whether Barth's Christology is merely an attempted repristination of a traditional Christology, i.e., a restoration of its original form, or whether it may in some sense be called a critical Christology. Apart from the fact that the last four volumes of his monumental *Church Dogmatics* were devoted to the doctrine of atonement, within which framework he also discusses the doctrine of the incarnation, his entire *Church Dogmatics* has a Christological approach, as indicated by the fact that Christology is discussed already in the prolegomena. In a work that spans over ten thousand pages and was written and published over a period of more than thirty years, there are great possibilities for nuances and development of the topic, but also possibilities for elucidation and changes of course. Here I will only discuss a few aspects of Barth's Christology in *Church Dogmatics,* above all his dependence on the Christological tradition as well as his transformation of it. My discussion is thus not comprehensive in any respect—I instead only want to highlight those aspects that are relevant for my study here. I therefore want to indicate critical aspects of Barth's Christology aimed at the tradition as well as at the liberal Christology of his time, and not least (indirectly) at earlier conceptions of his own Christology, and attempt to show that in Barth it is not a matter of a reiteration of historical Christology, but rather an interpretation

23. Karl Barth, *Church Dogmatics,* vol. 1: *The Doctrine of the Word of God,* part 2, trans. G. T. Thomson and Harold Knight (Edinburgh: T. & T. Clark, 1956), p. 132.

24. On the relationship between Barth's Christology and patristic Christology, see E. P. Meijering, *Von den Kirchenvätern zu Karl Barth: Das altkirchliche Dogma in der 'Kirchlichen Dogmatik'* (Amsterdam: Verlag J. C. Gieben, 1993), pp. 106-56, 340-88.

of it on the basis of the modern turn to subjectivity. In a certain sense Barth may be seen both as an antipode to and a continuation of Schleiermacher's Christological mission: like Schleiermacher, he believed that a theological discourse about God or the world apart from the relationship between God and the world becomes abstract, but unlike Schleiermacher Barth wanted to emphasize the divine rather than the human pole in this relationship.

One aspect of Barth's theology in *Church Dogmatics* that is appropriate as a starting point for my analysis is its Christological grammar. Christological grammar is not a concept that Barth himself uses, but applied to Barth, it means that Christology as theological doctrine is neither mythology nor speculation any more than in Schleiermacher.[25] We should note that the theology that Barth describes in his work is intended to be a critical corrective to something that precedes it, and that it is thus not in itself the conclusive form for Christian discourse about God. Dogmatics requires a Christian life-world where there explicitly or implicitly exist concepts, analogies, metaphors, and similes that govern the Christian life in discourse, text, and action. What Barth's dogmatics attempts to get at and critically study is

---

25. Cf. Ingolf U. Dalferth, *Jenseits von Mythos und Logos: Die christologische Transformation der Theologie* (Freiburg: Herder, 1993). Why call this a "grammar"? The point of this comparison is the difference between language and grammar. Language and grammar are not identical. A language can be used without its grammar being articulated, but it always implies a grammar. The grammar can be said to be the self-reflection of language, but it can never replace the use of language itself, and so does not constitute a competitor. Dalferth can also say that grammar shares the distance to its context (language, *mythos*, the life-world) with *logos*, but that it at the same time can never give up the relationship to its specific context and rise to a higher degree of universality. Every language has a rationale of its own that characterizes its grammar. Dogmatics as grammar thus involves a distance from the obvious of the religious life-world, but not a more universal replacement for it. Dalferth writes in *Jenseits*, pp. 195–96, "Grammatiken sind also rationale Orientierungsinstrumente, aber weder im Sinn der analogisierenden Verfahren der Mythen noch im Sinn des generalisierenden Logos neuzeitlicher Wissenschaft." This citation clearly illustrates Dalferth's idea that the theology of Christology as grammar finds itself beyond *mythos* and *logos*. The Christian life-world can be understood as a semiotic system, i.e., as syntactic, semantic, and pragmatic sign relationships, which follow certain grammatical rules. Thus this characterizes the Christian life-world as a whole and not only its texts. The Christian life-world is itself the text/context for dogmatics as grammar. Dogmatics as grammar is thus the system of rules for the semiotic activities of the Christian life-world. Theology is then a theoretical activity that is created by the practical problems and needs of the Christian life-world, for example, the problem of how Christian practices will continue under new or alien circumstances. Theology's attempt to set up rules for legitimate Christian discourse about God through dogmatics is not an attempt to formulate statements of the first order, but an attempt to specify those rules that these first-order statements must follow in order to be able to claim to be "genuinely Christian."

the structured cohesion between ideas, analogies, metaphors, and similes. Dogmatics will thus attempt to critically reconstruct the deep structure of the Christian life-world, i.e., its grammar. For Barth, the core structure of the Christian life-world is the Christological grammar of the biblical texts, and he bases this theologically on the fact that the revelation in Christ is a part of God's eternal predetermination.[26]

Thus it is Christology that structures Barth's theology, and here we find the basis for the criticism that has been expressed in several "classic" studies of Barth's theology, namely that it is christomonist.[27] So Christology does not function simply as an individual doctrine in Barth, the doctrine of Christ distinct from the doctrine of the Father and the doctrine of the Spirit. Moreover, Christology constitutes the standard on the basis of which all these doctrines are construed. It is on the basis of Jesus Christ that all these concepts that are used within the discourse of the theological life-world get their meaning.[28] The Christological grammar transforms the meaning of those concepts that are taken from outside theological discourse, but also governs the use of theological concepts within the same. The person who, within the Christian life-world, wants to speak and act in a correct way (which does not necessarily mean in an unambiguous way) does so, *if* she or he follows the rules for discourse and action that are formulated by the Christological grammar. Barth's Christology can thus be interpreted functionally, as a suite of rules for a correct Christian language. Christology is, in Barth, the grammar that regulates the semiotic universe of the Christian life-world. This does not mean that meaning in the Christian life-world is completely unambiguous, but instead that its semiotic universe interacts with the semiotic universes of other life-worlds in different ways by being influenced by them, coming into conflict with them, and transforming them.

According to Barth's theology, the Christological grammar ought to characterize dogmatics, since it characterizes the biblical testimony about

26. See Karl Barth's interpretation of the doctrine of predestination in *Church Dogmatics*, vol. 2: *The Doctrine of God*, part 2, trans. G. W. Bromiley, J. C. Campbell, Iain Wilson, J. Strathern McNab, Harold Knight, and R. A. Stewart (Edinburgh: T. & T. Clark, 1957), pp. 94–194.

27. See, for example, Hans Urs von Balthasar, *The Theology of Karl Barth: Exposition and Interpretation*, Communio Books, trans. Edward T. Oakes (San Francisco: Ignatius Press, 1992); G. C. Berkouwer, *The Triumph of Grace in the Theology of Karl Barth: An Introduction and Critical Appraisal*, trans. Harry R. Boer (Grand Rapids: Eerdmans, 1956); Gustaf Wingren, *Teologiens metodfråga* (Lund: Gleerups, 1954).

28. Cf. Bruce Marshall, *Christology in Conflict: The Identity of a Saviour in Rahner and Barth* (Oxford: Basil Blackwell, 1987), p. 163.

Jesus. The point of Christological dogmatics is that it makes criticism possible, since it gives "guidelines, directions, insights, principles and limits for correct speech by human estimate."[29] It therefore fills precisely the function of being able to assess which use of images, metaphors, and similes expresses the Christian message in a trustworthy and faithful way. The Christological deep-grammar that characterizes scripture thus makes it possible for dogmatics to relate critically both to preaching and to itself. It is thus not primarily the Christological grammar that is the standard for Barth, but Christ himself. There is accordingly a relativizing and self-critical feature within dogmatics itself. However, the standard for correction and improvement is not a changeable historical situation or an extra-theological logic, but Jesus Christ himself understood as an "epistemological principle."[30] Christology is the instrument the Christian church has for criticizing its own life-world, inclusive of the articulation of its dogma.

In light of this, it is hardly surprising that Christological thought is found in two different places in *Church Dogmatics,* more comprehensively in the volumes that make up the fourth volume, which treats the doctrine of reconciliation, and already in the first volume, which contains the prolegomena. For Barth the prolegomena entails discussing the reality and possibility of the revelation on the basis of the revelation itself, and so is not a neutral or extra-theological justification of theology's conditions of possibility.[31] Instead, the conditions of possibility are given in and with the revelation itself, and we thereby also find in the very justification of dogmatics a developed doctrine of the Trinity and Christology. The doctrine of the triune nature of God gives an answer to the question of the subject of the revelation that scripture testifies to, while Christology, in light of the objective reality of the revelation in Christ, discusses the objective conditions of the possibility for what Barth calls "God's freedom for Man."[32] Barth then also discusses the subjective conditions of possibility, "the freedom of humanity for God,"

29. Karl Barth, *Church Dogmatics,* vol. 1: *The Doctrine of the Word of God,* part 1, second edition, trans. G. W. Bromiley (Edinburgh: T. & T. Clark, 1975), p. 86.

30. Karl Barth, *Church Dogmatics,* vol. 4: *The Doctrine of Reconciliation,* part 1, trans. G. W. Bromiley and T. F. Torrance (Edinburgh: T. & T. Clark, 1956), p. 21. See also Karl Barth, *Church Dogmatics,* vol. 3: *The Doctrine of Creation,* part 2, trans. Harold Knight, G. W. Bromiley, J. K. S. Reid, and R. H. Fuller (Edinburgh: T. & T. Clark, 1960), pp. 21, 25.

31. Barth does not thereby argue for some simple "evil circle." On Barth's theology of revelation, see Bent Flemming Nielsen, *Die Rationalität der Offenbarungstheologie: Die Struktur des Theologieverständnisses von Karl Barth* (Århus: Aarhus University Press, 1988).

32. Barth, *Church Dogmatics* I/2, pp. 1–202.

within the framework of pneumatology. So Barth finds the objective conditions of possibility for a divine revelation in Christ, and thus the vision of Christ becomes vital for a revelation theology of Barth's sort.

The Christology we meet in the prolegomena is of a rather traditional kind. Barth explicitly affirms the Christological definitions and doctrine of two natures, but points out that there is no single formula, and that the different formulas must be understood as commentaries on the confession of Christ, not as the confession itself.[33] It is Christ himself, not some theory about him, who is the substance of the New Testament.[34] One should therefore neither attempt to harmonize what the different New Testament writings say about him, nor do violence via the Christological definitions to the character of mystery of the revelation.[35] Christological thinking does not consist in a system, but in a path—but it is a path that the dogmaticist leaves only at the risk of her or his own degradation. "As a whole, i.e., in the basic statements of a church dogmatics, Christology must either be dominant and perceptible, or else it is not Christology."[36] Barth believes that the work of dogmatics has strayed from this standard not only in the modern period, but that the ground was already laid even in the age of orthodoxy, yes, even during the Middle Ages and among the church fathers. At the same time, it is clear that Barth is above all critical of contemporary liberal theology and its criticism of traditional Christology. In one of the sharper formulations in a discussion of the traditional confession of Christ as "truly God and truly human," Barth criticizes modern Christology for "a horror of *physis,* of externality, of corporeality," suggesting that it is only capable of breathing the thin air of moralism—in other words, that its Christology is reduced to a vision of Jesus Christ as a moral role-model.[37] In part, one might imagine that Barth's use of the traditional Christological creeds is motivated by his critique of liberal theology. His general critique of this, which concerns its Christology as well, is that it attempts to understand theology on the basis of concepts and representations that are not taken or derived from the revelation itself, and that it thereby makes itself guilty of "natural theology," i.e.—to put it briefly—understanding God on human terms.

The North American theologian and Barth scholar George Hunsinger has called this Christological grammar in Barth's dogmatics a "Chalcedonian par-

33. Barth, *Church Dogmatics* I/2, p. 13.
34. Barth, *Church Dogmatics* I/2, pp. 14–15.
35. Barth, *Church Dogmatics* I/2, pp. 16–25, 131.
36. Barth, *Church Dogmatics* I/2, p. 123.
37. Barth, *Church Dogmatics* I/2, p. 130.

adigm" that informs the structure of the entire *Church Dogmatics*.[38] Through the Chalcedonian paradigm, which functions both implicitly and explicitly in Barth's theology, Barth conceptualizes, according to Hunsinger, a number of central dogmatic concepts, such as, for example, divine and human agency.[39] The Chalcedonian paradigm entails, put succinctly, that the person does not have any autonomy in relation to God (against Pelagianism), but that God, on the other hand, does not determine her actions (against determinism), even if God has the initiative (against a dialectical identity between the grace of God and the freedom of the person). This is one way to articulate how Barth understands grace as a theological category. Barth maintains this paradigm all the way through *Church Dogmatics,* thus giving a structure for understanding the relationship between God and human, along with their respective agency.

A Narrative Christology

Even if Barth's theology may thus be said to be christocentric throughout the entire *Church Dogmatics,* and so in one way or another to exhibit the Christological grammar that I have spoken of here, there are clear shifts in the understanding of Christology between the earlier and the later portions. As the Irish theologian David F. Ford has shown, Barth understood the revelation up through volume I, part 2 of *Church Dogmatics* as essentially a meeting between an I and a You.[40] However, in §59, "The Obedience of the Son of God," from volume IV, part 1 of *Church Dogmatics,* Barth seems to argue that the best explanation of the passion story is its retelling. He begins the entire paragraph with the following:

> The atonement is history *[Geschichte]*. To know it, we must know it as such. To think of it, we must think of it as such. To speak of it, we must tell

38. George Hunsinger, *How to Read Karl Barth: The Shape of His Theology* (New York/Oxford: Oxford University Press, 1991), p. 85. Cf. also pp. 286–87, n. 1.

39. Hunsinger, *Karl Barth,* pp. 185–88, 201–18.

40. David F. Ford, *Barth and God's Story: Biblical Narrative and the Theological Method of Karl Barth in the 'Church Dogmatics,'* 2nd edition (Frankfurt am Main/Bern/New York: Peter Lang, 1985), p. 24. Cf., for example, Barth, *Church Dogmatics* I/2, p. 103: "In the New Testament, too, revelation breaks in from above, from an altitude which is not that of a so-called historical peak." In his narrative interpretation of Barth Ford is inspired by Yale theologian Hans W. Frei. Cf. Frei's *The Identity of Jesus Christ: The Hermeneutical Bases of Dogmatic Theology* (Philadelphia: Fortress, 1975).

it as history. To try to grasp it as supra-historical or non-historical truth is not to grasp it at all. It is indeed truth, but truth actualised in a history and revealed in this history as such—revealed, therefore, as history.[41]

The meaningfulness of the incarnation can therefore, according to Barth, only be determined through reference to the account. Thus even the idea of revelation has changed in Barth's dogmatics from a dialogical to a narrative concept. Where in the prolegomena Barth could say that the entire revelation consists in the *name* Jesus Christ, it is said in the fourth volume of the Christology that this name without exception means the *story* of Jesus Christ.[42] The narrative focus in his later Christology means that its dynamic character becomes clearer.

The story of Christ is, according to Barth in this fourth part, identical with the story of how God does not want to be God without humanity.[43] Thus the story of Christ becomes the account of how a mutual story for God and humanity takes place in Christ. This story is mutual to both God and humanity because God makes it mutual. God's initiative is thus still primary, and the human's part in this story is her historical response to God's initiative. Even here we can recognize the Chalcedonian paradigm, if with a certain shift in emphasis. Before I return to this difference, let me first say something more general about Barth's Christology in volume IV.

It becomes clear here that Barth is not interested in discussing the doctrine of the incarnation apart and abstracted from the doctrine of atonement. On the contrary, the meaning of the incarnation first becomes clear in and through the exposition of the atonement. Barth notes that the distinction between "Christology" and "atonement" is a customary way to proceed within dogmatics, but he believes that such an abstraction is hardly trustworthy in light of the New Testament testimony: "In the New Testament there are many Christological statements both direct and indirect. But where do we find a special Christology?"[44] This does not mean that Barth does away with the patristic Christology: "We cannot avoid the old formula: very God, very man, very God-man."[45] For

41. Barth, *Church Dogmatics* IV/1, p. 157.

42. Barth, *Church Dogmatics* I/2, pp. 10–12; Barth, *Church Dogmatics*, vol. 4: *The Doctrine of Reconciliation*, part 2, trans. G. W. Bromiley (Edinburgh: T. & T. Clark, 1958), p. 107.

43. On the understanding of history in Karl Barth, see primarily Kjetil Hafstad, *Wort und Geschichte: Das Geschichtsverständnis Karl Barths*, Beiträge zur evangelischen Theologie (Munich: Chr. Kaiser, 1985).

44. Barth, *Church Dogmatics* IV/1, p. 124.

45. Barth, *Church Dogmatics* IV/1, p. 138.

Barth it is instead about understanding the traditional doctrine of incarnation within the framework of the story that Christ is. It is the very abstraction of these themes that Barth wants to counter, and that which he is most critical of is the presentation of the doctrine of atonement as an addition to or one implication of the doctrine of incarnation.[46] Barth is careful here to note that the opposite is not possible either, namely to let the formulations of the doctrine of incarnation fall away. Briefly, his justification involves the fact that the course of events of atonement would in that case be presented as a course of events without a subject. Thus the same aim as that of the theologians of the ancient church, but also as that of Schleiermacher—if carried out in a very different way—returns here in Barth, namely to avoid imagining Christ as something abstract, or approaching the matter in a speculative way, outside of the relationship of those who receive Christ.

Thus Barth as well comes to engage critically with the classical Christological definitions, insofar as they lead theology to the view that it is possible to formulate a doctrine of the person of Christ independent of his deeds. Apropos these classical definitions, Barth writes:

> In Himself and as such the Christ of Nicaea and Chalcedon naturally was and is a being which even if we could consistently and helpfully explain His unique structure conceptually could not possibly be proclaimed and believed as One who acts historically because of the timelessness and historical remoteness of the concepts (person, nature, Godhead, manhood, etc.). He could not possibly be proclaimed and believed as the One whom in actual fact the Christian Church has always and everywhere proclaimed and believed under the name of Jesus Christ. An abstract doctrine of the person of Christ may have its own apparent importance, but it is always an empty form, in which what we have to say concerning Jesus Christ can never be said.[47]

At the same time, and here we find a feature in the very configuration of Barth's Christology in the volume on the doctrine of atonement that is shared with the Christology of the prolegomena, Barth does not want to do without these traditional Christological definitions, but points out that the intent with these was never to provide building blocks for the construction of an abstract doctrine of the person of Christ. Instead, one must understand

---

46. Barth, *Church Dogmatics* IV/1, pp. 138–39.
47. Barth, *Church Dogmatics* IV/1, p. 139.

them contextually, as polemical, critical, but also clarifying and delimiting statements in line with which one can understand the person of Christ. For Barth's part, Christology is about being able to see how incarnation and atonement are associated, even joined, and thereby doing away with the traditional distinction between them, a distinction that seems to presume that it would be possible to divide the one from the other. The critique of an abstract understanding of the Christological definitions is one side of the coin, the other side of which in Barth represents the emphasis on the concreteness in the story of Jesus. So Barth emphatically argues that the Word did become "flesh" in the greatest general sense, but specifically "Jewish flesh"—this was written in 1953 against the background of Barth's own struggle during the Second World War against "Deutsche Christen," i.e., the movement within the German Protestant churches that allied itself with Nazism.[48] This means that Jesus Christ must be understood in light of the Old Testament and the history of Israel in order to be understood at all. Every attempt to speak about Jesus as "the human in general" thus risks falling into the pitfall of Docetism, in that one thereby looks away from his concrete, historical place in world history—or perhaps a better way to put it: world history within the framework of the concrete place and time that God had chosen to be revealed in. Docetism is the position that the humanity of Christ was merely a phantom humanity, a position that was sharply rejected by the tone-setting theologians of the early church.

Barth thus makes claim to continuity with the classical Christological creeds. The most comprehensive discussion of Christ's two natures is in the second part of the fourth volume. Here Barth treats the other aspect of the doctrine of atonement, the movement of the person towards God, or "the servant as Lord."[49] In §64, "The Exaltation of the Son of Man," we find a comprehensive discussion of the doctrine of two natures. The starting point for this discussion is that which is intended with the profession of Christ as *vere homo* (i.e., "truly human," or more literally, "human in truth"). To begin with, Barth rejects the idea, in accordance with his approach in the Christological grammar, that it is a matter of a humanity derived from a general anthropology.[50] The anthropology that underpins the understanding of the *humanitas* of Christ cannot be retrieved anywhere else than from Jesus Christ

48. Barth, *Church Dogmatics* IV/1, p. 181. On Barth's relationship to the Jewish people, see Eberhard Busch, *Unter dem Bogen des einen Bundes: Karl Barth und die Juden, 1933–1945* (Neukirchen-Vluyn: Neukirchener Verlag, 1996).

49. Barth, *Church Dogmatics* IV/2, pp. 3–377.

50. Barth, *Church Dogmatics* IV/2, pp. 26–31.

himself. Christ is namely the human who turns in gratitude to the grace of God. Here Barth wants to avoid an abstract representation of human nature, and attempts instead to deduce the meaning of *humanitas* from the Gospels' accounts of Jesus. As I mentioned apropos the Christological grammar, the meaning in the theological concepts is something that is governed by the language game of the theological life-world, and not something that one may establish "in general" apart from one or another language game. We know what true humanity is, speaking theologically, only through the true human, Jesus Christ. Barth further emphasizes, on the other hand, that the *humanitas* of Jesus is not something he is second-hand, but rather both his divinity and his humanity are necessary in order to understand Christ. Christ has no history apart from this human history.[51] It is in this human way that the Word exists as God, without, through its human existence, ceasing to be God because of this.

The formulation of the doctrine of two natures that Barth favors is "that in the one Jesus Christ divine and human essence were and are united."[52] Even here Barth emphasizes that this is not a speculative position regarding the possibility of joining that which it is impossible to join, but instead a reference to a concrete story where that which may not be joined is in fact joined. This joining, this *unio hypostatica,* does not entail a denial of the Alexandrian mission in the Chalcedonian creed, that it is one and the same Christ who functions in two natures (unity), or of the Antiochian mission in the same creed, that this does not entail any confusion of the two natures (differentiation).[53] The subject of the incarnation, in accordance with the Chalcedonian paradigm that I mentioned above, is nevertheless God, and the asymmetry in the hypostatic union is maintained as well. In a section in volume IV/2 Barth emphasizes as well that the concepts that are used in order to explain the doctrine of two natures are dependent on the concrete story that the New Testament attests to.[54] Barth must therefore deliver his Christology in a different form than the historical church did. The union of God and human in Christ does not actually have to do with the union of two "things," but with story and the course of events.

To sum up, one can note that Barth, in his discussion of the question of the two natures of Christ, does not intend to start from any more or less traditional, general representations about what constitutes divinity or humanity in

51. Barth, *Church Dogmatics* IV/2, p. 35.
52. Barth, *Church Dogmatics* IV/2, p. 60.
53. Barth, *Church Dogmatics* IV/2, pp. 63–66.
54. Barth, *Church Dogmatics* IV/2, pp. 106–12.

order to then apply them to the Gospel accounts. Instead, he wants to deduce the essence of the two natures from the evangelical accounts, and thus let the unique become the starting point for the more general. Using the concept of "grace," Barth wants to explain how the two natures can be united in Christ without the divine and human natures being confused.[55] The potential difference in Barth vis-à-vis a traditional Christology is primarily his emphasis that an abstract interpretation of the traditional definitions is not capable of satisfying the concrete revelation in and of Jesus Christ, but instead results in a phantom. I speak here of a "potential" difference, since my interpretation of the central historical Christological creeds emphasizes precisely that these do not replace the Bible's accounts, but should rather be seen as a commentary on these accounts, in other words, a kind of grammar. At the same time, it is clear that they have often been applied, not as "commentary," but as "primary text," and thereby have resulted in a Christological speculation that has been more or less cut loose from the accounts of Jesus from Nazareth. To the degree to which this happens, they have, according to Barth, failed in their function. The Christological creeds, to attempt to summarize Barth's perspective on this, are thus not some ahistorical, abstract truths, but contextually conditioned commentaries on the confession of Christ, commentaries that have nevertheless shown themselves to be of worth as landmarks for later periods as well, but on the other hand not as infallible criteria for a true confession. The Christological truth, if one may put it that way, is therefore, according to Barth, not in the Christological creeds themselves, but in Jesus Christ alone, and Christological creeds fulfill their function when they point to this truth. However, the dynamic character of the Christological creeds that Barth strives for becomes, according to my interpretation, not only a critique of other christologies than his own, traditional or liberal, but also a criticism of his own Christology (in earlier volumes of *Church Dogmatics*), insofar as he starts from a personalistically understood meeting between I and Thou.

Christology and the Concrete Human Being

Throughout Barth's theology one finds a desire to avoid making the human being the starting point for theology. Even in Christology Christ is the one

---

55. Barth, *Church Dogmatics* IV/2, p. 99: ". . . in the existence of this man we have to reckon with the identity of His action as a true man with the action of the true God. The grace which comes to human essence is the event of this action."

who confronts the person with the truth about herself. The relationship between God and human being is, according to Barth, asymmetrical. The theologian Charles T. Waldrop has argued that Barth's Christology has a fundamentally Alexandrian character, rather than Chalcedonian.[56] This means that Christ is primarily divine in his being, not because of his God consciousness, or because of some action that he carried out as a human, and definitely not because people impute this to him. At the same time, Waldrop points out that Barth also pursues an Antiochian mission by emphasizing that Jesus Christ is a true human as well. However, Waldrop's question comes to be whether Barth succeeds in doing justice to this true humanity. It is the divine nature of Christ that bears the human nature, and thus Barth's Christology is conferred an almost Apollinarist appearance. The problem with the Christology of Apollinaris, as I discussed in the previous chapter, is that the humanity of Christ is devalued and tends to disappear in the divine. Since the divine nature is dominant, the human nature tends to be understood as something entirely instrumental, dependent, and without a will of its own. Waldrop writes of Christ's human nature in Barth: "It is so integrally taken up and assumed into God's being that its purely human existence is denied."[57] Christ's human nature is thereby reduced to only one aspect of God's action. As a consequence of this, the humanity of the rest of humankind is also threatened, since it exists, according to Barth, in and through the humanity of Christ. The ultimate consequence is, according to Waldrop, that the historicity of salvation itself is threatened when the entirety of Jesus' human life becomes one aspect of God's eternal predetermination.

There are a number of views that may be presented regarding the question of whether Barth's Christology is Alexandrian or not. In accordance with my argument above, I would like to argue that Waldrop's characterization fits the Christology of the earlier volumes better than that of the later ones. Unlike the Christological grammar of the first volume, the more narrative Christology of the fourth volume shows more clearly how the human is involved in God's salvation history. The fourth volume thus provides resources for a constructive Christology that links to the traditional formulations, but avoids interpreting them in a static way. At the same time, David F. Ford has warned that the typological method of interpretation that Barth makes use

---

56. Charles T. Waldrop, *Karl Barth's Christology: Its Basic Alexandrian Character,* Religion and Reason 21, ed. Jacques Waardenburg (Berlin/New York/Amsterdam: Mouton Publishers, 1984).

57. Waldrop, *Christology,* p. 174.

of in *Church Dogmatics* threatens to swallow the entirety of human history and turn it into a backdrop for Christology.[58] In one sense, it seems as though everything significant has already happened with the crucifixion and resurrection, in that human history is typologically interpreted into these events. This can be illustrated with reference to Barth's critical discussion of the Catholic theologian Hans Urs von Balthasar's books on French saints, among others Thérèse of Lisieux and Elisabeth of Dijon. Here Barth believes that von Balthasar risks obscuring the view of that which these saints represent, namely Christ.[59] According to Barth, Christ does not need "to be repeated," a concept found in von Balthasar, since Christ is present in his own truth and power. Christ's unique position can be threatened if he can be replaced by those who follow in his footprints. The risk in this would be that God's grace would be able to be identified and domesticated. But at the same time one may ask whether Barth actually manages to do justice to the truly human reception of the Gospel, or whether he, in spite of everything, reduces humanity to an abstract category.[60] An additional indication that this is the case is when Barth, as I mentioned above, names Christ an "epistemological principle" and standard for theology, which seems to imply that there could be a knowledge of Christ that is not discursively mediated via a specific and historically situated interpretation of Christ—so, one Christology or another.[61] But such an unmediated knowledge of Christ is, I contend, not possible, since every interpretive act, including the theological, is situated in a concrete time and in concrete circumstances.[62]

The principal problem with Barth's Christology that all these objections point to is the sense in which his theology imagines the human as an independent being. Barth's theology can in a sense be described as a gigantic attempt to come to terms with what he understood as the self-centeredness of the modern human, and with the inability of contemporary philosophy

58. Ford, *Barth*, pp. 168–72.

59. Barth, *Church Dogmatics* IV/2, pp. 756–57. Cf. Hans Urs von Balthasar, *Two Sisters in the Spirit: Therese of Lisieux and Elizabeth of the Trinity,* trans. Donald Nichols, Anne Englund Nash, and Dennis Martin (San Francisco: Ignatius Press, 1992).

60. Cf. a similar critique of Barth's ecclesiology in Nicholas M. Healy, "The Logic of Karl Barth's Ecclesiology: Analysis, Assessment and Proposed Modifications," *Modern Theology* 10, no. 3 (1994): 253–70.

61. Cf. Graham Ward's critical discussion of Barth in *Christ and Culture,* pp. 1–2, 6–15, as well as in *Cultural Transformation and Religious Practice* (Cambridge: Cambridge University Press, 2005), pp. 19–57.

62. Cf. my argument about this in the first chapter.

and theology to be confronted with the radically different—but the question is whether his theology comes to terms in the same way with his own threatening idealism. If not, even Barth's Christology becomes, ironically enough, just another way to avoid being confronted with the other in terms of human history, creativity, subjectivity, and not least, embodiment. To avoid reducing Christology to an idealistic speculation about the human, what is needed, beyond what Barth managed to supply in his theology, is a critical and constructive dialogue with other fields like phenomenology, ethnography, sociology, et cetera. Even if these do not constitute the norm for theology's understanding of the human, here there is a knowledge about the human in her concrete existence; without this knowledge theology risks speaking only of an abstract human being. Put simply, one may describe Barth's Christological problem as the fact that, in spite of everything, he does not succeed in overcoming Schleiermacher's conception of human subjectivity; the difference consists only in the fact that in Barth it is Christ who becomes the absolute subject. Without a phenomenological, hermeneutic, sociological, and historical supplement that takes seriously the fact that the human who receives Christ is concretely situated, even Barth's Christology remains abstract.

This completes the investigation of Barth's theology, and I turn now to a Christology that works with entirely different philosophical and theological assumptions than either Schleiermacher or Barth, namely to the Christology one finds among those theologians involved in the book *The Myth of God Incarnate.* Yet even they pose the question of whether the doctrine of the incarnation manages to live up to the true humanity of Christ.

Incarnation and Language

One of the most influential books regarding the problem of incarnation that has been published in the Anglophone world during the twentieth century is *The Myth of God Incarnate,* from 1977, edited by the British philosopher of religion John Hick.[63] The first edition of the book sold out in a day, and during the first eight months after its publication sold over 30,000 copies.[64] The book comprises a number of essays by several well-established theolo-

---

63. John Hick, ed., *The Myth of God Incarnate* (London: SCM, 1977).

64. According to Ingolf U. Dalferth, *Der auferweckte Gekreuzigte: Zur Grammatik der Christologie* (Tübingen: J. C. B. Mohr [Paul Siebeck], 1994), p. 1.

gians at different English universities. They had met regularly at seminars over three years, which resulted in their collaborative book. Hick (born 1922), who was the book's editor, is one of the leading representatives for the analytical tradition within Anglo-American philosophy of religion, and was professor in Birmingham at the time of the book's publication. What these authors have in common is a critical attitude towards the traditional doctrine of incarnation, but they are not equally agreed about exactly what is problematic with it, and even less about what constructive theology can replace it. Much of that which is expressed in *The Myth of God Incarnate* had already been claimed earlier, partly by the liberal theological tradition, but also in Wolfhart Pannenberg's classic work from 1964, *Grundzüge der Christologie.*[65] With regard to the specifically English history of theology, *The Myth of God Incarnate* nevertheless had an impact that was more dramatic than Pannenberg's book; both are, in a way, a revival of certain Christological questions that had earlier been rejected by Barth and Bultmann, for example on the theological relevance of the question of the historical Jesus. The aspect of the critique from *The Myth of God Incarnate* that I want to focus on here, however, concerns the nature of the language that we find in the traditional doctrines of incarnation, above all Chalcedon. If this mythological language is to be understood literally, it will, according to the foundational thesis of the theologians in *The Myth of God Incarnate,* unavoidably function in an alienating way for the contemporary person who does not share the early Christian church's worldview. However, my critical question for *The Myth of God Incarnate* is, after the presentation of its thesis, whether this really is a reasonable understanding of the language of Chalcedon and the traditional doctrines of incarnation.

The Doctrine of Incarnation as Myth, Metaphor, and Metaphysics

A central critical point for the group surrounding *The Myth of God Incarnate* is that the traditional doctrine of incarnation is docetic (an accusation that traditional Christology typically directs against, for example, a Gnostic Christology), which means that in practice, if not always, it in principle denies the humanity of Jesus. Frances M. Young expresses it in the following way in her contribution to the book:

65. Wolfhart Pannenberg, *Jesus – God and Man,* 2nd edition, trans. Lewis L. Wilkins and Duane A. Priebe (Philadelphia: Westminster Press, 1977).

A literal doctrine of the incarnation, expressed in however sophisticated form, cannot avoid some element of docetism, and involves the believer in claims for uniqueness which seem straightforwardly incredible to the majority of our contemporaries.[66]

Young's polemic is directed above all against a "literally" understood doctrine of incarnation, and she herself, along with Maurice Wiles in the same book, wants the account of Jesus as the incarnation of God in time and space to be understood "mystically." In a similar way, John Hick prefers to speak about the incarnation of God in Jesus as a metaphor. The problem with a "literally" understood doctrine of incarnation is, according to the quotation above, both that it has the appearance of Docetism, and that it seems unthinkable for our contemporary period, due to the claims for Christianity's unique status that it implicates. The doctrine of incarnation has certainly always been docetic, he claims, but according to these theologians yet another complication has been added in the modern period, namely its claim to uniqueness. However, the intention with *The Myth of God Incarnate* is not—at least for these three authors—to reject all conceptions of incarnation, but rather to pose the question of whether and how these should be conceived, as "myths" or as "literal truths."

The polemic is primarily directed against a literally understood doctrine of incarnation that says that Jesus Christ is truly human, but also truly God, the second person in the Trinity.[67] Such an interpretation of the significance of Jesus for the believer might have been suitable for the time it arose in, but in our time it is no longer convincing. "We," i.e., the modern person, do not share in the "old-fashioned" idea that supernatural divine intervention might be possible, and we do not think, as they did in ancient times, that the Gospel of John could possibly be historical testimony.[68] Moreover, the doctrine of incarnation as formulated by, for example, the council in Chalcedon, has never been expounded in a way that has made it apprehensible. I will here give an account of Young, Wiles, and Hick's Christological discussions in *The Myth of God Incarnate*. Common to all of them is that they want to base their Christology on the historical Jesus.

To begin with, in her investigation of the sources for the representations of incarnation Young establishes that the New Testament Christology has

66. Frances M. Young, "A Cloud of Witnesses," in *The Myth of God Incarnate,* p. 32.
67. Maurice Wiles, "Christianity without Incarnation?" in *The Myth of God Incarnate,* p. 1.
68. Wiles, "Christianity," pp. 4–5; Young, "Cloud," p. 31.

taken over its own contemporary cultural categories in order to design its Christology, a Christology that aims to articulate a response to the experience of salvation through Jesus. What is common to the many formulations of this response is that they have seen Jesus as God's active initiative towards the human. Young believes that the New Testament presents Jesus as the embodiment and the fulfillment of all God's promises, rather than as an incarnation.[69] It is first in the patristic period that conceptions of incarnation in the strict sense became relevant for the questions that were then posed. This is in itself not a dramatic assertion, which has hopefully become clear in my previous chapter, but Young asserts as well that this later development led to "the blind alleys of paradox, illogicality and docetism."[70] The understandings of incarnation that were based on Nicea's *homoousios* and the Chalcedon formula do not manage to account for the relationship between God and the world in an apprehensible way. Even the church fathers themselves admitted that this was a mystery that human reason was not able to comprehend.

There is therefore no reason to view the historical doctrines of incarnation as timeless and incontestable if we want to formulate our own Christology, argue the authors of *The Myth of God Incarnate*. This does not mean that we do not share certain of the church fathers' questions about the importance of Jesus, but our reply cannot build on a philosophy that sees supernatural interventions as both possible and expected.[71] For example, Young speaks of the historical understanding of the incarnation in terms of a supernatural intervention: Paul is "our first witness to the belief that a supernatural agent of God entered the world in Jesus Christ."[72] She distances herself from a doctrine of incarnation that sets an ontological equal sign between Jesus and God, but at the same time recognizes that this is not what the Christian tradition has taught.[73] In our time we cannot make any such identifications, but we must realize that all of our discourse about how God relates to the world has to do with "mythological truths" rather than "literal facts."[74] It is not entirely clear here whether Young means that it is the oldest Christian tradition that has blended together myths with facts, or if it has to do with how historical theology's doctrine of incarnation has

69. Young, "Cloud," p. 19.

70. Young, "Cloud," p. 29. Cf. as well her article "Two Roots or a Tangled Mass?" in *The Myth of God Incarnate*, pp. 87–121.

71. Young, "Cloud," p. 31.

72. Young, "Two Roots," p. 103.

73. Young, "Cloud," p. 35.

74. Young, "Cloud," p. 34.

come to be understood today by its defenders. She suggests, however, that it is possible for her as a believer to agree with the traditional formulations that we see God in Jesus, so long as these are not taken literally. Young's conclusion in the form of her own Christological creed is that Jesus is the one who embodies the salvation of God, if not in an exclusive way.[75] This creed may be formulated in different ways, and there is value in this diversity, Young suggests.

In one of his contributions to *The Myth of God Incarnate* Wiles devotes himself to discussing the role of the myth in theology. Wiles notes several different ways in which the term has been used. He himself believes that the classification of a theological doctrine as myth does not need to mean that it is deprived of all truth value. An example is the creation myth. If the universe is a self-sustaining system that is not dependent on anything other than itself for its evolution, one may say that the creation myth is false, but if the universe is instead actually dependent on a transcendent, creative source, one may say that the myth is correct or true.[76] Wiles suggests that it is often difficult to establish whether a myth is true or false, or whether these categories are applicable to the myth in question; the point is that the question of truth is not *a priori* meaningless. The criterion he suggests is that there must be "some ontological truth corresponding to the central characteristic of the structure of the myth," a criterion that he himself admits can often be difficult to apply.[77]

When Wiles turns to the question of the incarnation, he wants, like the book's other authors, to reject what he calls a "direct, metaphysical" understanding of the incarnation in favor of "less direct" interpretations. Applied to a mythological understanding of the incarnation, the above criterion would require a correspondence between the mythological expression and an ontological seed of truth. Against the incarnation understood as a mythological expression, Wiles can suppose that there is a real "union of divine and human at the heart of the human personality."[78] What this union involves he describes no more comprehensively than this. Wiles additionally believes that the question of how the myth of incarnation corresponds to what we know of the historical person of Jesus is important. If this knowledge were to belie the realization of the union of human and divine at the

75. Young, "Cloud," p. 42.
76. Maurice Wiles, "Myth in Theology," in *The Myth of God Incarnate*, p. 159.
77. Wiles, "Myth," p. 161.
78. Wiles, "Myth," p. 161.

center of the human personality in a complete way in the life of Jesus, this would argue against the correctness of the myth of incarnation itself.[79] The myth of incarnation could therefore include a historical element, and does not then need to be understood as a truth that is independent of all history. Although Wiles can see certain problems with the application of this insight to the mythological character of the incarnation, he suggests that it stands for a more creative perspective than a literal understanding of the incarnation can manage.[80]

Incarnation as Exclusivism

The polemic against a Christian exclusivism is the most important mission in John Hick's article in *The Myth of God Incarnate,* "Jesus and the World Religions," an article that he followed up and broadened in 1993 in the book *The Metaphor of God Incarnate.*[81] Hick argues as well that the doctrine of incarnation must be understood as a mythological expression of the importance of Jesus for the Christian. In the book he formulates this myth in the following way:

> The myth of God incarnate is the story of the pre-existent divine Son descending into human life, dying to atone for the sins of the world, thereby revealing the divine nature, and returning into the eternal life of the Trinity.[82]

Hick compares this myth of incarnation to how the human Gautama came to be understood within Mahayana Buddhism as a divine, preexistent Buddha. The earlier literal understanding of the doctrine of two natures, as it had been formulated by Nicea and Chalcedon and had become normative for the Christian church, is no longer meaningful or understandable, and must be interpreted as expressive rather than indicative. An expressive understanding of the doctrine of two natures would mean that it is supposed to express a certain attitude towards Jesus in the believer,

79. Wiles, "Myth," pp. 162–63.

80. Wiles's argument is presented more fully in his book *The Remaking of Christian Doctrine* (London: SCM, 1974), pp. 41–82.

81. John Hick, *The Metaphor of God Incarnate: Christology in a Pluralistic Age* (Louisville: Westminster/John Knox Press, 1993).

82. Hick, *Metaphor,* p. 105.

while an indicative understanding would mean a descriptive statement about Jesus.[83]

Hick thus wants to replace a literal understanding of the doctrine of incarnation with a metaphorical one, and he formulates this in his book in the following way: "We see in Jesus a human being extraordinarily open to God's influence and thus living to an extraordinary extent as God's agent on earth, 'incarnating' the divine purpose for human life."[84] Hick believes as well that the step from the New Testament writings to patristic Christological thought entailed that the metaphorical Son of God became a metaphysical Son of God; thus the doctrine of incarnation hardened into a technically defined doctrine. The problem in our time with a literally understood doctrine of incarnation, apart from the fact that it is not understandable on the basis of our understanding of reality, is that it brings with it an exclusive claim that the Christian faith is the only path to eternal life (so, the same two reasons for rejecting the traditional doctrine of incarnation that run throughout the book). Such exclusive claims are not convincing in our pluralistic world. Hick himself presents here a pluralistic theology of religion with a theocentric focus.[85] Everyone is saved by God, Hick says, but not everyone is saved by Jesus of Nazareth. Even if it is possible to argue that God was revealed to Christians in a special way in Jesus, there are parallel revelations in other religions, for example in Buddha.

The conclusion of Young, Wiles, and Hick is that there is a great need for a reformulation of the Christian church's Christology, one that no longer clings to the obsolete and unintelligible formulas that served to present Christianity as exclusive. This does not mean that Jesus has played out his role for the Christian church. Wiles probably speaks for all these authors in the following sentence: "It would still be possible to see Jesus not only as one who embodies a full response of man to God but also as one who expresses and embodies the way of God towards men."[86] Gone, however, are all metaphysical, literal, and exclusive representations of the incarnation of God in Jesus Christ. Christology does not necessarily have to be Christology of incarnation, or to formulate it differently, an adequate Christology of incarnation does not need to and cannot assert more than that God has taken a special initiative in Jesus Christ for the sake of the

83. Hick, "Jesus and the World Religions," in *The Myth of God Incarnate*, p. 178.

84. Hick, *Metaphor*, p. 12.

85. For an overview of different sorts of theologies of religion, see Gavin D'Costa, *Theology and Religious Pluralism: The Challenge of Other Religions* (Oxford: Basil Blackwell, 1986).

86. Wiles, *Remaking*, p. 8.

people.[87] As I mentioned, Young, Wiles, and Hick articulate a criticism of representations of incarnation that are found in other authors as well, and their criticism can therefore be assumed to formulate a more widespread critique than just their own circle of theologians. In spite of this, I believe that their critique rests on several incorrect assumptions and therefore falls short. I will take up some of these critical objections against Young, Wiles, and Hick, not primarily from the contemporary critique that they met from the direction of conservative theology, but from points of view that fit in neither the standards that the circle surrounding *The Myth of God Incarnate* polemicize against nor that they themselves represent.[88] I limit myself to discussing the question of language and ontology, and so leave the no less important discussion of Christianity's claims to exclusivity for another occasion.[89]

Chalcedon and Apophatic Language

One of the assumptions that I believe is misleading concerns the language of the doctrine of incarnation as mythological. It seems as though the group surrounding *The Myth of God Incarnate* polemicizes against a conception of incarnation in which the second person of the Trinity is identified with the person Jesus in a way that depicts a story, where *logos* departs from heaven to earth in order to become human in Jesus of Nazareth, in order to then return to heaven, like a traveler from outer space. Such a representation of the incarnation is naturally strongly mythological, as Bultmann had already observed, but the question is whether or not the same insight existed during the time of the classical Christology as well. That there were mythological christologies during the patristic period does not mean that the church fathers did not know better than to take these for literal truth in the Christological doctrines. Rowan Williams writes in a direct polemic against such a view:

87. See Sarah Coakley, *Christ without Absolutes: A Study of the Christology of Ernst Troeltsch* (Oxford: Clarendon Press, 1988), p. 104.

88. For the conservative critique, see Michael Green, ed., *The Truth of God Incarnate* (London: Hodder & Stoughton, 1977).

89. For the latter, see instead Gavin D'Costa, ed., *Christian Uniqueness Reconsidered: The Myth of a Pluralistic Theology of Religions* (Maryknoll, NY: Orbis, 1990). I myself have a short discussion of this question in the chapter "Den andres religion" in *Kärlekens skillnad: Att gestalta kristen tro i vår tid* (Stockholm: Verbum, 1998), pp. 223-55.

Pace Wiles and many others, including nearly all of the contributors to *The Myth of God Incarnate,* incarnational doctrine is not to be reduced to the narrative of a heavenly being coming down from his native habitat, uneasily combined with an undifferentiated assertion of *identity* between Jesus of Nazareth and the divine Word. No professional theologian from 451 to (say) 1850 would have recognized that as an account of what the doctrine claimed.[90]

Even the church fathers were intensely conscious of the issue of anthropomorphism, according to Williams. They realized the risk in mythological representations and knew of the ambiguity in those metaphors they used. The Christological doctrines, unlike many of the expressions that conceptions of incarnation took on, attempted to regulate the motley and often contradictory diversity of Christological forms of expression in a quest for truth. This does not mean that they attempted to translate these into what the authors of *The Myth of God Incarnate* call a "literal" understanding of the incarnation, or that they attempted to fix Christological definitions once and for all, but rather concerns the fact that "dogmatic Christological definition sets out to establish the conditions for telling this truth in the most comprehensive, least conceptually extravagant, and least idly mythological language."[91] Insofar as our time must also pose ontological questions and not only functional ones to the Christological material, we do not escape the sort of problems that, among other things, Chalcedon attempted to process—and as I noted above, Wiles wants to pose these questions as well. The aim of the church fathers is not, however, to establish facts about God through the doctrine of incarnation or to see the incarnation as an aspect of the biography of God.

Williams's critique of *The Myth of God Incarnate* implies that the classical doctrines of incarnation should not be identified with a docetic representation of Christ. The doctrines of incarnation, rightly understood, say nothing about the life of Jesus, but about the *significance* of the life of Jesus. To say, like the Chalcedonian formula, that Jesus Christ was truly God and truly human does not mean comparing two magnitudes that exist, so to speak, on the same plane. When Young claims that "modern discussions have in-

---

90. Rowan Williams, "Doctrinal Criticism: Some Questions," in *The Making and Remaking of Christian Doctrine: Essays in Honour of Maurice Wiles,* ed. Sarah Coakley and David A. Pailin (Oxford: Clarendon Press, 1993), p. 251.

91. Williams, "Doctrinal Criticism," p. 251.

sisted on the impossibility of treating God as a thing like other things about which factual statements can be made," one can object that this has hardly been something that only *modern* discussions have noted, but that it has in fact been a fundamental understanding for thousands of years of Christian theology.[92] Thomas Aquinas insisted, for example, that God is not an existence, but existence itself, and that it is therefore not possible to say what God is, and similar assertions can be found among, in principle, all theologians worth the name before Thomas.[93] It is not until the modern period that God has at all come to be presented as an object or a thing, about which it is in principle possible to formulate unambiguous (univocal) statements. God, like the incarnation, is a mystery. Nevertheless, for early theology the fact that the discourse of God cannot be reduced to unambiguous statements did not mean that one could only speak nonsense about God.[94]

The importance of the question of God for the understanding of the incarnation cannot be underestimated. To put it rather drastically: if God is understood as an existence like others—but "bigger"—then the hypostatic union in Christ will in its turn be understood as an unequal competitive relationship, where the divine nature makes itself pertinent at the expense of human nature. On the other hand, if the emphasis lies instead on God as different, i.e., transcendent, the relationship between the divine and human must not be considered as a problematic competitive relation. On the basis of such a latter understanding, the German theologian Walter Kasper can write the following:

> [T]he greater the union with God, the greater the intrinsic reality of the man. Precisely because (and not despite the fact that) Jesus knew himself wholly one with the Father, he had at the same time a completely human consciousness, asked human questions, grew in age and wisdom (cf. Lk 2.52).[95]

The hypostatic union was not understood by historical theology as a competitive relation, where the emphasis on the divine nature meant a diminishing

---

92. Young, "Cloud," p. 41. Cf. Herbert McCabe, *God Matters* (London/New York: Mowbray, 2000), pp. 54–61, 67–74.

93. McCabe, *God Matters*, pp. 59–60.

94. Cf. Herbert McCabe, "Aquinas on the Incarnation," in *God Still Matters,* ed. Brian Davies (London/New York: Continuum, 2002), pp. 102–14.

95. Walter Kasper, *Jesus the Christ,* new edition (London/New York: T. & T. Clark, 2011), p. 236.

of human nature. This does not mean that there can be no cause to question how patristic Christology vis-à-vis Chalcedon manages to do justice to the humanity of Christ. What it does mean, however, is that one ought to present more clearly than the theologians in *The Myth of God Incarnate* the complex relationship with and the difference between Chalcedon's contemporary task and our contemporary conception of the human vis-à-vis the divine.

Proceeding from this latter understanding of the relationship between divine and human in the incarnation, we ought to return to the question that *The Myth of God Incarnate* brought to the fore concerning the language that is used in order to speak about the incarnation. Could it be that, in spite of everything, Chalcedon's language ought to be called "metaphorical" in order to defend Chalcedon against the abuse implied in understanding this language as literal, thus doing violence to the mystery of the incarnation? I am nevertheless skeptical that turning from an allegedly "literal" understanding to a "metaphorical" understanding of the incarnation solves the problem that Hick and others want it to solve. Or formulated in another way: How shall we understand "literal" vis-à-vis "metaphorical" in relation to Chalcedon's definition of the incarnation? As Sarah Coakley has pointed out in a discussion of Hick's view of the incarnation, his understanding of metaphors seems to require that they involve a "recession from reality," and so have almost a noncognitive status.[96] According to Hick, the original sense of Chalcedon was literal, but such an understanding has shown itself to be impossible: "in the case of divine incarnation the initial idea has proved to be devoid of literal meaning and accordingly identified as metaphor."[97] To use metaphorical language about the incarnation would thus mean less firm (or no?) ontological suppositions than what the literal language implies. But such an understanding of metaphor as noncognitive is not self-evident. It is rather the case that recent theory of metaphor does not set metaphorical language in opposition to literal language in so simple a way as Hick and his colleagues do in *The Myth of God Incarnate*.[98]

A metaphorical language should hardly be set in contrast to a language that wants to make assertions about reality. On the contrary, a metaphorical language can carry strong claims for speaking about reality, precisely

---

96. Sarah Coakley, "What Does Chalcedon Solve and What Does It Not? Some Reflections on the Status and Meaning of the Chalcedonian 'Definition,'" in *The Incarnation: An Interdisciplinary Symposium on the Incarnation of the Son of God*, ed. Stephen T. Davis, Daniel Kendall, and Gerald O'Collins (New York: Oxford University Press, 2002), p. 153.

97. Hick, *Metaphor*, p. 104.

98. Cf., for example, Jacques Derrida, "White Mythology," in *Margins of Philosophy*, trans. Alan Bass (Brighton, UK: Harvester Press, 1982), pp. 207–71.

through the fact that this language can involve a new and fresh perspective on this reality.[99] Even the mystical tradition within Christianity, which has been eager to emphasize the elusiveness of God, has done this from a realistic position.[100] Metaphorical language—irrespective of whether this is the correct language for speaking about the incarnation—is a way to relate to reality, and cannot be reduced to a looser, more ontologically unassuming language. Apart from the fact that it is questionable whether those who formulated Chalcedon and debated its meanings in antiquity made "literal" claims—in the sense of Hick and his colleagues—on their way to the creed, in principle a "metaphorical" understanding of incarnation sets before us the same dilemma as the "literal," namely, how one should understand the presence of God with, in, or through the person Jesus. The "literal" in the patristic creeds consists in the fact that they wanted to make claim to speaking truth, but this did not, however, mean for them that it was possible to create a precise and unambiguous definition in the modern sense.[101] The distinction itself between "literal" and "metaphorical" language is thus not a self-evident distinction that may be applied to Chalcedon in the way that the theologians in *The Myth of God Incarnate* supposed.

So now even if the patristic theologians did not want to defend a mythological understanding of the incarnation, Hick and his colleagues thus do not solve the problem with what could be an adequate Christology for our period. With Coakley I instead want to characterize the language of Chalcedon as "apophatic," i.e., a language that means to set a boundary for how God's action of salvation through Christ shall be interpreted, if one wants to avoid doctrinal misunderstandings (like "Apollinarism, Eutychianism, and extreme Nestorianism"; cf. the previous chapter) without, on account of that, claiming to be able to exhaustively understand or explain the reality that the confessional language wants to point to.[102] As I argued in previous chapters, one could say—put simply—that Chalcedon came to be, not in order to replace the biblical writings or the previous creeds from Nicea and Constantinople, but in order to protect them from unproductive misunderstandings. Chalcedon is and remains, in the words of Karl Rahner, "not end but beginning," or should, perhaps even more appropriately, be understood "as end *and* as beginning," or in Coakley's own words: "strictly speaking *neither* end *nor* beginning, but rather a transitional

---

99. See Janet Martin Soskice, *Metaphor and Religious Language* (Oxford: Clarendon Press, 1985), pp. 118–41.

100. Soskice, *Metaphor,* p. 152.

101. Cf. Coakley, "Chalcedon," pp. 158–59.

102. Coakley, "Chalcedon," p. 161.

(though still normative) 'horizon' to which we constantly return."[103] The gist of my argument is that the Chalcedonian creed is itself to a certain degree contextualized and relativized, for example in my indicating the limitations regarding the scope of its *own* claims and the many questions that Chalcedon leaves unanswered. The Chalcedonian creed is thus, whatever else it might be, not a *sufficient* ground for a contemporary Christology. *In itself* Chalcedon is far too abstract to offer an especially interesting Christology or anthropology, but *in its context* it becomes clearer what the creed is interested in. As I mentioned earlier in the previous chapter, Chalcedon actually says very little about Christ. Its function is not to furnish certain "biographical facts" about him—that he, along with being, say, brown-eyed, left-handed, and 165 centimeters tall, was also the Son of God, the second person of the Trinity—but rather to show that God is constitutive for who Christ is in such a way that we cannot speak of Christ without at the same time speaking of God.[104] The language that is used by Chalcedon can admittedly, placed in a certain context, be understood as mythological, and thereby seem alienating for the modern person, but I do not accept the view that this would be the only, or even the accepted usage of its language. In order to be able to know who Christ is, it is thus not enough to turn to Chalcedon, and that has never been the case. Instead, it is with the aid of Chalcedon that we turn to the New Testament writings, but also to the prayers, the hymns, and the liturgies. There is thus already in Chalcedon a critique of mythological views of the incarnation and a realization of the need for multiple means of expression for the understanding of Christ—and perhaps even an implicit understanding of the need for multiple Christological means of expression for an understanding of the human.

But is the problem with traditional Christianity not primarily its mystical mode of expression, but rather its androcentrism? Such is the argument of one part of the feminist critique, to which I now turn.

Incarnation and Sex

In recent times the doctrine of incarnation has been seriously challenged not so much by its mystical language, but rather by its exclusivity, as has also

103. Karl Rahner, "Current Problems in Christology," in *Theological Investigations*, vol. 1: *God, Christ, Mary and Grace*, trans. Cornelius Ernst (New York: Crossroad, 1982), pp. 149, 150, together with Coakley, "Chalcedon," p. 162.

104. Cf. Rowan Williams, *On Christian Theology*, Challenges in Contemporary Theology (Oxford/Malden, MA: Blackwell, 2000), pp. 25–26, 156–57.

been pointed out by the authors of *The Myth of God Incarnate*—in this case, however, not primarily an exclusivity in relation to other religions, but an androcentric exclusivity. In the book *Sexism and God-Talk: Towards a Feminist Theology* from 1983, Rosemary Radford Ruether poses the famous question of whether a male savior can save women, a question that could be said to be the rubric for much of feminist theological reflection on Christology.[105] If Jesus is the central person, symbol, or account in the Christian tradition, then does this not mean that the Christian tradition has always claimed that a man stands at the center of the relationship between God and human? Does this not mean that the Christian tradition is androcentric beyond all hope of rescue? Ruether believes that some form of feminist Christology is possible, and that such a Christology thereby makes it possible for her to remain in the Christian tradition. Others, like Mary Daly, believe that feminism must go "beyond christolatry," and she has therefore chosen to leave the Christian church.[106] If the traditional doctrine of incarnation is understood by modern Christology as a denial, or a least a devaluation of the genuine humanity of Christ, and so of human subjectivity, the question posed by feminist Christology to both traditional and modern Christology is whether it entails a denial of the subjectivity of the *woman,* and whether the humanity that is discussed by both traditional and modern Christology is implicitly identified with a male subjectivity.

The question of whether a male savior can save women is not only a matter of whether the man Jesus had a certain set of chromosomes. The discussion is primarily a matter of the concepts and the language that have traditionally been used in order to understand the importance of Jesus in the Christian tradition, concepts like "Son of God," "Son of Man," etc., which, intentionally or unintentionally, have situated the relationship between Jesus and God or Jesus and other people in a framework that, in a patriarchal culture, has inevitably and in various ways excluded women and their experiences. There are many questions that are brought to the fore by feminist Christology, but here as in the previous section I will limit myself to examining a feminist critique of the representations of incarnation, and then not least the doctrine that was formulated at the council in Chalcedon.

105. Rosemary Radford Ruether, *Sexism and God-Talk: Towards a Feminist Theology* (London: SCM, 1983), pp. 116–38. She also pursues her critique from the earlier book in her article "Can Christology Be Liberated from Patriarchy?" in *Reconstructing the Christ Symbol*, ed. Maryanne Stevens (Mahwah, NJ: Paulist Press, 1993), pp. 7–29.

106. Mary Daly, *Beyond God the Father: Toward a Philosophy of Women's Liberation*, new edition (London: The Women's Press, 1986), p. 71.

As I pointed out earlier in chapter 1, the idea of a divine incarnation in Christ should not be conflated with Chalcedon, and it is also clear throughout much of feminist Christological thought that it is not primarily the idea of God's incarnation that is criticized, but rather the way in which it has been understood in and by the tradition.

Chalcedon and Sex

According to Ruether (who will be the first of my conversation partners), the Chalcedonian Christology is the outcome of a long patriarchalization of a Christology that from the start entailed a questioning of all hierarchies, and as such is practically a betrayal of the message Jesus wanted to convey:

> To encapsulate Jesus himself as God's "last word" and "once-for-all" disclosure of God, located in a remote past and institutionalized in a cast of Christian teachers, is to repudiate the spirit of Jesus and to recapitulate the position against which he himself protests.[107]

Traditional Christology thus became the center in a system whose function was to hold down all who did not conform to the emerging Christian order, to which category belonged the women. Women are certainly a part of the body of Christ, but they could not represent Christ. Combined with an Aristotelian biology, traditional Christology would come to reinforce the androcentrism in the Christian tradition, in that the male sex was seen as normative, as the only sex that represented the human in general. Christ as the *logos* of God is the male offspring and revelation of a male God. The orthodox Christological formulations go hand in hand with the institutionalization and patriarchalization of Christianity. Access to Christ is no longer a matter of the Spirit "blowing as it will," as in the original charismatic congregations, but is regulated by the male episcopacy, Ruether says.

For Ruether the patriarchalization of Christology does not mean that Christ is irretrievably lost for women, either in history or in the present. A part of what she means is that there have always been alternative christologies, and she mentions two: "androgynous christologies" and "spirit christologies." Both have their roots in the fundamental Christian assertion that Christ saves the entirety of human nature, man and woman. According

107. Ruether, *Sexism*, p. 122.

to Ruether we find the androgynous Christology primarily in the mystical tradition, where it is said that sexual difference is thwarted on a spiritual level in redeemed humanity. So long as the male is the normative humanity, however, even androgynous christologies will be clearly androcentric. The spirit christologies, on the other hand, have found their *locus classicus* in the prophetic tradition. Christ becomes a force that permeates both men and women through the Spirit and gives them strength to critique the institutionalized church and its Christology. It has often been combined with or transformed into radical political movements.

Ruether herself argues that a feminist Christology is possible on the basis of a prophetic Christology. The humanity of Jesus has, speaking theologically, "no ultimate significance."[108] On the other hand, his sex has symbolic importance in that he represents through his lifestyle a new humanity that is critical towards these hierarchical privileges. Jesus, as the liberating Word of God, "manifests the *kenosis of patriarchy*," i.e., its retreat.[109] This patriarchal order is demystified by the man Jesus, who breaks with this order. In a similar way the female sex of the socially and religiously discarded who receive the message is symbolically significant, since it testifies to the same system that Jesus criticizes. However, Ruether is careful not to make this relationship between the saving Christ and the saved woman absolute. With that she would once more risk reinforcing the conventional sexual hierarchy. The solution she finds instead in a dynamic relationship between redeemer and redeemed: "The redeemer is one who has been redeemed, just as Jesus himself accepted the baptism of John. Those who have been liberated can, in turn, become paradigmatic, liberating persons for others."[110] In other words, Christ, the liberating Word of God, should not be identified with the historical Jesus. The incarnation, the presence of God in human form, is realized in the Christian community, and it is thus possible for us to meet Christ, as Ruether writes in a significant formulation, "in the form of our sister."[111] "Jesus is Christ," as Anne-Louise Eriksson summarizes Ruether's position, "but not the Christ-incarnation's exclusive possibility."[112]

Elisabeth Schüssler Fiorenza, another prominent German-American theologian with a feminist mission, has advanced a similar criticism of the

---

108. Ruether, *Sexism*, p. 137.

109. Ruether, *Sexism*, p. 137.

110. Ruether, *Sexism*, p. 138.

111. Ruether, *Sexism*, p. 138. Italics in the original.

112. Anne-Louise Eriksson, *Kvinnor talar om Jesus: En bok om feministisk kristologisk praxis* (Nora, Sweden: Nya Doxa, 1999), p. 55.

classic Chalcedonian doctrine of incarnation in her book *Jesus: Miriam's Child, Sophia's Prophet: Critical Issues in Feminist Christology* from 1994, and her more detailed arguments deepen Ruether's critique.[113] According to Schüssler Fiorenza, "Christological discourses" can best be understood as "social rhetorical practices that produce and reconstruct religious-theological identity in an ongoing intertextual and intercultural process."[114] While for many scholars it has been crucial to understand and evaluate a specific Christological creed's ontological pretensions, on the basis of her interest in a constructive feminist rereading of the Christological tradition Schüssler Fiorenza believes that it is important to examine the pragmatic function of Christological discourse.

Ruether's feminist critique of traditional Christology is, according to Schüssler Fiorenza, important but insufficient.[115] The problem is that Ruether's dependence on the historical Jesus, along with her idea of a "new humanity," still remains within traditional conceptions of sex. The "new humanity" does not mean the abolition of patriarchal power, but only accomplishes the "kenosis of patriarchy." Schüssler Fiorenza points out that one can only forgo what one has, and if Jesus' lifestyle entails that he forgoes privileges, as Ruether claims, he is thus construed by her as a man. The woman becomes the one who receives and serves this message, and thereby the cultural understanding of what it means to be a woman is also preserved. By this the conception of sex as something biologically given is maintained, and man remains the norm for what is seen as human. It may be possible to raise Schüssler Fiorenza's objections to Ruether against Schüssler Fiorenza's own Christology, but I will not follow this line of thought here, since my point is not to examine which feminist Christology is the most productive, but instead to focus on some anthropological aspects of the feminist critique of the doctrine of incarnation. What is important here, however, is Schüssler Fiorenza's critique of the Chalcedonian Christology.

Schüssler Fiorenza believes, like Ruether, that traditional Christological doctrine was formulated at the same time that the Christianity that came to be known as orthodox succeeded in winning power in the Constantinian church, and that it thereby shares its political ambition for uniformity and control: "Classic Christological dogma expresses the imperial desire for the

---

113. Elisabeth Schüssler Fiorenza, *Jesus: Miriam's Child, Sophia's Prophet: Critical Issues in Feminist Christology* (New York: Continuum, 1994), pp. 18–24. Her "classic" work is *In Memory of Her: A Feminist Theological Reconstruction of Christian Origins* (London: SCM, 1993).

114. Schüssler Fiorenza, *Jesus*, p. 34.

115. Schüssler Fiorenza, *Jesus*, pp. 46–47.

unification and control of a church created by the diverse understandings of Jesus developed in the beginnings of Christianity."[116] The diversity of christologies that characterized the early Christian movement was reduced and made uniform by a church with imperial ambitions, or one that at least let itself be used for such ambitions. The Chalcedonian formulation of the doctrine of incarnation is, according to Schüssler Fiorenza, a good example of how "kyriocentrism" and "kyriarchy" reinforce each other. By "kyriarchy" Schüssler Fiorenza means every form of domination where a superior governs a subordinate.[117] Schüssler Fiorenza has deliberately chosen this term instead of patriarchy in order to avoid a generalizing picture in which the superior is always a man and the subordinate a woman. "Kyriocentrism" is the ideology that legitimates the prevailing dominance or kyriarchy.[118] In the case of the Chalcedonian council, its Christological formulations become simply a legitimizing ideology for a "kyriarchal" political order. Let us now look a bit closer at Schüssler Fiorenza's critique.

To begin with, she takes up the term *oikonomia* from the council definition, a term that is used there three times, and has often been translated into Latin with the term *incarnatio,* the term that ever since, in the entirety of Latin Christianity, has constituted the center of Christology.[119] The term *oikonomia,* which reverberates in our word "economy," is, however, a merger of the words *oikos,* which means house/household, and *nomos,* which means law/order/government. A better translation of *oikonomia* would therefore, according to Schüssler Fiorenza, be "management/governing/administration of the household," which I translate here with the shorter word "householding." Such a demystification would show that the "mystery of the incarnation" *(to mystērion tēs oikonomias)* that the Chalcedonian definition speaks of actually has to do with the power of the kyriarchy, since the governance of the State and the whole universe was, during Antiquity, compared to how "the lord of the house" governed the household. "The mystery of householding" is in other words nothing other than the political system of the Roman Empire. Schüssler Fiorenza's interpretation of these Greek terms is rather speculative; she does not explain how *oikonomia* had been able to become *incarnatio* in Latin, for example.

116. Schüssler Fiorenza, *Jesus,* p. 18.
117. Schüssler Fiorenza, *Jesus,* p. 14.
118. Schüssler Fiorenza, *Jesus,* p. 14.
119. See the council text in *Decrees of the Ecumenical Councils,* volume one: *Nicaea I to Lateran V,* ed. Norman P. Tanner (London/Washington, DC: Sheed & Ward/Georgetown University Press, 1990), pp. 84–85.

In the council texts there is, according to Schüssler Fiorenza, a far-reaching connection between theology and policy.[120] The Chalcedonian Christology was added as a direct consequence of political pressures from the Roman Empire, which may also be seen in several of its formulations where the interest of the Roman emperor in preserving the *pax romana* takes on the dignity of salvation history. The Roman emperors are said to have called the council on divine orders.[121] Together with a long list of what Chalcedon condemns, this emphasizes that the Christological definitions do not lead to any discrepancies from the established Christological norm. Furthermore, at the purely theological level, there is the same problem, in that the divine origin of Christ is associated with the Father and his human origin with the Virgin. Schüssler Fiorenza gives some quotations from the Chalcedonian definition:

> begotten before the ages from the Father as regards his divinity *[pro aiōnōn men ek tou Patros gennēthenta kata tēn theotēta]*

> and in the last days the same for us and for our salvation from Mary, the virgin God-bearer as regards his humanity *[ep' eschatōn de tōn hēmerōn ton auton di' hēmas kai dia tēn hēmeteran sōtērian ek Marias tēs parthenou tēs theotokou kata tēn anthrōpotēta]*[122]

The kyriarchal order is therefore identified with a clear sexual hierarchy where paternity and masculinity are associated with eternity and divinity, and maternity and femininity with temporality and humanity. Thus the "mystery of housekeeping" is confirmed by the orthodoxy that has been established by the church of the Roman Empire in order to secure the *pax romana* and its religious power. The result of Chalcedonian Christology is not primarily a reflection on the relationship between divine and human, but rather a mystification of a kyriarchal order.

Schüssler Fiorenza's critique of Chalcedon not only targets a historically important definition of Christology, but is directed above all against the significance that Chalcedon still has for Christological thought today. Since Chalcedon became a landmark of Christological thought in all churches

---

120. Schüssler Fiorenza, *Jesus,* pp. 20–23.

121. Schüssler Fiorenza says in *Jesus,* p. 21, that *thespisma* in the introduction to the definition of the faith ought to be translated "divine decree." Cf. the council text on p. 83 of *Decrees of the Ecumenical Councils.*

122. *Decrees,* p. 86.

(with the exception of the non-Chalcedonian churches, for example, the Coptic Orthodox church), Christian identity continues to be shaped as a "kyriarchal" identity. It often functions as an unspoken frame of reference even for biblical investigations and feminist studies of Christological questions, and so can shape these in an unreflexive way.

However, in the end Schüssler Fiorenza observes, apropos a comment she found from dogma historian Aloys Grillmeier, that the final formulations of Chalcedonian Christology took place in a chapel consecrated to the holy Euphemia.[123] Historically this is not significant information, Schüssler Fiorenza says, but at the same time one can see it as symbolically important, since it shows that kyriarchal discourse needs "to construct the ideological space of the cultural-religious 'feminine' as the enabling ground of their articulation."[124] For the feminist critique of Christology it is thus not simply a matter of displaying and exposing the hierarchical relationships that are expressed by a kyriocentric Christology, but also about showing how these relationships construe the female as a condition for the kyriarchal ideology. Criticism of Christology is thus not only about an ideology-critical theory, but also about alternative practices.

Beyond Christological Inclusivism

A feature common to both Ruether and Schüssler Fiorenza that they also share with other contributions to feminist Christology is a critique of an abstract and timeless Christology that does not take its reception into consideration, i.e., an ontological Christology remote from the function of Christology. If Christological doctrine were understood in such a way, it would implicate an understanding of the human being as unilaterally passive in relation to the doctrine, and so repeat the base problem that much of feminist theology deals with (as with feminist critical theories generally), namely the construction of the man as active and the woman as passive. If modern Christology has generally criticized traditional Christology for having construed the divine as active and the human as passive, feminist theology adds a dimension and construes the relationship between these

---

123. Schüssler Fiorenza, *Jesus,* p. 23. Cf. Aloys Grillmeier, *Jesus der Christus im Glauben der Kirche,* vol. 1: *Von der apostolischen Zeit bis zum Konzil von Chalcedon (451),* 3rd revised and expanded edition (Freiburg: Herder, 1990), pp. 753-54.

124. Schüssler Fiorenza, *Jesus,* pp. 23-24.

two as an analogy of proportionality: the relationship between divine and human relates proportionally to the relationship between the sexes on the interpersonal level, and so the divine and the male inevitably come to be associated with each other. We find such a critique, by way of example, in two Swedish feminist christologies.[125]

Cristina Grenholm has argued in her book *Barmhärtig och sårbar. En bok om Kristen tro på Jesus [Merciful and Vulnerable: A Book on Christian Faith in Jesus]* that the traditional doctrine of two natures, as it was formulated by, among others, Chalcedon, takes its starting point in "Aristotelian philosophy," and that it is "that period's way of explaining the substance of Christian faith in Jesus."[126] The guiding point of departure for her book is her own experience of Jesus, but she nevertheless endeavors to relate to the tradition in that she affirms "the becoming human of God" and "the doctrine of incarnation," and asserts that its core is that "God became a human being like us."[127] I want to make use of one aspect of her argument, namely the emphasis on the incarnation as God's embodiment in Jesus and the connection to our common, human embodiment.[128] Grenholm also links her emphasis on embodiment to the rejection of a heteronomous understanding of Mary. The picture of Mary as the unilateral receiver is false, Grenholm says, and needs to be supplemented with and strongly modified by the image of the mother and of the one who practices compassion. The reception of the divine Word happens in, with, and during the conditions of everyday life, and is something that informs these conditions in a crucial way, which means that the Word is in some way embodied where the human being is active.

In her book *Kvinnor talar om Jesus [Women talk about Jesus]* Anne-Louise Eriksson also wants to speak of the incarnation of God as the way in which God takes form in everyday, human circumstances, and she is skeptical as well of the traditional Christological formulations.[129] One of the points that Eriksson takes up in her book is a critique of the tendency to passiviza-

---

125. I repeat here portions of a discussion that I presented in the article "Kristus och människan: Om inkarnationen och kärleksbegreppet," *Svensk Teologisk Kvartalskrift* 77, no. 2 (2001): 66–76.

126. Cristina Grenholm, *Barmhärtig och sårbar. En bok om kristen tro på Jesus* (Stockholm: Verbum, 1999), p. 61.

127. Grenholm, *Barmhärtig och sårbar*, p. 52.

128. Grenholm, *Barmhärtig och sårbar*, pp. 60, 62–63, 66–78. Aspects of this question are found as well in Cristina Grenholm's later book *Moderskap och kärlek: Schabloner och tankeutrymme i feministteologisk livsåskådningsreflektion* (Nora, Sweden: Nya Doxa, 2005).

129. Eriksson, *Kvinnor*, pp. 164–66; 200; 205; 206.

tion that has adhered to certain christologies. For her, a crucial criterion for a relevant Christology for our time is that it does not suppress or conceal the experiences of women. These have been concealed by traditional patriarchal Christology, which thus does not necessarily present the only truth about the accounts of Jesus. These accounts have an emancipatory potential for women as well, and it is therefore a challenge for contemporary Christological thought to liberate this potential in various ways. Among other possibilities, this occurs through breaking with the prevailing patriarchal language, for example, by speaking of Jesus as the *sophia* of God, i.e., the Wisdom of God. Eriksson does not want to argue that a Christology should *start* from particular experiences, for example women's experiences, in part because it is difficult to decide precisely which experiences ought to be ascribed such authority, and in part because it is all too generalizing to argue that a certain sort of experience is shared by all women. It is thus not about privileging women's experiences where previously men's experiences had been privileged. Instead, it is simply about not letting men's experiences (which should not be generalized either) be the only ones that count.

We get a clear example of this from Eriksson when she dedicates a few paragraphs to the sin of pride, or the attempt to set oneself in the place of God.[130] According to Eriksson this sin has occupied the interest of theologians through the centuries, and it has, among other things, resulted in a Christology where the boundary between God and human has been maintained by the understanding of the human being as essentially passive. However, this sin has primarily been a problem for men, since it is men who, by their "likeness with God," have been tempted to commit this sin. With this the other half of humanity has been represented as finite and limited. In other words, the man has been seen as active and the woman as passive.

In addition, both Grenholm and Eriksson express a certain skepticism before the classical formulations of the doctrine of incarnation. This is partially tied up with the fact that these formulations were in the service of a patriarchal Christianity, and there is an important critical task here. But it also seems to be partially tied up with a suspicion of "speculative" or "metaphysical" arguments. Here, I believe that it is important for a feminist Christology, just as for any other Christology, to look into those issues that these "speculations"—such as, for example, the Chalcedonian creed—actually raised, namely the question of what we mean when we profess Jesus as in some sense divine. In other words, I do not believe that feminist Christology,

---

130. Eriksson, *Kvinnor,* p. 200.

any more than other christologies, escapes the more ontological problems insofar as these christologies also want to reflect on the relationship between the divine and human. On the other hand, in its criticism of a unilaterally ontological Christology feminist Christology has a legitimate concern that this approach completely disregards Christology's inevitable functional—or perhaps existential—aspects.

Paradoxically enough, in this context the feminist critique encounters some problems that it has in common with the Christological reflection of the ancient church. To begin with, it thus criticizes the idea that it is possible to differentiate between theory and praxis in the way that a lot of modern theology takes for granted.[131] Furthermore, it reiterates—but with a difference—the question of the relationship between activity and passivity in Christ. For traditional Christology, this problem was within the scope of the relationship between divine and human nature. Was the human nature of Christ merely a passive instrument for the divine will? Just as the critics of monothelitism, i.e., the position that Christ had only a single divine will, questioned whether Christ can actually be said to be a true human if he cannot also be said to have a true human will, feminist Christology questions the construction of the female as passivity and the male as activity. They thus pursue a traditional Christological issue, and so, in a sense, also end up in the position that was victorious in that debate, namely the elevation of dyotheletism, the doctrine that Christ has two wills, to dogma at the sixth ecumenical council in Constantinople, 680–681. There are obviously also differences between contemporary feminist Christology and traditional patristic Christology, and one of these is the clearer articulation by contemporary feminist Christology of the context dependence of all theology.

One strategy of feminist Christology has been to point out that the masculine metaphors—Ruether's choice of words—that articulate the relationship between Jesus and God must be complemented by feminine metaphors. The point of this is not the replacement of one unilateralism with another unilateralism, but, as Ruether puts it, that the use of feminine metaphors "deliteralizes metaphors for the second person of the Trinity, revealed in Christ as 'Son of God.'"[132] Through this the register for speaking about this relationship is increased, and it thus becomes more difficult to understand any metaphor, for example, Son of God, as more literal than another. The

---

131. Cf. Mark A. McIntosh, *Mystical Theology: The Integrity of Spirituality and Theology,* Challenges in Contemporary Theology (Oxford: Blackwell, 1998), pp. 24–30.

132. Ruether, "Christology," p. 14.

ontological link between the man Jesus and a male God can thus be broken. In connection with the argument in the previous section, I want to point out that Ruether does not notice that in her striving for the "deliteralization" of traditional Christology she in a certain sense has the patristic Christology on her side, even if one does not contrast "literal" versus "metaphorical" language there in the way that Ruether does. However, Ruether and many others have pointed out that the biblical testimony, like the tradition, is not as one-sided as it has sometimes been presented. For example, the relationship between Jesus and God in the time of the New Testament could be formulated with the aid of "Wisdom" (as I noted in previous chapters), a metaphor that, in the biblical tradition, bears feminine features.[133] During Christian Antiquity and the Middle Ages there were also a number of ways to speak of Jesus as "mother," even as the "breast of the Father" that gives suckle to his children, an expression that breaks with an essentialized understanding of the sexes (as I will further illustrate in chapter 10).[134] Sex was a much more fluid concept for the premodern church, more social than biological, but the modern period's essentializing conceptions of sex have contributed to these traditions being forgotten or receiving a marginalized significance.

I believe that such a demystification of the masculine metaphor for Jesus' relationship to God in certain ways goes beyond an inclusive strategy. If an inclusive strategy tries to simply exchange sex-specific metaphors for more general ones, for example, "man" for "person," it thereby risks hiding the historical fact that the masculine has often been made the norm for humanity. Of course, this depends on the way that it is done, but arguing that sex should not be constitutive for the Christian doctrine of incarnation can hide the fact that sex has often been and still is something constitutive for many representations of the incarnation.[135] The feminist theologian Eleanor McLaughlin thus writes, entirely correctly:

> . . . if there is to be found or constructed a feminist Christology which includes woman as well as man in the icon of God, the male hegemony

133. Cf., for example, Ruether, "Christology," pp. 14–15, but especially Schüssler Fiorenza, *Jesus,* pp. 131–62, together with Elizabeth A. Johnson, "Wisdom Was Made Flesh and Pitched Her Tent among Us," in *Reconstructing the Christ Symbol,* ed. Maryanne Stevens, pp. 95–117.

134. On *logos* as the Father's breast in Clement of Alexandria, see Verna E. F. Harrison, "The Breast of the Father," in *Feminism & Theology,* Oxford Readings in Feminism, ed. Janet Martin Soskice and Diana Lipton (Oxford/New York: Oxford University Press, 2003), pp. 327–32.

135. Cf. Johnson, "Wisdom," p. 108.

must be deconstructed such that the image of God made Flesh is seen and experienced as female as well as male.[136]

McLaughlin thus suggests that a feminist Christology is in need of a symbolic, female embodiment of Jesus. She believes that the transvestite is a literary critical paradigm for this. Namely, the transvestite attempts to overstep the dualism between male/female:

> The transvestite . . . is a revealer of the cultural construction of gender categories making "clear," by the very ambiguity of the presentation, that gender, to a significant extent, is symbolic and lies in the eyes of the beholder, who is responding to a set of cultural clues.[137]

The transvestite thus links to the earlier tradition of the sex-transcending representations of Jesus that I mentioned in the paragraph above. These can help us understand that sex is something fluid, a social construction, and so make possible a transformed construction of sex. The hermeneutic potential in this is that we can also find a productive symbolic significance even in the texts from the past that had arisen and existed within the framework of a patriarchal culture. Thus it becomes possible to avoid an abstract, disembodied, and sexless Christ that additionally conceals women's experiences of their embodiment. If we castrate Christ, I believe that it becomes difficult to speak about incarnation at all.[138] A passable strategy would be to instead point out the symbolic significance of the male genitalia of Jesus (according to Luke 2:21 Jesus was circumcised on the eighth day), and the fact that this significance is not at all self-evidently masculine in a social sense, and since biological sex is something socially mediated (which I argue in chapters 8 and 10), the significance of Jesus' biological sex depends on its horizon of interpretation.

Christology as Practice

It is clear that a transformed discourse is not sufficient for a feminist Christology, and as Eriksson points out, the awareness of the need for a transformed

---

136. Eleanor McLaughlin, "Feminist Christologies: Re-Dressing the Tradition," in *Reconstructing the Christ Symbol*, ed. Maryanne Stevens, p. 121.

137. McLaughlin, "Christologies," p. 138.

138. Cf. Graham Ward, "Divinity and Sexuality: Luce Irigaray and Christology," *Modern Theology* 12, no. 2 (1996): 228.

Christological practice is something that reconciles otherwise very different feminist christologies.[139] Many of the more feminine metaphors that are used in order to speak about Jesus' relationship to God have been able to exist for a long time in more or less harmony alongside a patriarchal church, and thereby served in the worst case to strengthen stereotyped representations of sex. Feminine metaphors will thus not automatically lead to a more inclusive Christology. Conversely, one may also argue that masculine representations and concepts do not by definition need to lead to a sex-exclusive Christology, even if they have historically often been used in such a way. The crucial issue instead is which concrete practice constitutes the basis for the interpretation of these ideas and concepts. Schüssler Fiorenza's remark that the council in Chalcedon made its final resolution in a chapel consecrated to the holy Euphemia is therefore important, since it symbolically points to the dependence of the interpretation on the practices they are a part of. I would therefore like to argue that neither masculine nor feminine ideas and concepts in themselves constitute the problem or the solution to the Christological dilemma that feminist Christology has observed, even if feminist Christology's demystification of the masculine language is necessary for the establishment of a Christology that is not exclusive in relation to the female sex. This demystification must, however, be accompanied by transformed practices, and is thus an issue that goes beyond the purely linguistic critique. Most likely, transformed figurations of Christ in art, liturgy, preaching, etc., must accompany and influence a discursive transformation.[140] As McLaughlin writes: "[W]e may need ritual and visual symbols as well as words. Only thus can this be a Christology, a way of imaging Jesus Christ, which can be prayed and ritualized by the people of God."[141] Christology thus includes what we can quite simply call the reception of Jesus among men and women.

Speaking theologically, the incarnation is thus not something that is finished with Jesus, but we must instead, in accordance with these arguments, imagine that it extends to and includes people's reception of Jesus. The risk with understanding the presence of God in the human Jesus on the basis of the idea of an autonomous modern subject (whether the subject is the modern person as with Schleiermacher, or Christ himself as with Barth)

---

139. Eriksson, *Kvinnor,* p. 165.

140. Cf. Teresa Berger, "A Female Christ Child in the Manger and a Woman on the Cross, Or: The Historicity of the Jesus Event and the Inculturation of the Gospel," *Feminist Theology* 11 (January 1996): 32–45; and Doris Dyke, "Crucified Woman: Art and the Experience of Faith," *Toronto Journal of Theology* 5, no. 2 (1989): 161–69.

141. McLaughlin, "Christologies," p. 129.

is that one thereby contributes to an abstract, atomistic understanding of the incarnation, and disregards the fact that the incarnation must be understood as a relationship (which both Schleiermacher and Barth were also after). In her meditative reflection on the incarnation titled "The Crucified One," Luce Irigaray writes that "this god-man does not exist in a triumphant self-sufficiency. Always he is in society, in company, loved, helped. Living in a society of living people, from which he does not emerge as a solitary man. Sharing needs and desires with mortals."[142] Thus Jesus cannot be abstracted from the history in which he constitutes the primary node. I will return to the question of sex, embodiment, rite, and sociality in the chapters on the body (chapters 8–12), but what I want to finally highlight at this point is that feminist Christology, among many other things, clarifies the relationship between incarnation and human embodiment, and also points out the need for an understanding of the embodiment of the person in order to understand the incarnation, in a way that has not been equally clear in earlier theology (written by men), perhaps least of all in the modern period. So of the different Christological discourses I have examined in this chapter, it is feminist Christology that most clearly succeeds in avoiding the abstract characteristics that, as I established above, overshadow even modern Christology. This likely has to do with shifts in the understanding of subjectivity in relation to Schleiermacher as well as Barth and the theologians surrounding *The Myth of God Incarnate*. With the feminist theologians in general—and in particular with several of the theologians I have discussed in this section—the modern subject's self-determining status has not been denied, but certainly modified by a clearer emphasis on the human (the male as well as the female) subject's embodiment and sociality, or, if you prefer, our concrete historical, social, and cultural existence.

The Abstract Luster of the Christological Discourses

What reconciles these different modern christologies, in spite of their considerable theological differences, is the effort to safeguard the human in Jesus Christ. The implication is that the humanity of the human being as such is at stake in Christology. A lopsided Christology risks denying or diminishing the human being as such, and thereby giving a lopsided or

142. Luce Irigaray, "The Crucified One," in *Marine Lover of Friedrich Nietzsche*, trans. Gillian C. Gill (New York: Columbia University Press, 1991), p. 182.

unproductive understanding of the relationship between human being and God. Common to the four (in different ways) critical theologies that I have examined in this chapter is a greater or lesser critique of traditional Christology, above all as it has come to be formulated by the council of Chalcedon. However, as I have tried to show, such a critique has seldom succeeded in freeing itself from the issues that the Chalcedonian Christology raises—if this has in fact ever been a goal in itself. A reason for this may be that the Chalcedonian schema has become so decisive for the theological (and philosophical) history of effect that it is all but impossible to imagine any sort of Christological reflection independent of it. Another reason may be that Chalcedon's issues are more or less inevitable—not in the way that Chalcedon formulated the Christological creed, but in essence—and that they therefore continually return in one way or another. If one imagines the worth of Chalcedon more in terms of the questions that the definition opens up than as a last word, then the continued, critical question of this humanity as such would therefore not lie beyond the horizon of Chalcedon at all. Neither has the modern critique entirely succeeded in avoiding a character of abstraction in its own Christological contributions. Let me make a brief summary of this chapter in order to thereby come to my conclusion regarding where this places us in relation to the question of how a Christology would be able to recognize the human in its concrete historical existence.

Friedrich Schleiermacher emphasized Christian subjectivity as the criterion for an adequate contemporary Christology. The uniqueness of Christ consisted in that his God consciousness was not dimmed, as with us. The salvation of the human consists in that believers get to share in the God consciousness of Christ, which is mediated through the community of believers. The problem with traditional Christology was, according to Schleiermacher, that it gives the impression of speaking about God and the world individually abstracted from the concrete relationship between God and the world. The problem with Schleiermacher's Christology of subjectivity is, however, that it becomes difficult to see whether there is any real discontinuity between Jesus' God consciousness and the Christian self-awareness in a way that allows Christ to exercise a critical function vis-à-vis the Christian. Does a given understanding of human subjectivity not threaten to become the norm and starting point for Schleiermacher's Christological thought? Does the subjectivity of the human not thereby come to be the absolute (and so relatively abstract) horizon against which all her different ways of relating to God must stand out?

With Karl Barth we find a richly differentiated Christology with different emphases than Schleiermacher. Especially in the latter parts of *Church Dogmatics* Barth wants to show that real Christology does not consist in a formal definition, but in the exposition of the story of Jesus Christ. Christology cannot point to Christ through a static formula, but only through a dynamic retelling of Christ's own story. Although Barth is restrained in his critique of the traditional doctrine of incarnation and its reception throughout the history of theology, he wants to understand it within the framework of the story that Christ is, and so an at least indirect critique is directed against every form of abstract Christology. Here Barth finds himself not so far from Schleiermacher. Unlike Schleiermacher, however, he does not want to concede that the traditional creeds are ahistorical, abstract truths. He instead sees them as contextually conditioned commentaries on the confession of Christ, landmarks for later periods as well, but not infallible criteria for a true confession. The problem with his Christology is, however, the opposite of Schleiermacher's emphasis on the Christian self-awareness. Barth endeavors to avoid making the subjectivity of the human being the starting point for Christology, but the consequence of this strategy is that Christ is at times presented as a modern subject in relation to other human beings. So the problem has simply been moved over from one pole to another, and so we find an abstract luster lying over the humanity of the human even in Barth's narrative Christology. The history, creativity, subjectivity, and embodiment of the human tend to be reduced by Barth to functions of Christology, and so it becomes difficult to see how Barth manages to do justice to the human in her concrete, historical existence.

For the theologians surrounding the book *The Myth of God Incarnate* the critique of the traditional doctrine of incarnation is a question of its mythological style. On the one hand, it is unintelligible for a modern person, not least because it has characteristics of Docetism, i.e., the position that the humanity of Christ was only a phantom humanity. On the other, its claim that Christ is the unique revelation of God is not compelling in a time that is more conscious of religious pluralism. As regards the first critical point, Hick, Wiles, and Young believe that the "literal" understanding of the traditional doctrine of incarnation must make way for a "metaphorical" understanding. There is thus a greater capacity for formulating an adequate Christology for our time that takes more consideration for the humanity of the human being. I wonder, however, whether the critique itself in *The Myth of God Incarnate* is a matter of a misunderstanding. Hick and the others seem to ascribe to the traditional doctrine of two natures mythological features that it hardly has, and their understanding of the distinction between "literal" and "metaphorical" language takes place against a modern horizon that the theologians who formulated the traditional Christology did not share. Insofar as the circle around *The Myth of God Incarnate,* as with the traditional Chalcedonian Christology, want to make *some* sort of ontological claim, their distinction is not especially productive, since it can then hardly be understood as a distinction between having certain ontological claims and not having them. The traditional doctrine therefore *must* not seem alienating for our contemporary understanding of reality. What *The Myth of God Incarnate* makes clear is that Chalcedon is not *sufficient* in order to formulate an adequate Christology for our time, which does justice to the genuinely human. But at the same time we may ask, contrary to the arguments in *The Myth of God Incarnate,* whether an apophatic understanding of Chalcedon does not involve—and in principle always involved—a critique of a mythological understanding of the incarnation, and should thereby be seen as a defense of a concrete understanding of the human being rather than the opposite.

The other critical point in *The Myth of God Incarnate* becomes acute in feminist Christology. In 1983 Rosemary Radford Ruether posed the question of whether a male savior can in fact save women. She thereby focused on the androcentric exclusivism that, according to the feminist critique, adheres to the traditional Christology. Jesus Christ, the unique revelation and incarnation of God, is male, and so the masculine has been presented as normatively human. Christ as the *logos* of God is thus the male offspring and revelation of a male God. Another theologian, Elisabeth Schüssler Fiorenza, in an interpretation of the resolution at the council in Chalcedon, has accused this conception of constituting in its Christological formulations a legitimating ideology for a "kyriarchal" political order. Christology thus becomes a way to legitimate theological and religious androcentrism. The humanity of the woman becomes subordinate to that of the man, becoming a humanity in only a derivative sense. A potential feminist Christology should, apart from criticizing androcentric Christology, emphasize the woman as active and the human as a concrete, historical being. As with Schleiermacher and Barth, a more concrete representation of the human is thus called for within a feminist-oriented theology. Unlike these, however, feminist Christology is sensitive to sexual difference and manages to revalue the concrete human experience within the framework of theology as well. A feminist Christology is thus entirely possible, even if it acknowledges that Jesus had a male set of chromosomes. More important is the symbolic significance of the sex. Is it possible to shape symbolic representations of Christ that transcend the dualism between male/female?

Feminist Christology has additionally emphasized the need for a concrete, transformed praxis as a further development of the incarnation, and this emphasis, I want to argue, involves an important step away from that abstract luster that has plagued much of even modern Christology. The importance of the incarnation does not lie, therefore, only in Jesus Christ, but also in the reception of him. One might say that feminist Christology calls for precisely that which is missing in Barth (among others), namely a conception of the human in her concrete, historical existence as it is studied by phenomenology, ethnography, and sociology. This does not need to mean that feminist Christology must fall to the same critique that I leveled against Schleiermacher, namely that the subjectivity of the human thereby becomes an unproblematized norm and starting point for theology. Because feminist Christology starts from an understanding of subjectivity as embodied and social, it is always already decentered, and thus cannot constitute an unambiguous or absolute pole in the relationship between divine and human. As the British theologian Nicholas Lash has pointed out, the starting point for a Christology can hardly be either God *or* the human, since neither constitutes a self-evident, transparent starting point that is at our disposal in an uncontroversial way.[143] The relational understanding of the incarnation called for by both Schleiermacher and Barth has been realized by feminist Christology in a clearer way, and contains theological potentials that I will attempt to realize in the following chapters.

A characteristic trait in the christologies I have investigated in this chapter is undoubtedly that they strive to give an account of the humanity of Jesus Christ in a distinct way. Even if, as we have seen in previous chapters, this was not an unknown task for patristic Christology either, modern Christological reflection has consistently considered this earlier Christology rather ponderous. In his analysis of different christologies Lash writes that

> [t]here is no doubt that, throughout the history of Christianity, there has been a tendency to allow the 'weight of the absolute' to press upon, obscure or obliterate the specific, contingent particularities constitutive of the persons, events and series of events from which Christian reflection takes its origin.[144]

143. Nicholas Lash, "Up and Down in Christology," in *New Studies in Theology I*, ed. Stephen Sykes and Derek Holmes (London: Duckworth, 1980), pp. 30–46.
144. Lash, "Up and Down," p. 37.

What Lash wants to figure out is how to come to terms with the formal, abstract characteristic of many theological concepts about the human that has weakened many christologies—as we have even seen a bit of with the modern christologies. Lash mentions the German theologian Karl Rahner, who claims to be able to trace a Monophysite undercurrent in a large portion of popular Christology, but who argues that Chalcedon was a *defense* against such undercurrents, and so also of the human nature of Jesus.[145] As I attempted to show above, the distance between several of the modern critics of Chalcedon and Chalcedon itself is not absolute. Perhaps the critique is more a critique of the popular reception of Chalcedon than of Chalcedon itself. Irrespective of how it relates to this, it does not, however, seem as though it is possible within the framework of Chalcedon to come to terms with the endemic abstract character of the theological concept of the human. But neither does modern Christology, with its emphasis on the subjectivity of the human being, always manage to recognize the human in its concrete existence.

Now if the Chalcedonian creed was never intended to furnish an independent Christology, and if modern Christology's emphasis on the subjectivity of the human does not succeed either in escaping certain abstract characteristics, there is no need to choose the one over the other, or even to assume they are competitors. In order to come to terms with the abstract character of the anthropology in Christology, I want to suggest another strategy, and in accordance with this I will in the following chapters examine what concrete consequences the reception of Christology has had for the theological anthropology that has influenced the Christian self-image—a task that exists implicitly, among others, in feminist Christology's search for a greater awareness of the need for a transformed Christological practice. So what seems to be required—which is in line with Chalcedon, but which I have primarily found in feminist Christology—is a reflection on what, in this study's formulation of purpose, I have called the anthropological implications of the doctrine of the incarnation for the human mode of being-in-the-world, or in other words, how Christ has been received in concrete, human practices. But if Christology is in need of an anthropological supplement so as not to become abstract, one can also say that the reverse applies: a theological anthropology that wants to thematize the God-relationship of the human independently of Christology becomes abstract as well (in relation to the Christian tradition). Christology and anthropology presuppose

145. Rahner, "Current Problems in Christology," p. 188.

and follow from each other. By focusing on the gaze and embodiment from a theologically anthropological perspective, as well as how they have been shaped over the ages, a clearer image of the strengths and shortcomings in Christology should stand out. Both the gaze and the body are fundamental for the human being's concrete relationships to her surrounding world (and to herself), and the understanding of gaze and embodiment also influences how we humans can envisage our relationship to God. In the following eight chapters I will carry out one such investigation, but not from a strictly historical perspective. Instead, I will pursue a critical theological discussion with the aid of different phenomenological, critical theoretical, sociological, ethnographical, and other perspectives. The point is thus not simply to highlight different theological perspectives on gaze and embodiment, but above all to pursue a critical and constructive argument about how a contemporary theology of the gaze and the body might appear, as an experiment in working further with some of the issues that I reviewed above that we can find in modern Christology. Accordingly, in these eight chapters I will primarily approach the Christological questions from a clearer anthropological perspective than in this and the previous chapter. But in the Christian tradition theological anthropology has always been influenced by Christology, and so offers, I want to argue, the concrete reception of Christology in different significant practices, or, if one wants, it offers the supplement that is required in order to avoid a luster of abstraction in the Christological discourses.[146] As a first step towards such a theological anthropology I will therefore turn to the question of how the God-relationship of the human being has been given form through her gaze.

146. Cf. Graham Ward, "Introduction," *Christ and Culture,* pp. 1–26.

PART II

THE GAZE

4. On the Art of Seeing

In his book *Ways of Seeing* John Berger argues that our gaze is never independent of our social and historical context.[1] Sight, which we may think is a self-evident biological fact, is in fact historically and culturally conditioned. Sight is not something that is given, something that is constant and independent of circumstances. This means, in brief, that how we see differs between different places and times. Without the biological conditions there would obviously be no sight, but these biological conditions are intimately entangled with historical, cultural, social, and religious circumstances. One of today's foremost theoreticians of the visual, Jonathan Crary, writes: "There never was or will be a self-evident beholder to whom a world is transparently evident. Instead there are more or less powerful arrangements of forces out of which the capacities of an observer are possible."[2] In order to separate the biological conditions for sight from their historical and cultural conditions, we can speak of the latter as the person's "gaze."[3]

How we see the things we turn our gaze towards is dependent on our experience and our understandings. It becomes even more complicated when we turn our gaze towards another person. Then we can exchange gazes, and through the gaze alone perform a range of different relations,

1. John Berger, *Ways of Seeing* (London: BBC/Penguin Books, 1972).

2. Jonathan Crary, *Techniques of the Observer: On Vision and Modernity in the Nineteenth Century* (Cambridge, MA/London: MIT Press, 1990), p. 6.

3. The word "gaze" has a range of different connotations within different disciplines. I have no intention of confining myself to any particular one of them, even if my use of the concept is influenced by art history and critical theory rather than psychoanalysis. For a sort of concise explanation of the term from various perspectives, see Marita Sturken and Lisa Cartwright, *Practices of Looking: An Introduction to Visual Culture* (Oxford/New York: Oxford University Press, 2001), pp. 355–56. Cf. also pp. 72–108.

from passionate love or genuine indifference to hate. Sight has a dimension of reciprocity that is unavoidable, even if it is a matter of viewing a lifeless thing. Looking at something always entails that it is possible for us to be seen from the position of the thing. We can even be caught in the act of looking. Through our gaze we stand in an active relationship to the things and persons around us. Berger writes: "We never look at one thing; we are always looking at the relation between things and ourselves."[4] Through our gaze we place ourselves in relationship to the world, or rather, we have already been placed in relationship to the world.

Even images represent a way to look at the world. An image is never a self-evident reproduction of reality, but is always dependent on certain more or less conscious choices by the photographer or the painter or the illustrator, who decides what is depicted—if the image is representational— as well as how it is depicted. "Every image embodies a way of seeing. Even a photograph."[5] Photography has often been understood as a sort of image that is more mechanical, less dependent on human choice of perspective than, for example, a painted image. But this is a truth with a big qualification. Even if we bracket off for the moment the whole discussion of the post-photographic era, which we are said to be in now, it is clear that every photograph is dependent on the choices of the photographer—the choice to photograph one motif rather than another, to do it from one particular spatial perspective with a particular focal length on the camera's lens, to expose with a particular shutter speed and a particular aperture, as well as pushing the trigger at a particular moment. So for several reasons that I will return to, a photograph is not an innocent way of looking at the world that simply registers what it "sees."

Let us linger a while with photography as an illustration of the art of seeing. Crucial for our way of looking at a photograph is not only the fact that it embodies the photographer's way of seeing, but also the way in which we look at it. Berger takes as an example a group photograph where Sheila is one out of twenty, but for personal reasons our eyes only see her. But it is not only personal reasons that play a role in how we look at an image. The context for the viewing is crucial as well, and social institutions play a large role here. The museum is a socially established institution with great significance for how we view an image that has been placed in its auspices. When the artist Marcel Duchamp in 1914 exhibits a bottle rack in a museum, this

4. Berger, *Ways,* p. 9.
5. Berger, *Ways,* p. 10.

Ready-Made is "transformed" from a utilitarian object to art, thanks to the new context in which it is placed. In its original context the bottle rack would likely have escaped our investigative gaze, but when it suddenly becomes "art," it captures our attention in a whole other way. Even the pop art of, for example, Andy Warhol, indicates the significance of context for how we look at pictures. Warhol has made silkscreen prints of pictures taken from popular culture: Campbell's Soup and Marilyn Monroe are probably the most famous. Warhol's representations of famous artifacts and people have since been spread back into popular culture in the form of cheap posters in a way that has made them just as popular as the original soup can or actress (and has additionally challenged the distinction between "popular culture" and "art").

I have begun this chapter with several observations intended to suggest how our seeing is dependent on personal as well as cultural factors, and how every gaze and every image is thus situated in a context that has significance for *how* we see or *what* we see. What I have wanted to very briefly show is that our gaze is never innocent or neutral. The point of this chapter is to introduce a theological discussion of the gaze, which shall then continue in the following three chapters. In order to show how the gaze can be understood from a theological perspective as a concrete reception of Christology in a significant practice, I have chosen to begin this portion on the gaze with several more general historical and philosophical investigations of the gaze as both embodied and relational. If all gazes in some way express a relationship, I will here pay attention to several different sorts of gazes, which will soon clarify what is specific to the theological gaze that I want to advocate. By way of introduction in this chapter I want to investigate how cultural and historical factors affect our way of seeing. Such an investigation cannot be more than schematic here, given how steeped our culture and history are in different visual practices, different understandings of sight, the gaze, and the eye, as well as the visual and ocular metaphors at different levels of our language.[6] The theme that is indicated by the words sight, gaze, vision, eye, is too large to be encompassed in its entirety, but it is also too important to be neglected, which is why, in spite of everything, I risk this schematic investigation. In other words, I want to say something about how the relationship between the human being and her existence has been configured by different ways of seeing, or to use Christian Metz's expression, by different

---

6. Cf. Martin Jay, *Downcast Eyes: The Denigration of Vision in Twentieth-Century French Thought* (Berkeley/Los Angeles/London: University of California Press, 1993), pp. 1–2.

"scopic regimes."[7] Then I will also discuss the question of possibilities of the gaze for positioning us in relation to the world from a phenomenological perspective, rather than a historical one. I take my starting point here from several philosophers who have reflected on what it implies for human sight and gaze that the human is an embodied creature. The theological discussion continues in the next chapter on the New Testament's perspective on sight and in chapter 6 on the gaze of the icon. In these two chapters I want to both bring to the fore the contribution of the theological tradition to a contemporary theology of the gaze, and indicate the mutual interdependence of the gaze and its object. My more systematic conclusion comes in chapter 7 on the embodied, relational, and erotic gaze. But first, a short account of three different scopic regimes.

The Curious Eye

The gaze has a history. The way in which we concentrate ourselves on seeing something is influenced by our place in history. Every scopic regime carries its own unspoken cultural rules for what and how we shall see.[8] Among the historians of art, the historians of ideas, and others, a number of investigations have been implemented on precisely the way of seeing in different epochs.[9] This does not mean that a particular epoch would accommodate one and only one overall way of seeing. Rather, one can speak of a more or less open conflict between different ways of seeing, where there can nevertheless very well be a way of seeing that dominates during a particular period. In other words, it is as unbelievable that modernity, for example, would be a cohesive epoch as it is that its scopic regime would be one and only one. Nor is there just one single field of human activity that completely determines the scopic regime. The key to an epoch's visual culture is not its compatibility with science, but its comprehensibility. An example of this is the fact that perspective, that is, a system of converging lines that gives an impression of depth in a two-dimensional representation, is not the way early modern science imagines sight, but is instead, as the prominent representative for

7. I found this via Martin Jay, "Scopic Regimes of Modernity," *The Visual Culture Reader,* ed. Nicholas Mirzoeff (London/New York: Routledge, 1998), pp. 66–69.

8. Jay, "Scopic Regimes," p. 9.

9. See primarily Jay, *Downcast Eyes;* Jonathan Crary, *Suspensions of Perception: Attention, Spectacle, and Modern Culture* (Cambridge, MA/London: MIT Press, 1999); Crary, *Techniques of the Observer.*

"Visual Theory" Nicholas Mirzoeff puts it, "a hybrid of medieval theories of vision with the modern need to picture the world."[10] These reservations serve to show that the question of an epoch's scopic regime is never a question of a single explanation of the way of seeing, and that it is also hardly a question of a single sphere of human activity that is determinative for all the others. Every attempt at summary that is made, for example by myself in this chapter, is a refinement, in my case motivated by pedagogical considerations. To begin with I shall say something here about early modernity as a scopic regime.[11]

Let us begin with the question of perspective. Perspective painting began to be developed by Renaissance artists during the 1400s. One of the theoreticians of perspective who is still relevant in our time is the author, philosopher, linguist, and architect Leon Battista Alberti (1404–1472).[12] Perspective painting involves an attempt to reproduce the human being's three-dimensional visual impression in two-dimensional painting. The predecessors of the Renaissance artists during the Middle Ages had separated out background from foreground as well, but there the difference between these was often motivated by the worth that was attributed to the depicted. Thus an important person could be depicted as larger than someone less important. Or one could also let the depicted objects overlap each other in such a way that it showed what was foreground and what was background. The perspective artists, on the other hand, wanted to depict their motifs from a perspective where the starting point was the eye of the beholder, and where converging lines measured the observer's distance from the observed. If one imagines the image or the field of sight as divided by a grid, and from that grid draws converging lines away from the horizon and allows the proportional distance between the lines to be maintained, the depicted objects will successively shrink the more they near the horizon point. The closer to the point of the gaze the depicted object finds itself, the larger it is depicted. So the size of the depicted object is in proportion to its distance from the point of the gaze vis-à-vis the point of the horizon.

10. Nicholas Mirzoeff, *An Introduction to Visual Culture* (London/New York: Routledge, 1999), p. 38.

11. On the earlier history of vision, see Jay, *Downcast Eyes,* pp. 21–49; Janet Martin Soskice, "Sight and Vision in Medieval Christian Thought," in *Vision in Context: Historical and Contemporary Perspectives on Sight,* ed. Teresa Brennan and Martin Jay (New York/London: Routledge, 1996), pp. 29–43.

12. Leon Battista Alberti, *On Painting: A New Translation and a Critical Edition,* ed. and trans. Rocco Sinisgalli (Cambridge: Cambridge University Press, 2013).

An easy way to visualize perspective is to imagine it as the view one has from a window. The window frames what can be seen and what cannot be seen. Berger describes perspective in the following way:

> The convention of perspective, which is unique to European art and which was first established in the early Renaissance, centres everything on the eye of the beholder. It is like a beam from a lighthouse—only instead of light travelling outwards, appearances travel in. The conventions called those appearances *reality*. Perspective makes the single eye the centre of the visible world. Everything converges on to the eye as to the vanishing point of infinity. The visible world is arranged for the spectator as the universe was once thought to be arranged for God.[13]

So is perspective a convention? Mirzoeff points out that perspective is not "important because it shows how we 'really' see . . . but because it allows us to order and control what we see."[14] Perspective is not a mirror of the outer world in art, but a way of interpreting and thinking of the world visually. In other words, perspective is not the "natural" way to see—even if it has often been understood thus in the West since the fifteenth century—but a historically conditioned way to visualize reality from a particular point of view. Mirzoeff points out that the paintings of the Renaissance and early modern high-culture often took the king, the prince, or some other authority as the ideal as well as the actual observer, i.e., both the observer whom the perspective of the picture is oriented towards and the observer for whom the picture is made.[15]

The observer is the center of the perspectival view, but this is a matter of the observer's view*point,* which Martin Jay describes as "a monocular, unblinking fixed eye (or more precisely, abstract point), rather than the two active, stereoscopic eyes of embodied actual vision, which give us the experience of depth perspective."[16] This entails a practice where the painter's as well as the observer's living body is replaced, at least in principle, by an eye

13. Berger, *Ways,* p. 16.

14. Mirzoeff, *Introduction,* p. 40. For a philosophical critique of perspective realism, see Nelson Goodman, *Languages of Art: An Approach to a Theory of Symbols,* 2nd edition (Indianapolis/Cambridge: Hackett, 1976), pp. 10–19.

15. Mirzoeff, *Introduction,* p. 41. Martin Jay (*Downcast Eyes,* pp. 60–61) points out that Dutch art emphasized the materiality of the canvas and the presence of the observer in the work of art more than Italian art.

16. Jay, *Downcast Eyes,* p. 55.

made eternal, beyond the course of time. The observer withdrew from the seen. In contrast to the ancient Greek understanding of *theōria,* this eternal gaze was not involved in the world of the observed.[17] This gaze was instead distanced, active, and ordering.

Perspective painting retained its grip on art even when the physiological understanding of sight changed. The Dutchman Thomas Kepler was the first who argued that the eye's lens gave an inverted image on the retina. But it was primarily René Descartes in his *Discourse on Method* from 1637 who broke with the established understanding of sight.[18] In the Middle Ages there was a lengthy discussion on whether the eye intercepted light rays from outside of its visual impression, or whether it sent out light rays itself which were intercepted by the object in the field of vision. In addition it was believed that light was a spiritual medium. Descartes broke with tradition when he argued that light was a material substance with a concrete existence. He compared light to a cane for the blind in an attempt to explain its function with common metaphors—sight likened to touch[19]—and he used mathematics in order to understand how it functioned. Descartes believed that sensation itself was a function of the brain, not the retina. It was consciousness rather than the eye that saw. The sensory perceptions were interpreted in the brain, and it was here that the representations of the outer world were located. So there was the possibility that these sensory impressions deceived us. Our understandings of the objects in the world did not build on resemblance to these objects, but were a representation of them. Resemblance was preserved in the sense that the form of the object that was seen was preserved by its representation. Thus perspective was of great significance for Descartes as a way of mediating between representation and resemblance. Descartes points out in *Discourse on Method* that engravings in accordance with "the rules of perspective" often represent circles with ovals, squares with rhombuses, etc.[20] An object is thus sometimes represented better by something that is not like the object itself, in accordance with the "rules of perspective." The same process takes place in the brain, when it interprets sensory

17. Hans-Georg Gadamer says that *theōria* involves presence, participation. See *Truth and Method,* 2nd revised edition, translation revised by Joel Weinsheimer and Donald G. Marshall (London/New York: Continuum, 2004), p. 122.

18. See the relevant section in René Descartes, "Optics," in *The Visual Culture Reader,* pp. 60–65.

19. Crary, *Techniques,* p. 59: "From Descartes to Berkeley to Diderot, vision is conceived in terms of analogies to the senses of touch."

20. Descartes, "Optics," p. 64.

impressions, as when the engraver interprets the object in the engraving in accordance with the "rules of perspective." Perspective, like representation, was in other words elevated to a sort of natural law.

Descartes's understanding of sight would come to have great influence among scientists and philosophers, so great that Descartes is often seen as the founder of the modern scopic regime.[21] Jay wants to call the scopic regime of early modernity a "Cartesian perspectivalism" in view of its great impact.[22] Characteristic of this scopic regime was a disembodied eye in accordance with Descartes's dualism between body and soul. Descartes writes in *Dissertation on Method:* "Thus, this 'I', that is to say, the soul through which I am that which I am, is entirely distinct from the body."[23] The eye of consciousness is distanced from the objectified field of vision. We get a summary of such a "Cartesian perspectivalism" from Paul Ricoeur, who argues that it is "contemporaneous with a vision of the world in which the whole of objectivity is spread out like a spectacle on which the *cogito* casts its sovereign gaze."[24] Thus the Cartesian *cogito*'s gaze becomes a fundamentally disembodied gaze (cf. my discussion of Descartes's view of embodiment in chapter 8).

The scopic regime of early modernity is an expression of a rationalization of sight.[25] In this period the visual was detached from the textual—the book of creation became independent of the book of the Bible—and so the world came to be understood as an observable object, but without meaning, rather than as an intelligible text.[26] As Jay expresses it: "[S]pace was robbed of its substantive meaningfulness to become an ordered, uniform system of abstract linear coordinates."[27] The homogenization of space created the possibility of surveying and mastering this space. Curiosity became a highly valued virtue, in contrast to the devaluation of this faculty by an

21. Cf., for example, Richard Rorty, *Philosophy as the Mirror of Nature* (Oxford: Basil Blackwell, 1980), pp. 45–46.

22. Jay, *Downcast Eyes*, p. 70.

23. René Descartes, *Discours de la méthode/Discourse on Method,* a bilingual edition, translated and introduced by George Heffernan (Notre Dame/London: University of Notre Dame Press, 1994), p. 53.

24. Paul Ricoeur, "The Question of the Subject: The Challenge of Semiology," trans. Kathleen McLaughlin, *The Conflict of Interpretations: Essays in Hermeneutics,* ed. Don Ihde (London: Continuum, 2004), p. 232.

25. Jay, *Downcast Eyes*, pp. 49ff.

26. Cf. Michel Foucault, *The Order of Things: An Archaeology of the Human Sciences,* translated from the French (London: Routledge, 1986).

27. Jay, *Downcast Eyes*, p. 52.

earlier Christianity.[28] For medieval Christianity the curious gaze had been an expression of hubris and arrogance. Curiosity now implied an active intervention in the state of things, rather than a passive contemplation. As Jay writes: "[M]odern men and women opened their eyes and beheld a world unveiled to their eager gaze."[29] The gaze met a new and previously unknown land, in the same way as when Christopher Columbus "discovered" America.

We get what is possibly one of the most expressive examples of the modern scopic regime's mastering of space via the gaze from Jeremy Bentham's panoptic prison, which Michel Foucault has described in *Discipline and Punish*. According to Foucault, a coordination of two power-mechanisms arose in the eighteenth century. The first was the division between normal and not-normal; the second was techniques for disciplining the not-normal, making it normal. The architectonic expression of this coordination is Bentham's panopticon. Bentham imagined a round building with a tower raised in the middle. The round building is divided into cells with two windows. One window lets in light from the outer side of the building, the other faces the tower. The tower has corresponding windows that face the cells. Consequently a single warden in the tower can supervise all the people in the cells, since they stand out in the backlight. Everyone who is locked up in the cells plays a little one-person theater for the solitary viewer—the warden in the tower. A single person can thus, unseen, exercise complete control over many people. The inhabitant of the cell, on the other hand, "is seen, but he does not see; he is the object of information, never a subject in communication."[30] At the same time that the warden is guaranteed full control over the inhabitant of the cell, he is marked off from those who occupy the surrounding cells. This facilitates control as well. Discipline via the panoptic exercise of power is a node in the rationalization of society. The key word for the new exercise of power is no longer physical violence, but discipline, normalization, control. This entails a whole new order in human diversity.

On the whole modernity associated light and knowledge with each other, which is apparent not least in the terms "Enlightenment," "Aufklärung," "upplysning," or "les Lumières" that were used by a large

28. Hans Blumenberg, *The Legitimacy of the Modern Age,* trans. Robert M. Wallace (Cambridge, MA: MIT Press, 1983), part 3; together with Karsten Harries, *Infinity and Perspective* (Cambridge, MA/London: MIT Press, 2001).

29. Jay, *Downcast Eyes,* p. 69.

30. Michel Foucault, *Discipline and Punish: The Birth of the Prison,* trans. Alan Sheridan (New York: Vintage Books, 1977), 200; Jeremy Bentham, *The Panopticon Writings,* Wo es war, ed. Miran Božovič (London: Verso, 1995).

number of thinkers during the eighteenth century and are of course still the designation of this epoch. In common for several of them was a belief in the transparency of existence, that it would make itself available for the Enlightenment's curious and inquiring eye.[31] On the title page of the first volume of Diderot and d'Alembert's *Encyclopédie* one could see how the philosophers of the Enlightenment tore the veil of truth, so that it would show itself to the philosophers in all its nakedness. A less cocksure philosopher, such as Jean-Jacques Rousseau, for example, could yet remain ambivalent towards sight. But it was not until the nineteenth century onwards that the hegemony of Cartesian perspectivalism began to be seriously questioned. This had to do with several technical innovations, not least the camera and chemical photography.

The Mechanical Eye

The birth-year of photography—and the opening of the photographic era—is usually set at 1839.[32] Joseph Nicéphore and Isidore Niépce had then, together with Louis Jacques Mandé Daguerre in France and William Henry Fox Talbot in England, independently of each other developed exposure methods where the physical light itself could inscribe the picture instead of the hand of a person. Already in 1826 Nicéphore and Niépce had succeeded in capturing a view from a window with an exposure time of eight hours. Together with Daguerre, Nicéphore and Niépce developed the so-called daguerreotype, through which a photograph could be produced on silvered copperplate. In 1839 Niépce and Daguerre received pensions from the French government in exchange for not making any claims for a patent for their invention. Thus photography was public domain from the start. Talbot's foremost contribution consisted in the invention of a type of negative, which became the foundation for the modern photographic technique by which a picture could be reproduced, in contrast to the daguerreotype. His invention was patented in 1841. At the start, the negative—Talbot called it the "Calotype," from the Greek *kalos*, "beautiful," and *typos*, "imprinting"—was

31. Jay, *Downcast Eyes*, pp. 83–113.
32. See Graham Clarke, *The Photograph*, Oxford History of Art (Oxford/New York: Oxford University Press, 1997); Mary Warner Marien, *Photography: A Cultural History* (London: Laurence King Publishing, 2002); Jay, *Downcast Eyes*, pp. 124–47; Mirzoeff, *Introduction*, pp. 65–90. On why photography should not be seen as an extension of earlier forms of visual representation, for example through a *camera obscura*, see Crary, *Techniques*.

not at all as detailed as the daguerreotype, but the ease with which it could be reproduced contributed to the fact that it soon dominated.

The feature of photography that is popularly seen to be the most characteristic is its realism. A photograph presents, it has popularly been held, a bit of reality as it actually was. Mirzoeff writes:

> The newness and importance of photography stems from its most obvious capability: its rendering of a precise moment in time. The click of the shutter captures a moment of time that is immediately past but is nonetheless the closest thing there is to a knowledge of the present. The experience of modernity is contained in this paradox.[33]

On account of the realistic picture that was reproduced on the negative via the solitary eye of the camera, it has sometimes been suggested that the camera was a further reinforcement of the scopic regime of modernity. The perspective of the camera was identified with the understanding of sight that was accepted in modernity as natural law. As Jay formulates it: "The camera eye, as monocular as that of the peephole, produced a frozen, disincarnated gaze on a scene completely external to itself."[34] In contrast to Descartes, the sense of sight in the nineteenth century was no longer associated with touch, and so the "deincarnating" gaze of photography was primed at a purely cultural level.[35] Because of this, photography could, in a way, be imagined to be produced without human involvement, in the sense that that which was recorded through the camera's lens was not dependent on human technical skill or imaginative capacities.

The confidence in the ability of photography to represent the world as it actually was has been enormous, despite the fact that early on people had already began to experiment with retouchings and double exposures in order to present illusory effects. This confidence has of course been varied: a photograph that illustrates an important piece of news in a respectable newspaper has probably always been expected to be a more faithful depiction of the subject than the picture in a fashion magazine, where more or less comprehensive retouching belongs to the accepted order of things. But if we do not have an explicit reason to expect something else, we suppose—or we have at least earlier supposed, see below—that a photograph has not been

---

33. Mirzoeff, *Introduction,* p. 69.
34. Jay, *Downcast Eyes,* p. 127.
35. Crary, *Techniques,* p. 19.

modified. The human experience of reality thus comes to be understood as a photograph, since the photograph claimed to capture a moment in a way that could not be challenged. A famous example of this is when the British photographer Eadweard Muybridge in 1878 succeeded in capturing the different moments of a horse's motion with the help of twelve cameras.[36] He could thus show that its legs did not point forwards and backwards in a gallop, as had been represented for centuries in art. He could also show that all four of the horse's legs were in the air simultaneously.

Several critics have also connected the realism of photography with death. Susan Sontag writes the following in her book *On Photography,* a critical take on the phenomenon:

> All photographs are *memento mori.* To take a photograph is to participate in another person's (or thing's) mortality, vulnerability, mutability. Precisely by slicing out this moment and freezing it, all photographs testify to time's relentless melt.[37]

By recording that something *has been* in the past, the photograph is witness to the fact that this unique moment has already passed, and so has become vanished time. Through the inevitable distance in time between the subject of the photograph and the viewer of the photograph, the photograph becomes a witness to death. The French cultural theorist Roland Barthes in his book on photography *Camera Lucida* has also emphasized precisely the point that the present moment of the photograph cannot return, and so the photograph becomes a recording of *flat* death. Barthes draws a parallel between the photograph and the deritualization of modern society:

> Contemporary with the withdrawal of rites, Photography may correspond to the intrusion, in our modern society, of an asymbolic Death, outside of religion, outside of ritual, a kind of abrupt dive into literal Death. *Life/ Death:* the paradigm is reduced to a simple click, the one separating the initial pose from the final print.[38]

36. Marien, *Photography,* pp. 212–16.

37. Susan Sontag, *On Photography* (London: Penguin Books, 1979), p. 15.

38. Roland Barthes, *Camera Lucida: Reflections on Photography,* trans. Richard Howard (New York: Hill & Wang, 1981), p. 92. Cf. as well Barthes's thoughts on photography in "Le message photographique," *Communications* 1 (1961): 127–38.

Death was desacralized during the emergence of industrial society in the West, becoming increasingly privatized. As a part of this, death came to be one of the privileged subjects for photography, not simply its metaphor.[39] Through the photograph one could preserve a memory of the departed at home on the mantelpiece.

One aspect of photography's history and its significance for the scopic regime of late modernity is its popularity. Right from the start photography had a big impact with the general public, and it would almost be funny to assert today that photography is popular. Cameras have become cheap appliances that may be found in virtually all Western homes. It is said that forty-one million pictures were taken every day in the USA in 1991.[40] While that figure is old now, it gives us an idea of the number of photographs involved in a normal day. The twentieth century is the best-documented century so far, thanks to photojournalists who took advantage of the ever-more manageable technology and the immediate power of the image, which often far exceeds the effect of other media.[41] The popularity of the photograph has been discussed by many critics. Among others, Walter Benjamin suggested in a famous essay from 1936 that the new mass accessibility of the image would popularize art, but that the art would on the other hand lose its aura through the reproducibility of the photograph.[42]

But despite the realism and the neutrality associated with photographic technology, it is far from innocent. Photographs do not have to do so much with how the world is, as with how we have chosen to see it. Thus photographs have been able to play a large role in the processes of collective memory over the last century.[43] It may be that no picture symbolizes the Spanish Civil War better than Robert Capa's photograph of the dying Republican soldier Federico Borrell García from 1936.[44] Even if the photograph has come to be the way in which we view the world, and so has come to be understood as

---

39. Mirzoeff, *Introduction*, p. 75.

40. Mirzoeff, *Introduction*, p. 71.

41. See for example Bruce Bernard, ed., *Century: One Hundred Years of Human Progress, Regression, Suffering and Hope* (London: Phaidon Press, 1999).

42. Walter Benjamin, "The Work of Art in the Age of Its Technological Reproducibility: Third Version," in *Selected Writings*, vol. 4: *1938–1940*, trans. Edmund Jephcott and others (Cambridge, MA/London: Belknap Press, 2006), pp. 251–83.

43. William J. Mitchell, *The Reconfigured Eye: Visual Truth in the Post-Photographic Era* (Cambridge, MA/London: MIT Press, 1992), p. 59.

44. The authenticity of this photograph has been challenged, however. See Richard Whelan, "Robert Capa's Falling Soldier: A Detective Story," *Aperture* 166 (Spring 2002): 48–55, which argues for its authenticity.

self-evident and given by nature, the photographic way of seeing is a scopic regime just as much constituted by the instruments and techniques we make use of as it is a result of how we use these instruments and techniques for our own aims. Thus the photograph becomes, in the words of literary scholar and art historian Graham Clarke, "the replication, not so much of an objective reality, as of a subject framed by a set of ideological assumptions and values."[45] As I stressed in the introduction to this chapter, photography is a way of looking at the world, a way that is dependent on those conventions that determine its scopic regime, and so is not a naked mirror of the state of things in an objective reality.

One of the consequences of the photograph is thus that the view of what is real has changed. The example above with Muybridge's photographs of a horse in motion demonstrated for the people of the time that the camera's way of understanding movement differed from the eye's way. This initiated a deconventionalization of the visual experience up to that point. Photography opens a path to the "optic-unconscious," according to Benjamin.[46] The eye could not see that the legs of a galloping horse do not point forwards and backwards. In other words, the photograph does not depict static formulas—the way people have visualized a horse—but movement.[47] This entailed a departure from the scopic regime of Cartesian perspectivalism. The camera transformed the way in which people saw, in that time became a part of the visual experience.[48] Even the metaphorical connection to death mentioned above contributed to emphasizing the significance of time for the photographic scopic regime. It was thus clear that human vision was not a "view from nowhere," to borrow the expression of philosopher Thomas Nagel.[49] The visible became evasive and the gaze incarnated in space and time.[50] Through this, photography would constitute a break with the central perspective, rather than a continuity, since the human body makes itself relevant in the theoretical arguments surrounding the gaze.[51] The scopic regime that was characterized by the photograph thus

45. Clarke, *The Photograph*, p. 23.
46. Walter Benjamin, "Little History of Photography," *Selected Writings*, vol. 2: *1927–1934*, trans. Rodney Livingstone and others (Cambridge, MA/London: Belknap Press, 1999), p. 512.
47. Cf. Paul Virilio, *The Aesthetics of Disappearance*, trans. Philip Beitchman (New York: Semiotext[e], 1991), pp. 16–18.
48. Berger, *Ways*, p. 18.
49. Thomas Nagel, *The View from Nowhere* (New York: Oxford University Press, 1986).
50. This affected visual art as well. See Berger, *Ways*, and Jay, *Downcast Eyes*, pp. 136–40.
51. Crary, *Techniques*, pp. 25–66, 97–136. Crary argues that the person as a perceiving

in a certain way entailed both the reinforcement of the earlier scopic regime and its eventual fall. The camera could give an illusion of a gaze unbounded by time and space, a purely registering gaze, through its technical possibilities. Such a conception of the camera's unhindered gaze was, however, nothing but an illusion. If the human being was subject to time, rather than its master, and if her gaze was challenged by the camera itself, her claim to a knowledge uncorroded by time could be challenged. But even the close association of photography with realism would come to be doubted.

The Virtual Eye

The history of the photographic epoch was rather short, about 150 years. Several critics suggest that in 1989 we left the scopic regime of the photographic epoch to begin the post-photographic era. The difference between the photographic and the post-photographic epoch is that the subject of the photograph seems to have disappeared in the digital revolution. It is no longer necessary to imagine that the subject we see in a picture really *was there* when the photograph was taken. It is entirely possible to create pictures where it is impossible to determine whether that which the picture presents actually exists or has existed in the world outside the picture. This means that the photograph is no longer an index to reality, but has become virtual.[52] The interest of the post-photographic image creators has thus shifted from the subject of the camera to the possibilities of the medium itself.

The post-photographic era might be said to be the era when virtuality made itself relevant in a significant way. What is meant then by virtuality? Mirzoeff gives a short definition: "By definition, virtuality is an image or space that is not real but appears to be. In our own time, these include cyberspace, the Internet, the telephone, television and virtual reality."[53] The telephone is an example of virtual reality, or more specifically, an example of the "space" that arises when one speaks with someone on the telephone. This "space" is located neither where I am nor where the person I am speaking with is, but is a "placeless" space. It exists, it is real, but it is nevertheless located "nowhere in particular." Another example he mentions is that a large

---

subject becomes more significant for the understanding of the gaze during the nineteenth century. The gaze lost its transcendent foundation and became autonomous.

52. Mirzoeff, *Introduction,* pp. 88–89.
53. Mirzoeff, *Introduction,* p. 91.

amount of the money we concern ourselves with is virtual. Through different sorts of charge cards a store can send electronic impulses to my bank, which consequently transmits money from my electronic account to the store's account. It is only when I take out money from an ATM that it materializes. The ATM can be seen as a sort of transition station between reality and virtuality. These examples show that virtuality is not an entirely new invention. The telephone has more than a century of history, and the ATM has existed for several decades. What is new in our time is that virtuality no longer consists in our passive contemplation of it, but has become interactive. We can now affect and be affected by virtual reality.

Possibly one of the most influential virtual realities is television.[54] Through the TV it is possible for people all over the world to see the same pictures—it is reckoned that three-fourths of earth's population have access to TV. Large sporting events like the Olympics and the World Cup can thus count their audiences in the billions. In the West TV watching takes up several hours per day for a large portion of the population. It is probably no exaggeration to suggest that in our time the television creates a large portion of our shared experiences, at a national as well as a global level. The funeral of Princess Diana on September 6, 1997 was sent over the whole world, and was followed by an estimated two and a half billion people.[55] The French sociologist Pierre Bourdieu, who is very critical of television, writes (and even said in a TV broadcast):

> We are getting closer and closer to the point where the social world is primarily described—and in a sense prescribed—by television.[56]

Given TV's possibilities for sending programs throughout the whole earth, the TV medium is perhaps the most impactful medium today, not least when it concerns influencing the human representational world, our way of looking at the world.[57]

Besides the globalization of television, there is yet another tendency, namely the fragmentation that is the result of cable television, satellites, and the digital channels. These have meant a greater range of channels (if not

54. Mirzoeff, *Introduction,* pp. 96–101. For a critical discussion of the possibilities and limitations of television, see Pierre Bourdieu, *On Television,* trans. Priscilla Parkhurst Ferguson (New York: New Press, 1996).

55. Mirzoeff, *Introduction,* p. 253.

56. Bourdieu, *On Television,* p. 22.

57. Cf. Sturken and Cartwright, *Practices,* pp. 151–88.

necessarily an increased variety in programming), and an attendant clicking between channels. In other words, the globalization of networks by CNN and others is accompanied by a fragmentation of channels at the local level.[58] There is much to say about this, and about TV's place in a post-photographic culture, but let me instead turn to the more theoretical question of what characterizes the post-photographic image, in order to investigate how sight is affected by the scopic regimes of the post-photographic era.

If, to begin with, I pose the question of what constitutes the difference between the photographic era and the post-photographic era, it is undoubt-edly the case that one of the most crucial questions is that of the picture's eventual correspondence to something outside the picture. In his book *The Reconfigured Eye,* William J. Mitchell takes up just this question of visual truth in the post-photographic epoch. He argues that a digital picture can certainly appear similar to a traditional photograph, but that in spite of that the differences between them are as great as between a traditional photo-graph and a painting, and that they have equally different logical and cultural consequences.[59] Mitchell is thinking of three differences. Firstly, the digital picture differs precisely in the fact that it is digital. A traditional photograph is an analog representation of a subject, which entails, for example, that the transition between dark and light in a photograph is continuous, i.e., it passes through all grades of intensity. A digital picture, in contrast, is made up of a definite number of pixels, where every pixel has its own numerical value that corresponds to its placement in a tone- or color-scale. If one enlarges a digital picture sufficiently, it can be seen that what appear to be smooth curves and continuous transitions in tone are themselves broken up by individual pixels.

Secondly, the traditional photograph differs from the digital picture with regard to its reproducibility. A traditional photograph is a copy from a negative. In principle any number of copies can be produced from the nega-tive, since the negative constitutes an original. One can of course photograph a photograph, but such a "secondhand photograph" is of somewhat poorer technical quality than the original photograph. The difference between copy and original is, however, not meaningful when it comes to digital pictures. A digital "copy" cannot be distinguished from its electronic "original," since it is identical with the original. I can send an image file from my computer to another via email, and with that the recipient gets an identical copy of my original image file, which still remains on my computer.

58. Mirzoeff, *Introduction,* p. 100.
59. Mitchell, *Reconfigured Eye,* p. 4.

Thirdly, there is an expectation—if we do not have reason to believe otherwise—that a traditional photograph will not be manipulated. It is certainly possible, but the technical difficulties with manipulating chemically produced photographs are many, if not insurmountable. The digital picture, however, is characterized by the fact that it can be easily manipulated on a computer. The information in a pixel is easily changed out for other information, and so we get a different picture. It is significant that, for the digital picture, the term "manipulation" itself can be put within quotation marks, since it is uncertain whether the term is applicable to the digital picture as such. A digital picture can just as well have its origin in a traditional photograph, which has been scanned and then modified, as in an altogether digital creation without any photographic model. The capacity of the home computer is so great that computer-produced pictures that, without starting from a traditional photograph, are difficult or impossible to tell from something that *might* be reality are no longer uncommon. With the digital image we have entered into "the age of the electrobricolage," as Mitchell puts it.[60]

These three differences point to a question that must come up, namely the question of the credibility of the image. Is an image real, or only virtually real? As I mentioned above, traditional photography claims to refer to reality, but the digital image brackets off the question of whether there really is a referent.[61] With these endless possibilities for manipulation questions open up regarding the relationship between the digital picture and that which the photographic epoch called reality, but we also meet the more ethical questions of who owns the rights to an image and whether this ownership is forfeited when the image is manipulated. With Mitchell we can argue that the image has thus discarded the gold standard and is no longer a guarantee for a stable visual truth.[62] In other words, the connection between "media," "image," and "viewer" has been renegotiated in such a revolutionary way that the post-photographic gaze can hardly be said to resemble the gaze that characterized the scopic regime of the photographic era.

It is not only the possibilities for manipulating the image itself that have been transformed, but also the conditions for its distribution. The interpretation of an image is not given by the picture itself, but by the way it is contextualized. One of the examples in the previous section may be used here as well: I, and others with similar cultural repertoires, automatically

60. Mitchell, *Reconfigured Eye*, p. 7.
61. Mitchell, *Reconfigured Eye*, p. 52.
62. Mitchell, *Reconfigured Eye*, p. 57.

expect—because we have learned to do so—different things from fashion photography and from documentary photography as regards their correspondence to reality. But the easily distributed digital photograph increases the possibilities for images to be contextualized in different ways, and so a specific image can shape meanings in a number of different, eventually incommensurate ways. The difference from the photographic epoch here lies not so much in the possibility of recontextualizing images, as in the ease with which it can be done. Mitchell believes that digital technology—including the increased memory capacities for data storage—means that the dissemination of the image is accelerated in a way that will affect our institutions and social practices: "A worldwide network of digital imaging systems is swiftly, silently constituting itself as the decentered subject's reconfigured eye."[63] When images become almost ubiquitous, power is shifted to contextualizing images, and so the visual system is reconfigured. The scopic regime, within which the central position of the photographic image supported its claim to depict reality, is displaced in favor of a "polyscopic" regime, where eventually the pretension to truth is instead a question of the particular contexts where the picture is used, rather than a pretension to truth that resides in the image.[64]

A further step within the framework of the post-photographic era is taken by that which often goes by the name virtual reality, which, in brief, entails a simulated world that is experienced as real, not only visually in three dimensions, but also tactilely. Virtual reality makes it possible to, so to speak, climb into someone else's skin, whether it has to do with another real person or an electronically constructed avatar. The "hyper-Cartesian" consequence of this is that our consciousness is loosed from our embodied existence.[65] This paradox is certainly nothing new—every photograph that we view is in some sense an invitation to see that which someone else has earlier seen with *their* eyes. What is new is instead the scope and intensity that this "out-of-body-experience" may achieve through the new media, which are as yet half idea, half reality, as well as through the possibilities for interactivity.

63. Mitchell, *Reconfigured Eye*, p. 85. On pages 222–23 Mitchell compares photography's "powerful orthodoxy of graphic communication" with the processes of production of the digital image, which are "less subject to institutional policing of uniformity, offer more opportunities for human intervention, and are far more complex and varied in their range of possible representational commitments."

64. See Ella Shohat and Robert Stam, "Narrativizing Visual Culture: Towards a Polycentric Aesthetics," in *The Visual Culture Reader,* pp. 27–49.

65. Mitchell, *Reconfigured Eye,* p. 134.

This "hyper-Cartesian" consequence is likely modified by the fact that virtual reality, as we know it now, is not at all radically equal, but structured according to sex and class. There is talk of equality and freedom on the Internet, but this is a freedom above all for those who have money to get connected, and to a higher degree for those who have money to connect at a higher speed than others. Speed of accessibility to the Internet may be a transient problem in the West, a West that just now is completely dominant on the net. The risk is that there will arise a new class distinction between those who are connected and those who are not connected, a class distinction that has to do with things such as access to information and the possibility of communication. Even the virtual reality of the net is structured by sex and class, and is, if modifiable, not independent of these classifications. In other words, these socio-structural complexities make themselves relevant even in this virtual society, and so this "disembodiment" is questionable. It is thus highly doubtful whether this "disembodiment" could be the key to understanding the scopic regime of the post-photographic era, or at least the primary key.

Several critics have highlighted the visual culture of the post-photographic era as a critique of earlier and later modernity's "monoscopism," and with them it is common to emphasize the embodied nature of sight in contrast with a "hyper-Cartesian" disembodiment. One philosopher who delivers this sort of critique is Donna J. Haraway. She believes that the monoscopic regime is identical with "the standpoint of the master, the Man, the One God, whose Eye produces, appropriates, and orders all difference," or "the god-trick of seeing everything from nowhere."[66] The field of vision is not innocent and transparent for the probing gaze, but is always already constructed and constituted by the visual pre-understanding that the observer both carries and is a part of. This pre-understanding is structured by beliefs, desires, languages, and institutions, which means that the "god-trick of seeing everything from nowhere" is an ideological illusion.

What Haraway and others with her want to stress is that the gaze is never innocent, that it is always a gaze from someone and with some sort of purpose.[67] Research does not "happen" to see what it sees, but is looking to find what it is researching for, and so in a certain sense constructs its

66. Donna J. Haraway, "Situated Knowledges: The Science Question in Feminism and the Privilege of Partial Perspective," *Simians, Cyborgs, and Women: The Reinvention of Nature* (London: Free Association Books, 1991), pp. 193, 189.

67. See, for example, Irit Rogoff, "Studying Visual Culture," in *The Visual Culture Reader,* p. 22.

own object. This concerns the scientific gaze as well as the gaze of art or the everyday gaze. Every gaze is active and so represents a way to see, that is to say, a way to be-in-the-world. In the same article that the quotation above is taken from Haraway gives her alternative, namely to emphasize that sight is embodied, and so at least "stereoscopic." Sight as a source of and metaphor for knowledge can be "objective" precisely because it is situated, not by claiming to be transcendent and monoscopic. Such an objectivity is never innocent, but precisely because of its embodied status can become a responsible knowledge, that is, a knowledge that it is possible to localize and so bring to account.[68] This objectivity does not deny that there are different ways to see depending on where one finds oneself, or that one must in a certain sense learn to see, but precisely by its situatedness it avoids, Haraway believes, the "irresponsibility" that characterizes every supposed view from nowhere, whether this has to do with the gaze of the "god-trick" or with the gaze of relativism.[69] The situated objectivity that Haraway advocates is always "interpretive, critical, and partial" in its effort to find the common between different perspectives.[70]

For a critical theology of the gaze, as I will formulate in this study, it is important to show that a monoscopic gaze such as Haraway criticizes must *not* be identified with the theological gaze. Her critique of the "god-trick" is not primarily directed against theology, but it undeniably hits a theology that identifies its own gaze as the monoscopic gaze of objectivity, and thus gets out of the situated character of every gaze. The conception of the incarnation, however, implies that other gazes are available besides this gaze of the "god-trick." It is therefore important to present several paradigmatic instances for the understanding of the gaze in the theological tradition in the New Testament and the icon tradition. Before I come to these in the following chapter, I will however first show how Haraway's embodying gaze has parallels in phenomenology's investigations of human sight, and how these can cast light on the possibilities for sight after the fall of the monoscopic regime. I now turn from this summary of different historical scopic regimes to the more theoretical question of the eye's ability to see.

68. Haraway, "Situated Knowledges," p. 191.

69. Haraway says that relativism is just as bad with regard to irresponsibility ("Situated Knowledges," p. 191): "Relativism is a way of being nowhere while claiming to be everywhere equally."

70. Haraway, "Situated Knowledges," p. 195.

The Possibilities of the Eye

So if the gaze is historically and culturally constituted, is it possible to see anything at all? Few would contest that we really see something other than our own sight in seeing. The emphasis on the cultural construction of sight does not imply a denial of these biological dimensions, but instead acknowledges that biology and culture are mutually dependent in a way that makes it difficult or all but impossible to separate them. The task that shows up in the wake of a postmodern "crisis of representation" then is not finding the distinction between what is biologically and what is culturally conditioned in sight, but rather to investigate questions like how it is possible, in spite of everything, to differentiate between sight and that which sight sees, but now within the framework of an understanding of the gaze as embodied. This relationship between the perception and the perceived as configured by the gaze must also be investigated. With the help of a phenomenological framework, in this section I will attempt to show how the understanding of the sense of sight as embodied is linked to the question of the sense of sight as passive vis-à-vis active. In the extension of these questions, there are several larger questions that relate to the discussion around realism versus idealism. It is not possible here to do justice to this larger context, so I limit myself to saying something about perception and the relationship between subject and object, which shows how biological visual impressions are intertwined with our historically and culturally conditioned gaze.

As a convenient entry into this problem, I will turn to a discussion of Empedocles' theory of perception by the philologist Jesper Svenbro. By way of introduction, Svenbro differentiates in his article "Voir en voyant: La perception visuelle chez Empédocle" between a seeing that he describes as an optical registering and a seeing that also sees the meaning in what is seen at the moment. When Greek speaks of seeing letters in the first meaning of seeing, it often speaks of *grammata,* while letters that are joined together into a meaningful whole through reading are called *stoicheia.*[71] But, Svenbro notes, even perceiving letters as *grammata* as though one were illiterate, that is to say, as a collection of letters without any specific meaningful order, assumes that the viewer is something other than a purely passive receiver of visual impressions, since the understanding itself of *grammata* as precisely letters assumes some sort of active understanding that manages to differen-

---

71. Jesper Svenbro, "Voir en voyant: La perception visuelle chez Empédocle," *Métis: Anthropologie des mondes grecs anciens* 2 (2004): 50.

tiate between, for example, letters and ink stains. All perception of a thing thus seems to be a perception of a thing *as* a thing, and so assumes an act of interpretation, however rudimentary it may be.

In his continued discussion of several particular formulations in Empedocles specifically, Svenbro points out that the ancient Greeks did not differentiate between physical light and the light of understanding. This implies that for Empedocles seeing was "neither a purely active sending out of light nor a purely passive reception of light, but the result of the 'interaction' of active and passive seeing."[72] In other words, for Empedocles perception is an interaction between a movement from external world to consciousness and a movement from consciousness to external world. The interaction entails, according to Svenbro, a sort of continuous shift of aspect, where we can only focus on one of these aspects at a time. Empedocles' fundamental insights are not as obsolete as one might believe. It is hardly a self-evident move to posit with the modern (in Svenbro's discussion primarily Cartesian) understanding of perception only a passive registering of visual impressions, given the everyday experience of where optical perception cooperates with understanding in order to make sensory impressions comprehensible.

Empedocles and the ancient Greek tradition thus differ from a modern scopic regime for which sight primarily consists in a passive registering of an external world independent of consciousness. As I have reviewed above in the section on the curious eye, the modern idea of sight presupposed a gaze that was distanced from, rather than involved in the world that it watched. According to Cartesian optics, the retina intercepted impressions from the external world. These sensory perceptions were then interpreted by the brain, which thereby formed the person's perceptions. The idea in ancient and medieval optics of light-rays that emanated from the eye to the object in the field of vision is thus impossible to understand on the basis of the conceptions of modern optics. The eye of consciousness was thereby distanced from the objectified field of vision, and sight was understood as essentially passive. It is of course this Cartesian perspectivalism that came to be challenged by the photographic, and later also the post-photographic, era.

At the same time this fundamental passivity in sight contributed to the different scopic regimes of modernity coming to describe the field of vision as an object for the curious gaze of the person, like a lifeless material that on the one hand makes itself available for the person's use, but on the other hand is everything that exists to see. The question of the modern scopic

72. Svenbro, "Voir en voyant," p. 67.

173

regime is: What can we do with this world that sight passively registers? The world is perceived as something given: it exists there and it allows itself to be used for our scientific, artistic, voyeuristic purposes. Ever since the scientific revolution nature has been attributed an immanent causality without any purpose outside itself. Nature has been seen as regulated by laws, and so possible to master.[73] On the other hand, human consciousness has been understood as the origin of the transcendental categories that can put the world in order.[74] Nature has no meaning of its own, but is given meaning by human activity. The question is then no longer whether nature is good or not, but what it is good *for*. How this development has taken place is a long story that will not be retold here.[75] What essentially happens, however, is that the thought of a transcendent God, or transcendence at all, is struck from the possibilities of human experience. But if the gaze now becomes a way to master the world, then is the possibility of seeing another human as different not threatened as well, and likewise the possibility of seeing the nonhuman environment as something that is responsive rather than passive, and thus something "other"?[76]

Perhaps the problem with the modern scopic regime lies in too sharp a distinction between the sense of sight as a passive ability and human consciousness as an active ability. In an extension of Svenbro's exegesis of Empedocles one might instead argue that even a contemporary understanding of sight presupposes both these aspects. The act of perception ought to be seen as a synthesis, impossible to dissolve, between sight and other sensory perceptions together with consciousness's interpretation of these perceptions, and so between passivity and activity. Consciousness is not a *tabula rasa*—it is not a mirror image of nature—on which the world leaves its imprint. This is not to say that there is nothing other than consciousness, and thus nothing "external." Even if the distinction itself between consciousness and the external world is a distinction that is immanent in the human understanding of the world, this does not at all mean that the distinction is meaningless. Let us therefore turn to several ways of making this distinction philosophically productive.

73. See Amos Funkenstein, *Theology and the Scientific Imagination from the Middle Ages to the Seventeenth Century* (Princeton: Princeton University Press, 1986).

74. Cf., for example on Kant and the perceptions, Howard Caygill, *The Art of Judgement* (Oxford: Basil Blackwell, 1989).

75. See Louis Dupré, *Passage to Modernity: An Essay on the Hermeneutics of Nature and Culture* (New Haven/London: Yale University Press, 1993).

76. See Emmanuel Levinas, *Totality and Infinity: An Essay on Exteriority,* trans. Alphonso Lingis (Pittsburgh: Duquesne University Press, 1969).

The different scopic regimes essentially have to do with different ways of visualizing the relationship between human consciousness and world. Seeing the world as an object for our purposes is *one* possibility among many, and does not exhaust our relationship to the world. Seeing the world as an object for our purposes presupposes other relationships to the world, as a sort of background for the possibility of perceiving the world in this way, or in other words as a life-world (see chapter 1). The Canadian philosopher Charles Taylor has argued that in our relationship to the world around us we should understand ourselves as embodied agents who are engaged in the world:

> We can ponder distant events, or theoretical perspectives on things, because we are first of all open to a world which can be explored, learned, theorized about, and so on. And our primary opening to this world, the inescapable background to all others, is through perception.[77]

Because we are embodied agents, we experience the world as a field for possible action. Taylor understands this as something different than experiencing the world as a theoretical object. The world is not exhausted by our theoretical gaze. According to this understanding, learning how we should inhabit the world is a practical activity rather than a contemplative activity. By relating to the world as a field for our action, we learn to be responsive in the world, rather than to control it. Somewhat in the way a soccer player has to be mindful of the other players on his team, but also of what the other team is up to, we must be able to respond to what happens in the world around us when we act. In a sense we can say that we "play" with the world, respond to its actions, to whatever happens next.[78] Through the processes of perception we understand ourselves as agents *in* the world rather than *outside* of it, and we understand the world as a field of possibilities. We perceive the world as open to us, and not as a predetermined path that we must follow. Thus we also understand the world as something "other" than a product of our perception or our consciousness.

From the perspective of such an embodied understanding of the relationship between the human being and the environment, the relationship between that which perceives and the world that is perceived by the gaze

77. Charles Taylor, "The Validity of Transcendental Arguments," in *Philosophical Arguments* (Cambridge, MA/London: Harvard University Press, 1995), pp. 22–23.
78. Cf. what Gadamer writes on "das Spiel" in *Truth,* pp. 102–10.

no longer needs to be understood as a distanced relationship. Things do not primarily exist as identical with themselves in order to then make themselves available for our perception of them. Neither is our sight primarily empty, in order to then be filled with content by the things around us. According to the French phenomenologist Maurice Merleau-Ponty (whose philosophy I will discuss more closely in chapter 8), that which exists is "something to which we could not be closer than by palpating it with our look, things we could not dream of seeing 'all naked' because the gaze itself envelops them, clothes them with its own flesh."[79] We learn to recognize the world by allowing our gaze to palpate it. To palpate does not imply attempting to master the world from above, through a gaze that is not itself a part of the world, but rather existing in the world and learning to find our way in the world by responding to what one learns about it through the senses. What Merleau-Ponty argues is that the eye is an organ that recalls the hand. We can imagine ourselves with closed eyes, attempting to grope our way forward only with the help of our hands. Seeing is a sort of palpating, so to speak. It is in such ways we learn to find our way in the world, and it is in this way we perceive the world. We are always already *in* the world when we perceive it. Merleau-Ponty writes: "We have to reject the age-old assumption that put the body in the world and the seer in the body, or, conversely, the world and the body in the seer as in a box."[80] Visual perceptions are always already embodied perceptions; there is no perception in and of itself.

The reason that the world cannot be reduced to something preexistent or be exhausted by interpretation is not, according to this way of reasoning, that consciousness's construction of the world is arbitrary, and so the number of ways that it can be construed inexhaustible. It is instead the case that

79. Maurice Merleau-Ponty, *The Visible and the Invisible: Followed by Working Notes*, trans. Alphonso Lingis (Evanston, IL: Northwestern University Press, 1968), p. 131. In "Eye and Mind," however, Merleau-Ponty remains critical towards Descartes's comparison of the sense of sight with a blind person's cane. However, as far as I can tell it is a matter here of a critique of the idea that light is not something that functions from a distance, but through contact, and that the understanding of light as something from "outside" thereby disappears. At the same time Merleau-Ponty polemicizes against Descartes's view of the body as an "instrument" for the soul, rather than its "domicile," which ought to speak for the fact that it is a matter of a critique of "disembodied" seeing rather than seeing as a palpation. See Maurice Merleau-Ponty, "Eye and Mind," in *The Primacy of Perception: And Other Essays on Phenomenological Psychology, the Philosophy of Art, History and Politics*, Northwestern University Studies in Phenomenology & Existential Philosophy, trans. Carleton Dallery (Evanston, IL: Northwestern University Press, 1964), pp. 159–90.

80. Merleau-Ponty, *Visible and Invisible*, p. 138.

we, as embodied agents in the world, find it "pregnant" with possibilities. Because consciousness perceives this objective inexhaustibility, it cannot do anything but admit this as a dimension of existence in a particular thing in the world or in the world as a whole. The visible is, according to Merleau-Ponty, "the surface of an inexhaustible depth."[81] With Merleau-Ponty as well as Taylor I want to avoid reducing the world to an object for our investigative gaze, or alternatively reducing the gaze to a passive registering of what is present. Our relationship to the world ought to instead be described in a more fundamental way, where even the gaze is understood as embodied and responsive, i.e., both active and passive.

The consequence of such a reasoning is that neither can we reduce the thing we see to an object. Things are perceived against the background of their own inexhaustibility. According to Martin Heidegger in his lecture "Das Ding" from 1950, a thing is not just an object, but "that which stands forth." This "standing forth" has two meanings:

> First, standing forth *[das her-Stehen]* has the sense of stemming from somewhere, whether this be a process of self-making or of being made by another. Secondly, standing forth has the sense of the made thing's standing forth into the unconcealedness of what is already present.[82]

The immediacy of the thing is a standing forth from somewhere—what I termed its "inexhaustibility"—in the unhidden. Heidegger rejects the scientific reduction of things to objects—it is only one way among many to experience the thing. A thing, *as* a thing, is something that concerns a person, something that is important for her in its possibilities. In his essay Heidegger gives us a phenomenological account of a jug and shows how the jug carries a complex meaning in the human life-world, as a possibility for pouring a libation offering to the gods: "The jug's jug-character consists in the poured gift of the pouring out."[83] This possibility belongs to the jug's character of being a jug, and is not simply an area of use for the jug. The libation offering shows that heaven and earth, mortals and gods, belong together and brings them together. The jug makes this association present. "Das Ding dingt Welt"—"The thing things world"—Heidegger writes in one of his more enigmatic sentences.[84] In a jug

---

81. Merleau-Ponty, *Visible and Invisible*, p. 143.

82. Martin Heidegger, "The Thing," in *Poetry, Language, Thought*, trans. Albert Hofstadter (New York: Harper & Row, 1971), p. 166.

83. Heidegger, "The Thing," p. 170.

84. Heidegger, "The Thing," p. 178.

the whole world seems to be made present. The thing's possibilities for standing forth as thing, instead of as object, are not something that we humans provide. What we can do in order that the standing forth of the thing as thing will take place is, according to Heidegger, to watch: "The first step back toward such vigilance is the step back from the thinking that merely represents—that is, explains—to the thinking that responds and recalls *[das andenkende Denken]*."[85] Such a vigilance demands a sort of thinking that is responsive rather than manipulative in relation to that which it thinks. But Heidegger concludes by arguing that the number of things is smaller than the number of objects. What Heidegger gives us here, in his own mythopoetic language, is a different account of the perception of the thing, a perception that allows the thing to carry meaning that is given to us rather than produced by us.

However, it is still possible to understand the appearance of things as things as an event that is brought about by the vigilance of the human being. But this would be to misunderstand Heidegger. If we instead turn to another well-known lecture by Heidegger, "The Origin of the Work of Art," we can cast further light on this question. Here Heidegger introduces the term *"Lichtung,"* which has been translated as "clearing" (in Swedish *ljusning*, brightening). In order for the thing to stand forth as thing for us, we and it must meet in the clearing or brightening, where the light falls on the thing such that it may manifest itself for us as thing. It is not we or our gaze that is the source of the light, but the light already falls on us; it is we who come into the light. The clearing or brightening is the possibility we are given to perceive the "standing forth" of the thing. Heidegger writes:

> The being can only be, as a being, if it stands within, and stands out within, what is illuminated in this clearing. Only this clearing grants us human beings access to those beings that we ourselves are not and admittance to the being that we ourselves are. Thanks to this clearing, beings are unconcealed in certain and changing degrees.[86]

We are drawn into this manifestation. At the same time the being that is manifested draws away and is hidden. This hiding can be understood in several ways. Either it can stand for the refusal of things to give themselves to us, or the fact that they dissemble. The reason that Heidegger simultaneously speaks

85. Heidegger, "The Thing," p. 179.
86. Martin Heidegger, "The Origin of the Work of Art," in *Poetry, Language, Thought,* pp. 51f.

of the unhiddenness and the hiddenness in the clearing is, if I have understood it right, that even in the manifestation that the clearing is, we do not *own* the truth. We do not master things as things through our theoretical gaze. To cite Heidegger once more: "the open place in the midst of things, the clearing, is never a fixed stage with a permanently raised curtain on which the play of beings enacts itself."[87] We may not reduce the thingness of things, which are manifested in this clearing, to something familiar or something ordinary. The ordinary is extraordinary, Heidegger argues. Even if the clearing takes place in the midst of the world, it takes the ordinary world with it out of its usualness.

Heidegger's way of expressing himself about this clearing strongly recalls the theological conception of revelation, and it is perhaps not unbelievable that we can trace here some echoes of Heidegger's background in theology.[88] Following Heidegger, the French philosopher Paul Ricoeur has spoken of truth as manifestation, and he makes the connection between this manifestation and the religious sphere even more clearly.[89] Ricoeur namely believes that there exists a correlation between the manifestation of the holy and an approach to being: "To see the world as sacred is at the same time to *make* it sacred, to consecrate it. Thus to every manifestation there corresponds a manner of being-in-the-world."[90] Even if the manifestation of the holy or the standing forth of the thing in the unhidden is a manifestation, an event that is given to us and that we ourselves have not brought about, this does not imply that the manifestation happens independently of our attitude or the way in which we exist in the world. Perhaps one may speak of the significance of "vigilance" or "watchfulness" as a sort of "spiritual practice," as a condition of possibility so that the manifestation can be experienced. In other words, our way of seeing is not independent of our attitude at large. Ricoeur speaks in context about the correlation between the manifestation and the way of existing in the world as a correlation between manifestation and ritual.

---

87. Heidegger, "Origin," p. 52.

88. See Jayne Svenungsson, *Guds återkomst: En studie av gudsbegreppet inom postmodern filosofi*, Logos/Pathos 3 (Göteborg: Glänta, 2004), pp. 71–96.

89. See Paul Ricoeur, "Manifestation and Proclamation," in *Figuring the Sacred: Religion, Narrative, and Imagination*, trans. David Pellauer (Minneapolis: Fortress, 1995), pp. 48–67. Ricoeur's discussion of the manifestation recalls what Heidegger writes in "Origin." According to Heidegger truth is unhiddenness, *alētheia*, i.e., truth is a manifestation. However, Heidegger later modifies his earlier identification of truth and *alētheia*. See Martin Heidegger, "The End of Philosophy and the Task of Thinking," in *On Time and Being*, trans. Joan Stambaugh (New York: Harper & Row, 1972), p. 70.

90. Ricoeur, "Manifestation and Proclamation," p. 51.

The conclusion I want to draw from these phenomenological insights is partly that activity and passivity are more intertwined in gaze than a conventional understanding of the gaze tends to take for granted, and partly that there exists a correlation between certain rituals—in a broad sense—and certain ways of seeing.[91] This should in its turn imply that a reflection on how visual experiences are possible is not independent of a reflection on how we live, including the question of which rituals form our lives. The experience and the understanding that are needed for a particular way of seeing can demand long periods of "practice" in order to be able to be embodied, especially if this way of seeing runs counter to the sight conventions of the dominant scopic regime. Avoiding perceiving the world as solely an object for our theoretical gaze can involve practice in watchfulness, or in theological terminology, an ascetic practice. If our being-in-the-world is essentially as embodied agents rather than as disembodied, transcendental subjects or as epiphenomena of an immanent causality, our relationship to the world is always already both passive and active. We therefore do not need to *a priori* set any boundaries for what it is possible to perceive.

The scopic regime of modernity, with its theoretical gaze, does not set the boundary for the visible. To reduce the world to that which is visible for the theoretical gaze is to seek to control it. Through this reduction other ways of relating to the world are obscured. This does not mean that these other ways of seeing do not exist, but only that the theoretical gaze does not allow them to be perceived. The demystified world of Max Weber probably appears thus to the theoretical gaze that does not acknowledge that any other light falls on the world besides its own.[92] But, as I have argued above, we do not necessarily need to imagine that this is the only way to perceive the world. I shall now, after the above attempt to argue for the gaze as historically and culturally conditioned, as well as for the eye's possibilities for

---

91. It would have been exciting to investigate whether the phenomenological tradition that I have inclined towards here actually builds upon more or less explicit theological assumptions. However, such a task will have to wait for another occasion.

92. See Max Weber, "Science as a Vocation," in *The Vocation Lectures,* trans. Rodney Livingstone (Indianapolis/Cambridge: Hackett, 2004), p. 30. See also in this context Heidegger's essay "The Age of the World Picture," in *Off the Beaten Track,* ed. and trans. Julian Young and Kenneth Haynes (Cambridge: Cambridge University Press, 2002), p. 71: "The fundamental event of modernity is the conquest of the world as picture. From now on 'picture' means: the collective image of representing production *[das Gebild des vorstellenden Herstellens]*. Within this, man fights for the position in which he can be that being who gives to every being the measure and draws up the guidelines."

seeing in a different way than what the modern scopic regime allows, turn to a theological reflection on the possibilities of sight in the three following chapters. After first having turned to the question of the view of sight in the New Testament in the next chapter, in chapter 6 I will account for the historical development of the Christian tradition's attitude towards images and the Christological motivation for the use of icons. In chapter 7 I will then offer a theological formulation of the specific gaze of faith on the basis of the previous chapters, above all with respect to the question of God's incarnation in Jesus Christ. Through these three chapters I want to formulate a theology of the gaze as a concrete, anthropological reception of the doctrine of the incarnation, and thus linked to an embodied way of being-in-the-world; a theology that in a constructive way attempts to relate to both the theological tradition and to the intellectual challenges of the post-photographic scopic regime.

5. The Eyes of Jesus

In this chapter I will investigate what the New Testament has to say about sight, eyes, and gazes in connection with its portrayal of Jesus of Nazareth. The more traditional Christological reflections that the New Testament also offers, and I have already discussed in chapter 2, constitute a prerequisite for this chapter. This review is not comprehensive, but attempts to present the significant features of the New Testament's perspective on sight. Nor will I attempt to formulate my own theology of the gaze yet—that task can wait until chapter 7. The purpose of this chapter is to begin an investigation into the relationship between incarnation and the gaze—as the concrete anthropological reception of Christology—and to take note of some historical resources for a productive understanding of this relationship.

The question of the perspective on sight—and the gaze—in the New Testament runs into several problems for obvious reasons. To begin with, the different texts of the New Testament are not, as I have already mentioned, theoretical dissertations, and they are moreover authored in a different time than our own. For these two reasons we cannot expect to find a reflection on the differences and overlaps between sight and the gaze, i.e., between biology and history, and neither can the scholar take for granted that these texts answer the questions that she or he wants to pose. In the investigation I undertake here it is not primarily a matter of a historical exegesis of the account of sight in the New Testament texts, even if I am influenced by such an exegesis in my understanding of the texts, but rather of a phenomenological approach that attempts to determine what sort of being-in-the-world the New Testament gazes offer. This is how the Christian theological tradition has read these texts in practice, and they can offer the reader a resource for theological reflection on the gaze even in our time. The risk of relating "improperly" to the original errand of the New Testament texts is thus a risk I am prepared to take, a risk that in a certain sense exists in every attempt to bring any historical text up-to-date. From a hermeneutic starting point this risk is a prerequisite for what hermeneutics considers "understanding" at all, and thus also a prerequisite for more consistent historical work.[1] The risk of perpetrating anachronisms is thus not reserved for a phenomenological or theological reading of the New Testament, but characterizes historical work as well, and even the New Testament literature itself as an interpretation of the original, historical Jesus-event. The question is whether any historical work at all is possible without the nerve to perpetrate anachronisms. The possibility of productive anachronisms does not, however, mean that historically exegetical work should be seen as theologically uninteresting or irrelevant. On the contrary, it provides the opportunity for the theologian to test her or his phenomenological or theological interpretations and thereby remind us that not all interpretations are fruitful just because they claim to be theological.[2]

Furthermore, one may ask oneself whether there even is anything like a perspective on sight in the New Testament. Even if we leave room for variations in the perspective on sight between the different New Testament texts, and thereby, hopefully, avoid harmonizing the different biblical statements more than the texts themselves give reason for, the question still remains whether sight really is such a central theme for the New Testament texts that it is justifiable to speak of a specific perspective on sight. I want to argue that sight really is a central theme in portions of the New Testament, more so than what Lutheran tradition, with its concentration on hearing—and God's word as *viva vox*—has perhaps thought. As I will attempt to show below, several of the New Testament writings, primarily the Gospel of John, are characterized by a "scopophilia" that gives us reason to investigate their attitude toward sight, both as a biological and as a cultural phenomenon—or rather: how biological body and cultural meaning exist interwoven in those gazes that are so central to, for example, the message of the Gospel of John.

As I mentioned already in the introduction to chapter 1, the central function of the gaze in the New Testament entails the privileging of the perspective of a seeing person. Professor of Religious Education John M. Hull, who has himself become blind in old age, has pointed out in his book

---

1. Cf., for example, Hans-Georg Gadamer, *Truth and Method,* 2nd, revised edition, trans. Joel Weinsheimer and Donald G. Marshall (London/New York: Continuum, 2004), p. 296.

2. Hans Weder, *Neutestamentliche Hermeneutik,* 2nd revised edition (Zürich: Theologischer Verlag, 1986).

In the Beginning There Was Darkness that the Bible is a book written by seeing people for seeing people.[3] Therefore much that is found in the Bible can
seem alienating for a blind person. As Hull also points out, however, several
of the biblical authors are conscious of the limited validity of the language
that is used about God—God is in actuality beyond both gaze and blindness.[4]
There is thus a need for pursuing this (at least implicit) internal critique of
the ocularcentrism of the biblical texts. But instead of undertaking a task so
urgent in its own right, I will recall my decision to limit myself and focus
only on the sense of sight and its metaphoricity. A more complete review of
how the human senses of perception are represented in the New Testament
would emphasize not least how hearing and touch belong as well to the
human's fundamental way of being-in-the-world and of relating to God. The
aim here is thus not to establish, or reinforce, a biblical ocularcentrism, but
merely to implement a partial theological investigation of the perspective
on sight as *one of* the fundamental ways in which we create and visualize our
human relationships.

I have divided my review of the perspective on sight in the New Testament into four different sections. To begin with, I will very briefly take up
the passages in the Gospels where Jesus' own gaze is spoken of, and in this
way show that there are fundamental opportunities to find at least rudimentary grounds for a phenomenology of the gaze in the Gospels' depiction
of Jesus. I then continue by investigating how Jesus, as he is represented
in the New Testament, has taught about sight and what this means for the
understanding of sight in several of the New Testament texts. In a third
section I move on to describing how Jesus heals the blind, a practice that
touches sight as a biological as well as a spiritual capacity to see, and is thus
intimately associated with Jesus' parables. Finally, I take up how the New
Testament visualizes the way that the sense of sight has to do with the very
perception of the saving presence of God in Jesus Christ. Through these four
sections I want to show in part how central the sense of sight is for the New
Testament's perspective on salvation in Jesus Christ, in part how there is
also a continuity between sight and gaze, i.e., between biological sight and
theological content, in the New Testament. The latter is especially central
for my entire investigation in this section on the gaze—not to mention the
entirety of the project of this book—in that it gives us a hint regarding how

3. John M. Hull, *In the Beginning There Was Darkness: A Blind Person's Conversations with
the Bible* (London: SCM Press, 2001), p. 67.

4. Hull, *In the Beginning*, p. 76.

the Christian tradition imagines the relationship between transcendence and immanence, between eschatological salvation and its concrete presence here and now, between God and human, and this without allowing one pole to dominate the other. Because sight and gaze are held together by the New Testament texts—and because my focus is on the continuity between them both—I will in this chapter largely follow this language and, in other words, will not take pains to terminologically differentiate the gaze from sight where it is often a matter of both. Let me first, very briefly, turn to Jesus' own gaze according to the Gospels.

The Gaze of Jesus

It is significant that the narrative style of the Gospels is rather spare in the description of Jesus. One finds no trace of the inner dialogue or psychologizing style of the modern novel. Something of Jesus' "psychic life," in the sense of his relationships with other humans, nevertheless comes forth in the few places where the character of Jesus' gaze is defined with the help of words that describe Jesus' emotional state. There are two different sorts of accounts: on the one hand those where an emotional state is the effect of what Jesus sees, on the other hand those where the gaze itself is attributed an emotional expression. There are no more than seven significant places altogether in the Gospels, and so I highlight them all together here.

In Matthew 9:36 it is said that Jesus is filled with compassion *(esplanchnisthē)* for the people when he sees how badly battered and helpless they are. In 14:14 as well, i.e., right before the miracle of the bread, he is filled with compassion *(esplanchnisthē)* when he sees the people. Even in the second account of the healing of the two blind men in the Gospel of Matthew it is said that Jesus is filled with compassion *(splanchnistheis)* at the sight of these blind men (20:34). The verb *splanchnizomai*—and this is the form of the verb that is used in this context—is related to the noun *to splanchnon,* which denotes a person's internal organs, but is also used for the seat of the emotions, "the heart," or emotion itself. So it is said here that Jesus' gaze has the effect that he is moved in his "heart." Jesus' "compassion" is not just an expression in the Gospel of Matthew, but an emotion that Jesus demonstrates with his miracles of healing and is the foundation for his action.[5]

---

5. Ulrich Luz, *Matthew 8–20: A Commentary,* trans. James E. Crouch (Minneapolis: Fortress Press, 2001), pp. 313–14.

A compassionate gaze is not the only gaze we find with Jesus in the Gospel of Mark. Mark writes in 3:5 that Jesus met a man with an atrophied hand in a synagogue, and then "he looked around at them [i.e., the Pharisees] with anger *[met' orgēs]*, grieved *[syllypoumenos]* at their hardness of heart." The prefix *syn-* (here *syl-* on account of assimilation) serves here to emphasize the intensity of the emotion, i.e., "deep sorrow." Here it is more a matter of what the gaze expresses than of the effect on Jesus of what he sees. Later in the Gospel of Mark we find another expressive gaze. When the man who owned much comes up to Jesus and asks what he should do in order to achieve eternal life, Mark writes in 10:21 that Jesus "looking at him, loved him" *[emblepsas autō ēgapēsen]*. However, we also find in Mark the effects of what Jesus sees on his "heart": in 10:14 Jesus becomes annoyed *(ēganaktēsen)* when he sees the disciples turn the children away.

The Jesus of the Gospel of John is also emotionally affected by what he sees. In John 11 it is told how Jesus visits Bethany at the invitation of two sisters, Mary and Martha, because Lazarus has died. Jesus goes to Lazarus' grave and there Lazarus' two sisters cast themselves at Jesus' feet. In verse 33 John writes: "When Jesus saw her weeping, and the Jews who had come with her also weeping, he was deeply moved in his spirit and greatly troubled *[enebrimēsato tō pneumati kai etaraxen heauton]*." That Jesus is "distraught" means that he is angry.[6] The wrath directs itself against the rule of Satan, whom he finds himself face to face with here, represented by the death of Lazarus.

So in three of the four Gospels we find evidence of a number of different emotional states that are connected to the sense of sight. Jesus is filled with compassion, but he can also become annoyed, distraught, and shaken by what he sees. His gaze can express wrath, deep sorrow, and love. Given the Gospels' scanty descriptions of sight and emotion, it is probably not possible to draw any especially far-reaching conclusions about the relationship between these different gazes and the phenomenology of the gaze in Jesus. I will therefore be content with pointing out that Matthew, Mark, and John hold the sense of sight and emotion together. What the Jesus of these Gospels sees moves him, and his gaze expresses what he feels. The Gospels contain a number of references of the sort "Jesus saw," but most of these texts give no emotional attribute to these gazes. This should not be taken to mean that Jesus is represented with a gaze without emotional charge in all texts besides those I have mentioned in this section, but instead may be taken to

---

6. Raymond E. Brown, *The Gospel according to John: I–XII,* vol. 1 (London: Geoffrey Chapman, 1971), p. 435.

mean that the authors of the respective Gospels—excluding Luke—did not find it important to highlight the emotional life of Jesus apart from significant passages. I will therefore now turn to my investigation of the perspective on sight in the New Testament, going from Jesus' teaching on sight to the New Testament's different teachings on the vision of Jesus, an investigation that will give significantly richer results regarding the understanding of sight and the gaze in the New Testament.

Jesus Teaches about Sight

In the New Testament Jesus gives instructions in the art of seeing. In several places sight is central in the more moral as well as the more theological instruction that Jesus conveys. It is a matter of the person's way of relating to God, to him or herself, other human beings, and the rest of the environment. This instruction in the art of seeing is clearest in the Sermon on the Mount in Matthew 5–7.[7] Here the moral teaching is identical with Jesus' teaching about the coming kingdom of God. The question becomes, how will the sense of sight relate to the kingdom of God? What characterizes the sight that has been freed by the arrival of the kingdom of God? The sermon itself begins with Jesus looking at the people, and because of this he sits down and begins to teach the disciples who come up to him. Jesus states in the Beatitudes that "the pure in heart" shall "see God *[ton theon opsontai]*" (5:8). Purity of heart is a Jewish expression for undivided obedience to God.[8] This purity of heart that reveals God is set against the covetous gaze that "looks *[blepōn]* at a woman with lustful intent" and has thus committed adultery in his heart (v. 28). In this textual context "woman" can hardly be interpreted as any woman at all, but as a married woman: you commit adultery by "coveting your neighbor's wife" (cf. Exod. 20:17). This means that Jesus' message is not a matter of condemning all human desire as such, but of condemning the desire that attempts to take possession of its object, the desire that is greedy. Thus Jesus argues that the gaze can tempt, and that this can have serious consequences, which he inculcates through the hyperbolic statement in 5:29: "If your right eye causes you to sin, tear it out and throw it away."

7. There are many parallels to the texts of the Sermon on the Mount in Mark and Luke, but Matthew in his gospel has consistently collected various of Jesus' words into coherent discourses.

8. Ulrich Luz, *Matthew 1–7: A Commentary*, trans. Helmut Koester (Minneapolis: Fortress Press, 2007), p. 196.

The consequences of a covetous gaze are such that it is better for the gaze to cease. The gaze can namely become an instrument of adultery.

In addition to these covetous gazes another sort of gaze is mentioned in the Sermon on the Mount, namely the gaze with which the "others" see the "good works" of the disciples and thus "give glory" to God (v. 16). We can call this gaze a "generous" gaze in opposition to a covetous gaze. But having presented this generous gaze, in the following text Jesus seems to take back what he has just said about it. The disciples are namely warned about doing good works "before other people" (6:1) or like the hypocrites who "stand and pray in the synagogues and at the street corners, that they may be seen by others" (v. 5). Good works and prayer should instead be done "in secret" or "in your room." This does not make the good works completely invisible, since God "sees *[blepōn]* in secret" and can reward these good works and answer these prayers (vv. 4, 6). Even when one fasts one should avoid letting people see that one fasts—the only one who needs to see this is, again, the Father, who "sees in secret" (v. 18).

This does not, however, need to be interpreted as a contradiction of the statement that people praise God when they see the good works of the disciples. What the Gospel of Matthew and the Sermon on the Mount want to inculcate with the warning not to do good works "before other people" is that good works depend on the whole person, and not only what other people see of what the person does. In other words, the person should not pretend to be good and pious in order to attract attention: "Thus, when you give to the needy, sound no trumpet before you" (v. 2). The reference to God who sees what is done in secret might be interpreted as though it meant that since God will see, the person will receive another, subtler reward for her or his good and pious works. But the reference to the fact that God sees what is done in secret is probably used here in order to unmask the secret intention of certain good works, namely human self-affirmation.[9] The point is not to exchange the affirmation of human gazes for an affirmation from a heavenly gaze, but to warn against good works that are performed with consideration for a gaze—whatever sort of gaze that may be—rather than for the inherent value of the goal of those good works. Likewise when prayer has a purpose other than saying something to God.[10]

9. Luz, *Matthew 1–7*, p. 300.

10. Cf. Karl Barth, *Church Dogmatics,* vol. 3: *The Doctrine of Creation,* part 4, 2nd edition, trans. A. T. Mackay et al. (Edinburgh: T. & T. Clark, 1961), p. 88: "Prayer as a demonstration of faith, as disguised preaching, as an instrument of edification, is obviously not prayer at all. Prayer is not prayer if it is addressed to anyone else but God."

Then Jesus returns to the idea that the eyes are the key to true life in the parable of the lamp of the body: "The eye is the lamp of the body *[ho lychnos tou sōmatos estin ho ophthalmos]*. So, if your eye is healthy, your whole body will be full of light, but if your eye is bad, your whole body will be full of darkness. If then the light in you is darkness, how great is the darkness!" (vv. 22–23). Here as well it is a matter of the relationship of the person to her environment, rather than her inner being. The word "eye" is often used metaphorically in Judaism, and the exegete Ulrich Luz writes that "[a] person's character and moral quality are reflected in the eyes."[11] This does not mean that the eye should constitute a self-sufficient source of light for the body. That the eye is "healthy"—*haplous* literally means "simple"—indicates that it is a matter of the person's moral attitude, and also connotes generosity, which the context of the text suggests (cf. vv. 19–21, 24).

This generosity also finds expression in a text from the Sermon on the Mount that has to do with forgiveness. In 7:3–5 the disciples are exhorted not to judge: "Why do you see *[blepeis]* the speck that is in your brother's eye *[tō ophthalmō tou adelphou]*, but do not notice the log that is in your own eye? Or how can you say to your brother, 'Let me take the speck out of your eye,' when there is the log in your own eye? You hypocrite, first take the log out of your own eye, and then you will see clearly *[diablepseis]* to take the speck out of your brother's eye." The emphasis here is that the one judging becomes the one judged. One's own moral shortcomings prevent the person in question from seeing sufficiently clearly to be able to judge the moral shortcomings of another in an objective way. In the modern period the text could perhaps be understood as a defense of private integrity, namely that no one should meddle in the affairs of others. The Gospel of Matthew, however, does not argue in terms of a private sphere, but is precisely about relationships between people. In this case it is not about excusing the "speck in your brother's eye" and so also one's "own log," but about an attitude that is characterized by forgiveness and the effort to restore relationships in a way that fits with the coming kingdom of God. Sight is once again used as a metaphor for relationship with other people.

On the basis of these texts we can see that the sense of sight stands in a variety of different relationships. To begin with, we can differentiate between the person's covetous and generous gazes. The covetous gaze, i.e., the gaze that attempts to take possession of its object, thereby sets itself in a relationship that 1) involves an illegitimate ownership, and 2) consequently

---

11. Luz, *Matthew 1–7*, p. 333.

"commits adultery." The comparison of the eye to the lamp of the body shows that the ability to see is also associated with the person's attitude towards her possessions, and not only with her relationship to other people. Yet again it is a greedy attitude that is discarded in favor of a generous attitude.

The covetous gaze is rejected by Jesus. This gaze leads to darkness in the body and thereby misses out on the beholding of God. Throughout Christian history this beholding of God has been understood on the basis of a Platonic and Aristotelian model as a "spiritual beholding," but the text of the Sermon on the Mount clarifies that this spiritual beholding is at least associated with, if not identical to, the physical, embodied ability to see.[12] The physical gaze expresses the spiritual attitude of the person, and thus is not understood as a neutral, registering gaze. How one looks at other people is correlated to the beholding of God.

The generous gaze is the gaze with which people observe the good works of the disciples, and are thus led to praise God for these works. Such a gaze does not "reward" the tendency to self-assertion that may exist as motive for the good or pious deeds of the disciples. One might say that this gaze is generous in the sense that it can acknowledge what is good in the works that others do, and forgive what is not good. It is thus not a begrudging gaze. But this gaze can also be called generous in the sense that it leads the thoughts to God as the source of all good works. The generous gaze does not stay at home by itself, but reaches out towards the other, without wanting to either annihilate or own her. With this a relationship free from self-centeredness and the desire for control is expressed. The gaze that characterizes a disciple of Jesus—so might one summarize Jesus' teaching about sight in Matthew—is not a gaze that controls, not a gaze that attempts to master and own its object, but a generous gaze. I return to this in chapter 7.

Jesus Heals the Blind

In the Gospels' description of the activity of Jesus, the sense of sight is not only a means of teaching, but also of concrete action. Many of Jesus' miracles of healing are connected to the ability to see. But these miracles of healing ought to be understood in relation to Jesus' parables, not least when it concerns the ability to see. When the New Testament speaks of a blind person [typhlos] this can be understood purely literally, but there are often second-

12. Luz, *Matthew 1–7*, pp. 199–202.

ary accents on a more comprehensive "inner," "spiritual," or "metaphorical" blindness. In the Synoptic Gospels, to be blind in a spiritual sense was to not know in which direction one should look in order to see the arrival of the kingdom of God, and thereby not find a right relationship to Jesus. When Jesus came to heal, it was thus not simply a matter of healing a physical blindness, but also of healing the spiritual blindness that led people astray. Jesus is the one who restores the true gaze to the people, not just the one who teaches about the true gaze, and this happens through the miracles of healing as well as through the parables.

Jesus heals the blind in two places in the Gospel of Matthew. The first is in 9:27–31, where two blind men are healed. Here it is their faith that heals them. The Gospel of Matthew's account is probably based on the parallel account in Mark 10:46–52. In the Gospel of Mark it is a blind beggar who is healed. His name is given as Bartimaeus, son of Timaeus. A corresponding account is also found in Luke 18:35–43. In opposition to the Gospel of Mark's "making concrete" of the account of healing, Matthew's version is more "standardized."[13] It stands as an exemplary narrative of how Jesus heals the blind. For Matthew the blindness is of a metaphorical significance. Already in the Old Testament being blind meant not understanding, or living in the old era.[14] According to the prophet Isaiah (29:18) it is a sign of the coming kingdom of God that the deaf shall hear and "the eyes of the blind shall see." Thus there are probably already such overtones in Mark's account of the healing of Bartimaeus. In Matthew 23:16–26 Jesus returns five times to the blindness of the Jewish leaders and speaks of "blind guides," "blind fools," and "you blind men." In 15:14 it has already become clear that such leaders are not capable of leading the people: "they are blind guides. And if the blind lead the blind, both will fall into a pit." In other words, the metaphorical ability to see is also a condition for "seeing clearly" with regard to how one will become a part of the kingdom of God. For Matthew the metaphorical ability to see is clearly connected to the salvation of the people, and thus to Jesus as God's Messiah, which is already announced in the Gospel's first chapter (cf. vv. 20–25).

In Matthew's first account of the healing of the blind it is clear that the blind men's confession of their faith precedes their receiving back the ability

13. On the text in Mark, see Joachim Gnilka, *Das Evangelium nach Markus: Mk 8,27–16,20*, 2nd volume, Evangelisch-Katholischer Kommentar zum Neuen Testament vol. II/2, ed. Josef Blank, Rudolf Schnackenburg, et al., 3rd revised edition (Zürich/Einsiedeln/Neukirchen-Vluyn: Benziger Verlag/Neukirchener Verlag, 1989), pp. 108–12.

14. Luz, *Matthew 8–20*, p. 47.

to see: "Jesus said to them, 'Do you believe that I am able to do this?' They said to him, 'Yes, Lord.'" In the second account as well, 20:29–34—which goes back to the same account in the Gospel of Mark as the first, but retells it more concretely—sight and faith are linked.[15] But in this version the emphasis in the account lies not so much on the faith of the blind men, but rather on the fact that Jesus touches them. Jesus meets the two blind men outside of Jericho, and they ask him to have mercy on them. When Jesus asks what they want him to do for them, they answer (20:33–34): "'Lord, let our eyes be opened.' And Jesus in pity touched their eyes, and immediately they recovered their sight and followed him." So the order in the verses is the following: Jesus touches them, they see, and they follow him.

In early Christianity these miracles of healing were interpreted metaphorically—the blindness was a spiritual blindness. As we have seen, the Gospel of Matthew itself opens with the possibility of such an interpretation, even if Matthew, above all in the second version of the account, emphasizes the connection to concrete, physical blindness. The physical miracle, that the blind can see, reflects the metaphorical miracle, namely that through Jesus people receive understanding and knowledge about the kingdom of God. When, according to Matthew 11:2–6, the imprisoned John the Baptist asks his disciples who Jesus is, they convey the following message to John from Jesus: "Go and tell John what you hear and see: the blind receive their sight and the lame walk, lepers are cleansed and the deaf hear, and the dead are raised up, and the poor have good news preached to them" (vv. 4-5). Here the coming kingdom of God is associated with a number of physical miracles.[16]

At the same time the Gospel of Matthew makes a connection to the metaphorical meaning of blindness in chapter 13, where in the Parabolic Discourse Jesus explains the purpose of the parables. He first says that "this is why I speak to them in parables, because seeing they do not see, and hearing they do not hear, nor do they understand" (v. 13).[17] In verses 14–15 Jesus sees this as a fulfillment of the prophet Isaiah (6:9–10):

> "You will indeed hear but never understand,
>   and you will indeed see but never perceive."
> For this people's heart has grown dull,
>   and with their ears they can barely hear,

---

15. Luz, *Matthew 8–20*, pp. 548–51.
16. Cf. Luke 7:21f.
17. Cf. Luke 8:10.

and their eyes they have closed,
lest they should see with their eyes
and hear with their ears
and understand with their heart
and turn, and I would heal them.

Then those blessed "eyes that see" are praised (Matt. 13:16). What the disciples have gotten to see is something that "many prophets and righteous people" have "longed to see" (v. 17).[18]

The purpose of Jesus' parables is not that the listeners would misunderstand them, but that they would instead constitute a confirmation of the people's (spiritual) deafness and blindness that explains for the disciples why the message is not received. The practical actions, i.e., the miracles of healing, become concrete, physical signs of the coming kingdom of God, and the meaning of these miracles of healing is expounded for the disciples through the parables. Or one might just as well argue that the miracles of healing function as illustrations of the parables. The point is the same with both works and parables, namely to show the imminent arrival of the kingdom of God, which is both a linguistic and a physical event.[19] In contrast with the people who do not see, the eyes of the disciples have gotten to see, and so their eyes can be praised as blessed. What have they gotten to see? The object of their gazes is presumably the healings of Jesus, which portend the coming kingdom of God (cf. 11:5). But this kingdom of God becomes present in Jesus himself. The vision of Jesus is thus crucial for the New Testament perspective on sight.

Beholding Salvation

It is not uncommon for the New Testament to speak about sight in connection with salvation. In the Gospels it is as important to see what Jesus did as to hear what he said. It is then a matter of both seeing Jesus and beholding salvation— these are intimately associated with each other, illustrating the connection between incarnation and the gaze. The sense of sight thus has to do with the perception of God's saving presence itself. As in large parts of ancient Greece,

---

18. Cf. Luke 10:23f.

19. Cf. Hans Weder, *Die Gleichnisse Jesu als Metaphern: Traditions- und redaktionsgeschichtliche Analysen und Interpretationen,* 3rd revised edition (Göttingen: Vandenhoeck & Ruprecht, 1984), pp. 282-83.

sight is not understood in the New Testament as a passive sense, but as a way to actively interpret, understand, and thereby relate oneself to that which one sees.[20] The eyewitness was a participant in what she saw, and to see Jesus, with a particular gaze, was to also behold salvation. In this section I will show how the Gospels understand this beholding in the accounts of Simeon at the Temple and of Jesus on the Mount of Transfiguration from the Synoptic Gospels, and then in the Gospel of John as well, which of all the Gospels perhaps articulates the most developed interest in the sense of sight.

Simeon at the Temple

We find one of the earliest associations of sight and salvation in Luke 2, in what is usually called the "Song of Simeon," which we find in the larger narrative of Simeon at the Temple. Simeon, a man who is described in verse 25 as "righteous and devout" and who waited for the "consolation of Israel," received according to verse 26 a revelation of the Holy Spirit that "he would not see death before he had seen the Lord's Christ." According to the Gospel of Luke Simeon then went into the temple in Jerusalem at the same time that Joseph and Mary brought forth "the child Jesus, to do for him according to the custom of the law" (v. 27). In his song of praise Simeon says: "for my eyes have seen your salvation *[hoti eidon hoi ophthalmoi mou to sōtērion sou]* that you have prepared in the presence of all peoples, a light for revelation to the Gentiles and for glory to your people Israel" (vv. 30–32). The vision promised several verses earlier is fulfilled here. According to Luke Jesus is the one who is the "consolation of Israel," the answer to Jewish expectation. The Swiss exegete François Bovon writes about this biblical scene:

> The divine oracle is fulfilled not only by 'seeing' (vv. 26, 30), but in 'touching.' The relationship between Simeon and Jesus is a microcosm of the relation between the messianic expectation of the people of Israel and its fulfillment. . . . Jesus' reception by Simeon is a global behavior and attitude, in which the entire person of the old man, his body and inner self, his thoughts and feelings, become active.[21]

20. Cf. Samuel Byrskog, *Story as History—History as Story: The Gospel Tradition in the Context of Ancient Oral History*, Wissenschaftliche Untersuchungen zum Neuen Testament 123 (Tübingen: J. C. B. Mohr [Paul Siebeck], 2000), pp. 146–48.

21. François Bovon, *Luke 1: A Commentary on the Gospel of Luke 1:1–9:50*, trans. Christine M. Thomas (Minneapolis: Fortress Press, 2002), p. 101.

In other words this account in the Gospel of Luke is not merely a transitional narrative passage, but carries deep significance for the entirety of the theology of the Gospel of Luke, not to mention for the whole issue of incarnation, the gaze, and embodiment.

Here Luke takes up a thematic motif that is not unknown in other biblical writings. When the aging Jacob gets to see his son Joseph again after many years he exclaims: "Now let me die, since I have seen your face and know that you are still alive" (Gen. 46:30). When Tobias in the book of Tobit from the apocryphal scriptures sees his mother Hannah again, she exclaims: "I have seen you, my child; now I am ready to die" (Tobit 11:9). Tobias's father Tobit receives his sight back thanks to a remedy that Tobias gives him, and he breaks out in a song of praise as well (vv. 14–15). Likewise Moses gets to see the promised land before he dies (cf. Deut. 32:49–52; 34:1–5). In contrast with these thematic parallels, it is not his son that Simeon gets to see in the Gospel of Luke, but the Messiah; nor does the beholding constitute a form of punishment, as in the case of Moses, but the similarities between the accounts are nevertheless striking.

What sort of beholding is attributed to Simeon in the Gospel of Luke? It is not a matter of seeing God, since God remains invisible. To "behold salvation" is instead a matter of seeing God's concrete action in history, and it is precisely this action that becomes visible in Jesus, God's Messiah. That this liberating action of God will become visible has already been spoken of in the Old Testament scriptures (cf. Ps. 98:3; Isa. 40:5; Bar. 4:24), and in later passages the Gospel of Luke will speak of the possibility of seeing God's saving action in history. In Luke Jesus himself "saw Satan fall like lightning from heaven" (10:18), and he praises the blessed eyes of the disciples for what they see (v. 23). According to Bovon this likely has to do with the person's receiving of salvation: "Salvation occurs independently of human striving; but the individual should react to this objective reality with subjective appropriation of it. Though objective, it is not readily available. Salvation is only visible as a sign."[22] The relationship between the person's sight and the divine in the Gospel of Luke thus implies that one can receive God's salvation via sight, but this appropriation does not mean that she controls this salvation. The gaze does not constitute its object—it is instead a matter of a sort of "discipleship of the gaze" that includes the person's gaze and involves it in the seen.[23] In

---

22. Bovon, *Luke 1,* p. 102.

23. Cf. Eberhard Jüngel on the discipleship of thought in *God as the Mystery of the World: On the Foundation of the Theology of the Crucified One in the Dispute between Theism and*

the accounts of the Gospel of John salvation cannot be reduced to an inner, private process that only takes place in the person's consciousness, but is dependent on these external, concrete events, and the primary manifestation of these external, concrete events is God's action in Jesus. The account of Simeon at the Temple thus depicts how salvation becomes concretely visible in the baby Jesus.

Jesus on the Mount of Transfiguration

The account of Simeon at the Temple is found only in the Gospel of Luke, but the account of Jesus on the Mount of Transfiguration is reproduced in all three Synoptic Gospels (Matt. 17:1–9; Mark 9:2–10; Luke 9:28–36). The essentials of the account consist of Jesus taking his disciples Peter, James, and John up a mountain—in order to pray, according to Luke. Once there, Jesus is transfigured. His clothes become white and shining, and the disciples see him stand and speak with Moses and Elijah. Peter suggests that the disciples should make tents for them. A cloud sinks over them and they hear God's voice from the cloud, which in Mark's version says: "This is my beloved Son; listen to him." Then when the disciples look around, there is no one besides Jesus with them. They go down from the mountain and the disciples are silent about what they have seen—at the direct urging of Jesus, according to Matthew and Mark.

An immediate association for the original Jewish and Jewish-Christian readers or listeners to the account of Jesus on the Mount of Transfiguration is doubtless the account in Exodus 24 of Moses, who climbs up Mount Sinai and receives the law. With him he has Aaron, Nadab, and Abihu, and "seventy of the elders of Israel" (v. 1), but only Moses may draw near the Lord. In this account as well a cloud rests over the mountain when Moses finds himself there, and the Israelites who stand below can see "the glory of the LORD . . . like a devouring fire on the top of the mountain" (v. 17). Likewise, there are probably echoes of the other account of how Moses went up on Sinai in order to receive the stone tablets with the law in chapter 34. When Moses came down from Sinai a second time, "the skin of his face shone because he had been talking with God" (v. 29). Jesus' face is mentioned in

---

Atheism, trans. Darrell L. Guder (Edinburgh: T. & T. Clark, 1983), pp. 167–68. What Jüngel writes on the discipleship of thought also applies, *mutatis mutandis,* to the discipleship of the gaze, even if Jüngel himself might be skeptical towards ascribing the gaze this role.

the account of the Mount of Transfiguration by Matthew and Luke, and in Matthew—but only there—it is said that "his face shone like the sun," a clear association with the radiance from Moses' face. Likewise the account undoubtedly recalls a coronation ceremony when the voice of God proclaims from the cloud that Jesus is God's "beloved son" (cf. Ps. 2:7).[24] Other associations are also raised for the first readers of the account, but the account of Moses on Mount Sinai together with the coronation ceremony ought to have been the clearest.[25]

There are many questions to pose to these three parallel versions of the account of Jesus on the Mount of Transfiguration, not least with regard to their mutual compositional and textual differences, but let me limit myself to taking up the question of what it was the evangelists thought the disciples saw. The rhetorical style attests to the fact that it has to do with a beholding of Jesus in his "heavenly glory." The white and shining clothes Jesus suddenly wears are the clothes of the angels and the blessed.[26] In other words it is a matter of the coming kingdom of God becoming visible here and now in the form of Jesus. Matthew (17:2) and Mark (9:2) use the verb *metamorphoō* in passive form aorist, while Luke (9:29) uses another linguistic construction which may be literally translated "the appearance of his face became different *[egeneto . . . to eidos tou prosōpou autou heteron]*," but which—as with *metamorphoō*—has often been translated as "transfigured" (the English Standard Version has "altered" in the Luke passage). The use of the passive form of the verb *metamorphoō* indicates that what happens should be understood as a divine action with Jesus as the object, i.e., that Jesus does not make himself "luminous," but that the light of God falls on him. Regarding Luke, Bovon has written a commentary on the "transfiguration" that boils down to the fact that it has to do with Jesus' relationship rather than Jesus' identity. This is worth quoting in somewhat more detail, as it concerns the question of *what* was transformed:

What becomes 'different' is not the identity, which is envisaged in τὸ πρόσωπον *[to prosōpon]*, but its appearance, which is expressed by τὸ εἶδος *[to eidos]* ('form'). The word ἕτερον *[heteron]* ('other' of two) expresses a change not in essence but in the relationship of Jesus to the others, and of the others to him. According to Luke, Jesus does not become

24. Luz, *Matthew 8–20*, pp. 395–96.
25. Luz, *Matthew 8–20*, pp. 395–97.
26. Gnilka, *Markus*, p. 33.

different from what he was before, but for a moment his appearance becomes a divine sign to humanity, the sign of his true identity. In Luke this Christological observation remains embedded in the doctrine of God; 'the different appearance' does not express Jesus' divine nature, but a relationship of God to him, just as he stands, not in prayer, but in the right relationship to God.[27]

Through this transformation or transfiguration that Jesus goes through on the mountain it becomes clear—for the disciples in the Gospels—that Jesus should be identified with God's definitive revelation.[28] The revelation of Jesus' relationship to God that is expressed in the account of Jesus on the Mount of Transfiguration has to do with how the disciples appropriate this insight into this relationship through sight. Ulrich Luz comments on Matthew's version of the account in the following way: "It is a vision of Christ in the future glorious appearance of the Risen One."[29] Joachim Gnilka writes of the experience of the disciples as depicted by Mark: "They experience an anticipation of the heavenly glory."[30] The account therefore has just as much to do with a "transformation" of the disciples as with a transformation of Jesus. Their gazes become different—they now see Jesus in different light.

How should we understand an account like this? Is it an account of a historical, supernatural event—if such a thing is possible—or is it an invention of the authors of the Gospels? The earliest church understood the account as a historical event, while modern exegetes have either chosen to explain the account as a historical but natural event, or as a theologically motivated construction. Another way to interpret the account is to see it as a summation of the disciples' experience of Christ in light of his eschatological significance.[31] In other words, the account is a Christological reflection over Jesus' theological significance. It is then not a matter of a "physical beholding" but of a "spiritual beholding," an "insight" into the historical Jesus whom the disciples have seen with their own, physical eyes in light of his resurrection. The point of the account is thus to show that the journey with Jesus towards the cross does not end with the cross. In Matthew as well as in Mark and Luke, the account of Jesus on the Mount of Transfiguration is preceded by

27. Bovon, *Luke 1*, p. 375.
28. Bovon, *Luke 1*, p. 379.
29. Luz, *Matthew 8–20*, p. 398.
30. Gnilka, *Markus*, p. 34.
31. Gnilka, *Markus*, pp. 36–37.

a passage on discipleship's requirement to take up one's cross. Matthew explicitly mentions the suffering of the Son of Man in the story itself (v. 12).

What I want to bear in mind is the fact that a visual terminology is used in order to speak about the relationship between Jesus and God and about Jesus' eschatological significance. For the three disciples the insight into Jesus' identity is something that is conveyed to them through both sight and hearing—and that the evangelists convey further in their texts. According to Luz hearing is most important for the Gospel of Matthew, but it is relevant that for all the Gospels both senses are allotted a crucial significance for the disciples' relationship to Jesus.[32] The disciples are involved in what happens through both sight and hearing. The initiative is described as God's rather than the disciples', and the conveying happens through Jesus, who both is transformed physically and is "annotated" by God's voice from the cloud. The Synoptic Gospels describe the insight into Jesus' eschatological significance as a beholding, but even in accounts that primarily have to do with a spiritual beholding this spiritual beholding is never described independently of the concrete, physical act of sight. For the synoptics it is a matter of—and this was already clear in the previous section on the healings and parables—understanding what one sees, and not least understanding that eschatological salvation is concretely related to Jesus. This means that salvation is not described as only an inner mental occurrence, and that spiritual understanding is not independent of the concrete, historical gaze of the disciples.

"Whoever has seen me has seen the Father"

For the Gospel of John as well—and perhaps not least—the beholding of Jesus is crucial for salvation.[33] There are several examples in the Gospel of John of how faith is associated with the sense of sight. In a certain sense, in this Gospel it is only through Jesus that one can relate to God. Already in the prologue of John chapter 1, verse 18, it is established: "No one has ever seen [heōraken] God. The only God, who is at the Father's side, he has made him known." That it is impossible to see God apart from Jesus is emphasized in a number of passages in the Gospel of John: "His [the Father's] voice you have

---

32. Luz, *Matthew 8–20*, p. 394.

33. See here, among others, Franz Mussner, *Die johanneische Sehweise und die Frage nach dem historischen Jesus,* Quaestiones Disputatae 28 (Freiburg/Basel/Vienna: Herder, 1965).

never heard, his form you have never seen" (5:37); "not that anyone has seen the Father except he who is from God; he has seen the Father" (6:46). This is a theme that is already present in the Old Testament portion of the Bible. In Exodus 33:18 Moses asks to be allowed to see God's glory, but God replies that "man shall not see me and live." When the prophet Isaiah is allowed to see the Lord in a vision he exclaims "Woe is me! For I am lost . . . for my eyes have seen the King, the LORD of hosts!" (Isa. 6:5). In the Hellenistic world as well it was thought that God was invisible.[34] That the Son has seen God thus emphasizes the intimate as well as the unique in relationship between the Father and his son Jesus.

The possibility of understanding the will of the Father thus lies in seeing who Jesus is, because he has seen the Father. Jesus becomes the one through whom the Father's actions become visible. The Gospel of John says of Jesus: "He who comes from heaven is above all. He bears witness to what he has seen and heard, yet no one receives his testimony" (3:31-32). Jesus says of himself: "the Son can do nothing of his own accord, but only what he sees *[blepē]* the Father doing. . . . For the Father loves the Son and shows *[deiknysin]* him all that he himself is doing" (5:19-20). In a discussion with several Jews Jesus said: "I speak of what I have seen *[heōraka]* with my Father" (8:38). In all of these cases the qualification for the Son's ability to testify to humanity about the Father is that he himself has seen. The Son becomes the one who conveys his vision to the rest of the people. In his farewell discourse Jesus thus says to the disciple Philip: "Whoever has seen me has seen the Father *[ho heōrakōs eme heōraken ton patera]*. How can you say, 'Show *[deixon]* us the Father'?" (14:9). In this last sentence it seems as though it is possible to see the Father—in contrast to what was said in chapter 1, verse 18—but as the context makes clear, it is again a matter of an "indirect" beholding of the Father, because the one who has seen Jesus has also seen the Father. Jesus is not only the one whose sight extends beyond the natural sight given through the earthly existence of the human being, but he is the only one who has seen the Father and thereby understood his will in a genuine way. Because he has seen the Father, and moreover does only what he has seen the Father do, Jesus becomes the Father's visible testimony.

The Gospel of John thus links believing in Jesus with seeing Jesus. But it is not just any gaze that is capable of seeing the testimony of the Father in Jesus. As the exegete Samuel Byrskog writes:

34. Brown, *Gospel,* p. 36.

The real object of seeing is hidden from those who observe only with their eyes. On many occasions seeing is a spiritual seeing describing the encounter with Jesus in faith, with little or no immediate connotation of a direct sensual seeing of the Jesus of history.[35]

This becomes clear in chapter 6, among others. Here the Gospel of John describes a number of miracles: Jesus feeds 5000 people and walks on water. For those who can see, this is a sign of the arrival of the kingdom of God in the person of Jesus. When Jesus has disappeared the next day, the people look for him, but he says that they come because they are hungry, not because they have understood the signs he has done: "But I said to you that you have seen *[heōrakate]* me and yet do not believe" (v. 36). The people have not achieved this true beholding, for then they would also believe: "For this is the will of my Father, that everyone who looks on *[ho theōrōn]* the Son and believes in him should have eternal life" (v. 40). In this passage we can see a distinction between two terms for sight that go back to two verbs: on the one hand *horaō* and on the other *theōreō*, where *horaō* designates purely physical seeing, while *theōreō* designates a spiritual insight. This is an observation that extends only to these two verses, however, not a general conclusion about semantic fields of different verbs in the Gospel of John.[36] Three additional verbs are used by John regarding the ability to see: *blepō, eidon* (if one does not consider *eidon* the aorist of *horaō*), and *theaomai*. Nonetheless, we can state here that the Gospel of John differentiates between different sorts of sight, or different intensities of sight, by using two different designations. This also means that there can be space for a distinction between seeing and faith, in spite of what I wrote above. In 19:35 the eyewitness account is highlighted as a reason for believing, and with this the Gospel of John displays an awareness of the temporal difference between the story of Jesus and the actual circumstances of faith in Jesus.[37] In the very distance between the historical actions of Jesus and the contemporary situation of the author of the Gospel of John a possibility is also opened for a productive understanding of this story, a way of entering more deeply into its meaning.[38] Genuine sight in the Gospel of John is a matter of understanding that in Jesus the Father is revealed, rather than simply a physical beholding of Jesus' physical form.

---

35. Byrskog, *Story,* p. 235.
36. Cf. Brown, "Appendix I," *Gospel,* pp. 501-3.
37. Byrskog, *Story,* p. 236.
38. Mussner, *Sehweise,* p. 15.

I have already mentioned above how the beholding of the Father is an indirect beholding mediated through Jesus. This is clearest in the Gospel of John's farewell discourse, where we find a rather intricate account of this "beholding." Jesus argues that it is through him that one sees the Father, and he mentions as well that the Father will send another helper besides himself, namely the Spirit of truth, "whom the world cannot receive, because it neither sees [theōrei] him nor knows him" (14:17). The "world" is in this case made up of those who have not beheld the Father in Jesus. The ability to see is related to faith. But according to this farewell speech neither is Jesus visible always and for all: "Yet a little while and the world will see [theōrei] me no more, but you will see [theōreite] me. Because I live, you also will live" (v. 19). The world will not be able to see Jesus, but the disciples will. Jesus returns to the theme in the middle of the farewell discourse: "A little while and you will see [theōreite] me no longer; and again a little while, and you will see [opsesthe] me" (16:16). So there seem to be at least two different distinctions between different ways of seeing. The one would then consist in the difference between a physical beholding that perceives who Jesus is (the disciples) and one that does not perceive who he is (the world). The other distinction, which is a difference in different types of sight in those who perceive who he is, emphasizes that not even those who perceive who he is will always see him. Should one understand the second distinction on the basis of physical or spiritual seeing? In other words: Does Jesus' temporary invisibility mean that he retreats from physical beholding, or that the insight of the disciples fails? It seems to me that the interpretation of these passages most ready to hand involves Jesus retreating from visibility as a physical person, and another sort of beholding thus becoming possible thanks to the helper that the Father sends. The question is whether this other beholding should be understood as a purely spiritual beholding, i.e., without connection to the physical beholding, or whether it exists intertwined with a physical beholding. Let us see whether there are further indications of how the relationship between different sorts of beholding should be understood in the Gospel of John.

When the Gospel of John talks about the resurrection of Jesus there is even there a sort of dialectic between his visibility and his invisibility. To begin with, the Gospel of John mentions that one of the disciples who saw the empty tomb and the bandages and the shroud that lay there "saw and believed" (20:8). More detailed is the account of Mary Magdalene, as she also visited the tomb. She first got to see two angels (v. 12), but when she turned around she saw [theōrei] Jesus standing there without initially understanding that it was he (v. 14). When he addressed her she understood who it was and went to the disciples in order to tell them she had "seen *[heōraka]* the Lord" (v. 18). So it was necessary for Mary to be personally addressed to understand that it was "the Lord" that she saw. To physically see that something is there—as elsewhere in the Gospel of John—is not identical with "perceiving" what one sees. In order to "perceive," something more is needed, a divine intervention that goes beyond the purely natural capability. The gaze that was necessary in order to see the resurrected Lord as precisely the resurrected Lord was thus not spontaneous for Mary Magdalene. We thus understand from the context that she must have seen *someone;* otherwise the remark that she did not recognize Jesus would be meaningless.

A third narrative on the same theme at the end of the Gospel of John is the account of Doubting Thomas. When Jesus comes to the disciples later that same day, the disciple Thomas did not come in time and missed his visit. The other disciples then said to him: "We have seen *[heōrakamen]* the Lord" (v. 25). Thomas did not believe them but said, "Unless I see *[idō]* in his hands the mark of the nails, and place my finger into the mark of the nails, and place my hand into his side, I will never believe." When he gets to do so a week later, Jesus says to him (v. 29): "Have you believed because you have seen *[heōrakas]* me? Blessed are they who have not seen *[mē idontes]* and yet have believed." Here it is clearly a question of a physical beholding on the part of Thomas. When Jesus here sets those who believe without having seen before those who see and believe, the seeing in this case is a matter of physical seeing. This might suggest that the Gospel of John does not simply want to establish a distinction between physical and spiritual beholding, but also to differentiate them by establishing a hierarchy of value. This distinction is analogous to the distinction between the horizontal and the vertical eschatological lines in John, i.e., between salvation history and the unique divine intervention through Jesus.[39] But just as the Gospel of John never separates salvation history from God's intervention—and so never leaves room for a completely "gnostic" interpretation—so the physical and the spiritual beholding, in spite of everything, hold together in that Thomas is presented as though he really does both see and touch Jesus. The point of the Gospel of John's exposition on the visibility and invisibility of Jesus thus does not seem to be to discard physical beholding for the benefit of the purely spiritual.

39. Brown, *Gospel*, pp. cxv-cxvi.

Such a conclusion is reinforced by another passage from the Johannine literature that we find in 1 John, whose prologue (1:1–4) constitutes a meditation of several verses on seeing and visibility:

> That which was from the beginning, which we have heard, which we have seen with our eyes *[ho heōrakamen tois ophthalmois hēmōn]*, which we looked upon *[etheasametha]* and have touched with our hands, concerning the word of life—the life was made manifest *[kai hē zōē ephanerōthē]*, and we have seen *[heōrakamen]* it, and testify to it and proclaim to you the eternal life, which was with the Father and was made manifest *[ephanerōthē]* to us—that which we have seen *[heōrakamen]* and heard we proclaim also to you, so that you too may have fellowship with us; and indeed our fellowship is with the Father and with his Son Jesus Christ. And we are writing these things so that our joy may be complete.

Here the author of 1 John explains that he (i.e., "we," the Johannine fellowship) have both heard, seen, looked upon, and touched "that which was from the beginning," and thus can pass on the testimony of eternal life, which results in fellowship with the Father and the Son.[40] In other words, the author of the epistle of John holds the historical and embodied existence of Jesus—the prerequisite for the seeing as well as the touching—together with its more than historical meaning. Eternal life has become visible in history, and this constitutes the prerequisite for preaching and testimony.

No fewer than four verbs that describe sensory impression are used to emphasize that the author claims to be an eyewitness to Jesus' activity. Additionally, these four verbs are reproduced with heightened intensity: to hear, to see, to behold, to touch. The difference between "seeing" *(horaō)* and "beholding" *(theōreō)* may designate the difference between a purely physical seeing and the deeper beholding that is found in those who believe in Jesus (cf. 20:29 above). However, this does not contradict the fact that the author of the epistle has specifically the physical sensory impressions in mind, and so is not making a metaphorical circumlocution for a purely spiritual beholding or touching, such as Origen, for example, would later propose.[41] In other words, the relationship to the Father is, according to the

40. Cf. Hans-Josef Klauck, *Der erste Johannesbrief,* Evangelisch-Katholischer Kommentar zum Neuen Testament vol. XXIII/1, ed. Norbert Brox, Rudolf Schnackenburg, et al. (Zürich/Braunschweig/Neukirchen-Vluyn: Benziger Verlag/Neukirchener Verlag, 1991), pp. 53–78. Klauck also treats the question of whether the author really could have been a historical witness.

41. See, for example, Origen, *Against Celsus,* in *The Ante-Nicene Fathers,* vol. 4, *Tertullian,*

author of 1 John, mediated in such a way that it may be physically perceived. It is admittedly a matter of an indirect relationship to the Father, since the Father is presumed to be invisible (otherwise the life would not need to become visible through Christ, cf. v. 2), but this relationship goes *through* the physical, rather than *past* the physical.

Now if the Gospel of John, and so also 1 John, does not want to abandon physical beholding in favor of the spiritual, where then do we find the purpose of the clear distinction that the Gospel of John nevertheless raises between these two? The motivation behind this distinction appears to be in the Gospel of John's effort to, so to speak, not only present the earthly story of Jesus, but also to interpret and construe its significance for a different time. The exegete Franz Mussner believes that this looking back on the historical Jesus in the Johannine literature serves as an anamnesis that "makes possible the transposition of history to kerygma."[42] This looking back is no "mechanical reproduction" of the historical Jesus or the story of Jesus, but is the Spirit-inspired exposition of the reception history of Jesus.[43] There is in fact no opposition between the proclaimed Christ and the historical Jesus in the Gospel of John, Mussner argues, because the reception history is a part of the story, according to the understanding of the Gospel of John. The physically visible Jesus also becomes visible in his reception history among the disciples, albeit in a different way. Thus the distinction between physical beholding and spiritual beholding is probably not intended to create an opposition between these two, but serves instead to show how spiritual beholding at once both presupposes and fulfills physical beholding. In other words, physical sight does not fix Jesus in the past. For the one who has received the Spirit-given gaze as a gift, Jesus is visibly active even in the present (this also concerns representations of Jesus' embodied resurrection, which I discuss more closely in a section in chapter 11).

The Gaze of Grace

This review of the New Testament's different ways of looking at sight, from Jesus' teaching on sight to the New Testament's teaching on the seeing of

---

Part Fourth; Minucius Felix; Commodian; Origen, Parts First and Second, ed. Alexander Roberts and James Donaldson, revised by A. Cleveland Coxe (Grand Rapids: Eerdmans, 1956), book 1, chapter 48, and book 7, chapter 34.

42. Mussner, *Sehweise,* p. 40. Italics in original.

43. Mussner, *Sehweise,* p. 44.

Jesus, has primarily concerned the Gospel texts. However, it is not only in the synoptics and the Johannine literature that salvation and sight are associated in the New Testament. Even Paul does so in his own way, for example in 2 Corinthians 4:4, where he speaks of Christ as the image of God, a text that has been significant for the icon theology I will give an account of in the next chapter: those who do not believe do not see "the light of the gospel of the glory of Christ, who is the image *[eikōn]* of God." Even the Deutero-Pauline epistle Colossians speaks of Christ as "the image of the invisible God *[eikōn tou theou tou aoratou]*" in 1:15. In the second letter to the Corinthians, as well as in the hymn in Colossians, a very close association between Christ and God is represented.[44] In the sense that these authors use the word, an image is not a "reproduction," i.e., something that is distinguished from that which is depicted, a copy that represents the depicted in its absence, but a representation—or rather a *presentation*—of the presence of the depicted. "Image of God" in this context signifies instead "manifestation of God" or "representative." So even in the Pauline literature such an intimate relationship between God and Christ is expressed that the beholding of Christ—for those who really "look" and do not just "see"—indirectly becomes a beholding of "the invisible God."

There are several examples that could be cited regarding how the Pauline literature associates salvation and sight (cf. Rom. 1:19–20; 11:8–10; 1 Cor. 2:9–10; 2 Cor. 3:18; 4:17–18; Gal. 3:1; Eph. 1:18), but let me limit myself to one more example, which casts light on the question at issue in this chapter, namely 1 Corinthians 13:12: "For now we see *[blepomen]* in a mirror dimly *[di' esoptrou en ainigmati]*, but then face to face. Now I know in part; then I shall know fully, even as I have been fully known." In this verse Paul wants to articulate the fact that the beholding that is possible here and now in the earthly form of existence is of an indirect, mediated character, in contrast with the later "direct" and "unmediated" beholding.[45] The point is not

44. See Victor Paul Furnish, *II Corinthians,* translation with introduction, notes, and commentary, Anchor Bible vol. 32A (New York/London: Doubleday, 1974), pp. 215, 222, together with Eduard Schweizer, *Der Brief an die Kolosser.* Evangelisch-Katholischer Kommentar zum Neuen Testament vol. XII, ed. Josef Blank, Rudolf Schnackenburg, et al., 3rd revised edition (Zürich/Braunschweig/Neukirchen-Vluyn: Benziger Verlag/Neukirchener Verlag, 1989), pp. 56–58.

45. Wolfgang Schrage, *Der erste Brief an die Korinther: 1 Kor 11, 17–14,40,* 3rd volume, Evangelisch-Katholischer Kommentar zum Neuen Testament vol. VII/3, ed. Norbert Brox, Joseph Gnilka, et al. (Zürich/Braunschweig/Neukirchen-Vluyn: Benziger Verlag/Neukirchener Verlag, 1999), pp. 309–15, 351–59.

that we do not see clearly, but precisely that our knowledge of God will later match God's knowledge of us, or in other words, that the relationship between us human beings and God will be intensified.[46] In 2 Corinthians 5:7 Paul expresses himself somewhat differently—"we walk by faith, not by sight"—but even here the emphasis lies on the difference between earthly existence and the final eschatological beholding.[47] This does not mean that Christ as the one who mediates the beholding of God to the human being will no longer be necessary in eternity. Paul is not discussing the indirect beholding through Christ here. First Corinthians 13:12 instead finds itself in a polemical context where Paul is discussing prophetic gifts, and the text should instead be understood as Paul indicating the limited character of the knowledge that prophecies can convey. What abides is not the prophecies, but love (cf. v. 8). With Paul the connection between sight and salvation here is that it is not until the eschatological completion that we will truly see "face to face," i.e., directly, without mediation (whatever that might entail).

Let me briefly summarize my conclusions so far. To begin with, the fact that sight plays a prominent role in the New Testament is perhaps not especially surprising. The primacy of sight was deeply rooted in the ancient Greek view of knowledge. Most Greek historians concurred, in the words of Heraclitus, that "[e]yes are surer witnesses than ears," and the authors of the New Testament shared this socio-cultural attitude as well.[48] Sight was thus the primary way to be involved in what happened around one, something that is clear in the New Testament testimony.

Additionally we notice that the New Testament represents the gaze, if only occasionally in connection with Jesus, as a way to express emotions. However, the material is not sufficient for an especially developed phenomenology of the gaze. The Synoptic Gospels are clearer in their teaching on sight. Through, for example, the Sermon on the Mount in the Gospel of

46. Schrage, *Korinther*, p. 315: "Das menschliche *epignoskein* wird dem göttlichen entsprechen, insofern es ein ganz von der Liebe geprägtes und nicht mehr durch Vermittlung gebrochenes Erkennen und Anerkennen sein wird." I am here not entirely certain what Schrage wants to say with the contrast between mediated and unmediated beholding.

47. Cf. Friedrich-Wilhelm Marquardt, *Was dürfen wir hoffen, wen wir hoffen dürften? Eine Eschatologie*, vol. 1 (Gütersloh: Chr. Kaiser/Gütersloher Verlagshaus, 1993), p. 125: "*Eschatologie ist kategorial theologische Ästhetik*, nicht Lehre von der Erkenntnis, sondern von Wahrnehmung des Wirklichen. Das Sinnliche ist das Element der Eschatologie."

48. Heraclitus, *The Art and Thought of Heraclitus: An Edition of the Fragments with Translation and Commentary*, trans. Charles H. Kahn (Cambridge: Cambridge University Press, 1979), p. 35 (xv). Cf. Byrskog, *Story*, pp. 64, 73-82, 93.

Matthew a distinction is raised between a covetous or greedy gaze and a generous gaze. With this it becomes clear that the gaze can be an instrument for controlling and owning, something that Jesus' teaching in the Sermon on the Mount clearly shuns. The person's spiritual attitude can thus be expressed through her physical gaze, an attitude that, according to the Gospel of Matthew, does not only have consequences for her relationship to other humans, but also for her relationship to God.

It is also clear in the Synoptic Gospels' representation of Jesus' miracles of healing and parables that the gaze is a way to relate to other people and to God, and thereby expresses a spiritual posture. In both the miracles of healing and the parables the physical gaze can become a trope for the spiritual attitude; physical blindness is associated with (without being blamed for) spiritual blindness. Spiritual blindness can become a hindrance to beholding the coming kingdom of God. When Jesus heals the blind, this is thus represented as both a physical and a spiritual healing, i.e., a way to set right the person's relationship to God.

The generous gaze that allows the person to behold the coming kingdom of God is, in the synoptics as well as in the Gospel of John, intimately associated with Jesus. Jesus is both the one who grants the prerequisites for seeing the kingdom of God by "healing the blind" and so giving the generous gaze as a gift, and the one in whom one may behold the coming kingdom of God. Common to the account of Simeon at the Temple in the Gospel of Luke and of Jesus on the Mount of Transfiguration in all three Synoptic Gospels is that they hold the physical gaze and the spiritual gaze together. Spiritual beholding is never described independently of the concrete, physical act of sight. Seeing Jesus, the paradigmatic historical manifestation of God's action of salvation, is represented as a necessary but not sufficient condition for beholding salvation. In addition to "seeing" him with one's physical eyes, insight is thus also needed, which comes from seeing Jesus in the light that God grants as a gift (cf. the argument regarding the possibilities of the eye in the previous chapter). Jesus is an essential condition for understanding God's action in the Gospel of John as well. In accordance with the high Christological expositions in the Gospel of John, it is only through the Son that we can have knowledge of the Father. In contrast with the synoptics, however, the Gospel of John seems to want to differentiate between physical and spiritual sight. The purpose with this is not to deny physical sight in favor of the spiritual, but rather to show how Jesus is visible after the resurrection in a different way, a way that is not immediately recognizable for human sight without the help of the Spirit. Beholding salvation is therefore not possible without the gaze of grace, if "of grace" is understood here as both objective and subjective genitive, i.e., both the gaze that is transformed by being the object of God's grace (objective genitive) and the gaze that sees and thereby relates with grace to all the dimensions of existence (subjective genitive). Sight is, for the New Testament generally, a spiritual attitude, not "spiritual" in contrast to "physical," but as a way to be-in-the-world. The gaze becomes an expression for the person's relationality towards other people as well as towards God.

In other words, the New Testament seems to give grounds for a specifically "spiritual" gaze, which is nevertheless not independent of social and historical context. In the Christian theology of the image it becomes clear how this gaze has been more explicitly related to concrete physical beholding and its spiritual significance more generally throughout history, since an image implicitly embodies a particular gaze, a particular way of being-in-the-world. Throughout history the theology of the image has been central for the Christian tradition's attempt to understand the relationship between divine and human, and has been a part of its discussion of the theology of incarnation. It has also had far-reaching practical and theoretical significance as a concrete reception of Christology in a significant practice. In the next chapter I therefore turn to a historical and systematic-theological discussion of the Christian theology of the image.

6. The Eyes of the Icon

In this chapter I will discuss the representation of Christ in visual images. Such an investigation of the relationship between gaze and incarnation provides yet another resource for my effort to clarify the concrete reception of Christology in a significant praxis by formulating a theology of the gaze as an embodied way to be-in-the-world. If the previous chapter on the perspective on sight in the New Testament focused to a large degree on the gaze itself as such, this chapter on the theology of the image will instead discuss images and the gazes they embody. In the section on the possibilities of the eye in chapter 4 I argued that the embodied human gaze is both active and passive, which means that in reality the gaze and the object of the gaze cannot be separated. Perceiving and perceived go inseparably together, yet without being blended together because of that. Because of this, neither can we isolate distinct perspectives on the gaze with respect to the image—just as a particular gaze implicates a particular relationship to its object, a particular image will also both configure and address a particular gaze. Both gaze and image are concepts of relationship. The reflections of the historical theology of the image are, as we will see, conditioned by the doctrine of the incarnation, and so it is relevant for my theology of the gaze to investigate which gazes are embodied by different images.

The pictorial depiction of Christ is without a doubt one of the most common motifs in the cultural history of the West. Ever since the rudimentary representations of Christ in the early catacomb paintings, the desire to imagine Christ visually has been an incentive for image creation, an incentive that has been deeply involved in central theological problems and far from uncontroversial. It is above all within the theology of the icon that these problems have been formulated in a clear way. The question has been posed whether, on the basis of the Christological creed that was formulated at the council in Chalcedon in 451 (cf. chapter 2), it is possible to represent Christ pictorially. What does one represent in such a case: only Christ's human nature, or his divine nature as well? If the divine nature is also represented, has one then not depicted that which cannot or may not be depicted? What did Christ look like? How should his suffering be portrayed such that it has clear significance for us? The theological thought surrounding the being or nonbeing of the icon is intimately bound up with the questions of incarnational theology. But even apart from icon painting in the strict sense, the issue of the image of Christ has posed and poses theological questions that are of great significance for the understanding of the incarnation.

The diversity of Christ images, in all imaginable genres over nearly two millennia, makes the topic almost unmanageable. However, my purpose here is not to describe the history of the Christ image. I can thus let the selection be guided by the theological problem of the incarnation. This means that I will discuss the Christ images from a theological perspective, not from an art history perspective. In other words, the chief interest lies not in *how* different artists have represented Christ pictorially, but *what theological problems* have confronted the artist who has wanted to represent Christ pictorially. This does not mean that these artistic and theological problems must be independent of each other. But for those artists tasked with representing Christ pictorially in order to show the mystery of the incarnation, artistic skill was primarily a medium for expressing this mystery, rather than for self-expression. We find ourselves here largely in the time "before art," where the context of an image was the liturgy or private devotions, rather than the museum.[1] But even after the development of art as an autonomous institution, there are images whose purpose is to show the mystery of the incarnation either in relation to an autonomous art institution or independently of it. It is then not primarily a matter of differentiating between two well-delimited groups of Christ images—those that are produced with a primarily theological purpose and those with a more aesthetic purpose—but equally about in which context an image is shown. Even if the artist's intention with a particular image was not primarily theological, the image can still function theologically, partly dependent on the Christ motif

1. See Hans Belting, *Likeness and Presence: A History of the Image before the Era of Art,* trans. Edmund Jephcott (Chicago/London: University of Chicago Press, 1994). Belting has since given out an additional work that treats the questions I take up in this chapter, as well as in several other chapters. Unfortunately it came out too late for me to have the possibility of considering his discussion to a greater extent here. See, however, Hans Belting, *Das echte Bild: Bildfragen als Glaubensfragen* (Munich: C. H. Beck, 2005).

that has been retrieved from the tradition and therefore inevitably links a specific Christ image to the broader tradition of Christ pictures, and partly dependent on the context—church, devotional book, etc.—where a specific image is shown.[2]

In this chapter I will first account for the prehistory of the theology of the image up until the eighth century, when the debate over the theology of the image reached a special intensity. The second section of the chapter will be a historical account of the Byzantine iconoclastic controversy, and then in the third section the theology of the icon is discussed from a more systematic perspective. Finally, the question of image and incarnation in the West is also posed, for a comparative and partially contrastive perspective. The theological emphasis will be on the latter two sections, since these more immediately serve my purpose of investigating the relationship between the gaze and incarnation.

The Prehistory of the Theology of the Image

The icon has a long history, from Christianity's beginning, to the production of a normative theology of the icon at the second council in Nicea in 787, where the theology of the iconoclasts was rejected and image veneration explained for the faithful, to the Byzantine Empire's eventual ceasing of its iconoclastic policies in 843. The icon's purely conceptual origin exists already in the Pauline literature of the New Testament, which I mentioned in the previous chapter. Both in 2 Corinthians 4:4 and Colossians 1:15 Jesus is spoken of as "image [eikōn] of God." In the New Testament the idea of the image/icon is usually contrasted with the "idol" (in Greek: eidōlon), and the difference between these can be described as the difference between an image (material images as well as conceptual) that represents something other than ourselves (the icon) and an image that is a reflection of ourselves (the idol)—a distinction that I return to more fully in the next chapter.[3] The New Testament conception of the icon, however, did not immediately give

2. I have previously touched on these issues briefly in the chapter "Att förestålla sig Kristus" in *Hungerns väg: Om Gud, kyrka och mångfald* (Lund: Arcus, 2000), pp. 111–27.

3. This concise way of contrasting idol and icon is taken from Jean-Luc Marion, "Idol and Icon," in *God without Being: Hors-Texte*, Religion and Postmodernism, trans. Thomas A. Carlson (Chicago/London: University of Chicago Press, 1991), pp. 7–24. For an illustration of the contrast between the two, see Bruce Ellis Benson, *Graven Ideologies: Nietzsche, Derrida & Marion on Modern Idolatry* (Downers Grove, IL: InterVarsity Press, 2002), p. 22.

rise to a developed theology of the image—this was instead a product of a long historical development whose main features I will give account of here.

The earliest Christians represented Christ through signs and symbols rather than in figurative images.[4] At gravesites and in catacombs people would write a Christ-monogram, XP, the Roman alphabet's transliteration of the two initial letters X and P in the Greek *[Christos]*. One could also draw a simple fish, which symbolized Christ. The fish was associated with the water of baptism, with Communion, and with the disciples as fishers of men. The Greek word for fish, *ichthys,* made an acrostic of the first letters of the Greek words for Jesus/Christ/Son of God/Savior. By drawing a fish one could show a symbolic sign, which pointed to Christ rather than representing Christ through a direct depiction. The fish became a visualization of a metaphor with symbolic resonance. One could thus visually refer to Christ without breaking the prohibition of images that is articulated in the second of God's ten commandments that Moses, according to the Hebrew Bible, received on Mount Sinai (Exod. 20:4; cf. 34:17): "You shall not make for yourself a carved image, or any likeness of anything that is in heaven above, or that is in the earth beneath, or that is in the water under the earth." Initially directed against the polytheism of the surrounding world, this command would eventually come to be interpreted by the Jews and the early Christians as a strict order not to attempt to produce a representation of God, because God neither wanted to nor could be represented. God was beyond all human understanding and could only be proclaimed in words, not depicted. In Romans 1:23 Paul had already noted that the heathens had exchanged "the glory of the immortal God for images resembling mortal man and birds and animals and creeping things," and so in order to avoid all heathen idol worship, one avoided direct pictorial representations of Christ.[5] The early Christians, including such theologians as Irenaeus, Tertullian, and Clement of Alexandria, therefore rejected

4. See, for example, Gabriele Finaldi et al., *The Image of Christ: The catalogue of the exhibition* Seeing Salvation, introduction by Neil MacGregor (London: National Gallery Company, 2000), pp. 8–43.

5. The polemic against pagan idolatry was partially misplaced, since intellectual pagans like Celsus and Porphyry did not perceive statues as gods, but as symbols for the eternal thing. Through images one could reach the divine prototype. These arguments came to be repeated by the Christians of later periods in defense of their own images. See Paul J. Alexander, *The Patriarch Nicephorus of Constantinople: Ecclesiastical Policy and Image Worship in the Byzantine Empire* (Oxford: Clarendon Press, 1958), pp. 23–30. Cf. p. 30: "In Porphyry's work the symbolic theory of religious images had reached its climax. They were not what the 'utterly unlearned' called them: wood or stone. They were images suited for human perception, images that lead the spectator on to the conception of the deity."

all use of images for representing Christ (which does not mean that they opposed the use of all images in general).[6] Even Origen thought that Christ could not be depicted, since the body of Christ is a divinely made body that therefore cannot be represented figuratively.

That theologians were skeptical of all image use did not, however, mean that all Christians avoided figurative representations of Christ. There is certain evidence that people broke with this rule as early as the year 200. One finds depictions of Christ on the walls of the catacombs, on the sides of the baptismals, but also on the sarcophagi and even in the form of statues. These early images often served catechetical purposes. How did this happen? Was this a deviation from the authentic Christian prohibition of images? Probably not. In the following I will briefly summarize how the thought of the theological legitimacy of the Christ image grew over a number of centuries.

The fundamental reason for the growth of the Christian use of images, and eventually the Christian theology of the image, is formulated by the Scottish art scholar Neil MacGregor: "Unlike Muslims and Jews, Christians (or at least the early Christians) have *seen* their God; for Christianity is the religion of the Word made flesh, and, largely as a consequence, it is also a religion of the image."[7] The emerging reflection on the incarnation, God's becoming human in Christ, went hand in hand with a reflection on the possibility of representing Christ in an image. One might say that a historiography that ends its account of Christology with the council in Chalcedon in 451 is misleading, as the continued discussion of the theology of the icon up until the second council in Nicea in 787 is in fact a reflection on the possibility of representing God's word in visible form, and thus precisely a reflection on the problem of incarnation.

As said, this does not mean that the story begins with something other than image skepticism. A synod in Elvira (near modern Granada in Spain) during the first decade of the fourth century forbade all use of images in churches.[8] The synod probably had little impact on the actual use of images. An early authority within the theology of the image was Eusebius of Caesarea (ca. 263–340).[9] He wrote a much-discussed letter—not all researchers

6. Gervais Dumeige, *Nicée II,* Histoire des conciles oecuméniques vol. 4, ed. Gervais Dumeige (Paris: Éditions de l'Orante, 1978), pp. 17–23.

7. Neil MacGregor with Erika Langmuir, *Seeing Salvation: Images of Christ in Art* (London: BBC, 2000), p. 13.

8. Dumeige, *Nicée II,* pp. 23–24.

9. Dumeige, *Nicée II,* pp. 26f., together with Christoph Schönborn, *God's Human Face: The Christ-Icon,* English translation (San Francisco: Ignatius Press, 1994), pp. 57–80.

are completely convinced of its authenticity[10]—to the sister of Emperor Constantine, Constantia, where he answers her request for an image of Christ with a sharp no, which he also justifies theologically. He asks himself in the letter what such an image of Christ would depict: Christ's divine nature? That would be impossible, since only the Father knows this. Christ's human nature? That would also be impossible, since the human nature was blended with the divine glory at the Transfiguration and the Ascension, and therefore cannot be reproduced with lifeless colors. The body was totally transformed by the divine nature with the Resurrection. There is thus no possibility for producing a depiction that resembles the depicted. On the other hand, Eusebius is probably not disallowing symbolic and allegorical images that point to Christ, since these images do not lay claim to a likeness with their object; they are not depictions. It is, however, the question of the images' likeness to the original that would later come to be debated during the image controversy. Eusebius moves within the framework of a spiritualized theology where every imagining of the divine with the senses must entail a reduction of the divine to something not divine, and thus in practice entail a denial of the divine.[11]

Athanasius of Alexandria (ca. 295–373) did not show any interest in images, but nevertheless delivered a text and a theology that came to have significance for the later image controversy, and in its content finds itself far from the theology of Eusebius. In *Orationes adversus Arianos* we find a passage about the image of the emperor.[12] For Athanasius the relationship between the emperor and the image of the emperor is parallel to the relationship between the Father and the Son in the Trinity. The one who honors the image of the emperor also honors the emperor himself, since the image bears the form of the emperor and shows his features. This example will later come to be a fixed expression for the relationship between the image and its archetype, and is cited, among other places, by the second Nicean council. However, what separates Athanasius from Eusebius is not only this example, but also the meaning that "image" has in Athanasius's theology. That the Son is an image (i.e., *eikōn*) of the Father entails no subordination of the Son

---

10. Which leads Schönborn, *God's Human Face*, pp. 56–57, n. 39, to declare its authenticity.

11. Within Christology Eusebius radicalizes an Origenist standpoint, which I gave an account of in chapter 2. See also Frances M. Young, *From Nicaea to Chalcedon: A Guide to the Literature and Its Background* (London: SCM, 1988 [1983]), pp. 1–23.

12. Athanasius of Alexandria, *Against the Arians*, in *Nicene and Post-Nicene Fathers*, ser. 2, vol. 4: *Athanasius: Select Works and Letters*, ed. Philip Schaff (Grand Rapids: Eerdmans, 1978), p. 396 (III, 23, 5).

under the Father, as in Eusebius's semi-Arian theology, but the Son is called the "image" of the Father because the Son is of the same being as the Father.[13] "Image" is used here analogically. In the sphere of the created, an image's difference from that which it depicts is always greater than its likeness, but in the being of God "image" and "archetype" are completely alike in their being, according to Athanasius. The fact that Christ is a perfect image of the Father entails a legitimatizing of the Christ image: God is present in such a way in the created world that the created—the humanity of Christ—is not denied or transformed such that it would no longer be possible to depict it. Even in his humanity Christ is an image of the Father. This indicates a different perspective on the relationship between God and the world than the one Eusebius has, and this will be of significance for the theology of the icon.

With the three Cappadocian fathers one finds further building blocks for what would later come to be the normative doctrine of the image.[14] They were invoked by John of Damascus as well as by the second council in Nicea as evidence for the orthodoxy of the veneration of images. For Basil of Caesarea (ca. 329/330–379) the images had above all a didactic worth. In his work *De Spiritu Sancto* one finds a statement that the iconophile party will later invoke: "[T]he honour paid to the image passes on to the prototype *[prōtotypon]*."[15] Just as with Athanasius, we find this statement in a Trinitarian context that has to do with the relationship between the Father and the Son. He who praises the Son thereby praises the Father. The Son is an image of the Father by nature *(physikōs)*, while the created can be an image of God through mimesis *(mimētikōs)*. According to Basil there is thus a likeness as well as a difference between the Son as the uncreated image and created images. We do not find any doctrine of the image in the later sense in any of this, even if Gregory of Nazianzus and Gregory of Nyssa claim that the image can have a pedagogical use similar to that of the word, namely to "paint" a biblical scene for the hearer/viewer. The splendor of the image can then be even greater than that of the word. This more positive attitude towards the

---

13. Athanasius, *Against the Arians*, p. 318 (I, 6, 21). See Schönborn, *God's Human Face*, pp. 8–14.

14. See Dumeige, *Nicée II*, pp. 28–31; Günter Lange, *Bild und Wort: Die katechetischen Funktionen des Bildes in der griechischen Theologie des sechsten bis neunten Jahrhunderts*, Schriften zur Religionspädagogik und Kerygmatik vol. VI, ed. Theoderich Kampmann (Würzburg: Echter-Verlag, 1969), pp. 28–36.

15. Basil of Caesarea [Basil the Great], *On the Spirit*, in *Nicene and Post-Nicene Fathers*, ser. 2, vol. 8: *Letters and Select Work*, ed. Philip Schaff (Grand Rapids: Eerdmans, 1996), p. 28 (18, 45).

pedagogical worth of the image may depend on the Cappadocian fathers' background in a more image-positive literary-rhetorical tradition influenced by Hellenistic thinking.[16] The difference from the iconophiles in later times consists rather in the fact that the *function* of the images will be different for them—not only pedagogical, but also doxological.

The art of the mosaic was spread over the entire Roman Empire during the fifth century. It is not known what Christian laymen made of images, but in general it is thought that they were positively inclined towards them. The attitude of bishops towards images was often determined by pastoral views. Somewhat later, i.e., during the sixth and seventh centuries, the Christ images had been spread over the entire Christian world. During these centuries something new occurred, namely, in some areas the images became objects for cult, i.e., for a sort of worship (Greek: *proskynein;* Latin: *adorare*). They came to be a part of the liturgy. People began to carry pictures with themselves that could give protection. Even if the use of images was thus accepted throughout the entire Christian world, no uniform doctrine of the image existed; however, a distinct praxis existed in the sense that in the East as well as the West people created and used images. The greatest source for iconophilic statements during the seventh century is, typically enough, writings that are directed against the Jews' powerful critique of the adoration of images and the worship of the cross.

Byzantine Iconoclasm

During the eighth century the discussion of the theological status of images would reach a special intensity. This discussion primarily took place in the Eastern church, which had the consequence that it would develop a more reflective, articulate, as well as different theology of the image than the Western church. In the East we namely find a number of theological and political conflicts that arose around the being or nonbeing of images. There are far-reaching discussions of whether these conflicts ought to be understood primarily theologically or politically. Such a distinction is probably not pertinent to these conflicts. As one of the historians of the theology of the image, Jaroslav Pelikan, writes: "[T]he conflict over Iconoclasm was always much

---

16. Lange, *Bild und Wort,* p. 38. See also Jaroslav Pelikan, *Christianity and Classical Culture: The Metamorphosis of Natural Theology in the Christian Encounter with Hellenism* (New Haven/London: Yale University Press, 1993), pp. 15–16.

more than a political struggle; at the same time, it was certainly never less than political."[17] Before the eighth century there had existed an image praxis that was more or less recognized, but not explicitly theologically treated to the degree that the iconoclasm would lead to. The iconoclasm is usually said to encompass the time between 726 and 843. During this time a number of emperors, patriarchs, monks, theologians, and, for us, anonymous laymen are intensively engaged in this conflict, which had its center in the Byzantine Empire's capital Constantinople. In addition to the outer historical framework, I will present here the three theologians who have meant the most for the Orthodox church's theology of the image, namely John of Damascus, the patriarch Nikephoros of Constantinople, and Theodore the Studite.[18]

An important date is 717, when Leo III (ca. 685–741) became emperor and thereby ended thirty years of anarchy. The Byzantine Empire recovered its military strength when Leo defeated the Saracens in 718 and broke the siege of Constantinople. Eventually, by the end of 724 and the beginning of 725, it was clear that Leo III was an iconoclastic emperor.[19] A volcanic eruption the summer of 726 gave rise to a new island between Santorini and Crete, and this was seen by Leo III as an expression of God's wrath; he therefore intensified his fight against images. He cleared out all the Christ images in his own palace, first and foremost the Christ image over the entrance to the imperial palace, and attempted to influence the popes Gregory II and Gregory III in Rome in the same direction, though without succeeding in fostering any sympathy for his iconoclastic policies. The bond between Rome and Constantinople was broken.

One of the early defenders of the use of images was John of Damascus (ca. 650–750). John came from a Christian Arab family in Damascus. His father was the finance minister at the court of the Caliph, and John himself also came to be employed in the administration of the Caliphate. However, around the year 700 he moved to the Mar Saba monastery in the Judean desert, and it was here that he came to formulate his most famous contribution to the controversy, namely his "three discourses against those who

17. Jaroslav Pelikan, *Imago Dei: The Byzantine Apologia for Icons,* The A. W. Mellon Lectures in the Fine Arts, 1987, Washington, DC. Bollingen Series XXXV: 36 (Princeton: Princeton University Press, 1990), p. 7. Cf. pp. 7–39.

18. These three are discussed together by Kenneth Parry, *Depicting the Word: Byzantine Iconophile Thought of the Eighth and Ninth Centuries,* The Medieval Mediterranean Peoples, Economies and Cultures, 400–1453, vol. 12 (Leiden/New York/Cologne: E. J. Brill, 1996).

19. The motive behind this is discussed by Schönborn, *God's Human Face,* pp. 141–47. On Leo, see also Dumeige, *Nicée II,* pp. 58–68, 75–77.

denounce images."[20] John's contribution to the iconoclastic controversy thus comes from a place outside the Byzantine Empire. He takes up several of the threads that the theological tradition before him had prepared—among others Basil of Caesarea—and brings them together into an explicit theology of the image. With John we find a definition of the image for the first time.

According to John the image was both like and unlike that which it depicted. The likeness establishes a relationship between the image and the depicted, while the difference means that the image and the depiction cannot be identified with each other. The Son is an image of the Father that is identical in being with the depicted, but a difference remains between all other images and their eternal idea. When someone venerates the Christ images, this veneration does not appertain to the image in itself—which would be idolatry—but to the image's original, Christ himself. If God himself has now become human in Christ, why should one not then make oneself an image of Christ? In his first discourse John writes the following:

> In former times God, who is without form or body, could never be depicted. But now when God is seen in the flesh conversing with men, I make an image of the God whom I see. I do not worship matter; I worship the Creator of matter who became matter for my sake, who willed to take His abode in matter; who worked out my salvation through matter. Never will I cease honoring the matter which wrought my salvation![21]

The decisive twist in salvation history is that God becomes visible in flesh and blood for the sake of humanity. The prohibition on images is still in force for that which is not included in the incarnation. The invisible God cannot be represented in image, and it is not right to venerate the image as God himself. But the theological basis for an absolute prohibition on images has fallen away in and with this becoming human. The human being is constituted through her or his embodiment and senses, and through images and scriptures Christians of later times can experience Christ with their senses as well. John of Damascus can therefore be said to occupy a clearly anti-spiritualistic standpoint.

20. John of Damascus, *On the Divine Images,* trans. David Anderson (Crestwood, NY: St. Vladimir's Seminary Press, 2000). On John, see Dumeige, *Nicée II,* pp. 68–74; Lange, *Bild und Wort,* pp. 106–40; Schönborn, *God's Human Face,* pp. 191–200, but primarily Andrew Louth, *St John Damascene: Tradition and Originality in Byzantine Theology,* Oxford Early Christian Studies (New York: Oxford University Press, 2002).

21. John of Damascus, *Images,* p. 23 (I, 18).

Because John wrote his treatises outside the Byzantine Empire, they had no great immediate effect on the iconoclasm in Constantinople. After the death of Leo III his son Constantine became emperor.[22] Constantine V continued and intensified Leo's iconoclastic policies. Moreover, according to the Byzantine chronicler Theophanes, Leo's son had polluted the baptismal as a child, and so received the nickname Kopronymos (i.e., "the shit") from his opponents. In the year 754 Constantine summoned a synod that would deal with the image question. This synod took place in Hieria, between Chrysopolis and Chalcedon. Constantine also wanted to direct the negotiations via a text he had authored, which brought the iconoclastic controversy up to a higher plane of argumentation. In this, Constantine claimed that a true image is alike in essence to that which the image represents. He writes: "The icon of someone does not depict his nature but his person [prosōpon]."[23] A Christ image is therefore not possible, because the person Christ is of both divine and human nature, and the divine nature cannot be depicted. To depict Christ would therefore be to commit one of two heresies (as the synod in Hieria explicitly maintained): either to dissociate Christ's two natures ("Nestorianism") or to intermingle Christ's two natures ("monophysitism"). The Eucharist is the only true image of Christ, according to Constantine, because only it is of the same being as Christ himself. The veneration of images was accordingly a Christological heresy.

In accordance with Constantine's will, the synod in Hieria denounced the veneration of images, and condemned John of Damascus as well. Following the synod the persecutions from Constantine became even more intense. The monasteries were plundered and iconoclastic church decorations (i.e., decorative images with motifs from nature) were installed. The established image policy would not be alleviated until the son, the later emperor Leo IV, took power together with his wife Irene (ca. 752–803) after his father's death in 775.

In 769 Constantine V had given his son the Athenian Irene in marriage. Irene was both politically savvy and had a positive view of images.[24] However, she kept her iconophilia hidden until her father-in-law had died. Then she could influence her husband the emperor to alleviate the persecutions. Leo IV died already in 780. He had then already appointed his son Constantine VI (born 771, dead by 805) as his successor. He was only nine years old at

22. See Dumeige, *Nicée II*, pp. 78–98, and Schönborn, *God's Human Face*, pp. 168–78.

23. Constantine V quoted from Nikephoros of Constantinople, *Antirrhetici tres adversus Constantinum Copronymum*, Patrologiae Cursus Completus, Series Graeca, vol. 100, ed. J. P. Migne (Paris, 1865), col. 297 A (book 1, chapter 39).

24. Dumeige, *Nicée II*, p. 98.

his father's death, which meant that Irene acquired more influence over the empire's affairs. She delayed a while in implementing her reforms, but when the patriarch Paul IV renounced his office in 784, Irene and Constantine VI sent a missive to Pope Hadrian with the request that he convene an ecumenical council. The layman Tarasius, the empress's secretary, was chosen as the new patriarch. He got started with the preparations and the council met the first of August 786, in the Church of the Holy Apostles in Constantinople. This council disbanded the imperial bodyguard that had remained loyal to the earlier iconoclastic policy. In May 787 they met again in Nicea. Tarasius was the president of the council.

The second Nicene council argued that both scripture and the oral tradition as it had been conveyed through Christian praxis showed that God allowed images.[25] This was also evident through the—as they believed—authentic depictions of Christ that existed, and the miracles that occurred thanks to these images. Nicea II argued that Constantine V's synod in Hieria was a heretical synod. Against its iconoclasm they cited quotations from the fathers that showed the orthodoxy of the use of images. The council established that there was a difference between venerating *(proskynein)* and worshiping *(latreuein)* an image.[26] Worship was due only to the very being of God, while veneration was an appropriate attitude towards the images, since this veneration went back to that which the images depicted (citing Basil): "the honour paid to an image traverses it, reaching the model *[prōtotypon]*; and he who venerates the image, venerates the person *[hypostasin]* represented in that image."[27] The more one views the images, the greater the remembrance of and longing for the prototype.[28] The theological foundation

---

25. For the crucial definitions, see *Decrees of the Ecumenical Councils,* volume one: *Nicaea I to Lateran V,* ed. Norman P. Tanner (London/Washington, DC: Sheed & Ward/Georgetown University Press, 1990), pp. 133–37. The second Nicene council is discussed by Dumeige, *Nicée II,* pp. 99–150.

26. Undertaking such a semantic distinction between *proskynein* and *latreuein* was not a given, considering the fact that the Septuagint uses both of these Greek terms in parallel in the classic passage for the prohibition of images, Exodus 20:5: *ou proskynēseis autois oude mē latreusēs autois,* where the pronoun referred to *eidōlon* and *homoiōma.* In the translation (from the Hebrew) of the ESV: "You shall not bow down to them or serve them." It is thus not until Nicea II that the distinction is conceptualized as such.

27. *Decrees of the Ecumenical Councils,* volume one, ed. Norman P. Tanner, p. 136.

28. The second Nicene council established that it is legitimate to venerate images, not that it is obligatory. The obligation was first asserted at the anti-Photian council in 869–870. See Leonid Ouspensky, *Theology of the Icon,* vol. 2, trans. Anthony Gythiel and Elizabeth Meyendorff (Crestwood, NY: St. Vladimir's Seminary Press, 1992), p. 212.

for the possibility of the images was God's becoming human in Christ. The one who represents Christ in human form in a picture does not dissolve the unity between Christ's human and divine nature, but testifies that the Word of God really, and not just seemingly, became human.

Nicaea II's decision was translated into Latin and sent to the Western church. However, a misunderstanding arose when the document was translated from Greek to Latin, which was one of the reasons that Nicea was strongly criticized by the West. This criticism first occurred in the writing *Capitulare de imaginibus,* which is also called *Libri Carolini,* and later in the condemnation of the council by the synod summoned by Charlemagne in Frankfurt, 794.[29] This was an expression of imperial rather than papal politics—Pope Hadrian I defended the decision of the second Nicene council. In the West people were relatively unaware of the Christological issues that Nicea II was focused on. Nicea II was chiefly criticized by the Franks and Charlemagne because images were not found in the Gospels. Images served only for decoration and instruction, they argued. Nicea II was thus interpreted in the West from an entirely different understanding of images; with its cult of relics, the West emphasized physical rather than figurative likeness.[30]

Nicea II entailed neither the end of the iconoclasm, nor a definitive theology of the image. Even if the council in Nicea was a successful undertaking with regard to the restoration of the veneration of images in the empire, Irene and her son Constantine VI's remaining policies were in many ways a failure. In 790 Constantine dethroned his mother, but after two years he made her his co-empress. Irene eventually had his eyes gouged out, after which he went into exile. Irene could then rule alone until she was deposed in 802. Her finance minister and chancellor Nikephoros (ca. 760–811) was proclaimed emperor. When the patriarch Tarasius died in 806, emperor Nikephoros I appointed an imperial employee who was also named Nikephoros (750–829) to patriarch. This patriarch Nikephoros would come to be one of the foremost theologians of the image. His time as patriarch was short, however, as an iconoclastic emperor would come to replace his namesake on the throne, namely emperor Leo V, who had ascended to the throne in 813 when emperor Nikephoros I's son-in-law and successor Michael I Rangabe abdicated. With Leo V's ascension the war against images flamed up again, and in 815 he called an anti-Nicene synod

29. Dumeige, *Nicée II,* pp. 154–57.
30. Belting, *Das echte Bild,* p. 153.

in Constantinople, which would reinstate Hieria. Patriarch Nikephoros criticized the imperial image policy and chose to abdicate and go into exile in 815, rather than support the emperor's policy.

Patriarch Nikephoros devoted himself in the years between 811 and 828 to contemplating the image problem.[31] He emphasized the relationship between word and image, hearing and sight, especially strongly. According to Nikephoros, the words and images of scripture are equated with each other by the tradition. In addition to their use for those who cannot read, the images have a special significance for conveying the faith to people. Sight still has its primacy over hearing. Namely, that which one sees conveys its message more thoroughly, more quickly, and more immediately than that which one hears, which is fleeting and easy to forget. Through sight, the gospel is communicated in a more tangible way. The image is also a symbol for Christ's saving work, in that it makes it present in a dynamic way.[32] The image thus finds its function in relation to the word—and vice versa. Both aim to make present, i.e., bring to life the same message. They differ in terms of technique, but are united by the same theme and goal.

Nikephoros also highlighted how the doctrine of the image hung together with the question of salvation. To argue—as the image critics, and not least Constantine V, did—that Christ as the Word become human cannot be described with regard to his human nature would be a denial of the reality of the incarnation. Then Christ would have only seemingly become human, and so the salvation of the person would be compromised, because—in the words of Gregory of Nazianzus—"For that which He has not assumed He has not healed; but that which is united to His Godhead is also saved."[33] Christ's two natures belong indivisibly together, without being blended together, and thus a painted image of Christ can refer to the prototype without the image being made divine either, which would be idolatry, or being disconnected from its prototype, which would make the Christ images more or less meaningless. Now if Nikephoros is correct, the images are necessary in the sense that their legitimacy follows from both the saving action of God and from theological anthropology.

---

31. See Alexander, *Patriarch,* as well as Dumeige, *Nicée II,* pp. 166–70 and Lange, *Bild und Wort,* pp. 201–16.

32. Lange, *Bild und Wort,* pp. 206–7.

33. Gregory of Nazianzus, "Epistle 101," in *Nicene and Post-Nicene Fathers,* ser. 2, vol. 7: *S. Cyril of Jerusalem, S. Gregory Nazianzen,* ed. Philip Schaff (Grand Rapids: Eerdmans, 1977), p. 440 (32).

Theodore the Studite (759–826) is also counted among the foremost theologians of the image.[34] He was abbot for the Stoudios monastery in Constantinople from 789, where he took a stand for the images, with the result that he had to go into exile as well. In his three *Antirrheseis,* Theodore argued that the Christ images were as old as the Gospels. Christ himself had sent an image of himself to King Abgar from Edessa, and thus the Gospels as well as the images could be traced back to Christ himself. As with the books of the Gospels, the images could be venerated, but not worshiped. Theodore's theology of the image was further characterized by the fact that he made a qualitative distinction between a natural depiction and an artificially produced image. Only *one* natural image exists, namely the Son as a depiction of the Father. Here the depiction does not differ from the prototype in substance. In contrast with this natural depiction, the produced image exhibits both likeness and difference with regard to its prototype. If the difference between prototype and depiction were complete, no depiction would be possible. But because Christ has become human, the Word has thereby become visible and possible to represent as an image. If this were not possible, i.e., if it were impossible to represent his embodied form, he would not be a true human. The possibility and legitimacy of the images go together with the saving action of God, according to Theodore, and the one who denies the images therefore also denies God's salvation.

What is it then that is depicted? Here Theodore brings a crucial innovation in the theology of the image, which will come to be normative for its later formulation: it is not the human nature itself, nor the divine nature that is depicted, but Christ's *person (hypostasis)*. He writes: "When anyone is portrayed, it is not the nature *[hē physis]*, but the hypostasis *[hē hypostasis]* which is portrayed."[35] An image that represents a human is a depiction of a person, because human nature always occurs in concrete individuals with their specific attributes, and never in general. The universal may be understood through reason, but sensory perceptions only apprehend the particular.[36] Such is the case with Christ as well, and that makes it possible to depict him.[37]

34. See Dumeige, *Nicée II,* pp. 170–74, Lange, *Bild und Wort,* pp. 217–32, and Schönborn, *God's Human Face,* pp. 219–35.

35. Theodoros Stoudites, *Antirrhetici tres adversus Iconomachos,* Patrologiae Cursus Completus, Series Graeca, vol. 99, ed. J. P. Migne (Paris, 1860), 405 A; St. Theodore the Studite, *On the Holy Icons,* trans. Catharine P. Roth (Crestwood, NY: St. Vladimir's Seminary Press, 1981), p. 90 (III, 34).

36. Stoudites, *Antirrhetici,* 397 A; p. 83 (III, 15).

37. Stoudites, *Antirrhetici,* 396D–397A; pp. 82f. (III, 15, 16).

According to the Christology that was adopted by the council of Chalcedon in 451, Christ is one person in two natures, and Theodore makes use of this when he asserts that it is the person that is depicted. He also goes back to the council on images in Nicea, which asserted that it was the person that was represented in the image, though without giving this a theologically considered motivation—Theodoros was the first who provided such.

Theodore claimed that Christ is present in the Christ image through the relationship that is established between the image and the depicted person.[38] In other words, the Christ image is not a relic, it is not veneration-worthy in itself, except through its relationship to Christ. It is thus important as well that the name of the depicted is written on the image. Through this the relationship between the image and that which is depicted is unambiguous, which is necessary for the veneration that shall be shown the image.[39] One might say that for Theodore, as for other iconophiles, the image is a medium for being able to contemplate something beyond the image. But in Theodore's case it is not a matter of contemplating a purely spiritual reality, but of contemplating Christ who became human. Just as God's becoming human was not a step on a path to a higher, bodiless reality, the contemplation of the image is not a step on a path away from a physical vision towards a higher, spiritual vision. Physical sight does not need to be overcome, even if it does need to be purified. Visible images are thus not only for the "primitive." One cannot reach higher than the God who humbled God's own self in Christ, according to Theodore. It is the iconoclasts who stand for a devaluation of the material creation, not the iconophiles.

The iconophiles would eventually leave the iconoclastic controversy victorious. Leo V was murdered in 820 in Hagia Sofia by partisans of Michael II, but Michael, who became the new emperor, continued an iconoclastic policy even if the persecution of the iconophiles ceased.[40] Michael's son Theophilus (ca. 812–842), who became the new emperor in 829 (after having been co-regent since 821), also continued the principal iconoclastic policies, but resumed the persecution of the iconophiles as well. It was not until after Theophilus's death in 842, as well as the fact that his widow Theodora became the empire's leader as the guardian of his son Michael III (840–867), that image veneration was reestablished as the official stance of

---

38. Stoudites, *Antirrhetici*, 344 BC; p. 33 (I, 12).
39. See Lange, *Bild und Wort*, pp. 224, 244–45.
40. Dumeige, *Nicée II*, pp. 174–89.

the Byzantine Empire.[41] As emerges from this account of the most intensive period in the history of the theology of the image, the question of the
images was at the same time theologically profound and politically inflam-
matory. From our contemporary perspective this may seem like a tragic confusion, but we ought to nonetheless remind ourselves that this conflict was
not "only" about religious images, but about how one ought to understand
human relationality—to God, to other humans, and to one's own embodiment—and that it therefore inevitably touches to some degree on what we
now call politics.

The Theology of the Icon

Once the veneration of images became the Byzantine Empire's official stance,
the production of images could take place without fear of intervention by the
state against the artists. The theology of the image that had been formulated
now came to be guiding for the production of images in the Eastern church.
This did not mean that the images themselves had no story. There is a rich
history to the development of the Christ image, with many twists and turns
leading up to what today are usually called icons. I will not treat this history
here, however, but will instead say something more about the theology of
the icon as it has been understood by classical and contemporary theologians
of the image. I have already gotten into the theology of the image through
several of its classical representatives—John of Damascus, the patriarch Nikephoros, and Theodore the Studite. Here, however, I will give an account of
the theology of the icon from a systematic rather than a historical perspective.

By way of introduction it may be worth pointing out that an icon need
not be painted on wooden paneling with tempera paint.[42] Icons that have
been executed on or through other materials, for example, textiles, mosaic, ivory, metal, and stone, are of the same theological dignity as icons on
wooden paneling, even if it is these that are often called icons in everyday
speech. Additionally, the idiom of the icon is generally strongly stylized with
fields of uniform color. The icon's background symbolizes the light of divine
glory, often represented with golden pigment.[43] White is related to gold,

41. For the continued debate around images within the Orthodox church, see Ouspensky,
Theology of the Icon, vol. 2.

42. A good introduction to the history and theology of the icon is given by Ulf Abel,
Ikonen—bilden av det heliga (Hedermora, Sweden: Gidlunds Bokförlag, 1989).

43. See Ouspensky, *Theology of the Icon,* vol. 2, pp. 495–96.

and can also be used to represent the divine light. Even red and blue often have their specific meanings. Along with form and color, the icon painter's method of production is mandated by the tradition as well: the icon painter's devotional life at his icon painting, how the colors that are used should be produced, etc. For the icon painter, in contrast with the Romantic artist, it is not a matter of expressing oneself in one's painting, but of finding one's freedom by submitting to a relatively well-defined tradition that regulates how a particular sort of Christ icon should be produced.

The starting point for the icons and their theology is the Chalcedonian Christology. A contemporary theologian of the icon, Leonid Ouspensky, writes the following in his book *Theology of the Icon*:

> The icon of Jesus Christ, the God-Man, is an expression of the dogma of Chalcedon in image; indeed, it represents the person of the Son of God who became man, who by His divine nature is consubstantial with the Father and by His human nature is consubstantial with us, 'similar to us in everything except sin,' in the expression of Chalcedon.[44]

The icon is an attempt to express the Chalcedonian Christology as an image, and its theology follows Theodore the Studite when he asserted that the icon does not depict Christ's natures, but Christ's person. That Christ can be represented as an image is dependent on the fact that Christ is the second person in the Trinity, the one who adopted human form. The Father—it is claimed—it is not possible to depict, because the Father has not been incarnated, and therefore remains invisible. Through the incarnation, the Son has let himself become possible to represent, and it is God's own initiative that gives this possibility. The Spirit can be represented as it has been manifested: as a dove at Jesus' baptism, as tongues of fire at Pentecost. Here it is a question of manifestation rather than incarnation, i.e., the Spirit cannot be said to *be* a dove in the same way that the Son *is* human in Christ.

But it is not Christ's person in general that is depicted, but the glorified Christ, Christ as it was thought that the disciples saw him on the Mount of Transfiguration (see chapter 5). Why? The theological reason probably lies in the fact that the icon attempts to depict not only how the human being appeared in her Adamic original sinlessness, but even more what the result of the divinization of the human being will be, her "transfiguration"

---

44. Ouspensky, *Theology of the Icon*, vol. 1, trans. Anthony Gythiel and Elizabeth Meyendorff (Crestwood, NY: St. Vladimir's Seminary Press, 1978), p. 152.

or realization of that which Adam did not know how to achieve, namely a perfect harmony between human nature and divine nature. Ouspensky explains the transfiguration in the following way:

> The transfiguration is a manifestation, perceptible by the whole human being, of the divine glory of the second person of the Holy Trinity, who, in His Incarnation, is inseparable from His divine nature, common to both the Father and the Holy Spirit.[45]

But it is not only that God has become human in Christ, but that the human being shall also become divine.[46] The transfiguration or the making divine of us humans is a part of the restoration and transformation of the entire cosmos, and it includes the embodied and material as well as the spiritual. It is also because of this that salvation can be made visible, so to speak, through the icons. Through this it namely becomes clear that physical sight cannot be separated from spiritual sight. The salvation of the human is, if you will, not something that happens apart from her embodiment, but even *through* her embodiment and *with* her body. The transfiguration of the human entails, according to Ouspensky, a transformation of her corruptible embodiment into an incorruptible embodiment. The characteristic features of human embodiment are retained, but it becomes, so to speak, transilluminated thanks to the relationship to God. The icon's ambition is not artistic naturalism, but to convey "the perception of the spiritual world."[47]

Ouspensky also states that the icon does not represent the divine, but instead indicates the person's participation in the divine life.[48] Does this mean that Ouspensky contradicts himself and says that the icon is not a Christ-representation? I do not believe that this is the case, but instead understand it as a qualification of what sort of representation an icon is. The icon's utmost aim is not to portray Christ as a sort of reference for what Christ looks like. It has no interest in "the human Jesus" independent of the entirety of salvation history, inclusive of the viewer's relationship to this story.[49] The aim is rather to indicate, i.e., point to, the salvation of the human being and to make it present. Expressed otherwise: according to the theology of the

45. Ouspensky, *Theology of the Icon*, vol. 1, p. 159.
46. Pelikan, *Imago Dei*, p. 96.
47. Ouspensky, *Theology of the Icon*, vol. 1, p. 178.
48. Ouspensky, *Theology of the Icon*, vol. 1, p. 166.
49. Cf. Vladimir Lossky, *The Mystical Theology of the Eastern Church* (Cambridge: James Clarke, 1957), p. 242.

icon, the right relationship to the icon is not a viewing at a distance, but an involved veneration, where the one who sees the icon becomes experientially participatory in that which the icon wants to communicate. It is therefore also not correct to say that an icon wants to graphically represent a doctrine or dogma, if this is understood as a theoretical proposition. According to Ouspensky, the task of the icon is the same as that of the Gospel, to "reveal the true relationship between God and man."[50] This aim is existential, rather than intellectual.

The icon could be said to be a sort of symbol. A symbol contains—according to Paul Evdokimov, another Russian-Orthodox theologian from Paris—"in itself the presence of what is symbolized. It fulfills the function of revealing a meaning and at the same time it becomes an expressive and effective container of the 'presence.'"[51] The presence that the symbol presents is always represented indirectly. The icon thus becomes a sort of sacrament, as it becomes the medium for God's personal presence.[52]

With many icons we also find a "reverse perspective." This may be compared to the perspective painting that emerged from the Renaissance on, where the eye of the beholder was made the starting point for the way the view of the depicted was perspectivized (see chapter 4). In contrast, in the icon it is those who are depicted who have a perspective on the viewer. Thus the icon does not attempt to bring about the three-dimensional effect of depth that the art of perspective strives for, but is a relatively "flat," two-dimensional display that thereby even attempts to "denaturalize" the world that the person inhabits in favor of another world. The reverse perspective, however, means that the viewer of the icon also becomes the one who is viewed: "The world of the icon is turned *toward man*."[53] If the perspective of Alberti and other Renaissance artists can be compared to the view one has from a window, one might say that the icon can be compared to a window where the light falls in on us. The perspective does not vanish away into a distant horizon, but is opened towards the one who views the icon. One might say that the icon's "third dimension," its space, lies before rather than behind it, i.e., in the actual space in front of the icon. Thus the persons who are represented by the icon are united with the people who view the icon by

50. Ouspensky, *Theology of the Icon*, vol. 2, p. 491.

51. Paul Evdokimov, *The Art of the Icon: A Theology of Beauty*, trans. Steven Bigham (Redondo Beach, CA: Oakwood, 1990), p. 167.

52. Evdokimov, *The Art of the Icon*, p. 178. Cf. Pelikan, *Imago Dei*, pp. 95-96.

53. Evdokimov, *The Art of the Icon*, p. 225. Cf. Ouspensky, *Theology of the Icon*, vol. 2, pp. 491-95.

virtue of a shared spatiality. This lies in line with the icon's endeavor to place the person in a world other than the one she normally belongs in.

That the icon wants to display another world does not preclude, according to Orthodox theology, the possibility that the icon represents the earthly Jesus correctly. Reference is often made to a representation of Christ that is *acheiropoiētos,* "not painted by human hand."[54] This is sometimes also called *mandylion,* which means "linen cloth." This icon shows Christ's face on a piece of cloth, and has given rise to a vast number of reproductions. The legend behind this icon is that a King Abgar from Edessa wanted to have a portrait of Christ, and so sent a painter to depict him. But the radiance that went out from Christ's face made it such that the painter was not able to paint him. Then Christ took a cloak and pressed it against his face and sent it with the painter to King Abgar. We therefore know what Christ looked like, and the first icon thus has its origin with Christ himself. This legend is first mentioned in the fifth century, and is retold by, among others, John of Damascus. The piece of cloth itself, on which Christ is supposed to have left an impression of his face, has disappeared, probably destroyed, since the crusaders plundered Constantinople in 1204, where the icon had been moved to from Edessa in 945. There are beliefs that the evangelist Luke had painted several icons of Mary together with the baby Jesus. Parallel legends also exist within Western Christianity, which speaks of a piece of cloth with Christ's face, the so-called *vera icona,* i.e., "the true image." According to one version of the legend about this, Saint Veronica (the name is an amalgamation of *vera icona*) gave Christ a cloth to dry his sweat with on the way to Calvary. When she got the kerchief back, his facial features had fastened to it. These different "true images" have resulted in the establishment of a tradition about what Christ looked like, a tradition that has had a very great impact within Eastern as well as Western Christianity, and has thus made it possible to recognize in radically different images at least a family likeness between some of these early depictions. What connected the Abgar image to the Veronica image was the idea of an authentic depiction, which did not exclude the possibility that this idea could be realized in a number of different ways.[55] For example, there exist a number of interpretations and paraphrases of "not painted by human hand," the icon

54. For discussions of both "that not painted by human hands" and the Luke images and the Veronica image see Belting, *Likeness,* pp. 49–57, 208–24; Gabriele Finaldi et al., *The Image of Christ,* pp. 86–96; Ouspensky, *Theology of the Icon,* vol. 1, pp. 51–64; Alex Stock, *Poetische Dogmatik: Christologie: 2. Schrift und Gesicht* (Paderborn: Schöningh, 1996), pp. 105–37.

55. Belting, *Likeness,* pp. 222–24.

that, if anything, has the very "prototype" for the collective tradition of paintings.[56] For the early use of images, these "true images" guaranteed the exact correspondence between depiction and original—especially "not by human hand" and the Veronica image, since here no painter comes between depiction and original.

So even if there is an attempt to paint Christ's "true image," the "realism" of these representations is minimal, because the icons do not strive for any naturalism when they depict Christ or any other person, nor do they relate those depicted to their historical context. This does not mean that the representation is without context, but that it is another sort of context. It is not the person independent of her relationship to God that is the focus of the icon's interest, but the divinely made humanity, the humanity that is revealed in Jesus on the Mount of Transfiguration.[57] The theological interest in likeness to the original in the authentic Christ depiction can therefore be said to be motivated by the idea of Christ's presence via the icon, rather than by an independent interest in Christ's features. The context, the perspective on the person Jesus of Nazareth, one might say, is constituted by the background of gold that represents the divine light. Only this light allows us to see Jesus, as well as all other humans, in their proper light. Thus the icon wants to bring about a "recontextualization" of the "familiar" world, a new way to look at the world with a definite purpose. Rowan Williams writes of this purpose: "The point of the icon is to give us a window into an alien frame of reference that is at the same time the structure that will make definitive sense of the world we inhabit."[58] To formulate it in a different way: the icon expresses how the Christian church understands Christ liturgically.[59] I will return to this in the next chapter.

In summary, I want to conclude this portion by stating that that which characterizes the Christ image according to the theology of the image is that it wants to make the human, inclusive of her embodiment, participatory in the divine life by inserting her world into another context—another relationality—than her more mundane context. The gaze that the icon both configures and calls for is a gaze that both engages and is engaged—both active and passive.

---

56. Belting, *Likeness,* p. 235.

57. Lossky, *The Mystical Theology,* p. 243.

58. Rowan Williams, *Lost Icons: Reflections on Cultural Bereavement* (Edinburgh: T. & T. Clark, 2000), p. 2.

59. Evdokimov, *The Art of the Icon,* p. 195.

Image and Incarnation in the West

The Western church's theological reflection on the image—and even its concrete, painted images—has a somewhat different history than the Byzantine.
There is no equivalent to the Byzantine iconoclasm, even if there are discussions over the being or nonbeing of the images in the Western church as well.
The Reformation is usually named as an example of a period where a similar
iconoclasm occurs, but at the same time the iconoclasm of the Reformation
differs from the Byzantine in that the contrast between word and image had
come to be different, partially contingent on the development of the art of
printing.[60] Images were not quite as controversial for Lutheranism as for
the Reformed theologians and the radical reformers. Nor do we find any
icons or contributions to the theology of the image like those of the Byzantine iconoclasm. For the Orthodox church the image has, ever since Nicea
II and even earlier, taken a unique position that hardly has its like even in
the iconophilic portion of the Western church. This does not mean that the
Western church in practice would be without images and reflection on the
theology of the image, only that this would look different.

Church historian Arnold Angenendt believes that one may roughly divide ancient and medieval iconography into three periods: Antiquity, which
let Christ take form as liberator and savior; late Antiquity up until the twelfth
century, which fashioned Christ as God and judge; and the high and late
Middle Ages, whose Christ image was the groom and the suffering Christ.[61]
The emphasis on Christ's divinity within theology, as well as in pictorial representations, would obscure Christ's humanity for a long time in the Middle
Ages. Even if one in principle assented to Chalcedon's confession of Christ
as "truly God and truly man," the emphasis was different than that in, for
example, the New Testament.[62] However, the twelfth century marks a shift
in epoch, where Christ's humanity, as well as the human as such, came to
be revalued.[63] The one who initiates the new interest in Christ's humanity

---

60. Cf. Bengt Arvidsson, *Bildstrid Bildbruk Bildlära: En idéhistorisk undersökning av bildfrågan inom den begynnande lutherska traditionen under 1500-talet,* Studia Theologica Lundensia
41 (Lund: Lund University Press, 1987), together with Belting, *Das echte Bild,* pp. 150–216.

61. Arnold Angenendt, *Geschichte der Religiosität im Mittelalter* (Darmstadt: Wissenschaftliche Buchgesellschaft, 1997), p. 123.

62. Angenendt, *Geschichte,* pp. 138–41.

63. Cf. M.-D. Chenu, *Nature, Man, and Society in the Twelfth Century: Essays on New
Theological Perspectives in the Latin West,* new edition, selected, ed. and trans. Jerome Taylor
and Lester K. Little (Chicago: University of Chicago Press, 1979).

is usually said to be the French Cistercian monk Bernard of Clairvaux (ca. 1090–1153).[64] With him one finds an emphasis on the suffering of Christ as well as on human discipleship. Christ has become human, in order that humanity will be able to follow in his life path.

Francis of Assisi (1181/82–1226) has probably become even more significant for the emphasis on Christ's humanity.[65] Francis contributed to the revaluation of human nature during the twelfth century, which also meant a new interest in both Christ's humanity and in the human condition in general. Francis came to identify himself with Christ's suffering on the cross to such a degree that he received the stigmata. In addition, Christmas as the days celebrated in commemoration of Christ's birth came to play a large role for Francis and for the piety that emanated from him. That Christ was born as a human meant that Christ came to share the human condition. At Christmas 1223 Francis erected the first nativity scene in a cave in the town of Greccio in central Italy, and he thus made the birth of Christ concrete in a way that would have great repercussions—still significant in our time—for how Christ was represented in images by the western church. Art scholar Neil MacGregor writes:

> The Franciscan emphasis on the Incarnation re-humanized Christ. It also restored the Christ Child to the poor. The main point of this child was not that he was worshipped by rulers representing the whole of creation. It was his acceptance of the mean grubby business of life on earth. And so the very first visitors to the manger are rehabilitated: after centuries spent in the shadow of the Kings, the shepherds could now star in their own Adoration.[66]

Christ becomes a child who, just like other children, needs to be taken care of and attended to, and thus can arouse compassion. At the same time, Francis's highlighting of the Christ child and his innovative use of Christ's manger did not involve any sentimentalization of Christ. The understand-

---

64. Cf. Peter Dinzelbacher, *Bernhard von Clairvaux: Leben und Werk des berühmten Zisterziensers*, Gestalten des Mittelalters und der Renaissance, ed. Peter Herde (Darmstadt: Wissenschaftliche Buchgesellschaft, 1998).

65. See Jaroslav Pelikan, *Jesus through the Centuries: His Place in the History of Culture* (New York: Perennial Library, 1987), pp. 133–44. See also Pelikan's *The Illustrated Jesus through the Centuries* (New Haven/London: Yale University Press, 1997), pp. 143–55, which offers a somewhat abbreviated version of the text in the former work, but with more images.

66. MacGregor and Langmuir, *Seeing Salvation*, p. 53, cf. pp. 45–59.

ing that this child was born to suffer and die on a cross existed the whole time in Francis's awareness. This thus becomes God's identification with the human condition both in the vulnerability of the human at birth and with her suffering in life.

The Renaissance of the fifteenth and sixteenth centuries was interested in the humanity of Jesus as well. The Renaissance has often been interpreted as a naturalistic revolt against sterile medieval theology and its orientation towards the divine rather than the human. In his presentation of the theology of the icon Ouspensky also claims that the Western Renaissance is naturalistic, which in his eyes is a criticism of its images as potential bearers of piety.[67] There is, however, the possibility of seeing a greater continuity between late medieval piety and Renaissance art, not least as regards the emphasis on the humanity of Christ. Art scholar Leo Steinberg has advanced a controversial thesis in his book *The Sexuality of Christ in Renaissance Art and in Modern Oblivion,* namely that what modern eyes see as naturalism in fact did not at all appear to Renaissance contemporaries to be a revolt against Christological speculations.[68] On the contrary, the interest in naturalistic renderings of Christ should be understood against the background of the incarnational piety that permeated the society of the time. Steinberg writes: "Lifelikeness posed no threat, because these Renaissance artists regarded the godhead in the person of Jesus as too self-evident to be dimmed by his manhood."[69] The fact that Renaissance art is perceived by modern eyes as being without reference to a transcendent dimension depends instead on the fact that we no longer share the religious frame of reference that was a matter of course for the Renaissance artists and Renaissance people in general. What we perceive as a natural gesture, for example when the baby Jesus touches Mary's chin, is for the Renaissance a ritually shaped rendering of spiritual fellowship.[70] But for the Renaissance artists, who worked against the background of the entirety of the previous image tradition with its emphasis on the divinity of Christ, there was no need to feature this divinity since it constituted a presupposition for the representation of Christ. Compared to, for example, the Orthodox icon, the greater naturalism is a consequence of a different theological emphasis. Steinberg writes:

67. Ouspensky, *Theology of the Icon,* vol. 2, p. 486.

68. Leo Steinberg, *The Sexuality of Christ in Renaissance Art and in Modern Oblivion,* 2nd revised and expanded edition (Chicago/London: University of Chicago Press, 1996).

69. Steinberg, *The Sexuality of Christ,* p. 6.

70. Steinberg, *The Sexuality of Christ,* pp. 3–6, together with the excurses pp. 110–18.

Where the maker of a Byzantine cult image enthroned the incarnate Word as an imperial Christ, satisfied that the manhood assumed was sufficiently evident in his filiation from Mary, the art of the West sought to realize that same manhood as the common flesh of humanity. Realism, the more penetrating the better, was consecrated a form of worship.[71]

Even if there is reason to be critical of Steinberg's view of the "Byzantine cult images," I believe that his point regarding the Renaissance is insightful: "naturalism" stood, so to speak, in the service of theological expression.

More precise is Steinberg's thesis that there is a range of depictions of the baby Jesus where the genitals are presented in a similar way that cannot be a coincidence. We find such representations from 1260 onwards, and they come into their flowering in the Renaissance.[72] This fact has been neglected for a half millennium, Steinberg claims. There are, however, theological grounds for these genital references in pictorial representations. Namely, they intended to seal the fact of the incarnation in image: "to profess that God once embodied himself in a human nature is to confess that the eternal, there and then, became mortal and sexual."[73] That the Christ child was naked was therefore not (or at least not only) motivated by an interest in nude paintings influenced by Antiquity, but was primarily for the sake of incarnational theology. The tiny penis of the baby Jesus symbolized the fact that the Word had become human in Jesus Christ in fact, rather than only apparently. A sexless human being would not be a genuine person.[74] What separates the Renaissance's depictions of the naked baby Jesus from Antiquity's nude painting is the further dramatizing of the nakedness of the baby

71. Steinberg, *The Sexuality of Christ*, pp. 10–15. Cf. p. 11: "But for a Western artist nurtured in Catholic orthodoxy—for him the objective was not so much to proclaim the divinity of the babe as to declare the *humanation* of God."

72. Steinberg, *The Sexuality of Christ*, pp. 28–30.

73. Steinberg, *The Sexuality of Christ*, p. 15. Cf. pp. 15–18. Steinberg also says that the artists attempted to present Christ as the one whose sexuality was unaffected by the Fall, something I do not discuss here. However, Hans Belting is skeptical that Steinberg's thesis would be especially revolutionary—see *Das echte Bild*, pp. 109–13. Jesus is of course not depicted as someone who *exercised* his sexuality, which differentiates him from other human bodies.

74. This undoubtedly leads to Jesus being clearly identified as a *man*, which has led to a critique of Steinberg's thesis from Caroline Walker Bynum, who says that Jesus is often represented as androgynous in the later Middle Ages. See Bynum's critique in "The Body of Christ in the Later Middle Ages: A Reply to Leo Steinberg," *Fragmentation and Redemption: Essays on Gender and the Human Body in Medieval Religion* (New York: Zone Books, 1992), pp. 79–117, together with Steinberg's reply, "Ad Bynum," *The Sexuality of Christ*, pp. 364–89.

Jesus, Steinberg claims. Jesus' nakedness is often depicted through the active removal of a loincloth or similar piece of cloth.[75] This symbolizes an active unveiling or revelation of Christ's humanity.

This audacity in the depiction of the sexuality of Christ as evidence of his authentic humanity will be actively forgotten from the sixteenth century on, Steinberg says.[76] It was no longer seen as acceptable to exhibit Christ's genitals. Alberti's text on the art of painting—which I referred to in chapter 4 apropos the significance of perspective—exhorts artists to "let the indecent parts of a body and all those that are less graceful be covered by a cloth, or by fronds, or by a hand."[77] With this, one forfeited certain insights from what Steinberg sees as a theologically unique pictorial art. He writes:

> Because Renaissance culture not only advanced an incarnational theology (as the Greek Church had also done), but evolved representational modes adequate to its expression, we may take Renaissance art to be the first and last phase of Christian art that can claim full Christian orthodoxy. Renaissance art—including the broad movement begun c. 1260—harnessed the theological impulse and developed the requisite stylistic means to attest the utter carnality of God's humanation in Christ.[78]

The naturalism as well as the nakedness in the representations of Christ are theologically motivated by the doctrine of the incarnation, which was a self-evident background for the art of the Renaissance, and which the Renaissance artists managed to express in a unique way.

Steinberg primarily backs up his thesis through an overwhelming body of images, not least in the second edition of *The Sexuality of Christ*. The textual sources themselves are silent about this theological stress among the Renaissance artists.[79] Steinberg's thesis has, not unexpectedly, been perceived as controversial, which has forced him to defend his position in a longer retrospective postscript to the second edition. Let me leave these controversies for now and instead refer to the fact that historian of theology Pelikan in his account of Jesus' place in cultural history has seen Steinberg's thesis as a subtler interpretation of the naturalism of the Renaissance than

75. Steinberg, *The Sexuality of Christ*, pp. 33–45.

76. Steinberg, *The Sexuality of Christ*, pp. 45–46.

77. Leon Battista Alberti, *On Painting: A New Translation and a Critical Edition*, ed. and trans. Rocco Sinisgalli (Cambridge: Cambridge University Press, 2013), p. 61 (book 2, §40).

78. Steinberg, *The Sexuality of Christ*, pp. 70–71.

79. Steinberg discusses this more thoroughly in *The Sexuality of Christ*, pp. 330–44.

the earlier contrastive interpretation.[80] Thus there is reason to believe that it actually is possible to find an objective continuity between the earlier Bernadine and Franciscan emphasis on Christ's humanity and the Renaissance representations of it.[81] Whether the incarnation had thus found its consummate mode of representation in the Renaissance, which is moreover characterized by "full Christian orthodoxy," is another question, where I remain more skeptical than Steinberg.

It was probably not such a great leap for Western pictorial art to depart from the sort of "theological naturalism" that Steinberg discusses in his book. This departure does not have to do so much with a fading interest in the representation of Christ in images, but rather with the changed conditions for such a representation. As I touched on in chapter 4, the gaze has a history, and this history also takes place within the history of the Western representation of Christ. In a chapter of her book *Black Sun: Depression and Melancholia,* the Romanian-born psychoanalyst and author Julia Kristeva discusses Renaissance artist Hans Holbein the Younger's painting *The Dead Christ in the Grave* (1521/1522, Öffentliche Kunstsammlung, Basel).[82] It is this painting that Dostoevsky writes about in his novel *The Idiot,* and there he lets Prince Mysjkin say that "[a] man could even lose his faith from that painting!"[83] Kristeva seizes on Dostoevsky's statement in *The Idiot* and claims that Holbein's painting is a dead Christ without the least hope of resurrection: "[T]here is not the slightest suggestion of transcendency."[84] Holbein's painting is an altarpiece that measures 30.5 by 200 centimeters, and is executed with oil on wood in dull, earthy colors. Its unusual dimensions are a part of its message: the dead Christ is portrayed full-length from the side and lies stretched out on a white cloth. The head is partially turned towards the viewer, and the entire right arm is visible. The body is covered only by a loincloth, and it is emaciated and tortured. According to Kristeva this is a painting that represents Christ without any hope of atonement, salvation, or resurrection. Christ is alone, nearly trapped in his crypt. The naturalization of Christ in painting has reached a high point here, and instead of hope there remains only a melancholy viewing of death. The dead Christ that Holbein

---

80. Pelikan, *Jesus through the Centuries,* pp. 147–48.

81. See John W. O'Malley, "Postscript," in Steinberg, *The Sexuality of Christ,* p. 214.

82. Julia Kristeva, "Holbein's Dead Christ," in *Black Sun: Depression and Melancholia,* trans. Leon S. Roches (New York: Columbia University Press, 1980), pp. 105–38.

83. Fyodor Dostoevsky, *The Idiot,* trans. Richard Pevear and Larissa Volokhonsky (New York: Vintage Classics, 2003), p. 218.

84. Kristeva, "Holbein's Dead Christ," p. 110.

paints is a completely demystified, or rather, de-iconized Christ who in no way presents a window on the divine. Death was no longer a moment on the way to something other, but merely life's inevitable terminus.

As theologian Alex Stock has noted, Holbein's painting is not rejected as a "Western heresy" because the church in both the East and the West professes Christ's "real and embodied" suffering.[85] However, this Christological doctrine is represented here in a way that would harass a person's faith, in that the utmost consequence of this suffering is graphically presented before the eyes of the beholder. In Dostoevsky's novel a simple domestic icon appears as the only possible "counter-image" to the atheistic crisis that Holbein's image triggers, Stock says. The potential possibility of an icon as such a "counter-image" would, we might imagine, lie in its different "relationality" compared to Holbein's painting. Even if Holbein's painting of Christ's body is intended as an altarpiece, and thus set in a liturgical context, it seems despite this to express a completely secularized and naturalized relationship between the observer and Christ. Compare this with the icon's striving, not primarily for "realism," but rather to see existence from the perspective of the divine light. The icon presupposes and expresses a different relationship between God and human being than the increasingly naturalistic depictions, as, for example, with Holbein's painting of the dead Christ.

The increasing naturalization of the image in the West during the eighteenth and nineteenth centuries partially goes together with the fact that the image exchanges, so-to-speak, ritual contexts, from the church to the museum, and thereby comes to be viewed with an aesthetic rather than a liturgical gaze. This change is significant because it entails a "subjectivizing" of the gaze of the viewer, an increased emphasis on the viewer's active imagination. As the French philosopher Luc Ferry has pointed out about the early modern aesthetic, this envisioned beauty not as something that existed in the object we view, but rather as something that had its ground in human consciousness.[86] The beauty of existence was not to be found in the harmonious ordering of the external world, as the ancient and medieval philosophers and

---

85. Alex Stock, *Poetische Dogmatik: Christologie. 3. Leib und Leben* (Paderborn/Munich/Vienna/Zürich: Schöningh, 1998), pp. 208–11.

86. Luc Ferry, *Homo Aestheticus: The Invention of Taste in the Democratic Age,* trans. Robert de Loaiza (Chicago: University of Chicago Press, 1993), pp. 7–32. Cf. what Diarmaid MacCulloch writes apropos the rise of the art of printing and the increasing literacy during the early sixteenth century in *Reformation: Europe's House Divided 1490–1700* (London: Allen Lane, 2003), p. 75: "[W]ithout any hint of doctrinal deviation, a new style of piety arose in that increasingly large section of society which valued book-learning for both profit and pleasure."

theologians imagined it. We do not experience pleasure because an object is beautiful in itself, but we call it beautiful because it gives pleasure.

But the change that led to the naturalization of the image is not only a matter of the "discovery of taste." The "secularizing" of the image, if I may express myself thus, also entailed that its production context became different, when the position of the painter in relationship to the painting changed from that of the craftsman to that of the artist. As Stock writes: "Art goes its own way outside the protectorate of religion."[87] Likewise, the horizon of understanding for image creation itself (as for image interpretation) changes; the universe is no longer interpreted theologically, but naturalistically. Even when artists relate to an earlier iconographic tradition by, for example, representing an image of Christ, this involves different overtones than before, and implicates a different relationship between the image and religion, not least because such an image often claims to be precisely a solitary, unique image, which should not be understood in relationship to the entirety of the "image cosmos" that the liturgical use of images refers to. The question is whether this contrast does not pertain to the Renaissance paintings that Steinberg discusses as well. If this is the case, the continuity between ancient and medieval incarnational theology in these images is challenged by a break with the gaze that was its condition. During the Renaissance the pictorial representation of Christ became increasingly dependent on the expressiveness of the individual artist, an expressiveness that comes between, so to speak, the pious viewer and God. This is of significance for the understanding of the incarnation if one wants to avoid a theological-historical idealism that isolates the significance of the image at the expense of the gaze.

A further radical twist regarding the representation of Christ in image occurs with the invention of the photograph during the nineteenth century, and this in certain ways reinforces the tendencies that already exist with Holbein.[88] It is not uncommon for Christ to be represented in photography, often with direct reference to earlier religious iconographic traditions. Believing photographers like Julia Margaret Cameron wanted to create meditative images for the edification of the faithful with the help of this recently invented medium, while these religious associations were used by critics of religion like the surrealist Man Ray in order to undermine

---

87. Alex Stock, *Zwischen Tempel und Museum: Theologische Kunstkritik—Positionen der Moderne* (Paderborn/Munich/Vienna/Zürich: Schöningh, 1991), p. 11.

88. See Nissan N. Perez, *Revelation: Representations of Christ in Photography* (London: Merrell, 2003).

the Christian faith. Even in our immediate present the representation of Christ often occurs in photography, and is often controversial.[89] While photography is hardly the endpoint for the representation of Christ in images—one could also get into films about Jesus or digital representations of Christ as two further media[90]—I will conclude this chapter with a few short notes regarding how the art of photography has also entailed a change with theological implications for the representation of Christ in images.

Photography differs from earlier media for image production in that, as I touched on in chapter 4, it makes a direct claim to mimetic realism, which has consequences not least for the representation of Christ. A photograph of Christ—that is, a photograph that alludes to conventional ways of representing Christ—carries an inherent tension, since it obviously is not Christ himself who has been photographed, but a contemporary person who personifies him. As examples we can take the many photographs of crucified women that have been produced since the nineteenth century, a motif that otherwise had not been especially common in painted pictorial art. Such motifs can have several simultaneous aims. One aim in allowing a woman to give shape to Christ is subversive, a way of pointing out the gender oppression of the Christian church, while another (which need not contradict the previous) is the need to indicate the universality of the saving work that took place on the cross. With this the question inevitably comes up of the relationship between what is intended and what is actually depicted. The realistic associations that the photograph generally evokes and the obvious nonrealism of a photograph of Christ run up against each other within the creativity of the photographer. We have thereby departed from the liturgical context of the icon painter for a more artistic, or even technical, context. If the photograph additionally (see chapter 4 again) implies a metaphorical connection to death, we are, in spite of all photographic representations of Christ, very far from the gaze, i.e., the perspective on the relationship between God and human being, that formed the basis for the traditional icons. As Martin Golding writes apropos photography's mimetic realism as well as its connection to death:

89. See, for example, Elisabeth Ohlson, *Ecce homo,* photographs by Elisabeth Ohlson 1996–1998 (Stockholm: Ecce homo, 1998), together with Serge Bramly and Bettina Rheims, *INRI* (Munich: Gina Kehayoff Verlag, 1998).

90. Cf. Tomas Axelson and Ola Sigurdson, "Om frälsaren, filmstjärnan och samtidsmänniskan: Jesus på vita duken," *Film och religion: Livstolkning på vita duken,* ed. Tomas Axelson and Ola Sigurdson (Örebro, Sweden: Cordia, 2005), pp. 119–49.

For Barthes the literalness of the photograph is the literalness, accordingly, of death: the photograph, by its poignant, insensible and absolute dependence on something that once, and only once, took place, is by that token a sign of an absence that is irredeemable.[91]

Thus this mimetic realism is in a sense dearly bought; it is bought at the price of the representation of dynamic, living presence in favor of a momentarily grasped, static presence in a specific, past instant—the photograph "has no metaphysics; it constitutes a world purely of things."[92] The reason that one looks *at* a painting but *through* a photograph is, according to Golding, that the concrete questions in front of the painting never have to do with "who" or "what."[93] With photographs, one is never in dialogue with the circumstances. In front of the photograph of Christ, the observer occupies a position that is unavoidably affected by its function as a sign of absence. The observer looks *through* the photograph onto the inexorably departed instant when it was taken. The photograph therefore exhibits, in spite of its other advantages, hardly any relationship to the *living* Christ, which is the whole point of the icon. In a certain sense one looks *through* the icon as well, though not to the earthly life that Christ lived 2000 years ago, but instead to the resurrected, contemporary Christ. The photographic representation of Christ gets stuck, one might say, in the same place as Holbein's *The Dead Christ in the Grave,* namely, in the grave with a Christ who lies there without any hope of resurrection and transcendence. If the icon calls for a gaze that is both involved and engaged, one might in a bold generalizing contrast argue that the gaze of Renaissance art and of the photograph are more distanced and evaluative. The implicit relationality in these different images thereby differs in a way that is theologically interesting.

To contend that art after the Renaissance, inclusive of photography, did not immediately present a scopic regime corresponding to that established by the gaze in relation to the icon by no means entails denigrating either modern painted art or photography, nor their relationship to a theological horizon. The point is rather to indicate how these differ from the Christian gaze as a concrete attitude, and so are not immediately a part of the Christian attempt to understand in theory and practice the way of being-in-the-world

---

91. Martin Golding, "Photography, Memory and Survival," *Literature and Theology* 14, no. 1 (2000): 52.

92. Golding, "Photography," p. 58.

93. Golding, "Photography," pp. 58–59.

that is given by the incarnation. In the next chapter I will attempt to present a more systematic theological formulation of the specific gaze of faith. It would undoubtedly be interesting as well to conduct a discussion of how late Renaissance painting vis-à-vis the art of photography appears in light of this, but I will not take it upon myself to perform such a task here.[94] This chapter has had to do with the theological motivations for different representations of Christ in visual images, as well as the theological implications of different representations. What remains in my investigation of the gaze as a significant practice for the concrete reception of Christology is to attempt in the next chapter to systematize and build on those insights into incarnation and gaze that I have gained in this and the two previous chapters.

94. Cf. instead, for example, Jean-Louis Chrétien, *Hand to Hand: Listening to the Work of Art,* Perspectives in Continental Philosophy, trans. Stephen E. Lewis (New York: Fordham University Press, 2003). An additional perspective is given by Sigurd Bergmann, *I begynnelsen är bilden: En befriande bild-konst-kultur-teologi* (Stockholm: Proprius, 2003). Any explicit theological reflection around the art of photography is unfortunately conspicuous in its absence, but see nevertheless Vilém Flusser, *Towards a Philosophy of Photography,* trans. Anthony Mathews (London: Reaktion Books, 2000).

7. The Eyes of Faith

In this chapter I will formulate a theology of the gaze as an embodied way of being-in-the-world, a theology that attempts to relate in a constructive way to both the theological tradition and to the intellectual challenges of the post-photographic scopic regime. In other words, I am on the lookout for how the doctrine of God's incarnation in Jesus Christ has been received in the scopic regime of faith. The opening, and foundational, question of whether a specific scopic regime of faith actually exists is answered by the Danish theologian Svend Berg in the following way: "Christian faith entails a specific gaze on the world, a particular way of looking, yet nothing so special that this particular vision of faith would not be found in the extension of our natural vision."[1] If we proceed from my "denaturalizing" and historicizing of vision in chapter 4, one may indeed ask oneself what "our natural vision" would be, but I believe—and wonder if this is not also Bjerg's point—that the vision of faith is not independent of other scopic regimes that exist parallel to it in the same time and place. Sight is one of the means by which human identity—a relationally conceived identity—is constituted, and how one sees is constituted by a range of different cooperative, antagonistic, and mutually influencing scopic regimes.[2] The believing person's relationship to God is established through her beholding of God, or, to perhaps put it more properly, this beholding affirms, from the side of the human, the relationship to God that has, according to Christianity, already been established by God. How this relationship to God, seen from the perspective of the gaze, appears I have already touched on in chapter 5 with the discussion of what I there

---

1. Svend Bjerg, *Synets teologi* (Frederiksberg, Denmark: Anis, 1999), p. 20.
2. Cf. Wesley A. Kort, *Bound to Differ: The Dynamics of Theological Discourses* (University Park: Pennsylvania State University Press, 1992).

called the gaze of grace. I will return to this theme more systematically in this chapter, but this time under the rubric "the erotic gaze," since it is necessary to consider Christian love specifically in order to understand how the Christian tradition imagines the gaze of grace.[3]

The gaze of faith is characterized by the fact that it sees more than what reveals itself for the eye, in other words, that it beholds the invisible in the visible.[4] The paradigmatic theological example of how the invisible occurs in the visible is "the incarnation of the invisible God in the visible Jesus."[5] As we saw in the previous chapter, the icon and theological reflection have been ways whereby the Christian tradition has attempted to imagine the gaze for the invisible in relation to the incarnation. On the basis of the theological doctrine of the incarnation it is possible to imagine that the relationship between visible and invisible does not need to be understood as a competitive relationship or as a dialectical negation. In a section on the gaze for the invisible below I will deepen the trains of thought I have already touched on regarding how the visible can be open to the invisible and how the making visible of the invisible does not need to mean that its invisibility is reduced to nothing. In other words, a gaze does not necessarily constitute a potential threat to the invisible in its putative effort to make everything visible in its lust to dominate.

Such a relationship to God and such a beholding of God, as made possible through the erotic gaze and the gaze for the invisible, do not proceed from some sort of disembodied gaze that floats around independent of the cultural context in which it is incarnated. The relationship to God is, according to the Christian tradition, an embodied and historical relationship of the highest degree — more on that in the following four chapters — and so also are the erotic gaze and the gaze for the invisible. In a third section in this chapter I will discuss the liturgical gaze, that is, the way in which the scopic regime of the Christian tradition is ritually formed. With the help of contemporary cultural anthropology I will attempt to show that the specific way that believers experience the world is ritually constituted through the praxis of faith and the worship of the church. There the specific gaze of faith is both interpreted and shaped.

---

3. By "erotic gaze" I do not mean the same gaze that Laura Mulvey criticizes in her classic article "Visual Pleasure and Narrative Cinema," in *Feminism and Film,* Oxford Readings in Feminisms, ed. E. Ann Kaplan (Oxford/New York: Oxford University Press, 2000), pp. 34–47. In contrast with the gaze that is criticized by feminist film scholarship, the "erotic gaze" that I discuss here is a relational and incarnated gaze, not a voyeuristic gaze.

4. Bjerg, *Synets teologi,* pp. 20–30.

5. Bjerg, *Synets teologi,* p. 30.

The aim with this chapter is accordingly to formulate, in a more systematic than historical way, a theology of the gaze as an embodied way of being-in-the-world. I will discuss the way in which the gaze sees what it sees (with a generously erotic desire), but also what this gaze sees (the invisible in the visible) and how it comes to see what it sees (through the liturgy in a broad sense). On the basis of this discussion I will account in the final section for how the gaze of faith relates to other gazes. But first, then, let us take up the question of the way in which the gaze sees what it sees.

The Erotic Gaze

With what gaze do the eyes of faith look at God? Precision is important here, as it indicates the way in which the person considers herself to stand in relation to the divine. There are several clues in Jesus' teaching on sight in the Gospels (see chapter 5). Here there are, for example, explicit warnings against certain types of gazes. Those gazes that express desire (in the sense of wanting to possess the object of the gaze) and self-centeredness are condemned, while gazes that express generosity are highlighted as the gaze of the pure-hearted person. Insofar as Jesus' own gazes (as they are depicted by the Gospels) express the latter attitude, they show a number of modulations of what I call the generous gaze, namely wrath, deep sorrow, and love. Even wrath may thus indirectly be an expression of generosity, in that the wrathful gaze expresses wrath over the obduracy of others, that is to say, their lack of generosity.

The theological appraisal of different gazes proves at length to be parallel to another way of speaking theologically about the human being's relationship to God, namely the question of—as Lundensian theologian Anders Nygren formulated it—"the Christian concept of love." In a broadly encompassing conceptual history Nygren sharply differentiated between two concepts of love, namely *eros* and *agape,* where *eros* designated the non-Christian desiring, self-centered love, while *agape* designated the self-giving, generous love.[6] These two basic motifs have often been blended together in their historical figurations, but purely in terms of content they ought,

---

6. See Anders Nygren, *Agape and Eros: The Christian Ideal of Love,* trans. Philip S. Watson (Chicago: University of Chicago Press, 1982). I have discussed problems in Nygren's distinction in the article "Kristus och människan: Om inkarnationen och kärleksbegreppet," *Svensk Teologisk Kvartalskrift* 76, no. 2 (2000): 66–76. I repeat several of these arguments here.

Nygren believes, to be kept distinct. Christianity's *agape* contains none of the self-centered features of the Greek and Hellenistic *eros*-love. *Agape* stands for a theocentric attitude towards life, while *eros* stands for an egocentric one. *Agape* is thus identified as the love with which God loves the people and sends them salvation in Christ, while *eros* means that the person herself attempts to fill the lack of God that characterizes her being, and so attempts to achieve her salvation herself. Through this distinction Nygren wanted to emphasize that the person's salvation in Christ is not a matter of her own achievements, but that it is wholly and fully a gift from God, which the person cannot contribute to. This sharp distinction is nevertheless problematic.

On the one hand the erotic gaze, according to Nygren's determination, looks at its object with desire, a desire that wants to use the object in order to fill a lack in its own constitution. Such a gaze could thereby be equated with the desiring and covetous gaze that is condemned by Jesus in the Gospels (see chapter 5). The agapeic gaze—the gaze of grace—on the other hand, should then correspond to the gaze of the pure-hearted, those who do not perform good works for the sake of their own self-interest and who look with love at their object, a love that is love not because the object can fill the lover's lack, but because the object should be loved for its own sake. It is possible to describe the two gazes in such a way that a correspondence between Nygren's schema and Jesus' teaching on the gazes in the Gospels may be seen. But this is only an apparent correspondence. Let me give an example.

When Jesus condemns those who look at a woman "with lustful intent" in Matthew 5:28 and asserts that in and with this they have committed adultery in their hearts, does he then also mean that every gaze that is filled with desire is reprehensible? The lust that is discussed in this verse in the Gospel of Matthew is designated by a Greek verb with the same stem as the noun *epithymia,* which is usually translated with desire or lust. Neither the verb nor the noun in itself expresses a positive or negative valuation of this desire.[7] There are several places in the New Testament where the term is used in a positively charged context (see below). In this specific case, however, the term seems to designate a sexual desire that is blameworthy. Now the object

7. See William F. Arndt and F. Wilbur Gingrich, *A Greek-English Lexicon of the New Testament and Other Early Christian Literature: A translation and adaptation of the fourth revised and augmented edition of Walter Bauer's Griechisch-Deutsches Wörterbuch zu den Schriften des Neuen Testaments und der übrigen urchristlichen Literatur,* 2nd edition, revised and expanded by F. Wilbur Gingrich and Frederick W. Danker from Walter Bauer's 5th edition, 1958 (Chicago/London: University of Chicago Press, 1979), p. 293.

of the desiring gaze in this case is not just any woman at all, but specifically a married woman—otherwise her marriage could not be broken—and one might therefore draw the conclusion that the problem in this verse is not desire in itself, but that which is desired, that is to say, the—implicit—will to violate the married woman's marriage. Now it is doubtless not so simple as its merely having to do with the wrong object for the desiring gaze. If the desiring gaze means that the one who looks at the married woman implicitly violates her marriage "in his heart," then there is something askew in the desiring gaze as well, since it hangs together with the center of the personality itself, namely—according to biblical usage—the heart. This gaze would probably not have been justified even if the object of its lust had been an unmarried woman. The problem lies in the attitude in the heart that the gaze gives expression to—only the "pure in heart" shall "see God," according to chapter 5, verse 8.

What then is the problem with the gaze filled with *epithymia*, if *epithymia* does not necessarily have negative connotations, that is to say, if the problem does not necessarily lie in the gaze itself or in the object of the gaze? Let me approach this question by observing another passage in the Gospel of Matthew where *epithymia* has positive connotations, namely 13:17. Here Jesus mentions that "many prophets and righteous people longed to see what you [the disciples] see." The same verb that is translated "lust" in 5:28 is translated here with "longing." So here as well a gaze is mentioned that is associated with *epithymia,* but whose object in this case is presumably the kingdom of God foretold in the healings of Jesus (see chapter 5). The term occurs only in these two places in the Gospel of Matthew. What then is the difference between these two gazes at the level of phenomena? I believe that an essential distinction is constituted by the attitude of the respective gazes to their objects. In the example where the woman is viewed with *epithymia* it is not only a matter of desire in the most general sense, but of a desire that, to articulate it with modern terminology, does not respect the integrity of the other, but incorporates the other within the framework of the gaze's own lustful project. This speaks to the fact that *epithymia* in the second passage in Matthew can hardly be about these prophets and righteous people incorporating the kingdom of God within the framework of their own project, since in that passage "many prophets and righteous people" are said to long to get to see the kingdom of God. The kingdom of God comes to the righteous as a gift, and can only be received by the righteous as a gift if its character of being precisely *God's* kingdom does not collapse. Those whose hearts have grown "dull"—that is to say, impervious to grace—cannot see and hear, and thus do not receive the kingdom of God, and vice versa (cf. Matt. 13:15). The gift-character of the kingdom of God, and the gaze whose *epithymia* respects this gift-character, thus implies a different attitude of the "heart" than the gaze that looks at the married woman with *epithymia*. The ESV translates this distinction with "longing" versus "lust." I want to capture the same distinction by speaking of a covetous *epithymia* respective a generous *epithymia*, as both may characterize a person's attitude towards life and thereby also express a person's "heart" through her "gaze."

In other words, Jesus' words about the desiring gaze in Matthew 5:28 do not necessarily mean that every erotic gaze as such is reprehensible.[8] If it is possible to argue for the existence of an erotic gaze that does not intend to unilaterally take possession of its object, this speaks for the potential theological legitimacy of the erotic gaze. What Nygren and other like-minded theologians find problematic with *eros*-love, and thus by extension with an erotic gaze, may be summed up in the covetous potential of this gaze. But if I begin to reverse the argument and instead ask how a love and a gaze would be possible that are completely without any characteristic of desire in the sense of wanting to possess their object, such a thought appears equally problematic. A purely giving, unilateral love can appear as a strangely indifferent form of love, since it does not seem to matter for such a love what the result of that love is. Any hint that the giving love would prefer that this love be reciprocated in one particular way rather than another would speak of calculation, which would thwart the unilateral character of this love. But here I believe that one can insert a distinction between a calculating love—which would thwart this love's character as love—and an *eros*-love that does not deny that it loves something that is worthy of love, and which therefore in some sense gets something back, but which nevertheless is not a calculating love, but hopes that the love will be returned without prejudice and without calculation. This would open up the possibility of an *eros*-love that is not strictly possessive in the sense of calculating, and the possibility

---

8. L. Williams Countryman, in *Dirt, Greed and Sex: Sexual Ethics in the New Testament and Their Implications for Today* (London: SCM Press, 2001), pp. 158–59, says that it is possible to interpret the statement hyperbolically, as the idea that every erotic gaze as such is reprehensible, which means that none are free from sin. His other possibility is to interpret this gaze as an expression of avarice, which is the interpretation that I prefer. Considering Countryman's other arguments for the idea that sin consists in avarice *(pleonexia)* in the New Testament, his second alternative interpretation has a certain precedence, since the general orientation supports this argument. Countryman also points out in several places that *epithymia* does not have to be identified with negative connotations; see *Dirt, Greed and Sex,* pp. 99–101.

of an *agape*-love that is not strictly unilateral (I will return to aspects of this question in chapter 10).[9]

One of the many philosophers who have treated the question of human desire in recent times is the Irish philosopher Richard Kearney. He believes that within the Western history of religion there are two primary ways to desire God.[10] The first he calls (after Martin Heidegger) the ontological way.[11] This characterizes desire as lack (cf. Nygren's understanding of *eros*-love), a lack that strives to be obliterated in the nearness of plenitude. Kearney says that this desire is "the desire of the eyes *[hē epithymia tōn ophthalmōn],*" following 1 John 2:16, and *concupiscentia oculorum* following Augustine in *Confessions:*

> It is a vain inquisitiveness dignified with the title of knowledge and science. As this is rooted in the appetite for knowing, and as among the senses the eyes play a leading role in acquiring knowledge, the divine word calls it 'the lust of the eyes' (1 John 2:16).[12]

Such a curiosity as wants to fill its lack consumes the desired object with its eyes, seizes it. This desire is a form of covetous love. If this desire is the only desire that exists, it will be difficult to find a positive theological legitimization for desire, but in my exegesis above I have hinted that it is possible to look at desire in another way. Kearney and the philosophers and theologians he invokes have also done so.

Kearney calls the second way the eschatological way. In contrast with ontological desire, Kearney believes that eschatological desire is not characterized by striving for security, but builds on expectancy. This hope is also a desire, Kearney says, but it is a desire that attempts "to transcend our imprisonment in all that is *(ta onta)* in favor of another desire—a desire for something that the eye has never seen and the ear has never heard"; in other

---

9. For a discussion of how this does not need to mean a denial of the idea of grace, see my argument in *Kärlekens skillnad: Att gestalta kristen tro i vår tid* (Stockholm: Verbum, 1998), chapter 3, pp. 125–47, together with *Hungerns väg: Om Gud, kyrka och mångfald* (Lund: Arcus, 2000), chapters 1, 9, and 14, pp. 9–31, 134–40, 180–200.

10. Richard Kearney, *The God Who May Be: A Hermeneutics of Religion* (Bloomington: Indiana University Press, 2001), pp. 60ff.

11. See Martin Heidegger, "The Onto-Theo-Logical Constitution of Metaphysics," in *Identity and Difference,* trans. Joan Stambaugh (New York: Harper & Row, 1969), pp. 42–74.

12. Augustine, *Confessions,* trans. Henry Chadwick (Oxford/New York: Oxford World Classics, 2008), p. 211 (10, 54).

words, following Paul in Romans (8:25), it is a matter of hoping "for what we do not see."[13] Kearney expounds eschatological desire using Emmanuel Levinas's possibly most famous work *Totality and Infinity*.[14] Here Levinas discusses the ambiguity of love, an ambiguity that entails that love oscillates between an immanent love for other human beings and a desire for the infinite that transcends our immanent love. Levinas writes:

> Love remains a relation with the Other that turns into need, and this need still presupposes the total, transcendent exteriority of the other, of the beloved. But love also goes beyond the beloved. This is why through the face filters the obscure light coming from beyond the face, from what *is not yet,* from a future never future enough, more remote than the possible.[15]

Levinas then speaks of a simultaneity between immanence and transcendence, between need and desire, between greed and desire. This striving for "a future never future enough" is what Kearney speaks of as an eschatological desire. Levinas goes further by speaking of a "phenomenology of the caress."[16] The caress seeks the other, but not as a thing. Even if the caress is physical, sensual, it still seeks that which goes beyond the physical. The caress does not capture the beloved in a hard grip that forces her/ him into obedience, but on the contrary, the caress can never clasp the beloved, who in a certain sense remains "untouchable" or even "virginal." Levinas writes:

> The caress aims at the tender which has no longer the status of an "existent," which having taken leave of "numbers and beings" is not even a quality of an existent. The tender designates *a way,* the way of remaining in the *no man's land* between being and not-yet-being.[17]

The desire that is expressed in the caress thus lies beyond every conceptualization or objectification. Levinas speaks of an *"intentionality without vision"* or of a "pure" or "blind" experience.[18] An additional quotation may

13. Kearney, *The God Who May Be*, p. 62.
14. Emmanuel Levinas, *Totality and Infinity: An Essay on Exteriority,* trans. Alphonso Lingis (Pittsburgh: Duquesne University Press, 1969).
15. Levinas, *Totality,* pp. 254–55.
16. Levinas, *Totality,* pp. 256–66.
17. Levinas, *Totality,* p. 259.
18. Levinas, *Totality,* p. 260.

illuminate what Levinas means: "Eros is not accomplished as a subject that fixates an object, nor as a pro-jection, toward a possible. Its movement consists in going beyond the possible."[19] The eschatological desire Levinas speaks of thus lies beyond every possibility—Levinas seems to speak of a sort of dark night of desire where it is purged of every human conception that would be able to objectify the aim of desire. In another text, *Time and the Other*, Levinas says that the erotic lies beyond every form of "knowing," "possessing," or "grasping."[20] What is it then that this erotic desire actually desires?

According to Levinas, the desire that goes beyond all need is a desire that cannot be consummated and thereby quenched. Desire is like the good, the good that in Plato's words in *The Republic* is "beyond the present" *(epekeina tēs ousias)*, the good that is not satisfied but deepened.[21] It nourishes itself with its hunger. This desire is thus a desire for the good beyond being, for the transcendent, the invisible. But this does not mean that this eschatological desire is completely disembodied. In his presentation of the phenomenology of the caress Levinas attempts to show how even this eschatological desire is related to the embodied environment and is not an escape from time and from embodiment.[22] When the beloved is not reduced to embodiment and objectified, this desire that transcends every desire to own arises between the lovers. In the caress (for example) there is opened (a path to) the impossible possibility of a future that is never future enough, and thereby overcomes the partner relationship's *égoisme à deux*.[23] As Kearney writes: "This erotic epiphany is the portal to ethics itself, the carnal trace of *goodness*."[24] The desire that Levinas speaks of is no covetous desire—the lovers instead lose themselves in each other in the play of love (cf. "kär-*leken*," from Swedish *kärlek*, "love"): "Nothing is further from *Eros*

---

19. Levinas, *Totality*, p. 261.

20. Emmanuel Levinas, *Time and the Other,* trans. Richard A. Cohen (Pittsburgh: Duquesne University Press, 1987), pp. 88–90.

21. Levinas, *Totality*, pp. 34–35. Plato, *Republic*, Books VI–X, trans. Paul Shorey, The Loeb Classical Library; Plato VI (Cambridge, MA/London: Harvard University Press, 1994), 509b.

22. According to Kearney, with this Levinas goes beyond Plato (*Republic*, p. 64). According to Catherine Pickstock, on the other hand, it is not at all certain that this is going "beyond Plato"; see *After Writing: On the Liturgical Consummation of Philosophy* (Oxford: Blackwell, 1998), pp. 3–46.

23. Cf. Kearney, *The God Who May Be*, p. 65, and Emmanuel Levinas, *Entre Nous: Thinking-of-the-Other,* trans. Michael B. Smith and Barbara Harshav (New York: Columbia University Press, 1998), pp. 18–19.

24. Kearney, *The God Who May Be*, p. 66.

than possession. In the possession of the Other I possess the Other inasmuch as he possesses me; I am both slave and master."[25] In a certain sense Levinas wants to resolve Hegel's dialectic between master and slave by *intensifying* it.[26] The mutual dependence between master and slave is transformed in the caress of love-play (kär-*lekens*) to a simultaneous activity and passivity. At the same time this transformed relationship is also transcended by this desire going beyond the possible.

Thus desire is not stilled (and does not stop) in the caress. The future that is not future enough takes place through the child. The child could be said to be the "consequence," "product," or "project" of the caress, if it were not for the fact that these words are often connected with something that lies within the framework of human possibility. The child comes from a future that lies beyond the possible: "The relation with such a future, irreducible to the power over possibilities, we shall call fecundity."[27] Bringing terms such as "child" and "fecundity" into a discussion of desire does not mean that Levinas wants to reduce the question of desire to biology (or economy).[28] He instead wants, with the help of well-known phenomena, to speak about something that has a greater scope than purely physical procreation, but which is expressed, among other places, in this—not only, but also—biological phenomenon. The child stands for an impossibility that cannot be reduced to the subject's own project, because the child breaks up the subject's self-centeredness from the future. Firstly, the caress is a condition for the child. Secondly—and perhaps more importantly—the child is at the same time both related to and the progeny of the parents, and someone completely other: "My child is a stranger (Isaiah 49), but a stranger who is not only mine, for he *is* me. He is me a stranger to myself."[29] The relationship of fecundity is, in contrast with the caress, an asymmetrical

25. Levinas, *Totality*, p. 243.

26. Cf. G. W. F. Hegel, *Phenomenology of Spirit*, trans. A. V. Miller (Oxford: Oxford University Press, 1977), pp. 111–19.

27. Levinas, *Totality*, p. 267.

28. Levinas has been criticized for the sexist implications of his use of the terms "fecundity," "fatherhood," "motherhood," et cetera. See for example Luce Irigaray, "Questions to Emmanuel Levinas: On the Divinity of Love," trans. Margaret Whitford, together with Catherine Chalier, "Ethics and the Feminine," both in *Re-Reading Levinas*, ed. Robert Bernasconi and Simon Critchley (Bloomington/Indianapolis: Indiana University Press, 1991), pp. 109–18 and 119–29. Luce Irigaray has also criticized Levinas in "Fécondité de la caresse: Lecture de Lévinas *Totalité et infini*, section IV, B, 'Phénoménologie de l'éros,'" *Éthique de la différence sexuelle*, Collection "critique" (Paris: Les Éditions de Minuit, 1984), pp. 173–99.

29. Levinas, *Totality*, p. 267.

relationship. The relationship with the child is not a desire that is fulfilled and quenched, but a desire that, so to speak, goes beyond itself through its fecundity, and thereby goes further to a future that lies beyond what can be calculated. Desire engenders a desire that is not just more of the same, that does not simply continue to express those possibilities that the person controls, but which is a transcendence of immanent desire.[30] Levinas attempts to balance on this narrow boundary—I have in another place attempted to speak of this boundary as "love's difference"[31]—between a desire that is merely a desire for more of the same, and so never meets anyone other than itself in that which this desire wants, and a desire that is completely possessed by the other, and therefore completely abandons itself without any thought of resurrection (as, for example, with Nygren's *agape*-love, and possibly with Levinas himself in his later writings).[32] In fatherhood desire is preserved as "insatiate desire, that is, as goodness."[33] Or, to return to the terms I have used above, the desire Levinas speaks of is not a covetous desire, but a generous desire.

Kearney notes that there are a number of objections to Levinas's phenomenological investigation of desire. One of these is the question of whether there really is a phenomenology that Levinas presents in his exposition of desire, or whether it is in fact a matter of a specific interpretation of desire on the basis of Biblical and Talmudic expositions.[34] Because I am not ultimately aiming for a phenomenological, but rather a theological understanding of desire in this book, such an objection is less important to me. Another more serious objection is whether Levinas's conception of eschatological desire is actually plausible. Is it not the case that this "future never future enough" means that this eschatological desire is a desire for something that is constantly postponed, and is therefore never realized in the human world? Does it not become an unbridgeable gulf between the desire that is expressed in the human caress and eschatological desire? Is there ever a concrete child who becomes the chosen child, who is Messiah, or will we always wait for another? Additionally: Is the desire that Levinas speaks of a blind desire that wanders without aim? Does Levinas's eschatological desire not become an aimless desire that seeks out the destructive just as much as the good in its effort to avoid the calculable and every form of fulfillment or

---

30. Levinas, *Totality*, p. 269.
31. Ola Sigurdson, *Kärlekens skillnad,* primarily chapter 2.
32. Cf. Levinas, *Totality*, pp. 283–85.
33. Levinas, *Totality*, p. 272.
34. Kearney, *The God Who May Be*, p. 69.

fullness, whether it consists in finding the first principle or the quintessential objective of the human?[35]

The Danish philosopher Peter Kemp believes that the above objections are a misinterpretation of what Levinas argues. It is not a question of a continually postponed eschatology, but of a realized eschatology:

> Lévinas's eschatology is thus not inscribed as an end to world history, but is a "realized eschatology," where every moment is the "last" in the sense that it bursts the bounds of the reality that we have attempted to shut up in a closed world encompassing everything that exists.[36]

Kemp interprets Levinas's position in *Totality and Infinity* as in substance close to what one finds in, for example, Franz Rosenzweig's *Der Stern der Erlösung* from 1921 and Karl Barth's *Der Römerbrief,* second edition from 1922. Because every moment is the last, this future constitutes a presence that is, however, not comprehensible or calculable. But the question is whether a reading of Levinas in which his eschatological desire is interpreted as a realized eschatology really solves the problem. Certainly there exists a critical potential in this desire that does not let itself be stilled or quieted by an immanent fulfillment, but which breaks up every immanent structure. But is this a constructive desire that has an intrinsic relationship to the human desire for the spiritual, for example in the caress? Can eschatological desire be incarnated in some form of human structure, however tentatively and provisionally this incarnation must be understood?

I want to complement Kearney's typology of two different sorts of desire—the onto-theological and the eschatological—with a third type, namely the Trinitarian. This is in a certain sense not a critique of Kearney's typology—which is phenomenological—but rather a shift to a more dedicated theological perspective. One possible starting point for such an exposition of a theological desire is precisely a Trinitarian theology. In the love relationships of the Trinity the theologian finds support for speaking of a human desire that exceeds both the onto-theological desire as a lack and the eschatological desire as continually postponed—apart from whether this is a proper interpretation of Levinas or not—and is instead generous and eternal. This divine desire is

---

35. For a nuanced discussion of the relationship between closure and openness in the eschatological telos, see Paul S. Fiddes, *The Promised End: Eschatology in Theology and Literature,* Challenges in Contemporary Theology (Oxford: Blackwell, 2000).

36. Peter Kemp, *Lévinas: En introduktion,* trans. Rikard Hedenblad (Göteborg: Daidalos, 1992), p. 60.

understood on the one hand as an intra-Trinitarian desire, where the different persons exist ecstatically through each other and thereby allow their unity to exist precisely as this ecstasy. On the other hand this desire is understood as an extra-Trinitarian desire in the sense that the intra-Trinitarian desire is not restricted to the divine mode of existing, but overflows in its ecstasy and is thereby also able to encompass nondivine reality. Rowan Williams formulates this in a pregnant way in the article "The Body's Grace":

> The whole story of creation, incarnation and our incorporation into the fellowship of Christ's body tells us that God desires us, as *if we were God,* as if we were that unconditional response to God's giving that God's self makes in the life of the trinity. We are created so that we may be caught up in this; so that we may grow into the wholehearted love of God by learning that God loves us as God loves God.[37]

In other words, God wants to draw us into the movement of dynamic love that the triune God essentially is. While our identity as human beings is by necessity constituted by the fact that other humans look at us, and even desire us, according to Williams God does not, so to speak, need to wait on that which is not God in order to be God.[38] In this sense God is beyond need, which is expressed in the doctrine of *creatio ex nihilo* (a creation out of nothing). But at the same time God wants to be God even for that which is not God. The intra-Trinitarian love overflows to that which is not God. Williams can thus assert with a provocative formula that God creates for the sake of God, but because God is overflowing love, this *is* to create for our sake. Even if the love of God is unilateral in the sense that it, and no other, is the love that creates and redeems the human, the human is nevertheless made participatory in this love through the fact that the intra-Trinitarian love extends beyond itself and thereby draws in and embraces that which is not God in this dynamic of love. Nor should God be understood as indifferent with regard to the object of this love, as though it were a question of a giving without consequences for the recipient. The human being is created desirable by God, and God also desires the human being's response as though it were God's own response.

37. Rowan Williams, "The Body's Grace," *Our Selves, Our Souls & Bodies: Sexuality and the Household of God,* ed. Charles Hefling (Cambridge, MA: Cowley, 1996), p. 59.

38. Rowan Williams, "On Being Creatures," *On Christian Theology,* Challenges in Contemporary Theology (Oxford: Blackwell, 2000), pp. 73-75.

In this economy of desire even human desire finds its place as a response to God's desire for the human being. Understanding oneself as created and thereby as receiving one's own existence as a gift entails that a person is not her own cause. Human love must therefore be understood as an *eros*-love. Supposing a unilateral love from the human side entails either a person who only receives, and therefore never herself becomes someone who gives—an infantile perspective—or a person who only gives, and before such a person we have to ask ourselves what makes it such that she is not able to receive.[39] To be human is instead to remain in a continual giving and taking. Williams can thus call this grace in the theological sense that someone desires us as the people we are, our bodies and our souls in indissoluble union.[40] But to want to be desired entails existing for the other. One may ask oneself whether a unilateral human love in contrast to divine love is what we mean by love at all. The love for our neighbor, that we are liberated to through God's love, is thus not a matter of a unilateral love, if Williams is correct, but of generosity, a love that does not calculate with regard to what it gets back and so nullify the character of love as a gift. Human desire for the (nondivine) other, which has been formed by God's desire for the human being, and the human desire for God can resemble God's desire in a generosity that is not calculating. So this does not mean that love is completely unilateral, but rather that there is no fixed exchange rate by which one would be able to calculate and compare the love one gives and the love one receives.[41]

By focusing on such a theological desire, which both characterizes God's desire for the human being and the human being's desire for other people and God, the reciprocal in the economy of desire is emphasized—it seems to me—more clearly than in Levinas, even if in the relationship between God and human being it is a matter of an asymmetric relationship. From his phenomenological perspective Kearney suggests something similar—his "tentative summary hypothesis" in his discussion of the desire of God goes like this:

39. Williams, "On Being Creatures," p. 69.

40. Williams, "The Body's Grace," pp. 59–64.

41. In other words, I am critical of a unilateral understanding of the gift, as seems to be found in, for example, Jacques Derrida, *The Gift of Death*, Religion and Postmodernism, trans. David Wills (Chicago: University of Chicago Press, 1995). I instead orient myself following Marcel Mauss, *The Gift: The Form and Reason for Exchange in Archaic Societies,* trans. W. D. Halls (London/New York: Routledge Classics, 2002), and John Milbank, "Can a Gift Be Given? Prolegomena to a Future Trinitarian Metaphysics," *Modern Theology* 11, no. 1 (1995). More on this in chapter 3 of *Kärlekens skillnad.* But also see Robyn Horner, *Rethinking God as Gift: Marion, Derrida and the Limits of Phenomenology* (New York: Fordham University Press, 2001).

While God's lovers always continue to seek and desire him whom their soul loves, they have always already been found, because already sought and desired, by him whom their souls love. Their eros occupies a middle space, a two-way street between action and passion, yearning and welcome, seeking and receptivity.[42]

Kearney does not develop the significance of this further, but my understanding is that he wants to emphasize more clearly than Levinas that desire, on the part of the human, should not be unilaterally understood as giving. That the human "longs" and "seeks" implies that there is an authentic lack in human desire, which does not need to blossom into a half-desire that attempts to take possession of its object, but is instead a constant absence that coexists with an ecstatic generosity that is not looking out for itself.

In other words, I believe that one may argue the possibility of an erotic gaze that is not covetous. Desire in itself is not covetous in the sense that it wants to dominate and domesticate its object. Desire instead has a positive meaning as the driving force that brings the human being towards God and towards other humans. There is a desire, a longing, or a craving for the other that is not covetous, but instead strives for a relationship that preserves the integrity of the other. The gaze is not necessarily an expression of a unilateral will to power. This is a reason for remaining skeptical about the animosity towards the sense of sight that can be traced in, for example, Levinas.[43] For him sight is itself totalizing, and he speaks of "the avidity proper to the gaze" as though this greed were an essential property of the gaze.[44] For Levinas the caress is more fundamental—and has more positive connotations—than the gaze.[45] The tactile sense is thus set against the visual sense. Thus Levinas reiterates a historically common distinction between sight and feeling,

42. Kearney, *The God Who May Be,* p. 79.

43. See Martin Jay, *Downcast Eyes: The Denigration of Vision in Twentieth-Century French Thought* (Berkeley/Los Angeles/London: University of California Press, 1993), pp. 543–86.

44. Levinas, *Totality,* p. 21. Cf. also p. 103.

45. Besides Levinas's treatment of the embrace in *Totality,* see also *Time and the Other,* pp. 84–90. The theme is also treated by, among others, Edith Wyschogrod, "Doing before Hearing: On the Primacy of Touch," *Textes pour Emmanuel Lévinas,* ed. François Laruelle (Paris: Jean-Michel Place Éditeur, 1980), pp. 179–203. In "Language and Proximity," in *Collected Philosophical Papers,* trans. Alphonso Lingis (Dordrecht/Boston/Lancaster: Martinus Nijhoff, 1987), p. 118, however, Levinas writes the following: "Sight is, to be sure, an openness and a consciousness, and all sensibility, opening as a consciousness, is called vision; but even in its subordination to cognition sight maintains contact and proximity. The visible caresses the eye. One sees and one hears like one touches."

where sight more or less in its essence designates a distanced relationship between subject and object, while feeling instead designates a relationship of nearness and intimacy.[46] But I believe that it is possible to imagine a greater similarity between sight and feeling. Maurice Merleau-Ponty, whom I have previously mentioned in chapter 4, is an example of a philosopher who does not think that there is any conflict of essence between sight and feeling. For him sight is also a hand by which the person extends herself in order to get to know the world. Seeing is a way of touching something. Both the hand and the eye can occupy a dominating as well as a responsive stance. A hand can both strike and caress, and an eye can both indifferently survey and marvel at the surrounding world. It is not sight or feeling in themselves that are the problem versus the solution, but certain of their modulations. The erotic gaze does not need to stand in opposition to the caress, but can be an embodied gaze that is both active and passive. It can be a part of the caress that also sees and lets itself be seen by the beloved. In other words, the erotic gaze is not a monoscopic gaze that attempts to master its object, but instead represents a whole other way of being-in-the-world. But as the previous chapter has shown, it is not simply a matter of the gaze, but also of the image, i.e., the world. Now that I have shown "how" the Christian gaze sees its object, I will turn to the question of "what" it sees. In what way is the erotic gaze a gaze for the invisible?

The Gaze for the Invisible

As I demonstrated in chapter 5, there is in the New Testament a strong emphasis on the beholding of salvation. Seeing the earthly Jesus with the eyes of faith means not only seeing his physical body and its actions, but also beholding God's action in this body and its actions, that is to say, perceiving God's invisible presence in the world with physical senses in Jesus' concrete person. The texts that bear John's name often tend to be presented as the New Testament scriptures that more clearly emphasize physical as well as spiritual beholding, but as I showed in chapter 5, the idea of such a beholding is not at all limited to the Gospel of John or the other Johannine texts. The account of Simeon in the Gospel of Luke, the synoptics' account of Jesus on the Mount of Transfiguration, and the Pauline epistles also contain clear references to the person's physical and spiritual beholding of salvation.

46. Jay, *Downcast Eyes,* p. 557.

Characteristic of the gaze that can be found in a large portion of the New Testament scriptures is the fact that the person appropriates salvation through sight, without possessing it as one's property because of that. Through sight the person relates to God in such a way that the initiative for the relationship is still understood as the work of God. In other words, it is not a purely registering gaze with which people in the New Testament regard Jesus, but a loving gaze that desires, but does not want to possess its object—an erotic gaze in the sense I have explained above. This is shown not least by the fact that the beholding of Jesus viewed as a physical person is ambivalent—some believe when they see him, some see him without believing. It is not until God's intervention, as, for example, in the three parallel accounts of Jesus on the Mount of Transfiguration, that Jesus' eschatological and theological significance becomes clear. In the Gospel of John Jesus is presented as the only one who has seen the Father, that is to say he is the one who stands in a unique relationship to the Father, and thus can indirectly convey the beholding of God to other people. It is not possible to see God, the Gospel of John claims, except through Jesus who is the visible testimony of the invisible Father.

It is also interesting that the spiritual beholding in the Johannine literature, that is to say, the understanding of who Jesus is and what he does, is not presented as independent of physical seeing. It is certainly possible to see Jesus with the physical eyes without understanding who he is, but the understanding of who he is is not independent of the physical seeing. On the one hand, to physically see is not identical with "understanding" what one sees. It is thus presented as entirely possible—humanly speaking—to not see anything other than a particular person when Jesus' contemporaries saw him. The basis for the understanding of who he is was a divine intervention (in some sense). On the other hand, to "understand" what one sees does not mean that Jesus was constantly before the disciples' (physical) eyes; Jesus says that the disciples will believe without seeing during the farewell discourse, and Jesus points out to the doubting Thomas that they are blessed who have not seen—in the physical sense—but still believe. So despite the fact that there is a significant difference between sight and understanding in the Johannine literature, this does not mean that the relationship between the two is dissolved. The doubting Thomas gets to see and touch Jesus, and receives back his faith, and 1 John contains a meditation on the relationship between physical seeing, tactile perception, and spiritual understanding. Even if the relationship to God is thus not directly dependent on sight and the tactile perception of Jesus, that is to say, dependent on immediate contemporaneity with the earthly Jesus, this relationship cannot be conceived as though it were possible to go around the physical or leave the physical behind. The relationship to God is mediated in and through the reality that can be perceived with the senses, not to the side of them, even if this visible reality is not identical with the divine reality.

In other words, Jesus' person and deeds are, according to the New Testament, of an epiphanic character: they reveal God's presence for the human senses. Faith is not a direct, intuitive beholding of the divine reality, but happens through an indirect beholding that is dependent on the human senses.[47] Among these, sight plays a prominent role. Then does the absence of the earthly Jesus not mean a qualitative change in the conditions of the Christian faith in the way that understanding is robbed of its basis in physical seeing? Not really. According to the New Testament tradition Christ is present for his disciples in their loving relationship to each other and Jesus (John 15:4), in Communion (John 6:56), and in the fact that the Father sends the Helper, through whom the disciples will behold Jesus even during his physical absence (John 14:15–31).[48]

We also find an insightful reflection on the presence of God in the image tradition. John of Damascus believed, as we remember from the previous chapter, that there exist both likeness and unlikeness in the relationship between the image and its prototype. Likeness preserved, so to speak, the presence of God with the created, while unlikeness preserved the qualitative difference between God and the created. In the icon one may perceive an aura that is God's own dynamic presence. The material image mediates an embodied beholding that one perceives only with a spiritual understanding that is a direct consequence of the incarnation. The second Nicene council established that the person who pictorially depicts Christ's human form does not dissolve the unity between Christ's human and Christ's divine nature, but testifies that God's Word actually, and not only apparently, became human. Thus, one could with the patriarch Nikephoros argue that the one who denies the legitimacy of the images also denies God's saving work in Christ. God is present in the image of Christ as well, without the painted

47. Cf. my discussion of the knowledge of the angels in "Varför änglar inte kan vara kloka: Om klokhet som en mänsklig dygd," *Penelopes väv: För en filosofisk och teologisk pathologi*, ed. Mats Rosengren and Ola Sigurdson, Logos/Pathos 1 (Göteborg: Glänta, 2003), pp. 101–17.

48. Cf. Jean-Luc Marion, "They Recognized Him; and He Became Invisible to Them," trans. Stephen E. Lewis, *Modern Theology* 18, no. 2 (2002): 145–52, together with the response from Shane Mackinlay, "Eyes Wide Shut: A Response to Jean-Luc Marion's Account of the Journey to Emmaus," *Modern Theology* 20, no. 3 (2004): 447–56.

image being confused with the depicted Savior because of this. Theodore the Studite believed the same, also arguing that Christ is present in the image through the relationship that is established between the image and the depicted person, and where the name of the depicted, written on the image, makes the relationship unambiguous. The theologians of the icon defend themselves against every attempt to confuse depiction and prototype and so argue that the icon in itself possesses some "magical" power, and simultaneously against every attempt to differentiate between depiction and prototype in such a way that the presence of the depicted in the image becomes impossible. The theology of the image thereby becomes an interpretation of the relationship between God and human in the extension of the doctrine of incarnation as it was formulated by the council in Chalcedon in 451: Christ is "truly God and truly man," whose two "natures" are both impossible to blend together and to separate. Christ's presence in the image was never an identification with the material image, at the same time that this difference did not entail the undoing of the material image. With this the material world is also preserved from being undone in a higher, spiritual world, since through the incarnation the material world has shown itself to be capable of revealing God. This means that the Christian tradition in principle believes that the salvation of the person is not something that happens apart from her embodied constitution.

In other words, the icon can be said to express a sort of oscillation between representation and presentation in the sense, for example, that it represents the earthly Jesus in his absence at the same time that it presents Christ as present with the one who views the icon. Even its not-quite naturalistic style serves this purpose, namely to point to the salvation of the person rather than to the appearance of the human Jesus, or to the human as such, abstracted from the salvation history that involves God as well as the human. The French philosopher and theologian Jean-Luc Marion has concerned himself with the phenomenology of the icon, and he believes that the icon's relationship to the divine should on the whole not be understood as a representation or as a mimetic relationship.[49] Marion's discussion of the icon, and even the idol, has met with great debate and great interest in our time, and I will therefore devote a large portion of my exposition on the gaze for the invisible to giving a critical account of Marion's theology of the icon, above all as it is expressed in a text from 1991, "The Prototype and

---

49. Jean-Luc Marion, "The Prototype and the Image," in *The Crossing of the Visible*, trans. James K. A. Smith (Stanford: Stanford University Press, 2004), pp. 66–87.

the Image." It is in this that Marion primarily touches on the relationship to the traditional theology of the icon, and it will be my primary text, even if it is supplemented with other texts by Marion and other philosophers and theologians.

The icon should, according to Marion, be compared to the cross on which Christ was crucified. The cross as such has no likeness with Christ, and therefore neither does the icon. Marion writes:

> For the icon only gives Christ to be seen in his holiness in the same way that the Cross gives to be seen—renders visible—the divine holiness of Christ. The question thus remains to be asked: Just what does the Cross actually give to be seen? Does it offer the type of a prototype? This fitting together of two pieces of wood raised up as a gallows gives nothing as such to be seen of the least holiness or the least divinity—except a human body that one may have perhaps already seen before he had been put to death.[50]

In other words, the icon shares the status of the earthly Jesus: it is not obvious that one directly beholds the divine in him. Only if one sees in the icon or in Jesus a sign or a type that refers outside of itself to something invisible does the icon function as an icon. It does this for the one who has eyes to see, that is to say, for the one who has faith.[51] The icon opens outwards and frees the gaze from stopping at an idolatrous reflection of itself. The icon is therefore, Marion says, radically nonmimetic.[52] With terms taken from the philosopher Nelson Goodman, one may say that according to Marion the icon *denotes* Christ rather than *depicts* Christ.[53]

A skepticism towards a mimetic understanding of the icon resembling Marion's has also been articulated by the Danish theologian Svend Bjerg. He writes:

> A mimetic approach easily brings about an aesthetic seduction through the icon, so that it is transformed into an idol. Between the prototype and

50. Marion, "Prototype," p. 72.

51. Jean-Luc Marion, *The Idol and Distance: Five Studies,* Perspectives in Continental Philosophy, trans. Thomas A. Carlson (New York: Fordham University Press, 2001), p. 172.

52. As Svend Bjerg (*Synets teologi,* p. 114) points out, there is a corresponding account of the critical function of the cross in Paul Tillich. See his *Systematic Theology,* vol. 1: *Reason and Revelation: Being and God* (Chicago: University of Chicago Press, 1951), p. 136.

53. Nelson Goodman, *Languages of Art: An Approach to a Theory of Symbols,* 2nd edition (Indianapolis/Cambridge: Hackett, 1976), pp. 3–10.

the type the "aesthetic" likeness can come to hide the "sacral" unlikeness. The likeness makes it so that the image closes in on itself, the unlikeness makes it so that the image opens itself to a transcendent reality.[54]

The critique of mimetic thinking in both Marion and Bjerg hangs together with a defense of the icon as revelatory force. The mimetically construed relationship between type and prototype continually threatens to transform the relationship into an identification that shuts out the transcendent and thereby transforms the invisible into something visible and tangible. With a certain degree of generalization one might argue that the Christian tradition has continually attempted to avoid that the invisible either out-competes the visible or is devoured by it. In other words, we find the invisible not apart from the visible, but *in* it.

In the New Testament tradition as well as the Orthodox image tradition we find an emphasis on the fact that the relationship to God is mediated by the visually perceptible world. It is in the visible that the person beholds the invisible. Without the visible, the possibility of relating to the divine also disappears. In her book *Image as Insight* the theologian Margaret R. Miles emphasizes that "[f]igurative 'seeing' is dependent on literal seeing, and the religious life must be conceived and articulated by the use of metaphors based on natural objects if its concepts are not to remain lifeless."[55] But is it a sufficient argument to assert with Miles that metaphors that do not ground themselves on natural objects are lifeless? Can one not in a more Platonic spirit argue that the ascent of the human being begins in the concrete, the material, but eventually leaves that behind?[56] Marion has discussed precisely this question.[57] Could it be that the independence of the icon from the mimetic logic of the image in order to be able to be completed in its relationship to the invisible actually exposes it to two objections? The Platonic objection would be that it would be better to free oneself from such an ambiguous intermediary, when the veneration of the images must nevertheless transcend the visible icon in order to reach the invisible prototype. The second objection, more inspired by Nietzsche, argues that by drawing itself back from the

54. Bjerg, *Synets teologi*, p. 104.

55. Margaret R. Miles, *Image as Insight: Visual Understanding in Western Christianity and Secular Culture* (Boston: Beacon Press, 1985), pp. 2–3.

56. Cf. Plato's dialogue *Phaedrus*, in *Plato in Twelve Volumes, 1: Euthyphro, Apology, Crito, Phaedo, Phaedrus*, Loeb Classical Library, trans. Harold North Fowler (Cambridge, MA/London: Harvard University Press, 1914).

57. Marion, "The Prototype and the Image," pp. 78–83.

likeness-relationship, the original of the icon, its prototype, reduces the icon to a common and unassuming visibility. This means that the type replaces its prototype—the visible has primacy over the invisible—in an inversion of the classical schema. Both objections, Marion believes, are nevertheless examples of a "metaphysical iconoclasm" that does not lead to the freeing of the gaze, but to a reinforced idolatry. The gaze that has done away with the idea of an invisible prototype meets nothing other than itself in the images that it views. It stops in the visible, because it feels well at home there. Having broken with its prototype, the image becomes even more subject to its viewer. The image world becomes an expression of the human will to power, a sort of self-deification. In order to connect to my discussion of scopic regimes in chapter 4, one might say here on the basis of Marion's argument that the post-photographic scopic regime entails the downfall of the image, since the gaze does not find anything that offers resistance to itself in the images.

The icon is in a sense a defense against the downfall of the image and the will to power of the gaze. The logic of the icon is namely, according to Marion, that a gaze meets me from the icon before I gaze back.[58] I become visible for and seen by a gaze that is invisible for me, even if it is represented by the visible. Marion says that this is an utterly erotic relationship, face to face through two invisible gazes that cross each other through the visible testimony of the bodies.[59] The invisible and the visible coincide and are aesthetically reiterated by the icon, in the same way that Christ's divine and human natures coincide in the hypostatic union. Christ is the paradigm for the painted icon, not such that visible and invisible are dissolved in each other, but on the contrary, through the fact that the relationship is fulfilled without them being dissolved in each other or radically separated through a mimetic relationship. Iconoclasm does not succeed in safeguarding this, since it works from a foundational dualism between invisible and visible,

58. Marion, "The Prototype and the Image," pp. 83–85. The icon is one of the "saturated phenomena" that transcend the person's capacity for objectifying and making comprehensible. Marion discusses saturated phenomena in the article "The Saturated Phenomenon," in Dominique Janicaud et al., *Phenomenology and the "Theological Turn": The French Debate* (New York: Fordham University Press, 2000), pp. 176–216, and more thoroughly in *In Excess: Studies of Saturated Phenomena*, Perspectives in Continental Philosophy, trans. Robyn Horner and Vincent Beraud (New York: Fordham University Press, 2002). For a discussion of "saturated phenomena" in Marion, see Jayne Svenungsson, *Guds återkomst: En studie av gudsbegreppet inom postmodern filosofi*, Logos/Pathos 3 (Göteborg: Glänta, 2004), pp. 160–65.

59. Marion, "The Crossing of the Visible and the Invisible," in *The Crossing of the Visible*, p. 21.

which Marion wants to avoid. The icon should be understood according to the paradigm of the incarnation, and the difficulty of seeing the invisible in the icon reiterates the difficulty of recognizing Christ as God's son. Marion writes:

> The difficulty of recognizing on the painted wood of the icon the invisible gaze of Christ precisely reproduces the absolute difficulty of confessing that on the wood of the Cross the divine nature of the Son of God dies according to his humanity, the mortal sufferings of invisible holiness in the horror of visible sin.[60]

The icon can thus be understood no more than Christ himself as merely an object for the human gaze. The icon raises the claim to be a "conversation partner" and meets the viewer face-to-face. To meet the icon as icon entails becoming involved in the mutual exchange of gazes that the icon manifests. An agapeic gaze, in the sense of a gaze that is only unilateral, cannot do the icon justice as icon, for only a loving gaze, which expresses an involved love, meets the icon as icon. Meeting the icon as icon does not mean fixating on the material artifact itself, but letting it serve as a sign that points beyond itself towards the invisible. The visible and the invisible penetrate each other here since they do not compete as mimetic rivals. "Rather than being merely an object, the image then becomes the site of a reciprocal transition, thus the instrument of a communion."[61] So through the icon a fellowship is established that does not reduce the other to an object for one's own gaze. The person's veneration of the icon makes her relationship to the divine possible.

In contrast to the theology of the icon that I described in chapter 6, Marion accentuates the difference between type and prototype through his nonmimetic understanding of the icon. It is not that the medieval theologians of the icon had a mimetic-thinking behind their understanding of the icon—on the contrary, John of Damascus, for example, differentiates between icon and imitation.[62] But as I mentioned in the previous chapter, there existed, and still exists, the idea of an authentic image, something that finds expression in representations of Christ that "are not painted by human

---

60. Marion, "The Prototype and the Image," p. 84.
61. Marion, "The Prototype and the Image," p. 86.
62. John of Damascus, *On the Divine Images,* trans. David Anderson (Crestwood, NY: St. Vladimir's Seminary Press, 2000), III, 21.

hand" *(acheiropoiētos)*, understood as a direct depiction of Christ, but also in legends of King Abgar from Edessa, and in Western Christianity's conception of *vera icona*. Here a mimetic characteristic of the theology of the icon comes forth that conflicts with Marion's understanding of the icon. His argument, however, proceeds from the cross that refers to Christ without being like Christ, and he takes the thought of the cross from the definition of holy images in the second Nicene council in 787.[63] Marion thereby differentiates himself from the earlier icon tradition in that he wants to emphasize the difference more clearly, and because of this rejects every mimetic understanding of the icon. Here we find a number of problematic aspects of Marion's theology.

One objection that has been directed against Marion is that his argument about the icon as mediator of God's revelation would lead to an "ontic fundamentalism," in that it privileges the icon at the cost of other possible places for this revelation.[64] All other phenomena would thereby be subordinated to the icon, and the result would be an indiscriminate uniformity. It is, however, clear from the above that Marion's argument not only touches the icon as such, but also touches his perspective on subjectivity, God, and knowledge. Marion has, for example, been critical towards the idea of a modern subject, understood primarily as activity, and has instead argued that the subject is constituted primarily by the fact that it receives a "call" that it is not itself the source of.[65] The subject is thus constituted by something outside itself, and the person therefore exists primarily as "receiving" or "addressed." Marion does not even want to go along with the idea that the human being exists ecstatically, that is to say by "standing outside herself," because ecstasy still proceeds from a self that it overcomes, and so does not entail a radical decentering.[66] He speaks instead of the constituting "address" as a "surprise" for the subject, a radical "surprise" that also robs the subject of its ecstasy. It is significant for Marion's theology that the subject is constituted outside of itself, since Marion is anxious that human conditions should not get to set the measure for the experience of God. So all of Marion's thinking is,

---

63. Marion, "The Prototype and the Image," p. 68.

64. Such a critique is advanced by Phillip Blond, "Introduction," *Post-Secular Philosophy: Between Philosophy and Theology,* ed. Phillip Blond (London/New York: Routledge, 1998), pp. 34–35.

65. See, for example, Jean-Luc Marion, "The Final Appeal of the Subject," in *The Religious,* Blackwell Readings in Continental Philosophy, ed. John D. Caputo (Malden, MA/Oxford: Blackwell, 2002), pp. 131–44.

66. Marion, "Final Appeal," pp. 141–44.

one might say, saturated with the opposition between idol and icon, since the essential problem with the idol is precisely that it sets the conditions for the experience of God, and thereby limits God's infinity to what will fit within the human gaze. The icon, on the contrary, is the sign that manages to point beyond itself. The designated thus does not allow itself to be restricted by the limitations of the sign. The opposition between idol and icon is, in Marion's thought, not limited to painted images or other images, but these constitute two fundamental phenomenological categories that refer to the entirety of human existence. Thus I do not believe that Marion's argument about the icon should be understood as the idea that the painted icon and no other phenomenon in the world is a privileged place for the visibility of the invisible. It is rather the case that the entire world can adopt an iconic character under certain conditions. I believe that Marion instead wants to argue that the icon should be understood as a paradigm for how one ought to perceive God's dynamic presence—but possibly not at all the only or even unique paradigm, since Marion emphasizes the difference between Christ's presence in the icon and the Eucharist. Only in the Eucharist can one speak of Christ's real presence (I discuss Marion and real presence more closely in chapter 11).[67] In other words, God is incarnated first and foremost in Christ, not in the icon.

Another, more serious, objection to the coherence of Marion's project we get from the English theologian Graham Ward. He believes that Marion ends up dangerously near a Kantian dualism between the noumenal (i.e., the thing-in-itself) and the phenomenal (i.e., that which it is possible to experience). This threatens to reduce the transcendent to the sublime in Kant's sense, namely, something that it is impossible to represent, and thereby becomes a contrast to that which is concrete and materially visible (for Kant the sublime is in effect not something that it is possible to represent visibly, but an idea of reason).[68] In that case, the Cross in Marion's theology would

---

67. Marion, "The Prototype and the Image," p. 77: "The incarnation, which delivers the person of Christ and the divine nature, only prolongs the presence of this nature in the Eucharist, where no face accompanies it, and vice versa: it grants legitimacy to the icon, a perpetual visage of Christ waiting for his return, with the sacramental accompaniment of the divine nature." For Marion's further treatment of communion, see Jean-Luc Marion, "Of the Eucharistic Site of Theology," and especially "The Present and the Gift," in *God without Being: Hors-Texte*, Religion and Postmodernism, trans. Thomas A. Carlson (Chicago: University of Chicago Press, 1991), pp. 139–58, 161–82.

68. Graham Ward, "The Beauty of God," *Theological Perspectives on God and Beauty*, John Milbank, Graham Ward, and Edith Wyschogrod, Rockwell Lecture Series (Harrisburg, PA/

stand merely for a break with the order of the visible, its unrepresentable boundary and barrier that prevents the visible from being transformed into an idol, that is to say, a reflection of ourselves. The invisible as the boundary of the visible would then further entail that the invisible does not permeate the visible, but instead exists apart from it. Thus the visible and invisible would not exist united with each other, but only in a dialectical contrast that would threaten the entire time to turn over in one direction or the other—to Docetism or Nestorianism, that is to say, either to visible existence becoming only an apparent existence, or to visible and invisible existing side-by-side without any actual mediation. Ward finds support for this understanding in certain of Marion's more extreme statements, for example, when Marion argues that on the cross "nothing is more exhibited that the unnamable, than what cannot be named in any language," or when he contends that the only gaze that contemplates the icon in the right way is the one that venerates it as "the stigmata of the invisible."[69] If Ward is right in his interpretation, he points out a problem with the whole of Marion's conception of the theology of the icon, namely whether the icon itself manages to appear in a visible way, or whether the visibility of the icon is not in fact erased.[70] That which is concrete and material in the icon would thereby disappear in favor of the icon as a sublime idea of the unrepresentability of the invisible, or, as Ward writes, "the physical is metaphorised, then iconised and finally vaporised."[71] Such a dissolving of the physical is hardly compatible with the incarnational theology maintained by the traditional theology of the icon. Just as God's becoming human was not a step on the path to a higher, bodiless reality, the contemplation of the icon is not a step on the path away from a physical vision to a higher, spiritual vision. In other words, Marion would be a secret iconoclast.

I believe that there is a certain justification for Ward's critique. At the same time, I hesitate a bit to accept it altogether, since Marion's critique of the modern subject seems to contradict the idea that he would risk reducing the icon to a sublime idea. A crucial part of his critique of the subject was, as

London/New York: Trinity Press International, 2003), pp. 40–41 n. 7, 48–49. Cf. Immanuel Kant, *Critique of the Power of Judgment,* The Cambridge Edition of the Works of Immanuel Kant, trans. Paul Guyer and Eric Matthews (Cambridge: Cambridge University Press, 2000), §23.

69. Marion, "The Prototype and the Image," p. 67.

70. Ward, "The Theological Project of Jean-Luc Marion," in *Post-Secular Philosophy,* p. 232.

71. Ward, "Theological Project," p. 233.

I mentioned above, the understanding of the subject as constituted outside of itself, so that human conditions would not get to set the measure for the experience of God. Would Marion not thus be conscious of the risk that the invisible icon of the human's idol-worshiping gaze would be reduced to an idea of her consciousness (like the sublime in Kant), and so to an idol? I therefore want to suggest the possibility of another interpretation.[72] Such an interpretation would be able to argue with Marion that it is rather a matter of an "emphasis on the cross" with the beneficial effect that the gaze is directed both towards the difference that safeguards the invisibility of the invisible in the visible, and towards the integrity of the visible (the Antiochian business at the council in Chalcedon; cf. chapter 2). In this case Marion's errand would be a different *emphasis* within the framework of a Chalcedonian Christology, rather than a fundamentally Gnostic or dualistic Christology that manages to hold neither divinity and humanity together, nor invisible and visible. If the icon tradition emphasizes the incarnation more, one can say that Marion more clearly emphasizes the cross. Since incarnation and cross go together in the story of Jesus, so also should like-ness and unlikeness, presence and absence be held together. Bjerg writes, apropos a similar reasoning:

> Just as incarnation and cross should be thought together, so also should likeness and unlikeness in the image. Likeness is the incarnational feature that allows God to come near. Unlikeness signals that it is God, and not an extraordinary human, who is near.[73]

What I want to seize on in this quotation is precisely the possibility of different emphases. Aside from the fact that there might be a point to Marion's indirect critique of mythological elements in the earlier icon tradition, one might also find in him a clearer emphasis on the risk of the idolatry of the gaze.

According to Ward's critique of Marion, there is no idol—it is merely a fantasy.[74] He supports himself here with statements from the iconophiles

---

72. David Bentley Hart says in *The Beauty of the Infinite: The Aesthetics of Christian Truth* (Grand Rapids: Eerdmans, 2003), pp. 237–40, that Marion is rather ambiguous (p. 239): "To the degree that Marion reduces the iconic liberty of the divine to a gaze that seems to emanate from an invisible sublimity merely outside the fold of ontological difference, he lapses into dualism. Insofar, however, as God's gaze, for Marion, belongs indeed to an icon, his thought shows the way past this peril."

73. Bjerg, *Synets teologi,* p. 116.

74. Ward, "The Beauty of God," p. 65 n. 73.

that were made in connection with the second Nicene council, and assert that the "representation of things which have no being is called idolatrous painting."[75] The idol is therefore merely a phantom. Against this one can set statements in Marion that say that the idol "closes itself to every other" and that it "never deserves to be denounced as illusory since, by definition, it is seen."[76] Because Marion thinks that the idol is a creation of the human gaze rather than an autonomous entity—"the gaze alone characterizes the idol"—it seems right here as though Ward and Marion are speaking past each other.[77] Marion hardly says that the idol has the same ontological status as the icon, but this does not mean that it can be dismissed as an illusion so long as the idolatry of the gaze is a possibility. The question is whether Ward himself, while it is hardly his intention, does not here risk approaching a theology of glory that does not take seriously the unfinished state of salvation (the gaze as *simul iustus et peccator*—"at once righteous and sinner"). Marion's entire philosophy is a polemic against all forms of idolatry, intellectual as well as visual, and one might understand the emphasis on this difference as a moment in this polemic, what Marion also calls "the crossing of the visible" or an "endless hermeneutic," which both indicate how the human gaze never manages to *capture* the invisible via the visible.[78] Marion's theology of the icon might then be interpreted as a theology that attempts to more clearly incorporate the ideology-critical posture of iconoclasm within the framework of the affirmation of icons in general.[79]

Whether such an alternative interpretation can also explain the more dualistic character of Marion that Ward highlights I will not attempt to determine here, and I thus have no definitive answer to the question of whether Marion is a closet iconoclast or only attempting to avoid a particular sort of idolatry. What I have wanted to show with this discussion of Marion's phenomenology of the icon is above all that the icon is a dynamic phenom-

---

75. The quotation is found in Ambrosius Giakalis, *Images of the Divine: The Theology of the Icons at the Seventh Ecumenical Council,* Studies in the History of Christian Thought vol. 54 (Leiden/New York/Cologne: E. J. Brill, 1994), p. 89.

76. Marion, "The Prototype and the Image," p. 67, as well as Marion, "The Idol and the Icon," in *God without Being,* 9.

77. Cf. Marion, "The Idol and the Icon," p. 10.

78. The former references the title *The Crossing of the Visible,* the latter the expression in a chapter on the icon (primarily as the human face, inspired by Levinas) in Marion, *In Excess,* pp. 104–27.

79. On iconoclasm and ideology criticism, see William J. T. Mitchell, *Iconology: Image, Text, Ideology* (Chicago/London: University of Chicago Press, 1986), pp. 196–208.

enon. What is phenomenologically critical with the icon is not what it *is* but what it *does*. From Marion's phenomenological perspective the icon is not really an "it," that is to say, a thing, but a certain way of appearing for different phenomena. A painted icon would, according to Marion's argument, be able to function as an idol for certain people. The icon as a way of appearing instead designates an event that allows the invisible to emerge in the visible and thereby allows the person to receive the world through her gaze in a new way, a way that does not reduce the world to an object for the person's curious gaze, but instead sees it as glorified, responsive, and inexhaustible (cf. chapter 4).[80]

By way of conclusion let me tarry a bit here with the relationship between the visible and the invisible. According to my argument above apropos Marion, the visible and the invisible are not each other's rivals. The relationship between the visible and the invisible is connected in an intimate way to the corresponding relationship between transcendence and immanence, and I therefore want to reiterate and clarify my conclusions above through a short discussion of the relationship between these concepts. The question is whether it is possible to understand how experiences of transcendence can be possible without reducing transcendence to anthropological categories—so without reducing the invisible to the visible. In modern times transcendence has come to stand for something that is the opposite of immanence, that is to say, something that is "far away." A transcendent God, according to this way of understanding transcendence, is not a God who is worthy of humanity, because we need a God who is "near" us.[81] If transcendence means that something is remote this is correct, but if transcendence could be understood as "difference," it is hardly the opposite of presence or immanence.[82] According to Thomas Aquinas God is not an existence, but existence itself, and God's transcendence can thus be God's way of being present in the world.[83] This is a theological

---

80. Here is the starting point for a theological aesthetics. I will not develop any such viewpoints here, but will refer to David Bentley Hart, *The Beauty of the Infinite,* as well as Hans Urs von Balthasar, *The Glory of the Lord: A Theological Aesthetics.* Vol. 1: *Seeing the Form,* trans. Leiva-Merikakis Erasmo (Edinburgh: T. & T. Clark, 1982).

81. Cf. Sallie McFague, *Models of God: Theology for an Ecological, Nuclear Age* (London: SCM, 1987).

82. See Rowan Williams, "The Nicene Heritage," in *The Christian Understanding of God Today,* ed. James Byrne (Dublin: Columba Press, 1993), p. 46.

83. Thomas Aquinas, *Summa Theologica* (Paris: Sumptibus P. Lethielleux, Bibliopolae Editoris, 1939), Ia, q8, a 1, resp. Cf. also the account in Walter Lowe's article "Second Thoughts

understanding of "transcendence as difference," but such an understanding of transcendence is not necessarily theological in a confessional sense. Maurice Merleau-Ponty has argued that the invisible, as a condition for our being able to experience the visible, is not something absolutely invisible, but rather "the invisible *of* this world, that which inhabits the world."[84] Plato had a similar understanding of transcendence in *The Republic* and in *Phaedrus*.[85] Let me here give a concluding summary of transcendence via Plato.

If with Plato we understand the good as an "inaccessible and inexhaustible plenitude," this means that the presence of the good can be understood as the gift of existence.[86] To borrow a term from Jacques Derrida, we can say that the good, according to Plato, is "disseminated" through existence. Where does one meet the good? Even if the good, according to Plato, is "other from all being," this does not mean that one must say goodbye to time and space in order to meet it. Because goodness is disseminated in time, it is through time that one can experience the good, says the English theologian Catherine Pickstock: "[T]he good arrives through time, and therefore time is not merely a ladder of access which can be kicked away, its job performed."[87] Experiences of the good are not a retreat from this world, even if every single case of "making present" of the good will fall short before the inexhaustibility that exists in its transcendental source. This understanding of transcendence as difference does not represent transcendence as the world's second floor, but instead as something that spreads its light throughout the world, even as something that is embodied in the world. Transcendence makes up the luster of the world. According to Plato, transcendence reveals itself in the beautiful, but does not thereby nullify the world or the beauty of the world. The adequate reception of the good that shines through the world—the adequate way to perceive it—is through the doxology (in the sense of praise) a way to be-in-the-world, according to Pickstock: "Praise of

---

about Transcendence," in *The Religious,* ed. John D. Caputo (Malden, MA/Oxford: Blackwell, 2001), pp. 241–51.

84. Maurice Merleau-Ponty, *The Visible and the Invisible,* Northwestern Studies in Phenomenology & Existential Philosophy, trans. Alphonso Lingis (Evanston, IL: Northwestern University Press, 1968), p. 151.

85. Catherine Pickstock, *After Writing,* pp. 3–46. Pickstock's reading of Plato is an overall critique of Jacques Derrida's reading of Plato's *Phaedrus* in "Plato's Pharmacy," in *Dissemination,* trans. Barbara Johnson (London: Athlone Press, 1981), pp. 61–172.

86. Pickstock, *After Writing,* p. 11.

87. Pickstock, *After Writing,* p. 13.

the beautiful is the supreme ethic, the route to the transcendent good which does not circumvent situatedness and contingency, and remains open to difference and multiplicity."[88] The possibility of receiving the beautiful, that is to say, perceiving it, thus lies in a certain way of relating to the beautiful, namely the doxological.

Understood thus, transcendence is not identical with the negation of time, space, history, and language. Transcendence is not the downfall of the human, but rather her consummation, and this is an important insight. Instead of being the negation of human or nonhuman nature, transcendence means that there exists a "deeper" or "higher" dimension to the world's existence. Transcendence is embodied in the world and allows us to glimpse something that is not the world through the world itself. If one understands the presence of the invisible in the visible—or for that matter, the presence of God in the world—according to this model, the errand of the iconoclasts also becomes comprehensible, namely to avoid at any cost identifying the Creator with the creation. Through the presence of the invisible in the visible the difference between the two threatens to escape notice, and with this we would get a fatal confusion of invisible and visible, which would lead to the reduction of both, but also to idolatry. The theologically legitimate errand of the image prohibition—and of the iconoclasm as well—was of course to prevent the created from being deified and so becoming an idol.[89] With this its iconic luster would be exchanged for something other than itself. The understanding of transcendence that I have outlined, however, wants to offer an alternative to both iconoclasm, which warns against confusing visible and invisible, and the other extreme, namely contrasting invisible and visible by understanding God's revelation as the negation of the visible world. For the theology of the icon it is not a matter of the negation of the material world, but rather, as John of Damascus has indicated, of a "glorification of matter."[90] The gaze that manages to behold the glorification of matter is not just any human gaze at all, but an embodied and involved gaze, a gaze that is simultaneously both passive and active. But gaze and image cannot be separated, and the erotic gaze that manages to perceive the invisible in the visible is therefore also a liturgically informed gaze, a gaze that is participatory in the doxological practices.

88. Pickstock, *After Writing*, p. 45.
89. Bjerg, *Synets teologi*, p. 37.
90. John of Damascus, *On the Divine Images*, I, 16.

The Liturgical Gaze

Critical questions for the Christian scopic regime are not only which gaze Christianity strives for or what it sees, but also how it comes to see what it sees. As I have argued above in chapter 4, the gaze is not given by nature, but is socially and historically conditioned. On the basis of a discussion of scopic regimes, I attempted to show how the conditions for sight vary with different epochs, cultures, and social communities. But even if it is possible to describe scopic regimes or epochs of sight in the way I have done above, this should not be understood as though the gaze were wholly determined by its scopic regime. There is never one and only one scopic regime, which, so to speak, determines from above how people see, but within a given scopic regime there exists a constantly open possibility for deviant or critically questioning gazes. There are always other influences besides that of the dominant culture, which may lead to hybrids and creative syntheses between different scopic regimes. The question then becomes how one learns to see within a particular scopic regime and how the dominant regime is questioned by other ways to see. How can the social encoding of the individual's gaze be altered or replaced? It is not a matter of an individual act of will, but rather the fact that deviant and critical gazes are also socially conditioned, even if they may be conditioned in a different way than the dominant perspective. In addition, I believe that the social "training" that results in the individual learning to see differently is a question of which social practices she or he is participatory in. For the Christian church it is a matter of the praxis of faith and the worship of the church, that is to say, of ritual practices like prayer, worship, Bible reading, and meditation.

These ritual practices are named with language taken from church and the theology of the liturgy. The French theologian Louis Bouyer defines liturgy in a succinct way: "that system of prayers and rites traditionally canonized by the Church as her own prayer and worship."[91] Implicit in such a definition is that liturgy and prayer cannot be separated by means of the oppositional pairs external and internal or public and private. The public prayer of the church and the private prayers of the solitary believer are mutually dependent on each other. This means that the liturgy cannot be seen as an empty ceremony, but is of essential and constitutive significance for the faith of the believer, both in the sense of *fides qua creditur*, "the faith by which I

---

91. Louis Bouyer, *Liturgical Piety* (Notre Dame: University of Notre Dame Press, 1955), p. 1. Italics in the original.

believe," that is to say the personal relationship to God, and *fides quae creditur,* "the faith that is believed," that is to say the content of faith. It is through the liturgy that *fides qua* and *fides quae,* that is to say the "subjective" and the "objective" dimensions of faith—if these concepts are not understood too absolutely, or as competing—meet in a dynamic relationship, and it is here that the believer's specific way of experiencing the world is constituted. The liturgy is thus primary in the relationship to doctrine as well as to the theological exposition of the same. Liturgy is, according to philosopher and theologian Jean-Yves Lacoste's more phenomenological definition, a name for everything that embodies the person's relationship to God.[92]

Through the liturgy the believer experiences the world as God's world. These experiences should not be understood as though they were a retrospective interpretation of already-given facts. The Dutch theologian Edward Schillebeeckx attempts, following hermeneutic phenomenology, to explain how the Christian faith can be unilaterally understood neither as a subjective experience nor as an objective fact, taking the example of seeing a chair as an analogy.[93] In the visual perception of a chair, Schillebeeckx says, one does not *interpret* the thing before oneself as a chair, one *sees* a chair, even if this seeing is inevitably an interpretation. Every act of sight that sees something sees this something *as* something, and thus the act of sight is itself an interpretive act. It is the same with faith. Faith is not primarily experienced as an interpretation of an already-stated fact that has in some way already been established before and independently of faith; faith is the *specific way* in which religious people actually *experience* what is happening. Schillebeeckx means that the person experiences actively, through her entire way of being-in-the-world, and it is therefore not possible to separate faith as subjective experience from faith as an objective fact other than purely conceptually. It is not only Christian words, but also images and embodied acts that both articulate the meaning of "God" for Christianity and form the Christian experience.[94] The liturgies of different churches thereby come to form different

---

92. Jean-Yves Lacoste, *Experience and the Absolute: Disputed Questions on the Humanity of Man,* Perspectives in Continental Philosophy, trans. Mark Raftery-Skehan (New York: Fordham University Press, 2004), pp. 2, 26f. The entirety of Lacoste's study could be called a "phenomenology of the liturgy."

93. Edward Schillebeeckx, *Christ: The Christian Experience in the Modern World,* trans. John Bowden (London: SCM, 1980), 32–33.

94. Cf. John Milbank, "Postmodern Critical Augustinianism: A Short *Summa* in Forty-two Responses to Unasked Questions," in *The Postmodern God: A Theological Reader,* Blackwell Readings in Modern Theology, ed. Graham Ward (Oxford: Blackwell, 1997), p. 269.

experiences. While I will get into these differences a bit more closely in the coming chapter on embodiment, I will touch on the question from a more general perspective here.

In order to somewhat deepen the understanding of how the ritual can be a way of constituting the person's interpretive acts, I will now turn to several central strands within cultural anthropology and the study of rites. The American anthropologist Clifford Geertz is one of those who has attempted to define the concept "culture" in relation to issues of the sort I have outlined above (and here we will recognize the discussion from the phenomenology of the life-world that I presented in chapter 1). In one of these definitions he writes:

> [Culture] denotes an historically transmitted pattern of meaning embodied in symbols, a system of inherited conceptions expressed in symbolic forms by means of which men communicate, perpetuate, and develop their knowledge about and attitudes toward life.[95]

If the Christian church is understood as such a culture, its liturgy is the symbolic form through which the Christian faith is handed down, both as knowledge and as a way of orienting oneself in life. The one who participates in the liturgy of the church will thereby cultivate certain distinct dispositions for experiencing the world. Geertz also says that the conviction that religious conceptions and religious instructions are trustworthy is generated through ritual. He writes in an oft-cited formulation: "In a ritual, the world as lived and the world as imagined, fused under the agency of a single set of symbolic forms, turns out to be the same world"—and the ritual thereby produces a transformation of the perception and experience of reality.[96]

---

95. Clifford Geertz, *The Interpretation of Cultures: Selected Essays* (New York: Basic Books, 1973), p. 89.

96. Geertz, *Interpretation of Cultures*, p. 112. How do the concepts liturgy and ritual relate to each other? They are likely often understood as correlatives to the concepts particular and universal, so that liturgy is a particular making concrete of the more general concept rite. Such a division is problematic, however, since it is not obvious that "the ritual" as a universal category for human experience really is universal. No form of typologizing is neutral, and the appearance of the concept ritual within the framework of the European cultures' transformation of their self-understanding in relation to other cultures and religions during the nineteenth century speaks for the fact that the concept is governed by the interests that arose during this epoch. My praxis will be that I follow the terminology of those authors whom I refer to. Among theologians the concept of liturgy is the most common, but scholars of rite—from "Religious Studies"—instead make use of the concept rite. I will draw on insights from both

In the ritual a symbolic union of the person's *ethos*—in the sense of ethical character—and her worldview, that is to say, reflection on this character, occurs. Geertz says that it is not always easy to differentiate between cultural and distinctly religious practices, and it is precisely my point that such a distinction is difficult. It is not a matter of specific religious rituals constituting people's specifically religious attitudes to life, but that *ethos* and the reflection on this *ethos* are united in the ritual—even as regards purely secular practices. As Geertz puts it, in the ritual not only is a model *of* what the participants believe created, but also a model *for* what the participants believe.[97] This is presumably the case with both religious and secular cultural practices.

Even if there is thus no point in separating out religious rituals as unique examples of the union of *ethos* and worldview, this does not mean that it is impossible to differentiate between the religious or cultural context of different rituals. Geertz further indicates that most believers do not live more than momentarily in the symbolic world that the religious symbols formulate. The everyday world with its everyday objects and practical actions is the world that most humans are most rooted in. The symbolic world that the religious rituals establish is, however, not completely distinct from this more everyday world, but "colors"—to use Geertz's expression—the individual's conception of this everyday world.[98] Geertz is not completely clear here, but I do not believe that he wants to argue that the everyday world is naturally given in a way that the religious world is not, but quite simply means that it is more "ordinary," i.e., that, for most people and for the most part, it constitutes a self-evident condition. He notes that a person can be religiously insensitive, but that it is difficult to survive without some sort of sense for the everyday. But the question is, of course, where the boundary between "the religious" and "the everyday" goes. I want not so much to question the differentiation between respective spheres as to argue that the differentiation between them does not generally need to allot "the religious" to a distinct sphere, even if in particular cases it can of course behave in such a way. It is not only conceivable, but also probable that "the everyday" in certain cultures is "religiously" conditioned in a way that it is not possible to separate "the religious" from other practices and conceptions. Catherine Pickstock writes: "[M]edieval

---

in this section, and therefore follow their own terminology in order to mark the disciplinary differences—which also becomes a difference in perspective. More on this problem is found in both of Catherine Bell's books, referred to below.

97. Geertz, *Interpretation of Cultures*, pp. 113–14.
98. Geertz, *Interpretation of Cultures*, pp. 119–23.

social practice was definitively ritual or liturgical in character. There simply was no duality of the liturgical and the mundane, just as the dichotomy of public and private was foreign to the medieval mind."[99] The existence of religiously indifferent individuals is possible even in such a culture, but it is then most likely primarily a matter of individuals who are indifferent towards the actual faith content of the religion. With Geertz it can sometimes sound as though the separation between "the religious" and "the everyday" were clear, at the same time that he expressly wants to keep them together. Among other places, this is clear in the following quotation:

> Having ritually "leapt" . . . into the framework of meaning which religious conceptions define, and the ritual ended, returned again to the common-sense world, a man is—unless, as sometimes happens, the experience fails to register—changed. And as he is changed, so also is the common-sense world, for it is now seen as but the partial form of a wider reality which corrects and completes it.[100]

Here it is assumed—at least conceptually—that "the religious" and "the everyday" are two distinct spheres that are united thanks to the ritual. Again, I do not mean to dispute that humans often believe themselves to live in differentiated spheres, or that "the religious" and "the everyday" may be perceived as two distinct spheres, which is probably the case in certain late-modern European societies, such as, for example, Sweden. What I want to argue is quite simply that any distinctions between different spheres originate in historically contingent reasons, and that "the religious" per definition hardly has to be understood as a distinct sphere in an analysis of society. The relationship between religion and everyday life may appear very different depending on which society one is thinking of, but also depending on which religion one has in mind, which Geertz is conscious of as well.[101] In

---

99. Pickstock, *After Writing*, p. 146. Cf. pp. 140–58, together as well with Talal Asad, *Genealogies of Religion: Discipline and Reasons of Power in Christianity and Islam* (Baltimore/London: Johns Hopkins University Press, 1993), pp. 55–79, as well as Arne Rasmusson, "En gång fanns inte det sekulära—Social teologi från Ernst Troeltsch till John Milbank," in *På spaning efter framtidens kyrka*, ed. Sune Fahlgren (Örebro, Sweden: Libris, 1998), pp. 105–30.

100. Geertz, *Interpretation of Cultures*, p. 122.

101. Geertz, *Interpretation of Cultures*, p. 122: "The nature of the bias religion gives to ordinary life varies with the religion involved, with the particular dispositions induced in the believer by the specific conceptions of cosmic order he has come to accept." In some of Geertz's statements it seems as though there is an interpretation of religion as a worldview distinct from

summary, one can say that the significance of religion for an anthropologist like Geertz is that it is both a source of conceptions of the world, the self, and the relationship between them (religion as a model *of*), as well as a source of deep-lying distinct mental dispositions for how the world is experienced (religion as a model *for*). Religion both interprets and forms the experiences of existence. Both of these aspects are united in the ritual.

Rituals have garnered ever-greater interest in recent times in academic as well as in other contexts.[102] One of the foremost within the field is religious scholar Catherine Bell from the USA. In two books she has studied not only rites, but also rite research.[103] In these she takes a critical stance towards Émile Durkheim's perception of religion as a question of primary beliefs and secondary rites (even if he also highlights the significance of the rite for the handing down of collective convictions). Rites are not only an expression of certain beliefs that exist prior to and independent of these rites, but are also a formative practice in which beliefs are shaped. Thought and practice are, according to Bell, mutually dependent, and she wants to show how these concepts are dichotomized in the discourse on ritual, for example, in Geertz.[104]

Bell is also more skeptical than Geertz regarding the possibility of bringing together a culture's beliefs and its rituals. Symbolic actions, however central they may be for a culture or religion, are more ambiguous for the participants than many theoreticians have been willing to recognize.[105] They therefore do not function in any simple way as a medium for transmitting particular beliefs. In other words, they do not constitute a distinct knowledge

---

a particular *ethos,* and as though religion's shaping significance for intellectual, emotional, and moral experiences would come secondhand (see *Interpretation of Cultures,* pp. 123; 127). Such an understanding of religion is, however, historically developed, and most characteristic of a contemporary West marked by Christianity, and does not constitute a universal category that can be applied to all religions, always and everywhere. See Talal Asad, *Genealogies of Religion* as well as Arne Rasmusson, "En gång."

102. From a reformed, theological perspective, see Bent Flemming Nielson, *Genopførelser: Ritual, kommunikation og kirke* (Copenhagen: Anis, 2004).

103. Catherine Bell, *Ritual Theory, Ritual Practice* (New York/Oxford: Oxford University Press, 1992), together with *Ritual: Perspectives and Dimensions* (New York/Oxford: Oxford University Press, 1997). Bell is also critical towards talk of "ritual" as an autonomous and universal category, and therefore prefers to speak of ritualization as a distinguishable phenomenon in the human life-world. She writes in *Ritual Theory, Ritual Practice,* pp. 222–23: "'Ritualization' attempts to correct the implications of universality, naturalness, and an intrinsic structure that have accrued to the term 'ritual.'" It is therefore not given that "rituals" are something obsolete for the post/modern Western person. See *Ritual,* pp. 138–69.

104. Bell, *Ritual Theory, Ritual Practice,* pp. 25–35. Cf. pp. 48–49.

105. Bell, *Ritual Theory, Ritual Practice,* pp. 183–84.

for the participants, since the meaning of the ritual is often overdetermined. Now this does not need to mean that they do not communicate any meaning at all, that they are mute, but rather that this overdetermination can lead to what Paul Ricoeur calls "a surplus of meaning," that is to say, the semantic possibilities that a rite gives rise to cannot be collected under a particular category.[106] One might imagine that the rituals establish a conceptual world that may be related to and behaved in in various ways, depending on the participants' individual dispositions and histories, rather than providing a system of knowledge, some sort of outlook. Additionally, it is certainly possible for rites, whose structure is different from the majority culture's, to question the surrounding culture's values and ways of understanding life by undermining its linguistic, ritual, and perceptual conventions. In brief, one might contend that the rituals establish a *doxa* (here in a philosophical rather than a theological sense), rather than some form of *epistēmē,* that is to say, a historically situated knowledge rather than an absolute, atemporal knowledge.[107]

That something constitutes a rite—in opposition to another human practice—says nothing in itself of its effectiveness in creating and maintaining a meaning. Bell writes: "Whatever the commonalities among ritual in general, we must conclude that ritual practices can encode very different ways of being in the world."[108] How and with what sort of success a concrete rite establishes a conceptual world (including dispositions for perceiving, assessing, and characterizing existence in a particular way) is probably dependent on which concrete rite we have in view. This leads to the question of the relationship between icon and liturgy, which is also a concrete example of a rite. It is assumed without any doubt that the ritual and/or cultural context is critical for how one experiences an image. Marita Sturken and Lisa Cartwright write the following in their introduction to visual theory:

> An image creates meaning in the moment that it is received by the viewer, and interpreted. Hence, we can say that meanings are not inherent in images. Rather, meanings are the product of a complex social interaction among image, viewers, and context.[109]

106. Paul Ricoeur, *Interpretation Theory: Discourse and the Surplus of Meaning* (Fort Worth: Texas Christian University Press, 1976), pp. 45–69.

107. Cf. Mats Rosengren, *Doxologi: En essä om kunskap* (Åstorp, Sweden: Rhetor förlag, 2002).

108. Bell, *Ritual,* pp. 190–91.

109. Marita Sturken and Lisa Cartwright, *Practices of Looking: An Introduction to Visual Culture* (Oxford/New York: Oxford University Press, 2001), p. 47.

The Russian-Orthodox icon that is found in a museum is thus in a certain way a different image than one that is found in a Russian-Orthodox worship service or placed in a Russian-Orthodox church. The question is whether the icon may be understood as icon without its liturgical setting.

According to theologian Nikolaus Thon, who has investigated the connection between icon and liturgy in the Orthodox church, the two are intimately connected. Thon illustrates their connectedness with the image of two branches from the same root.[110] To perform the liturgy is nothing other than to create a living icon, and to paint or perceive an icon is a liturgical action. Both icon and liturgy are adapted ways for human beings to know God and thereby embody faith—the one through form and color, the other through sound and movement. So there is a sort of likeness both in terms of form and content between icons and liturgy since both point to God's action of salvation. Thus in Orthodox theology, the image of the icon is not thought to function outside of or independently of the liturgy. The liturgy is the icon's working and primary context, and provides, according to the formulation of theologian Steven Grimwood, "the rhythm, spaces, syntax and grammar around which they articulate their meaning."[111] Those who participate in the liturgy thus become a part of the whole of the symbolic world that is articulated by icon, liturgy, and assembly together. As Grimwood has indicated, this is a critical point in relation to Marion's understanding of the icon: one can ignore neither the materiality of the image nor the relationship of the viewer to the image when one speaks of the icon. The icon is not only something that quite simply surprises or overtakes the viewer, but is something that interacts with the viewer, who is thereby actively involved in the relationship to the icon.[112] My aim with this section is precisely to emphasize that the gaze that can perceive the invisible in the visible is a liturgically informed gaze, and that only through this can there exist a social basis for a distinctly theological scopic regime.

It was thus of great significance when, during the iconoclasm, the ecumenical tradition rejected Constantine V's iconoclastic synod in 754, which argued that the Eucharist was the only necessary and legitimate image of Christ.[113] The argument that the Eucharist should be the only legitimate

---

110. Nikolaus Thon, *Ikone und Liturgie,* Sophia: Quellen östlicher Theologie vol. 19, ed. Julius Tyciak and Wilhelm Nyssen (Trier: Paulinus-Verlag, 1979), p. 28.

111. Steven Grimwood, "Iconography and Postmodernity," *Literature and Theology* 17, no. 1 (2003): 83.

112. Grimwood, "Iconography and Postmodernity," pp. 88–89.

113. Hans-Joachim Schulz, *Bekenntnis statt Dogma: Kriterien der Verbindlichkeit kirchlicher Lehre,* Quaestiones Disputatae 163 (Freiburg/Basel/Vienna: Herder, 1996), p. 148.

image of Christ was hyperrealistic: only the Eucharist was of the same being as Christ. For the iconophiles, on the other hand, the Eucharist was not any sort of "image" at all. The image opponents saw the Eucharist as wholly autonomous, while the iconophiles saw it as the culmination of a liturgy whose entire practice revealed Christ. The images had their place in this liturgy as well. What primarily legitimated the role of the images theologically in tradition was not legends of images not painted by human hand *(acheiropoiētoi)*, or of miracles in connection to images, but the place of the images—as well as of the church building—in the liturgy.[114] Through images and symbols the liturgy can produce a representation/presentation of God's action of salvation in a dynamic way that human senses can perceive.

Here we can enlist the help of the argument above regarding Geertz. In this case, the liturgy is both a source of ideas about God, the world, the self, and the relationship between them—Geertz's understanding of religion as a model *of*—and a source of deep-lying distinct mental dispositions for how the world is experienced that, among other things, come to shape the participants' experiences of the icon—Geertz's understanding of religion as a model *for*. In other words, the liturgy both interprets and shapes experiences of existence. It is by being involved in this liturgy that the person learns to see and experience the invisible through the visible. Seeing the icon as icon is not something given by nature, but must be learned like every other way of seeing. Through the liturgy the participants learn the right codes in order to be able to see the icon as icon.[115] The Danish theologian Bent Flemming Nielsen compares the liturgy to a "reenactment": "The ritual actions open up a different focus for consciousness by virtue of the body's repetition of the prescribed movements. This can be understood as a renewed contextualizing, as the establishment of a new space and a new time."[116] The perception of the icon is in other words not a purely cognitive, intellectual activity. In some ways it cannot be reduced to a visual activity either—the church's rite, the liturgy, involves more or less all of the person's senses. Participation in the liturgy is thus participation on the part of the whole body. It is with the whole body, and not just with the eye, that one looks at an image, and the placement of the icon within the liturgy clarifies how this also applies to the icon—one might argue that it applies to the icon eminently.[117]

114. Schulz, *Bekenntnis statt Dogma,* p. 149.

115. Bjerg, *Synets teologi,* p. 105.

116. Nielsen, *Genopførelser,* p. 101.

117. Jean-Louis Chrétien, *Hand to Hand: Listening to the Work of Art,* Perspectives in Continental Philosophy, trans. Stephen E. Lewis (New York: Fordham University Press, 2003), p. 18.

So a particular gaze is required in order to see the icon as icon, and this gaze is rehearsed in the liturgical event. This claim is supported by the liturgy's character as doxology, that is to say, its theological significance as worship of God. The liturgy configures a distinct way to both understand existence and to relate to existence.[118] The doxological posture goes beyond both a "mimetic realism" that ascribes the person a complete and definite— and autonomous—identity and a "secular irony" that configures a continually distanced and alienated identity.[119] The doxology instead configures an identity that remains open to diversity and difference without renouncing its situated and contingent existence. Through the liturgy, and above all through the liturgy of communion, a posture is configured where the person relates both actively and passively towards God, fellow humans, and the rest of creation.[120] The gaze that is cultivated by the doxology is not an agapeic gaze in Nygren's unilateral sense, but an erotic gaze in the sense that I have described earlier in this chapter. To celebrate communion is to stand in a line of endless improvised variations on one and the same theme, which is not given prior to the improvisations, but rather in, with, and under them.[121] Through the liturgy of communion the lives of the communion participants are related to the crucified and risen Christ, at the same time that the bread and the wine—as symbols for what all humans live on, food and drink—connect them to their everyday, earthly life. Through the liturgy the (for the church) foundational interpretation context is also established, and the sermon should thus not be understood as an altogether discursive activity in contrast with a ritual.[122]

In a theological sense, the doxological person is a person who understands her existence as a fundamental relationality, not as a religious, national, or ethnic politics of identity, and as a gift, not in terms of a competitive or exchange economy. David F. Ford speaks of communion as a "condensation of the Christian *habitus*"[123] and in this borrows a concept from the French sociologist Pierre Bourdieu (I will return to Bourdieu's concept of the *habitus* in the next chapter). By *habitus* is meant a way of being and acting that structures and generates dispositions, tendencies, and

---

118. Pickstock, *After Writing*, p. 39: "Liturgy is . . . not a constative representation now and then of what is praise-worthy, but constitutes a whole way of life."

119. Pickstock, *After Writing*, p. 45.

120. Pickstock, *After Writing*, pp. 176–77.

121. David F. Ford, *Self and Salvation: Being Transformed,* Cambridge Studies in Christian Doctrine (Cambridge: Cambridge University Press, 1999), pp. 107–281.

122. Nielsen, *Genopførelser,* pp. 100–103, 195–208.

123. Ford, *Self and Salvation,* p. 140.

inclinations in the thinking and acting of the person, at the same time that the *habitus* is shaped by earlier structures and actions. The *habitus* concept is appropriate for describing the participant in the liturgy, since it contains both a passive, socializing dimension and an active, striving dimension: the person is indeed shaped by the liturgy, but by participating in it she has also chosen to be shaped by it, and can relate reflexively to this shaping as well. A Christian *habitus,* as Ford terms it, can therefore be a training in a specific relationality, not being possessed by one's own person, but rather living responsively towards Christ and towards other people.[124]

Now the liturgy's habituation of the participants for seeing existence in a certain way should not be understood as something that occurs automatically. Bell has warned against drawing conclusions that are too far-reaching about the effectiveness of rituals for socializing, resocializing, and desocializing those who participate in them.[125] That they function in a socializing way—or rather, in a habituating way—is not questioned by Bell, but she does wants to bring in other factors, such as the degree of participation, the frequency of ritual participation, and how the values that are encompassed by the deep-structure of the rite are supported by other areas in social life. The rite, Bell says, is embedded in a rich configuration of understandings, traditions, practices, and tensions that affect its function. Translated into more theological terms, the liturgy is not independent of the larger context of religious life and doctrine that it is a part of—but the dependence is mutual. One ought to additionally keep in mind the fact that the habituation of both the person's gaze and of her total way of being-in-the-world that occurs through the liturgy for a contemporary late- or postmodern human being hardly takes place within the framework of a liturgy.[126] Meaning is instead shaped by practicing worship-service participants in the relationship between the liturgy and the context of our more everyday lives. In other words, the liturgy also has a context, and the meaning, the dispositions and interpretations it eventually creates, occurs in a negotiation with the surrounding context. The meaning of the liturgy is produced in the negotiation between the conducting of the liturgy and the cultural context of the recipients in a complex social interaction, and so is no more something that exists within the liturgy than the meaning of the icon is something that exists in the icon itself.

124. Ford, *Self and Salvation,* p. 140.

125. Bell, *Ritual,* p. 252.

126. See Graham Hughes, *Worship as Meaning: A Liturgical Theology for Late Modernity,* Cambridge Studies in Christian Doctrine (Cambridge: Cambridge University Press, 2003), pp. 220–21.

In summary, the liturgy is the way by which the believing person learns to perceive the world as God's world. This means that her entire way of being-in-the-world is shaped by the liturgy. As the American theologian David Bentley Hart writes: "It is a way of seeing that must be learned, because it alters every perspective upon things; and to learn it properly one must be conformed to what one sees."[127] This does not occur in any infallible, predetermined, or absolute way.[128] Learning to see the world as God's world, and so to exercise one's gaze for the invisible, is not a momentary process, but a process that builds on repetition and deepening. What I have wanted to show in this section is thus not that the liturgy inexorably comes to force the practitioner to understand the world in a certain way. Rather, I have wanted to clarify how the way in which we perceive the world, not least through our gaze, has a social context that is not given by nature. Thus our gazes can actually be transformed, and we therefore do not need to presuppose a particular way of seeing the world, be it the majority perspective or not, as a given way of seeing. The gaze thereby becomes both an ethical and a political question, since it concerns fundamental ways for the person to relate to herself, her surroundings, her fellow humans, and God. How we come to see what we see is thus significant both for *what* we see (the visible and the invisible) and *how* we see (covetously or generously). I will now leave the question of the liturgical gaze—but will return to the question of the liturgical body in chapter 9—in order to finally return to the question of the scopic regime of Christianity and how its gaze configures a specific way to be-in-the-world.

The Scopic Regime of Christianity

In this chapter I have offered a reflection on the gaze determined by Christianity. This reflection has not only—from a theological perspective—dealt with the way in which the gaze sees what it sees (with a generously erotic desire), but also what this gaze sees (the invisible and the visible) and how it comes to see what it sees (the liturgy as the embodiment of the human being's relationship to God). Finally, I shall attempt to summarize the consequences of this for the scopic regime of Christianity in dialogue with the issues and the different scopic regimes that I outlined in chapter 4. How does the gaze of faith relate to other gazes?

127. Hart, *The Beauty of the Infinite*, p. 337.
128. Jean-Luc Marion, "The Blind at Siloah," in *The Crossing of the Visible*, pp. 64–65.

285

In his book *Simulacra and Simulation* from 1981 the French philosopher Jean Baudrillard argues that the iconophiles were "the most modern minds, the most adventurous" because they had understood that the icons, beneath the mask of representing the presence of God pictorially, in fact staged God's death.[129] It was thus the iconophiles rather than the iconoclasts that had understood the true worth of the images, namely to function as a simulacrum for God: "[W]hat if God himself can be simulated, that is can be reduced to the signs that constitute faith?"[130] The iconoclasts feared that the icons replaced the pure idea of a transcendent God with a visible spectacle. The fear was not so much conditioned by the idea that the icons would be misleading or incomplete images of God, Baudrillard says, but this fear instead originates in the suspicion that the images do not refer to anything. The images would then become idols, that is to say, representations of something nonexistent, "perfect simulacra, forever radiant with their own fascination."[131] Baudrillard says that it is indeed the iconoclasts who saw through the threat from the images, and to a certain degree realized that they did not refer to anything, but at the same time it was the iconophiles who were boldest in letting the sign take the place that belonged to the designated, and thereby allowing a simulation of God. Baudrillard sets simulation against representation and believes that the entire religious system becomes a free-floating system that does not refer to anything other than itself, just as Disneyland in our time constitutes a simulated and mummified dream image of an America that no longer exists—and has never existed.[132] Such simulations should not be understood as ideologies in the sense that they give a skewed image of reality, but rather they serve to hide the fact that reality itself is no longer real, but has become a hyperreality, a virtual reality without any anchoring outside of the endless, self-referencing chain of the sign: "a liquidation of all referentials."[133] Baudrillard's conception of a free-floating hyperreality recalls the outline of the virtual eye or the post-photographic scopic era that I presented in chapter 4.

Paul Virilio, another French philosopher and cultural theoretician, has also connected the virtualization of reality to the disappearance of the divine referent, if in a less cynical interpretation of the iconophiles. In his book *The Vision Machine* he writes the following:

129. Jean Baudrillard, *Simulacra and Simulation,* trans. Sheila Faria Glaser (Ann Arbor: University of Michigan Press, 1994), p. 5.
130. Baudrillard, *Simulacra,* p. 5.
131. Baudrillard, *Simulacra,* p. 5.
132. Baudrillard, *Simulacra,* pp. 12–14.
133. Baudrillard, *Simulacra,* p. 2.

We have all had enough of hearing about the death of God, of man, of art and so on since the nineteenth century. What in fact happened was simply the progressive disintegration of a faith in perception founded in the Middle Ages, after animism, on the basis of the unicity of divine creation, the absolute intimacy between the universe and the God-man of Augustinian Christianity, a material world which loved itself and contemplated itself in its one God. In the West, the death of God and the death of art are indissociable; *the zero degree of representation* merely fulfilled the prophecy voiced a thousand years earlier by Nicephorus, Patriarch of Constantinople, during the quarrel with the iconoclasts: 'If we remove the image, not only Christ but the whole universe disappears.'[134]

Where Baudrillard thought that the iconophiles anticipated the future "society of the spectacle" and actively affirmed it, Virilio on the contrary argues that the patriarch Nikephoros anticipated the zero point of representation, and moreover warned against it.[135] This interest in medieval Byzantine discussions of icons among French philosophers might be surprising, but since the Russian Revolution there have existed in Paris a number of influential Russian-Orthodox theologians in exile, which may have contributed to a greater awareness of the problem of the icon among more secular thinkers as well. The point for Baudrillard or Virilio is, however, not to say so much about icons and iconophiles in themselves, but to illustrate, with the help of the theology of the icon, their contemporary analyses; nevertheless, their arguments about the icons provide a reason to bring in the idea of a Christian scopic regime in relation to the contemporary conceptions of the gaze and the three scopic regimes that have been outlined in chapter 4.

I want to begin by pointing out that the theologically determined gaze has a whole lot in common with the critique of monoscopism in modernity in all its phases. This has been criticized for dissolving the body, for being a "view from nowhere," for being "monoscopic," if not "monotheistic." Donna J. Haraway speaks, as we have seen in chapter 4, of "the god-trick of

---

134. Paul Virilio, *The Vision Machine,* trans. Julie Rose (Bloomington/Indianapolis: Indiana University Press, 1994), pp. 16–17.

135. The term "society of the spectacle," *la société du spectacle,* is taken from situationist Guy Debord's book *The Society of the Spectacle,* trans. Donald Nicholson-Smith (New York: Zone Books, 1995), and designates the social order of capitalism as a state of complete unreality.

seeing everything from nowhere."[136] Haraway's critique is not exclusively directed against a theological gaze, but can just as well be read as a theological critique. What I have attempted to plead for in this and the two previous chapters is that this is a critique that does not affect a theological gaze understood on the basis of the incarnation. The erotic gaze as an incarnated, involved gaze does not hover imperturbably apart from its visual object, but attempts to establish a generous relationship to what it sees. The erotic gaze attempts neither to dominate nor to domesticate its object, whether by devouring it as the covetous gaze does, or by relating indifferently to it as a purely registering gaze. The erotic gaze is not a "monoscopic" gaze, but rather an embodied gaze, and thus a gaze that allows itself to be found, positioned, and through this can be held responsible. The "deincarnated gaze," on the contrary, can never be held responsible because it can never be found. The Christian gaze based on an incarnational theology should thus be able to agree with Haraway's critique of a monoscopic regime, a critique that can indeed affect modern abstract theism, but does not affect incarnational theology in the same way. It relates to existence, to use Michel de Certeau's image, as a pedestrian relates to the city, rather than as a voyeur who creates a distanced overview from the highest tower of the city (or, one might add, through Bentham's panopticon).[137]

An additional feature of the theological gaze I have outlined in this chapter has to do with its perspective. If the perspective artists during the Renaissance (see chapter 4 again) imagined perspective as the view one has from a window—where the window frames what can and cannot be seen—we find a different, reversed perspective with the icon. If we also imagine the icon as a window here, then it is a window where the light falls in on us, not a window where we are the source of light (see chapter 6). In the icon it is those who are depicted who have a perspective on the viewer, not the viewer who has a perspective on that which is depicted. As the Swiss icon theologian Michel Quenot writes in one of his books on the icon:

> This means that the focus point actually moves out away from the icon toward the beholder, and the icon figures come forth to 'meet' him. The

136. Donna J. Haraway, "Situated Knowledges: The Science Question in Feminism and the Privilege of Partial Perspective," *Simians, Cyborgs, and Women: The Reinvention of Nature* (London: Free Association Books, 1991), p. 189.

137. Michel de Certeau, *The Practice of Everyday Life,* trans. Steven Rendall (Berkeley/Los Angeles/London: University of California Press, 1988), pp. 91–93.

result is an opening, a radiating forth, while the vanishing point in ordinary paintings results in a convergence that closes up.[138]

Where the icon opens towards the viewer, goes to meet her in order to involve her in its event, central perspective becomes, as Quenot has in mind in the quotation above, a way to capture and bar. The inverted perspective of the icon, as well as the icon's nonrealistic way of depicting what is portrayed, entails a different spatial awareness than that given by the curious gaze of modernity. The erotic gaze is not a gaze that investigates a strictly delimited space from a distance, but is instead a gaze that at once both views and is involved in this space. The icon has also been compared with a postmodern installation that the viewer can step into, interact with, and become a part of.[139] At the same time the erotic gaze is, one might say, a liturgical gaze, since the worship service is an alternative symbolic world that the viewer, as with the postmodern installation, can step into, and can interact with and become a part of. The erotic gaze, the eyes of faith, are an involved gaze.

But is there not a risk in this postmodern dissolution of central perspective, namely, that the scopic regime of the digital eye also dissolves every distinction between biological sight and cultural gaze, and so every partial standpoint, in an indifferent virtuality, which ironically reiterates modernity's "monoscopism" through a "polyscopism" without limit? According to Marion the self-referential image, that is to say, the image without reference to anything original, is still an idol, since it thereby receives as its highest aim, the gratification of the visual desire of the viewer.[140] With this the gaze of the viewer becomes self-referencing and the image is transformed into an idol. Expressed otherwise: How can a gaze inspired by the theologies of the incarnation and the icon avoid the indirect critique that Baudrillard directs against it, namely, that this would constitute a disguised disintegration of reality, a simulation of God via an iconic representation that disguises the fact that reality is simply an effect, a free-floating hyperreality? In chapter 4 I have shown how the gaze is both active and passive, and how it is thus possible for the gaze to see something other than itself. It can thereby avoid being reduced to an idol in Marion's sense above, as a reflection of itself, a mirror image. The content of the phenomenological argument in chapter

---

138. Michel Quenot, *The Icon: Window on the Kingdom,* trans. a Carthusian monk (Crestwood, NY: St. Vladimir's Seminary Press, 1991), p. 106.

139. Grimwood, "Iconography and Postmodernity," p. 82.

140. See Marion, "The Blind at Siloah," pp. 46–65.

4 was that the things we see cannot be reduced to a visible object that it is possible to master without doing violence to them. It is first and foremost the invisible light that makes the thing visible as thing. The thing, according to Heidegger, is not an object, a statically existing entity that it is possible to explore and map, but rather something that *does something* with its viewer by entering into relationship with her or him. Similarly, the icon represents the world as glorified, responsive, and inexhaustible in that the invisible appears here in visible form.

In this context I want to again highlight the icon as a thing where visible and invisible do not compete with each other.[141] Just as Christ's divine nature in the hypostatic union should not be understood as a rival of the human (cf. Chalcedon's "no confusion") or vice versa—as Baudrillard seems to suppose—the visible and invisible should also not be understood as rivals. The function of the icon is to "puncture" the self-sufficiency that characterizes the idol, the simulation, and the limitless gaze by gesturing to something that transcends the merely given. Steven Grimwood makes an interesting comparison with two concepts that Roland Barthes makes use of in the book *Camera Lucida,* namely *studium* and *punctum. Studium* constitutes the conventional codes we find in a photograph—background, attire, poses, etc.—by which we can understand and interpret a photograph, but never enter into relationship with it. *Punctum,* on the other hand, designates in a photograph that which goes beyond these codes, "a kind of subtle *beyond,*" which does not determine the viewer's response, but allows her to enter into relationship with the object of the photograph, that which saves the photographed thing from becoming an object and the viewer's gaze from being determined by the object.[142] The *punctum* is a pinprick from the photograph that strikes the viewer, or in the formulation of film scholar Astrid Söderbergh Widding, "an opening towards the unknown in the midst of the well-known."[143] Where *studium* dominates an image, its meaning is closed, but where *punctum* comes through, the viewer is invited "not just to view

141. Cf. Grimwood, "Iconography and Postmodernity," pp. 86–92.

142. Roland Barthes, *Camera Lucida: Reflections on Photography,* trans. Richard Howard (New York: Hill & Wang, 1981), p. 59.

143. Astrid Söderbergh Widding, *Blick och blindhet,* Bonnier Alba Essä (Stockholm: Bonnier Alba, 1997), p. 21. Cf. her account of how Barthes's insights can be applied to film as well as photography, pp. 21–24. Söderbergh Widding returns to the theme in a more specifically theological context in her article "Att gestalta det osynliga i det synliga medium," *Film och religion: Livstolkning på vita duken,* ed. Tomas Axelson and Ola Sigurdson (Örebro, Sweden: Cordia, 2005), pp. 77–95.

but also to 'speak,'" as Grimwood puts it.[144] Grimwood finds an analogous *punctum* in the icon, and he writes:

> The icon breaches the limits of the coded space by opening it up to a beyond—a transfigured, eternal space, into which the observer is brought into relation. This is not to claim any supernatural powers for the icon; rather that the icon, through its rich visual language and artistic conventions aims to show forth the divine reality within which *all* sensible things participate.[145]

The icon is a way of allowing the invisible to become visible in the visible without imagining these two as competing and thereby risking—to express myself in a schematic and typologizing way—either reducing the invisible to the visible as with the gaze of modernity, or allowing the visible to swallow the invisible—"the murderous power of images"—as with Baudrillard.[146] In other words, Grimwood affirms the quotation from patriarch Nikephoros that Virilio cited above, that "[i]f we remove the image, not only Christ but the whole universe disappears." The scopic regime of Christianity thus does not have to do with determining the gaze, but rather with its liberation. It is thus probably doubtful whether the word "regime" is applicable here, at least in its more negative connotations of "authoritative control." If the word is instead interpreted as "way of life," it is clearer what is meant, since by extension a "scopic regime" concerns the entirety of a person's way of being-in-the-world.

This second meaning of the word "regime" is also clear in Grimwood's continued distinction between the scopic regime of the digital eye and the eyes of faith. The gaze for the invisible is namely not given outside of a fellowship that cultivates what I have above called the liturgical gaze. Even if the erotic gaze is a gaze of grace that does not attempt to bring about an endpoint of the gaze, but in fact the opposite, this does not occur independently of a consciously cultivated way of life. The icon's meaning is generated in relationship to the Christian fellowship that also relates to different texts and practices, and encompasses both the viewer and the icon.[147] The gaze for the invisible is generated in the ongoing process that is the liturgy of the church.

---

144. Grimwood, "Iconography and Postmodernity," p. 88.
145. Grimwood, "Iconography and Postmodernity," pp. 89–90.
146. Baudrillard, *Simulacra*, p. 5.
147. Grimwood, "Iconography and Postmodernity," pp. 90-91.

It is not the icon in itself that saves them from becoming a spectacle or a mirror—it is instead by being included in this visually and ritually rich context as it opens towards the invisible. What the gaze sees and in which way it sees it are not independent of how it comes to see it. Or put differently: the erotic gaze as the gaze for the invisible is not independent of the liturgical gaze.

For the Christian scopic regime it is clear that this gaze is an incarnated gaze. The human being's way of relating to her environment is directly dependent on her embodied constitution in a way that makes it such that a discussion that focuses on the gaze easily becomes abstract. The gaze has often been understood by its critics as the sense organ that distances rather than holds together. I have in this and the three previous chapters attempted to show how the gaze is anything but abstract; instead it is culturally, historically, and not least physically situated. The gaze is a way of establishing relationships of different sorts; it *is* in fact a relationship. Not least the gaze of faith, whose theology I have formulated in this chapter, is a relational gaze, a gaze that takes its specific configuration from the Christian doctrine of God's presence in the person Jesus Christ, that is to say, from the doctrine of incarnation. The gaze is therefore an example of a concrete practice in which Christology has been received. I will now continue along the same path with the question of Christology's reception in additional significant practices by—again in four chapters—theologically investigating how the Christian tradition has imagined the embodiment of the human, as well as how a theology of the body could be formulated in our time. Gaze and embodiment go intimately together in the human way of being-in-the-world. These following chapters can thus be seen as a broadening and a deepening of the argument I have already brought apropos gaze and incarnation, at the same time that I hope the discussion of embodiment will make it even clearer how involved the human is in her life-world—and how embodied her gaze actually is.

PART III

EMBODIMENT

8. The Philosophical Body

As a first step on the path to a theology of the body, in this chapter I will discuss how the body as theme has returned in a distinct way in the contemporary philosophical debate. In chapter 1 I suggested that few specific theologies of the body have been developed historically. Even if there are now a number of different attempts at such, it would be wrong to argue that theological interest—at least so far—has matched the philosophical interest that has provided the opportunity to speak of the return of the body within philosophy.[1] There is therefore every reason for theology to listen to this philosophical conversation, and in this chapter I will describe different aspects of the philosophical interest in the body, in part as a background to my own theological investigation of the body, but also as an aid for generating insights and questions that may be useful in the formulation of such a theology.[2] Even if the questions that philosophy

---

1. Some attempts at a theology of the body from different perspectives and with different depths of attention may be found in Lisa Isherwood and Elizabeth Stuart, *Introducing Body Theology*, Introductions in Feminist Theology 2 (Sheffield: Sheffield Academic Press, 1998); James B. Nelson, *Body Theology* (Louisville: Westminster/John Knox Press, 1992), as well as Mary Timothy Prokes, *Toward a Theology of the Body* (Edinburgh: T. & T. Clark, 1996).

2. The point with such an investigation is not to establish a theology of correlation in Paul Tillich's sense. My division between a philosophical and a theological discussion of the body should not be understood as something principally expressive of a difference in essence between philosophical and theological pursuits. When it comes to a topic as controversial and elusive as a philosophy or theology of the body it is safest to avoid all too self-confident localizations of one's own discourse, not least given how these disciplines have been woven together in many different ways over the course of history, including in the discussion of the body. My division reflects only one such—in this instance—pragmatically accepted by standard descriptions of the subject and the self-descriptions of various thinkers. For an interesting typology of the relationship between theology and philoso-

offers are not entirely unknown to theology, I still believe that they can contribute both to achieving a distance from the prevalent ways of representing Christian embodiment and to preserving constructive insights within the theological tradition. This chapter will thus be of a primarily introductory character, even if I will indicate my theological interests more clearly in a few places.

What then does philosophy have to say about human embodiment? Gender theory and other critical theories of the last decades, in combination with the growing suspicion of the partiality of reason, have entailed an enormous interest in the body and its representations—an interest that in large part builds on earlier phenomenological studies of the body by the German philosopher Edmund Husserl, but perhaps above all on the French philosopher Maurice Merleau-Ponty. Even where feminist theory has found reason to criticize Merleau-Ponty for his ostensibly sex-neutral philosophy of the body, it has to a large degree been able to further develop his thought. However, as I touched on in chapter 1, referring to the body within a philosophical discourse is not self-explanatory. According to the English theologian Sarah Coakley, the interest in the body can be interpreted as a way to attempt to find an "Archimedean stable point" in a present where no "grand narrative" is still trustworthy. But even "the post-modern 'body,'" Coakley continues, "becomes subject to infinitely variable social constructions."[3] What is it we speak of when we refer to the body? It is a question whose answer is not at all self-evident. The body is formed *in* society and history, but also *by* society and history, and so a discussion of the body cannot be detached from its social and historical context. "The body is many," writes historian of ideas Karin Johannisson: "the desiring body, the disciplined body, the narcissistic body, the modern machine body of industrial society, the body of pain and illness, the unemployed body. The body as shell, exterior, language, myth, and locality."[4] To say something about the body today thus means that one ventures into the whole postmodern debate over the dissolution of the subject and the social construction of knowledge.

---

phy, see Ingolf U. Dalferth, *Theology and Philosophy*, Signposts in Theology (Oxford: Basil Blackwell, 1988).

3. Sarah Coakley, "The Eschatological Body: Gender, Transformation, and God," in *Powers and Submissions: Spirituality, Philosophy and Gender* (Oxford/Malden, MA: Blackwell, 2002), pp. 154–55.

4. Karin Johannisson, *Kroppens tunna skal: Sex essäer om kropp, historia och kultur* (Stockholm: Bokförlaget Pan, 1998), p. 10.

This new interest in the body within feminist and critical theory can at a fundamental level be said to have two claims. The first is that our body is never "given" to us in an immediate way. Even our consciousness of our relationship to our own body is mediated through representations of the body that are socially constituted. The second is that there is no "natural" body "underneath" or "behind" all these discursive representations. This means that the body is not only socially represented, but also socially constructed. In other words the body—just like vision—has a history, a history of different ways in which the body has been constructed.[5]

This chapter is divided into four sections, where I begin by discussing the basis for the return of the body, namely, the fact that it has in some sense been absent.[6] What does the absence of the body entail, what are its historical roots, and what reasons are there behind this absence? Then I will transition to describing what the return of the body as a living body in Merleau-Ponty's philosophy entails, and how this living body differs from other bodies. After the section on Merleau-Ponty I take up a critique that is directed against his phenomenology, namely, that it has not sufficiently taken into account the social construction of the human body. Following poststructuralist and feminist theory, I attempt to understand what the construction of the body means for the understanding of the human body, and whether this means that one has removed oneself from the materiality of the body, as is sometimes argued. Finally, I take up a thread from the section on the constructed body, namely the question of the relationship between the private person's physical body and the social body and the societal body. From a historical perspective, there have existed intimate connections between the human body and the societal body, connections that will be interesting to view from a theological perspective as well in later chapters. But I begin accordingly with the questions of what distinguishes the absent body.

---

5. See Michel Feher, "Introduction," *Fragments for a History of the Human Body,* Part One, ed. Michel Feher with Ramona Naddaff and Nadia Tazi (New York: Zone Books, 1989), pp. 11–17. It is significant that this volume, together with the other two parts of the work, constitutes not less than 1500 pages, and is still not more than a "fragment" of the history of the body.

6. I will investigate the absence of the body in a *philosophical* discourse. As Karl-Heinrich Bette has pointed out, modern society is characterized by a simultaneous constriction *and* fixing of the body. See Karl-Heinrich Bette, "Wo ist der Körper?" in *Theorie als Passion: Niklas Luhmann zum 60 Geburtstag,* ed. Dirk Baecker, Jürgen Markowitz, Rudolf Stichweh, Hartmann Tyrell, and Helmut Wilke (Frankfurt am Main: Suhrkamp, 1987), pp. 600–628.

The Absent Body

How then might the body be absent? Is the body not something that we—so to speak—always carry with us, or put more strongly, that we always are? What this section is about, however, is the question of the body as theme for a philosophical or other intellectual reflection. Several different epochs of thought may be traced here. People often refer in a general way to the dualism between body and soul that characterizes Plato, the Gnostics, Antiquity, Christianity, the Middle Ages, or Descartes, a dualism that also entails valuing the soul more highly than the body. Even if all these thinkers, epochs, and traditions can be said to be characterized by some sort of dualism between body and soul, the distinction is all too simple to be especially apt. It is easy to argue that all thought up to the materialism of the 1700s was dualistic in the above sense, and that materialism overcame the earlier contempt for the body. However, one actually finds a number of attitudes towards the body over the course of history, and towards its relation to the soul, spirit, consciousness, or whatever one now sets it in contrast to. In this section I will look more closely at the conceptions of the body in several thinkers. I will dwell especially on Descartes, since he has often appeared both as a prominent figure in the modern dualism between body and consciousness, and as the one whom contemporary philosophers choose to contrast themselves with. I will also—with the help of philosopher and physician Drew Leder—take up several phenomenological reasons for the "absence of the body" in Descartes. Descartes and other thinkers have not been without grounds for their philosophy of the body. Even if we have since then come to view dualistic philosophies of the body as deficient, there is reason to look over the grounds that might exist for differentiating between body and soul, or between body and consciousness. Otherwise we run the risk that our own understanding of the body becomes merely a dependent contrast to the earlier understanding.

The Body in Ancient Philosophy

The ancient history of Western philosophy is usually described as a dark chapter with regard to the body. Plato's (427–347 BC) statements about the body as the grave of the soul are well known. In the early dialogue *Phaedo* Socrates argues that the pre-philosophical soul is "entirely fastened and welded to the body and is compelled to regard realities through the body as through prison bars, not with its own unhindered vision, and is wallowing in utter ignorance."[7] In another early dialogue, *Gorgias,* there exists an alliterating word collocation that has become classic: *sōma-sēma,* i.e., "the body is our tomb" *(to sōma estin hēmin sēma),* and which according to Plato has an older origin.[8] But this quotation says hardly anything about Plato's view of the body. In the dialogues *Symposium* and *Phaedo* physical beauty is an important moment in the ascension of the soul to the idea of the beautiful.[9] There is thus no absolute dualism between soul and body in Plato, unlike within the more radically dualistic Gnosticism.[10]

On the whole, there is no unilaterally negative view of the body within the Platonic tradition. Plotinus (ca. 205–270), for example, thought that the beauty of bodies was a trace or a likeness of pure beauty, and so he wanted to introduce a hierarchy of the ontological value of levels of existence.[11] Plotinus's disciple Porphyry claimed in his biography of the master that Plotinus was ashamed to exist physically. But neither did Plotinus imagine that body and soul were two distinct substances. According to Plotinus the body would not be able to exist without the soul, since the body without the soul would not have any life, and would thereby completely fall apart. All matter thus has a shadow of a soul, without which it would be completely formless, and so would lack any real existence. Even if the soul is higher than the body, and can exist independently of the body, body and soul are in the human thus not two different substances, but are related to each other.

Similarly, Aristotle (384–322 BC) said in book 2 of *On the Soul,* much earlier than Plotinus, that body and soul are intimately connected. His argument in *On the Soul* is not only about human bodies, but also about the

---

7. See Plato, *Phaedo,* in *Plato in Twelve Volumes, 1: Euthyphro, Apology, Crito, Phaedo, Phaedrus,* Loeb Classical Library, trans. Harold North Fowler (Cambridge, MA/London: Harvard University Press, 1914), p. 289 (82e).

8. Plato, *Gorgias,* in *Plato in Twelve Volumes, 3: Lysias, Symposium, Gorgias,* Loeb Classical Library, trans. W. R. M. Lamb (Cambridge, MA/London: Harvard University Press, 1925), p. 415 (493a).

9. Plato, *Symposium,* in *Plato in Twelve Volumes, 3: Lysias, Symposium, Gorgias,* pp. 200–208 (210a–212a).

10. Kurt Rudolph, *Gnosis: The Nature and History of Gnosticism,* trans. Robert McLachlan Wilson (San Francisco: Harper, 1987).

11. See here Stephen R. L. Clark, "Plotinus: Body and Soul," in *The Cambridge Companion to Plotinus,* ed. Lloyd P. Gerson (Cambridge: Cambridge University Press, 1999), pp. 275–91, together as well with Margaret R. Miles, *Plotinus on Body and Beauty: Society, Philosophy, and Religion in Third-Century Rome* (Oxford: Blackwell, 1999), pp. 162–82.

bodies of plants and animals. The body—whichever body we may speak of— is composed of matter on the one hand, which is its possibility of existing as a body, and of soul *(psyche)* on the other, which constitutes its form, and thus its realized existence. For Aristotle, matter is a possibility for something, while the form "is that precisely in virtue of which a thing is called a this."[12] It is primarily through the union of matter and form that we have a concretely existing object. Translated to body and soul, this means that the soul is the being of the body, the actualization of a specific body, the life of the body—in other words, that which makes the body the sort of object it is, i.e., a body. In his definition of the soul Aristotle writes that it is "substance in the sense which corresponds to the account of a thing. That means that it is what it is to be for a body of the character just assigned."[13] The definition of the soul thus says what the body is.

So it is not the case that a soul can "inhabit" any body at all—in that case the soul would not be able to be the essence of a specific body.[14] The soul always exists in a body acquired in a certain way. The actuality of a given thing can only be realized in a way that is closed in its potentiality. The soul of a duck can never be found in the body of a human. Without a soul, a living body would not be what it is. On the other hand, it would not be meaningful to speak of a soul without a body, since the soul is precisely the realization of a specific body (possibly with the exception of the soul as thought or reason *[nous]*, which does not seem to be dependent on the body in order to be realized).[15] A specific body's specific material and specific form (its soul) belong intimately together, but it is not entirely clear how Aristotle imagines the difference between a material and a formal description of a living body (a problem that nevertheless falls outside the bounds of my review). The question of whether body and soul are *one* Aristotle consequently designates as unnecessary—it would be like asking whether wax and its form are one. Aristotle thereby connects body and soul to each other more intimately than Plato and the Platonic tradition, even if the differences should not be exaggerated.

12. Aristotle, *On the Soul*, in *The Complete Works of Aristotle*, vol. 1, ed. Jonathan Barnes, The Revised Oxford translation (Princeton: Princeton University Press, 1995), p. 656 (412a 8). Cf. Stephen Everson, "Psychology," in *The Cambridge Companion to Aristotle*, ed. Jonathan Barnes (Cambridge: Cambridge University Press, 1995), pp. 168–94.

13. Aristotle, *On the Soul*, p. 657 (412b, 10–12).

14. Aristotle, *On the Soul*, p. 659 (414a, 21–29). Cf. 649–50 (407b, 14–26).

15. Aristotle, *On the Soul*, p. 682 (429a, 19–429b, 5).

The Cartesian Body

It is hopefully clear from this short review that the philosophers mentioned are not embedded in the modern discussion regarding how consciousness and body—the mental and the physical—ought to be related to each other. For Aristotle the question is instead what distinguishes the living from the dead. In order to understand the modern conception of the body, it is important to realize that we are here moving within a, for the most part, very different discussion. Between Antiquity and modern philosophy lies more than a millennium of Christian theological influences (a subject I return to in the next chapter). René Descartes (1596–1650), who will represent here the modern conception of the body, advocated a dualism of a different sort than the dualism of ancient philosophy—insofar as ancient philosophy actually was dualistic. He strove to find certain knowledge beyond all quagmires of ambiguity. Where does the immovable knowledge exist that could constitute a ground for all other knowledge? Not in the perceptions of the senses. The senses can deceive us. The body's experiences are not reliable; they are, on the contrary, subject to everything from madness to dreams. In the second, lightly revised edition of *Meditations on First Philosophy* from 1642 (originally 1641) Descartes writes:

> But even if the senses would perhaps sometimes deceive us about certain minute and more remote things, there are still many other things that plainly cannot be doubted, although they be derived from the same senses: such as that I am now here, that I am sitting by the fire, that I am clothed in a winter robe, that I am holding this piece of paper with the hands, and similar things. Truly, by means of what reason could it be denied that these hands themselves and this whole body are mine? Unless I were perhaps to compare myself with—I know not which—insane people, whose brains the stubborn vapour of black bile so weakens that they might constantly assert that they are kings when they are very poor, or that they are clothed in purple when they are nude, or that they have an earthenware head, or that they are—as wholes—pumpkins or made of glass. But these people are without minds, nor would I myself seem less demented if I were to transfer something as an example from them to me.[16]

16. René Descartes, *Meditationes de prima philosophia/Meditations on First Philosophy,* a bilingual edition, trans. George Heffernan (Notre Dame/London: University of Notre Dame Press, 1990), p. 89.

Descartes thus rhetorically asks himself how he would be able to doubt his embodied senses and whether his hands and body are really his. Would he then not be as crazy as those who believe they are pumpkins or made of glass? But prior to this in *Discourse on the Method* from 1637 Descartes has argued that he can imagine himself without his body.[17] Even in *Meditations* he argues that a naïve affirmation of sensory impressions can lead us astray, since even our hands and our body are perhaps different than how we perceive them.[18] Certainly the similarity between the bodies we see in our dreams and the bodies we see while awake indicates the trustworthiness of the sensory impressions in this case, but the possibility itself of imagining bodies through dreams and fantasies sows doubt with regard to the reliability of the sensory impressions. Descartes eventually comes to doubt the existence of the living body, in favor of a more general body that can be investigated with respect to size, place, and time—in other words through a mathematical analysis.[19] Mathematical relationships are the same whether we dream them or think about them while awake. But the consequence of Descartes's "indubitable" body in *Meditations* is that the living body with all its experiences is dissolved in favor of a "de-souled" body, characterized primarily by the fact that it can be weighed and measured, i.e., by its extent. Descartes's argument for a certain knowledge then continues at the end of his first meditation, where he hypothetically imagines himself "as not having hands, not eyes, not flesh, not blood, not any senses, but rather as falsely opining that I have all these things."[20] By hypothetically ridding himself of the body and its senses, Descartes can also avoid the root of these potential illusions—perhaps my embodied existence is a delusion caused by an evil spirit?—in order to end up at the impossibility of doubting the subject's own existence.[21]

Descartes's philosophy of the body is primarily known for its radical distinction between *res cogitans* and *res extensa,* i.e., between thinking substance and extended substance. The person's actual self was her thought, while the body belonged to the extended world that is understood purely mechanically. Consciousness was autonomous, the body purely material. It

17. René Descartes, *Discours de la method/Discourse on the Method,* a bilingual edition with an interpretative essay, trans. George Heffernan (Notre Dame/London: University of Notre Dame Press, 1994), p. 51. Cf. Descartes, *Meditationes,* p. 97.
18. Descartes, *Meditationes,* p. 91.
19. Descartes, *Meditationes,* p. 93.
20. Descartes, *Meditationes,* p. 97.
21. Descartes, *Meditationes,* pp. 99–105.

is possible to argue that Descartes's conceptualization of the body is tied to several changes that took place in medical science during his time.[22] Blood, for example, came to be a central symbol for the understanding of the body in Descartes.

The English doctor William Harvey (1578–1657) published in 1628 the text *On the Motion of the Heart and the Blood in Animals*, where he said that the circulation of blood constituted a closed system, where the heart pumped the blood around in the blood vessels, and that it thereby passed through the lungs in order to pick up oxygen. It was thus the same blood that was pumped around, and not, as was previously believed, new blood that was produced. Nor did the warmth of the blood cause it to flow through the body. The circulation of blood was autonomous; the heart seemed like a machine. This meant a scientific revolution with regard to the understanding of the body, a revolution that not only led to a new understanding of the body, but also of society. The new understanding of the body as described in the writings of Harvey and others occurred simultaneously with the growth of modern capitalism and individualism. Sociologist Richard Sennett writes:

> Adam Smith's *Wealth of Nations* first reckoned what Harvey's discovery would lead to in this regard, for Adam Smith imagined the free market of labor and goods operating much like freely circulating blood within the body and with similar life-giving consequences.[23]

Thus a biological revolution in the science of the body was significant for the understanding of the societal body (and vice versa one may imagine), but also for the philosophical understanding of the body in Descartes.

Harvey retained features of an Aristotelian vitalism, but Descartes still benefited from Harvey's research results about the circulation of blood for his conceptions of a mechanical, autonomous body. This entailed a complete reconceptualization of the body, according to historian of philosophy, art, and literature Dalia Judovitz:

> The body is no longer a mirror of the larger cosmos; it is a mere object whose mechanical logic and material definition reflects [Descartes's]

---

22. See Dalia Judovitz, *The Culture of the Body: Genealogies of Modernity* (Ann Arbor: University of Michigan Press, 2001).

23. Richard Sennett, *Flesh and Stone: The Body and the City in Western Civilization* (London/Boston: Faber & Faber, 1994), p. 256.

philosophical understanding of nature as inanimate, defined purely as matter, extension and motion.[24]

There is thus no essential difference between the human body and an automaton. And it was nature itself that produced automatons, whether it was a matter of the human being or the animal. The bodies of human beings and animals were conceived as mechanical marvels without intrinsic meaning. As with a mechanical clockwork, their meaning existed in the purpose that they were produced for, thus, in the intent of the designer. What makes the human being a human being is simply her thinking. In contrast with his precursors, Descartes did not really conceive of the body as alive. The body that became paradigmatic for the understanding of the body was the dead body—the corpse. Descartes was quite zealous in attempting to understand the mystery of life by examining dead bodies. The philosopher Drew Leder writes of Descartes's philosophy: "The living body is not fundamentally different from the lifeless; it is a kind of animated corpse, a functioning mechanism."[25] The life-principle was the person's consciousness, the rational soul—the body's administrator and tender. This rational soul, however, existed as a whole other substance than the body, which led to an acute problem: explaining how these two so different substances could interact. How could a disembodied soul guide a mechanical body?

Descartes's subject in *Meditations* is, however, not entirely bodiless. After having imagined a bodiless existence and having come to the idea that the essence of the human being consists in being a thinking thing, the body is reintroduced. It is, however, described in a dispassionate way in the second meditation: "Namely, it occurred to me, first, that I had a face, hands, arms and this whole machine of members such as it also shows itself in a corpse and which I designated by the term 'body.'"[26] The body is compared to a machine and a corpse. The function of the body in *Meditations* is, so to speak, to assure the subject of an existence as a specific entity. The subject's general existence might be so general that it would not be able to relate to itself as something that could be localized—and so the certain ground of knowledge would once more be at risk.[27] The body is thus reintroduced not

24. Judovitz, *Culture of the Body*, p. 70.
25. Drew Leder, "A Tale of Two Bodies: The Cartesian Corpse and the Lived Body," in *Body and Flesh: A Philosophical Reader*, ed. Donn Welton (Malden, MA/Oxford: Blackwell, 1998), p. 119.
26. Descartes, *Meditationes*, p. 103.
27. Judovitz, *Culture of the Body*, pp. 91–92.

as an agent, as something active, but as pure passivity. The body as corpse corresponds to the mechanical body as the instrument of consciousness. The body can also be compared to a piece of wax, since it is plastic and its only permanent characteristic is extent.[28] But with this the wax ceases to be an entity in the phenomenal world. The disappearance of all properties that can be perceived leads to the mathematical virtualization of wax.[29] Descartes's recovered body thereby becomes merely a phantom of the living body. The nearest analogies are a machine or a corpse. Descartes returns in his sixth meditation to the body and the material world, but their existence is purely mathematical—the material thing is "the object of pure mathematics"[30]— and the emphasis lies the whole time on consciousness as the real essence of the human. The body is certainly present for the person's imagination *(imaginatio)*, but this imagination differs from her pure intellect *(pura intellectio)*.[31] But imagination—in contrast with the intellect—does not belong to the essence of the human. One might say that the imagination faces the body, and precisely because of that differentiates itself from pure intellect. Sensory impressions and the body are in the same way as imagination not a part of the essence of the human: "[M]y essence consists in this one thing: that I be a cogitating thing *[res cogitans]*."[32] This fact separates the person's consciousness from her body:

> And although I might perhaps (or rather, as I shall soon afterwards say, for certain) have a body which is very closely joined to me, because I have— on the one hand—a clear and distinct idea of me myself, in so far as I am only a cogitating thing and not an extended one, and because I have—on the other hand—a distinct idea of body, in so far as it is only an extended thing and not a cogitating one, it is still certain that I am really and truly distinct from my body, and that I can exist without it.[33]

In other words, the human being's true self is self-contained and not dependent on the body for its existence. Her subjectivity is essentially not embodied. Even if Descartes in his passages in *Meditations* seems to want to cling to a certain union between body and consciousness, this is not

28. Descartes, *Meditationes*, pp. 109–13.
29. Judovitz, *Culture of the Body*, p. 95.
30. Descartes, *Meditationes*, p. 185.
31. Descartes, *Meditationes*, p. 185.
32. Descartes, *Meditationes*, p. 197.
33. Descartes, *Meditationes*, p. 197.

convincing given the absolute distinction he makes between thinking thing and extended thing. The mechanical, passive, sometimes even outright ghostly virtual body is not identical with the living, experiencing body in the phenomenal world, and no bold philosophical attempt by Descartes to reunite consciousness and body will resuscitate the body that he has done away with earlier in his meditations.[34] But the reduction of the body in Descartes's philosophy to merely a contextless object does not mean—as we have seen—that it completely disappears. The body instead constantly haunts Descartes's philosophy as a ghost.

The question, however, is how one should interpret Descartes's dualism. According to historian of philosophy Lilli Alanen, the point of *Meditations* is to show how the body appears from the perspective of contemporary science, not to substitute what we in our time might call a more phenomenological perspective on the body. An indication that suggests such an interpretation is the fact that in 1649 Descartes published *Passions of the Soul,* where embodiment is illustrated from a different perspective than that in the earlier writings which became definitive for the reception of Descartes's philosophy, *Discourse* and *Meditations*.[35] These latter writings would thus be aimed at illuminating certain aspects of human embodiment, not at offering a systematic and contradiction-free philosophy of the body. Descartes's understanding of human nature and the relationship between body and soul was, Alanen says, Aristotelian, rather than a substance dualism.[36] But even if Descartes's philosophy of the body in *Discourse* and *Meditations* leaves the possibility open for a phenomenological investigation of the body, it is embodiment understood within the frame of *scientia* rather than within the frame of a life-world that has *de facto* come to be Descartes's philosophical heritage.

A plausible explanation for this is that the reception or nonreception of a philosopher or a philosophy does not take place in a social vacuum. A particular time can therefore be more amenable to certain thoughts than

---

34. Judovitz, *Culture of the Body,* p. 104.

35. See Lilli Alanen, *Descartes's Concept of Mind* (Cambridge, MA/London: Harvard University Press, 2003), especially pp. 44–77 and 165–207, together with René Descartes, *The Passions of the Soul,* trans. Stephen Voss (Indianapolis/Cambridge: Hackett, 1989). Cf. Lilli Alanen, *Concept of Mind,* p. 53: "To qualify as an object of science in Descartes's sense, the body must be considered as mechanically moved extended matter. Important aspects of human nature and experience are thereby left outside the scope of scientific explanation when that explanation is limited to what fulfills the requirements of a mechanistic or physicalistic science of nature."

36. Alanen, *Concept of Mind,* p. 166.

others. Descartes's philosophy of the body in *Discourse* and *Meditations,* for example, lies in line with the social events that took place in France during his time. This can be illustrated with the playwright Pierre Corneille (1606–1684), whose drama *Le Cid* was performed the same year as the publication of Descartes's *Discourse,* 1637.[37] *Le Cid* is a literary equivalent to Descartes's philosophy of the body. Both *Le Cid* as well as Descartes's philosophical work mirror an ongoing consolidation and centralization of the king's power, something that had been begun under Cardinal Richelieu and implemented by Cardinal Mazarin. According to Judovitz, one sees here an "emergent emphasis on social identity and the recuperation of the individual as agent and instrument of the state."[38] The body is "reorganized" in *Le Cid* in order to be better incorporated into the body politic of the absolute monarchy. The physical body is no longer a microcosm of the State's macrocosm, but an instrument for the social reproduction of the State. In other words, the body bore no meaning in itself, but was valued on the basis of its social function. The most striking correspondence to Corneille's representation of the body in *Le Cid* is, according to Judovitz, Thomas Hobbes's *Leviathan* from 1650, where Hobbes "describes man as a mechanism and the state as an artificial mechanism that embodies to a higher degree the principles of incorporation that the individual body possesses in only a limited fashion."[39] The true body is the social body, not the physical body, and the social body is understood as a machine.

After Descartes, the body's situation in philosophy becomes precarious. Among the materialists the body is seen as a machine or automaton, and human consciousness is understood as an epiphenomenon of the purely materially understood body. Among the idealists the body disappears, since thought can be understood as the ground for human subjectivity. In many respects the battle between materialism and idealism is a battle played out on Descartes's premises, a battle over what shall be reduced to what: *res cogitans* to *res extensa,* or *res extensa* to *res cogitans.* But even resolutely monistic philosophers come to be haunted by the excluded or reduced, so the monism is seldom or never stable. Perhaps it is first with Friedrich Nietzsche (1844–1900) that a different understanding of the body makes itself relevant within philosophy.[40] Nietzsche is known for his critique of idealism, but he

---

37. Judovitz, *Culture of the Body,* pp. 109–30.

38. Judovitz, *Culture of the Body,* p. 111.

39. Judovitz, *Culture of the Body,* p. 129.

40. Éric Blondel, *Nietzsche, the Body and Culture: Philosophy as Philological Genealogy,* trans. Séan Hand (Stanford: Stanford University Press, 1991), pp. 200–238.

does not replace idealism with materialism, but with *interpretation*. Éric Blondel writes:

> Nietzsche's apparently biologizing texts, far from reducing the ideal to body, are merely attempts to bring culture (conceived of *as* a body) to the fundamental interpretation, the physiological body being one case of interpretation among others.[41]

Here the body is no longer a given object, but part of a fundamental and ongoing interpretive activity. I will not elaborate more on this here, but instead will take up the thread from Nietzsche in the coming section on the constructed body and the social body. But first back to Descartes.

The Three Types of Bodily Absence

That there exists a social context that exhibits parallels to Descartes's understanding of the body does not mean that Descartes's philosophy should be understood as merely an expression for Zeitgeist. Certainly our understanding of the body is shaped by social practices—about which I will say more below—but that also means that this relationship could be reciprocal, i.e., that bodily experiences can be involved in creating social practices and philosophical insights. Although in his book *The Absent Body* North American philosopher and doctor Drew Leder has strongly criticized Descartes's philosophy of the body (above all as it is expressed in *Discourse* and *Meditations*), he has at the same time wanted to demonstrate different phenomenological grounds for such a philosophy of the body as can exist.[42] He says that we experience our body both as present and as absent, and it is this experience of bodily absence that makes a dualistic philosophy of the body like Descartes's experientially credible— even if it is undermined by other experiences. Leder takes his critique of Descartes's dualism from, among others, Merleau-Ponty, but since I will discuss Merleau-Ponty more closely below, I will limit myself to Leder's discussion of the experience of bodily absence. More particularly, Leder finds three principal sorts of bodily absence: the ecstatic body, the recessive body, and the dysfunctional body.

41. Blondel, *Nietzsche,* p. 219.
42. Drew Leder, *The Absent Body* (Chicago/London: University of Chicago Press, 1990).

Leder begins by describing the experience of the ecstatic body, i.e., the body as it is directed outward, away from itself towards different projects in the world.[43] Through the surface of the body we extend ourselves out towards the world with the help of our senses, sight as well as feeling. But this outgoing movement makes the origin of our perceptions invisible. Because we perceive everything that we perceive from a particular perspective, the starting point of that perspective is itself invisible. Leder finds the prototype for this disappearing in the eyes, which see the world around themselves but do not see themselves. Through sight I orient myself in the world, but my own placement in the world is the point—spatial as well as temporal—from which I orient myself. My own body—in this example the eyes—becomes an absent presence without which I cannot understand my perceptual field. Certainly I can see my eyes in a mirror, but as a number of philosophers have pointed out, I do not really see my eyes as looking in the mirror, but my eyes as objects in the world with certain properties. The perception does not coincide with that which perceives. But the invisibility of the eye in the visual field that it generates is only one sort of bodily absence in the ecstatic body.

The ecstatic body shows itself as another form of bodily absence when certain bodily regions disappear from focus because they are not engaged. An example of this can be when we close our eyes in order to better perceive something with hearing, so that the sense of sight is in practice turned off and so becomes an unemployed background for our actual bodily perceptual activity. Different regions of the body are engaged by different bodily activities—not only perceptual activity in the limited sense—and with this, other bodily regions end up in the background. Bodily absence is, however, not limited to these two sorts. Under the same rubric Leder also discusses the skills and technologies of the body. To be able to swim, or to use a tool, a cane for the blind, or a telephone, are skills and technologies that we can have incorporated into bodily skills even to the point where we do not need to reflect on them. The body is, Leder says, a living process that continually reacts and relates to its environment. Certain regions or skills become present while others disappear from focus. The different modalities in the absence of the ecstatic body constitute the absence of a body that is engaged in the world and thereby becomes more or less invisible to itself.

Another sort of bodily absence is what Leder calls the recessive body, i.e., a body that is secluded through its depth.[44] This depth has both a

43. Leder, *The Absent Body*, pp. 11–35.
44. Leder, *The Absent Body*, pp. 36–68.

physical and a phenomenological aspect. Purely physically, the body has a depth through the viscera (liver, spleen, kidneys, etc.) and through bodily processes (metabolism, sleep, respiration, etc.), which—normally—are neither visible to the naked eye, nor conscious. A philosophy of the body that does not take into account this physical depth risks becoming a philosophy without bones or guts, and so does not do complete justice to human embodiment. Phenomenologically, this means that the human being is dependent on processes that are beyond her conscious control. But these processes affect us fundamentally, and Leder exemplifies this with a phenomenological analysis of digestion, which for the most part takes place apart from our awareness, even if it makes itself felt through certain signals. The bodily absence of the recessive body differs from the absence of the ecstatic body in that the body as recessive houses a depth that is in part impossible to experience. According to Leder, experiences of the depth of the body are not entirely impossible, even if it is a matter of an indirect experience. For example, our digestion and metabolism are experienced through physical hunger, which also colors our experience of the world in clear ways in our ecstatic project. However, Leder also reminds us that there is not only a spatial depth to the body, but also a temporal depth. Sleep and birth are such temporal depth phenomena as are unavailable to our experience. I will not take up Leder's description of these right now. For Leder the crucial point in discerning this recessive bodily absence is that our living body cannot be reduced to either perceiving or being perceived. There exist anonymous bodily depths that make themselves felt, but only indirectly. These constitute a second form of bodily absence.

The third sort of bodily absence is what Leder calls the body's "dysappearance."[45] This differs fundamentally from the other forms of absence in that it actually has to do with a thematic focusing on the body, but a focusing on the body as the other. The body appears for us, but the Greek prefix *dys-* designates "bad," "harsh," or "sick"—as in "dysfunctional"—and signals here that the body appears in a way where it is not simply available—like the ecstatic body—but asserts itself for its own sake. Leder's examples are pain and sickness, but also hunger, thirst, wrath, depression, etc. Here Leder finds one of the explanations for the fact that Descartes did not depend on the body, namely that it makes itself felt precisely in its limitations and its deficiency. The "dysfunctional"—in the absence of a better term—body is a body that stands out in several ways. It stands out from our "normal" health, and

---

45. Leder, *The Absent Body*, pp. 69–99.

thereby gives a feeling of being deprived of a normal, desirable, or at least immediately comfortable state (for example, childbirth can be both normal and desirable, without because of that being especially "comfortable"). It also stands out in such a way that it may be experienced as something subject to an alien will, a different will than our own. Our body is not experienced as identical with our self, but at the same time it is a difference that arises within our self, within our own organism. Leder also takes up temporal aspects of this "dysfunctionality," namely age, menstruation, and pregnancy. Leder does not mean by this that these are "dysfunctional" states in themselves—as Iris Marion Young has pointed out, it is primarily grown men in the middle of life who perceive health as the body's normal state[46]—but that they are often at least states of a heightened attention to the body. Leder believes that these different states of heightened attention are a second-order absence, since they are an absence of an absence, in that the body is absent from its usual, or at least more unproblematic, absent existence as an ecstatic or recessive body. The "dysfunctional" body may be said to make a "claim" for attention, a claim that receives existential significance as well since it questions our normal understanding of ourselves. This is why the body has often come into focus for philosophical and other attention specifically in its dysfunctional mode.

These are the main features of Leder's phenomenology of the absent body in three important modalities. The point with these discussions of bodily absence is that they show that there exists a tendency in the body itself to hide itself, which may be one of the grounds for the body disappearing in philosophy with—and even more so after—Descartes. Bodily absence constitutes a phenomenological explanation for why a philosophy of the body of Descartes's type can seem plausible. Leder writes:

> Philosophical doctrines arise out of the life-world and attain popularity and credibility only to the extent that they harmonize with lived experience. In this the Cartesian doctrine is no different; though long criticized by phenomenologists of the lived body, it carries within itself a hidden phenomenology.[47]

46. Iris Marion Young, "Pregnant Embodiment," *Body and Flesh,* ed. Welton, p. 282: "The dominant model of health assumes that the normal, healthy body is unchanging. Health is associated with stability, equilibrium, a steady state. Only a minority of persons, however, namely adult men who are not yet old, experience their health as a state in which there is no regular or noticeable change in body condition."

47. Leder, *The Absent Body,* p. 125.

It is this hidden phenomenology that Leder attempts to uncover, not as an attempt to defend a Cartesian philosophy of the body, but as a step in the search for a better. In other words, Leder wants to argue that there are reasons that the body has disappeared or been devalued in earlier philosophy, and not only with Descartes. Its anonymity, its physical fragility and perishability, together with its epistemological fallibility have contributed to it having been dethematized or devalued. Leder nevertheless believes that there exist other experiences of the body that remain dethematized in Descartes's philosophy, and these experiences make it so that his philosophy ultimately does not manage to phenomenologically correspond to the lived body. The double absence of the dysfunctional body is not the only reason that the body appears in a particular way for our consciousness. It also appears in our cultivated pleasures, abilities, rituals, and sports activities. In order to do the body justice a less reductive phenomenology is required than that which is implicated by Descartes's philosophy, and Leder sees his own book as a contribution to a phenomenology of the lived body, inspired by Maurice Merleau-Ponty.

Against this background one may ask oneself to what extent the Christian theological tradition also maintains a dualistic conception of the relationship between body and soul. Is such a dualism in this case a consequence of the reception of Descartes, or is the Christian body characterized by a different sort of dualism? I also want to ask myself, in light of Leder's discussion of bodily absence, whether certain forms of what is usually called "contempt for the body" can possibly have to do with different dimensions of human embodiment that then do not start from some form of spontaneous "affirmation of the body." Such issues will be interesting in the following chapter, but for now I will turn to Merleau-Ponty.

The Living Body

The French philosopher Maurice Merleau-Ponty (1908–1961)—Jean-Paul Sartre's long-term colleague at the journal *Les temps modernes*—strove throughout his entire philosophical career to present a philosophy for the concrete, embodied human life. His philosophy of the body is often associated with his most known work, *Phenomenology of Perception* from 1945, where there is a longer section on the phenomenology of the body. For Merleau-Ponty's part, however, the question of the body was not settled in and with the publication of this phenomenological classic, but he instead continually returned to the question. One of the most important texts for his thoughts on the body is the posthumously published *The Visible and the Invisible* from 1964, where his philosophy of the body has undergone great revisions. Because Merleau-Ponty—possibly justifiably—considered himself to be breaking new ground within philosophy, his philosophical prose is often difficult to decipher. He often relies on insights that he claims to find primarily with artists and authors, rather than with philosophers. His way of writing has made it such that his interpreters, especially of his later philosophy, have diverged from each other.[48] My interpretation limits itself to his philosophy of the body—which certainly does not make it any less disputed—and seeks to make his thought useful for my theological aim in this book.

Maurice Merleau-Ponty and Phenomenology

Merleau-Ponty worked with a phenomenological method in large part inspired by the German philosopher Edmund Husserl.[49] According to the foreword of *Phenomenology of Perception,* the phenomenological method has to do with describing, not with explaining or analyzing. It seeks to describe the human and her environment in their actual existence, and proceeds from a life-world—see the discussion of the life-world in chapter 1—that always already exists there before reflection begins. Every analysis, reflection, or description is secondary in relation to the world that is given the human in her experience of existing, and then not only by existing in general, but concretely in a specific time and a specific space. The world is the permanent horizon for human thought and action: "The world is not what I think, but what I live through. I am open to the world, I have no doubt that I am in

---

48. Different possibilities for interpreting his later philosophy are given in Fred Evans and Leonard Lawlor, eds., *Chiasms: Merleau-Ponty's Notion of Flesh,* SUNY Series in Contemporary Continental Philosophy (Albany: State University of New York Press, 2000).

49. Maurice Merleau-Ponty, *Phenomenology of Perception,* trans. Colin Smith (London: Routledge, 1992), pp. vii–xxi. For a concise account of Merleau-Ponty's intellectual background, see Dermot Moran, *Introduction to Phenomenology* (London/New York: Routledge, 2000), pp. 406–12, as well as Anna Petronella Fredlund, "När tanken tar kropp—om Merleau-Pontys filosofi," in *Lovtal till filosofin* (Stockholm: Brutus Östling, 2004), pp. 7–40. Donn Welton says that the phenomenology of the body in, for example, Merleau-Ponty is limited to the perceiving body, while the desiring body remains unthematized. See Donn Welton, "Affectivity, Eros and the Body," in *Body and Flesh,* ed. Welton, pp. 181–206.

communication with it, but I do not possess it; it is inexhaustible."[50] The world is thus not an object for our subjectivity; we exist always already as a part of the world, and so our relationship to the rest of the world cannot be exhaustively described as an objectifying gaze where our subjectivity exists, so to speak, beside, above, or beyond the world. In other words, Merleau-Ponty is strongly critical of Descartes's philosophy, which of course construes the subject as a *res cogitans* in contrast with the environment as *res extensa.* But he is also critical of his earlier friend and colleague Jean-Paul Sartre's philosophy in *Being and Nothingness,* since the subject is there described as a negativity in contrast to the rest of the world, and so is ultimately world-less in Sartre as well.[51] Merleau-Ponty strives to get away from the dichotomy between subject and object. The person's world is always already given, and so we are also "condemned to meaning," since we receive the world by continually giving a response to its address, and do not simply ascribe the world meaning from a transcendental position outside of the world.[52] On the other hand, this does not, according to Merleau-Ponty, mean that the task of philosophy is to reflect on a truth that exists before reflection. Rather, it is a matter of, like art, allowing the truth to enter into existence.[53]

Even if Merleau-Ponty had much in common with other phenomenologists of his period, there is no doubt that he has pursued the most intensive reworking of the questions of the body's phenomenality. Before I focus on this I will briefly account for the effort that can be said to be common both to Merleau-Ponty's different philosophies of the body and to his phenomenologically oriented colleagues, namely the fact that they all want to reach the "pre-theoretical field" on which different theoretical attitudes could be based, and without which they would be groundless. According to Merleau-Ponty, the sciences are a second-order expression

50. Maurice Merleau-Ponty, *Phenomenology,* pp. xvi–xvii.

51. See Maurice Merleau-Ponty, "The Battle over Existentialism," in *Sense and Non-Sense,* trans. Hubert L. Dreyfus and Patricia Allen Dreyfus (Evanston, IL: Northwestern University Press, 1971), pp. 71–82, but especially "Interrogation and Dialectic," in *The Visible and the Invisible,* Northwestern Studies in Phenomenology & Existential Philosophy, trans. Alphonso Lingis (Evanston, IL: Northwestern University Press, 1968), pp. 50–104.

52. Maurice Merleau-Ponty, *Phenomenology,* pp. xviii–xix.

53. If you perceive echoes of Hegel here, you are not imagining things. Merleau-Ponty was influenced by Kojève's Hegel-lectures and was thereby provided with a more "existential" Hegel. See Maurice Merleau-Ponty, "Hegel's Existentialism," in *Sense and Non-Sense,* pp. 63–70. Cf. p. 65.

of a first-order experience.[54] His phenomenology is thus an effort to describe this experience without reducing it to what one believes it must be on the basis of what science teaches or epistemology requires. Here—as in several other places—Merleau-Ponty's project recalls the phenomenology of Edmund Husserl, especially as it is expressed in his late text *The Crisis of European Sciences and Transcendental Phenomenology: An Introduction to Phenomenological Philosophy,* which I mentioned in chapter 1.[55] It goes more or less without saying that this is a difficult task, if it is not only a matter of describing a fixed field of experience, but also of reckoning with the different theoretical attitudes that always assert themselves already in the attempt to speak and write about this pre-theoretical field. Because of the dominant position of the gaze of modernity, these attitudes can very well be more immediate for the contemporary person than the perception of her experience of being engaged with actions as well as senses in her world. With his phenomenological analysis Merleau-Ponty wants to attempt to restore this theoretical level, not in order to uncritically return to a naïve view of the world, but in order to get a perspective on the human as an embodied, engaged creature, together with how her world is present for and with her as a prerequisite for her reflection. It is thus not a matter of denying the modern sciences, but rather of ascertaining their actual basis, the horizon, background, or relief against which the person's perceiving, thinking, and acting play out. In *The Visible and the Invisible* Merleau-Ponty compares what he says about the world to what Augustine says about time in *Confessions,* namely that it is completely obvious to us at first, but it is a riddle as soon as we explain it for someone else.[56]

---

54. Merleau-Ponty, *Phenomenology,* pp. viii–ix. Cf. p. ix: "Scientific points of view, according to which my existence is a moment of the world's, are always both naïve and at the same time dishonest, because they take for granted, without explicitly mentioning it, the other point of view, namely that of consciousness, through which from the outset a world forms itself round me and begins to exist for me. To return to things themselves is to return to that world which precedes knowledge, of which knowledge always *speaks,* and in relation to which every scientific schematization is an abstract and derivative sign-language, as is geography in relation to the countryside in which we have learnt beforehand what a forest, a prairie or a river is."

55. Edmund Husserl, *The Crisis of European Sciences and Transcendental Phenomenology: An Introduction to Phenomenology,* trans. David Carr (Evanston, IL: Northwestern University Press, 1970).

56. Merleau-Ponty, *The Visible and the Invisible,* p. 3.

The Phenomenology of the Body

The object of Merleau-Ponty's investigations is the living body, not the corpse, as with Descartes. This means that the philosophical understanding of the body is dependent on the person's experience of her embodiment, but not by the attempt to abstract thought from embodiment or by taking a detour through scientific studies of the body. A precursor to Merleau-Ponty's way of reasoning is the French philosopher Gabriel Marcel, who says that we do not *have* a body, but *are* a body, as well as Husserl, who makes a distinction between the body as a lifeless physical object *(Körper)* and as living and animated *(Leib)*.[57] Merleau-Ponty writes in *Phenomenology of Perception:* "To be a body, is to be tied to a certain world, as we have seen; our body is not primarily *in* space: it is of it."[58] The body is a part of the world, and it cannot be investigated independently of how the subject of the investigation herself experiences the world: "Thus experience of one's own body runs counter to the reflective procedure which detaches subject and object from each other, and which gives us only the thought about the body, or the body as an idea, and not the experience of the body or the body in reality."[59] In other words, the body always exists, like perception, as situated. Here it is also clear that Merleau-Ponty wants to overcome the dichotomy between subject and object with his philosophy of the body—a theme he will return to later, dissatisfied with his first attempt.

Perception is important for Merleau-Ponty, since it is the beginning of human knowledge. In contrast with what the Cartesian philosophy of representation claims—see my discussion in chapter 4—Merleau-Ponty says that the sight of a house does not mean that a house is represented for me in my consciousness, but that I in some sense actually see the house. To see something is to "inhabit" the object of vision, and that assumes that the visible object makes itself available for my gaze.[60] This means that the gaze is neither passive nor active, but both-and. The gaze gives a sort of reply to the fact that the thing makes itself available in perception. It is primarily by

---

57. Gabriel Marcel, *Journal métaphysique* (Paris: Gallimard, 1927), pp. 236–37, as well as Edmund Husserl, *Ideas Pertaining to a Pure Phenomenology and to a Phenomenological Philosophy: Second Book: Studies in the Phenomenology of Constitution,* Edmund Husserl Collected Works vol. 3, trans. Richard Rojcewicz and André Schuwer (Dordrecht/Boston/London: Kluwer Academic Publishers, 1989).

58. Merleau-Ponty, *Phenomenology,* 148.

59. Merleau-Ponty, *Phenomenology,* pp. 198–99.

60. Merleau-Ponty, *Phenomenology,* p. 68.

this that the sensory impression becomes comprehensible. In order to be able to see something as something, however, it is also necessary that the object of my sensory impression be outlined against a horizon. Without the horizon against which I perceive different objects, it would not be possible to differentiate them. And this horizon is not directly visible. Even if I do not see all the sides of the house at the same time, those sides that I do not perceive exist alongside as an assumption, an assumption that can moreover be brought to the fore as needed. The house's—for the moment—invisible sides Merleau-Ponty calls the deep horizon. The object of my perception can thus not be thought independently of its horizon—horizon and object shape each other in the same way as the relation between figure and ground.

When it comes to our own body, it is not uncommon that we perceive it as one object among many other objects in the world; it is in fact commonplace. The prerequisite for perceiving the body as an object, however, exists in an embodiment that is more fundamental than the objectified body. In order to come at this more fundamental level, Merleau-Ponty to begin with differentiates between the objectified body *(le corps objectif)* and the more original phenomenal body *(le corps phénoménal).*[61] A description that Merleau-Ponty makes of the phenomenal body is the following: "The body is the vehicle of being in the world, and having a body is, for a living creature, to be intervolved in a definite environment, to identify oneself with certain projects and be continually committed to them."[62] That we nevertheless tend to perceive the body as an object has to do with the fact that we become aware of our body through interaction with other bodies and objects in the world. The experience of the phenomenal body as the condition or horizon of the objective body can thus easily become invisible. Our experience of the body is thereby transformed to a representation of the body—from a phenomenon comes a psychic fact.[63]

The phenomenal body is, however, not condemned to invisibility. Certain phenomena constitute reminders of its existence, and Merleau-Ponty uses amputated body parts and piano playing as examples. Certain practical fields belong to the person's phenomenal embodiment, as, for example, being able to play the piano. For the piano-playing person who has recently amputated an arm, piano playing remains a practical field even after the amputation, even if it is in practice impossible. In other words, the phenomenal

61. Cf. Moran, *Introduction,* p. 419.
62. Merleau-Ponty, *Phenomenology,* p. 82.
63. Merleau-Ponty, *Phenomenology,* pp. 94–95.

body also consists of embodied habits, skills, and possibilities. The absence of the physical possibility of playing piano makes the phenomenal body visible in its very absence. Piano playing exists, so to speak, in the body, even when it is physically impossible to carry it out.

In order to explain the phenomenal body, two categories are important for Merleau-Ponty: spatiality and mobility. Turning first to the spatiality of the body, we find that it differs from the spatiality of the thing. Merleau-Ponty takes his own arm as an example, resting on a desk beside an ashtray and a telephone.[64] The arm's way of being located beside the ashtray differs from the way that the ashtray is located beside the telephone. In contrast with the ashtray and telephone, the arm is namely not primarily characterized by a "spatiality of position," where various things may be placed within a coordinate system. The body is always oriented towards an actual or potential task, and the arm is therefore characterized by what Merleau-Ponty calls a "spatiality of situation." On the basis of Merleau-Ponty's example we can imagine that the arm moves itself towards the telephone in order to lift the receiver if it suddenly rings. This being oriented towards the world as a task belongs to the person's fundamental embodiment, to the phenomenal body.

Spatiality of situation is further explained by the relationship that my body parts have to each other. They are not located side-by-side like the ashtray and the telephone. Instead one may say that they are contained in each other. My experience of the body is the experience of a whole that I possess undivided, not as a conglomeration of distinct entities.[65] The body I experience is in other words not five fingers attached to a hand that sits on an arm connected to the trunk, etc., but a whole body. Through my body image I perceive where my various limbs are located in relation to each other. It is thus also possible that different parts of the body are emphasized in different situations, without my losing the implicit perception of the body as a whole because of that. To make use once more of Merleau-Ponty's example of the desk, my hands thus come to be emphasized when I lean against the desk, while the rest of my body follows suit, but remains unemphasized. Or my feet are emphasized when I carefully go down a steep staircase cluttered with papers and books. In another analogy Merleau-Ponty compares this emphasis with the darkness that is needed in a theater for the light of the performance to be visible. In these examples the light falls on the hands and the feet, while the rest of the body lies in relative darkness.

64. Merleau-Ponty, *Phenomenology,* p. 98.
65. Merleau-Ponty, *Phenomenology,* p. 100.

Situational spatiality serves to orient us in the world. The spatiality of the body cannot be reduced to an objective spatiality without thereby denying the phenomenon of experience itself, and so also human knowledge. Merleau-Ponty says that "there would be no space at all for me if I had no body."[66] Positional spatiality is indeed also a factor in human embodiment, but it is an abstraction if the human body's situational spatiality is taken away. Situational spatiality is namely a sort of third factor in every relation between figure and ground. The figure—i.e., the objective body—stands out not only against the background of its physical position in space, but also against the background of the relation of possibilities that the body finds itself in vis-à-vis the world in its situational spatiality.

We thereby come to the second category that explains the phenomenal body, its mobility. Merleau-Ponty describes movement as an active seizing of space and time. Mobility therefore becomes the body's way of inhabiting space. For mobility to become visible, however, spatiality is assumed as its background. At the same time, it is in movement that spatiality exists. Figure and ground cannot be separated. Merleau-Ponty writes:

> The background to the movement is not a representation associated or linked externally with the movement itself, but is immanent in the movement inspiring and sustaining it at every moment. The plunge into action is, from the subject's point of view, an original way of relating himself to the object, and is on the same footing as perception.[67]

Movement can also be described as a fundamental dimension of human intentionality. It is through movement that we orient ourselves towards the thing and our environment, either through a concrete movement in the world as it is given, or through an abstract movement as an orientation towards possibility. Here Merleau-Ponty means that the body and consciousness are intimately tied to each other. Consciousness is namely "being-towards-the-thing through the intermediary of the body."[68] By moving our body we orient ourselves towards the thing. Movement itself is thus a part of the phenomenal body.

How then should one understand the distinction between the spatiality and mobility of the phenomenal body? To begin with, I want to establish

66. Merleau-Ponty, *Phenomenology*, p. 102.
67. Merleau-Ponty, *Phenomenology*, pp. 110–11.
68. Merleau-Ponty, *Phenomenology*, pp. 138–39.

that for Merleau-Ponty the two belong together primarily as fundamental intentionalities in the person's being-in-the-world. The experience of them is not of two distinct phenomena; the description is thus in a certain sense an abstraction. However, the spatiality of situation has to do with aspects of the spatial relationship that exists between the body and the thing. With regard to the pole of the body it is, for example, a matter of which emphasis I give to a particular body-part: the hands when I lean against the desk, the placement of the feet while walking down the staircase. With regard to the pole of the thing, it is a matter of differences in the relationship between my body and things, which can in fact be located at the same physical distance, but which are charged with different significance: the telephone that might ring any time at all offers different possibilities than the empty and thereby uninteresting coffee mug on my desk. Mobility, on the other hand, has to do with the fact that I am on my way in time towards or from the thing: the hand on the way to the telephone that rings, the feet on the way down the steep staircase, the gaze on the way away from the coffee mug. My different tasks, like answering the telephone or retrieving something from a different floor, implicate both spatiality and mobility.

That I can bodily orient myself in time and space thus presumes a phenomenal body. In relation to the physical body, the phenomenal body constitutes the condition of possibility for our being able to understand what it means to have a body. The distinction between physical body and phenomenal body also makes it possible to, at least partially, get a view of the phenomenal body through, for example, the fact that the concrete, physical possibilities for piano playing cease through the amputation of an arm, but that piano playing still remains as an action inscribed in the phenomenal body of the pianist. The orientation of the body in time and space is therefore not primarily a matter of being able to indicate the coordinates of the body in an objective space and an objective time. Phenomenal space and phenomenal time constitute a region for our intentions and our bodily actions, and this region is therefore phenomenologically primary. And this phenomenological time-space, or phenomenal space, is formed by habit. Merleau-Ponty says:

> To get used to a hat, a car or a stick is to be transplanted into them, or conversely, to incorporate them into the bulk of our own body. Habit expresses our power of dilating our being-in-the-world, or changing our existence by appropriating fresh instruments.[69]

69. Merleau-Ponty, *Phenomenology*, p. 143.

These habits are neither intellectual nor instinctive abilities. Merleau-Ponty's example is the art of typing. For the one who can type, this art is neither a matter of thinking about which key ought to be hit in order to write a particular letter, or of a conditioned reflex being triggered by the sight of a particular letter. The art of typing lies, so to speak, in the hands, and makes itself known precisely through the writing itself. To be able to type does not at all need to be connected to the ability to explain how one types. Instead, the art of typing is a knowledge that has been acquired through practice and has been transformed into a habit and into what has additionally become one ability among the repertoire of bodily possibilities of the individual. Through the fact that the practical skill of being able to type is found neither in consciousness as such nor in instinct, knowledge here comes to be a matter of experiencing "the harmony between what we aim at and what is given, between the intention and the performance—and the body is our anchorage in a world."[70] The body mediates a world, in this case the world of the typewriter. The repertoire of possibilities that Merleau-Ponty says exists in the phenomenal body extends from the simplest gestures needed to keep ourselves alive to complicated artistic expressions like, for example, dance.

This discussion leads to the general conclusion, for Merleau-Ponty's part, that the body "is our general medium for having a world."[71] It is through the body that we relate to the environment in our human existence, and it is through the body that existence becomes meaningful for us. Space is not an empty container and time not a linear time. Space and time are existentially significant, and it is on this that the human being's understanding of space and time is founded, an understanding that also makes it possible for us to orient ourselves in existence. Or, to link to the concept of the life-world that I previously discussed in chapter 1: the lived world precedes the person's thought world, and its obviousness is so great that it is often overlooked. The thought world is, however, fundamentally dependent on the lived world.

The spatiality and temporality of the phenomenal body are thus fundamental categories for Merleau-Ponty, but they are not the only aspects of this embodiment. In *Phenomenology of Perception* he also discusses how the human being's bodily being-in-the-world is both erotically and linguistically structured. Through sexuality, which is not a matter of a particular part of embodiment but of a dimension of the entirety of the human being's bodily being-in-the-world as such, different attitudes towards existence are

70. Merleau-Ponty, *Phenomenology,* p. 144.
71. Merleau-Ponty, *Phenomenology,* p. 146.

formed.[72] Likewise, the human being's status as a linguistic creature is a dimension of the entirety of a person's being-in-the-world, not merely a specific ability. The primary function of language is that it orients the person in her life-world, not that it creates a correspondence between thought and thing.[73] With a theologically colored word, Merleau-Ponty argues that language "transfigures" the human body.[74] One way to understand what Merleau-Ponty means by this is that the body communicates through its linguistic capacity and thereby clarifies how the human being's embodiment is always more than a naked factuality. Language is thus not something that lies to the side of the body, but is an aspect of the phenomenal body.

The phenomenological description of the phenomenal body is an attempt on Merleau-Ponty's part to thematize the pre-theoretical world that is itself the basis for both human action and reflection. Before the distinction between subject and object we find the life-world as the basis for the distinction itself. For Merleau-Ponty the life-world is a pre-theoretical world that is meaningful for the person, not a world that is organized on the basis of purely quantitative structural relationships. The person does not view existence from the perspective of eternity or of a spectator, but lives in a world that she does not understand from above and cannot survey, a world that encloses her on all sides. Her relationship to her environment is not monocular or ostensibly disembodied, to link to the discussion I have given in chapter 4, but we instead have a polyscopic, embodied perspective on the environment. Merleau-Ponty's philosophy thus does not pose as an absolute system of knowledge either, but imagines knowledge as perspectival and situated, or, in other words, incarnated.[75] Even variables such as breadth, depth, and height—but also time and the thing—are primarily existential categories.

This does not mean that our world is entirely subjective, or all too familiar, i.e., a world that we bring completely into harmony with our intentions. The world we live in is, to begin with, the world as we perceive it, not the

---

72. Merleau-Ponty, *Phenomenology*, pp. 158–59.

73. Merleau-Ponty, *Phenomenology*, pp. 191–92.

74. Merleau-Ponty, *Phenomenology*, p. 197.

75. He has been accused by his critics of resurrecting the relativistic philosophy of the Greek philosopher Protagoras; cf. for example Moran, *Introduction*, p. 430. How justified such a critique is I will not discuss here, but will content myself with stating that a Protagorian theory of knowledge does not necessarily need to have especially much to do with relativism in the general sense of the word. See Mats Rosengren's new reading of Protagoras in *Doxologi: En essä om kunskap* (Åstorp, Sweden: Rhetor, 2002).

world as we want it to be.[76] It is instead a matter of the world having at least some sort of order, such that it is not completely inhospitable for the human inhabitant.[77] The body makes it such that we are at home in a somewhat regular world, at the same time that the world is alien to us, in that it exposes us to the gazes of others who see both us and, independently of us, things. Secondly, Merleau-Ponty's phenomenology is not a matter of describing a world completely congruent with human intentions. In order to formulate this with reference to theology: the person's being-in-the-world as it is described by Merleau-Ponty assumes neither that the world is created by God, and fixed by God as congruent with the person's intentions, nor that it is not congruent with her intentions in the absence of a divine creator. Both positions—the world is meaningful or the world is meaningless—assume a view on things that is not possible on the basis of the contingent perspective of the human being. The entirety of Merleau-Ponty's philosophy involves rejecting such an apocalyptic view from nowhere. What Merleau-Ponty wants to express instead is that there is meaning, however ambiguous it may be.[78] Here and now the world seems to be relatively trustworthy in a very fundamental but relatively modest sense. It is thus not a matter of discussing a world created for the human being or not, but instead of the fact that we can to some extent depend on our everyday experiences of what it means to live a human life.

The Invisible Flesh

As I have mentioned above, Merleau-Ponty eventually came to be unsatisfied with his attempt at a philosophy of the body in *Phenomenology of Perception*, and so he returned to the problem in his posthumously published *The Visible*

76. Cf., for example, what Merleau-Ponty says about Cézanne's paintings in "Cézanne's Doubt," in *Sense and Non-Sense*, pp. 9–25.

77. Apropos this problem Samuel Todes writes in *Body and World,* Introductions by Hubert L. Dreyfus and Piotr Hoffman (Cambridge, MA: MIT Press, 2001), p. 41: "But in practice we cannot help believing that since the human subject has both a dependable body and undependable circumstances, his experiences are moderately ordered. This implies that there is at least a moderately dependable regularity in appearances of things in the world, because the world, as the body's world, must be at least a somewhat habitable world. Any other view is incredible in practice."

78. Merleau-Ponty, "Metaphysics and the Novel," in *Sense and Non-Sense*, p. 34: "All life is undeniably ambiguous, and there is never any way to know the true meaning of what we do. Indeed, perhaps our actions have no *single* true meaning."

and the Invisible. The main problem in *Phenomenology of Perception* was, according to himself, that there he proceeded from a dichotomy between consciousness and object that he in fact wanted to overcome.[79] He is even more critical towards a distinction between nature and culture—or between realism and idealism—that would differentiate between what is naturally given and what is culturally conditioned in the human: "[E]verything is cultural in us (our Lebenswelt is 'subjective') (our perception is cultural-historical) and everything is natural in us (even the cultural rests on the polymorphism of the wild Being)."[80] In *The Visible and the Invisible* Merleau-Ponty attempts to write a different philosophy of the body, or perhaps rather to write a more general philosophy of the flesh for which the human body is only a prototype. This time it is not a matter of the phenomenology of the body, but rather the ontology of the flesh. Primary for understanding the ontology of the flesh was "perceptual faith."

Merleau-Ponty said, as I have stated above, that the person lives in a pre-theoretical and pre-scientific life-world.[81] We inhabit this world with our bodies and we presuppose it with a certainty that makes it such that we do not differentiate our world from our understanding of the world.[82] That which we perceive, we also perceive as true, without differentiating between the presumption of truth and the act of perception itself. It is therefore a question of a faith, rather than a knowledge: "[I]t is therefore the greatest degree of belief that our vision goes to the things themselves."[83] The world is, as the basis for our perceptions, beyond our affirmation or rejection of it; it is beyond all opinions we have of it. The same thought is formulated in an earlier work: "Each of our perceptions is an act of faith in that it affirms more than we strictly know, since objects are inexhaustible and our information limited."[84] This perceptual faith means that we, even in our scientific and philosophical reasoning, presuppose that our experience of and with the world in this moment stands in continuity not only with the moment before and after, but also with how others experience the world.[85] The problem with science and philosophy is, according to Merleau-Ponty, not that they question this perceptual faith—such a faith ought not be a

79. Merleau-Ponty, *The Visible and the Invisible,* pp. 200–201.
80. Merleau-Ponty, *The Visible and the Invisible,* p. 307.
81. Merleau-Ponty, *The Visible and the Invisible,* pp. 48–49.
82. Merleau-Ponty, *The Visible and the Invisible,* pp. 31–48.
83. Merleau-Ponty, *The Visible and the Invisible,* p. 48.
84. Merleau-Ponty, "Faith and Good Faith," in *Sense and Non-Sense,* p. 179.
85. Merleau-Ponty, *Phenomenology,* p. 54. Cf. pp. 321–22.

blind faith.[86] The problem consists instead in that science and philosophy have forgotten their origin in the pre-theoretical world, as well as the fact that they presuppose this perceptual faith. Through this forgetfulness they have believed themselves to be self-contained and independent. For a critical reflection it is therefore necessary for philosophy—and here Merleau-Ponty argues in a way that recalls Husserl—to return to this pre-theoretical world. As Merleau-Ponty writes in *Phenomenology of Perception:*

> The first philosophical act would appear to be to return to the world of actual experience which is prior to the objective world, since it is in it that we shall be able to grasp the theoretical basis no less than the limits of that objective world, restore to things their concrete physiognomy, to organisms their individual ways of dealing with the world, and to subjectivity its inherence in history.[87]

What separates Merleau-Ponty from Husserl, however, is that he does not want to find the ground for this philosophy in some sort of transcendental subjectivity. The activity of philosophy begins instead with the perception—thereof Merleau-Ponty's interest in the same—of concrete existence, inclusive of the reflection on this existence itself. Philosophy is therefore the perceptual faith that interrogates itself about itself.[88] Perceptual faith thus constitutes the foundation for Merleau-Ponty's ontology of the flesh, which is a reworking or an enlargement of his philosophy of the body.

The concept of the flesh *(chair)*—which Merleau-Ponty argues has no name in any philosophy—can be seen as a further development of the thought of the body schema in *Phenomenology of Perception.*[89] But in con-

---

86. Merleau-Ponty, "Faith and Good Faith," pp. 178–80.

87. Merleau-Ponty, *Phenomenology,* p. 57.

88. Merleau-Ponty, *The Visible and the Invisible,* p. 103.

89. Merleau-Ponty, *The Visible and the Invisible,* pp. 139–40, 147–48, 205–6. Cf. Alphonso Lingis, "Translator's Preface," in *The Visible and the Invisible: Followed by Working Notes* (Evanston, IL: Northwestern University Press, 1968), p. liv. Merleau-Ponty has been criticized for the Christian connotations of terms like flesh and chiasm (i.e., the incarnation and the cross). Since I am ultimately interested in a theological understanding of the body and do not intend in this chapter to establish a theologically neutral philosophy, such a critique—justified or not—plays less of a role. See Gilles Deleuze and Félix Guattari, *What Is Philosophy?* trans. Hugh Tomlinson and Graham Burchell (New York: Columbia University Press, 1994), p. 178. However, according to Dominique Janicaud, *The Theological Turn of French Phenomenology,* in *Phenomenology and the "Theological Turn": The French Debate,* Dominique Janicaud et al. (New York: Fordham University Press, 2000), Merleau-Ponty is, in contrast to, for example,

trast with the phenomenal body, the flesh cannot be limited to one side of the relationship between the one who sees and the seen. The philosophy of the body in *Phenomenology of Perception* risks, according to Merleau-Ponty's own belief, creating a dichotomy between body and world. By arguing that our human body stands in relation to the world, he has brought in a distinction that more or less involuntarily repeats the distinction between subject and object. The flesh is brought in in order to transcend this distinction. It is compared by Merleau-Ponty to an "element," i.e., a sort of general thing that lies halfway between an idea and an entity in time and space, "a sort of incarnate principle that brings a style of being."[90] The flesh is neither horizon nor object, neither background nor figure, but that which makes it so that these can enter into relationship with each other. The possibility of perception is found in the flesh, since the flesh is a medium that does not allow itself to be reduced to mutually exclusive categories like consciousness and object or seeing and seen. In contrast with the body, the flesh cannot stand in relation to the world, since this would presume a distinction between flesh and world. In the philosophy of the body the human can still be understood as someone who is defined as a negation in relation to her environment, as though embodiment constitutes a sort of contrast to the thing. In his later philosophy Merleau-Ponty wants instead to emphasize the "chiasm," i.e., the intertwining of that which is visible and that which perceives the visible.[91]

The argument about the flesh is in other words a way for Merleau-Ponty to reject every form of dichotomy between consciousness and object, where these could be imagined to exist independently of each other, and where the one or the other pole would be able to dominate the relationship. Our gaze palpates things rather than masters them, it clothes them with its own flesh, and we therefore do not meet "naked" things that primarily exist for themselves and then also give themselves to our perception.[92] The gaze can—to highlight another metaphor in Merleau-Ponty—be said to interrogate things

Levinas, a faithful steward of Husserl's heritage, and thus innocent of theology. That there exists some sort of theological interest in Merleau-Ponty is clear, however, not least in his essay "Faith and Good Faith," pp. 172–81.

90. Merleau-Ponty, *The Visible and the Invisible*, p. 139.

91. But perhaps even the idea of a chiasm or an intertwining presumes two separate elements that are woven together in a way that does not do justice to the more radical identification of the flesh. Thanks to Helena Dahlberg, University of Gothenburg, who pointed this problem out for me. I refer to her dissertation *Vad är kött? Kroppen och människan i Merleau-Pontys filosofi* (Göteborg: Glänta, 2013).

92. Merleau-Ponty, *The Visible and the Invisible*, pp. 130–35.

according to their own will. That this is possible depends on the chiasm, the intertwining between that which sees and the visible. Merleau-Ponty's paradigmatic explanation of this chiasm is that the hand that touches things can itself be touched, and therefore is one of the things. There thus exists a sort of given intimacy between person and thing that underlies her perception of the things around her. The movement of the hand with the touching of a thing incorporates it into the same universe as that which it investigates. The same is true of the sense of sight, which Merleau-Ponty does not see as a sense entirely independent of feeling. Feeling and sight each have their own complete maps, which, without merging, still overlap or cross each other. It is the same body that both touches and sees, and so Merleau-Ponty can without contradiction take metaphors from the region of the one sense in order to apply it to that of the other. This means that sight—which can be described as a palpation—does not exist in a disembodied way either: "He who looks must not be foreign to the world that he looks at."[93] I who see am at the same time the one who can be seen by some other person, and am thus myself a part of the visible world. In a side comment Merleau-Ponty says that the body as visible is what he earlier called the "objective body," and that the body as seeing is what he earlier called the "phenomenal body."[94]

Between the one who sees and the thing that is seen there exist both nearness and distance, and the same nearness and distance are found between people as well. Distance is "synonymous" with nearness, since distance is not understood as an empty space between the perceiver and that which is perceived, but as the flesh between the perceiving and that which is perceived, that which makes communication between them possible. Distance is thus both that which makes it such that something can stand in relation with something else, and that which makes it such that they differ from each other. Both the perceived thing in the world and the perceiving body have a "depth," Merleau-Ponty says, and for the body's part this consists in the fact that it is not only perceiving, but perceivable. The depth of things consists in that they do not open themselves for the gaze that surveys them from above, but only for the gaze that exists together with them in the same world. The depth of the things also means that they are never given in a single glance, that they are always "pregnant" with their possibilities. With regard to things, we only see their "exterior," but their total visibility exists behind or after or between the aspects of them that we see. The coexistence of things

93. Merleau-Ponty, *The Visible and the Invisible*, p. 134.
94. Merleau-Ponty, *The Visible and the Invisible*, pp. 136–37.

and the body can therefore not be compared to an existence where the thing is only seen and the body only sees. Sight is not in the body as though in a box, nor is the body in the world as though in a box. On the basis of such an outlook it is not entirely correct to speak of "embodiment," since it seems to presume an at least semi-autonomous existence of the consciousness.[95] But what Merleau-Ponty strives for is a perspective on the relationship between consciousness and body that is not a dichotomy. The relationship between people as well—an intercorporeal relationship rather than an intersubjective relationship—is characterized by both distance and nearness. Fred Evans and Leonard Lawlor write the following:

> The invisible of the flesh is like the soul of the other into which I can never see, onto which I can never hold, and most important, which I can never know. The other is absent, crossed out. Yet, since the soul has been incarnate, I can still feel it, feel with it, feel into it—*Einfühlung*—and believe.[96]

Because the person's soul is incarnated in—intertwined with—the whole of her body, her soul may be perceived through the whole of her physical and phenomenal body. Such an entanglement between body and consciousness corresponds as well to the entanglement between sight and that which is seen, hearing and that which is heard, etc.[97]

However, seeing things is, according to Merleau-Ponty, not only a matter of seeing the visibility of things as they are intertwined with us, in the flesh. This primary visibility is accompanied by a secondary visibility of fields and lines of force, and one can therefore not see "the massive flesh" because it does not come "without a rarefied flesh, the momentary body without a glorified body *[un corps glorieux]*."[98] What Merleau-Ponty is trying to articulate with this strange theological-sounding statement—the term *glorieux* is associated with, for example, the accounts of Jesus on the Mount of Transfiguration (cf. chapter 5)—is how one ought to understand the relationship between body and thought. Merleau-Ponty wants to avoid imagining an idea as existing in another world—a world of ideas—separate

95. Which is pointed out by Tina Chanter, "Wild Meaning: Luce Irigaray's Reading of Merleau-Ponty," in *Chiasms,* ed. Evans and Lawlor, p. 222.

96. Fred Evans and Leonard Lawlor, "Introduction: The Value of Flesh: Merleau-Ponty's Philosophy and the Modernism/Postmodernism Debate," in *Chiasms,* ed. Evans and Lawlor, p. 11.

97. Merleau-Ponty, *The Visible and the Invisible,* pp. 143–44.

98. Merleau-Ponty, *The Visible and the Invisible,* p. 148.

from the world of phenomena we perceive through the senses. That would be to deny the very foundation of his philosophy. We would not understand ideas better if we were bodiless. On the contrary, we could never understand them without our body, since these ideas are also embodied. Our embodiment gives us not only the opportunity to perceive these ideas, but also gives them their authority. As an example, Merleau-Ponty takes the way the essence of love is communicated to Swann in Marcel Proust's *In Search of Lost Time* through a little musical phrase from the Andante movement in Vinteuil's sonata for violin and piano.[99] Swann meditates on its meaning for himself:

> Even when he was not thinking of the little phrase, it existed latent in his mind on the same footing as certain other notions without material equivalent, such as our notions of light, of sound, of perspective, of physical pleasure, the rich possessions wherewith our inner temple is diversified and adorned.[100]

The "little phrase" does not exist without its factual, physical performance, even if it can be thought of as independent of the performance itself, just like the other ideas Merleau-Ponty speaks of here: "[T]hey could not be given to us *as ideas* except in a carnal experience."[101] They cannot be explained without their inscrutable essence foundering, even if the forms through which they are manifested may be spoken of.[102] Swann views musical motifs as "actual ideas, of another world, of another order, ideas veiled in shadow, unknown, impenetrable to the human mind, but none the less perfectly distinct from one another, unequal among themselves in value and significance."[103] The obscurity that is spoken of here, at least in Merleau-Ponty's version, is not a synonym for vagueness, but rather for an inscrutability regarding the invisibility of these ideas, the impossibility of viewing them in a direct act of perception.[104] Their inscrutability does not make them invisible in the sense that they would hide behind other objects or that they would

---

99. Merleau-Ponty, *The Visible and the Invisible,* pp. 149–50. See Marcel Proust, *In Search of Lost Time,* vol. 1: *Swann's Way,* trans. C. K. Scott Moncrieff and Terence Kilmartin, revised by D. J. Enright (New York: The Modern Library, 1992), pp. 475–83 *et passim.*

100. Proust, *In Search,* p. 479.

101. Merleau-Ponty, *The Visible and the Invisible,* p. 150.

102. Proust, *In Search,* p. 477.

103. Proust, *In Search,* p. 478.

104. Merleau-Ponty, *The Visible and the Invisible,* pp. 150–51.

be invisible in principle. They are "the invisible *of* this world."[105] Merleau-Ponty again uses the sonata as an illustration of the fact that we do not own these ideas—the ideas own us. Musicians who perform the sonata do not produce or reproduce the piece of music, but find themselves at its service; it is through her or him as medium that the sonata sings out. The ideality that Merleau-Ponty speaks of here gives the flesh its lines, its depth and its volume. In other words, it is not a question of an ideality independent of the flesh and the world, even if its flesh is of another sort than that which is directly visible—a more transparent flesh. Thought and body form a chiasm; they exist interwoven with each other in the flesh.

When Merleau-Ponty speaks of the flesh, it is thus not in order to dissolve the physicality of the human body, or, conversely, to see thought as a pure epiphenomenon of the material, but in order to, more radically than in *Phenomenology of Perception,* imagine the affinity between thought and body, vision and the visible, and the invisible and the visible, without because of this wanting to dissolve the distinction between them. In other words, he wants to overcome the two modern alternatives of materialism and idealism. One might say that the physical body and the phenomenal body have an interactive relationship, such that they both give the possibility for each other without the one pole being able to be reduced to the other. The flesh is as "spiritual" as it is "material," since "the real" is indissolubly intertwined with its "meaning." Arguing with Max Weber that the environment is meaningless in itself and that it is the human who imbues it with meaning runs counter to Merleau-Ponty, since this would be to introduce the Cartesian dualism between a lifeless and meaningless body on the one hand and a transcendental and meaning-giving consciousness on the other.[106] But the human is one with the world, both as body and consciousness, through the flesh, and the world bears within itself, according to Merleau-Ponty, an ideality (a depth and a volume) that exists intertwined with its materiality. There is no dualism between what is seen and sight, but their continuity—a continuity that transcends the existence of the human being—is found in the flesh. Nor do our bodies or other things exist as absolutely discrete entities: the surface of our bodies does not constitute an absolute boundary for our bodies, since the flesh unites everything that may be perceived into a single (differentiated) surface.

---

105. Merleau-Ponty, *The Visible and the Invisible,* p. 151.

106. Max Weber, "'Objectivity' in Social Science and Social Policy," in *The Methodology of the Social Sciences,* trans. Edward A. Shils and Henry A. Finch (Glencoe, IL: Free Press, 1949), p. 81.

Merleau-Ponty's revision of his philosophy of the body into a philosophy of the flesh in the unfinished work *The Visible and the Invisible* does not mean that *Phenomenology of Perception* should be a thing of the past in the discussion of the body. On the contrary, these two works together have been crucial for the continued discussion within philosophy and feminist theory. Despite the limitations that may be found in both works, they have served as a sufficiently articulated philosophy of the body to be able to be further developed, or to be resisted in the attempt to find an alternative philosophy of the body. It is therefore no exaggeration to claim that Merleau-Ponty's contribution to a philosophy of the body and to the return of the body within contemporary philosophy has been of crucial significance. In particular, his way of emphasizing the living body—both in its physical and in its phenomenal form—in opposition to the body as a dead, objectified object for the scientific gaze has meant a new orientation for philosophical discussions of the body.[107] It should be noted here that Merleau-Ponty's philosophy of the body did not mean anything entirely new compared to the philosophies of the body of earlier times—an interesting example is Michel de Montaigne.[108] But Merleau-Ponty remains the philosopher who has succeeded in a pioneering way in setting the body on the philosophical agenda, and who has systematically attempted to consider its constitution and possibilities.

More important in this context is the fact that Merleau-Ponty's philosophy of the body has a critical value for a contemporary theology of the body, and even if the following chapter will not be an explicit attempt to write a theology "after Merleau-Ponty," his ideas will have indirectly influenced much of what is said. An important lesson is that it is important to decide which body it is that we are discussing in a given context. Is it a dead body-object, or the living body that constitutes the human being's practical field in her life-world? Is it the body as an object for philosophical or theological arguments, or the body as the human being's practical and concrete relation to other human beings and to the divine? Especially in the wake of our understanding of the incarnation, it is important to reflect on *which* embodiment is meant in the different theological arguments about the meaning of the body. On the basis of the previous chapters on incarnation and gaze we can at least hypothetically suspect that for theology it is a matter of a body

---

107. On the dead body from a perspective inspired by Merleau-Ponty, see Suzanne Laba Cataldi, "Embodying Perceptions of Death: Emotional Apprehension and Reversibilities of Flesh," in *Chiasms*, ed. Evans and Lawlor, pp. 189–201.

108. Judovitz, *Culture of the Body*, pp. 15–40.

deeply engaged in the person's life-world, rather than a body as an isolated object for the person's theoretical gaze.

The gravity of what Merleau-Ponty had to say shows itself not least in the many attempts by his critics to further develop his philosophy of the body—inclusive of his ontology of the flesh, which bursts the confines of the philosophy of the body.[109] I will now turn to a few of these.

The Constructed Body

The continued discussion of Merleau-Ponty's philosophy of the body has not related uncritically to either the early or the late Merleau-Ponty. The critique has often involved the question of the significance of institutions for the meaning of the body in his philosophy. One critique (or a clarification?) that has been presented by the two Merleau-Ponty scholars Fred Evans and Leonard Lawlor is that in *The Visible and the Invisible* he has still overemphasized perception and language as the human being's primary relationship to the world. But perception and language are always embedded in institutions that specify what may be seen and said in accordance with their respective discursive structures. Perception and language never exist independent of the intrinsic logic of these institutions, and it is thus this intrinsic logic, rather than perception and language, that is primarily determinative for the human being's relationships to other human beings and to the objects surrounding her. Different institutions are what they are only in relationship to other institutions, and therefore occur in constant movement where new forms of life are produced. Evans and Lawlor write:

> Institutions fold themselves into subjects in conformity to their logic, but the incorporated subjects refold the institutions into an interplay of institutions and the sorts of exchanges that create new institutions and metamorphose the network of institutions.[110]

It is thus not perception or language that is primary, but institutions. Even phenomenology is a part of the play between institutions, and acts within

---

109. Samuel Todes thought that, in spite of everything, Merleau-Ponty did not succeed in escaping idealism. For Todes's own attempt at a nonidealistic philosophy of the body, see Todes, *Body and World* (Cambridge, MA: MIT Press, 2001).

110. Fred Evans and Leonard Lawler, "Introduction," p. 16.

the framework of one of these institutions, and can therefore not claim to be universally valid. Phenomenology is a part of the conflict between institutions. The flesh that Merleau-Ponty speaks of is, Evans and Lawlor say, precisely this interplay between institutions. There is thus every reason to dwell on the question of the socially constructed body in relation to these institutions.

The Institutional Body

One of the precursors when it comes to the idea of the social construction of the body is the anthropologist Marcel Mauss. In his article "Techniques of the Body" from 1936 Mauss says that the movements of one's own body are not something naturally given, but a socially learned ability.[111] Thus, for example, a way of swimming, walking, or resting varies significantly between different cultures and subcultures. Every technique of the body has its form that is specific to its society. One learns how the body ought to move by acquiring its society's *habitus*—Mauss uses the Latin term to more clearly point to the parallel to Aristotle's idea of *hexis,* i.e., an "acquired disposition."[112] Socially acquired body techniques, biology, and psychology exist intertwined in one and the same body, and are expressed in actions. Even "mystical states," Mauss argues, are linked with specific body techniques.[113] Because of this he says that "[t]he body is man's first and most natural instrument. Or more accurately, not to speak of instruments, man's first and most natural technical object, and at the same time technical means, is his body."[114] The body, its movements, and its postures are thus socially constructed, rather than given with a pre-social nature. Mauss's ideas of a bodily *habitus* have been further developed by a number of thinkers in France, among them Michel Foucault and Pierre Bourdieu. I will here pay attention to Foucault's view of the body and institution, and will also mention something of Bourdieu's *habitus*-concept.

111. Marcel Mauss, "Techniques of the Body," *Economy and Society* 2, no. 1 (1973): 70–88.

112. Mauss, "Techniques," p. 73. Cf. Aristotle, *Nicomachean Ethics,* Loeb Classical Library, trans. H. Rackham (Cambridge, MA/London: Harvard University Press, 1934), I xiii 20, II v.

113. Mauss, "Techniques," pp. 86–87. For a theological discussion of "the embodiment of mysticism," see Mark A. McIntosh, *Mystical Theology: The Integrity of Spirituality and Theology,* Challenges in Contemporary Theology, ed. Lewis Ayres and Gareth Jones (Oxford: Blackwell, 1998).

114. Mauss, "Techniques," p. 75.

The role of institutions for the construction of the body has been ana-
lyzed by Foucault in the book that I mentioned back in chapter 4, namely
Discipline and Punish. The chapter on "docile bodies" is what one might
call a lesser classic in this context.[115] Foucault says here that the classical period, i.e., Descartes's time, discovered the body as an object for power. They
wanted to make the body both understandable by studying it, and useful by
subjugating and exploiting it. Anatomy, philosophy, technology, and politics
were united in a desire to understand and tame the body. To get the body
to defer to power is certainly nothing new, Foucault says, but what is new is
the scale at which this control is carried out, the object of this control, and
the way in which this control is exerted. It is not the individual's control over
the body that will be strengthened, but society's "use" of the body that will
increase. Foucault writes:

> The human body was entering a machinery of power that explores it,
> breaks it down and rearranges it. A 'political anatomy,' which was also a
> 'mechanics of power,' was being born; it defined how one may have a hold
> over others' bodies, not only so that they may do what one wishes, but so
> that they may operate as one wishes, with the techniques, the speed and
> the efficiency that one determines. Thus discipline produces subjected
> and practiced bodies, 'docile' bodies.[116]

Power enters into a "micro-level," so to speak, by focusing on the body parts,
not as parts of a single physical or virtual body, but as parts of a larger me-
chanic of power. Through a minute observation of the body, through the
systematizing and ranking of the different facts about details that one obtains
in observation, one establishes a discipline that gets the body to function in
the most effective way for the political power. The modern discipline of the
body aims to generate an effective body rather than a virtuous or sensual
body. By placing the body of the human being into this context, the body
becomes an object for a new sort of knowing:

> It is the body of exercise, rather than of speculative physics; a body ma-
> nipulated by authority, rather than imbued with animal spirits; a body
> of useful training and not of rational mechanics, but one in which, by

115. Michel Foucault, *Discipline and Punish: The Birth of the Prison,* trans. Alan Sheridan
(New York: Vintage Books, 1995), pp. 135–69.
116. Foucault, *Discipline,* p. 138.

virtue of that very fact, a number of natural requirements and functional constraints are beginning to emerge.[117]

Power thus produces a new body and a new knowledge. Or rather it is a matter, according to Foucault, of an indissoluble connection between power and knowledge whose contemporary relations of strength are traced on the surface of the body. In contrast with the period before Classicism, the body was subjugated not through force, but through ideology.[118]

The premise for Foucault's argument about the "taming" of the "docile" body is that institutions form the person's body according to their own inner logic. The bodies are formed according to the ruling institutions' configuration of power/knowledge. The question, however, is whether one ought to read *Discipline and Punish* as a general philosophy of the body. The book is largely a critique of the ruling prison system, and hardly a general philosophy of human embodiment. In other words, it would be possible to imagine that there are alternative ways for people to configure their embodiment, ways that do not necessarily entail that these bodies are infinitely malleable—"docile"—or that these bodies are solely seen as passive objects.[119] Now if Foucault imagined *Discipline and Punish* as a contribution to French politics of imprisonment, we can imagine that he thereby represented an alternative politics of the body, which in some sense was "better" than that of his present time. Such a philosophy of the body and politics of the body would hardly argue that bodies can exist independently of institutions, but rather that there exists an interplay between institutions that may be taken advantage of by individual people. (Foucault will later present a proposal that moves in that direction in *The History of Sexuality,* which I return to in chapter 10.) What one can learn from Foucault more generally has to do, I believe, not with the body's infinite docility and plasticity—even if the critique of the consequences of such a politics/philosophy is important—but that the body is always already involved in institutions, that it does not exist as an atom or monad, independent of its environment, but that it is on the contrary always already woven into a larger context of practices and discourses that fight for its attention and form its desire. The body—regardless which body we speak of—is not only something signified, but is invariably

117. Foucault, *Discipline,* p. 155.

118. Foucault, *Discipline,* pp. 25–26 *et passim.*

119. Within feminist theory a critical attitude may be found regarding a pacifying of the human body that goes too far in Foucault. See, for example, Jana Sawicki, *Disciplining Foucault: Feminism, Power, and the Body* (New York/London: Routledge, 1991).

also a sign in a general economy of signs. What Foucault wants to say in *Discipline and Punish* is sententiously and elegantly captured in his loan of a Platonic maxim which he himself inverts: "the soul is the prison of the body."[120] The question is whether it is possible to transform the soul into something other than a prison.

Here I will enlist the help of Bourdieu.[121] With his *habitus*-concept— which is influenced by Mauss, among others—Bourdieu also wants to attempt to understand how the subjectivity of the person is always already socialized. For Bourdieu *habitus* is the very link between institution and subjectivity. Subjectivity cannot be understood without the "objective" structures that these institutions provide, but at the same time these structures do not exist independent of subjectivity. The relationship between the two can best be described as dialectical. A *habitus* is generated by the social structures in a particular milieu and gives rise to a number of dispositions in the individual, which thereby make possible her or his "improvisations" in a particular concrete situation for action. These improvisations, however, also harmonize with the way others act in the same situation, if they are habituated in the same way. The interpersonal relationship is thus, according to Bourdieu, never a direct interaction between two individuals, but always mediated by a *habitus* that has its origin in institutions that vary by class, occupation, sex, etc.

Bourdieu additionally says that the human being's habituation is above all bodily. A child will not only acquire a particular way of walking or different facial expressions by imitating other people's actions, but also a particular way of experiencing the world. In the command to "stand straight" or to "not hold the knife with the left hand," a whole "cosmology" is embodied, including an ethics, a metaphysics, and a political philosophy. The connection between the person's consciousness and the things surrounding her is thus very intimate, according to Bourdieu: "The mind is a metaphor of the world of objects which is itself but an endless circle of mutually reflecting

120. Foucault, *Discipline,* p. 30.

121. Bourdieu discusses the *habitus*-concept in a number of different places in his work, but I have chosen to proceed from the exposition that is found in *Outline of a Theory of Practice,* trans. Richard Nice (Cambridge: Cambridge University Press, 1977), pp. 72–95, which is a translation of a revised version of portions of *Esquisse d'une théorie de la pratique: Précédé de trois études d'ethnologie kabyle,* Travaux de droit, d'économie, de sociologie et de sciences politiques, no. 92 (Geneva: Librairie Droz, 1972). For an expanded discussion of *habitus* in Bourdieu see Donald Broady, *Sociologi och epistemologi: Om Pierre Bourdieus författarskap och den historiska epistemologin,* Skeptronserien (Stockholm: HLS Förlag, 1990), pp. 228–69.

metaphors."[122] A particular bodily habituation is thus at the same time a way of acquiring a particular way of understanding the world. But even if this habituation is beyond the person's own will and control, it is not a matter of creating a deterministic behavior. Bourdieu says that the freedom that the habituation gives rise to is about neither a behavioral determination of the sort stimulus/response, nor a voluntarily understood, spontaneous, and unbound freedom to do, but is instead a matter of a "subjective" possibility to improvise on the basis of the possibilities that are given by the "objective" social structures. One might say that Bourdieu imagines both a passively so-cializing *habitus*-function—as, for example, with the raising of a child—and a coveted and active choice, which thereby constitutes the entrance pass to a particular social field, for example, the academic milieu.[123] Thus it also becomes possible to change social structures as well as subjective disposi-tions, if not through a solitary act, since these structures and dispositions are sluggish. With his *habitus*-concept Bourdieu highlights more clearly than Foucault—at least in *Discipline and Punish*—the dialectic or interplay between the institution and the individual person. The point is thus not to deny the person's freedom of action, but rather to point out the institutional and dispositional conditions for this freedom. The problem that arises in this field of tension between institution, body, and freedom returns as well in the feminist and gender theory discussions of the body that I will now get into.

The Performative Body

How the body is formed and determined by its environment has been stud-ied in feminist theory in particular, and it may be appropriate here to recon-nect with my discussion of Merleau-Ponty above. A feminist critique of his philosophy of the body has been delivered from several directions, and boils down to the fact that Merleau-Ponty's supposedly neutral phenomenological account of embodied sexuality in *Phenomenology of Perception* is in fact an account of a male, heterosexual body.[124] The consequence of Merleau-Ponty's phenomenology is that he naturalizes a cultural construction of body, sex,

---

122. Bourdieu, *Outline of a Theory of Practice,* p. 91.

123. Cf. Pierre Bourdieu, *Homo Academicus,* trans. Peter Collier (Cambridge: Polity, 1988).

124. Judith Butler, "Sexual Ideology and Phenomenological Description: A Feminist Cri-tique of Merleau-Ponty's *Phenomenology of Perception,*" in *The Thinking Muse: Feminism and Modern French Philosophy,* ed. Jeffner Allen and Iris Marion Young (Bloomington/Indianap-olis: Indiana University Press, 1989), pp. 85–100.

and sexuality, and thereby universalizes a particular experience of the body. Certainly Merleau-Ponty does not say that sexuality is a natural sex instinct, but at the same time his account seems to imply that every individual encounters a natural sexuality that she then gives concrete embodied form in her own existence. Sexuality thus becomes historical by the fact that the individual appropriates it. But the question is whether this historically given sexuality that is thus taken for natural is not in fact a sedimented sexuality, such that the individual acts of appropriation are more a transformation of an earlier cultural form of sexuality into a contemporary culture's sexuality than a transformation of a natural sexuality into a historically specific sexuality. That we cannot imagine human existence and embodiment without sexuality is not argument for a sexuality given by nature. On the contrary, one can imagine that a historically developed and culturally contingent sexuality is *understood* as a naturally given sexuality. Merleau-Ponty would then instead advocate a weak form of historical situatedness where the possibilities of the subject are bounded, not where the subject is constituted by history. But the collective world, which sexuality places us in according to Merleau-Ponty, is rather a reification of social relations in a world where women are dominated by men, which gives these social relations a supposedly objective status. This depends on the fact that his method does not admit the historicity of sexualities and bodies. For a concrete description of lived experience, one must ask which sexuality and whose bodies are described, since "sexuality" and "body" remain abstractions if they are not first situated in concrete social and cultural contexts.[125]

The one who has delivered the above critique is the North American feminist philosopher Judith Butler. Despite this rather sharp critique of Merleau-Ponty, she believes—like other feminist philosophers—that it is still possible to build upon Merleau-Ponty's phenomenology with feminist aims.[126] This

125. Cf. my debate with Gösta Hallonsten about precisely this in "Sexualiteten och traditionen: Svar till Ola Sigurdson," *Svensk Teologisk Kvartalskrift* 80, no. 3 (2004): 120–23, together with Ola Sigurdson, "Vems tradition? Vilken sexualitet? Svar till Gösta Hallonsten," *Svensk Teologisk Kvartalskrift* 80, no. 3 (2004): 124–26.

126. In the same critical article as above ("Sexual Ideology," p. 98), Butler writes that "a feminist appropriation of Merleau-Ponty is doubtless in order." Cf. as well Iris Marion Young, "Throwing like a Girl: A Phenomenology of Feminine Body Comportment, Motility, and Spatiality," in *The Thinking Muse*, pp. 51–70; Young, "Pregnant Embodiment," in *Body and Flesh*, ed. Welton, pp. 274–85, as well as Young, "'Throwing like a Girl': Twenty Years Later," in *Body and Flesh*, pp. 286–90. An overview is given by Linda Martín Alcoff in "Merleau-Ponty and Feminist Theory on Experience," in *Chiasms*, ed. Evans and Lawlor, pp. 251–71.

is perhaps due to the fact that Merleau-Ponty's attention to concrete, bodily experience is something that a feminist philosophy can affirm in principle. With the help of Merleau-Ponty, feminist philosophy has also been able to recover the role of experience in the construction of sex, and has thereby avoided reducing this construction to the intersection between different institutions and structures. If we turn to Butler's own philosophy, which, besides Merleau-Ponty, has also been inspired by Foucault, among others, we find that she has engaged with the question of the body in several much-discussed books, among others *Gender Trouble* from 1990 and *Bodies That Matter* from 1993. Her primary interest is how social institutions construct sexuality, and for Butler's part this entails a direct interest in the relationship of embodiment to both biological and social gender. In *Gender Trouble* Butler takes up the question of whether it is a productive strategy for feminism to reference the term woman as a collective identity. Social gender is namely impossible to separate from the political and cultural intersections that produce and maintain it. There is no pre-social sexual ontology, for even "woman" is a discursive construction that is therefore produced by the society whose internal logic engenders a hierarchization as well as a reification of different sexual identities. But it is not only social gender that is a construction, according to Butler, but also biological gender. She writes:

> Gender ought not be conceived merely as the cultural inscription of meaning on a pregiven sex (a juridical conception); gender must also designate the very apparatus of production whereby the sexes themselves are established. As a result, gender is not to culture as sex is to nature; gender is also the discursive/cultural means by which "sexed nature" or "a natural sex" is produced and established as "prediscursive," prior to culture, a politically neutral surface *on which* culture acts. . . . This production of sex *as* the prediscursive ought to be understood as the effect of the apparatus of cultural construction designated by *gender*.[127]

Thus it is the social gender that produces the biological gender at the same time that it hides this production under a veil of natural givenness.

This means that the body as such is not something naturally given, that in a simple way "is there" prior to all its cultural meanings. The body is that which is produced by social gender. Butler rhetorically asks:

127. Judith Butler, *Gender Trouble: Feminism and the Subversion of Identity* (New York/London: Routledge, 1999), p. 11.

> Is "the body" or "the sexed body" the firm foundation on which gender
> and systems of compulsory sexuality operate? Or is "the body" itself
> shaped by political forces with strategic interests in keeping that body
> bounded and constituted by the markers of sex?[128]

Her answer is the latter. The body is never a passive and pre-discursive foundation that gives itself to all sorts of interpretations. The body does not exist
before interpretation. Butler says instead that one should understand the
sexed body as "performative"—a concept she borrows from philosopher
J. L. Austin[129]—i.e., as constituted and constructed through its actions, gestures, and other bodily signs. Its being or essence is a fabrication, a function
of a social discourse that also constructs its interior and gives the body the
appearance of being a stable core. The consequence is both a hierarchization of the difference male/female and a naturalization of heterosexuality,
which also continues to be reproduced by the ruling discourse. But revealing
the illusion of these ostensibly naturally given constructions means that the
possibility is opened for breaking with these naturalized sex identities by
parodically destabilizing them.

Butler has been criticized for her perspective in *Gender Trouble.* She
has been accused on the grounds that her refusal to speak of a stable female
identity would lead to political passivity, but also on the grounds that she
would dissolve the materiality of the body in a linguistic construction. One
of Butler's critics, Carol Bigwood, says that the poststructuralist body is so
fluid that it seems to be able to be embodied in infinitely different ways.[130]
It has no earthly weight. Thus the masculine alienation of the modern world
from nature is reinforced. An additional critique of Butler's discourse on
performative bodies is that she would thereby represent an almost volunta-
rist perspective on gender identity, i.e., the idea that our gender identity is
something that we can choose and change without major problems. In the
sequel *Bodies That Matter* Butler answers certain critiques of this sort and
clarifies what she means. She rejects the idea that she represents a volunta-
rist position by, among other things, arguing that it would in that case mean
that there exists a subject beyond this culturally contingent gender identity,

128. Butler, *Gender Trouble,* p. 164.

129. See J. L. Austin, *How to Do Things with Words: The William James lectures delivered
at Harvard University in 1955,* ed. J. O. Urmson and Marina Sbisà (Oxford: Oxford University
Press, 1976).

130. Carol Bigwood, "Renaturalizing the Body (with the Help of Merleau-Ponty)," *Body
and Flesh,* ed. Welton, pp. 102–3.

which would be able to choose one or another gender identity. But what Butler argued in *Gender Trouble* was that even the subject is a social construction, i.e., a product of social gender, not the contrary.[131] Butler wants to avoid both voluntarism and determinism when it comes to biological and social gender. The problem with determinism is that it makes transformation impossible. Her solution is to speak of the performative body as constituted by a ritualized repetition and mediation of norms, which in their turn produce and stabilize "not only the effects of gender but the materiality of sex."[132] To speak of sex as a social construction does not, according to Butler, entail a denial of the materiality of the body, of the fact that the constitution of the body has its inevitable restrictions or that there are certain features of sex identity that are stable over long periods.

The materiality of the body is sometimes invoked as evidence of sex differences.[133] But gender differences are always already formed by institutionalized discourses. "Gender" is a category that functions as a "regulative ideal" and thereby also produces gender differences. These differences are created through the ideal being mediated through ritual repetition. Butler says that it is a mistake to understand this ritualizing repetition or performativity as an isolated action. Performativity is rather "the reiterative and citational practice by which discourse produces the effects that it names."[134] The materiality of the body is a product of this performativity, and so nothing that should be perceived as a static place or surface. Butler's understanding of matter is more dynamic: "a process of materialization that stabilizes over time to produce the effect of a boundary, fixity, and surface that we call matter."[135] Through ritual repetitions a "normal" body is created, and a human subject, but also "abjective" bodies that fall outside of normality. Repetition namely creates a norm that sets a boundary for what is normal and what is not normal. Repetition thus creates both stability in the materiality of the body with respect to gender identities and the possibility for destabilization. Butler writes:

> As a sedimented effect of a reiterative or ritual practice, sex acquires its naturalized effect, and, yet, it is also by virtue of this reiteration that

131. Judith Butler, *Bodies That Matter: On the Discursive Limits of "Sex,"* 2nd edition (New York/London: Routledge, 1993), p. x.

132. Butler, *Bodies That Matter*, p. x.

133. Butler, *Bodies That Matter*, pp. 1–16 *et passim.*

134. Butler, *Bodies That Matter*, p. 2. Cf. pp. 107, 187, 225 *et passim.*

135. Butler, *Bodies That Matter*, p. 9. Italics in original.

gaps and fissures are opened up as the constitutive instabilities in such constructions, as that which escapes or exceeds the norm, as that which cannot be wholly defined or fixed by the repetitive labor of that norm.[136]

But at the same time Butler says that her position—that discourses or institutions are formative—does not mean that discourse "originates, causes, or exhaustively composes that which it concedes."[137] In other words, she does not imagine performativity as a creation out of nothing.[138] It is instead about the fact that there is no reference to a pure embodiment or materiality that does not at the same time create this body. "In philosophical terms," she writes, "the constative claim is always to some degree performative."[139] She thereby wants to reject the idea that she stands for the counterintuitive proposition that there is no "prior to" discourse. It is instead the case that we can never speak about this "pre-discursive" other than through discourse, and we are thus participatory in the materialization of the body and its gender. Thus "matter" or "body" cannot constitute a pre-discursive absolute ground for philosophical or political reasoning.

Butler takes up a (perhaps surprising) comparison to Aristotle's text *On the Soul* and compares his conception of the soul with what Foucault says in *Discipline and Punish*.[140] According to Aristotle the soul is the actualization of matter. Because matter *(hylē)* never appears without form *(schēma)*, it is pointless to speak of unformed matter other than as a sort of boundary concept. However, the problem with Aristotle's view of the body and soul is, according to Butler, that he advocates a natural teleology that, among other things, has entailed that women have been seen as belonging by nature to the private sphere. For obvious reasons, such a naturalized view of the body is not especially appealing to Butler. In line with Foucault, she therefore historicizes Aristotle's conception of form. Form in Butler's interpretation becomes the historically contingent, discursive formation of the body. Butler interprets Foucault's references to "soul" in *Discipline and Punish* as a revision of Aristotle's conception of *schema*. With Foucault it is the soul that forms, cultivates, and materializes the body—"the soul is the prison of the body"[141]—and thereby provides

136. Butler, *Bodies That Matter*, p. 10.
137. Butler, *Bodies That Matter*, p. 10.
138. Butler, *Bodies That Matter*, p. 107.
139. Butler, *Bodies That Matter*, p. 11.
140. Butler, *Bodies That Matter*, pp. 32–35.
141. Foucault, *Discipline*, p. 30.

the conditions for the possibilities for materialization, which are given with matter, to be realized.[142] Matter is in other words always already discursively formed. To appeal to embodiment or materiality as a ground for theory is therefore to appeal to a concrete "sedimented history of sexual hierarchy and sexual erasures" and not at all some ahistorical or pre-discursive foundation.[143]

To put a little more meat on the theoretical bones I have taken from Butler, I will very briefly turn to a noted book by Thomas Laqueur, *Making Sex* (1990), which may in part illustrate Butler's thesis.[144] Laqueur describes here how the understanding of the person as a sexual being has changed over the course of history. From perceiving sexual differences as differences of degree, with the woman presented as an abortive man, philosophers, scientists, and others began towards the end of the 1700s to imagine a qualitative difference between women and men. Premodern anatomy could, in accordance with the degree of difference between the sexes, depict the female genitals as everted male genitals. The woman's body was a version of the man's body. This meant that the pictorial representation of the body was (and is) also socially conditioned:

> The history of the representation of the anatomical differences between man and woman is thus extraordinarily independent of the actual structures of these organs or of what was known about them. Ideology, not accuracy of observation, determined how they were seen and which differences would matter.[145]

---

142. Butler asks herself whether Foucault's idea of the dependence of discourse and materiality on each other really can account for what is excluded from the discourse and what must be excluded in order for the system to sustain itself (Butler, *Bodies That Matter*, p. 35). However, I will not look any more closely at the problem here.

143. Butler, *Bodies That Matter*, p. 49.

144. Thomas Laqueur, *Making Sex: Body and Gender from the Greeks to Freud* (Cambridge, MA/London: Harvard University Press, 1990). One critique of Laqueur's thesis may be found in Arne Jarrick, "Har könen blivit fler med tiden? En kritik av Thomas Laqueur," in *Seklernas sex: Bidrag till sexualitetens historia*, ed. Åsa Bergenheim and Lena Lennerhed (Stockholm: Carlsson, 1997), pp. 22–38.

145. Laqueur, *Making Sex*, p. 88. Laqueur is somewhat unclear here. How does one come to the difference between how the organ "actually appeared" and how it came to be "perceived"? Does the determination of which differences "meant something" not imply that one actually perceived the organ on the basis of this determination and in some sense depicted them as they "actually appeared"?

Laqueur's account thus does not at all deal only with conceptions of social gender, but with anatomical and physiological investigations as well.

During the modern period biology has been used to defend sexual difference between women and men, and has thereby also constituted a basis for a politics of sex. But it has not always been thus. "Sex before the seventeenth century, in other words, was still a sociological and not an ontological category."[146] The reasons that conceptions about sex changed at this time were two.[147] For the first, there was an epistemological reason, namely, a changed view of the body: one no longer imagined the body as a microcosm analogous to the macrocosm, but as a closed system (see the section on Descartes above). For the second, the political order was changed in a way that contributed to the changing view of gender. When the theologically or transcendentally motivated social order was replaced and nature became the ground for the organization of society instead, biology became the battlefield where one fought over gender identity.[148] The new political order was also the prerequisite for being able to distinguish so sharply between biological and social gender.

Laqueur's own point is that everything that can be said about biological gender contains statements about social gender. Laqueur does not want to completely reject the distinction between the two—there is a space between the unreachable "transcultural body" and its representations that supports the distinction, and thereby provides an explanation for the fact that progress in the understanding of the body is actually possible, as with, for example, the discovery of gametes in the physiology of reproduction.[149] History teaches us, however, that conceptions of sex and body are always dependent on scientific and metaphysical paradigms. Thus even scientists' representations of biological sex cannot be said to be neutral. Philosophical discourses, scientific research, anatomical plates—they are all a part of a larger discourse where the representation of sex is not politically innocent. As the theologian Regina Ammicht Quinn writes apropos Laqueur's book: "A historical reflection on anatomy, however, shows that the body never says anything other than what a person is able to hear, and does not show anything other than what a person is able to see."[150] Nor is sex in Laqueur, who

146. Laqueur, *Making Sex,* p. 8.
147. Laqueur, *Making Sex,* pp. 10–11.
148. Laqueur, *Making Sex,* pp. 151–54.
149. Laqueur, *Making Sex,* p. 16.
150. Regina Ammicht Quinn, *Körper—Religion—Sexualität: Theologische Reflexionen zur Ethik der Geschlechter* (Mainz: Matthias-Grünewald-Verlag, 1999), p. 61.

with greater emphasis, but possibly less success, than Butler disputes that the construction of sex entails a denial of the materiality of bodies, something that may be described or spoken of outside of the play between institutions that produces the social gender and the social body.

The Technological Body

The question of the constructed body also sets before us an uncertainty about what constitutes the human in general. In the wake of the discussion of the construction of the body, but also of the technological and biotechnical "advances" over the last few decades, it is warranted to speak of the constructed body in an additional sense, namely, in the fusion of human and technology. In one sense this is not a new phenomenon. Even simple implements like a hammer or a cane for the blind, not to mention the telegraph and the telephone, constitute technological extensions of the person's body that have been completely incorporated into her body image—her repertoire of bodily possibilities. Thus what is new is hardly the fact that technology is incorporated into the person's body image, but the way in which it can do that. Can technology and the human body fuse together in such an intimate way that it can be a matter of a critical transformation of the human as such?[151]

The French architect and cultural critic Paul Virilio speaks in this context of a colonization of the human body:

> Having contributed for a long time to the colonization of the geographical expanse of the *territorial body* and the geological core of our planet, the recent progress in science and technoscience has today resulted in the gradual colonization of the organs and entrails of man's *animal body,* the invasion of the microphysical finishing off the job that the geophysical invasion began.[152]

Now we no longer send our technology just to other planets, but into our own bodies, Virilio says, and this is of epochal significance. With this the distinction between exterior and interior disappears as well, as the body's

---

151. An important text in this context is Donna J. Haraway, "A Cyborg Manifesto: Science, Technology, and Socialist-Feminism in the Late Twentieth Century," in *Simians, Cyborgs, and Women: The Reinvention of Nature* (London: Free Associations Books, 1991), pp. 149–81.

152. Paul Virilio, *The Art of the Motor,* trans. Julie Rose (Minneapolis: University of Minnesota Press, 1995), 99–100.

interior is adapted to the (previously) exterior technology. The boundary between the human body and the machine also disappears. The human being's
body image is transformed by this in a critical way. The body is no longer
an organism where its different parts support each other, but a mechanism
whose parts become interchangeable. Virilio sees a parallel between the
ethnic cleansing in Europe during the 1990s and a possible cleansing among
the human being's viscera as an expression of the endogenous tyranny of
neuroscience.[153] In both cases it is a matter of "cleansing" a particular environment in order to later colonize it anew. In the extension of this, the
question also arises whether the human body as such is not interchangeable
with another body. The body no longer needs to constitute a hindrance for
the technological curiosity of the human being. But then what do space and
time mean any longer for the person's situatedness? *"Will Earth soon become
humanity's phantom limb?"* Virilio asks himself—and Ammicht Quinn fills in
the question of whether the body then also becomes "the phantom limb of
the individual."[154] This scientific revolution or "microphysical colonization"
has led to a greater discussion of the "post-human."[155]

With a greater skepticism towards the actual possibilities of the post-
human, philosopher Don Ihde has asked himself how far the virtualization
of the body can really go.[156] Is not the thought of a body unhindered by its
physical limitations more a fantasy of getting rid of these boundaries than of
getting rid of the body in itself? One meets the same bodily effort that exists
in the real world in the virtual world as well, and the difference between their
respective life-worlds is thus not especially great. The search for the post-
human would then instead become an emphasis on already-existent features
in the human body image, not a radical transformation of it. Theologian
Nancy L. Eiesland, who in her book *The Disabled God* formulates a liberation theology for the handicapped, has been indirectly skeptical as well.
She points out that her own human body does not only consist of flesh and
bone, but also of plastic and metal.[157] For her the "normal" body is not the

153. Virilio, *Art of the Motor,* p. 114.

154. Virilio, *Art of the Motor,* p. 127; Regina Ammicht Quinn, *Körper—Religion—Sexualität,* p. 109.

155. See Elaine L. Graham, *The Representation of the Posthuman* (Manchester: Manchester
University Press, 2002).

156. Don Ihde, "Bodies, Virtual Bodies and Technology," in *Body and Flesh,* ed. Welton,
pp. 349–57.

157. Nancy L. Eiesland, *The Disabled God: Toward a Liberatory Theology of Disability*
(Nashville: Abingdon, 1994), p. 22. Cf. pp. 47 and 49–67.

physically conventional body, and through her book it again becomes clear that the question of the human body cannot be detached from the question of the human life-world. The body is simultaneously and indissolubly both physical and social.

But if I am to return at the end of this section to the question of how the relationship between nature and culture ought to be understood in relation to the human body—i.e., to the question of how constructed the body really is—I believe it is critical to realize that the human body is invariably both nature and culture, and that these are indissolubly intertwined with each other. It is therefore a question of the limitations of the human and whether the post-human person can arise at all. Butler, who according to my interpretation does not want to deny the materiality of the body, says, however, that this materiality needs to be an object of critical analysis, not the basis for critical analysis. Referring to the materiality of the body does not mean referring to something pre-theoretically or pre-linguistically fundamental, but quite simply referring to the "sedimented history of materiality."[158] What we are confronted with when we attempt to speak or write about the body is not the material body per se, but different human representations of the body. Our discourse does not create the body in some absolute sense, but what the body is for us, in all its materiality, becomes accessible only through all we write and say about the body.[159] What is uncanny about the being of the body is that it is simultaneously both nature and culture. It therefore escapes every attempt to unilaterally argue the one or the other.

For my part, I believe that every attempt to reduce the body—either to nature or culture, corpse or matter, spirit or discourse—expressly or in secret cries out for what has thereby been reduced away. When we speak of the nature of the body, we always indirectly refer to the body as cultural construction, without thereby rejecting the idea of the nature of the body. It is only possible to speak of the nature of the body within the framework of a particular institutionalized discourse ("the nature of the body according to Christian theology," etc.), and so its cultural construction is already given. For my theology of the body, this section actualizes questions about the Christian body as a gendered body, and about gender differences as stable identities. But these questions cannot be posed independently of the social institutions through which a theologically understood embodiment

---

158. Susan Hekman, "Material Bodies," in *Body and Flesh,* ed. Welton, pp. 67–68.

159. Edward Casey, "The Ghost of Embodiment: On Bodily Habitudes and Schemata," in *Body and Flesh,* ed. Welton, p. 208.

is mediated, and so the question also arises of the significance of the liturgy for the constitution of the Christian body. In which sense can the Christian liturgy be said to constitute these Christian bodies, their materiality in general and their sexuality in particular? What does this performativity mean for the idea of *imitatio Christi?* In other words, a theology of the body cannot only treat the question of the symbolization of the body in Christian discourse; it must also take up the question of the discipline of the body in and through the Christian institutions. The fusion of human and technology leads us into the question of what constitutes the human as such, for example in the transformation of the body that will take place at the resurrection according to the belief of the Christian church. The resurrection is about what the body shall *become,* and thereby also reveals what it is thought to *be.*

If the nature of the body shall not now be thought of as something given prior to or to the side of cultural discourse, and culture shall not be understood as existing only in the person's consciousness, as her processing of a given matter, we then come to the last of the issues that structure this chapter. I will give an image of how intertwined the thought of the person's physical body and the societal body have been by, as a concluding amplification of this section, turning to the question of the social body.

The Social Body

An important aspect of human embodiment that I have touched on at various occasions above, but which I will now focus on a bit more fully, is the question of the sociality of the body, i.e., the relationship between the body of the individual human and the social body. The conception of the constructed body entails that the person's body in a sense may always be said to be social, inasmuch as its material constitution as well as its cultural representation are inevitably social. There is thus—at least in this sense—no individual body, since the individual person's body is always dependent on its social context. But the person's body is also social in that the physical body has constituted a symbol system for the societal body or the body of the state. Social anthropologist Mary Douglas writes in her book *Purity and Danger:*

> The body is a model which can stand for any bounded system. Its boundaries can represent any boundaries which are threatened or precarious.

The body is a complex structure. The functions of its different parts and their relation afford a source of symbols for other complex structures.[160]

The body can thus constitute a symbol for society, and the dangers that threaten society may be compared to those dangers that threaten the body. Douglas notes here that rituals have an intermediary function: "The rituals work upon the body politic through the symbolic medium of the physical body."[161] In this section I will first say something in general about the dependence of the individual physical body in its social context, and then expand this to include what Douglas says about the relationship between the individual body and the societal body.

Transcorporeality

With regard to the first aspect, this mutual dependence between the physical body and the social body has led a portion of philosophers to speak of the "intercorporeality" or "transcorporeality" of the body. Philosopher Gail Weiss describes the former in the following way: "To describe embodiment as intercorporeality is to emphasize that the experience of being embodied is never a private affair, but is always already mediated by our continual interactions with other human and non-human bodies."[162] The latter term is used by theologian Graham Ward apropos a discussion of the French philosopher Jean-Luc Nancy. He explains "transcorporeality" in the following way: "The physical body of any one person does not end at its fingertips or toes. It is always a part of and extends into larger bodies than itself: the social body, the civic body, the ecclesial body, and the body of Christ, for example."[163] A consequence of both "intercorporeality" and "transcorporeality" is that the modern distinction between private and public, between ethics and politics, cannot be understood as a distinction between two independent spheres. Our everyday life instead constitutes a constant negotiation between different embodiments and body images,

---

160. Mary Douglas, *Purity and Danger: An Analysis of Concepts of Pollution and Taboo* (London/New York: Routledge, 2002), p. 142.

161. Douglas, *Purity and Danger*, p. 159.

162. Gail Weiss, *Body Images: Embodiment and Intercorporeality* (New York/London: Routledge, 1999), p. 5.

163. Graham Ward, *Theology and Critical Theory*, 2nd edition (Basingstoke, UK: Macmillan, 2000), p. 105.

a negotiation that does not leave space for any absolute distinction between private and public. One might say that the human body is always social—not "after" the body's existence as the individual body, but simultaneously. The sociality of this body can be thought of in several ways. I will here mention something of two such attempts that we find in the philosophers Jean-Luc Nancy and Gail Weiss. Weiss's "intercorporeality" will be the object of the investigation in the next section, and I begin here with "transcorporeality."

Nancy's essay (and later book) "Corpus" is an attempt to imagine just such a transcorporeality.[164] Nancy wants to return to a Greek and Christian metaphor of the body and see how the physical, social, and theological body are linked. "Corpus" is rich with Christian symbolism, not least its account of how people's bodies continually give themselves to each other, which may be seen as a "secular" iteration of the Christian doctrine of the church as *communio sanctorum*.[165] Nancy writes that there is nothing like the body in definite form, but on the contrary "there are patient and fervent recitations of numerous corpuses."[166] He says that our bodies are mutually dependent on each other in a sort of mimetic repetition without any real "original." All bodies are thus related to each other. It is not possible to determine once and for all where one body ends and the other begins—even if it is possible to draw provisional boundaries—since we as human beings are not stationary, passive, or quiet. There are thus no stable bodies; what we actually have

> is nothing other than the interlacing, the mixing of bodies, mixing everywhere, and everywhere manifesting this other absence of name, named "God," everywhere producing and reproducing and everywhere absorbing the sense of sense and of all the senses, infinitely mixing the impenetrable with the impenetrable.[167]

164. Jean-Luc Nancy, "Corpus," trans. Claudette Sartiliot, in *Thinking Bodies,* ed. Juliet Flower MacCannell and Laura Zakarin (Stanford: Stanford University Press, 1994), pp. 17–31. Here I use the article that Ward, Shapiro, and Gayatri Chakravorty Spivak refer to, but see also Jean-Luc Nancy, *Corpus,* Perspectives in Continental Philosophy, trans. Richard A. Rand (New York: Fordham University Press, 2008).

165. On the ecclesiological conception of *communio sanctorum,* see my article "Kyrkan som de heligas samfund: På väg mot en evangelisk *communio*-ecklesiologi," in *På spaning efter framtidens kyrka,* ed. Sune Fahlgren (Örebro, Sweden: Libris, 1998), pp. 49–72.

166. Nancy, "Corpus," p. 31.

167. Nancy, "Corpus," p. 22.

"God" stands here for an absolute identity where being and existence coincide—a *"logos"* where we reach the final meaning. But such a final meaning is not possible, according to Nancy, and we must instead imagine a *logos* spread out ("disseminated") in an endless chain of signs and bodies.[168] All bodies exist entangled in each other: "It is by touching the other that the body is a body, absolutely separated and shared."[169] Nancy speaks of an "indefinitely ectopic corpus."[170] A body or a body part is "ec-topic" (from the Greek *ek* which here instead denotes a separation, a standing out from something, and *topos,* i.e., place) because it stands out from its place and thereby touches other bodies or body parts. The body or body parts always exist indefinitely apart from themselves.

Nancy does not attempt to dissolve the materiality of the body, but instead imagines a more porous body, a body whose unity is not as given as that of the Cartesian corpse. Because these bodies are a part of the chain of signs, they are continually involved with each other through this communication—through this communication a communion, so to speak, is accomplished—and their composition with regard to the relationship of body parts to each other, as well as the relationship of bodies to other bodies, is not something that is given with a pre-discursive physical nature, but occurs in and through the discourse's continual circulation of meaning, with "God" as its sublime horizon.[171] Our understanding of the body is thus not as given as some of the references to a "natural" body imagine. The body gets its meaning—and produces meaning—in the context in which it is situated. So

168. Echoes of the doctrine of the incarnation and of *logos spermatikos* are not far off here. In "Corpus," p. 22, Nancy writes: "The *spirit* of Christianity is incorporated here in full. *Hoc est enim corpus meum* . . ." In contrast with the Christian doctrine of the incarnation Nancy does not seem to imagine any transcendence. It is instead a matter of a decapitated God, i.e., a blind God without any existence that transcends the immanent chain of signs and bodies. Cf. Ward, *Theology and Critical Theory,* pp. 112–15. This symbolism is challenged by Gayatri Chakravorty Spivak, "Response to Jean-Luc Nancy," in *Thinking Bodies,* pp. 32–51. See also Gary Shapiro, "Jean-Luc Nancy and the Corpus of Philosophy," in *Thinking Bodies,* pp. 52–62.

169. Nancy, "Corpus," p. 29.

170. Nancy, "Corpus," p. 29.

171. Not necessarily God in the Christian theological sense. Cf. Jean-Luc Nancy, "Des lieux divins," in *Qu'est-ce que dieu? Philosophie/Théologie. Hommage à l'abbé Daniel Coppieters de Gibson (1929–1983)* (Brussels: Publications des Facultés Universitaires Saint-Louis, 1985), p. 570: "Je ne sais si c'est encore, pourtant, à des dieux, à un autre dieu qui viendrait ou à 'pas de dieu' que se fait cet abandon. Mais il y a la mort comme nom générique, et une infinité de formes et d'occasions à travers notre vie." In Jean-Luc Nancy, *Au ciel et sur la terre: Petite conférence sur Dieu* (Paris: Bayard, 2004), "God" stands more for the person's openness to the unexpected.

we can conceive of a different order for the relationship of the body parts to each other without negating the materiality of the body. A different order becomes "conceivable" precisely through insight into the significance of language for embodiment and through the available means for thinking the unthinkable—the body as such is never thought in philosophy, Nancy says, but what we think are always representations of the body. But these representations never exist autonomously, apart from the physical body as such. Thus all speaking about the body of the human being is always already also a speaking about her social community at all levels: societal, political, ecclesiastical, theological. These social interrelationships can, in accordance with Nancy's understanding of the body and social community, be thought of as "intercorporeal" rather than "intersubjective."

Body and meaning go together, as with Merleau-Ponty, and so a simple distinction between the "literal" body (would that be the person's physical body?) and the "metaphorical" body (is that the social body?) is not possible. This may be a reason why Nancy borrows terms and concepts from Christian theology. There is a rich world of symbols here, where the symbolic connections between the body of the believer and the church as the body of Christ are clear and elaborated. There are resources here for understanding how the meaning of the body, the social as well as the physical, is interwoven with embodiment itself in a chiasm where it is not possible to separate the one from the other in an absolute sense. I will explore these aspects further in the following chapter.

Intercorporeality

To Nancy's transcorporeality I want to add Weiss's view of the body's "intercorporeality." Weiss makes use of the concept "body image"—a concept that recalls the body schemata or "phenomenal bodies" I discussed in my examination of Merleau-Ponty. She says that our body images must walk a difficult tightrope between formlessness and rigidity. Without some sort of stability we would completely lose orientation and not be able to distinguish a reasonably reliable "here and now." On the other hand, an all-too-stable body identity can lead to a rigidity that denies the plasticity of body images. Our body images are namely not private, but are socially mediated, and thus stand in a continual exchange with all the body images that surround us and that we live in and through. Certainly our individual body images are always particular, Weiss says; our individual body images are images of a particular body with all its idiosyncrasies. At the same time our particular body images are in large part anonymous. We do not think about how our gestures and movements are structured by our body image. Our individual body image must therefore be understood instead as a sort of intersection between the different body images that assert themselves in a society. There is never a single body image, but body images must instead be differentiated as male body images, female body images, white body images, black body images, etc.

Our body images can be distorted, Weiss says, as with the body image of the anorexic when she or he sees her- or himself as overweight, or with the schizophrenic's multiple body images.[172] But the possibility of such a distortion does not mean that there is an Archimedean point, a given body beyond or behind its representations. Weiss notes that it is no simple thing to say what it is that differentiates distorted body images from those that are not distorted, given that all body images—distorted as well as nondistorted—are culturally mediated. However, a way out would be to distinguish between those body images that are too rigid—as with the anorexic—and those that are too amorphous—as with the schizophrenic. The "harmonious" body image is not a static body image or a body image without tensions, but rather a body image that manages to house the tensions between different body images without it tipping over to one side. Weiss's "harmonious" body image is thus characterized by a sort of equilibrium rather than by an absolute normality. A distorted body image is a body image that represses parts of itself. On a social plane distorted body images function as normative for what should be seen as a "normal" body, and thereby cast out people with physiologically different bodies.

The nonrigid equilibrium between the different body images that claim us also means that there exists a possibility for resistance towards the dominant body images in a particular culture. We can actively work with our fantasies of body images and thereby make ourselves conscious of what those body images are that anonymously mediate our bodies to ourselves. Weiss writes:

> Changing the body image, I maintain, must involve changes in the imaginary which situates the body image within a vast horizon of possible significances. To change the imaginary, we must in turn create images of the body, dynamic images of non-docile bodies that resist the readily

172. Weiss, *Body Images,* pp. 90–102.

available techniques of corporeal inscription and normalization that currently define "human reality."[173]

Our bodies are according to Weiss apparently not totally "docile" in Foucault's sense; resistance is possible via conscious work with our body images. Changing body image does not, however, necessarily mean that the new body images are freer, since the fact that they are new is not a guarantee of anything. Such a change of body images is not an entirely "ideal" activity, as though these body images exist in a sphere apart from the physical. Our interpersonal relationships, including our conceptions of the body, are not only "intersubjective," but always "intercorporeal."[174] It is important, Weiss says, to recapture the understanding of how our social interactions are embodied, and what I in this chapter call "the return of the body" within philosophy is an essential moment in such an understanding.

The individual's relationship to her or his own body—and even to other bodies—is always already social, in that the image of the body is socially and culturally mediated. How is this? To take an example from another direction than Weiss's book, we can mention here Susan Bordo's investigation of the female body in contemporary culture in *Unbearable Weight* from 1993, and of the male body in *The Male Body* from 1999.[175] Here Bordo very concretely describes how men's and women's ideas about male bodies are governed by cultural expectations mediated through films, TV, advertisements, and newspapers. The beautiful man on a billboard constructs for both the man and the woman—though in different ways—cultural expectations of how the man's body ought to look, how his sexuality ought to be, etc. There is space here for a number of differentiations like class, sex, sexual orientation, race, but in common for all these images of the male body is that they govern

173. Weiss, *Body Images*, p. 67.

174. Weiss, *Body Images*, pp. 166–70.

175. Susan Bordo, *Unbearable Weight: Feminism, Western Culture, and the Body* (Berkeley/London/Los Angeles: University of California Press, 1993), together with *The Male Body: A New Look at Men in Public and Private* (New York: Farrar, Straus & Giroux, 1999). Bordo has been sharply critical of what she perceives as a denial of the materiality of the body in contemporary feminist theory. For a comparison between Butler and Bordo, see Hekman, "Material Bodies," pp. 60–70. Bordo comments on this comparison in "Bringing Body to Theory," in *Body and Flesh*, ed. Welton, pp. 84–97. Here she writes that "'materiality,' for me, is not *stuff*, not substance, not nature" (p. 90). The materiality of the body instead designates our finitude, which not only forms us, but bounds us. She is therefore critical towards postmodernism to the degree that it carries with it the dream of being everywhere. For further discussion of the male and the female body, see Quinn, *Körper—Religion—Sexualität*, pp. 66–97.

expectations of how the body ought to be, and are thereby also involved in shaping how its physiology is actually understood. We cannot get rid of the cultural conditions for how we perceive the body by making them conscious, but we can very well transform them to some degree, and above all acquire a more active relationship to them. The aim for Bordo is not so much to get rid of body images—as though that were possible—and reach the "naked" body, i.e., the body whose surface is not always already inscribed in culture, but to reach more productive body images that do not function oppressively. A theological sketch of such a view of the body I hope to be able to give in coming chapters, above all in chapter 12 on heavenly bodies and their eschatological horizon.

Political Bodies

What Nancy, Weiss, Bordo, and other researchers who write on the body point out is that our individual bodies are always political. How our bodies, i.e., we ourselves, relate to the environment, to other people, to the divine, but to ourselves as well, is a question of politics, since the body, according to the perspective reviewed above, is not individual or self-contained in any broad meaning. About the same thing has been pointed out by sociologists and historians of ideas who have studied the body in history: the history of the body of the individual person is intertwined with the history of the societal body. And with that we come to the other aspect of the social body in this section.

We can take one example from sociologist Richard Sennett. In a larger investigation of the relationship between bodies and cities he has attempted to show how different understandings of the human body have resulted in different sorts of cities.[176] The person is thus not only the microcosm of the city, as one might infer from Sennett's colleague Foucault, but the city is also the macrocosm of the human body. In *Flesh and Stone* Sennett's fundamental problem is how a city ought to be such that human bodies would be able to be present for each other. The late-modern city is characterized by a well-developed individualism, where the hastiness itself in the communication between people threatens to annihilate the places where people have the possibility to interact in a way that promotes people's accountability for each other. The modern city is to a great extent based on a thinking whose

---

176. Sennett, *Flesh and Stone.*

model is taken from Harvey's conception of blood circulation. This has resulted in a lack of functioning public places, which in its turn has pacified the human body. According to Sennett, the solution to this problem—in all briefness—is to recapture the idea of the suffering body, the body that is in conflict with itself, the body that is not whole, but dependent on other bodies.[177] In other words, Sennett attempts to get back to a conception of the human body as nonautonomous, in order to clarify that our cities must be built in a way that makes genuine interaction between people possible.

Sennett's description of ancient Athens around the time of the Peloponnesian war between Sparta and Athens is telling. Sennett shows how the city aimed to exhibit the human body.[178] Not all bodies were to be exhibited in this way, however, but only the bodies of free men. The bodies of women and slaves were distinguished from the bodies of citizens, since they had—people thought—a lower body temperature and so were effeminate. The social honor of the exhibited bodies of citizens went together with the shame of the body of lower standing. The *polis* of the citizens was thus a highly segregated city.

The human voice was highly valued, and people constructed buildings and squares in accordance with this. There were places here for theaters as well as public debates, both practices that were dependent on the voice. However, this prioritization of the voice would lead to a destabilization of the city-state, since the naked human voice could seduce the people, as they were manipulated by orators and politicians. Reason, as an ability to act rationally, was thus undermined. Rhetoric increased the person's body temperature and thereby created disunity. The architecture itself, modeled after the naked human body, became a cause of disunity. Sennett emphasizes that it is not a matter of pointing out that the democratic ideal in Athens could not live up to its own ideal, but rather of indicating the contradictions and tensions that "people experienced in a democracy which celebrated the human body in a particular way."[179] The problem with the understanding of the body in classical Athens was that its dominant image marginalized and excluded other bodies: those of women and slaves, but also that its metaphorical extension in the body of the city gave rise to tensions that this society was not able to handle.

177. Sennett refers to Elaine Scarry's acclaimed book *The Body in Pain: The Making and Unmaking of the World* (New York/Oxford: Oxford University Press, 1985). I discuss this book in chapter 11.

178. Sennett, *Flesh and Stone*, pp. 31–67.

179. Sennett, *Flesh and Stone*, p. 66.

Other conceptions of the body dominated during the Christian era and the modern era in the West, and gave rise to other exclusions from and tensions within the body of the city. For Sennett the point in describing how city and body go together is not to argue that one way is as good as another. Sennett's aim in showing how the *ethos* of bodies and the politics of the city go together is ethical and political. So he says, for example, that the way in which the suffering body was highlighted in the ancient tragedies and in the Christian concept of the suffering Son of Man created places for the suffering body in the city. These places made possible conceptions of the body that could harbor such difference within the walls of the city (even if the examples Sennett highlights are often examples of horrible failures), rather than separating bodies as in modernity. Sennett's hope for the city is, as he writes, that "those who have been exiled from the Garden might find a home in the city."[180] It is an experience of lack and deficiency in our own bodies, rather than good will or political integrity, that leads to civil compassion. It is not by becoming self-sufficient and complete that we—whether as individuals or as society— avoid unstable societies, but rather by admitting our need for each other.

My intention in taking up Sennett's book here is thus far something less far-reaching than Sennett's own aim. I want to show here how body and society go together, even in modern "autonomous" society. Sennett is, however, far from the only one who has pointed out this connection. Another example is the historian of ideas Karin Johannisson, who in her book *Kroppens tunna skal [The Thin Shell of the Body]*, in a chapter with the fitting title "political anatomy," has shown how public health during the heyday of the Swedish model linked "macrocosm" and "microcosm" together, i.e., the societal body and the individual body.[181] She notes that medical anatomy became the model science for the analysis of society as well. The societal body would be divided up into its constituent parts, and what was sick would be cut away. "The goal of political anatomy was a new body: fixed, strong, capable."[182] In principle this concerned both the individual body and the societal body. In order to achieve this political goal a new individual body was needed, and social hygiene thus went hand in hand with an increased emphasis on the hygiene of the individual. An enormous educational or disciplinary project would create the new person.

180. Sennett, *Flesh and Stone,* p. 27.

181. Johannisson, *Kroppens tunna skal,* pp. 221–57. See also Ola Sigurdson, *Den lyckliga filosofin: Etik och politik hos Hägerström, Tingsten, makarna Myrdal och Hedenius* (Stockholm/ Stehag: Brutus Östlings Bokförlag Symposion, 2000).

182. Johannisson, *Kroppens tunna skal,* p. 222.

> The body was sucked into *modernity*. It became modern, i.e., enlightened and rational, to view one's body as individual capital. The culture of the body corresponded to the idea of total social mobility. It had a progressive function by concentrating interest on the individual more than on the group/class, and the social attribute of nurturing and caring for one's body became a ritual in the name of social affirmation.[183]

So one's own person could appear as an individual project that converged with the greater project of society. Or conversely: the body was political.

Sennett and Johannisson show with all desirable clarity that the connection between the societal body and the individual person's body is not broken in modernity's emphasis on the autonomy of the body. Rather, it is the case that the passive—almost absent—body that is highlighted by modernity after Descartes is precisely the body that (more or less) harmonizes with the project of modern society. What Sennett, at least, explicitly calls for is a different body than the modern one, and the question of a different body is always a political question. With the help of Merleau-Ponty's conception of a body schema or of the phenomenal bodies that I accounted for above, one can understand how the body is always greater than its purely physical form. The living body stands in relationship with its environment in many different ways (as his critics have pointed out, these ways were more than those Merleau-Ponty wrote about). The possibilities for this body are therefore much greater than for the body that is reduced to an object or even a corpse. These possibilities, the body schema that we are and carry with us, are always—more than Merleau-Ponty perhaps conveyed—co-determined by the institutions that belong to our environment. It is thus reasonable to argue that our embodiment is socially constructed.

As I indicated earlier, I do not understand this as the idea that the materiality of the body would thereby be dissolved in an idealistic body, or that our bodies would be infinitely docile. It is instead the case that our bodies exist intertwined with our representations of the body. To refer to a "natural" body given prior to its discursive attributes would therefore be to refer to a specific discursive configuration of the body. Representations of the body are indissolubly intertwined with its materiality (cf. Nancy and Weiss above). Every transformation of the representation is a transformation of its materiality and vice versa. Something that seems to speak against my last statement is the fact that representations seem to be much simpler to form

---

183. Johannisson, *Kroppens tunna skal*, pp. 253–54.

than a physical body. But I believe that this is an all too "spiritualized" view of representations. It is rather a matter of attempting to understand how both materiality and representation are transformed over time, for example, by speaking of "performativity" like Butler, or perhaps even of the ritual body. The concept of "performativity" that Butler uses wants to show how transformations of the body, i.e., both of its materiality and of its representation, are not a question of any easy "choices," but of repeated actions that create a particular sedimentation, though not any absolute or ahistorical stability.

Nancy borrowed terms and concepts from Christian theology, since its symbolic world emphasizes the connection between the body of the believer and the church as the body of Christ. A crucial issue for the whole of this project is how we should understand the intertwining between individual bodies and social bodies from a Christian perspective. It is then not simply a matter of stating *that* such an intertwining exists, but at least as much of *which* discourses and institutions will affect the mediation of bodies. The sort of theory that I have described in this chapter will show itself to have a deep interconnectedness with issues that were particularly topical for historical theologians. If the *ethos* of bodies and the politics of the city go together, as Sennett argued, we then come to the question that Augustine posed in *The City of God,* namely, what sort of desire it is that shapes society.

The return of the body that I have described here within contemporary theoretical discourse in philosophy, sociology, and the history of science has to do with recapturing a way to speak of the body as something more than an object. The living body draws back from a reification that attempts to fix its surface by cutting off ties to language, history, society, and transcendence. But such a reification transforms the living body into a phantom body that only partially overlaps the embodiment of the person. The body that returns after modernity is a linguistic, historicized, and constructed body, but also a body that is to a significantly greater extent open for transcendence—or to put it more precisely: whose boundaries are no longer self-evident in any direction. The following three chapters, together with my concluding summary, will have to do with how such an embodiment can appear from a theological perspective.

9. The Liturgical Body

The body that returns after modernity is thus a lingual, historically situated, and constructed body, but also a body that is open to transcendence to a much greater extent. It is no coincidence then that the question of human embodiment has become very topical within contemporary theology. The previous chapter will have made clear the fact that the body is not something self-evidently given in philosophical or theological discourse. The body has a history, or more accurately, many histories. Talking about the body does not mean referring to some constant, pre-discursive, and naturally given entity beyond all linguistic, cultural, and social overlays. It is instead a matter of entering into a multilayered labyrinth of meanings, contradictions, and half-sensed connections. This chapter will discuss the body on the basis of the conditions given by the Christian church and by the reflection on its practice, i.e., theology. The primary purpose of this chapter, together with the two following chapters, is to present a theology of the body. Such a theology takes its starting point in the idea of the body of Christ. The body of Christ, understood both as the physical body of the earthly Jesus, and as the church (I return to the relationship between the two below), has been and is central to the understanding of individual Christian bodies. In other words, theological conceptions of human embodiment are intimately tied to different conceptions of the incarnation. The specific thesis that I pursue in this chapter is that there is always a ritual mediation between social and individual bodies. The relationship between incarnation and embodiment is therefore not simply a question of what different theologians have said or written about the body, but is, as I have previously argued in chapters 2 and 3, equally a question of the body's concrete life-world, i.e., how Christology has come to be received in and to influence various significant practices.

The philosophical issues that have been generated in the previous chapter for this continued theological investigation of conceptions of the body and bodily practices are the following: (1) the dualism between body and soul, and the Christian contempt for the body; (2) the representation of the body (i.e., "What sort of body?"); (3) the Christian body as a gendered body; (4) the constitution and construction of the body in the liturgy; (5) the relationship between the individual body and the social body; (6) the continuity between the earthly body and the heavenly body. In traditional theological terms, these questions deal with anthropology, ecclesiology, and eschatology. These questions have been brought to the fore—within theological discourse as well as within Christian practice—in different ways during different historical epochs and within different churches. In order to avoid a rhetoric that gives the impression that there is an "answer" to these questions that stands outside any historical context, I will therefore relate them to historical theologies and practices. In this chapter I will lay the foundation for a theology of the body by outlining a sort of historically grounded "fundamental somatology" on the basis of the topics mentioned above, and thereby show the historical plausibility of my thesis that there is always a ritual mediation between the social body and individual bodies, even if this mediation can appear in very different ways. I will begin by posing the question of human embodiment to several central texts from the Christian Bible. After this I will in turn discuss the Christian social body in light of a doctrine of the church, the individual Christian body in light of Christian practices like asceticism and mysticism, and finally the constitution and construction of the body—the mediation between social bodies and individual bodies—in the liturgy. In the two chapters that follow I will use this historically based foundation of fundamental somatology to present a theology of the body in the form of a discussion of the erotic and the grotesque body within the Christian tradition.

An additional point for my thesis in this chapter is to show that the Christian tradition's understanding of the body is not monolithic; there is no single idea that is handed down through the centuries—neither an antagonistic dualism nor a harmonious reciprocity between body and soul—but a multitude of different historical bodies, the constitution of which is dependent on social, economic, religious, and theological circumstances. Pointing out that Christian history is not monolithic in its conceptions of the body may seem trivial, but it is hardly so if one of our aims is to show that this differentiation raises the possibility of critically presenting a contribution to a theology of the body in our time. If history really were monolithic in this case, the argument for a transcultural constitution of the body would be

361

stronger, and so the possibility of a different, critical theology of the body for our time would be weaker. A particular representation and constitution of the body would be able to be understood as "natural" and so impossible to change. A common understanding of ancient and medieval Christian texts is that the body is represented there as—at best—a necessary evil. This is of course *also* true, but Christian history offers all too many differentiated understandings of the body for it to be captured in such simple categories. The differences between various conceptions of the body certainly cannot save that part of history that has been antagonistic towards the body or contemptuous of the body, but they can at least indicate possibilities for another theology of the body today.

Another reason to engage with the difference between various historical theologies of the body is that an attentiveness to these differences helps us avoid projecting our own culture's conceptions of the body onto the texts we investigate. The treatment of the body in ancient and medieval texts does not necessarily need to answer to the questions we consider most significant, but may have treated radically different questions in their own context. If we proceed from too naïve a conviction that we know what a body is and that those others from long ago were incurably contemptuous of the body, we easily risk an ideological reading that simply strengthens our biases and does not challenge them. Such a reading allows the texts of other cultures to be heard only according to the terms of our own culture, and so in its zeal to understand constantly risks misunderstanding.[1] What is needed is an approach that dares to be both critical and generous, that dares both to allow its own pre-understanding to be challenged by another horizon, and to critically assess the other horizon. In this chapter I will, among other things, discuss central Christian practices like asceticism and mysticism and show that, far from needing to be connected to contempt for and denial of the body, they indicate the existence of a different body than the one our time imagines as the only possible body. But for now I will turn first to the biblical bodies.

Biblical Bodies

An important starting point for the discussion of the body in the Christian tradition is the texts that have constituted the center of the Christian church

---

1. Cf. Johannes Fabian, *Time and the Other: How Anthropology Makes Its Object* (New York: Columbia University Press, 1983).

for nearly two thousand years. Even if these texts are, like all other texts, ambiguous, and have been used for a number of different purposes and to legitimate several different representations of embodiment, it is nevertheless important to reread these texts in order to indicate the (alternative) possibilities that they offer for the understanding of the body. I will begin by discussing from which perspective the biblical texts understand human embodiment, as well as very briefly mentioning something of the Old Testament's understanding of the same. Then I show how human embodiment is represented in the four Gospels, in order to finally turn to the most complex discussion of embodiment in the New Testament, that which is found in Paul and the Pauline texts. I will pay special attention here to the relationship between figurative and literal bodies in Paul. I believe, however, that there is something that binds together the understanding of the body in the New Testament, in the midst of all the different emphases, and it is this that I will turn to by way of introduction.

The Dramaticized Body in the Bible

The philosopher Donn Welton has pointed out that the biblical texts place the body in a theological context that is not exhausted by the ethical, psychological, sociological, and physiological contexts that have been treated by philosophers, sociologists, and others the last few decades. The Bible places "the body at the intersection of good and evil, life and death," and the question is whether an adequate understanding of all of the dimensions of the body is possible without placing the body, its desires, and actions in a theological context as well.[2] The biblical texts represent the body at the intersection between external powers that influence its structures of desire. In the conceptualization and narrativization of the conceptions of the body that take place in the biblical texts we reach a level, Welton says, that is not captured by Merleau-Ponty's reflections on the finitude of the body, but is actualized in the question of how the body is "fallen" and how it is "redeemed." Welton writes:

> We discover here not the sense in which the body is bound by its own essential structures but infected with a certain weakness, and the sense in

2. Donn Welton, "Biblical Bodies," in *Body and Flesh: A Philosophical Reader,* ed. Donn Welton (Malden, MA/Oxford: Blackwell, 1998), p. 229.

which it is cleansed and transformed with a certain strength or, perhaps, transformed by a certain weakness that is its strength.[3]

In other words, in contrast with the phenomenological investigation of the body, in the biblical texts it is not a matter of discovering the transcendental structures of the body, but about how it is included in an existential drama of salvation, which can also cast new light on the understanding of its transcendental structures. The body is in other words always already involved in ethical, psychological, and theological conflicts. Welton has thus noticed the features of the biblical writings that I highlighted in chapter 2 apropos the conceptions of incarnation that exist there, namely that these have an existential rather than a speculative or philosophical approach. A phenomenology of the body is thus not sufficient here, but a hermeneutic is needed as well, which interprets the signs, symbols, and narratives that place the body in the midst of the struggle.

I will most closely examine the two central understandings of the body, *sōma* and *sarx,* and their usage in the New Testament. It is, however, important to keep in mind the fact that the texts that constitute the New Testament are not conceptual studies, but narratives and letters, which may in their turn be divided up into a number of different genres. In the Gospels the body is not "explained," but "dramatized" and "symbolized." One particular feature of the Synoptic Gospels is, as I pointed out in chapter 2, that they narrate Jesus' life as a concrete, embodied life on earth. It is not a matter of a mystical heavenly form that comes to earth on a visit. The Passion story of Jesus' suffering on the cross constitutes a large portion of the scope of these three Gospels. In the Gospel of Luke Jesus is born in a stable (2:1–21), and in all three Gospels he dies on a cross. On the whole, all three Gospels are characterized by an account of a bodily existing person (as well as, though to a lesser degree, the fourth Gospel). The philosopher Luce Irigaray emphasizes, as I mentioned in chapter 2, that it is a bodily story that is recounted.[4] Even in Paul's letters, which perhaps account for the most detailed treatment of the body and the flesh, it is a matter of a concrete story, and not an attempt to establish a unified and especially precise terminology. The narrativization itself is, however, not a chronicle of specific dates in Jesus' life, but instead every narrative—in the four Gospels as well as in the references in the rest

3. Welton, "Biblical Bodies," p. 233.

4. Luce Irigaray, "Equal to Whom?" in *The Postmodern God: A Theological Reader,* ed. Graham Ward (Oxford: Blackwell, 1997), p. 203.

of the New Testament writings—is a theological interpretation of the significance of Jesus' life. In other words, the New Testament texts are both narration and interpretation at the same time.[5] With these qualifications regarding what we can expect when we investigate the biblical writings, I will now give an account of their conceptions of human embodiment. I begin by briefly mentioning something of embodiment in the Hebrew Bible, in order to then turn to the Synoptic Gospels and, above all, to Paul's letters. Here we will see that the biblical writings do not present a substance dualism like that of Descartes (or rather, the prevalent interpretation of Descartes), but that a different dualism is predominant.

In the Hebrew Bible the term *bāśār* is the most important term for designating the human being as "flesh" or "body," i.e., the human being in her entirety viewed from an external perspective.[6] Its semantic field is rather wide, and encompasses both the bodies of animals and dead human bodies, as well as, euphemistically, human genitals and the whole person. When the term is used of the person, *bāśār* often designates the outer person, in contrast to the person's heart (*lēb;* cf. Prov. 4:20ff.) or soul (*nepeš;* cf. Ps. 63:2). However, the fact that the term is used together with, for example, soul, does not mean that the Hebrew Bible implies an anthropological dualism. N. P. Brastiotis writes the following in his investigation of the term:

> It is impossible to miss the distinction intended in these passages, and yet we are not to think of it as a dualism of soul and body in a Platonic sense. Rather, *basar* and *nephesh* are to be understood as different aspects of man's existence as a twofold entity. It is precisely this emphatic anthropological wholeness that is decisive for the twofold nature of the human being. It excludes any view of a dichotomy between *basar* and *nephesh,* 'soul,' as irreconcilably opposed to each other, and reveals the mutual organic psychosomatic relationship between them.[7]

The term can also denote the person's fellowship with all other people, and the person's dependence on God. *Bāśār* designates several anthropological

5. According to Kari Syreeni, "Den sublimerade kroppen: Jesu kroppslighet som symbol i Johannesevangeliet," *Svensk exegetisk årsbok* 63 (1998): 203, narrativization and symbolization flow into each other most markedly in the Gospel of John.

6. N. P. Bratsiotis, "bâsâr," in *Theological Dictionary of the Old Testament,* vol. 2, revised edition, ed. G. Johannes Botterweck and Helmer Ringgren, trans. John T. Willis (Grand Rapids: Eerdmans, 1977), pp. 317–32.

7. Bratsiotis, "bâsâr," p. 326.

features of the person, namely that she is created and dependent on God, but also the fact that her constitution is weak, insufficient, and perishable.[8] A poetic expression for this is found in Isaiah 40:6–7: "All flesh *[kol-habbāśār]* is grass, and all its beauty is like the flower of the field. The grass withers, the flower fades when the breath of the LORD blows on it." *Bāśār* is thus often used in order to describe the predicament of the person in contrast to God. It also means, in the Hebrew Bible, that the person as flesh is prone to sin, which in itself does not imply an identification between the person's carnality—i.e., finitude—and sin as such. Finitude is constitutive of the person, but her sinfulness is contingent. Thus the person as flesh, i.e., her exterior aspect, as well as soul, is included in the battle between good and evil. Her carnal weakness admittedly makes her prone to sin, but as a creation of God, her flesh is something good and will also be redeemed.

The Bodies of the Gospels

In the Synoptic Gospels the *bāśār* of the Hebrew Bible often corresponds to the concept *sōma,* especially when the person is designated on the basis of her exterior aspect.[9] The Synoptic Gospels use *sōma* of the dead as well as of the living body.[10] In the Gospel of John, on the other hand, *sōma* is only used once to designate a living body and five times to designate dead bodies.[11] The most theologically significant use of the concept *sōma* in the synoptics is, however, in those texts that have to do with the establishment of communion. Here Jesus breaks the bread and gives it to the disciples with the words "Take; this is my body *[touto estin to sōma mou]*" (Mark 14:22; parallels in Matt. 26:26 and Luke 22:19). Then they drink together from the cup with the words "This is my blood" (Mark 14:24; Matt. 26:28; Luke 22:20). Jesus gives his life for the disciples, and so *sōma* should not be understood here in contrast to an immortal soul. *Sōma* instead denotes Jesus' whole existence, which is offered for the disciples—as the exegete Joachim Gnilka expresses

8. Bratsiotis, "bâsâr," p. 328.

9. See Eduard Schweizer and Friedrich Baumgärtel, "σῶμα, σωματικός, σύσσωμος," in *Theological Dictionary of the New Testament,* vol. 7, trans. and ed. Geoffrey W. Bromiley (Grand Rapids: Eerdmans, 1971), pp. 1044–48, 1057–59.

10. Cf. *sōma* as the term for the dead body, Matthew 10:28; 14:12; 27:52–53; 27:58–59; Mark 14:8; 15:43; Luke 23:52; 23:55–24:3; 24:22–23.

11. *Sōma* as the term for the living body: John 2:21, and *sōma* as the term for the dead body: 19:31; 19:38–40; 20:11f.

it: "Since *sōma* circumscribes the person, the word also lets itself be rendered with: this is myself."[12] In this offering the disciples are incorporated through communion into Jesus' existence in a more fundamental way than by a psychological identification, even if in the synoptic texts it is hardly a question of a doctrine of real presence in a more developed sense.[13]

When it comes to the other aspects of the embodiment of the human being, namely her mortality, weakness, and dependence on God, the concept *sarx* (which is often translated with "flesh" instead of "body") is particularly used in the New Testament.[14] In spite of this, the concept occurs relatively infrequently in the Synoptic Gospels.[15] The human being's limited knowledge in contrast with God's is indicated with the formulation "flesh and blood" in Matthew 16:17. Mark 14:38, which seems to imply a substance dualism—"The spirit indeed is willing, but the flesh is weak"—deals rather with different aspects of the human being, where "the body" in this case instead designates the human being in her inclination to sin.[16] The formulation in Luke 24:39, "flesh and bones," designates the human being's material, "earthly" constitution in contrast to a "spiritual," or rather, "ghostly" existence. These three places constitute the synoptics' entire usage of *sarx,* with the exception of several citations from the Hebrew Bible and the more universal formulation *pasa sarx* (approximately "all people").[17]

The Gospel of John's more marked use of *sarx* differs, as we will see below, from that of Paul. For John there are no connotations of sinfulness in the concept *sarx*. It instead designates the person as an earthly, and thereby

---

12. Joachim Gnilka, *Das Evangelium nach Markus: Mk 8,27–16,20,* 2nd volume, Evangelisch-Katholischer Kommentar zum Neuen Testament vol. II/2, ed. Josef Blank, Rudolf Schnackenburg, et al., 3rd revised edition (Zürich/Einsiedeln/Neukirchen-Vluyn: Benziger Verlag/Neukirchener Verlag, 1989), p. 244.

13. Ulrich Luz, *Matthew 21–28: A Commentary,* Hermeneia, trans. Helmut Koester (Minneapolis: Fortress Press, 2005), p. 379: "In all probability, for Matthew the idea of a substantial identity of the 'elements' of bread and wine with the body and the blood of Jesus was relatively remote. . . . On the other hand, it is not enough to speak of an explanatory 'parable,' for along with the bread that 'represents' Jesus' body there is the *ritual* of breaking, distributing, taking, and eating."

14. Eduard Schweizer, Friedrich Baumgärtel, and Rudolf Meyer, "σάρξ, σαρκικός, σάρκινος," in *Theological Dictionary of the New Testament,* vol. 7, pp. 124–44.

15. Schweizer, Baumgärtel, and Meyer, "σάρξ, σαρκικός, σάρκινος," p. 124.

16. Luz, *Matthew 21–28,* p. 397.

17. These passages are Matthew 19:5; 24:22; Mark 10:8; 13:20; and Luke 3:6. On the general usage of *pasa sarx,* see Schweizer, Baumgärtel, and Meyer, "σάρξ, σαρκικός, σάρκινος," p. 106.

finite creature.[18] Thus when Jesus in 8:15 says "You judge according to the flesh *[kata tēn sarka]*; I judge no one," the problem is that the Pharisees in this passage judge only according to the exterior, and so do not have any knowledge of where Jesus really comes from and where he is going (from and to God). To have knowledge of Jesus' genealogy is to have knowledge according to the flesh, in other words, an expression of the person's blindness (cf. chapter 5, "The Eyes of Jesus"). A person does not perceive who Jesus is by judging "according to the flesh," i.e., *kata sarka,* but only by judging *kata pneuma,* i.e., in a way that is inspired by the Spirit of God. For "It is the Spirit who gives life; the flesh *[hē sarx]* is no help at all" (6:63; cf. 3:6 and 1:12ff.). *Sarx* is the human and earthly sphere that neither has nor can convey any true knowledge of God, and it stands in contrast to the spiritual (pneumatic) sphere where true knowledge of God is conveyed. However, in John *pneuma* is not a substance, but rather a testimony of God.

Any suspicions of substance dualism in John ought to also come to naught through the clear reference to the importance in communion of eating Jesus' own body in order to partake in eternal life in 6:51–56. In verse 51 we read that "the bread that I will give for the life of the world is my flesh *[hē sarx mou estin],*" and Jesus mentions flesh an additional five times in these verses. This passage ought to refute all overly spiritualized interpretations of the humanity of Jesus, as well as of the flesh and blood of communion.[19] In verse 47 in the same chapter Jesus states that "whoever believes has eternal life," and in said passage the significance of closeness to Jesus for eternal life through the eating of his body and the drinking of his blood in communion is intensified (cf. v. 54). At the same time there is no "magical" meaning in the eating and the drinking, but this eating is instead coupled with faith. So even if the limited human sphere that John calls *sarx* can never partake in eternal life in a self-sufficient way, but must receive this life from elsewhere (cf. the whole discussion in 3:1–21), this does not then involve a rejection of *sarx* as such. On the contrary, John emphasizes God's solidarity with the whole of the sarkic sphere, seen most strongly in the fact that *logos* itself became "flesh" *(sarx)* in Jesus Christ (see chapter 2 on the incarnation).

Here the Finnish exegete Kari Syreeni has argued that the keyword for the understanding of the embodiment in the Gospel of John is sublimation rather than substance dualism:

---

18. Schweizer, Baumgärtel, and Meyer, "σάρξ, σαρκικός, σάρκινος," pp. 138f.

19. Raymond E. Brown, *The Gospel according to John: I–XII,* vol. 1 (London: Geoffrey Chapman, 1971), p. 292.

The strategy of sublimation makes it such that from the start one does not look at the bodily as something dangerous and alien to a true spirituality. The body does not need to be curbed by "forcing it into obedience" with rigorous asceticism. Instead, the body is experienced as a less important but developable givenness. This may be interpreted, allegorized, and transformed into something more.[20]

According to Syreeni this means that Jesus' embodiment is less human, despite the talk of incarnation in the prologue. Jesus' body in John is not as "passionate" and "existential" as in Paul, and at the crucifixion this is even characterized by an unbearable lightness.[21] The bodily death and resurrection that John also insists on nevertheless sets certain boundaries for the sublimation of the body:

> The concrete, individual and corporate body is . . . the starting point for the spiritual "added value." The Johannine writings reproduce a strong feeling that Christians are a social body, a family or flock, rather than isolated virtuosos of spirit and insight.[22]

Syreeni indeed finds something attractive in John's understanding of embodiment as well. In contrast with the Pauline social body, John's sublimated social body, a body that one may become participatory in through understanding, amounts to a more "democratic" assembly than the Pauline, which is based in the prophets and apostles (cf. John 10:11–16; 15:1–8). But the Johannine body never becomes, compared to the Pauline, as existentially engaged in the drama of salvation. It has less earthly weight, even if it does not entirely leave the earthly behind.

Now as Syreeni himself points out, the differences between the different New Testament texts are a question of nuances. Within the bounds of the Gospel of John's greater emphasis on a realized eschatology, embodiment indeed comes to take on a different form than, for example, in the Pauline writings, but the fact itself that John lets go, so to speak, of the (physical) body ought to suggest that John also expects, in some sense, a future transformation. As I have shown in chapter 5, "the beholding of salvation" in the person of Jesus is significant for the Synoptic Gospels as well. It certainly does not

20. Syreeni, "Den sublimerade kroppen," p. 212.
21. Syreeni, "Den sublimerade kroppen," p. 212.
22. Syreeni, "Den sublimerade kroppen," p. 214.

need to be wrong to call the Gospel of John more "Platonizing"—any more than it would be correct to set the Platonic heritage *against* the Christian in principle—but this then requires a rereading of the Platonic perspective on embodiment.[23] Inasmuch as we are dealing with a representation of the body—and where are we not?—then this representation will inevitably, as Syreeni writes, "be interpreted, allegorized, and transformed into something 'more,'" since *all* representations of the body are found within the framework of an interpretive practice. Referencing John's allegorizing of the body thus does not in itself suggest an argument that John's understanding of the body is more sublimated than any other. In every interpretive practice the physical body is always already something "more," as the previous chapter's discussion of Merleau-Ponty ought to have shown.

In other words, I want to argue that neither the Synoptic Gospels nor the Gospel of John build their understanding of the body on a substance dualism. They instead understood embodiment from the perspective of the drama of salvation, if with different emphases. The parts and dynamic of the body display the whole of a person's life. But there are exceptions to the rule, as, for example, when the heart is distinguished from the rest of the body, and where the "impurity" that comes from the heart, i.e., from "within," and "comes out of the mouth" is contrasted with that which "goes into the mouth," i.e., comes from "outside" and does not make the person impure, even if it is "expelled" (Matt. 15:15–20). In the Synoptic Gospels there is a continuum that stretches from the body being identified with the whole person to a situation where the heart stands in conflict with the body.

Figurative Bodies and Literal Bodies in Paul

We find the most complex discussion of the body and the flesh in the New Testament in the Pauline texts. I will not refer to all the passages that deal with the body and embodiment, but will limit myself to several of the most significant, namely Romans 6–8 on the flesh and the body, 1 Corinthians 12:12–31 on the body of Christ, and 1 Corinthians 10:16–18 and 11:17–34 on communion. The text on the resurrection in 1 Corinthians 15:35–58 could also go here, but I return to that in chapter 11.

23. For such a rereading, see Catherine Pickstock, "Justice and Prudence: Principles of Order in the Platonic City," in *The Blackwell Companion to Postmodern Theology,* ed. Graham Ward (Oxford: Blackwell, 2001), pp. 162–76.

In Paul neither *sōma* nor *sarx* designates an embodiment that constitutes a self-sufficient whole, a sort of microcosm, but both are instead relational concepts. This means that Paul is never especially interested in the physical materiality of the human being (which he nevertheless does not deny as constitutive for the human being), since it only describes the way in which the human being is formed. Instead, the human being's embodiment is more interesting for Paul as the way in which she relates to her Creator. *Sōma* designates the person in her relationship to God, sin, or neighbor. It is in *sōma* that the person's faith is lived out and in which she serves God.[24] *Sarx* can, as with John, designate the earthly sphere of the human being, which in itself is not sinful, but only limited (cf., for example, Rom. 1:3; 1 Cor. 1:26). When *sarx* is used of a person's exterior, i.e., that which is in purely concrete terms visible for other people, the term receives a negative use in the sense that the person trusts what is external (cf. Rom. 2:17–29). It is not anything bad in itself, but it plays a negative role in the sense that the person places her existential confidence in it. In the extension of such a confidence in the external, *sarx* can assume the form of a power that shapes the person. In Galatians 5:13 and 17, *sarx* becomes a self-sufficient power that overwhelms the person, but this way of delimiting the power of *sarx* does not mean that Paul imagined *sarx* as a mythological power independent of the person. This comes up more clearly in several chapters in Paul's letter to the Romans.

In Romans 6–8 it is clear that the embodiment of the human being should not only be understood in terms of the ethical contrast between righteous and unrighteous actions, but also in terms of the more fundamental distinction between life and death. Paul's exposition on the body *(sōma)* in chapter 6 sees it as situated between the fallen and the new creation. The body is a slave to sin, rather than the person to the body. It is by the fact that sin has taken power that the body becomes its instrument. It is by being crucified with Christ that the believer is identified with a new life, where sin no longer has power over the body (6:6). Instead of sin being able to use the person's limbs "as instruments for unrighteousness" Jesus will use the person's limbs as "instruments for righteousness" (v. 13). It is clear here that unrighteous and righteous actions are not the primary categories, but are the consequences of a more fundamental orientation in the whole person. So if the body is inserted into an ethical context, the question of who has power over the body is of a more fundamental significance, not least for the question of life or death. The critical question is thus whether the person lives

---

24. Schweizer and Baumgärtel, "σῶμα, σωματικός, σύσσωμος," pp. 1065–66.

according to the flesh or the Spirit. Paul writes in 8:5ff. that "those who live according to the flesh *[kata sarka]* set their minds on the things of the flesh *[ta tēs sarkos phronousin]*, but those who live according to the Spirit *[kata pneuma]* set their minds on the things of the Spirit. For to set the mind on the flesh *[to phronēma tēs sarkos]* is death, but to set the mind on the Spirit is life and peace." The Christian has received the Spirit through baptism into Christ (6:3ff.). It is thus not simply one aspect of the person—for example, her embodiment *in opposition* to her soul—that is affected by the context that governs her life, but her life as a whole.[25] The context that determines the person is also decisive for her (manifold) actions, and can therefore be seen as a single action.

But is there not a use of *sarx* in Romans 7:18 and 7:25 that resembles more of a substance-dualistic conception of the flesh in contrast to the human being's intrinsic self? In verse 18 the absence of the good "in my flesh *[en tē sarki mou]*" is contrasted with my impotent will *(thelein)*, which at least wants to do good, and in verse 25 "my flesh *[sarki]*" serves "the law of sin" while "my mind *[tō noi]*" serves "the law of God." Here there seems to be a clear contrast between the sinful flesh on the one side and a will and desire on the other that wants, but does not manage to serve God and the good. This passage should not, however, be understood as being about a tension between different parts of the anthropological constitution of the human being. Paul is not attempting to escape responsibility for his sinful actions by locating them in a quasi-external aspect of his person. In continuity with Paul's use of *sarx* in other places, it is instead a matter of an eschatological tension between the person's existence imprisoned in a sinful form of existence and the person's existence as liberated to eternal life with Christ. Both of these sides belong to the person's self. Further, this tension is not purely conceptual, but an experience the believer makes in her or his life.[26] In other

25. Schweizer, Baumgärtel, and Meyer, "σάρξ, σαρκικός, σάρκινος," p. 135.

26. There is an extensive debate whether the experience Paul speaks of is an experience that the person does before the conversion to Christ or after, whether the experience as such is interpreted before or after the conversion as well as whether Paul speaks from his own experience. Cf. Schweizer, Baumgärtel, and Meyer, "σάρξ, σαρκικός, σάρκινος," pp. 133-34; C. E. B. Cranfield, *The Epistle to the Romans: An Exegetical and Critical Commentary*, vol. 1: I-VIII, The International Critical Commentary, ed. J. A. Emerton and C. E. B. Cranfield (Edinburgh: T. & T. Clark, 1975), pp. 340-70; James D. G. Dunn, *Romans 1-8*, Word Biblical Commentary vol. 38A, ed. David A. Hubbard, Glen W. Barker, et al. (Dallas: Word, 1988), pp. 374-412; Ernst Käsemann, *An die Römer*, 4th edition, Handbuch zum Neuen Testament, 8a, ed. Günther Bornkamm (Tübingen: J. C. B. Mohr [Paul Siebeck], 1980), pp. 183-204; Ulrich Wilkens, *Der Brief an die Römer: Röm 6-11*, 2nd volume, Evangelisch-Katholischer

words, the Christian self is the divide between God and sin, but the division concerns precisely the self, and does not imply any anthropological dualism between the self and the flesh.

In chapter 8 it seems, in spite of everything, as though Paul advocates a dualism not only between *sarx* and *pneuma,* but also between *sōma* and *pneuma* (v. 10): "But if Christ is in you, although the body is dead *[to sōma nekron]* because of sin, the Spirit is life because of righteousness." Is the embodiment of the human being thus a part of the carnal nature that the human being will be liberated from in Christ? The verse immediately following, however, refutes such a possibility, as Paul writes that the same God that has raised Christ from the dead will also "give life to your mortal bodies *[ta thnēta sōmata hymōn]* through his Spirit who dwells in you" (v. 11). Further, in verse 23 Paul speaks of "the redemption *[tou sōmatos hēmōn]* of our bodies." *Sōma* is thus not something the person shall be redeemed *from,* but *sōma* is instead something that shall be redeemed. This redemption is accomplished primarily through the resurrection of the body by analogy with the resurrection of Christ from the dead (cf. 1 Cor. 15:35–58). Exegete Ulrich Wilkens's comments on human embodiment in relation to Romans can serve as a summary:

> It is not the materiality of embodiment that is the evil, but the veritable, inescapable reality of evil actions; and they are not evil because the person's appetites and suffering would fix her in her embodiment, but on the

---

Kommentar zum Neuen Testament vol. VI/2, ed. Joseph Blank, Rudolf Schnackenburg, et al., 2nd revised edition (Zürich/Einsiedeln/Cologne/Neukirchen-Vluyn: Benziger Verlag/ Neukirchener Verlag, 1987), pp. 62–117. The commentators discuss whether the second part of verse 25 (the one I discussed above) really is authentically Pauline and thereby serves as a summary of verses 7–25 or not. I follow Cranfield's and Dunn's "Christian," rather than Käsemann's, Schweizer's, and Wilkens's "pre-Christian," interpretation. Dunn writes on verse 18 (p. 408): "Paul is talking about himself in his belongingness to the world of flesh, the old epoch. However much he may also rejoice in his belongingness with Christ to the life beyond the resurrection, the new epoch, he recognizes with all seriousness that he is still flesh; that is, still inextricably bound up with the fallen world, an attachment which only death will sever, when the believer's identification with Christ's death has worked itself out completely." The question is also whether Paul's "I" in Romans 7 should be interpreted autobiographically, rhetorically, or both/and. Krister Stendahl in *Paul among Jews and Gentiles and Other Essays* (Philadelphia: Fortress Press, 1976), is doubtful while Stephen Westerholm in *Israel's Law and the Church's Faith: Paul and His Recent Interpreters* (Grand Rapids: Eerdmans, 1988) defends the autobiographical reading (which is found in, for example, Augustine and Luther). See also Wilkens, *Der Brief,* pp. 101–17.

grounds that they go against God's will and *therefore*—as a consequence of sin (Rom 6:21)—"bear fruit for death."[27]

The body with its limbs, functions, actions, and appetites will be freed in the resurrection from the quasi-autonomous power that has ruled it, and will thereby finally live a life that is determined by *pneuma*. But the body can be enlisted in service of God already in this life (12:1). The person will be freed from *sarx,* but not from *sōma.*[28] Thus for Paul the body is not something that can be separated from the person's real self, but is instead an aspect of a person's whole character in those relationships that she stands in.

One critique of Paul's understanding of human embodiment has come from a different direction. In an investigation of conceptions of human embodiment in rabbinic Judaism, where he notes that the body has a deeply positive significance, Jewish philosopher Daniel Boyarin has argued that Paul, even if he does not deny the positive meaning of the body, values the soul more highly.[29] Paul—and the later Christianity even more, but also a Jew such as Philo—has drawn anthropological conclusions that differ from those of rabbinic Judaism through a hermeneutic practice (allegory) that differs from the Jewish interpretive practice (midrash):

Their [Paul and Philo] allegorical reading practice and that of their intellectual descendants is founded on a binary opposition in which meaning exists as a disembodied substance prior to its incarnation in language, that is, in a dualistic system in which spirit precedes and is primary over body. Midrash, the hermeneutic system of rabbinic Judaism, seems precisely to refuse that dualism, eschewing the inner-outer, visible-invisible, body-soul dichotomies of allegorical reading. Midrash and platonic allegory are alternate techniques of the body.[30]

When Paul, as, for example, in Romans 7:5ff., differentiates between "flesh" and "Spirit," this has given rise to an interpretive practice that differentiates between "literal" and "figurative" interpretation.[31] Even if Boyarin has a point in his critique of how the Jews have been represented in Christian polemical

27. Wilkens, *Der Brief,* pp. 68–69.

28. Dunn, *Romans 1–8,* p. 391.

29. Daniel Boyarin, *Carnal Israel: Reading Sex in Talmudic Culture* (Berkeley/Los Angeles/Oxford: University of California Press, 1993), p. 5 n. 8.

30. Boyarin, *Carnal Israel,* p. 9.

31. Boyarin, *Carnal Israel,* p. 8. Cf. pp. 31–35.

writings, and even if his connection between anthropology and hermeneutics is insightful, I believe that he makes too much a point of the difference between allegory and midrash, at least when it comes to Paul's own position.[32] The biblical language—including the New Testament—functions on a level that comes before the later division and opposition between literal and metaphorical language. For Paul—just as for the rabbinic Jews of his time—the "body" is simultaneously understood both literally and figuratively.[33] Without a figurative understanding of the body, it would be reduced to something resembling Descartes's *res extensa,* a project that, in light of Merleau-Ponty and other phenomenologists' studies of the body, can no longer be viewed as especially meaningful, and certainly was not in Paul's time. The rabbinic bodies are thus embedded in a figurative interpretive practice as well, as Boyarin himself shows in his book. This is not to say that there are no differences between Paul and the rabbis, or that the Christian church has not all too often made itself guilty of an anti-Semitic polemic in its interpretive practice. My point in rejecting Boyarin's claim is simply to argue that Paul hardly privileges a figurative body over a literal one in the way that Boyarin suggests. As I have shown in chapter 5, the bodily constitutes no hindrance for the revelation of God in the New Testament; on the contrary, the divine revelation is mediated through the embodied and material creation. This "transfiguration" of reality is indeed "primary" in the sense that it is not a function of the creation (visible as well as invisible, material as well as immaterial), but a gift that "refigures" the created. But this relationship between the created and the divine should not be understood as a binary, contrastive difference.[34]

32. Boyarin has returned to this issue in *A Radical Jew: Paul and the Politics of Identity* (Berkeley: University of California Press, 1994). For a critique of Boyarin's thesis about Paul in the book, see Stephen Fowl's review in *Modern Theology* 12, no. 1 (1996): 131–33. On page 132 Fowl writes: "If, as Boyarin claims, Paul's allegorizing dissolves historical Israel, then Boyarin dissolves the Church." Cf. as well, on interpretive practices, Gerald L. Bruns, "Midrash and Allegory," in *The Literary Guide to the Bible,* ed. Robert Alter and Frank Kermode (Cambridge, MA: Belknap Press, 1987), pp. 625–46; Richard B. Hays, *Echoes of Scripture in the Letters of Paul* (New Haven/London: Yale University Press, 1989). I touch on the problem more thoroughly in the chapter "På återbesök i Aten och Jerusalem" in my book *Kärlekens skillnad: Att gestalta kristen tro i vår tid* (Stockholm: Verbum, 1998), pp. 95–124.

33. It is not until later that *veritas* and *figura* come to be contrasted with each other within the Christian interpretive tradition, which has to do with changes in the understanding of the ecclesial body in relation to Jesus' historical body and the sacramental body, which I return to in the following.

34. For a general discussion of this problem, see my book *Kärlekens skillnad,* as well as, for example, Jean-Luc Marion, *God without Being: Hors-Texte,* Religion and Postmodernism,

The question of the figurative vis-à-vis the literal body also comes up in a way in those texts that concern the Christian congregation as the body of Christ. Here Paul uses a spatial term to speak of the congregation, in contrast with a temporal term, like, for example, "people of God," and thereby emphasizes the contemporary presence of God's saving work.[35] Paul's most extensive use of the term "body of Christ" about the congregation is in 1 Corinthians 12:12–31 (but cf. Rom. 12:4ff. as well). In verse 27 the believers are identified with Christ's body: "Now you are the body of Christ and individually members of it *[hymeis de este sōma Christou kai melē ek merous]*." Here the question of the social body is brought to a head for theology. How should this be understood? Is Paul simply making use of a figurative expression when he identifies the believers with the body of Christ? For the modern imagination, the social body is a metaphor for the collective existence of individual bodies. But does Paul share this view? Or is it more correct to speak of a sort of "intercorporeality" or "transcorporeality" in Paul? For Paul, the latter is more appropriate, since he shared his period's understanding of the body as a microcosm. Thus Plato in the dialogue *Timaeus,* for example, conceived of not only the body as a cosmos, but the cosmos as a body, and here he was in agreement with many in his period.[36] With this, every sharp distinction between a figurative and a factual body, but also between a social and an individual body, disappears.

The text in 1 Corinthians deals in general terms with unity and difference in the congregation in Corinth.[37] In order to discuss this, Paul makes use of an organic conception of the body and its limbs that was widely spread throughout the rest of the ancient world as well. Paul points out for the readers that they all, whether they are "Jews or Greeks, slaves or free," have been baptized into "one body *[hen sōma]*" (v. 13). The body is one, but its parts are many, and none of the parts can replace any other or manage without

---

trans. Thomas A. Carlson (Chicago: University of Chicago Press, 1991) and Kathryn Tanner, *God and Creation in Christian Theology: Tyranny or Empowerment?* (Oxford: Basil Blackwell, 1988). For yet another discussion on Judaism and embodiment, see Louis Jacob, "The Body in Jewish Worship: Three Burials Examined," *Religion and the Body,* ed. Sarah Coakley (Cambridge: Cambridge University Press, 2000 [1997]), pp. 71–89.

35. Schweizer and Baumgärtel, "σῶμα, σωματικός, σύσσωμος," p. 1074.

36. Dale B. Martin, *The Corinthian Body* (New Haven/London: Yale University Press, 1995), p. 16.

37. Cf. Wolfgang Schrage, *Der Erste Brief an die Korinther: 1 Kor 11,17–14,40,* 3rd volume, Evangelisch-Katholischer Kommentar zum Neuen Testament vol. VII/3, ed. Norbert Brox, Joachim Gnilka, et al. (Zürich/Düsseldorf/Neukirchen-Vluyn: Benziger Verlag/Neukirchener Verlag, 1999), pp. 204–72.

it. Thus the Corinthians ought to also affirm their mutual dependence, not reject certain parts as unnecessary or of less worth. All gifts that anyone in the congregation may be imagined to have go back to the same Spirit, and belong, therefore, to the same Christ. The individual Corinthians belong to Christ in the same way that the limbs belong to their body. But this concerns not only a resemblance, but an identification: the congregation as the representation of Christ in the world.[38] The identification between the congregation as Christ's body and Christ does not, however, go so far that Christ thereby becomes a function of the congregation, or that Christology and ecclesiology become identical. The congregation may instead be described as incorporated into Christ's reception history.[39] On the basis of this, we can draw the conclusion that for Paul the body of Christ is primary in relation to the congregation, and not a result of the fact that people congregate.

In verses 14–26 Paul makes use of this classical organism analogy in order to argue for the fellowship of the congregation. The foot cannot say that it is not a hand, and so does not belong to the body. Even if they are different, they belong to the same body. Every body part has its own function. They can therefore not manage without each other. The eye cannot manage without the hand, nor the head without the feet. In the ancient world this organism analogy was used for the most part in a markedly conservative way to argue for the status quo with regard to society's hierarchies. While Paul also affirms differences within the body, it is doubtful that his use of the organism analogy should be taken as a defense of the status quo. The emphasis lies on mutual dependence, which can very well be understood as a relativization of ancient hierarchies. Verses 14–20 warn against all inferiority complexes, while 21–25 warn against ideas of superiority. Thus, through an organism analogy that was often used in ancient philosophy as a defense of the legitimacy of social hierarchies, Paul argues for an inversion of the usual hierarchies, and emphasizes that the "weaker" and "lesser" parts are those that God allows to be honored in a special way.[40]

We find two more of the most central passages for the understanding of Paul's conception of the body in 1 Corinthians, namely in those texts that deal with communion, 10:16–18 and 11:17–34. The immediate context for these texts is on the one hand the issue of idolatry (in chapter 10) and on the other the issue of how the congregants should behave towards each other

---

38. Schrage, *Der Erste Brief,* vol. 3, p. 212.
39. Schweizer and Baumgärtel, "σῶμα, σωματικός, σύσσωμος," p. 1069.
40. Martin, *Corinthian Body,* p. 96.

at the congregation's communion meals (in chapter 11). The question of the theology of communion is thus not something that Paul treats directly in these texts—it instead occurs only indirectly, as Paul has reason to enter into it in order to use the theology of communion as a contrastive example of what is taking place in the Corinthian congregation.

In chapter 10 Paul wants to try to persuade the members of the Christian congregation in Corinth of the fact that participation in heathen sacrificial and cult meals is not compatible with participation in the communion meal of the Christian fellowship. The meal namely adds the participant in the meal into a greater social body. This leads him to briefly reflect on the meal of the Christian fellowship. For the sake of clarity, I will cite the following three verses (16–18) in their entirety, since they show how Paul conceives of the relationship between the believers' individual bodies and the body of Christ:

> The cup of blessing that we bless, is it not a participation in the blood of Christ? The bread that we break, is it not a participation in the body of Christ *[koinōnia tou sōmatos tou Christou estin]*? Because there is one bread, we who are many are one body *[hen sōma]*, for we all partake of the one bread. Consider the people of Israel *[ton Israēl kata sarka]*: are not those who eat the sacrifices participants in the altar?

In these three verses Paul treats several of the themes that interest me in this chapter.[41] The bread that is broken and shared among the congregants becomes the means by which they receive fellowship with the body of the risen Lord. But just as a loaf of bread broken into several pieces can still be one and the same bread—so Paul conceives of it in this image—many people can also be "one body"—in this case "body" refers to the church as the body of Christ—and they become this by sharing of "one bread." Those who belong to Israel *kata sarka*, i.e., the recalcitrant Israel (cf. 10:1–10), not Israel *as* Israel, are used as a metaphor for the Christian: even they receive fellowship with their social body by eating of the sacrificial animal. The bread of communion thus becomes a means by which the Christian is incorporated into the body of Christ. In other words, there occur three sorts of bodies in this text: the body of Jesus Christ, identified with the bread of communion, the

---

41. For a commentary, see Wolfgang Schrage, *Der Erste Brief an die Korinther: 1 Kor 6,12–11,16*, 2nd volume, Evangelisch-Katholischer Kommentar zum Neuen Testament vol. VII/2, ed. Norbert Brox, Joachim Gnilka, et al. (Solothurn/Düsseldorf/Neukirchen-Vluyn: Benziger Verlag/Neukirchener Verlag, 1995), pp. 430–60.

bodies of the Christians, and the church as the body of Christ. How should the relationship between them be understood?

Paul hardly presents a developed doctrine of communion here, but at the same time it is clear here that he thinks Christ is present in some form in communion. The communion participants become, one might say, participatory in Christ's death and resurrection through communion in two ways: in part as an eschatological hope, but in part also through the fact that Christ himself is present in the meal. The gift cannot be separated from the giver, and so the participants in the communion table are dealing with Christ himself; this is how Christ offers his salvation and binds the participants to himself.[42] But the communion participants are not bound only to Christ himself, but also to the body of Christ that is the church. Through the *sōma* of communion they also become participatory in the *sōma* of the church.[43] Christ, the church, and the believers become "one body" in communion. It is thus not merely a question of a "figurative" integration, if figurative is set in opposition to literal. The church *is* a body, the body of Christ, not merely compared to a body.[44] Participation in communion has fellowship as its consequence.

This becomes clear in 11:17–34 as well, where Paul draws out the ecclesiological and ethical consequences of his understanding of communion (without expounding a systematic doctrine of communion here because of that).[45] In verse 24 Paul refers explicitly to the first communion and cites Jesus' words following the breaking of the bread: "this is my body *[touto mou estin to sōma]* which is for you" (basically an analogue to Luke 22:19). It is not obvious whether *sōma* should be interpreted Christologically here, i.e., as referring to Jesus' own person, or ecclesiologically, i.e., as referring to the church. It is a question of what "this" refers to: What is it that is designated, the broken bread or the whole rite of thanksgiving, inclusive of Jesus' person? Even here I believe that Christ's presence in the bread cannot be comprehensively described as a "figurative-symbolic" presence, but must be understood as a "real" presence, that the Lord himself is present in the bread, without it being possible because of this to pinpoint how Paul conceived of this presence. At the same time this presence is not understood as reified, but rather as a personal and dynamic event.[46] This gift belongs, in turn, together

---

42. Schrage, *Der Erste Brief,* vol. 2, p. 439.
43. Schrage, *Der Erste Brief,* vol. 2, p. 440.
44. Schrage, *Der Erste Brief,* vol. 2, pp. 441–42.
45. Schrage, *Der Erste Brief,* vol. 3, pp. 5–107, especially pp. 32–37, 50–52, 77–89.
46. Schrage, *Der Erste Brief,* vol. 3, p. 36.

with the church, as is emphasized in verse 29—"For anyone who eats and drinks without discerning the body *[to sōma]* eats and drinks judgment on himself"—where *sōma* probably, in the same ambiguous way as in 10:16ff., refers to both the sacramental meal and the church as Christ's body.[47] So for Paul, the person of Christ, the sacramental meal, and the church as the body of Christ belong intimately together. The emphasis in Paul on Christ's presence is not an individualistic interpretation of the sacramental event, but is on the contrary a social interpretation. If one brings together these two passages that deal with communion, 10:16–18 and 11:17–34, with the discussion of the church as the body of Christ in 12:12–31, one gets a relatively articulate picture of Paul's emphasis on the affinity between the person of Christ, communion, and the church as the body of Christ.[48] As I will show in the following three sections, this affinity will also play a critical role for the understanding of embodiment in the continued history of theology.

What can we say in summary then about biblical bodies? Firstly, that any sort of substance dualism is seldom or never brought to the fore by the biblical writings. The problem that is common to the different groups of biblical texts is instead how the person's body exists engaged in a battle between, to use the Pauline terminology, "the flesh" and "the Spirit." As I pointed out in the introduction to this section, according to the biblical writings the human body exists at the intersection between various more or less external powers that influence the structure of its desire. The understanding of the body is dramatic and existential rather than ontological or transcendental. When the biblical writings approach a more ontological determination of the person's being, it is often emphasized that the body is one aspect of the whole person, rather than a part of the person. Secondly, we find an emphasis on the affinity between individual bodies and the social body, above all in the Pauline writings. As I just mentioned, for Paul communion is the real presence of the crucified and risen Christ, and it is by participating in communion that individual Christians are incorporated into the body of Christ, that is, the church. In the later Deutero-Pauline epistles there is a tendency to extend the social body via the church to encompass the entire cosmos.

47. Schrage, *Der Erste Brief,* vol. 3, p. 51.

48. As regards the putative Deutero-Pauline epistles, in Colossians 1:18–24 and Ephesians 1:22–23, which I have not discussed here, there are tendencies to expand the term "body of Christ" until it not only encompasses the congregation, but the entire cosmos. Christ is said to be the head of the body that is the church, but also the head of the entire cosmos, and the one who redeems everything in the cosmos. The church is the body of Christ through which Christ goes out into the world.

It is difficult to find any great interest in the embodiment of the person as an individual or narrow phenomenon in the biblical writings, but through the fact that human embodiment is placed in a soteriological, sacramental, and ecclesiological context one may indirectly discern certain constant features of the biblical—here primarily New Testament—bodies. A person's embodiment is an integrated part of her existence, not something incidental, given in and through God's creation of the person. Her body is not, however, understood as a closed and smooth whole, but is communicative and expressive, in fact a medium through which the person relates to God as well as to other people. The individual body of the solitary Christian cannot be separated from the social body. Further, the body is open to change, such that even the body as body will be liberated from the power of the flesh in the future redemption. These aspects of embodiment are also, I believe, essential for a theology of the body for our time.

Starting from this biblical perspective, I will next discuss the understanding of human embodiment in later periods. To begin with, I will study the understanding of the social body that Paul calls the "body of Christ." Then I turn to the question of the individual body in order to finally look at the relationship between social and individual bodies by focusing on the liturgy (and within this communion) as the way in which the Christian tradition mediates the relationship between the social and the individual body. In principle it should be possible to begin with either the individual or the social body, but there may yet be a pedagogical reason for beginning with the question of the social body as a counterweight to our period's individualized understanding of both the Christian tradition and of the embodiment of the human being.

The Communal Body

The history of the body of Christ, the social body that is called the Christian church, is a long and multifaceted history. Since the relationship between a person's social body and her individual body is inevitable for anyone who wants to understand human embodiment, I will here concern myself with certain strands of this bodily history of the church, or, rather, the history of the Christian understanding of the social body. Parallels between the individual body and the social body were common knowledge in Antiquity. As I mentioned back in the previous section, in his dialogue *Timaeus,* which was very influential within the early Christian tradition, Plato argued that the cosmos constitutes a great body, the human creature a little body, and the life-giving principle for both is the rational soul.[49] An analogy existed between the two bodies, and so the key to understanding the cosmos existed within the person herself. Likewise, Paul imagined the conception of the church as the body of Christ not only as a metaphor or a symbol, but as an actually existing unity where Christ was really present, and which could not be reduced to its individual members. Out of all these shifts in how people have understood the body of Christ as a social body throughout history, I will focus on several significant periods: in the High and Late Middle Ages, and in the twentieth century. Discussing these periods is important because they describe a central problem for a theology of the body in a clear way and with an emphasis on the social body.

Corpus Mysticum

One of the most important contributions to the understanding of the history of the church as a social body during the twentieth century is the French Jesuit Henri de Lubac's book *Corpus mysticum* from 1944 (especially in its second, expanded edition from 1949).[50] De Lubac is one of the foremost representatives of a French theological school from the first half of the twentieth century, *la nouvelle théologie,* which is characterized both by a return to the sources and by an openness to the issues of its time, and whose critical front was directed against New Scholasticism. *Corpus mysticum* is a historical investigation of the referents of and connection between the terms *corpus mysticum* and *corpus verum.* One of the (for de Lubac) contemporary reasons for the book can, despite its historical character, be traced to the Catholic discussion at the start of the 1900s of the meaning of *corpus mysticum,* "Christ's mystical body," as a popular way to speak of the Christian (Roman Catholic) church.[51] *Corpus mysti-*

---

49. Plato, *Timaeus,* in *Timaeus, Critias, Cleitophon, Menexenus, Epistles,* Loeb Classical Library, trans. R. G. Bury (Cambridge, MA/London: Harvard University Press, 1929).

50. Henri de Lubac, *Corpus Mysticum: The Eucharist and the Church in the Middle Ages,* Faith in Reason, trans. Gemma Simmonds et al. (Notre Dame: University of Notre Dame Press, 2007). For a basic walk-through of the entirety of Lubac's thought, see Peter Bexell, *Kyrkan som sakrament: Henri de Lubacs fundamentalecklesiologi* (Stockholm/Stehag: Brutus Östlings Bokförlag Symposion, 1997).

51. See William T. Cavanaugh's summary of these trends in *Torture and Eucharist: Theology, Politics, and the Body of Christ,* Challenges in Contemporary Theology (Oxford/Malden, MA: Blackwell, 1998), pp. 207–12.

cum is often used as a counterweight to the emphasis on the institutional and juridical side of the Roman Catholic Church that had been dominant within Roman Catholic ecclesiology ever since the Counter-Reformation. From de Lubac's perspective the problem with *corpus mysticum* was, however, that the term implicitly or explicitly served a dichotomy between the church's "external" and "institutional" side on the one hand and the church's "inner," "mystical," "invisible" body on the other. The question was whether the church defined as *corpus mysticum* could be understood as a social body at all.

The Roman Catholic *corpus mysticum*–ecclesiology was in no way the only ecclesiology of the twentieth century that tended towards individualized and thereby incorporeal features—on the contrary, we find here a trend that includes the Protestant churches as well. Those who advocated a *corpus mysticum* ecclesiology, however, claimed that they relied on early sources of Christian history. De Lubac's investigation in *Corpus mysticum* shows that this is indeed the case, but that the church fathers and the early medieval theological tradition did not associate the term with the church. On the basis of the Pauline image of the body of Christ, people distinguished between three different aspects of this body.[52] One aspect was the historical body, i.e., Jesus of Nazareth's physical body. A second aspect was Christ's presence in communion, i.e., the sacramental body, and a third was the church, i.e., the ecclesial body. According to de Lubac, it was the sacramental body that was designated *corpus mysticum* while the ecclesial body was called *corpus verum*. During the 1100s, however, a change began such that towards the end of the century the sacramental body came to be identified with *corpus verum* and the ecclesial body with *corpus mysticum*.[53] An exchange of the terms' referents has thus taken place.

Another change lies in the understanding of the relationship between the different aspects. The church fathers and the early Middle Ages understood the Eucharist both as church and as the contemporary appearance of the historical body.[54] There was thus a dividing line between the historical body and its contemporary forms of manifestation. Theologian, cultural critic, and historian of mysticism Michel de Certeau, who, like de Lubac, was Jesuit, but belonged to the generation after him, writes apropos de Lubac's book:

52. De Lubac, *Corpus,* pp. 23–28.
53. De Lubac, *Corpus,* pp. 3–9.
54. De Lubac, *Corpus,* p. 256.

The sacrament . . . and the church . . . were joined . . . as the contemporary performance of a distinct, unique "event," the *kairos,* designated by the "historical body" (Jesus). The caesura is therefore of the temporal sort, in conformity with Augustinian theology. It separates from the original event the manifestation of its effects in the mode of the Church-Eucharist pair, which is the "liturgical" combination of a visible community of people *(laos)* and a secret action *(ergon)* of "mystery."[55]

The dividing line was of a temporal nature, but was transcended by the action of the mystical body, i.e., of the sacrament. However, with the referents of *corpus mysticum* and *corpus verum* changing place, the critical dividing line to draw comes to be between the historical and the sacramental body on the one hand and the ecclesial body on the other. This means, to begin with, that the Eucharist increasingly comes to be described as an objective and visible thing, not as a communication that established relationships.[56] The sacrament is objectified and the emphasis comes to rest on the miracle in the transformation of the elements as an isolated phenomenon, rather than as the edification of the church through the presence of Christ in communion. The church's visibility changed places with the sacrament, so that henceforth it was the sacrament that was the visible indicator of the invisible mercy that suffuses the church. With this, the visibility of the sacrament became more important than the celebration of the communal meal.[57] Eventually a spirituality was also developed that emphasized the beholding of the Eucharist, rather than the eating.[58] Communion became a *spect*acle, rather than a part in a greater liturgical event. In contrast to the patristic and early medieval understanding of the church as a visible manifestation of Christ in the world—*corpus verum*—the visibility of the Eucharist on the altar became central. The church as Christ's mystical body was relegated to a different plane of existence than the more concrete plane where the historical and the sacramental body were found.

55. Michel de Certeau, *The Mystic Fable: The Sixteenth and Seventeenth Centuries,* trans. Michael B. Smith (Chicago: University of Chicago Press, 1995), p. 83.

56. De Lubac, *Corpus,* pp. 65, 240–45. This also has consequences for the concept of truth. See Peter Bexell, *Kyrkan som sakrament,* pp. 180–82.

57. De Certeau, *The Mystic Fable,* pp. 83–84.

58. See, for example, Miri Rubin, *Corpus Christi: The Eucharist in Late Medieval Culture* (Cambridge: Cambridge University Press, 1991), pp. 55–63, together with Caroline Walker Bynum, *Holy Feast and Holy Fast: The Religious Significance of Food to Medieval Women* (Berkeley/Los Angeles/London: University of California Press, 1987), pp. 53–58.

A tripartite structure was exchanged for a binary structure, which had the result that the relationship between the different aspects of Christ's body was no longer understood as temporal, but as an opposition between visible and invisible. The historical body and the sacramental body were thereby understood as two authoritatively given facts (Bible and communion) rather than events within the framework of the divine plan of salvation.[59] These tendencies were separated in the Reformation, where the Protestant side of the Reformation prioritized the historical body, while the Catholic Reformation prioritized the sacramental. In relation to these immovable values or authoritatively given facts, the church was reduced to a secondary level.[60] It was no longer seen as an integrated part of the symbolic structure of the event of salvation through its participation in the sacramental body, but only as metaphorically embodied.[61]

This theological development went hand in hand with a historical and anthropological change.[62] The period between the thirteenth and the fifteenth centuries involved an increased specialization among the upper classes, while the great majority of the population in Europe was marginalized. Theological education was internationalized and specialized, which also served to reinforce the hierarchies within the church. The power of the priest was increasingly connected to his ability to present the miraculous Eucharist through the words of consecration. The priest was emphasized in his role as the only one who could ritually perform the sacramental actions.[63] As the Eucharist received this new and increased significance as an isolated phenomenon, the fear that the consecrated elements would be misused increased as well. Someone could drop the bread and it could break, or the wine could be spilled.[64] In order to avoid this, the chalice was withdrawn from the lay communion during certain times. The person's relationship to God became ever-more subjectivized. An authority on medieval political theology, Ernst H. Kantorowicz, comments on this development:

Official and popular piety, after the era of Saint Francis, became both more spiritualized and more material; and concomitantly there took place an

---

59. De Certeau, *The Mystic Fable*, pp. 83–85. Cf. as well Catherine Pickstock, *After Writing: On the Liturgical Consummation of Philosophy*, Challenges in Contemporary Theology (Oxford/Malden, MA: Blackwell, 1998), pp. 160–61.

60. Pickstock, *After Writing*, p. 161.

61. De Lubac, *Corpus*, pp. 114–15. Cf. Pickstock, *After Writing*, pp. 162–66.

62. De Certeau, *The Mystic Fable*, pp. 85–87.

63. Rubin, *Corpus Christi*, p. 50.

64. Rubin, *Corpus Christi*, pp. 70–73.

evasive and yet quite distinct, transformation of Christological concepts. Man's relation with God retired from the 'realism' of object-centered mystery to an inner haze of subject-centered mysticism characteristic of the latter Middle Ages.[65]

Separation of the real, objective, and visible from the mystical and invisible culminates in an absolutist structure, where a centralized power exercises authority over a homogenized social body.[66]

This transformation of the relationship between *corpus mysticum* and *corpus verum* thus not only had consequences for the liturgical life of the church, but also for the relationship between church and society in the late medieval period. Secular institutions were built up that had interests outside the jurisdiction of the church. At the same time the church came to increasingly resemble these secular institutions through an emphasis on the central administration. This meant that the term *corpus mysticum* became important for understanding the essence of the church. Parallel to this development, the twelfth century also strove to sanctify the secular governments and their administration.[67] This does not mean that the one caused the other, but that it was a part of the same ambitions and impulses that asserted themselves around the beginning of the 1100s. During the earlier Middle Ages the political sphere had been understood in accordance with Augustine's division between the two cities as an earthly and finite city, and a heavenly and eternal city. These two cities did not compete over a specific territory, but were separated with respect to the perception of time that governed their actions. The earthly, political city would be a functional way to manage temporal affairs, while the heavenly, theological city in the form of the church was responsible for the highest good of the human being, which was something beyond the political. The authority of the king did not exist "outside" the church, in another territory, but exercised a "liturgical" office as "Christ's deputy" in the temporal sphere.[68]

When king and bishop eventually came to stand against each other, this entailed a change in the view of both state and church. The emerging secular kingdom had spiritual ambitions and borrowed symbols and images from the church. It made claim to a competing perception of time

65. Ernst H. Kantorowicz, *The King's Two Bodies: A Study in Mediaeval Political Theology* (Princeton: Princeton University Press, 1997), p. 93.

66. Pickstock, *After Writing*, p. 162.

67. Pickstock, *After Writing*, p. 197.

68. Pickstock, *After Writing*, pp. 87–97.

by attributing to itself a sort of eternity, and could even make use of the idea of *corpus mysticum* as a characteristic of the state, since it was also seen as a body.[69] The state was transformed into a church, but the church was also transformed into a state through its increasingly centralized and organized administrative apparatus. Its jurists came to use the term *corpus mysticum* in order to emphasize the church's characteristic of being a juridical organization and in order to describe the relationship to the pope in Rome. This development did not mean that the church became more visible, that its body became more social, but the opposite: through the emergence of the sovereign state, the life of the church came to be internalized all the more. Invisible mysticism and visible institution came to be set against each other, and the Eucharist was no longer understood as a congregation's commemoration of the body of Christ, but as an individual's.[70]

In other words, this process meant that the Christian church was on its way to losing its social body. *Corpus mysticum* became an increasingly colorless sociological or juridical concept.[71] The church thereby came to resemble the secular political institutions, and the pope became more like an emperor. The sacramental and the ecclesial body were separated more and more. Where *corpus verum* came to live a life of its own with its own mysticism, supported by the doctrine of transubstantiation and the celebration of *Corpus Christi, corpus mysticum* became an ever-paler concept, quite simply synonymous with whichever institutional body at all.[72] When the emerging state took up a position beside and independent of the church, the difference between state and church was no longer understood in terms of time. Instead, both became competitors in the same territory, and even with the same terminology. When the church lost the battle for territory, this also meant a gradual spiritualization of the Christian message.

---

69. Pickstock, *After Writing*, pp. 207, 271. On the "eternity" of the state, see Kantorowicz, *Two Bodies*, pp. 275–313. This transformed perception of time eventually also brought about the idea of a king who never dies, even if every concrete personification of the king dies. This was interpreted with the help of Christological terms. See p. 446: "It was indeed a 'royal Christology' which the jurists established, and which they were almost bound to establish once they started to interpret consistently the relation between the individual king and his immortal Dignity by means of the metaphor of the 'two Bodies.'"

70. Cavanaugh, *Torture and the Eucharist*, p. 219.

71. Kantorowicz, *Two Bodies*, p. 202.

72. Kantorowicz, *Two Bodies*, p. 206.

Classical Bodies and Grotesque Bodies

To further illuminate the transformation of the conception of the social body during the Middle Ages, I want to highlight here a way of conceiving of the body that stood in (implicit) conflict with the contemporary late medieval church's centralization and individualization, and that we find in the female English anchorite Julian of Norwich (born ca. 1342, died after 1416). Julian's literary heritage consists of two versions of the book *Revelations of Divine Love* (the "short text" written sometime after 1393), and in this Julian articulates an understanding of the social body that differs radically from the social body that is manifested by the emerging secular state.[73] One can formulate the difference thus: if the state body is smooth and controlled, Julian imagines the ecclesial body as fractured and generative. Julian is certainly not untouched by the affective mysticism that characterized her time, but what is interesting is that she goes beyond the conception of Christ's historical body as an object for the pathos of devotions to a "text" that reveals a love that transforms the very way of conceiving of these social structures.[74] Salvation is being incorporated into Christ's suffering and generative body, a union that is as political as spiritual.

To clarify Julian's conception of the body of Christ, I want to refer with the American theologian Frederick C. Bauerschmidt to Mikhail Bakhtin's distinction between the classical body and the grotesque body in his study of folk culture in the Middle Ages and Renaissance. Bakhtin himself speaks of the "new bodily canon," but he says that there are roots back into Antiquity. According to Bakhtin, the classical body is characterized by being an "entirely finished, completed, strictly limited body, which is shown from the outside as something individual."[75] This body attempts to avoid or smooth out all protrusions and cavities in order to thereby close itself to the world:

> The basis of the image is the individual, strictly limited mass, the impenetrable façade. The opaque surface and the body's "valleys" acquire an essential meaning as the border of a closed individuality that does not merge with other bodies and the world.[76]

73. Frederick Christian Bauerschmidt, *Julian of Norwich and the Mystical Body Politic of Christ* (Notre Dame/London: University of Notre Dame Press, 1999), p. 2.

74. Bauerschmidt, *Julian of Norwich*, p. 36.

75. Mikhail Bakhtin, *Rabelais and His World*, trans. Helene Iswolsky (Cambridge, MA/London: MIT Press, 1968), p. 320.

76. Bakhtin, *Rabelais*, p. 320.

The smooth, controlled body does not enter into relationship with other bodies through the fact that it as a whole or through certain of its parts symbolizes something else. The classical body is a "finished body in the finished outside world."[77] The folksy, grotesque body is depicted by Bakhtin in a completely different way. Here it concerns "a body in the act of becoming":

> It is never finished, never completed; it is continually built, created, and builds and creates another body. Moreover, the body swallows the world and is itself swallowed by the world. . . . This is why the essential role belongs to those parts of the grotesque body in which it outgrows itself, transgressing its own body, in which it conceives a new, second body: the bowels and the phallus.[78]

The corporeal drama is played out at the boundaries of the body, and these are continually exceeded, so that it cannot be a question here of a body that is finished and clearly delimited with respect to other bodies. This body is generative, since it continually begets new life and thereby exceeds its own boundaries, and it is additionally cosmic and universal in that it is interwoven with the other bodies that surround it.

Even if Bakhtin's distinctions between the classical and the grotesque body are overly clear and perhaps not fully applicable to medieval culture, nor correspond to an "official" versus "folk" culture, he nevertheless gives an important insight into the social force of images of the body. Julian's vision of Christ's body can be interpreted as the vision of a grotesque body. She has a clear interest in the boundaries of the body, both individual and social, and in the vision of Christ these boundaries are exceeded. Thus she can speak of the person's feces as a reminder of her created nature and mortality and as a source of social humility, but also more positively as an asset for growth. The humble matter of physical existence is not grounds for shame, but for thankfulness, since God's love is revealed even in the simplest detail of the person's constitution.[79] But all such images of the person's situation appear against the background of the vision of Christ's body, which Bauerschmidt describes in the following way:

> It is the sight of Jesus' bleeding head that occasions Julian's hybridization of language, mixing high and low, majesty and familiarity, and indeed,

---

77. Bakhtin, *Rabelais*, p. 321.
78. Bakhtin, *Rabelais*, p. 317.
79. Bauerschmidt, *Julian of Norwich*, pp. 79–81.

Christ's crucified and risen body is the grotesque backdrop against which all of Julian's revelations take place. Christ's body is the site of the degradation of God, where the very interior of God is opened up to Julian and her fellow Christians, and as such is characterized, beyond all other bodies, as imbued with infinite generative power.[80]

This generative power is articulated by Julian in her descriptions of mutability in Christ's body. With the opening of his body to the suffering of the world, there are in principle no boundaries for its saving power. By being broken in the crucifixion, and thereby in a certain sense being a failed body in the classical sense, it is opened in order to generate salvation for the whole world. Julian speaks of Christ as "mother" and with this means that the "humble" and "low" status of the female body is suitable for the self-denial by which God saves and renews the world.[81] For Julian it is not a matter of emphasizing certain stereotypical "female attributes" like humility or tenderness, but of referring to a body that gives birth in pain and communicates its own substance. The consequence, however, is also a reinterpretation—in relation to her time—of what failure and emptiness, renewal and abundance, are. Bauerschmidt summarizes: "Christ's body is a body of flesh that desires our flesh, that indeed is shattered by desire for us, a body moist and labile, generative and nutritive. This is the home God has prepared for humanity."[82] The church is an extension of Christ's humanity. The world is transformed by the church into parts in the body of Christ in that it, as Bakhtin writes, "swallows the world and is itself swallowed by the world."

Julian's vision of the church is thus not of a "tolerant" or "egalitarian" body in the modern sense, i.e., a body that "respects otherness" and is "democratic" (and here she differs from Bauerschmidt). The generativity of the church is the historical extension of God's infinite generative power, and its purpose is the transformation of humanity into the image of God.[83] But the image of Christ's body that she gives is not the image of a body that is smooth and controlled, governed by a sovereign and almighty God at a distance from the common folk and their everyday lives. Christ's body is a crucified

80. Bauerschmidt, *Julian of Norwich*, p. 84.
81. Bauerschmidt, *Julian of Norwich*, p. 90. Cf. p. 91: "On the whole, women were thought to be physically, intellectually, and morally weaker and inherently more passive than men; the female body was, in short, a body characterized by lack."
82. Bauerschmidt, *Julian of Norwich*, p. 107.
83. Bauerschmidt, *Julian of Norwich*, p. 122.

body, and God can never, for Julian, be thought of as anything other than this broken, and thereby generative, body. Its boundaries are never closed, and it is therefore never a "finished body," but a body that continually exceeds itself. The church then becomes a community that is gathering rather than delimiting, and that will transcend every existing political, ethnic, social, or cultural community.[84] The church can thereby never be identified with a particular race or class, or a specific gender, or, for that matter, with the church existing at an actual point in time. It is a church whose skin is always permeable, but whose core is given, the crucified Christ.[85] For Julian this church's only authority is Christ, the incarnation of God, who allowed himself to be crucified, which results in a completely different view of what authority is than that prevalent in her own feudal period. For Julian's part, this thus becomes a question of transcending the boundaries for how language partitions into high and low in her period. The church could have been described by her as God's triumph through history, but for Julian it is never a question of any other triumph than the crucified one who conquers by losing, and who gathers the world together by allowing his body to be broken on the cross.[86] In other words, in Julian's vision the ecclesial body is formed by this drama.

The Disappearing Church

The shift in the perception of the church as described above did not only influence a theology of the church divorced from all other articles of faith, but came also to influence the view of God, of the human being, and of the relationship between them. As faith came to be individualized, the social dimensions of Christian salvation fell out of focus. It is not, however, a development that is entirely linear. The example of Julian of Norwich—as well as Bakhtin's investigations of the vernacular culture of the Middle Ages and Renaissance—shows that the development was not in any way unambiguous. The reason I have discussed both of these above is not primarily to show the historical development of the understanding of the church from the church as a social body to the church as a more intangible mystical body,

---

84. Bauerschmidt, *Julian of Norwich*, p. 120. Cf. Oliver O'Donovan, *The Desire of the Nations: Rediscovering the Roots of Political Theology* (Cambridge: Cambridge University Press, 1996), p. 175.

85. The image is taken from O'Donovan, *Desire of the Nations*, p. 176.

86. Cf. Bauerschmidt, *Julian of Norwich*, pp. 162–73.

but to show how these understandings of the church have also influenced the conceptions of the human being's embodiment within the Christian tradition. In the modern period the tendencies towards individualization are even clearer.[87] This individualization entails that the social body disappears from much of the field of view of modern theology, and this may be seen as a contributing factor to the fact that the Christian tradition *in the modern period* is understood as relatively bodiless. With the support of the previous chapter, I want to argue that a reduction of the social body entails the disappearance or reification of the individual body. Instead of the body being understood as the person's practical and concrete relation to other people and the divine, it has been increasingly understood as an object for philosophical and theological, or perhaps primarily biological and medical investigations, and so as something exterior in relation to our subjectivity as people. Before I turn to the question of the individual body as the body of the solitary person, I will therefore say some additional words about this individualization.

The connection between the social and the individual body coincides with the aim in de Lubac's book *Corpus mysticum,* namely, to show how sacramental realism and "ecclesiological realism" go together. The objectification of communion on the altar table on the one hand and the ever-more subjective communion devotion created an imbalance in the understanding of the relationship between communion and the church. Communion as a communal meal, and not merely as an object for individual exercises of devotion, had disappeared from view in this individualized and disembodied faith. De Lubac worked with the question of the sociality of the person and salvation in other books as well. Not least in the book *Catholicism,* whose first edition was published in 1938, de Lubac pleads that salvation is social, not a private story between God and the soul as it has come to be understood in the modern period.[88] The humanity of the person becomes intelligible once one understands her as a social being, and the very point of salvation is that God will restore the unity of humanity in the church. The sin of the person consists in the fact that she breaks with God, but this departure from God is at the same time a fragmentation of the unity of humanity.[89] Salvation

87. Cf., for example, Paul Heelas and Linda Woodhead, eds., *The Spiritual Revolution: Why Religion Is Giving Way to Spirituality,* Religion and Spirituality in the Modern World (Malden, MA/Oxford/Victoria: Blackwell, 2005).

88. Henri de Lubac, *Catholicism: Christ and the Common Destiny of Man,* trans. Lancelot C. Sheppard and Elizabeth Englund (San Francisco: Ignatius Press, 1988).

89. De Lubac, *Catholicism,* p. 33.

consists in the restoration of unity and agreement between God and humanity, and thus is in its essence social. Even the historical study *Corpus mysticum* can therefore be understood as a link in de Lubac's theological attempt to restore the social character of Christian salvation, and this in light of the different challenges that this ever-more individualized and individualizing society offers.

For a close, and for me, a very fruitful analysis of the relationship between the church and its contemporary society that proceeds from de Lubac's work, we turn to de Certeau. He has shown how the contemporary Christian church lacks a concrete "place," and so a "body," on the basis of which Christian discourse may be conferred some form of social authority.[90] Civil society first replaced the church's role when it came to defining people's functions and positions in society, and left only marginal possibilities for the church to correct or transcend its domains. Today the ecclesiastical space for defining a unified strategy for these margins has disappeared as well.[91] When the ecclesial body disappears, faith becomes ever-more individualized: "As the ecclesial 'body of sense' loses its effectivity, it is for Christians themselves to assure the articulation of this 'model' [of discipleship and repentance] with actual situations."[92] In other words, according to de Certeau the Christian faith as a collective phenomenon is on its way to falling apart. If this was a provocative diagnosis when it was posed in 1974, it has been borne out by later sociological studies.[93] For de Certeau, an impossible tactic given this situation would be to allow the Christian faith to "evaporate" into abstract, universal principles like goodness, truth, and beauty.[94] Such a tactic is quite simply a flight from, and an attempt to hide, this particularity, so necessary for the Christian church, which is a consequence of its faith in a God who is incarnated in history. Only this particularity allows the Christian church to

---

90. Michel de Certeau, "The Weakness of Believing: From the Body to Writing, a Christian Transit," in *The Certeau Reader,* ed. Graham Ward (Oxford/Malden, MA: Blackwell, 2000), pp. 214-43.

91. On de Certeau's use of the word "strategy" as a contrast to "tactic," see Michel de Certeau, *The Practice of Everyday Life,* trans. Steven Rendall (Berkeley/Los Angeles/London: University of California Press, 1988), pp. xix, 34-39.

92. De Certeau, "The Weakness of Believing," p. 226.

93. Jeremy Ahearne, "The Shattering of Christianity and the Articulation of Belief," *New Blackfriars* 77 (November 1997): 493. An example of such a sociological investigation—which Ahearne would of course not have been able to take account of—is Heelas and Woodhead, eds., *The Spiritual Revolution.*

94. Michel de Certeau, "Autorités chrétiennes et structures sociales," in *La faiblesse de croire,* ed. Luce Giard (Paris: Éditions du Seuil, 1987), p. 85.

become conscious of its own limitations.[95] Without limitations it becomes impossible to meet the other.

In contemporary, modern society, however, where civil society has seized the earlier place of Christianity, there no longer exists any ecclesial body, and de Certeau comes to be more pessimistic at the end of his life regarding the possibility of a Christian particularity achieving any breakthrough, or existing at all. Faith has become a private thing. There is no longer any other world than "the body of the world and the mortal body."[96] Christian experience is no longer converted primarily into different practices, but into "faith," i.e., certain beliefs, which mean that the "spiritual" and the "political" are located in different spheres. The church is no longer held together by visible, tangible ties, but by inner postures, by *"sentiment religieux."*[97] This is not a development that exclusively characterizes modern society, which I hope has become clear through the account above of de Lubac's thesis on the transformations of the term *corpus mysticum,* and which de Certeau has also made clear in his study of the mysticism of the sixteenth and seventeenth centuries. What de Certeau argues, however, is that during the twentieth century the ecclesiastical body is fragmented to a degree not previously surpassed. Everything that has been written on ecclesiology during the twentieth century, de Certeau seems to say, also shows the disappearance of the ecclesial body within modern society; the effect of ecclesiology is not a church that is discovered, i.e., a church that is already preset before it is discussed by ecclesiology, but a church that is produced by the discourse itself.

Thus the Christian experience today must continually define itself in relation to bodies other than the ecclesial body, and can express its Christian identity through critical and prophetic deviations from other bodies. The church is once again called to become a pilgrim people in earnest. But at the same time de Certeau asks himself whether a Christian practice may even be identified as Christian if there is no longer a church as an ecclesial body where a reasonably stable meaning for Christian language can be produced. Without this body, Christian language can be used for a range of different purposes, political, generally religious, and commercial.[98] Does the absence of a social body make any alternative to individualized and internalized

---

95. De Certeau, "How Is Christianity Thinkable Today?" *The Postmodern God: A Theological Reader,* ed. Graham Ward (Oxford/Malden, MA: Blackwell, 1997), p. 150.

96. De Certeau, "The Weakness of Believing," p. 229.

97. De Certeau, "Autorités chrétiennes et structures sociales," p. 100.

98. De Certeau, "Lieux de transit," in *La faiblesse de croire,* p. 244.

Christian experience impossible? However, this (to say the least) bleak picture of the future of the Christian church may be questioned, among other things because it seems to presuppose that the sort of Constantinian Christianity, which has ceased in and with the emergence of modernity, is the only Christianity that can have a body.[99] But why should a non-Constantinian Christian church be unthinkable after the Constantinian epoch any more than before it? Is the church's homelessness in contemporary society not both a curse and a blessing? I will not, however, immerse myself further into the meaning of the disappearance of the ecclesial body, but in conclusion I just want to emphasize the fact that the missing body constitutes a serious theological problem for our time. According to de Certeau, the primary theological question is not whether God exists, but what it means to exist as a Christian community.[100] The disappearance of the ecclesial body has consequences for the Christian representation of the individual body.[101]

The Individual Body

My starting point in the social body within the Christian tradition serves the purpose of establishing my thesis that individual or personal bodies find their meaning within the framework of the social body. Changes in the representation of the social body, for example, through the fact that *corpus mysticum* came to designate the church rather than communion, entail changes of the social configuration of the individual body. Body and society can thus never be separated, and as I have made clear in the two previous sections on biblical bodies and social (ecclesial) bodies, it is not sufficient to speak of the social body as a metaphor, if by this we mean merely a way of speaking about a collective of people. The intimacy between individual and collective is greater than this, and it is thus warranted to speak of some form of "inter-"

99. See Frederick Christian Bauerschmidt, "The Abrahamic Voyage: Michel de Certeau and Theology," *Modern Theology* 12, no. 1 (1996): 18–20. Cf. as well Bauerschmidt, "Walking in the Pilgrim City," *New Blackfriars* 77 (November 1996): 504–18, together with Jeremy Ahearne, "Shattering," pp. 493–504.

100. De Certeau, "How Is Christianity Thinkable Today?" p. 155.

101. For further discussion of the "placelessness" of contemporary religion and the "disembodiment" of theology, see Marcia Sá Cavalcante Schuback, "Philosophy and Religion," *Svensk Teologisk Kvartalskrift* 78, no. 3 (2002): 98–106, together with my answer "On Ghosts and Bodies: A Response to Marcia Sá Cavalcante Schuback," *Svensk Teologisk Kvartalskrift* 78, no. 3 (2002): 107–9.

or "transcorporeality" when one wants to speak of how the relationship between individual bodies and the social body appears in the Christian church.

The representation of the body that a particular epoch prefers also influences the possibility of talking about how individual and social bodies go together. The classical body in Bakhtin's description above, which is a smooth and controlled body, and does not readily enter into liaison with other bodies since it is a finished body, does not lend itself as well to the proposition of an intimate affinity between individual and social body. The grotesque body, on the other hand, offers much greater possibilities for speaking of "inter-" or "transcorporeality," since it is per definition not closed, but is continually woven together with other bodies. Because of this the grotesque body is not a limitless body, but a body whose protrusions and cavities make these boundaries much more fluid and porous than the smooth skin of the classical body. Now one of the implicit consequences of the previous chapter on the return of the body was that modernity's forgetfulness of the body had, among other things, to do with the fact that it represented an understanding of the body that to some degree resembled the classical, but that this hides how individual bodies are dependent on social bodies. In other words, I argue that the body—the individual as well as the social—in some sense is "grotesque," in the meaning unclosed, permeable, and excessive. There are several ways to flee from the grotesque body.

Throughout the history of the Christian church the temptation to flee from the grotesque body has for the most part not manifested itself in the attempt to create a classical body. The crucified Christ, with wounds in his head from the crown of thorns, nail-holes in hands and feet, and wounded from the soldier's spear that penetrated his side, has been far too powerful an image through the centuries for the Christian church to have been able to avoid some sort of image of the body as grotesque for any length of time. The temptation has instead lain in the attempt to flee from the material, concrete, contingent, historical reality by "spiritualizing" Christianity. If and when this has happened is naturally a historical question, and the answer to this question undeniably has much to do with the position from which we pose this historical question. There is a—possibly paradoxical—conception in our time (as I pointed out in the introduction to this chapter) that the Christian church's early and medieval history is characterized by an intrinsic contempt for the body connected to a substance-dualistic conception of the relationship between soul and body. What is paradoxical with this critical suspicion is that it is posed from the perspective of a time that is characterized, or at least until very recently has been characterized, by a fondness for an abstract universalism where the textual, the general, and the timeless—in other words: the bodiless—has been prioritized as the way to knowledge at the cost of the oral, individual, local, and time-bound.[102] Attempting to understand the Christian attitude towards the body during different epochs therefore does not mean that one should relate uncritically to it, but that one ought to be conscious of the cultural biases that assert themselves in the interpreter her- or himself, when she or he meets particularly different representations of the body.

In this section I will discuss the individual body in the Christian tradition. Choices must be made here as well, with regard both to the historical epochs and the aspects of the individual body. My selection of periods will primarily focus on Antiquity and the Middle Ages, and these aspects will involve asceticism, above all in the sense of sexual abstinence and mysticism as two bodily practices. Asceticism and mysticism are practices that, besides the fact that they illustrate the Christian attitude towards the individual body during the historical epochs mentioned, also have the "advantage" that they are practices that are often thought to stand in the service of contempt and hostility towards the body. However, as will become clear, these practices are more difficult to define than this. In these practices the body is not necessarily seen as something evil, but as a communicative medium, and the ascetic and mystical practices as a way to both relate to God and to exercise criticism towards contemporary society. In these practices individual bodies are embedded in a social context that makes them much more existentially significant than a simple dualism between contempt for the body and affirmation of the body can account for. Asceticism became a way for Christians to wring the body out of the grip of contemporary society, in other words, a way of transforming social bodies, in order to be able to strive for the transformation of the body through relationship with God. Similarly the mystic, at least in the epoch I describe here, was public and corporeal rather than private and spiritual. Several of the themes I deal with here I return to in the two following chapters on the erotic and the grotesque body. Even if, on the basis of my theoretical perspective, I can hardly differentiate between embodiment as such and its different erotic and grotesque modulations, I want to focus on the former in this section for pedagogical reasons. In the next chapter I will add more systematic perspectives on sexuality, while here one might say that, with the help of historical examples, I study the bases that a theology of the body has to start from.

---

102. Cf. Stephen Toulmin, *Cosmopolis: The Hidden Agenda of Modernity* (Chicago: University of Chicago Press, 1992), pp. 30-36, 187-92.

The Body of the Ascetic

In ancient society there were several competing conceptions about how the relationship between body, gender, sexuality, and society should be understood. Much of the early Christian theology of the body had to do with a critique of ancient society and culture. How did classical pre-Christian society see the embodiment of the person? Chastity, but also virility, were virtues sought by nearly everyone in classical antiquity, not only as an expression of contempt or affirmation for the body, but as a way to position one's own person in relation to the rest of society (which I will discuss more closely in the next chapter). Whether one was a man or a woman also played a critical role for the person's place in the social hierarchy. Men were seen as bearers of a greater energy than women, and for a man to be able to be chaste it was therefore important to hold this energy in so as not to lose self-control.[103] The aspiration for the civilized man was thus to maintain self-control, not only for his own sake, but because the discipline of the whole society, not least during the third century, was thought to rest on this control. At the same time, there was a tolerance for the male upper class's exploitation of the bodies of their male and female slaves. Women's energy was lower in contrast, and their self-control was not as reliable as the man's. For fertile women, childbearing threatened pain and, in the worst case, death. It is an important *memento* for every study of representations of the body in classical society, Christian or otherwise, that the question of embodiment was more charged than in our contemporary society. In daily life physical violence, as well as painful diseases and early death, were a much more palpable reality than in the Western world during the last century.[104] Consciousness of the body's frailty would have been more obvious in Antiquity than it needs to be in our time.

The basis for classical bodily practices in this case was an image of the human person that started from what historian Peter Brown calls a "benevolent dualism," where the body was subordinate to the soul, and so ought to be governed by the soul and not allowed to go astray in its own desires. The

103. Peter Brown, *The Body and Society: Men, Women and Sexual Renunciation in Early Christianity* (London: Faber & Faber, 1989), p. 20.

104. This is naturally a relative claim. Large groups in the contemporary Western world suffer from hunger, brutality, and pain. My point is only that in the general consciousness these phenomena are not as obvious in human life in the time and culture I live in. The advances of medical technology have also transformed the contemporary attitude towards pain, or perhaps rather the contemporary expectations of absence of pain as a desirable goal.

body could thus be refined: through its place in a "great chain of being" it could both degenerate to the bestial and reach towards the divine.[105] But its place was not only in this chain, but also in the family and the society that would govern the body and thereby determine to what degree its connection to the natural world was acceptable.

The Christian view of the body that emerged in this culture would, however, break with the classical view. The body was not only something that should be administered, but something that could actually be transformed. Even sexual restraint received a different meaning. Restraint could transform the body into something other than that which the discipline of the classical city wanted to shape it into.[106] It was therefore no longer the dualism between body and soul that was the fundamental conflict, but another dualism, one that concerned the person's relationship to God expressed in terms of the affinity of her heart. In Paul—as I have shown above—the fundamental dualism was that between "the flesh" and "the Spirit," and he was therefore not the least interested in a dualism between body and soul where the person is a link in a "great chain of being."[107] The big question was whether the person lived in rebellion against God or in the freedom of Christ. This does not mean that the body was neutral. The discipline of the body, which Paul and other classical Christian theologians also talked about, thus stood in the service of the transformation of the body that they all looked forward to. The celibate lifestyle that Paul advocated in 1 Corinthians indeed left a problematic legacy for the future church, since sexual lust came to be associated with sin, but Paul was hardly out to deny the legitimacy of marriage and children, but instead voiced what was at the top of his agenda as an apostle.[108] For the Christian leaders after Paul as well chastity stood high on the agenda, even if they had a number of different reasons for this.[109]

Renouncing sexuality could thus be a way of breaking with classical society, whose continued existence was dependent on the birth of children.[110] In the eyes of several Christian groups, classical society was doomed, since it stood under the judgment of God, and practicing sexual abstinence was

---

105. Brown, *The Body and Society*, p. 27.

106. Brown, *The Body and Society*, p. 31.

107. Brown, *The Body and Society*, p. 48.

108. Brown, *The Body and Society*, pp. 55–57. According to Brown, Pope Siricius (384–399) was the first in the Latin West who came to identify Paul's talk of "the flesh" exclusively with sexual activity. See Brown, *The Body and Society*, p. 358.

109. Brown, *The Body and Society*, pp. 57–64.

110. Brown, *The Body and Society*, pp. 83–102.

thus a way of breaking with this society. Sexual chastity created a possibility for free fellowship between people that did not build on blood ties. Nor was the body contemptible for the desert fathers.[111] The body was on the contrary intimately involved in the battle to transform the soul. Brown writes:

> The rhythms of the body and, with the body, his concrete social relations determined the life of the monk: his continued economic dependence on the settled world for food, the hard school of day-to-day collaboration with his fellow-ascetics in shared rhythms of labor, and mutual exhortation in the monasteries slowly changed his personality. The material conditions of the monk's life were held capable of altering the consciousness itself.[112]

The hard life in the desert served to strengthen the understanding of the close tie between body and soul, and sexuality made itself felt here as well, not because it was the worst temptation, but because it was so palpable in the body that now received a new focus. For Gregory of Nyssa (ca. 334–394) as well, asceticism was a way to break with a doomed society.[113] In contrast, the chastity of Christian women often did not take on the same dramatic expression as that of the desert fathers and other male ascetics. Female chastity had its origin in the Christian household, and it more often existed within the framework of the local church and in small groups of women who strove for holiness.[114]

Different attitudes among the early theologians can of course be traced. For Irenaeus of Lyons (died ca. 202) and Tertullian (ca. 160–220) chastity was an important virtue, but the motivation for chastity was primarily to be able to achieve the simplicity that would make it possible for the Christian to not need to share loyalty to God with other loyalties. At the same time, sexuality belonged to human nature—especially the woman's—and it was therefore not something that the Christian could hope to overcome in this life. However, the chaste would thereby be able to make themselves more available for God's purposes.[115] A distinct substance dualism was never topical for these two theologians. The Platonically influenced Origen (ca. 185–254) related more equivocally to the material cre-

111. Brown, *The Body and Society*, pp. 235–40.
112. Brown, *The Body and Society*, p. 237.
113. Brown, *The Body and Society*, p. 301. Cf. as well pp. 305–22, on John Chrysostom.
114. Brown, *The Body and Society*, pp. 254–89.
115. Brown, *The Body and Society*, pp. 65–82.

ation and body.[116] On the one hand he said that for the person, the material world was a consequence of a fall from a more original, angelic nature. The body constantly indicated her frustrating limitation in her love for God. Origen even had a two-stage doctrine of creation: first the spiritual being was created, who was shaped in God's image, then a material cosmos was created and those souls who had fallen from God were embodied.[117] On the other hand, the body was also one of the tools that existed for overcoming these frustrating limitations. Every person's body was attuned to her soul's need, and could therefore serve as a "sparring-partner" for her soul's path back to God. The body was thus in no way identified with an evil principle, but was quite simply lower. The body was a temporary moment in the purified soul's path back to God, and it was therefore not identified by its sexuality. The entirety of the material creation was only a pale echo of the richness of the spirit's communion with the invisible world and with God. The chaste body was therefore the uniquely free body, since it stood free from the sexuality and social roles of this world. It could become a physical symbol for the purity of the spiritual world.

Augustine (354–430) is a further example of the fact that for the early theologians the problem was not the body versus the soul. For him the deepest problem had to do with the person's alienated will.[118] It is this alien will that the person finds in the body, and that makes it such that it becomes a stranger for her. The person's fallen body must be disciplined, not because the bodily is in itself something negative, but because the person's distorted desires turn both body and soul into a battlefield. The person is thus more or less overpowered by lust. Augustine's ideal was not a person without a body, but a person whose body, soul, and society were not distorted by her alienated will. Even in the smallest details of the person's spiritual and physical life she was surrendered to a will that threatened to overpower her best intentions and so make her spiritually impotent. As with Paul, the flesh was not identical with the body, but with all that caused the person to choose her own will over God's will. In *City of God* Augustine explicitly writes that the person's carnal life depends on defects in consciousness just as much as in the body.[119]

---

116. Brown, *The Body and Society*, pp. 160–77.

117. Andrew Louth, "The Body in Western Catholic Christianity," in *Religion and the Body*, ed. Coakley, pp. 114–15.

118. Brown, *The Body and Society*, pp. 387–427. Cf. as well R. A. Markus, *The End of Ancient Christianity*, Canto (Cambridge: Cambridge University Press, 1998), *passim*.

119. Augustine, *The City of God against the Pagans*, Cambridge Texts in the History of Political Thought, trans. R. W. Dyson (Cambridge: Cambridge University Press, 1998), 14, 2.

In other words, sexual abstinence carried several different meanings, depending on which context it was practiced in. In Western, Latin Christianity chastity was focused on the male clergy and symbolized a "holy," i.e., separate status in relation to the Christian congregations. Certain groups, for example in Asia Minor, used chastity more as a way of breaking with what they understood as a doomed society. It was nevertheless the case throughout that the majority of Christians did not practice abstinence at all. This was reserved for a small elite. It has sometimes been argued that the strict sexual morality was a critique of the licentious earlier classical society, but such a view largely builds on a myth.[120] The Christian understanding of the body nevertheless came to break with the classical in a crucial way. Brown writes in summary:

> Christian attitudes to sexuality delivered the death-blow to the ancient notion of the city as the arbiter of the body. Christian preachers endowed the body with intrinsic, inalienable qualities. It was no longer a neutral, indeterminate outcrop of the natural world, whose use and very right to exist was subject to predominantly civic considerations of status and utility. God had created the human body and Adam had brought upon it the double shame of death and lust.[121]

But the Christian promise and hope was not that the body would be annihilated, but that it awaited a transformation. In other words, the body was not finished, but mutable, and asceticism served, in different ways for different ascetic trends, this future transformation. Even if a tendency to substance dualism existed in, for example, bishop Ambrose of Milan (333/334–397), it is not here that the emphasis lies in the ancient Christian representation of the body, but precisely on the transformation of the body.[122] Thus asceticism shared its orientation with the practice of mysticism.

The Body of the Mystic

To switch tracks from asceticism to mysticism, and so also historical epochs, I want to begin by stating that "mysticism" has often been understood as a

---

Here Augustine also rejects the dualism of the Platonic tradition, since it makes the body responsible for the moral deficiencies. Cf. 14, 5.

120. Brown, *The Body and Society*, pp. 208–9.
121. Brown, *The Body and Society*, p. 437.
122. Brown, *The Body and Society*, pp. 348–49.

phenomenon that transcends concrete, embodied traditions. This has, however, been a modern way of understanding mysticism. In one sense, one can say that mysticism as such is a product of modernity, inasmuch as it is early modernity that first defines a "mystical" discourse and distinguishes it from "theological" discourse. In mysticism one finds a distinct way of being religious, which is not inhibited by particular traditions and doctrines. This is, however, a tendentious understanding of the tradition of mysticism. Mysticism never exists in a cultural vacuum, but as one element in a given religious tradition. As Bernard McGinn, one of the foremost authorities on the history of mysticism, puts it: "No mystics (at least before the [twentieth] century) believed in or practiced 'mysticism.'"[123] For Augustine, Thomas Aquinas, Hildegard von Bingen, or Julian of Norwich there was no meaningful choice between theology and spirituality, between ecclesial exteriority and mystical interiority, between body and soul. The one could not be had without the other. During the High and Late Middle Ages one can certainly speak of an interiorization of mysticism, where it also loses its public meaning. The mystical authors of the sixteenth century no longer authorize their statements by referring to the Bible or tradition, but by referring to an "I" and to their own particular experiences.[124] The authority of the self emerges in connection with the transformation of the church from *corpus verum* to *corpus mysticum,* as well as in connection with the desacralization of the universe, when the world was no longer experienced as God's own discourse.[125] But neither was the inner mystical spirit completely independent from the outer body for these mystics. The context for their mysticism remained an existential drama, which may not be reduced to abstract or universal categories. It is not until the modern period that we get a mysticism that sees itself as wholly divorced from a specific tradition, and is thereby radically individualized.

Female piety during the late Middle Ages (1200–1500) is characterized by a particular somatic quality. There are several reasons for this. One was that women were associated with embodiment in a way that men were not. Other reasons were that this period conceived of the person as a psychosomatic whole, and that one therefore expected the resurrection of both the body and the soul at the end of time. During the Middle Ages, conceptions of

---

123. Bernard McGinn, *The Foundations of Mysticism: Origins to the Fifth Century,* The Presence of God: A History of Western Christian Mysticism (New York: Crossroad, 1991), p. xvi. Cf. as well Denys Turner, *The Darkness of God: Negativity in Christian Mysticism* (Cambridge: Cambridge University Press, 1998 [1995]).

124. De Certeau, *The Mystic Fable,* pp. 178–79.

125. De Certeau, *The Mystic Fable,* p. 188.

the body's resurrection at the end of time exhibit an "extreme materialism," not least in comparison to the religious sensibility of our time, and people emphatically emphasized the bodily continuity between the earthly body and the resurrected body (which I return to in more detail in chapter 11).[126] Additionally, male and female bodies were seen as a variation of one and the same physiological theme (cf. the discussion of this in chapter 8).[127] All these factors work together to allow men's and women's embodiment, and then especially the woman's embodiment, to represent the fullness of humanity for medieval people. Medieval historian Caroline Walker Bynum, who has specialized in female mysticism and embodiment, makes this point in the following way:

> To women, the notion of the female as flesh became an argument for women's *imitatio Christi* through physicality. Subsuming the male/female dichotomy into the more cosmic dichotomy divine/human women saw themselves as the symbol for all humanity.[128]

Given the woman's special association with embodiment in the Middle Ages, the incarnation as the life of God in the corporeal became a clear analogy to this embodiment, which thereby came to be a symbol for all of humanity (including for male authors). Relic cults, corporeal ascetic practices, and miracles in connection with communion were all important parts of contemporary devotion, and reinforced its somatic quality as well. The states of the female mystics in particular often took on bodily expression. Bynum tallies up a whole list of states that distinguish female piety over male piety:

> Trances, levitations, catatonic seizures or other forms of bodily rigidity, miraculous elongation or enlargement of parts of the body, swellings of sweet mucus in the throat (sometimes known as the "globus hystericus") and ecstatic nosebleeds are seldom if at all reported of male saints, but

---

126. Caroline Walker Bynum, *Fragmentation and Redemption: Essays on Gender and the Human Body in Medieval Religion* (New York: Zone Books, 1992), pp. 241, 253.

127. See here Caroline Walker Bynum, *The Resurrection of the Body in Western Christianity, 200–1336* (New York: Columbia University Press, 1995), together with Thomas Laqueur, *Making Sex: Body and Gender from the Greeks to Freud* (Cambridge, MA/London: Harvard University Press, 1990).

128. Bynum, *Holy Feast and Holy Fast,* p. 263. Cf. the entire chapter "Woman as Body and as Food," pp. 260–76.

are quite common in the *vitae* of thirteenth- and fourteenth-century women.[129]

Francis of Assisi's famous stigmatization thus constitutes an exception; stigmatization was otherwise far more common among women, according to Bynum. Disease and pain played a religious role more often in women's lives than in men's. But neither are these somatic qualities sufficient for describing the medieval female mystic. It was also the case that the descriptions of these mystical experiences or states had a more somatic quality in women's accounts than in men's—one example is Julian of Norwich, who was mentioned above. This also had consequences for those men whose experiences resembled those of the female mystic. They often understood themselves in feminine terms and learned their practices from women.[130] Generally, one can distinguish between a masculine mysticism that is characterized by stillness and a feminine mysticism that is characterized by heightened emotions or sensory impressions, which go beyond normal experiences. Hadewijch from the Netherlands (ca. 1150–1200) could describe the meeting or union with Christ as an orgasm.[131] Other common metaphors had to do with death and eating.

Eating in particular was intimately connected to yet another important feature of feminine piety during the Middle Ages, namely communion. Communion was an occasion to meet the humanity of Christ through the wine and the bread, symbols for the embodiment of Christ and so for his humanity.[132] Receiving the elements of communion was an "eating" of the humanity of Christ, a clear symbol for union with him and the communion participants, through the incorporation of Christ into one's own body and vice versa. There were highly developed conceptions of how the communion meal involved a union with the crucified Christ. Metaphors for this ecstatic union occurred that looked towards both asceticism and disease, which were understood as participation in Christ's suffering, and towards marriage and sexual consummation—at times these two metaphorical fields were blended. The Eucharistic devotion was thus yet another element in the somatic quality of medieval piety. One quite simply venerated "the divine *in the material.*"[133]

129. Bynum, *Fragmentation and Redemption*, p. 186.
130. Bynum, *Fragmentation and Redemption*, p. 191.
131. Bynum, *Holy Feast and Holy Fast*, p. 156.
132. Bynum, *Fragmentation and Redemption*, pp. 129–34.
133. Bynum, *Fragmentation and Redemption*, p. 144.

Like Bynum, we can ask ourselves whether the medieval association of embodiment with the woman should be seen as an expression of dualism and misogyny.[134] Her answer is that even if there indisputably are such tendencies, the tradition here is not univocal. The connection between the woman as bodily and God's embodiment in Christ could obviously not be seen as something unequivocally negative. This alleged medieval dualism is in large part a projection of modern physiological theories onto a material that does not fit these categories. Conceptions of gender were more fluid and more social than biological in the Middle Ages. The same body could be both masculine and feminine and men could emphasize their humility by speaking of themselves as feminine: "[M]edieval thinkers used gender imagery fluidly, not literally."[135] This does not only concern conceptions of social gender—the conceptions of the gendered nature of the biological body were fluid as well. Finally, conceptions also existed for how God inverted these social roles: precisely because masculinity was, from the human perspective, superior, God chose the lower feminine body as his primary instrument. Bynum writes:

> If the Incarnation meant that the whole human person was capable of redemption, then what woman was seen as being—even in the most misogynist form of the Christian tradition—was caught up into God in Christ. And if the agony of the Crucifixion was less sacrifice or victory than the redemption of that which is human (matter joined to form), then the Crucifixion could be imaged as death or as eating or as orgasm (all especially human—bodily—experiences). Women mystics seem to have felt that they *qua* women were not only *also* but even *especially* saved in the Incarnation.[136]

Incarnation was thus the material key to the embodiment of both creation and salvation. The emphasis on the incarnation promoted the spiritual empowerment of women, rather than the opposite. From the late twelfth century until the middle of the fourteenth century women's options for participating in specialized religious practices increased.[137] The number of convents increased and women—so-called tertiaries or beguines—gathered

134. Bynum, *Fragmentation and Redemption*, pp. 200–222, 108–14, 146–50, 151–79.
135. Bynum, *Fragmentation and Redemption*, p. 218.
136. Bynum, *Fragmentation and Redemption*, p. 150.
137. Bynum, *Fragmentation and Redemption*, pp. 59–60, together with Bynum, *Holy Feast and Holy Fast*, pp. 16–30.

in more unofficial communities as well. I do not want to explain away the strong tendencies to misogyny that existed in the Middle Ages any more than Bynum.[138] What is desirable instead is in part a more nuanced picture and in part an indication as well that the picture did not necessarily look the same from a female perspective as it did from the perspective of the male elite.

High medieval theology and piety emphasized the unity between body and soul more than the difference.[139] Even if one began with a (for that time) obvious dualism between body and soul, it was simultaneously obvious that a person really *is* her body. Thomas Aquinas (ca. 1225–1274), who is known in his time for, inspired by Aristotle, having launched a theory of the person as a psychosomatic whole, was far from the only one who emphasized this wholeness and unity. Even his opponents, who were more inspired by Plato, did so. Bynum says that those who followed a more Platonic, Augustinian, or Franciscan tradition than Thomas perhaps attributed the body even greater significance than he did. While Thomas advocated his Aristotelian-inspired hylomorphic doctrine of the soul as the form of the body, his opponents claimed that the body had its own form (i.e., that the soul was not the form of the body), and was thus more self-sufficient than Thomas's teaching allowed.[140] In other words, it is inaccurate to imagine that the Middle Ages were characterized by a pervasive contempt for the body: "[N]o other period in the history of Christianity has placed so positive (and therefore so complex and ambiguous) a value on the bodiliness of Christ's humanity."[141] But what then did the medieval authors mean by the body? Bynum has pointed out that the medieval conceptions of the body have more to do with fecundity and decay than with sexuality.[142] The ascetics, who also characterize the medieval relationship to the body, are not so much about contempt for the body, but about a—for modern sensibilities rather grotesque—elevation of the body as a means or instrument for communicating with God.[143] In other

138. Bynum, *Holy Feast and Holy Fast,* pp. 216–18.

139. Bynum, *Fragmentation and Redemption,* pp. 222–35. Cf. as well Bynum, *The Resurrection of the Body,* pp. 135–37.

140. Bynum, *The Resurrection of the Body,* pp. 271–76, together with Bynum, *Fragmentation and Redemption,* pp. 228–29. On Thomas's teaching on the body, see John Milbank and Catherine Pickstock, *Truth in Aquinas* (Oxford: Blackwell, 2001).

141. Bynum, *Holy Feast and Holy Fast,* p. 252.

142. For Bynum's opinions on the medieval view of embodiment and sexuality, see *Fragmentation and Redemption,* pp. 85–88.

143. Bynum, *Fragmentation and Redemption,* pp. 182, 194–95. On the iconography of the medieval body, see Lena Liepe, *Den medeltida kroppen: Kroppens och könets ikonografi i nordisk medeltid* (Lund: Nordic Academic Press, 2003).

words, the body had a particularly important role simply in the fact that it was through it, according to many mystics, that one related to God. How then should one understand this bodily relationship to the divine?

In the feminine mysticism of the passion of, for example, Hadewijch and Angela of Foligno (ca. 1248–1309) we can find a clear return to an earlier tradition where the process of knowledge and the constitution of the self were understood as dependent on incorporation into the body of Christ. The deepest fulfillment of the mystical drama can take place through the most bodily participation in a concrete historical event, namely, Jesus' suffering, death, and resurrection. For Julian of Norwich embodiment itself is a medium for communication and fellowship. Theologian Mark A. McIntosh expresses it thus:

> My suggestion is that *the bodily language of Christ's passion becomes the communicative medium in which divine meaning and human knowing are able to converse.* So bodies, as [Herbert] McCabe points out, are not "atomic units" but are intrinsically *communal* events of converse, of language and communion, and this means that bodily knowing in mystical theology is an inherently public and communal form of theological speech.[144]

The body that can be a medium for communication is not the physical body we are born with, but what I called the phenomenal body in connection with the discussion of Merleau-Ponty, i.e., the body that reaches out through linguistic media. The knowledge that comes from Jesus' embodiment is not a matter of being imprisoned in a world of physical sensations, but about these sensations constituting the structures of a new creation. This is a crucial dimension of a mystical theology, since it is a knowledge of the utmost mystery of God expressed in the flesh. Through the fact that Jesus' physical body reaches out in the phenomenal body, a new way of speaking and existing is created in the ecclesial body.[145] Mystical theology is therefore not a private and "spiritual" drama, but in the highest degree a public and bodily one.

144. Mark A. McIntosh, *Mystical Theology: The Integrity of Spirituality and Theology,* Challenges in Contemporary Theology (Oxford/Malden, MA: Blackwell, 1998), p. 79. Partial italics in the original. McIntosh refers to Herbert McCabe's article "Transubstantiation and the Real Presence," in *God Matters,* Contemporary Christian Insights (London/New York: Mowbray, 2000), p. 121.

145. McIntosh, *Mystical Theology,* p. 82.

A Public Body?

The examples of bodily practices I have chosen to illustrate the conception of the embodiment of the person, asceticism and mysticism, show that for the Christians of Antiquity and the Middle Ages the body was in the highest degree involved in the drama of salvation, and not only in a negative way. The body was embedded in a greater drama. From the start of the Christian church, Christians said that when praying one should stand up and turn to the east, where the sun rose and where they waited for Messiah to come.[146] This custom of standing up at prayer on Sundays and Easter received canonical authority at the council in Nicea in 325. The positioning of the body in a certain way and its orientation in a certain direction is a practical expression of the cosmic significance of the body and of the cosmic import of the coming redemption.

Something of the cosmic significance of the body apparently disappeared with Augustine, since he regarded the position of the body at prayer as less interesting, nor did he see the body as a microcosm. For Augustine, the most important journey was inward.[147] It was, however, not until the twelfth century that Augustine's opinions came to have much significance for the cosmic understanding of space and time. At that time the change in the understanding of the church occurs that I have spoken of above, and the idea of a "holy space" disappears.[148] The body is "liberated" from space and time and becomes instead—in a more Augustinian way—an outer expression of the interior of the human being, as with female mysticism and in the emphasis on the humanity of Christ that is found in Francis of Assisi (see chapter 6). From having seen the individual body as a microcosm that reflects the greater cosmos, the understanding of the body is changed in the Middle Ages to be an external interpretation of the interior of the person. The body quite simply loses its cosmic significance, which, however, does not mean that it is individualized and objectified in a modern way.

The emergent celebration of Corpus Christi during the High and Late Middle Ages is one example of the way in which the Eucharistic devotion had collective features.[149] This period shows an accentuated awareness of the

---

146. Louth, "The Body," pp. 113–14.

147. Louth, "The Body," pp. 118–20. Cf. what I have written on Augustine in *Kärlekens skillnad: Att gestalta kristen tro i vår tid* (Stockholm: Verbum, 1998), pp. 24–27.

148. Louth, "The Body," pp. 124–27.

149. Cf. Miri Rubin, *Corpus Christi,* together with Caroline Walker Bynum, "Did the Twelfth Century Discover the Individual?" in *Jesus as Mother: Studies in the Spirituality of the*

meaning of the collective, but also of the fact that within that social collective there exists a space for different, complementary roles. Bynum says that the twelfth century's movement inwards goes hand in hand with a feeling of group affiliation. The collective was necessary both in order to provide models for how life should be lived, and for salvation itself. She writes:

> A new sense of self, of inner change and inner choice, is precipitated by the necessity to choose among roles, among groups. A new sense of be- coming part of a group by conforming one's behavior to an external stan- dard is necessitated by a new awareness of choosing and interior self.[150]

According to Bynum the twelfth century is thus not the beginning of the individualization process that culminates in modernity, but on the contrary, the twelfth century was a century characterized by a flowering of new groups and communities for the exercise of piety. It was not until the Fourth Lateran Council that this development slowed, if not completely. It is not until then that individual experience breaks loose from or undermines the religious communities. This is, however, a slow and gradual development. Nor did the theologians of the early Reformation give up the individual and the social body, even if the emerging national states and the budding capitalistic eco- nomic system increasingly enlisted individual bodies for a different societal body.[151] The relative autonomy that was emphasized by the twelfth century was thus not automatically a competitor with the idea of a communal body.

Through the centuries the bodies of Christians have been embedded in different sorts of social bodies via different bodily practices. Asceticism, mysticism, and other bodily practices that I have not discussed here have been different ways to transform the individual body and to relate to the various social bodies that fight for dominion over these individual bodies.

High Middle Ages (Berkeley/Los Angeles/London: University of California Press, 1982), pp. 82–109.

150. Bynum, "Individual," p. 107.

151. Cf. David Tripp, "The Image of the Body in the Formative Phases of the Protestant Reformation," in *Religion and the Body,* ed. Coakley, pp. 131–52. Lisa Isherwood and Elizabeth Stuart write the following in *Introducing Body Theology,* Introductions in Feminist Theology 2 (Sheffield: Sheffield Academic Press, 1998), p. 12: "The Reformation encouraged people to experience their minds as separate from and superior to their bodies which in turn led to an individualistic view of life." Generalizing statements of this sort on the disembodiment of Protestantism are, however, grossly misleading. The question is rather which body, or which bodies Protestantism can fashion.

These practices may be described as the sort of habituation of bodies that Bourdieu speaks of, and as the origin of a certain way of experiencing the world. Rather than describe these practices as an expression of contempt for the body, it is more appropriate to speak of them as an effort to experience the world in a certain way, and so to break with other ways of experiencing it. I have paid attention to these bodily practices here, not to present them as normative for our contemporary church to imitate, but to show how these practices had a *different* (and perhaps for us alien) focus than the sort of contempt for the body that follows from a substance dualism. In the following two chapters I will return to several of the themes—among others, sexuality and pain—that have been brought to the fore here, but now from a more constructive theological perspective. I have also wanted to more generally illuminate how the Christian church has resulted in the understanding that the social and the individual body belong together by discussing asceticism and mysticism. The next section will focus on this affinity.

The Ascetic Body

"Asceticism" might be said to be a rubric for Christian embodiment in general, in the sense that it clearly articulates how Christian bodies are shaped by collective practices within the framework of the Christian sociality that is called the church. Asceticism should then not be understood as a contempt for the body or a way to become independent of the body, but as the way through which the Christian church shapes embodiment and thereby inserts these bodies into the communal drama of salvation. Asceticism is in this respect not exclusively the reserve of the Christian church. In a certain sense one might say that every social institution includes its own asceticism or its techniques of subjectivization. As literary scholar Geoffrey Galt Harpham writes: "In the tight sense asceticism is a product of early Christian ethics and spirituality; in the loose sense it refers to any act of self-denial undertaken as a strategy of empowerment or gratification."[152] Asceticism trains Christian bodies in how they should behave in the battle between good and evil, and what it is that constitutes the uttermost horizon of their embodiment. In the Christian church asceticism is in this sense intimately associated with the liturgy as the mediator of the relationship between the

---

152. Cf. Geoffrey Galt Harpham, *The Ascetical Imperative in Culture and Criticism* (Chicago: University of Chicago Press, 1987), p. xiii.

social and more personal dimensions of the body. Asceticism thus becomes a practice by which the individual creates and finds meaning in relation to the church as both a social and symbolic community. As I wrote in chapter 7, rites are not simply an expression of certain beliefs that exist prior to and independent of these rites, but they are also a formative practice in which beliefs are created, and so thought and practice come to be mutually dependent on each other.[153]

In this section I will summarize what I have given an account of above first by briefly illustrating the transformation of the body that is the goal of these ascetic practices in the Christian church. Then, with several examples from various Christian traditions, I show how such ascetic practices have been formed. Finally, I give several more general features of this "intertwining" of social and individual bodies. This theme has been treated in part in chapter 7 in my discussion of the liturgical gaze.

The Transformed Body

Common to the Christian bodily practices I have described above is the fact that they not only constitute a mediation between the individual and the social body, but they have also wanted to bring about some form of transformation of the body in order to be liberated from "the flesh" in the Pauline sense. The Christian body is not a finished body, but neither is its development aimless; it has a "bearing" that is a consequence of the Christian eschatological hope, namely, to realize in a pervasive way the human quality of being made in the image of God.[154] In their accounts of the political body several of the poststructuralist philosophers that have written about the body also seem to implicitly gesture towards some form of eschatological hope, or at least to a hope that transcends the boundaries of discursive and institutional practices. This hope becomes a motive for change or transformation. Nor is it a matter for Foucault, Bordo, Butler, Weiss, or Sennett in the previous chapter of merely stating how our bodies are formed by institutions, but it is also a matter of some form of liberation, some form of movement from an oppressive to a more emancipatory or less reductive attitude towards the body. In the transcorporeal process that bodies are embedded in, it is a

153. Catherine Bell, *Ritual Theory, Ritual Practice* (New York/Oxford: Oxford University Press, 1992), pp. 25–35. Cf. pp. 48–49.

154. Cf. de Lubac, *Catholicism*, pp. 351–66.

matter of forming a productive economy where the body does not simply remain a docile body. In other words, these authors seem to have some conception of a horizon or a bearing that saves their philosophies of the body from simply reinforcing the status quo. Sarah Coakley has made a similar point in her comparison of Judith Butler and Gregory of Nyssa.[155] The choice of Gregory of Nyssa is based on the fact that as early as the fourth century he said that the existing order of social gender was not something given by God, but something fluid and changeable, which involves continual changes in role on the person's path towards God. The social gender of one and the same person is thus mutable, and changes in role are invited.

According to Coakley there is a hidden eschatological longing in the preoccupation with the body in contemporary culture and philosophy. Butler's account is certainly resolutely secular, and often deeply pessimistic regarding the possibility for change, but at the same time there is an echo of theological conceptions in her account of the performativity of the body and of fluid social genders. With the help of an alternative practice Butler wants to transform the body and shape its future by pursuing the possibilities of the future here and now in a way that recalls ascetic practices, whose goal is also the transformation of the body into its divine *telos*. Both Butler and Gregory want to transcend the (in their respective cultures) prevalent stereotypical gender order, which implies an orientation in Butler towards an as-yet undefined goal. Both hope and opposition become possible through an asceticism. In other words, Coakley writes, Butler seems to gesture

> to an eschatological horizon which will give mortal flesh final significance, a horizon in which the restless, fluid post-modern "body" can find some sense of completion without losing its mystery, without succumbing again to "appropriate" or restrictive gender roles.[156]

Coakley seems to argue that some sort of eschatological horizon is necessary in order to maintain the possibility of hope as well as opposition. In Butler's case it is a matter of establishing an alternative practice, where the body is able to oppose the heteronormativity that characterizes the prevalent gender order.

155. Sarah Coakley, "The Eschatological Body: Gender, Transformation and God," in *Powers and Submissions: Spirituality, Philosophy and Gender,* Challenges in Contemporary Theology (Oxford: Blackwell, 2002), pp. 153–67.

156. Coakley, "The Eschatological Body," p. 166.

As mentioned above, in chapter 7 I had already gotten into the significance of rites and liturgy for human sight, and showed then how rites shape the way we see and thereby shape the person's spatial understanding and relationship to the rest of the environment. Here I will again turn to the question of rites and liturgy, but now I will instead focus on the question of the constitution and construction of the body in liturgy and rites, and then above all on how the rites become mediators between individual body and social body. This issue is brought to the fore not least with Judith Butler's "performative bodies," i.e., the idea that the sexuality and materiality of the body are produced by ritual repetitions that, precisely through their repetition, give rise to the idea of a stable, "natural" sexuality and materiality. The connection between a performative body and a ritual, or even a liturgical, body cannot be an odd thought; just as the sexuality and materiality of the body are produced by ritual repetitions, so can these repetitions produce a stable religiosity and sociality. What I want to clarify in this final section of this chapter is that the ritual repetitions that produce a particular bodily sexuality, materiality, religiosity, or sociality find their context in one or another particular tradition. In other words, every individual body is dependent for its very embodiment on the specific *corpus mysticum*—if the term will for the moment allow itself to be used in a very wide sense—that it exists within. This can in principle be a Christian church, a Jewish synagogue, a Muslim mosque, a Buddhist temple, or a secular mall, but all of them constitute some sort of *corpus mysticum* with a certain set of rituals both for entering into this community and for maintaining the community. However, in accordance with my purpose here, I will take my examples from different Christian traditions.

The Liturgical Construction of the Body

According to one definition, rituals may be described as conscious and voluntary repetitions of stylized symbolic bodily actions that bind the person together with cosmic structures and the presence of the holy.[157] Through rituals people can transcend their own individual selves and become participatory in a greater community, and also train their body in experiencing the world religiously. To change terminology somewhat, one can say that it

---

157. Evan M. Zuesse, "Ritual," in *The Encyclopedia of Religion,* vol. 12, ed. Mircea Eliade (New York: Macmillan, 1987), pp. 405–22.

is through rituals—understood in a broad sense—that the person's body is extended to linguistically encompass more than the purely physical body. From such a definition one may get the impression that the body, in spite of everything, in some sense exists prior to all rites, but I understand the definition instead as the fact that the body is shaped as body precisely through these rites. It is first through these that time and space receive a form that makes the experience of the world possible at all.[158] This does not mean that a person must experience the world in a religious way, but only, as I wrote apropos Merleau-Ponty and others in the previous chapter, that the person's understanding of time and space is primarily existentially anchored and ritually mediated. A newborn baby is habituated from the start through certain schematically given bodily actions that it internalizes and by which it becomes participatory in a specific human community, which cultivates certain dispositions with regard to behavior and understandings of the world.

The relationship between the person's embodiment and her ritual life becomes clear in the history of the Christian church, and I will take several examples from different traditions in order to clarify the relationship between body and liturgy. One example from history is Ephrem the Syrian (304–373), who understood the body as the context for how we come to know God and what we can come to know about God.[159] For Ephrem bodily experiences and expressions are epistemological tools, not only here and now, but also in eternal life. Apart from an epistemological role, the body also played an existential and an experiential role. The body is the place for God's revelation and for the battle against the powers of destruction, and it is additionally the medium through which the person expresses her relationship to God. For Ephrem it is essential that the body is not a medium that allows a distanced relationship to what it experiences. The person cannot distance herself through the senses from that which she experiences, in the way that she can through the intellect. Since we cannot get to know God by separating ourselves from God or by treating God as an object for our study, the body becomes the primary epistemological medium through which we get to know God. The body mediates a relational, rather than an objectified knowledge (cf. the discussion of the erotic gaze in chapter 7 and the erotic body in the next chapter).

---

158. Zuesse, "Ritual," pp. 406–9.

159. Susan A. Harvey, "Embodiment in Time and Eternity: A Syriac Perspective," in *Theology and Sexuality: Classic and Contemporary Readings,* Blackwell Readings in Modern Theology, ed. Eugene F. Rogers Jr. (Malden, MA/Oxford: Blackwell, 2002), pp. 3–22.

Early Syrian Christianity had a clear sense for the physical. The person is body and soul, and none of its constituent parts have any meaning without the others. The body was what God created in the beginning, and the body is the place in which the person exists after the Fall, and so God dealt with the person through the incarnation. The body is thus embedded in the cosmic drama where God works to restore and transform the human being's life in its wholeness. The ascetic life is therefore not a rejection of the body as such, but of a world that does not live up to God's original intention. Susan A. Harvey writes:

> The body is the place in which salvation happens and the instrument by which it is done. The body is more than the physicality of our existence; it provides the activity, or external expression, by which the salvific process takes place. Bodily acts express the believer's interior condition even as they display the living image of the body, individual and collective, redeemed.[160]

The body of the ascetic is thus a microcosm of the ecclesial body, the body that will be restored and transformed, but which is also the ground for God's battle with evil. In the extension of the central meaning of the body for our relationship to God, we accordingly find that bodily exercises and sacraments also become central for knowledge of God in a way that neither nature nor scripture (as different media for God's revelation) is capable of being. In other words, for Ephrem the body is constructed liturgically; it becomes a place for prayer and thanksgiving.

Another, contemporary example may be taken from Greek Orthodox Christianity. According to the Greek Orthodox theologian Kallistos Ware, it is the body of the Eucharist (communion) that is the mediator between the church, that is to say the ecclesial body, and the solitary believer's individual body. Without the Eucharist the church would merely be an external organization, but through the Eucharist it becomes clear that the church is a living and embodied organism.[161] This also becomes clear through the fact that the church, in Ware's understanding, does not primarily consist of theological doctrines of one sort or another, but of liturgy. The body becomes directly participatory through the liturgical actions. Ware counts

160. Harvey, "Embodiment," p. 10.
161. Kallistos Ware, "'My Helper and My Enemy': The Body in Greek Christianity," in *Religion and the Body*, ed. Coakley, p. 94.

eight different Greek Orthodox liturgical actions that weave into the person's embodiment in the Christian drama: (1) symbolic actions such as turning to face the east when one prays and making the sign of the cross; (2) fasting and sexual abstinence during certain periods; (3) the two main sacraments of baptism and communion; (4) anointing the body with oil; (5) laying on of hands at ordination and confession; (6) open casket and parting kiss at burials; (7) marriage; (8) solitary prayer (which, however, does not really belong to the liturgy).[162] Private prayer need not be only a mental, quiet prayer, but can often be accompanied by three physical aspects: proper posture, proper breathing, and seeking after "the heart" in the right way. After having counted up the first five liturgical actions, Ware additionally points out that they involve all five of the human being's senses, not just hearing and sight. Taste is actualized in communion, the sense of touch by the laying on of hands, anointing, and kissing, together with the smell of the oil and the incense.

Even if other denominations have a liturgy that differs in part from the Syrian or the Greek Orthodox, there is something universal in these descriptions that embraces the liturgies of most denominations. Different liturgies may be more or less stimulating for the senses, but all of them in one way or another actualize the body's participation in the Christian drama that they attempt to express. A ritual is not simply an expression, but also a way to both incorporate a representation of the body and to shape the body in a certain way. These descriptions of the liturgically constructed body within Syrian and Greek Orthodox Christianity show that conceptions of the body within a tradition are not only or primarily mediated through a theoretical discourse, but through concrete practices. It also shows that individual and social embodiment go intimately together. One objection to my assertions here might be that they are based on examples from historical theologians or specific denominations, such as the Orthodox. However, I would argue that the liturgical construction of the body is just as present in our time, if less thematized. Within the Lutheran tradition the word and the sermon have been emphasized as the foremost media of God's divine presence, and in the modern period social embodiment—and thereby the relationship between the social and the individual body—has disappeared from view. Within liturgical scholarship, however, one studies the liturgy's music, drama, aesthetics, homiletics, gesticulation, mimicry, kinetics, proxemics (i.e., the study of the person's perception and use of spatiality), etc., and so there exists

162. Ware, "'My Helper and My Enemy,'" pp. 102–7.

within liturgical scholarship a well-developed understanding of how the liturgy not only speaks to human consciousness, but engages the whole body with all its senses.[163] The reason that I have chosen Ephrem and the Greek Orthodox church as my examples is that these clarify an understanding of the relationship between social and individual body that the Protestant church has in many cases come to obscure, an understanding that, however, is also highlighted by several philosophers in our present period.

From a theological perspective it can be easy to fall into a theoretical approach to how the Christian faith is mediated. But the question is whether these bodily practices are not at least as significant for the Christian life. In accordance with such reasoning the German theologian Alex Stock has written a "poetic dogmatics," which is an attempt to expound a Christology not only with the help of traditional conceptual theology, but also with the help of liturgies, catechisms, devotions, sermons, images, and other cultural media. In volume 3 of *Poetische Dogmatik* it is therefore a matter of Jesus' "Leib und Leben," i.e., of the "mysteries" of Jesus' life.[164] Stock divides up these mysteries into eight chapters that treat the annunciation, the birth, the passion, Easter, the ascension, Corpus Christi, the heart of Jesus, and the transfiguration. These mysteries have played a large role during the liturgical year, and meditations on these themes have played a large role for religious culture, but—unfortunately, according to Stock—they have seldom been used in recent times as a source for more conceptually minded theology. In a time that is so interested in the body, as the contemporary discussion within cultural scholarship and cultural philosophy shows, it is remarkable that theology is involved to such a limited degree in this discussion, given that theology is in fact based on a religion that has the incarnation at its heart—but Stock wants to remedy this. The general insight that Stock articulates is that what is primary for the representation of the body and the shaping of the body within the Christian tradition cannot be identified with a specific conceptual formulation of a doctrine of the body in the writings of one theologian or another. Conceptions of the body are bodily mediated, in that images, music, sermons, devotions, etc., mediate a certain way of being in the world, a concrete bodily posture that one rehearses by participating in these practices.

---

163. Cf., for example, Aidan Kavanagh, *On Liturgical Theology* (Collegeville, MN: Liturgical Press, 1992), together with Frank C. Senn, *Christian Liturgy: Catholic and Evangelical* (Minneapolis: Fortress Press, 1997).

164. Alex Stock, *Poetische Dogmatik: Christologie: 3. Leib und Leben* (Paderborn/Munich/Vienna/Zürich: Schöningh, 1998), pp. 12–16.

The liturgy or the rite is thus not about a unilaterally cognitive process, as though it functioned by mediating a particular ideational content in as pedagogical and illustrative a way as possible. The liturgy is itself a communication, and what it communicates is instead a specific (if not entirely deterministic) way of being in the world. The prominent scholar of liturgy Aidan Kavanagh connects the liturgy to the incarnation, and says that since "God's most complete self-revelation was neither in words nor in print, but amid a people and in the flesh"—he is referring here to the incarnation in Christ—neither should God's self-revelation in the liturgy be reduced to word and text.[165] The liturgy does not primarily communicate something *about* God, but is a communion *with* God himself. It is thus impossible to pull a cognitive core out of the shell of concrete liturgical practice without transforming the meaning of the liturgy from fellowship with God to instruction. Liturgy as an act of communication is both a verbal and a nonverbal action. Or, to reiterate Jean-Yves Lacoste's definition from chapter 7, the liturgy is a name for everything that embodies the person's relationship to God.[166]

Intertwined Bodies

The understanding of the practical mediation of embodiment and sociality, as well as knowledge and the relationship to the divine, such as it is found in certain theologians from liturgically self-aware Christian traditions, has resulted in sociologists, anthropologists, scholars of rite, and others attempting to generalize this knowledge. Here the sociologist Paul Connerton has provided an important contribution in the book *How Societies Remember.* Connerton argues there that social collectives also have a sort of "memory," in that knowledge and conceptions of the past are mediated and maintained by rituals, and so by embodied practices.[167] Historical revelation is mediated to coming generations through various such rituals, for example through the sign of the cross: "The fact of the crucifixion is symbolized in each sign of the cross: itself a condensed commemoration, a narrative made flesh, an evocation of the central historical fact and the central religious belief

---

165. Kavanagh, *On Liturgical Theology,* p. 112.

166. Jean-Yves Lacoste, *Experience and the Absolute: Disputed Questions on the Humanity of Man,* Perspectives in Continental Philosophy, trans. Mark Raftery-Skehan (New York: Fordham University Press, 2004), pp. 2, 26–27.

167. Paul Connerton, *How Societies Remember* (Cambridge: Cambridge University Press, 1989).

of Christianity."[168] But the ritual is not simply a contingent medium for a historically "necessary" knowledge, and neither can it be reduced from a bodily practice to a linguistic meaning. The ritual can, in the religious case, in itself be the way through which a revelation expresses itself, the way in which one imagines that God's action of salvation makes itself present in history. Thus the Christian liturgy is not a communication of certain statements about God, but a communication of God's presence. Certain rituals, for example the sign of the cross or communion, do not only point back to a historical event, the crucifixion of Jesus, but make this historical event contemporary with the time and place in which the rite is performed. Connerton speaks of a "ritual *re-enactment*," "a fresh incarnation of the traditional" or a "mythical identification."[169] Even if this is a feature that can feel foreign in the modern period, with its emphasis on the unique status of the individual or the repetition of the statistically typical, it is still alive in public and semi-public ceremonies: the Olympics, the World Cup Finals, National Days, Royal Jubilees, etc. For the most part, however, these modern rites are deeply nostalgic, and emphasize formal, unchanging features even more than historical rites. They function as a compensation in that they attempt to hide the fact that a "mystical identification" is impossible for a society whose economic logic invariably emphasizes the new and hitherto never seen or heard, Connerton says.

If we go back to the historical rites, they additionally create, according to Connerton, a solidarity among those who perform them through the use of particular verbs and pronouns.[170] The liturgical "we" and "us" have a performative power in that they "create" the collective that they simultaneously intend. Additionally, in the liturgy individual bodies are "positioned" in relation to other bodies and in relation to the social body, and thereby find their relationship to the environment, their "choreographic instructions"; with this a life-world is mediated to the participants in these rites, a life-world consisting of both space and time.[171] To take an example that deals with proxemics, i.e., spatial perception, Connerton says that the orientation upwards, against gravity, establishes a spatial base for our values, which we express via binary pairs like "high" and "low," "to rise" and "to fall," "superior" and "inferior," "to look down at" and "to look up to." Thus we find in our human,

168. Connerton, *How Societies Remember*, p. 47.
169. Connerton, *How Societies Remember*, pp. 61, 63.
170. Connerton, *How Societies Remember*, p. 58.
171. Connerton, *How Societies Remember*, pp. 59, 73–74.

embodied, social existence the metaphors by which we think, assess, and live. When it comes to time, the past is reiterated and thereby made present through embodied rites.

A relatively thorough differentiation is of course needed between which rites are central and which are more peripheral, how formal or informal they are, etc. Liturgical rites and religious acts do not exist independent of the other rites that shape a society, but do not have any immediate religious purpose. In other words, meaning is not something that is constituted by the liturgical act in itself, but occurs instead in relationship to the surrounding society. This is perhaps especially relevant in late- or postmodern, Western, pluralistic society (see chapter 7).[172] This does not, however, limit the scope of the thesis of how bodies are incorporated into a life-world via rituals. Every social group, Connerton says, passes down its most central values and categories through rituals that are often so obvious that they are not viewed critically. Through these rituals "a habitual memory sedimented in the body" is created, which means that the social body is woven together with the individual.[173]

The consequences of this are, as I understand it, at least two. Firstly, the incorporation of the body into a life-world through ritual means that it is the ritual that binds the social body to the individual body. To link to Bourdieu in the previous chapter, we can say that the rite stands for the habituation that is the link between institution and subjectivity. Secondly, and more far-reaching, it is the case that rituals thereby, in a sense, "create" the individual body, since these rites exist right at the start of a human life. The individual, human body is, in a broad sense, never without a social body. It can of course be without a specific social body—not all bodies, sociologically understood, are parts of the Christian church—and it can exist at the intersection or overlap between two or more rival or complementary social bodies, for example, between the Christian church and modern society. But the individual body never exists without some sort of social body. Even modern or postmodern society has its rites that bind social and individual body to each other, even if these may not be designated as "rites," or are so universal that they are understood as "natural" to the human body. The conception of a bodily *habitus* helps us conceive of the person's body as "an assemblage of

---

172. See Graham Hughes, *Worship as Meaning: A Liturgical Theology for Late Modernity*, Cambridge Studies in Christian Doctrine (Cambridge: Cambridge University Press, 2003), p. 233. Cf. pp. 220–54.

173. Connerton, *How Societies Remember*, p. 102.

embodied aptitudes."[174] The question is thus not whether a "naturally given body" can take on cultural meaning, but how the body is formed and how its competence is developed through ritualized patterns of action. The body's meaning is produced, one might say, in the interaction between its physical constitution and its linguisticality and sociality (cf. again Bourdieu's concept of the *habitus*). Such a process is not something that occurs "after" its physical constitution, but the physical body is always already involved in such a process. The body is constituted precisely through this formative process in various practices, and this is especially relevant, as with Mauss or Bourdieu, in religious practices. Here liturgies and other bodily practices function as a mediation between individual and social bodies.

But perhaps the choice of the word "mediate" is not so appropriate in this context. The word seems to denote two independently existing entities. Is it better to speak of "merging," or even of "extracting"? Every word one chooses carries its own problems. Better to say something of how I imagine a "mediation" between bodies in this case. How one understands the mediation of bodies depends on how one understands these bodies: as "classical bodies" with exactly defined boundaries, or as "grotesque bodies" that are not closed. A mediation of "classical bodies" with each other and with the social body through rites is certainly imaginable, but can be compared to drawing a line between two closed circles. If we instead imagine bodies as grotesque, the individual bodies become more like individual nodes in a field linked by rites. On the basis of this understanding of the body, both the individual and the social, as outlined in this and in the previous chapter, the second description is more appropriate, not only from a theological perspective, but also from a phenomenological and anthropological perspective. The classical body, which is also the modern body, more resembles a fiction.

Rites have to do with how the phenomenal body, as Merleau-Ponty puts it, is constituted. The extent of the phenomenal body is namely not only linguistic, but also ritualistic. For the medieval mystic, Jesus' physical body reaches out linguistically in the social body. But this extension of Jesus' physical body is not only linguistic, but also ritualistic, which is especially shown in the Eucharistic devotion, so central for the female medieval mystics. Through the rituals of communion individual bodies are choreographed and thus woven together into a greater social body, namely the ecclesial body. The individual body thereby becomes in the highest degree a medium

---

174. Talal Asad, "Remarks on the Anthropology of the Body," in *Religion and the Body,* ed. Coakley, p. 47.

for communicating with God. It is thus not only words, but also images and bodily actions that articulate what Christians mean by "God."[175]

Now it is certainly the case that the social body looks different depending on whether we are speaking of an *ekklēsia* of the ancient church with roots in the Jewish synagogue, or the medieval *corpus mysticum,* a Lutheran national church, a congregation of believers of the free church, or the postmodern panopticon state, but what they all have in common is that they organize individual bodies through a sort of habituation. This organizing and choreographing of bodies is not necessarily something that happens through one and only one social body. Nor can it be said to be ethically and politically neutral. One can very well imagine that different social bodies irrupt into each other in a more or less violent way. My argumentation does not have to do—so far—with how a specific embodiment and a specific penetration look or ought to look, but is instead an attempt to establish at a more general level a theologically informed theory of how the constitution and construction of the body in liturgy, as well as the relationship between the individual body and the social body, come about. At the same time the above perspective on embodiment already entails certain criteria for a fruitful theology of the body, namely that its thematization must be tripartite: the individual body, the social body, and the liturgical mediation between them. If we start from the individualized understanding of Christian "faith" that is widespread today, a theology of the body that wants to be critically aware of ideology must account for the social and liturgical aspects of the person's embodiment— this requirement does not follow only from the historical perspectives on Christian embodiment, but also from the more philosophical argument I pursued in the previous chapter.

Finally, some words on the choice of bodily practices and theologies of the body taken from different ancient and medieval Christian traditions. The choice of these was not conditioned by any notion that we can in an unmediated way find in them an answer to the question of a contemporary theology of the body. However, I hold with Caroline Walker Bynum, who writes the following in her book on the significance of power in the Middle Ages: "If their images and values cannot become our answers, they can nonetheless teach us that we need richer images and values. Perhaps they

---

175. Anna Marie Aagaard, *Identifikation af kirken* (Frederiksberg, Denmark: Anis, 1991), p. 244, together with John Milbank, "Postmodern Critical Augustinianism: A Short *Summa* in Forty-two Responses to Unasked Questions," in *The Postmodern God,* ed. Graham Ward (Malden, MA/Oxford: Blackwell, 1997), p. 269.

can point the direction in which we should search."[176] Formulated in another way: the Christians of Antiquity and the Middle Ages lived in a time where the body was not displaced in the same way as in our period, but was instead understood as a medium for communication and fellowship. They can, like Merleau-Ponty, help us open our eyes for a richer understanding of our own embodiment by posing questions to us that are not those we would typically pose to ourselves on the basis of our own cultural horizon and our period's conceptions of the body. This will be my task in the two following chapters, where I will investigate the erotic and the grotesque body from a more systematic-theological perspective.

176. Bynum, *Holy Feast and Holy Fast,* p. 302.

10. The Erotic Body

When Friedrich Nietzsche writes in *Beyond Good and Evil* that "Christianity gave Eros poison to drink:—he did not die from it, but degenerated into a vice," one may ask oneself what he means and whether it is in fact true.[1] Could Christianity in Antiquity have caused *eros (erōs)* to become sick? To contend that the Christian church has had an ambivalent attitude towards human sexuality throughout history is hardly to overstate things, as has already become clear in the account of asceticism and sexuality that I undertook in the previous chapter. On the other hand, *eros* has continually been a central theme, an inheritance whose management by the church one can certainly dispute, as with Nietzsche, but whose presence is impossible to deny. It is not until more recent centuries that theological *eros*-love has fallen into disrepute. This has in part been a consequence of the fact that *eros* has come to be identified with sexuality in modern speech, in particular intercourse. For Augustine, Gregory of Nyssa, and others from the classical Christian tradition, *eros,* or its Latin equivalent *amor,* stood for love of God. A theological erotics was thus high on the theological agenda even with those theologians that had little use for sexual intercourse. In contrast, one can compare the often very negative attitude of modern theology—especially Protestant—towards *eros.* I have already dealt with Anders Nygren's attempt to completely separate *eros* and *agape (agapē)* in chapter 7, and his Swiss colleague Karl Barth can, despite several attempts to integrate *eros* into theology, drop comments about "sexual *eros*" as a "dangerous demon."[2] A

1. Friedrich Nietzsche, *Beyond Good and Evil,* Cambridge Texts in the History of Philosophy, ed. Rolf-Peter Horstmann and Judith Norman, trans. Judith Norman (Cambridge: Cambridge University Press, 2002), p. 72 (§168).
2. Karl Barth, *Church Dogmatics,* vol. 3: *The Doctrine of Creation,* part 1, trans. J. W. Edwards, O. Bussey, and Harold Knight (Edinburgh: T. & T. Clark, 1958), p. 314.

contributing reason for the problematic relationship of modern Protestant theology to the concept of *eros* is perhaps that it has come to be associated with human sexuality in a new way. Namely, between Augustine and Barth a critical historical change occurs in the points of contact between *eros* and sexual intercourse, a change that had theological consequences.

Through the emergence of a *scientia sexualis* in the seventeenth century, the development of medical science, and not least the widespread sexualization of Western society during the twentieth century, *eros* and sexuality have come to be identified with each other.[3] The year 1789 is also symbolic for the birth of sexuality in form and concept.[4] It was then that the Christian worldview was symbolically buried and capitalism was born. Sexuality in the modern period came to be secularized in the sense that the person's sexual intercourse came to detached from its connection to her religion. A quotation from historian Thomas W. Laqueur summarizes this development:

> [P]hysicians of the body, in their various ranks and strata from the eighteenth through the twentieth century, increasingly took on the mantle of earlier physicians of the soul; they welcomed every opportunity to become arbiters of morality and good order. As the authority of divine revelation became less convincing and that of nature ever more so, doctors became its voice.[5]

The secularization of the person's sexual intercourse, as Laqueur stresses, did not mean that it was simultaneously demoralized. On the contrary, one might say that medical science and its new form of knowing was at least as interested as the Christian tradition in setting up moral norms for sexual acts. Nor did secularization mean that the various religions, including Christianity, ceased to have opinions about the person's sexual acts, but with the development of a specialized knowledge of these acts—a specific knowledge of sexuality—the moral discourse of Christianity now had an external relationship to this other

---

3. Michel Foucault, *History of Sexuality,* vol. 1: *An Introduction,* trans. Robert Hurley (New York: Pantheon Books, 1978), pp. 53–73.

4. Volkmar Sigusch, *Kritik der disziplinierten Sexualität: Aufsätze 1986–1989* (Frankfurt/New York: Campus, 1989), p. 11. Reference taken from Regina Ammicht Quinn, *Körper—Religion—Sexualität: Theologische Reflexionen zur Ethik der Geschlechter* (Mainz: Matthias-Grünewald-Verlag, 1999), p. 253 n. 58. For a discussion of different aspects of modern sexuality, see Quinn, *Körper—Religion—Sexualität*, pp. 251–61.

5. Thomas W. Laqueur, *Solitary Sex: A Cultural History of Masturbation* (New York: Zone Books, 2003), p. 186.

special discourse. Instead of speaking of sexuality as such, theology was forced to speak about this other discourse. Even where moral theology retained those norms that it had inherited from earlier theology, the theological status of these norms was unwittingly changed, since the sexuality it now discussed was primarily understood medically, and only secondarily theologically.

When I discuss questions that concern human sexuality in this chapter, it is thus important to understand that sexuality is a concept that arose during modernity, and serves to organize different sorts of human experience in a certain way. Neither the concept nor the object that it is thought to designate is self-evident, however. Sociologist Jeffrey Weeks gives the following definition in the book *Sexuality,* which may also serve to enlighten us about the instability of the concept itself:

> [W]hat we define as "sexuality" is an historical construction, which brings together a host of different biological and mental possibilities, and cultural forms—gender identity, bodily differences, reproductive capacities, needs, desires, fantasies, erotic practices, institutions and values—which need not be linked together, and in other cultures have not been.[6]

Other contexts would sort these experiences in a different way—this has also been the case, for example, within the Christian tradition. "Sexuality" thus does not describe something given by nature, but is a historical construction that organizes a specific dimension of relations between people in a specific society. According to the French philosopher Michel Foucault, the concept itself is tied to the will to know, which is an heir to the pastoral power of the confessional system, but which has been transformed from theology to medicine and the social sciences during the emergence of modernity.[7] The purpose is to identify and manage the sexuality of society's citizens in an expedient way. The term itself is thus not politically innocent. If I nevertheless use it here, this is due to the fact that it is difficult or even impossible—in our time and in our culture—to conceptually organize the human sex life in a way that is not indebted to these categorizations of sexuality.

In this chapter I will formulate a theological understanding of human sexuality and gender against the background of the foundational theological understanding of the body that I outlined in the previous chapter. Sexuality and gender will thus not be discussed from a moral perspective in the

---

6. Jeffrey Weeks, *Sexuality,* 2nd edition (London/New York: Routledge, 2003), p. 7.
7. Foucault, *History of Sexuality,* vol. 1.

modern sense, but certainly as an "ethics," that is to say, a way of being in the world. As theologian Regina Ammicht Quinn has argued, it is of greatest importance for theology to "reintegrate sexuality into the person's life-world—and thereby also into the values that form this life world," rather than supporting the tendency to "partition off, fragment, bureaucratize sexuality in moral discourse."[8] The person's sexuality is not something that exists apart from and independent of her life-world, but is an integrated part of it, and every theology that tends to treat sexuality as merely a moral phenomenon risks reinforcing a modern dichotomizing between the "religious" and the "profane," but also reducing the complexity of the person's sexuality to an abstract question of which sorts of sex acts are allowed with which people, under which circumstances and with which purpose—as though a general answer to such questions were possible. It is impossible to understand the person's sexuality as a moral phenomenon without retaining the relationship to her life-world and the visions that undergird the values and norms that the life-world embodies. Nor can sexuality be limited to the act of sex, as it encompasses other dimensions of her relationships as well, like, for example, contact, emotional warmth, nearness, and the structure of the relationship between the genders. Sexuality is, in other words, a central dimension of the embodiment of the human being, and to disregard this would therefore be a way of transforming the idea of the person's bodily constitution into an abstraction. Sexuality is, in the words of my thesis in the previous chapter, a dimension of the ritual mediation between social and individual bodies.

My thesis is that the secularization of acts of sex through the emergence of sexuality is not something that Christian theology needs to lament. With this there has come a historic possibility for achieving a distance from the earlier theological integration of sex acts, and so to critically, self-critically, and constructively revalue its configuration of sensuality, gender, and desire. Below I will discuss a critical theological understanding of the person's sexuality against the background of a theological *eros*. I will treat in turn the ethics of sensuality in the Christian tradition, Christianity's view of the relationship between biologically gendered bodies, and heteronormativity in sexual relationships, to finally return to the central question of a theological erotics. With this I want to provide a theological contribution to the understanding of the erotic dimension of the embodiment of the human being, which includes her sexuality, but is not identical with it. First, then, I turn to the question of the place of sensuality in Christian theology.

8. Quinn, *Körper—Religion—Sexualität*, p. 329.

The Ethics of Sensuality

In order to understand how sensuality has found its place in the Christian tradition—or more accurately: how sensuality has not yet found its theologically legitimate place in the Christian tradition—I will begin by outlining the classical figuration of human desire as a technique of subjectification. This gives us a key to understanding the place of sensuality in Christian theology by pointing out the connection between sexuality and subjectivity. According to the French philosopher Michel Foucault in his groundbreaking work *The History of Sexuality,* there is a critical break between this technique of subjectification, this *ars erotica,* and the Christian hermeneutics of desire whose purpose was to regulate the Christian sexual life in a way that strove for virginal simplicity rather than masculine self-control. Christianity's hermeneutics of desire became increasingly interested in classifying sexuality, a heritage that has gone further with the modern period's *scientia sexualis.*

On the basis of Foucault's argument, the important question in the next section becomes whether a potential path to a theologically legitimate sexuality, one that is not simply an accommodation of the current cultural situation, would not be to once more speak of a sort of *ars erotica.* In the prayer praxis and liturgy of the Christian church there are resources for an erotic language whose purpose is not instrumental, and which could apply to physical sensuality as well. Finally, I will also pose the question of which institutions are constitutive for a contemporary theology of the sexuality of the human being, and how the relationship between these institutions and her sociality should be understood. The purpose of this section on the ethics of sensuality is thus to reach a constructive theological understanding of the relationship between sexuality, subjectivity, and sociality.

Sexuality as Technique of Subjectification

In the second volume of *The History of Sexuality* Michel Foucault investigates how human desire had been configured in Antiquity.[9] Foucault says here that the break between a freer pagan sexuality and a stricter Christian sexuality, as is often postulated, is not consistent with non-Christian Greek and Latin texts of Antiquity that attempt to regulate the person's sexual practices. This

---

9. Michel Foucault, *History of Sexuality,* vol. 2: *The Use of Pleasure,* trans. Robert Hurley (New York: Vintage Books, 1990).

does not, however, mean that classical pagan and classical Christian sexual ethics constituted a continuity. The difference between them lies in a different sphere than the contrast between a freer and a stricter ethic, namely in the place that the sexual practice occupies in the life of a free man. According to Foucault this place is constituted by the individual's relationship to himself, and he counts four areas where sexual practices were problematized in late Antiquity: the relationship to body and health, the relationship to the other sex, the relationship to one's own sex, and finally, the relationship to truth and the search for wisdom.[10] So even if a continuity may exist with respect to moral rules for behavior between classical paganism and Christianity, this does not mean that the same continuity exists between paganism's versus Christianity's way of constituting the subject through ascetic practices. The goal for these techniques of subjectification was different, and the means were determined and understood in different ways.

To begin with, the question that the Greeks posed was not which actions, pleasures, or desires were allowed, but with how much energy one was driven by them.[11] *Ta aphrodisia,* the pleasures, were not problematic in themselves, but what was problematic was the relationship to these pleasures, namely whether this was characterized by moderation or lechery. The problem was not whether one enjoyed "wrong" actions, actions that were "against nature" (*para physin;* cf. Rom. 1:26), but whether the frequency and intensity of these pleasures threatened to dominate the one enjoying them. Aside from immoderation, there was another threat to the free man's relationship to pleasures, namely passivity. To be an object instead of a subject in a sexual relationship was yet another way to forfeit domination and thus not to act in accordance with what was proper for a free man. The role of the free man consisted in "being active, in dominating, in penetrating, in asserting one's superiority."[12] What was critical was thus not how to avoid or extinguish pleasures—there was nothing "sinful" about them in themselves—but how one would use (*chrēsthai*) these in the proper way.[13]

In the meditations on the use of pleasure one may, according to Foucault, find a threefold strategy that reflects on need, legality, and status. The virtue of moderation (*sōphrosynē*) is dependent on the status that appertains

---

10. Foucault, *History of Sexuality,* vol. 2, p. 22.
11. Foucault, *History of Sexuality,* vol. 2, pp. 40–52.
12. Foucault, *History of Sexuality,* vol. 2, p. 214.
13. Foucault, *History of Sexuality,* vol. 2, pp. 53–62.

to a person's rank, position, and responsibility. It is thus not a universal law that encompasses all people in the same way—which Foucault says characterizes the Christian ethic—but an ethic that is dependent on position. A greater moderation is expected of the high person than of the low. The high person should be characterized by *enkrateia*, "an active form of self-mastery, which enables one to resist or struggle, and to achieve domination in the area of desires and pleasures."[14] Self-mastery is a prerequisite for moderation. Through self-mastery the individual manages to battle against pleasures, not because these are evil in themselves, but in order to retain dominion over them. This battle is fought within the subject himself, and is thus a matter of being master of oneself. The goal of this battle is not for the moderate man to completely extinguish desire, but, as Aristotle writes in *The Nicomachean Ethics,* to not go to extremes and to not be plagued by the absence of these pleasures other than to a moderate degree, and no more than one ought to in regard to what is appropriate at a particular point in time. The moderate man strives only for "the things that, being pleasant, make for health or for good condition," which "he will desire moderately and as he should."[15] Such a character trait requires training *(askēsis)*, but this training consists simply in the exercise of virtue itself. This asceticism is included in the free man's *paideia*—speaking approximately, his training as a citizen.

What then is the point in this moderation that the free man should strive for in relation to the use of pleasures? The aim is to achieve *sōphrosynē,* which involves a certain sort of freedom.[16] The one who is not moderate is not free in relation to his desires either, and therefore risks becoming their slave. Since the free man should lead and rule over others, he must also be able to lead and rule over himself. Self-mastery is therefore an active, "masculine" freedom that should not only be exercised over others, but also over one's own subject. "Self-mastery was a way of being a man with respect to oneself," in Foucault's formulation.[17] Conversely, immoderation was thought to be passive and feminine. So with regard to sexual actions, the problem for the free man was not a matter of loving both sexes. The problem arises in the moment he finds himself in an inferior, passive position in relation to his partner, since he would then lose his freedom. To master pleasures, on the other

14. Foucault, *History of Sexuality,* vol. 2, p. 64. Cf. pp. 63–77.

15. Aristotle, *Nichomachean Ethics,* in *The Complete Works of Aristotle,* vol. 2, ed. Jonathan Barnes, the revised Oxford translation (Princeton: Princeton University Press, 1991), p. 1766 (III, 2, 1119a).

16. Foucault, *History of Sexuality,* vol. 2, pp. 78–91.

17. Foucault, *History of Sexuality,* vol. 2, p. 82.

hand, is to subject them to *logos*. Moderation thus goes intimately together with truth. But, Foucault points out, it is not a hermeneutics of desire—an interpretation and classification of desires—that is the consequence of this relationship between moderation and reason, as it becomes in Christian spirituality, but an aesthetics of existence. A life that is lived in moderation and the love of truth contributes "to the maintenance and reproduction of an ontological order."[18] By relating properly to oneself and to the body, the person comes into harmony with the beauty of the cosmos.[19]

Christian sexual ethics thus does not differ so much from the Classical with regard to regulations and prohibitions. The big difference lies in the models for the subject—virginal in contrast to masculine self-mastery—and the ascetic techniques. Here Christianity recalls more the "care of self" of the Hellenistic erotics.[20] For Christianity, these ascetic techniques are not a matter of a technique for subjectifying the self associated with an aesthetics of existence, but are instead a matter of a hermeneutics—spiritual practices, confession—that gives an ever-more precise and codified regulation of desires. Within Classical sexual ethics a number of regulations were developed that attempted to conventionalize sexual actions through dietetics (the care of the health of the body), economics (the care of a harmonious household), and erotics (the care of proper love relationships), but none of these regulations were, according to Foucault, an attempt to regulate these actions in detail. The purpose was to cultivate and maintain moderation. For Christianity, in contrast, ethics took its starting point in "sin, the Fall, and evil."[21] Foucault describes Christianity's hermeneutics of desire as "a type of work on oneself that implies a decipherment of the soul and a purificatory hermeneutics of the desires; and a mode of ethical fulfillment that tends toward self-renunciation."[22] The emergence of Christianity thus entails a break with Antiquity in the issue of sexual ethics.

18. Foucault, *History of Sexuality*, vol. 2, p. 89.

19. Foucault uses the example of a dialogue between Socrates and Callicles in Plato's dialogue *Gorgias,* 506d–507d.

20. Michel Foucault, *History of Sexuality*, vol. 3: *The Care of Self,* trans. Robert Hurley (New York: Pantheon Books, 1986). On the relationship between Christianity and the Hellenistic eroticism, see pp. 39, 64, 141, 143–44, 183, 235–36, 239–40.

21. Foucault, *History of Sexuality*, vol. 3, p. 184.

22. Foucault, *History of Sexuality*, vol. 3, pp. 239–40. Unfortunately Foucault never got to complete the fourth volume of *History of Sexuality* where the question of the Christian hermeneutic of desire would have been treated more closely. Several fragments together with other relevant writings by Foucault have been collected in Michel Foucault, *Religion and Culture,* Manchester Studies in Religion, Culture and Gender, ed. Jeremy R. Carrette (Manchester:

Between Scientia Sexualis *and* Ars Erotica

In *The History of Sexuality* there is a recurrent assessment of Christianity that is not so much about its rigid system of laws, as about its striving for purity, innocence, virginity, and its hermeneutics of desire that ever more zealously comes to classify sexual actions. Historically, Christianity has certainly had an ambivalent attitude toward sexual practices. Theologians like Origen and Augustine have discussed whether the person's sexual actions are a consequence of the Fall, and thus not something that belongs to her original, paradisiacal constitution.[23] A life of complete abstinence has been advocated both within and outside of marriage. The question I want to pose here is not so much about how one ought to annotate the history of Christian sexual ethics, but rather whether or not there are resources for another sexual ethics within the framework of Christian theology. In other words, I want to argue that Christian sexual ethics as it has appeared by and large throughout the course of history is not a necessary consequence of Christian theology. Christianity's revaluation of the person's body through the doctrine of the incarnation, of the person's passivity through the doctrine of "an imputed righteousness," and of the person's relationship to other people through the doctrine of God's transcendence, but also through the doctrine of the church, should on the contrary be able to lead to other conclusions and consequences on the part of theology. If sexuality and subjectification go together in the way that I have described above with the help of Foucault, one would be able to imagine that there are resources for a *different,* less negative, view of sensuality to retrieve from the ideas and practices of the Christian tradition. I will pay attention to several of these here.

As I touched on in the previous chapter apropos the individual body, the church's view of sexuality was not directly conditioned by an antipathy towards sexuality and embodiment. Sexuality was, even for Christians, embedded in a context that had to do with the relationship to society and the body, but also to the hope that was expressed by the Christian congregation. Sexual chastity was thus seldom a direct, but instead an indirect goal, a step in the transformation of the entirety of human existence, so that it became more available for God's purposes. In other words, an interest in sexual

---

Manchester University Press, 1999). See also Jeremy R. Carrette, *Foucault and Religion: Spiritual Corporality and Political Spirituality* (London: Routledge, 2000).

23. For a presentation of Augustine's perspective on sexuality, see R. A. Markus, *The End of Ancient Christianity,* Canto (Cambridge: Cambridge University Press, 1998), pp. 45–62.

practices did not stand at the center of early Christianity, even if the attitude towards them was certainly ambivalent. This ambivalence was, according to Foucault's account, motivated more by a pursuit of virginal simplicity than of masculine self-mastery. Even if we read already in Paul of certain practical exceptions for those who are married and so engage in sexual relationships (1 Cor. 7:1–40), the ethical ideal was a life "apart from sex" in order to be able to follow Christ all the more devotedly.[24] When the techniques of subjectification, governed by this virginal ideal, came to be combined with a developed hermeneutic of desire, whose classifications were reinforced by confessional practices, this eventually meant a greater stereotypization of sexual actions as such. We already find such a confessional practice in what is perhaps the most famous work of Christian Antiquity, namely Augustine's *Confessions*, which was written sometime between 397 and 401. To take one illustrative example, the longing for the body of the beloved is described here as though the soul in "an ulcerous condition . . . thrust itself to outward things, miserably avid to be scratched by contact with the world of senses."[25] Augustine is not initiating anything new at the end of the fourth century, but following an early tradition.

Eventually these confessional practices would be developed into institutionalized practices, where a detailed classification system was also elaborated, on the basis of which sexual practices could be classified and judged.[26] Here abstract and general principles came to be elaborated regarding who got to do what with whom, and when, where, and how it could occur. Sexual practices were organized into systems for judgment, and so for moral evaluation. According to the American theologian Mark D. Jordan, there are two problems with such a systematizing and evaluation (as he himself has shown when it comes to "sodomy" as a categorization of sexual practices, which I return to below). The first problem he calls the "Vice of the Obligatory Answer."[27] The chief difficulty with this "sin" is that it presumes that Christian ethics should and can solve every moral dilemma that can be imagined. Jordan is, however, strongly critical of the idea that such princi-

24. See Mark D. Jordan's comments on this in *The Ethics of Sex*, New Dimensions to Religious Ethics (Oxford/Malden, MA: Blackwell, 2002), pp. 47–75.

25. Augustine, *Confessions*, trans. Henry Chadwick (Oxford/New York: Oxford World Classics, 2008), p. 35 (3, I, 1). Cf. Jordan's comments on this in *The Ethics of Sex*, pp. 4–5.

26. I have discussed this more closely in the article "Herdemakten och biktens hemlighet," *Res Publica: Hemligheter* 59 (2003): 56–65.

27. Jordan, *The Ethics of Sex*, pp. 6–9. In this section I am strongly influenced by Jordan's theological problematizing of the person's sexuality.

ples or rules actually exist, which manage to encompass every situation in a satisfactory way. The second problem with such an ethics Jordan calls the "Vice of Timeless Science," and here the problem is that Christian ethics are often conducted as though its categories and conclusions have no history. Rather than find "Vice" in different sexual practices, Jordan thus finds them in the ethical practice of the Christian church. This ethical practice, it has been supposed, would give expression to "a science or a law code or a perfect therapy."[28] He poses, however, the pertinent question of whether the ethical practice of the Christian church can actually live up to this ideal. Does such a goal not instead entail morally negative consequences, namely an ethics whose self-assurance and abstraction oppress rather than transform the person's desire by essentializing her identity in the effort to classify the essence of sin? The pursuit of transformation of the self degenerates here into identifying oneself with a predetermined identity. Could sexual actions, which are configured in a particular (sinful) way according to the interpretation of Christian sexual ethics, not be construed in an entirely different way?

We can also ask ourselves why traditional Christian sexual ethics in our Western contemporary period seem so outdated, even within the churches.[29] Why does a Christian sexual ethics play such a small social role, at least in Europe? The reason for this is not the so-called sexual revolution, but the fact that the nation-state has in large part taken over the role that the Christian church previously had in Western society. The discourse of the Christian church on sex has diminished in authority while the bureaucracies of the nation-state have gained in authority. Foucault writes the following in the first volume of *The History of Sexuality:*

> Sex was not something one simply judged; it was a thing one administrated. It was in the nature of a public potential; it called for management procedures; it had to be taken charge of by analytical discourses. In the eighteenth century, sex became a 'police' matter—in the full and strict sense given the term at the time.[30]

Sex should be useful, and must therefore be made public. Discourse about sex within demography, biology, pedagogy, politics, medicine, psychology,

28. Jordan, *The Ethics of Sex,* p. 9.

29. Jordan, *The Ethics of Sex,* pp. 131–54. Contra James B. Nelson, *Body Theology* (Louisville: Westminster/John Knox Press, 1992).

30. Foucault, *History of Sexuality,* vol. 1, p. 24.

psychiatry, and ethics thus flourishes as never before: "Sex was driven out of hiding and constrained to lead a discursive existence."[31] Through the fact that the state takes over responsibility for sexuality, the church has been successively forced to accommodate its understandings of the person's sexuality to the dominant culture of the national state, but often without recognizing this.[32] The modern state, on the other hand, has further developed the "will to know" of Christian confessional practice in an attempt to map out and regulate citizens' sexual practices. In other words, the Christian church as an institution has lost power over the person's sexuality, at least in Europe and the USA, even if the modern state has taken over, reinforced, and transformed the Christian institution of confession into a public, scientific discourse of sex.

Theology does not need to see this as a loss, but may see it as an opportunity for a new Christian sexual ethics. The understanding here must be that every sexual ethics is tied to a sexual politics—or, to express it with the help of Foucault's terms, the person's sexuality is dependent even in our time on techniques of subjectification, with the help of which sexuality is formed in and by the individual. These techniques of subjectification are institutionally anchored. The position that the Christian church finds itself in in our time is a more powerless position, which can lead to the understanding that it is not the pursuit of sensuality, but the pursuit of power that leads to the worst sins. The task of the Christian church is not to allow its sexual ethics to be conformed to the power of the state, but rather on the one hand to reconcile, in terms of its attitude towards sexuality, with its dark past, and on the other to recognize how the history of sexual ethics has influenced contemporary society's secular discourse of sexuality. "Christianity is," according to Jordan, "partly responsible for the particular shames felt by many members of the cultures that used to be Christendom. These shames are written into our laws and our daily languages."[33] The Christian church's ethical practice thus ought to avoid the illusory dream that its discourse of sexuality can have the same authority that it once had, but ought to also avoid reinforcing the modern state's continued use of this authority. In other words, the challenge of finding a discourse of human sexuality lies beyond every attempt at control and zeal for classification. For such a discourse to be possible, the language

31. Foucault, *History of Sexuality,* vol. 1, p. 33.

32. See Johanna Gustafsson, *Kyrka och kön—om könskonstruktioner i Svenska kyrkan 1945–1985* (Stockholm/Stehag: Brutus Österlings Bokförlag Symposion, 2004).

33. Jordan, *The Ethics of Sex,* p. 152.

must be especially restrained, as well as conscious of its fragmentary and hypothetical status.

In order to think theologically about sensuality in a productive way, we must begin by detaching sexuality from its rigid ties to reproduction, which have been implicit in the Christian tradition.[34] In Thomas Aquinas, to take only a single example, we find that the actions that are "against nature" are so on the grounds that they are not reproductive (and here Thomas is influenced by Aristotle).[35] Sex acts between people of the same genital configuration (to make use of an expression that does not immediately carry the same problematic connotations as "homosexuality") are "against nature" precisely on the basis of their incapacity for reproduction.[36] But this entails an instrumentalization of sensuality—it exists for the sake of reproduction—that is neither self-evident nor given in nature. Other language about sensuality that does not instrumentalize it in the same way, and can therefore be productive within a Christian discourse, already exists in the tradition of the church. It is namely clear that a strong tradition within the Christian church has widely used an erotically charged language to speak about mystical experiences and about prayer. But if an erotic imagery could be regarded as appropriate for describing union with God, one can argue that there exists a continuity between the more everyday erotic and these theological experiences. It ought to additionally be possible for this communication to be effective in the opposite direction: that our theological erotic experiences can influence our everyday erotic experiences.[37] In other words: if we use an erotically charged language to speak of experiences of prayer and union with God, we can also use a language taken from the sphere of prayer to speak about sexual relations. There are thus theological resources here, not only for describing spiritual and sexual erotic experiences, but also for giving counsel for how one should grow in one's prayer life or sexual life. Issues involving sexual self-satisfaction (onanism) and sado-masochism in sexual relationships can be illuminated on the basis of analogous phenomena within the prayer life: private prayers and physical asceticism. There is thus already a theological discourse here that treats questions of bodily sensuality. The Christian

34. Jordan, *The Ethics of Sex,* pp. 157–72.

35. Thomas Aquinas, *Summa theologiae* (Paris: Sumptibus P. Lethielleux, Bibliopolae Editoris, 1939), 1a2ae, 30:3.

36. Cf. Eugene F. Rogers Jr., *Sexuality and the Christian Body: Their Way into the Triune God,* Challenges in Contemporary Theology (Oxford/Malden, MA: Blackwell, 1999), pp. 91–139.

37. Jordan, *The Ethics of Sex,* p. 166.

doctrine of prayer is already an *ars amatoria*, i.e., an instruction in the art of love. Examples that touch bodily sensuality may be taken from many different fields of the practices of the Christian church: liturgy, music, preaching, and even the disciplined silence of the Quakers. Here we can find an important starting point for another way to speak about sensuality in human sexuality, a way that does not conform with an authoritarian zeal for classification, whether on the part of the church or the state. All these references to possible discourses and practices aim to establish a discourse that creates different sexual "identities" through different rhetorical choices than those that the earlier church made. According to Jordan such a discourse would

> emphasize, not dichotomies, but the drawing of all created goods toward Christ, the transfigurative union in Christ of apparent opposites. It would describe, not the sinful fixity of self-identities, but the graced capacity for learning, transformation, even exchange.[38]

Through such a discourse we can thus place human sexuality within the Christian existential drama of salvation in a new way.

What I want to accomplish with the help of the above argument is not to break with Christian discourse, but to use these resources in order to, so to speak, exchange symbolic backgrounds for Christian sexual ethics. The techniques of subjectification of the Christian tradition leave—at least this is my thesis—space for a theological conception of *eros* that is not poisoned by the dichotomies of the Christian tradition and that has not fallen prey to the sort of power hunger that attempts to master the person by classifying and manipulating her. In several places Foucault describes the difference between a *scientia sexualis* and an *ars erotica* or *ars amatoria* as an interest in the truth of a person's sexuality, rather than in how one approaches an intense sensuality.[39] Even if Foucault's historical contrast of a *scientia sexualis* and an *ars erotica* is somewhat exaggerated, it is nevertheless along the lines of the latter, understood as a type, that I will seek a new, discursive practice.[40] There has probably never been a theologically inspired art of love per se, apart from indirectly through other practices. Sexual practices have stood in the shadow of virginity or abstinence, but it is not a theological given

38. Jordan, *The Ethics of Sex*, p. 172.

39. Cf. Foucault, *History of Sexuality*, vol. 1, pp. 57–73, but also "Sexuality and Power," in *Religion and Culture*, selected and edited by Jeremy R. Carrette (New York: Routledge, 1999), pp. 119f.

40. Jordan, *The Ethics of Sex*, pp. 123–24.

that this should be the case. I will therefore search for a Christian *eros* that can inspire techniques of subjectification whose ideal is neither virginity, understood as sexual chastity, nor the masculine self-mastery of Antiquity, but whose analogies are instead found in the mystical traditions and in the prayer practice and liturgy of the church.

Sexuality and Sociality

The search for a theological *ars erotica* raises the question of which institutions are constitutive for a contemporary theology of human sexuality. It is not only the emergence of modern society and the secularization of sexual discourse that has influenced sexual practices in their formation of human sexuality, but also the logic of the society of consumption. There is in our immediate present an ever-clearer evocation of a connection between sexuality and religion, possibly as a backlash against the secularization of sexuality during the emergence of a scientific discourse of sexuality.[41] Speaking about sexuality, sensuality, and desire in general is not politically innocent. It is a critical question, which institutions our techniques of subjectification are cultivated within and which configuration and form of sexuality these give rise to. The risks that come with a theological discourse of human sexuality are many. Not only that such a discourse may contribute to legitimizing a continued oppression of certain sexual practices, and thereby to a continued authoritarian control of them, but also, paradoxically enough, the opposite, namely that a "liberal" or "modern," "liberated" discourse of sexuality would play into the hands of the ruling commercial reification of sexuality. Sex becomes a commodity, an object, rather than one of the person's fundamental ways of relating to other people.

Such a reification does not only occur through the fact that sexuality is privatized to a single person, the individual.[42] Even if conceiving of human sexuality in terms of an individual effort to maximize sexual pleasure is a reduction in perspective, it is no solution to, as the so-called traditional Christian emphasis on the family wants to do, shift the perspective to the idea of the couple. Sexuality namely breaks through the boundaries both

41. Cf. Graham Ward, *True Religion,* Blackwell Manifestos (Malden, MA/Oxford: Blackwell, 2003), pp. 129–33.

42. Linda Woodhead, "Sex in a Wider Context," in *Sex These Days: Essays on Theology, Sexuality and Society,* ed. Jon Davies and Gerard Loughlin, Studies in Theology and Sexuality 1 (Sheffield: Sheffield Academic Press, 1997), pp. 98–120.

of individual autonomy (through the desire not to be alone, but rather that the other would also be with one) and of the mutuality in togetherness (through the couple's relationships to family, friends, and society, and the possibility—in the heterosexual case—that the relationship leads to children). For the Christian, sexuality is also a part of the fellowship in the body of Christ, the church. In the previous chapter I emphasized how the social and the individual body is mediated through rites, and in an analogous way one may say that the body of Christ, according to the Christian tradition, constitutes the context for the person's sexuality. Christ's union with the church becomes an analogy for the sexual union of human beings, and the person's sexuality can therefore be seen as a spiritual path. From a Christian perspective (as, for example, from the perspective of the World Health Organization), sexual intimacy is not constituted only by the sex act itself, but is a practice that is more extended over time, quite simply a way to live together. To say the same thing in another way: the person's sexuality is always already political, since it concerns life in *polis* at large, and not only life as monads or dyads.

In order to understand the theologically motivated affinity between sexuality and sociality, we ought to pay attention to their relationship to the household economy and neighborhood politics.[43] A household can, partially in contrast to modern ideas of the nuclear family, be understood as open and socially reproductive. Where the (modern) family is characterized by being a safe harbor of intimacy in contrast to the technical and economic calculations of the market, the household is characterized by the fact that it is a way to allocate work and a place where one invests one's time. In our time the family is an institution for reproducing the individualistic values of the society of consumption and the nation-state, and ironically enough conceptions of romantic love and sexual intimacy serve to reinforce this reproduction. The difference between family and household is the difference between different ways to socialize our desire. In these different institutions we teach ourselves to love in certain ways instead of others, and for certain reasons and motives rather than others. The household habituates its members in different codes for love and sexual desire than the nuclear family, as it is configured in contemporary society. The nuclear family diminishes the social character of sexuality, raising children, love, etc., through its romantic understanding of intimacy, and thereby misses the social character of those

43. Cf. David Matzko McCarthy, *Sex and Love in the Home: A Theology of the Household* (London: SCM, 2001), pp. 1–10.

practices that can maintain and create conditions for sexuality, raising children, and love. Apropos the social dependence of sexuality the American theologian David Matzko McCarthy writes the following:

> Through any given sexual act, spouses might express love, desire, generosity, frustration, fatigue, or a manipulative intent, but they will do so in the semantic context of a day, week, a stage of life, and series of specific events, and all set within the broader context of a shared life.[44]

In other words, the sexual act needs a context in order to be comprehensible, where additional similar actions make it both comprehensible and unique. Depending on whether this context—the other practices that are regarded as meaningful for sexual practice—is understood narrowly or broadly, the context for the sexual act will be understood in different ways. With this the socialization of human desire will also be different. The theologically adequate context for understanding the sexual act is in other words a social practice, namely the household, not an individual or a personal practice.

The point, according to McCarthy, in emphasizing the household rather than the nuclear family as the context of sex acts is to not limit the understanding of sexuality to the idea of the couple.[45] Romance has come to be understood as an I-you relationship apart from more practical, everyday chores, but one thereby avoids the question whether love and sex actually are a product of cultural and economic reproduction, i.e, whether they arise through the complexities and ambiguities of social life. Through the fact that love and sexual relationships between people are "protected within the private harmony of idealized lovers," the understanding of love and sex not only becomes theoretically deficient, since it avoids the question of how these are dependent on the cultural and economic socialization of our desires, but also theoretically reductive, through the fact that sexuality's connection to the existential drama becomes unclear.[46] Returning to a more social understanding of love and sex is thus at the same time a return to understanding these from a more theological-dramatic perspective, where forgiveness and reconciliation are important ingredients, an understanding that is anchored in the earlier theological tradition.[47]

---

44. McCarthy, *Sex and Love in the Home*, p. 8.
45. McCarthy, *Sex and Love in the Home*, pp. 21–32.
46. McCarthy, *Sex and Love in the Home*, p. 25.
47. McCarthy, *Sex and Love in the Home*, pp. 26–32, 166–69.

An adequate theological perspective on sex ought to differ from contemporary culture, at least when sex in the modern sense becomes something restless.[48] For McCarthy restlessness is a characteristic of modern sexuality: "In the prevailing economy of desire, moments of satisfying pleasure ought to give way to a need for more, so that common standards of good sex are frequency, technique, and the power of pleasure to create a need for more."[49] Sexual desire is trained to continually search for new sensuality: "Consumer capitalism is less about what we have and more about desire for what we lack."[50] Against the market orientation of contemporary sexuality, traditional theological sexual ethics has indeed emphasized love and the sexual act as an authentic meeting between two persons. The problem with such a perspective is that it gives far too idealized an image of human sexuality, since it lifts this out of its everyday context. The sexual act comes to stand for something "beyond" everyday reality, a "true" meeting that symbolizes a love that transcends ordinary life. Romantic love, which also implicates a certain view of sexuality, becomes a relationship apart from all other everyday relationships.[51] With this the demand grows that the relationship to the other person will be able to result in a complete fellowship. The idea of the couple in romantic love comes to represent the only authentic relationship, while other social relationships to a greater or lesser degree come to be instrumentalized.[52] A context of more social practices is needed, however, for a theologically productive understanding of both love and sex, and this is provided, for theology, by the Christian church. It is here that the theologically significant mediation between individual and social bodies occurs.

If the context of love and sex is the social practices that constitute the Christian church, this does not mean the significance of specifically religious practices is maximized at the cost of everyday practices. It is precisely these everyday practices, which are developed through ordinary friendship and different obligations in neighborhood and household, that cultivate love.[53] In other words, it is through practices that are not focused on love in the conventional sense that love is cultivated. By finding its context in the wider

48. McCarthy, *Sex and Love in the Home,* pp. 33–49.

49. McCarthy, *Sex and Love in the Home,* p. 34.

50. McCarthy, *Sex and Love in the Home,* p. 40. Cf. here as well Graham Ward, "Suffering and Incarnation," in *The Blackwell Companion to Postmodern Theology,* ed. Graham Ward (Malden, MA/Oxford: Blackwell, 2001), pp. 192–208.

51. McCarthy, *Sex and Love in the Home,* p. 61.

52. McCarthy, *Sex and Love in the Home,* p. 123.

53. McCarthy, *Sex and Love in the Home,* p. 127.

context of the common practices and goals that characterize the household, love is no longer fragile, since it is not defined in contrast to these everyday practices. Marriage is in itself insufficient for maintaining love; it must instead be set within the framework of a complex network of social roles, functions, and practices.[54] And it is here that the church comes in. Understood as such a complex network—as a grotesque body in the sense that I suggested in the previous chapter and I return to in the next chapter—the church can imitate and embody God's love in the world, and through its presence transform the everyday practices that maintain the person's social life.[55] McCarthy also gives his view of the church along the lines of such an argument in an article on the relationship between bodies:

> The widest possible consideration of common life . . . is God's reconciliation with the world, which, in the gathering of the church, constitutes a body. This body, the body of Christ, is generative of a relationship of bodies, and within this network of common life, marriage is understood as an "embodied" theological hermeneutics, a synecdoche of God's redemptive activity. Marriage is mimesis.[56]

The key to understanding the church is that it is not identical with a specific building or a specific, easily identifiable social body, but with a grotesque body.[57] This grotesque body fosters the communal life—not only through marriage, but among other things through marriage—through a transformation and cultivation of the person's desire, which leads it along the paths of reconciliation. Thus the church as the body of Christ is not merely understood symbolically here, but is understood as a means for the reconciliation of the person through the fact that it empowers the person to new social relationships. The church can thus be said to function as a sort of "extended household." Of course, such an extended household does not

---

54. The very question of a theological understanding of marriage I do not touch on here, since it would carry us too far from the subject. For a start to such a discussion, see instead Mark D. Jordan, *Blessing Same-Sex Unions: The Perils of Queer Romance and the Confusions of Christian Marriage* (Chicago/London: University of Chicago Press, 2005).

55. McCarthy, *Sex and Love in the Home,* pp. 127–51.

56. McCarthy, "The Relationships of Bodies: A Nuptial Hermeneutics of Same-Sex Unions," in *Theology and Sexuality: Classic and Contemporary Readings,* Blackwell Readings in Modern Theology, ed. Eugene F. Rodgers Jr. (Oxford/Malden, MA: Blackwell, 2002), p. 201.

57. Cf. as well John Milbank, "On Complex Space," in *The Word Made Strange: Theology, Language, Culture* (Oxford/Cambridge, MA: Blackwell, 1997), pp. 268–92.

need to embrace only heterosexual marriage as the unique or only legitimate form of the person's sexuality. Same-sex marriages, as well as singles and voluntary celibates who live together, should obviously also be able to be considered a part of this household.[58] The inadequacy of all these forms of sexuality should not be understood as a lack in a negative sense, but instead constitutes a part of its social character and entails an openness towards other households and friends.[59]

The specific act of sex is a part of a wider social economy as well, rather than a privately understood economy. Sexual relationships receive their meaning in relation to other social relationships than the sexual, and so their significance is not limited to that of two partners. They are also participatory in the same risks and possibilities as other social relationships, and so become a way to negotiate and express belonging, power, identity, and status. In other words, sex is not private, as McCarthy has pointed out, if by private one means something that does not have significance outside the relationship between two people.[60] A sex act is a communicative act, and as with all other communication, it is social and dependent on the material bases that constitute the conditions for social life. It is because of this that sexual practices can find their place in an everyday and friendly togetherness between the marriage partners.[61] The place for sex is thus more "in the midst of" rather than "to the side of" everyday life. It is here that every sexual act—in itself without greater significance—can receive a greater significance by forming the lovers in a way that can communicate significant things. Thus the focus of the sex act does not need to be the intensity of the sensual pleasure, but its quality over time. By being a part of a marital relationship the sexual act does not need to live up to the contemporary demand to give a deep and unique sexual experience every time, but the often unsuccessful and clumsy character of sexual acts can instead find a redeeming context in sexual fidelity extended in time within marriage. If marriage is not seen as the singular social relationship of the marriage partners, but as one among several significant relationships, marriage in its turn does not need to bear the burden of fulfilling all a person's needs for intimacy and familiarity.

58. For McCarthy's argument for same-sex marriage, see "Homosexuality and the Practices of Marriage," *Modern Theology* 13, no. 3 (1997): 371–97, together with "The Relationships of Bodies," in *Theology and Sexuality,* ed. Rogers Jr., pp. 200–216.

59. McCarthy, *Sex and Love in the Home,* p. 174.

60. McCarthy, "The Relationships of Bodies," p. 204.

61. McCarthy, *Sex and Love in the Home,* p. 208.

The above argument opens the possibility of a theologically legitimate discourse on sensuality as well as reproduction. The reproduction that the social perspective on sexuality implicates does not, however, need to be understood as (exclusively) biological. It is not only the ability of the heterosexual couple to produce biological offspring that belongs to the understanding of the reproductive ability of the household, but social reproduction in a more extended sense: adoptions, social belonging for singles, help between neighbors as well as for temporarily visiting strangers and refugees. The emphasis on sensuality thus does not need to reiterate the focus of contemporary society on a sexual desire "liberated" from the possibility of having children. Instead, the emphasis on the social dimension of sexuality entails precisely an emphasis on reproduction, but then not limited to biological reproduction. The thought of marriage as a place where sexual intimacy is cultivated over time does not only mean that it can constitute a redeeming context for the relationship, but also a more directly cultivating aspect of sensuality. If the church constitutes, so to speak, the social context for a theological *ars erotica,* it becomes clear both how human desire is always already a habituated desire, and how the thought of a theological *eros* can avoid falling victim to the emphasis of contemporary sexuality on experiences.

A critical point for the argument about the church's role in human sexuality, which I have, however, not yet seriously dealt with, is sexuality's ambiguous history within this institution. What prevents the argument from quite simply becoming a reiteration of traditional gender hierarchies and condemnations of homosexuality? Referring to the church is, of course, never risk-free. But at the same time it is necessary to speak of the institutional side of the Christian tradition, if the discourse of sexuality is not to remain in the noncommittal rhetorical arena of generalizations, but instead become a reflection on possible techniques of subjectification, a draft of a sociology of faith. It is therefore necessary to discuss the theological questions of gender hierarchies and sexual orientation more closely. The question that arises in the wake of this theological discussion of sexuality, subjectivity, and sociality is thus the following: Can the theological tradition really avoid both androcentrism and heteronormativity?

The Gendered Body

Gender hierarchies—the asymmetrical relationship between genders—have looked very different in different periods. As I have mentioned in chapter 8, in the West up until the end of the eighteenth century people perceived the woman as an abortive man. This meant that the difference between man and woman was a difference of degree. From the end of the eighteenth century on this perception changed, and people came to perceive the difference as a difference of kind. In a way this has meant a clearer fixing of gender identities during the modern period than previously. Different attributes are ascribed to the respective genders that both stabilize and define gender identities. Philosopher Genevieve Lloyd says that modern Western philosophy contains a polarization of "male reason" and "female emotion": "Rational knowledge has been construed as a transcending, transformation or control of natural forces; and the feminine has been associated with what rational knowledge transcends, dominates or simply leaves behind."[62] This polarization corresponds to a polarization between active and passive, public and private, consciousness and body.[63] This section will discuss gender hierarchies primarily within the framework of theological questions, which deal with subordination and superiority, activity and passivity, as well as the transcending of these. My purpose is to show how a theological understanding of the body also holds potential for feminist theological interpretations, which want to assert a female subjectivity that is neither complementary to nor in competition with the subjectivity of the male. It will become clear here as well that the gendered dimension of the person's embodiment is, in Judith Butler's words, embedded in sedimented practices that constitute a mediation between social and individual body. I turn first to the division of humanity into passive and active beings, with the help of one of the most famous accounts of this problem, namely Simone de Beauvoir's study *The Second Sex* (1949), but also with the help of a discussion of contemplative prayer and doctrine of justification. In a second section I present Luce Irigaray's discussion of how one might conceive of a self-sufficient, female subjectivity that is neither complementary to nor competitive with the subjectivity of the male. By way of conclusion, in this discussion of the gendered body I show how Irigaray's philosophy can also inspire a theology of the woman's independent subjectivity and sexuality that both breaks with and makes use of portions of the androcentric theological tradition.

---

62. Genevieve Lloyd, *The Man of Reason: 'Male' & 'Female' in Western Philosophy,* 2nd edition (London: Routledge, 1993), p. 2.

63. Cf. Jean Bethke Elshtain, *Public Man, Private Woman: Women in Social and Political Thought,* 2nd edition (Princeton: Princeton University Press, 1993).

The Second Sex

In *The Second Sex* Simone de Beauvoir undertakes a longer analysis of gender differences as they are configured in different myths, cultures, sciences, and situations. The crucial difference between man and woman, according to de Beauvoir, is that the man has always been and is still represented as the normative and the normal:

> In actuality the relation of the two sexes is not quite like that of two electrical poles, for man represents both the positive and the neutral, as is indicated by the common use of *man* to designate human beings in general; whereas woman represents only the negative, defined by limiting criteria, without reciprocity.[64]

In relation to the man, the woman is the other, but the reverse does not apply. The man is self-sufficient, independent, and is not defined in relation to the woman. He, and only he, is autonomous.

De Beauvoir uses a number of terms to show how the woman relates to the man: passivity in relation to activity, immanence in relation to transcendence, object in relation to subject, body in relation to spirit, the Other in relation to the One. These terms are defined in relation to her "existentialist ethics."[65] According to *The Second Sex* this boils down, in brief, to the fact that the person becomes a subject through transcendence, understood as a movement where the person in freedom continually exceeds herself towards additional freedom. The authentic person continually transcends herself in her creative project, whether this is a matter of war, hunting, and fishing, or philosophy, art, and literature. The opposite is immanence, the identification of one's own subject with something preexistent and the identification of freedom with factuality. Instead of a transcendent and creative activity, here it is a matter of a preserving and reproductive activity. A "fall" into immanence can occur both by oppression and by acquiescence, but is in both cases "an absolute evil." This is because authentic human existence is to transcend oneself by consciously taking responsibility for one's own life, and not viewing it as something that simply befalls the person. Immanence,

---

64. Simone de Beauvoir, *The Second Sex,* trans. H. M. Parsley (London: Jonathan Cape, 1956), p. 15. For an introduction, interpretation, and analysis, see Eva Lundgren-Gothlin, *Sex and Existence: Simone de Beauvoir's* The Second Sex, trans. Linda Schenk (London: Athlone, 1996).

65. De Beauvoir, *The Second Sex,* p. 27.

understood as irregularity and objectification, has been the woman's lot throughout history:

> Every individual concerned to justify his existence feels that his existence involves an undefined need to transcend himself, to engage in freely chosen projects. Now, what peculiarly signalizes the situation of woman is that she—a free and autonomous being like all human creatures—nevertheless finds herself living in a world where men compel her to assume the status of the Other. They propose to stabilize her as object and to doom her to immanence since her transcendence is to be overshadowed and for ever transcended by another ego *(conscience)* which is essential and sovereign.[66]

Somewhat later in *The Second Sex* de Beauvoir points out that transcendence and immanence are indeed dependent on each other in every human existence, since this existence cannot transcend itself, but must in some sense be preserved.[67] But it is the transcending movement that is the proper one for the person's existence, that which separates her from a merely existing thing. Humanity is defined by de Beauvoir as transcendence, and so the identification of the woman with immanence becomes a major problem.

In book one of *The Second Sex* de Beauvoir traces the genealogy of subordination to the ancient Greeks. Already in *Metaphysics* Aristotle identified the woman with passive matter and the man with active form, and since then this hierarchical order has been handed down in a range of different forms. De Beauvoir gives the example of, among others, Hegel, and gives an illuminating quotation from him that deserves to be repeated here as well: "The man is . . . active; but the woman is receptive, since she remains in her undeveloped unity."[68] The examples could be multiplied, even from academic disciplines that lie outside those de Beauvoir investigates.[69] But this gender hierarchy does not only haunt theoretical subjects—*The Second Sex* covers fields such as social analysis, biology, religion, education, liter-

---

66. De Beauvoir, *The Second Sex*, pp. 27–28.

67. De Beauvoir, *The Second Sex*, p. 419.

68. G. W. F. Hegel, *Enzyklopädie der philosophischen Wissenschaften im Grundrisse: Zweiter Teil: Die Naturphilosophie*, Werke 9 (Frankfurt am Main: Suhrkamp, 1986), p. 519 (§369).

69. For example, within the history of theology. To mention one example, cf. Paul S. Fiddes, "The Status of Woman in the Thought of Karl Barth," in *After Eve: Women, Theology and the Christian Tradition*, ed. Janet Martin Soskice (London: Marshall Pickering, 1990), pp. 138–55.

ature, fashion, and sexuality in order to show how this hierarchization has saturated every area.

However, de Beauvoir does not see this gender hierarchy as fated. Anatomy is not the same as fate. "One is not born, but rather becomes, a woman," de Beauvoir writes in a famous sentence, and thus establishes that the "female" is a historically constructed category that thereby both can and will be transformed in every period.[70] Nor is the woman's embodiment something given, and here de Beauvoir refers to Merleau-Ponty. It is instead a situation in which the woman finds herself, i.e., a situation through which the world is related to her and through which she relates to the world.[71] Thus, according to de Beauvoir no person can be identified with her body as though it were merely a thing, a fate, an immanence. The identification of the woman's body with immanence is, in spite of everything, not an immediate immanence, but a mediated one, which means that it is in comparison with the man's transcendence that the woman is identified with her embodiment and, like the body, becomes an object. In a certain sense the woman thus becomes a paradox, namely, an object with subjectivity.

Is there any possibility of liberation for the woman from this crippling gender hierarchy? De Beauvoir is rather optimistic in this regard.[72] She says that women of today want to be acknowledged as existing in the same way as men, i.e., as transcendence. Only in this way can her existence become valuable, since it is precisely through this transcendence that the person creates the world. For this to become possible both abstract rights and concrete possibilities are needed. Abstract rights such as suffrage, autonomy in relation to the law, etc., can only lead to the emancipation of the woman if they are combined with concrete economic and sexual possibilities for independence. It is by being productive and active in the same way as the man that the woman subjectifies herself and wins her own transcendence. This transcendence is not a specific transcendence for the woman as woman, but a human transcendence. It is not until the woman is fully allowed to incarnate a human transcendence that she can be an authentic, active woman beyond gender differences: "The quarrel will go on as long as men and woman fail to recognize each other as equals; that is to say, as long as femininity is perpetuated as such."[73] In other words, that which is in common is much more

---

70. De Beauvoir, *The Second Sex,* p. 273.

71. De Beauvoir, *The Second Sex,* pp. 60–64.

72. De Beauvoir, *The Second Sex,* pp. 152–53, 159–60.

73. De Beauvoir, *The Second Sex,* p. 675. Cf. p. 671.

characteristic of human beings than that which separates them as gendered beings, according to de Beauvoir.[74]

How human activity versus passivity is related to masculine and feminine is, as I have discussed above, also historically a central point for the understanding of the relationship between the sexes. Foucault's account of techniques of subjectification within Antiquity shows in a relatively clear way that it is precisely the man who strives for self-mastery. To be a man was to be active, not only in relation to one's sexual partners, but also in relation to oneself. Passivity involved a forfeiture of self-mastery. Thus we find a strict hierarchization of masculine-active and feminine-passive. To submit to someone was seen as disgraceful for the ancient man. In homoerotic encounters, it was not the homosexual relationship itself that was disgraceful for the free man, but being the subordinate in a homosexual—or for that matter, heterosexual—relationship. For the same reason it was not advisable for the free man to read, since that was to submit oneself to someone else's thoughts.[75] In Antiquity there was thus a strongly normative character to the relationship between the sexes and their respective idealized character traits.

In this context it is interesting to note a crucial discontinuity between the Classical tradition—with certain exceptions—and the Christian tradition. The thought that a right relationship to God is established by receiving God's mercy as an "imputed righteousness" means that the person's relationship to God, both as creator and savior, is characterized by a fundamental passivity.[76] In relation to God, the person must give up the demand for autonomy and complete control. This does not necessarily mean that the essence of the human being is defined as passive. Receiving God's mercy was an active deed, at least in the sense that the person thereby actively accepted her passivity. By worshiping God the person could also, in a certain sense, restore God's gift with a return gift. This return gift of the person should, however, be understood as secondary in relation to God's primary gift. It is God who

74. De Beauvoir, *The Second Sex,* p. 836.

75. Jesper Svenbro, *Myrstigar: Figurer för skrift och läsning i antikens Grekland* (Stockholm: Bonniers, 1999), p. 21. As Svenbro shows, Socrates constitutes an exemption here in Plato's dialogue *Phaedrus* (pp. 24–29).

76. I have discussed the question of the relationship between activity and passivity on the bases of a theological anthropology in the chapter "Augustinus hunger," from an ecclesiological perspective in the chapter "Vilka är vi nu?" *Hungerns väg: Om Gud, kyrka och mångfald* (Lund: Arcus, 2000), pp. 180–200, and from a Christological perspective in the article "Kristus och människan: Om inkarnationen och kärleksbegreppet," *Svensk Teologisk Kvartalskrift* 76, no. 2 (2000): 66–76.

has the initiative, who establishes the conditions of possibility for the person's return gift as a response to God's gift. This has been expressed in several ways in the history of the Christian church and theology, for example, in the liturgy of communion. There God gives God's own self to the person, and the person gives herself to God in her worship, and with this, every simplified way of looking at the relationship between activity and passivity that has been common in the modern period (as well as during portions of the Classical period, we might add) will fall apart.[77]

So it is not self-evident in the Christian tradition that active penetration is the privileged approach. On the other hand, historical Christianity most often retained the symbolic connection between activity and masculinity and passivity and femininity. At the same time there was a lot of room for transcending these symbolic gender boundaries. In the discussion of the individual Christian body in the previous chapter I referred to the medieval female mystic, where it became clear that gender symbolism during the Middle Ages was more social than biological. A male mystic could understand himself in female terms, and vice versa. Even representations of the gendered nature of the biological body were fluid. There was thus an ambivalence within the gender hierarchy. Even if one often followed a conventional division between the masculine and active and the feminine and passive, it was theologically problematic to maintain this convention considering Christ's human, bodily nature, Christ's passive suffering on the cross, and the doctrine of salvation itself. At least at a theological, symbolic level, it was not self-evident that the man was superior to the woman. That there existed symbolic resources that were occasionally used in the Middle Ages is of course not an argument against the fact that there was an extremely real gender oppression then. It means, however, that there were several different possibilities for the understanding of the relationship between the sexes, and that gender boundaries were not perceived as something entirely static. Even if women were usually identified with the passive and the bodily, this identification was, in their own eyes, not always an expression of gender oppression, at least not as it concerned the relationship to God, since God himself had identified himself with the body through the incarnation. Thus women's connection to the bodily was perceived as a more immediate access to the divine incarnation.

For some corners of contemporary feminist theology the point is not to reiterate the contrast between active and passive, but neither is it to revalue

---

77. Catherine Pickstock, *After Writing: On the Liturgical Consummation of Philosophy,* Challenges in Contemporary Theology (Oxford: Blackwell, 1998), pp. 176–77.

the later conventional "feminine" traits, or, like de Beauvoir, to identify the human in general with activity and transcendence. Even if there is an especially legitimate pursuit of women's liberation and empowerment, and thereby a pursuit of the ability to conceive of women as active, this does not mean that they want to reiterate the dichotomization of active and passive, and, so to speak, return to Foucault's masculine self-mastery, if in a more inclusive variant. One who has argued for a more nuanced understanding of the relationship between active and passive from a theological perspective is Sarah Coakley. According to her the challenge is how one should conceive of "vulnerability and personal empowerment *together*," or how the paradox in the Bible verse "Whoever seeks to preserve his life will lose it, but whoever loses his life will keep it" (Luke 17:33) should be lived up to.[78] Coakley's example of what has held activity and passivity together in the Christian tradition is mystical practices, but as I will show, it is also possible to understand the Reformation's doctrine of justification in a similar way. With the help of mystical practices and the doctrine of justification, I will exemplify several ways in which the Christian tradition has represented a more complex view of activity and passivity and their relevance for a theology with a feminist errand.

One insight that this complex view brings with it is that passivity may not be played off against activity, as though human passivity really were something subordinate and of less worth for a true humanity.[79] This would only reiterate gender stereotypes, if with reversed overtones for women. Instead, it is important to conceive of passivity in a way that does not repeat these stereotypes and thereby obscure the fact that vulnerability, passivity, and suffering are not simply the result of people being victimized. Coakley finds an alternative in contemplative (wordless) prayer, where waiting on God functions as a way of leaving space for God, in that the person no longer sets the agenda for the relationship to him.[80] This waiting entails a certain sort of empowerment of the contemplative person, rather than an invitation to self-destruction or oppression. Prayer is a matter of giving the person a prophetic spirit and increased self-understanding. Of course, even contemplative prayer can be manipulated, but its purpose is not manipulative, but a way to transform the self. Contemplative prayer and other ascetic

---

78. Sarah Coakley, *Powers and Submissions: Spirituality, Philosophy and Gender,* Challenges in Contemporary Theology (Oxford: Blackwell, 2002), p. 5.

79. Coakley, *Powers and Submissions,* pp. 28–30.

80. Coakley, *Powers and Submissions,* pp. 32–39.

practices are different ways of attempting to reach a conception of human activity and passivity that follows neither conventional gender hierarchies nor gender stereotypes, but undermines them in a more complex practice. Contemplative prayer could very well be understood as a technique of subjectification in Foucault's sense, but without following the masculine model of self-mastery. It is instead a matter of allowing a *certain sort* of vulnerability—and thus not an independence from the other at any cost—to transform the person into a life where a *certain sort* of self-mastery serves the empowerment of the person.

Simone de Beauvoir has also treated Christian mysticism in *The Second Sex*.[81] She sees mysticism, together with narcissism and love, as a way for women to transcend a male structure. Whether love directs itself towards one's own self, towards the man, or towards God, however, these attempts at transcendence will be inauthentic, since they do not transcend one's female identity, but are instead an extension of it. When it comes to mysticism, God replaces the man in the absence of the man. Love for God as well as love for the man is a transcendence that is directed towards a "supreme person."[82] In other words, the woman is still captive in the attempt to find her transcendence through another and not through herself. That this other is God rather than the man makes little difference. De Beauvoir goes so far as to emphasize the role of incarnation for the female mystic: "[The female mystic] is overwhelmed to see that Man, Man-God, has assumed her role. She it is who is hanging on the Tree, promised the splendour of the Resurrection."[83] But neither is this indirect concession that even God (symbolically) transcends gender boundaries in the incarnation seen as a resource for the subjectification of women, since this transcendence occurs, so to speak, in the wrong direction: from the transcendent to the immanent. For de Beauvoir authenticity lies only in the transcendent, because of which she is sometimes criticized for quite simply taking over a masculine project.[84] For many of the medieval mystics embodiment is something that binds the woman to immanence, rather than something that serves her empowerment. Transcendence occurs in opposition to immanence, not in and through it.[85]

---

81. De Beauvoir, *The Second Sex*, pp. 633–40.

82. De Beauvoir, *The Second Sex*, p. 633.

83. De Beauvoir, *The Second Sex*, p. 639.

84. Cf. Lundgren-Gothlin, *Sex*, pp. 202–10, 230–42, together with Toril Moi, *Simone de Beauvoir: The Making of an Intellectual Woman* (Oxford: Blackwell, 1994), pp. 152–55.

85. De Beauvoir, *The Second Sex*, p. 597.

We can notice, however, apropos what de Beauvoir has written on mysticism, that there is a tension in her account between, on the one hand, the prioritization of transcendence, and on the other hand an awareness of the significance of the situation, which separates her from, for example, Jean-Paul Sartre's existentialist ethics.[86] So she can, for example, see the Carmelite Teresa of Avila as an example of a mystic with an active, and thereby genuine expression of her faith, a woman who has "lived out, as a woman, an experience whose meaning goes far beyond the fact of her sex."[87] Teresa's value for de Beauvoir comes from her ability to grasp freedom without any "reassuring ceiling over her head."[88] At the same time, she represents Teresa as a startling exception, which results in looking away from Teresa's contemporary social and religious context and transforms her into "a lone individual" and "an existentialist hero."[89] Apropos of this, medieval historian Amy Hollywood states that "Teresa's situation not only limited or denied her freedom, but also provided the means by which she was able to transcend at least some of its constraints."[90] Teresa was hardly an existentialist hero, however, but rather a Carmelite nun who is difficult to understand without also taking into account the central role that her relationship to God and her social and religious context play.[91] As a characterization of Teresa's life, Coakley's description of, among others, Carmelite mysticism is an attempt to hold "vulnerability and personal empowerment *together*" better than in de Beauvoir's attempt, as a pursuit of a freedom without a "reassuring ceiling over her head." This does not need to involve an absolute difference in relation to de Beauvoir's understanding of female emancipation, but can be understood as a critique of her at times dichotomous understanding of the relationship between activity and passivity, transcendence and immanence, spirit and body, in favor of a more complex intertwining of these inspired by her emphasis on the significance of the situation and women's concrete

---

86. Amy Hollywood, *Sensible Ecstasy: Mysticism, Sexual Difference, and the Demands of History,* Religion and Postmodernism (Chicago: University of Chicago Press, 2002), pp. 120–45.

87. De Beauvoir, *The Second Sex,* p. 636.

88. De Beauvoir, *The Second Sex,* p. 671.

89. Hollywood, *Sensible Ecstasy,* pp. 137, 144.

90. Hollywood, *Sensible Ecstasy,* p. 137.

91. On Teresa, see Rowan Williams, *Teresa of Avila,* Outstanding Christian Thinkers (London: Geoffrey Chapman, 1991). Williams writes on p. 166: "Teresa's spirituality is not to be reduced to a simple pattern of 'female' contemplative receptivity to God: there is a more complex interrelation of action and passion in both God and the female self before God."

possibilities. In order for men and women to be able to recognize each other as equals as de Beauvoir calls for, a more nuanced understanding is needed of the relationship between activity and passivity than what the unilateral affirmation of transcendence, activity, and spirit can give.

The Christian mystical tradition is, however, not the only possible way to discuss the intertwining between activity and passivity that I call for. Another example exists in the most central doctrine of Reformation theology, the doctrine of justification. In a discussion of justification and sanctification from the same perspective I have brought forth here, the North American theologian Serene Jones reminds us that according to Lutheran and Reformed theology justification and sanctification are not simply theoretical speculation regarding the person's relationship to God, but find their anchor in a concrete practice, namely, the preaching of the gospel in the church service.[92] Here the person is confronted with a "living word" that reveals and determines her relationship to God. "Doctrine" should not be associated here with "theory," but refers instead to an activity.[93] Even here it is a matter of the person as active and passive. In Luther's doctrine of justification the person relates passively in relation to God's mercy. Her self-righteousness and pride are challenged by an "alien righteousness," and she becomes aware that she is not able to save herself, but is dependent on God's mercy for her salvation. Jones says that Luther's doctrine as it is traditionally formulated does not affect women in the same way as men. For men—according to conventional gender stereotypes—it is pride that must be broken, while women, who have been defined as subordinate, do not have an arrogant ego that must be challenged. Jones's proposal is instead to begin with the doctrine of sanctification, i.e., the doctrine of the edification of the person. The woman's problem is not that she is too self-centered, but that she lacks a center—or that she exists immanently rather than transcendently, to refer to de Beauvoir's terminology. She must first be given a center, and then she can also be saved from making this center absolute:

> With sanctification at the beginning, the first word to meet the woman who enters the doctrine of the Christian life is the one that constructs her,

92. Serene Jones, *Feminist Theory and Christian Theology: Cartographies of Grace,* Guides to Theological Inquiry (Minneapolis: Augsburg Fortress, 2000), pp. 61–68.

93. Cf. *The Augsburg Confession,* in *The Book of Concord: The Confessions of the Evangelical Lutheran Church,* ed. Robert Kolb and Timothy J. Wengert, trans. Charles Arand et al. (Minneapolis: Fortress Press, 2000), pp. 42–43 (§7).

giving her the center and the substance she needs to become the subject then judged and graciously forgiven.[94]

Through this reversal of order in the doctrine of justification and sanctification, even the Reformed doctrine of God's mercy can be emancipatory for women, rather than yet another way to crush their self-confidence. For the woman who meets the gospel, the first thing she hears—according to Jones's way of seeing—is a word that makes her responsible, gets her to blossom as a person. The doctrine of justification in its turn involves a critique of traditional stereotypes that define the woman's nature. I would like to emphasize more than Jones does just how intertwined human activity and passivity are in relation to the gospel. In Jones's rereading of the traditional Reformation doctrines it is still a word that meets both woman and man, and thereby implies an image of the person as receptive, which is still a role where the person is both passive and active simultaneously, even if there may very well be strategic reasons to emphasize passivity or activity in a particular concrete situation. What I want to show with Jones's example is, however, primarily that there are resources within the Christian tradition for understanding the relationship between activity and passivity in a more productive way than the prevalent stereotypes suggest.[95]

From the starting point of these two examples (contemplative prayer and the doctrine of justification) I want to argue that the Christian tradition accommodates a more complex understanding of the relationship between activity and passivity than what has sometimes been the consequence of its concrete expression. If the doctrine of the incarnation is taken seriously, there is a potential deconstruction here of several dichotomies between activity and passivity, divine and human, male and female. But arguing that a more complex understanding of the relationship between active and passive is necessary in order to break with the hierarchization of gender that has been a part of the Christian tradition does not in itself count as an analysis and critique of its gender hierarchies. If a dialectical, rather than a hierarchical relationship between genders is to be possible, the question of the possibility for women to discern their own position, independent of and prior to this dialectic, arises. In what way will men and women interact? How will an in some sense genuine relationship between the genders, that

94. Jones, *Feminist Theory and Christian Theology*, p. 63.
95. Cf. as well Susan Frank Parsons, *The Ethics of Gender*, New Dimensions to Religion Ethics (Oxford/Malden, MA: Blackwell, 2002), pp. 97–112.

does not build on unilateral subordination, be understood? In the wake of de Beauvoir's theories in *The Second Sex,* feminist theory and feminist theology have posed the question of the woman's autonomy, of the possibility of a symbolic understanding of the woman that achieves a self-sufficient subjectivity that is not traced over man's.

The Philosophy and Religion of Gender Differences

One of the feminist theoreticians who has most clearly concerned herself with the question of gender differences and women's self-sufficiency within religiosity as well as sexuality is Luce Irigaray. Irigaray is trained in both psychoanalysis and philosophy, and belongs to a later generation of French thinkers than Simone de Beauvoir, with whom she is often compared.[96] Luce Irigaray says that equality between men and women is at best a doubtful ideal, since equality presupposes some sort of common yardstick, a comparative term. But what is this comparative term? Is not the consequence of the pursuit of the equality of women with men the fact that the man still constitutes the yardstick? In order for true equality to be possible, it is first necessary for the woman to become her own yardstick: "Equality between men and women cannot be achieved without a *theory of gender as sexed* and a rewriting of the rights and obligations of each sex, *qua different,* in social rights and obligations."[97] What Irigaray calls for is thus a possibility for realizing gender differences without them hardening into a hierarchy between the genders.[98]

For Irigaray there is no neutral arena where man and woman can meet on equal terms independent of gender differences. Science, politics, culture, language, religion, everything is a part of a gender-defined universe. With regard to science, for example, there are certain things that are taken up in research and others that are not.[99] There are gender-defined subject

96. Her work has been the occasion for an intensive theological interest. For an exciting discussion of Irigaray and the Christian conception of God as triune that I do not, however, take up here, see Gavin D'Costa, *Sexing the Trinity: Gender, Culture and the Divine* (London: SCM, 2000).

97. Luce Irigaray, "A Personal Note: Equal or Different?," in *je, tu, nous: Toward a Culture of Difference,* trans. Alison Martin (New York: Routledge, 1993), p. 13.

98. Luce Irigaray, "An Ethics of Sexual Difference," in *An Ethics of Sexual Difference,* trans. Carolyn Burke and Gillian C. Gill (Ithaca, NY: Cornell University Press, 1993), pp. 117–18.

99. Irigaray, "Ethics," pp. 121–25.

positions inscribed in the scientific paradigm itself, understood as a conglomerate of practices, which influence what science researches, its results, and the way these are presented.

> Given that the scientist, now, wants to be *in front of* the world: naming the world, making its laws, its axioms. Manipulating nature, exploiting it, but forgetting that he too is *in* nature. That he is still *physical,* and not only when faced with phenomena whose *physical* nature he tends to ignore.[100]

To judge from this quotation, and there are several similar passages in Irigaray's work, the man occupies the subject position that de Beauvoir terms activity, transcendence, and spirit. The man has forgotten or repressed the fact that he is body, and therefore occupies a subject position that is alienated from his being. This repression bases itself, according to Irigaray, on a primordial murder of the mother (in opposition to Freud's patricide).[101] The identity of the man is maintained precisely through the repressed difference in relation to the mother-nature, which has the effect that the man maintains a love to precisely that which avoids every fall back into this undifferentiated origin. The binary logic of science serves to maintain this separation. To adopt such a subject position would be fatal for the woman, since science would thereby be transformed into a new superego.[102] Similarly, it is the man's subjectivity that is defining in language itself, and that gets to pass for the universal position.[103] In her analysis of the woman's situation, Irigaray is in relative agreement with de Beauvoir. It is primarily in their views on the liberation of the woman that they differ.

Whether women enter into the masculine order or define themselves against it, they wind up at an impasse, according to Irigaray. If one wants to achieve a true equality, a dialectic between the sexes rather than a hierarchy, the only possibility is for women to develop a self-sufficient subjectivity that is neither complementary nor competitive. For women, it is thus a matter of beginning to speak their own language, which is easy to say but more difficult to accomplish, since women have long been doomed to silence precisely because they are women. Through their marginalization women

100. Irigaray, "Ethics," p. 125.

101. Luce Irigaray, "Body to Body: In Relation to the Mother," in *Sexes and Genealogies,* trans. Gillian C. Gill (New York: Columbia University Press, 1993), pp. 7–22.

102. Irigaray, "A Chance of Life," in *Sexes and Genealogies,* p. 203.

103. Irigaray, "The Language of Man," trans. Erin G. Carlston, in *Cultural Critique* 13 (1989): 191–202.

can, however, contribute to mirroring culture in a more "objective" way.[104] The prerequisite for this is, however, that women be given the possibility for building up their own structures, their own language, their own genealogies, and their own religions. Irigaray herself has set about attempting to upset the discourse of philosophy, since it is determinative for so many other discourses. The *logos* of philosophy, its reason, has had a singular success through its ability to reduce everything that is different to the same, and thereby erase all differences:

> A *sexed* subject imposes its imperatives as universally valuable, as if they alone were capable of defining the forms of reason, of thought, of meaning, of exchanges in general. This leads us back, still and always, to the same logic, to the only logic: of the One, of the Same. Of the Sameness of the One.[105]

Philosophy, Irigaray says, has the power to *"eradicate the difference between the sexes* in systems that are self-representative of a 'masculine subject.'"[106] Irigaray wants to try to check this machinery that reduces everything to univocality. In other words, for Irigaray it is a matter of revealing a sort of conceptual idolatry where static order locks down the meanings of words and thereby reduces and censures the reality they claim to describe, among other things the woman. Irigaray's own authorship thus oscillates between the strictly philosophical and the more literary in an attempt to break up the conventions that regulate access to the different discourses. At the same time she is very conscious of the fact that it is not possible to simply choose another language, one completely free from the phallic order of conventional language. The goal is an other language, which is different by not defining the man as the whole and the woman as lack, the man as subject and the woman as object, etc.[107] The means may be a subversive strategy, which makes use of the woman's marginalized position in order to undermine and destabilize the unproblematized presuppositions that androcentric philosophy builds on.

Irigaray does not only strive for a different language, but also for a different sexuality and a different religion. In the areas of both sexuality and

---

104. Irigaray, "A Chance of Life," p. 187.

105. Irigaray, "The Language of Man," p. 193.

106. Irigaray, "The Power of Discourse and the Subordination of the Feminine," in *This Sex Which Is Not One,* trans. Catherine Porter with Carolyn Burke (Ithaca, NY: Cornell University Press, 1985), p. 74.

107. Irigaray, "The Power of Discourse," pp. 78–80.

religiosity women have been defined on the basis of the man, but both areas are essential if nonhierarchical gender differences are to be established, and thereby also give the possibility of true equality. In true equality, the woman does not get to be the mirror image of the man, but must establish her own, self-sufficient subjectivity that takes into account the difference between men and women, but also between women.[108] In the area of sexuality the woman must find a sexual identity and pleasure that is unique for her. "The more or less exclusive—and highly anxious—attention paid to erection in Western sexuality proves to what extent the imaginary that governs it is foreign to the feminine."[109] Western sexuality is for the most part an expression of a masculine rivalry. A female sexuality would, according to Irigaray, not be based on a phallic symbolism of aggressive penetration, but on the woman's more tactile and manifold sexuality symbolized by the shape of her genitals, where two lips stand in constant contact. The woman is in herself always already two who embrace each other, and it thereby becomes impossible to separate activity and passivity. In female sexuality the difference is primordial, and so it cannot be made to conform with a phallic sexuality that follows the logic of the "a-lone" (Swedish *en-samma,* one-the same, a play on *ensam,* alone) rather than of difference.

Religion is important because religion constitutes the horizon for the aspirations of men and women. Irigaray is indeed critical towards Western patriarchal Christianity, but this does not mean that Christianity's symbolic resources are exhausted, or that religion is unimportant. Rather, it is one of the most important dimensions of the symbolic system that determines the relationship between the genders.[110] In her attempt to revive a feminine mythology and religion, Irigaray emphasizes the relationship to nature and the body. But it would be too simple to perceive this as an inversion of a masculine religion's emphasis on transcendence. Instead, Irigaray attempts to keep transcendence and immanence together, rather than seeing them as each other's opposites. An indication of this may be seen in a positive interest in the doctrine of the incarnation—and here she differs from de Beauvoir. Because Irigaray believes that the divine must be connected to human embodiment, the doctrine of the incarnation bears a tremendous

---

108. Serene Jones, "This God Which Is Not One: Irigaray and Barth on the Divine," *Transfiguration: Theology & the French Feminists,* ed. C. W. Maggie Kim, Susan M. St. Ville, and Susan M. Simonaitis (Minneapolis: Fortress Press, 1993), p. 121.

109. Irigaray, "This Sex Which Is Not One," in *This Sex Which Is Not One,* p. 24. Cf. pp. 23–32.

110. Irigaray, "A Chance of Life," pp. 190–91.

potential. To deny the importance of human sexuality is to give up the doctrine of the incarnation, Irigaray says—a viewpoint I have previously touched on in chapter 3.[111]

One critique that has sometimes been directed against Irigaray is that her feminist theory builds on an essentialist understanding of gender, i.e., the idea that there is a biologically founded gender difference.[112] However, such a critique misses the fact that Irigaray, firstly, is not looking to describe actually existing women, but the symbolism that is in part generated about the woman by masculine discourses and is in part generated by women's discourses in their attempt to find another language. Secondly, Irigaray starts with the fact that body, sex, and nature are historically changeable categories, and thus not given in any simple sense. One of the reasons she explicitly links to the body is, however, the fact that women have been associated with the body, and that women must therefore make use of a reinterpreted and reevaluated embodiment in order to be able to achieve their own subjectivity. Irigaray also seems to proceed from the symbolic connection between the individual body and the social body, and by making use of the specific in the female body she attempts to find an alternative metaphor that breaks with the conventional masculine metaphor, and thereby serves the process of women's own subjectification.[113] In light of the connection between social and individual embodiment that I highlighted in the previous chapter, Irigaray's purpose thus agrees well with the theological interpretation of embodiment that I pursue in this study. Nor is it especially surprising that Irigaray has also contributed to a theology of the self-sufficient sexuality of the woman.

A Clitoral Symbolic Economy

Irigaray is one of the feminist theoreticians who has inspired different theologians to discuss the sexuality (and subjectivity) of the woman independent of her motherhood. Motherhood has otherwise been the legitimate

---

111. Irigaray, "Equal to Whom?" in *The Postmodern God: A Theological Reader,* ed. Graham Ward (Oxford: Blackwell, 1997), pp. 203, 205.

112. For a detailed argument why Irigaray should not be understood as essentialist and an attempt to explain why her philosophy is often understood as essentialist in an Anglo-American context, see Tina Chanter, *Ethics of Eros: Irigaray's Rewriting of the Philosophers* (New York/London: Routledge, 1995).

113. Hollywood, *Sensible Ecstasy,* pp. 187–90.

place for a female sexuality within Christian theology. There the choice lay between the ideal of virginity and the ideal of reproduction, and as the ideal of virginity was usually seen as asexual, motherhood quite simply became the sole symbolically possible place for female sexuality. English theologian Tina Beattie has, however, pointed out that there are theological resources for expanding this symbolic spectrum. Taking inspiration from what Irigaray has written about the sexuality of the woman, as well as from what Pope John Paul II has written about the male body, as itself a bearer of a revelation, Beattie thus argues that the woman's clitoris can be interpreted in a theologically significant way.[114] Beattie is interesting for my purposes because she exemplifies a trend within contemporary feminist theology, namely, with full understanding of the androcentric history of Christian theology, to make the latent feminist potential within this same history productive. Beattie shares the strategy of focusing on a particular body party or bodily movement and interpreting it in theological-symbolic terms with large portions of the theological tradition. Augustine interprets the man's involuntary erection, and thus the way the man's sexual lust functions independently of his will, as a symptom of the Fall.[115] Even if the details in this particular concrete interpretation may be challenged, it is one example among many of how a gender-specific body part or bodily movement may be interpreted theologically (or philosophically). Beattie's strategy is to

> map bodily metaphors on to the female body as a way of prising them away from the masculine imaginary, with its feminine fantasies, in order to create a symbolic space that recognizes the existence of woman as body and not just as feminine ideal.[116]

The fight for the liberation of the woman stands, as with Irigaray, not only on de Beauvoir's abstract rights and concrete possibilities, but also on an alternative symbolic system that manages to set sexuality, religiosity, reason, and interpersonal relationships in a different light.

114. Tina Beattie, "Carnal Love and Spiritual Imagination: Can Luce Irigaray and John Paul II Come Together?" *Sex These Days,* ed. Jon Davies and Gerard Loughlin, pp. 177–81.

115. Augustine, *The City of God against the Pagans,* Cambridge Texts in the History of Political Thought, trans. R. W. Dyson (Cambridge: Cambridge University Press, 1998), pp. 623–30 (14, 23–26).

116. Tina Beattie, *God's Mother, Eve's Advocate: A Marian Narrative of Women's Salvation* (London/New York: Continuum, 2002), p. 7.

What Beattie herself wants to argue is that men and women are asymmetrically sexually embodied. With respect to the clitoris it should not—as with Freud—be understood as "a little penis," but as a self-sufficient sexual organ. Beattie believes that a symbolic interpretation of the clitoris can contribute to an understanding of the woman's sexuality that is not dependent on her motherhood. "This is an organ created purely for woman's delight, mercifully protected from the wounds of childbirth."[117] The clitoris is namely independent of the woman's reproductive function. She can reproduce without orgasm, and can orgasm without any reproductive function. This is in contrast with the man's sexuality, where ejaculation and physical fertilization cannot be separated. This difference can be illustrated with a quotation from philosopher Gayatri Chakravorty Spivak:

> Male and female sexuality are asymmetrical. Male orgasmic pleasure "normally" entails the male reproductive act—semination. Female orgasmic pleasure (it is not, of course, the "same" pleasure, only called by the same name) does not entail any one component of heterogeneous female reproductive scenario: ovulation, fertilization, conception, gestation, birthing. The clitoris escapes reproductive framing.[118]

Further, according to Beattie the woman's clitoris represents a sexual pleasure that is not dependent on the man, a pleasure that is apparently created without any reproductive function. An interpretation of the theological symbolism of the clitoris can therefore contribute two things: in part, a theological understanding of sensuality as a part of the goodness of creation independent of a reproductive function (see the first section of this chapter), and in part a female sexuality independent of the man's. The body can, as I wrote in chapter 8, serve as a source of symbols for other complex structures. With Beattie the symbolic meaning of the clitoris assumes cultural dimensions analogous to the cultural symbol of the penis, the phallus: "If the phallus can symbolize a culture of domination, aggression and power, the clitoris might even symbolize a culture that celebrates playfulness and nurtures small delights in the loving and patient encounters of daily life."[119] To anticipate the objection that this is to overestimate the symbolism of embodiment, Beattie

---

117. Beattie, "Carnal Love and Spiritual Imagination," p. 178.

118. Gayatri Chakravorty Spivak, "French Feminism in an International Frame," *In Other Worlds: Essays in Cultural Politics* (New York/London: Methuen, 1987), p. 151.

119. Beattie, "Carnal Love and Spiritual Imagination," p. 180.

further argues that female circumcision actually plays a greater symbolic role than one is often conscious of. Female circumcision—physically as well as psychically—signals that the woman's self-sufficient sexuality is perceived as a threat.

One objection to Beattie's interpretation of the clitoris as a cultural symbol (and of what Irigaray writes of the woman's labia as constantly touching) is that the interpretation carries associations of female self-satisfaction. The problem with this is not the autoerotic act itself, but its associations with the lack of a relationship (aside from the relationship to oneself), which in a certain way reiterates part of the problem with the phallus as cultural symbol.[120] Masturbation is intimately tied to modernity's ideal of autonomy, and is connected not only to sexual self-satisfaction, but at the same time signals a religious, ethical, and political posture that primarily comes to expression within the Enlightenment.[121] But even within the Enlightenment masturbation signaled a self-sufficiency that went too far even for its ideal of autonomy. It was by shaming and pathologizing the person's autoerotic actions that her sexuality would be socialized, and so prevented from running amok. It is not until the 1960s that masturbation ceases to be the threat towards the person's sociality that it had been ever since the beginning of the eighteenth century, and is instead transformed into a manifestation of human expressivity. The objection to a socio-symbolic interpretation of the clitoris should, however, not be understood as inspired by this modern history, but instead has its source in the theological idea that the person's sexuality should be understood as neither monadic nor dyadic, but finds its proper place in a social context, namely in the church.

However, the point of Beattie's metaphor is not antisocial, but is intended to emphasize the woman's sexual self-sufficiency within the framework of a greater theological symbolic horizon. If this self-sufficiency were to tip over into relationlessness, it would work against the very point of Beattie's metaphor. The problem may be generalized: What is primary, the difference or the relationship? It is no more a matter of denying the relational as a fundamental value in Beattie's case than in Irigaray's, but is instead a matter of establishing a more genuine relationality between man and woman, one that is not already inscribed in a masculine symbolism. What I want to show with the help of Beattie and Irigaray—as with the discussion of contemplative prayer and the doctrine of justification—is that it is impossible to

120. Cf. Gavin D'Costa, *Sexing the Trinity,* pp. 52–55.
121. Laqueur, *Solitary Sex,* p. 13. Laqueur's book is the definitive work on onanism.

conceive of the difference without the relationality, and vice versa, and thus neither is primary.[122] The reference to the clitoris should be understood as strategic rather than existential. In order to function in an actual emancipatory way, its symbolism must, however, be integrated into a fuller theological erotics, which does not potentially threaten to undermine relationality apart from oneself. The individual body and the social body must be held together for relationality not to disappear from sight.

A clitoral symbolic economy is not the only possibility for speaking of a self-sufficient female sexuality. Mariology may also be strategically used as a way to break with a masculine theological symbolism.[123] Mary has not unequivocally stood for a stereotyping of the woman's identity. She has also represented a sexuality independent of a woman's relationship to a man. Another possible practice that does not aim to avoid sexuality, but to express it in another way, is celibacy taken as a way to withdraw the woman's sexuality from her role as the man's partner.[124] So yet again I want to argue that it is possible to work within the Christian tradition while displacing its symbolic economy by bringing in viewpoints from feminist theory, and thereby developing a theological understanding of women's sexuality that does not follow conventional gender hierarchies.

Why would this be theologically significant? In part because in this we find a possibility for speaking about a self-sufficient female sexuality, and thereby dislodge the masculine theological symbolism. But also because we can thereby exploit both the dynamic and the subversive symbolic potential within a relatively traditional theology. It would be a mistake to represent feminist theology and the earlier theological tradition as antitheses, since the tradition is neither so homogenous nor so unequivocal as it has often been represented. Sexual metaphors and symbolism permeate the entire theological heritage, and this heritage thus itself carries the potential for a (relative to androcentrism) subversive interpretation. The thought of the incarnation itself can, through the fact that it brings together the divine and the human, turn established theological hierarchies upside down, as has in fact historically occurred. Beattie's works that attempt to exploit the dynamic as well as the subversive symbolic potential in a relatively traditional Catholic theology are an example of a feminist theology that in a critical

122. Cf. Irigaray, "This Sex Which Is Not One," pp. 31–32.
123. Beattie, *God's Mother, Eve's Advocate.*
124. Janette Gray, "Celibacy These Days," in *Sex These Days,* ed. Davies and Loughlin, pp. 153–56.

way attempts to reclaim and reuse the theological tradition.[125] Even if the Christian church bears a heavily androcentric heritage, we now live in a time where Christian feminism does not need to be an isolated and suppressed tradition within an androcentric church. Thus other possibilities exist for interpreting the Christian message anew by reusing insights that have previously influenced Western conceptions of the woman in a—in relation to androcentric theology—subversive way. The tradition that we meet in the Christian church is neither unchangeable nor unequivocal. Even if portions of the Christian tradition may be characterized as androcentric, at the same time it carries the potential for other interpretations, which may be taken advantage of in order to formulate a more radical theology. Note that this theological work does *not* in principle differ from the theology of earlier ages. Even historically theology has worked with its own tradition by highlighting and emphasizing certain parts at the cost of others. Today's feminist theology is thus not so essentially different from earlier (primarily ancient and medieval) theology as its detractors and supporters sometimes represent it. Through the emergence of feminism the possibility is given for discovering already existing but marginalized traditions within the tradition—and thereby in a certain sense saving the tradition from itself. Finding space for an autonomous female subjectivity and sexuality within the framework of the Christian tradition is not, however, simply a matter of making female subjectivity an object for theology, but also of women becoming the subject of theology in an authentic way—which is one of the greatest changes of the twenty-first century. Feminist theology is thus generally in need of what the feminist christologies in chapter 3 sought, namely a concrete, transformed practice as a further development of the incarnation. Although androcentrism has generally been prevalent within the history of the Christian tradition, I hope that with the above argument I have shown that it is not inevitable.

Love for the Same?

Alongside the question of the androcentrism of the theological tradition, during recent decades the question of its potential heteronormativity has been paid attention to, that is to say, the question of whether the hetero-

---

125. Cf. as well Tina Beattie, *Woman,* New Century Theology (London/New York: Continuum, 2003).

sexual couple has gotten to constitute in an uncritical way the norm for what legitimate sexual expression is. Different formulations of homo- and queer-theologies have presented everything from radical repudiations to optimistic rereadings of the Christian tradition and its apparently inevitable negative image of sexual relations between people of the same sex.[126] By making use of constructivist theories, however, historical research has increasingly come to show the problems with imagining that there would have existed an ahistorical "homosexual" or "sodomitic" essential identity during the Christian centuries. It is said—often in connection to Foucault's studies in *The History of Sexuality*—that it is not possible to easily identify, for example, what Paul says in Romans 1:27 about "men committing shameless acts *[tēn aschēmosynēn katergazomenoi]* with men" with what is called homosexuality in the West of our time.[127] The New Testament, the church fathers, and the medieval authors present a sexual ethics that is alien to our time, not only as regards the love between people of the same gender, but in general. This alienation depends in part on inevitable displacements of the horizon of expectations, but in part also on the critical understanding of the Christian tradition's dominant heteronormativity.[128] When it comes to sexual love between people of the same genital configuration, it is particularly doubtful that the majority of the people of the ancient or medieval world would have recognized themselves in the modern categorization. Every attempt to bring relevant historical texts to the fore must take into account the hermeneutic gap between our time and theirs, if we are to avoid naïvely reading in the questions and problems of our own time.

Such an "alienation" of the texts of the tradition has in its turn made possible a both critical and constructive new reading of the theological tradition, which in turn has opened up the possibility of a critical reclamation of its texts at the same time that their heteronormativity is challenged. It shows as well that the tradition is not as completely unequivocal as a more

126. For an overview, see Elizabeth Stuart, *Gay and Lesbian Theologies: Repetitions with Critical Difference* (Aldershot, UK: Ashgate, 2003).

127. For a discussion of Romans 1:26–27, see L. William Countryman, *Dirt, Greed and Sex: Sexual Ethics in the New Testament and Their Implications for Today* (London: SCM, 2001), pp. 100–103. On the problem of using the term "homosexuality" to designate sexual love between two persons of the same genital configuration, see John Boswell, *Christianity, Social Tolerance, and Homosexuality: Gay People in Western Europe from the Beginning of the Christian Era to the Fourteenth Century* (Chicago/London: University of Chicago Press, 1980), pp. 41–59.

128. Cf. my discussion in "Vems tradition? Vilken sexualitet? Svar till Gösta Hallonsten," *Svensk Teologisk Kvartalskrift* 80, no. 3 (2004): 124–26.

generalizing understanding would suppose.[129] When it comes to the biblical texts that constitute some of the most critical foundations for how Christianity has come to develop, it is not at all self-evident that they are directly condemnatory with respect to sexual love between people of the same sex, or that they in general discuss what in the modern period has come to be called "homosexuality." According to exegete L. William Countryman, the context for much of what the Hebrew Bible as well as the New Testament has to say about sexuality consists of conceptions of ritual and physical purity and specific conceptions of property ownership that have very little or nothing at all to do with the understanding of sexuality in our time.[130] This does not mean that the biblical texts or other significant texts from Christian history are meaningless for our period. What it means is that it is not possible to "translate" or "apply" these texts in an unmediated way. What is needed is a critical interpretation.[131] Rather than leaving these historically significant texts obsolete, their "alienation" amounts to a demand for a close and detailed interpretation, partly in order to avoid a generalizing view of the historical horizon, partly in order to make possible a critical perspective on those preconceptions that govern our own, contemporary horizon.

The task in this section is to critically discuss, with the help of these studies, the heteronormativity of the Christian tradition and to bring a theological contribution to what may in a sense be called a more genuine "heterosexuality" that embraces with the same obviousness sexual intercourse between people of the same genital configuration as between people of different configurations. To begin with, I will, with the help of Mark D. Jordan, say something about the emergence of the concept of "sodomy," which has been significant in Christian theology's (unsuccessful) attempt to relate to sexual intercourse between people of the same biological sex. The unsatisfactory nature of this theological category shows the need to find alternative theological understandings of same-sex love. In order to be able to do this, it is probably also necessary for the modern identification between desire and sexuality to be overcome, since this ties legitimate sexuality to an ideal of

---

129. It is a matter of, for example, so-called *adelphopoiesis,* i.e., "making brothers." See John Boswell, *Same-Sex Unions in Premodern Europe* (New York: Villard Books, 1994).

130. Countryman, *Dirt, Greed and Sex,* pp. 123–28.

131. Cf. my article "Bibeln som Skrift: Om bibelns anspråk på aktualitet och auktoritet i den kristna kyrkan," *Tolkning för livet: Åtta teologer om bibelns auktoritet,* ed. Anne-Louise Eriksson (Stockholm: Verbum, 2004), pp. 215–38, 271–73, and Jesper Svartvik's article "Vem vaktar väktarna? En undersökning av bibelbruket i debatten om homosexualitet," in *Tolkning för livet,* pp. 168–92; 260–67.

biological reproduction. If the modern understanding of sexuality as reproduction is abandoned, the possibility is opened for understanding sexuality
not as identical with desire, but with the desire for God as the horizon of sexuality. Through the Christian understanding of God the possibility is opened
for understanding love between people of the same genital configuration as
a genuine form of love for the other, not as a love of the same. Starting from
my constructivist understanding of sexuality, with this discussion I want
to attempt to shift the issue to my overall question of how the sexuality of
the human being in general should be understood theologically, rather than
finding a theological legitimacy for either a heterosexual or a homosexual
"orientation" in the modern sense.

Sodomy and History

Let me begin with the concept of sodomy. With Mark D. Jordan we can view
this concept as a medieval artifact. "Sodomy," which according to the glossary of the Swedish Academy means "sexual intercourse between people of
the same sex or between people and animals," did not start as a designation
for a particular sexual action; the word occurs in the account of the two
cities Sodom and Gomorrah in Genesis chapter 19.[132] Here two angels come
to visit Lot, who invites them to eat and sleep in his house. All of Sodom's
male inhabitants gather around Lot's house and demand that he send out
the two strangers (for that is how they perceive them) from the house so
that they can lie with them. Lot refuses, instead offering to send out his own
two untouched daughters, but Sodom's inhabitants insist. Finally, when they
attempt to force their way into the house the two angels grab hold of Lot and
close the door. Sodom's inhabitants are struck with blindness as punishment,
and the Lord later destroys Sodom in a rain of fire and brimstone.

On the basis of this account in the Hebrew Bible the word "sodomy"
has come to describe the sexual activity that was characteristic for its

132. The fact that "sodomy" *(sodomi)* according to the *Svenska Akademiens ordlista*
(SAOL) can designate both sexual relations between "people of the same sex" ("personer av
samma kön") and "between a person and an animal" ("mellan människa och djur") shows in
itself how the term is both instable and how different sexual activities have been able to be
combined under a common denominator. For a discussion of Genesis 19, see John Boswell,
Christianity, Social Tolerance, and Homosexuality, pp. 92–105, together with Mark D. Jordan,
The Invention of Sodomy in Christian Theology (Chicago/London: University of Chicago Press,
1997), *passim.*

inhabitants. Jordan has explained the long process that lies between the biblical account and the theological concept in his book *The Invention of Sodomy in Christian Theology*.[133] The concept of *sodomia* itself was minted in the eleventh century by the theologian Petrus Damianus as an analogy to *blasphemia,* that is to say, the sin of denying God. For *sodomia* to be able to become a theological concept, however, a long process of thinning and condensation must take place, as the biblical account, according to most exegetes, does not have the condemnation of "sexual intercourse between people of the same sex" as its point. Its point lies instead with the inhabitants' inhospitable treatment of passing travelers or strangers. During biblical times, the city Sodom came to be an example of a divine judgment, a trope for God's wrath over humanity. In neither the Hebrew Bible nor the New Testament is there any text that connects the judgment of Sodom with a condemnation of "sexual intercourse between people of the same sex." It is not until the end of the patristic period, that is to say, the end of the sixth century, and with Pope Gregory the Great that the account unambiguously comes to be associated with a sexual sin. Gregory the Great categorized this sin under *luxuria,* one of the seven deadly sins. According to Jordan *luxuria* has two functions with Gregory. On the one hand, it is a general sin that consists in self-centered deeds in both thought and action. On the other hand, it is a specific sin whose center is the person's genitals. Thus the idea itself of *luxuria* is filled with tension, and this is a tension that could be used in order to claim something general and something concrete simultaneously.

Eventually *luxuria* came to be further condensed to *sodomia.* The aim with this abstraction is to formulate the essence of sodomy and thereby classify actions in order to be able to punish them. This occurs in medieval penance books, manuals of a sort for confessors, which made it possible to identify a particular sin and determine the appropriate penance. This abstraction also serves to reduce the sin to a schematic caricature of more complicated actual deeds. When Petrus Damianus invents "sodomy" in the eleventh century, the word has undergone an abstracting process that has reduced all the various motives and circumstances that could have surrounded a number of different but similar actions. Sodomites are now those who perform sodomy. Through this process of abstraction, a distinct category has been created.

Inventing such a category, however, involves certain risks. To begin

133. Jordan, *The Invention of Sodomy.*

with, the author of the penance manual must avoid the impression that he himself knows the sin in question from his own experience. He must then also avoid representing the sin as so widespread that it appears as a universal or natural human feature. The very essentialization of sodomy threatens to make it a natural trait of certain people, and so challenges its objectionable character, or, challenges whether the sin may really be healed. Further, the author must avoid representing the sin as too interesting, either by saying too much or by saying too little, and thereby arousing the interest of the reader of the manual. The treatment itself of certain sins in these manuals can raise the question of why they actually are forbidden. Finally, the categorization of the sin risks arousing feelings of fellowship with those who are guilty of the same sin. The knowledge produced by inventing sodomy as an abstract category thus threatens to become a cause of sodomy. Eventually the anxiety over this will lead to sodomy becoming a sin that is powerfully condemned, but which may not be named (which differentiates it from other serious sins).

Jordan is especially critical of the way the category of sodomy has been formulated by medieval theology (which has also affected how people have come to speak of homosexuality in later moral theology). In itself sodomy has been an unstable term that has been able to mean whatever one has wanted it to mean. The consequence of this process of essentialization has been to create a knowledge of "the sodomite," but this knowledge has also created the identity it has pretended to identify. Jordan seems to mean that the historical origin of the contemporary discourse on homosexual identities lies in the penance manuals of the Middle Ages. The concept of sodomy is incoherent as well, and over the course of history has gotten to stand as a designation for a range of varied sexual actions. "'Sodomy,'" Jordan therefore concludes, "is not a name for a kind of human behavior, but for a failure of theologians. 'Sodomy' is the nervous refusal of theologians to understand how pleasure can survive the preaching of the Gospel."[134]

My point in recounting this history is not to point out what is doubtful in historical theology's stance towards "sexual intercourse between people of the same sex," even if this is also worth drawing attention to. What I want to seize on is rather how Jordan describes sodomy as a category that emerges through a process of confession and thereby establishes a knowledge. This knowledge constitutes a power relationship in Foucault's sense, a power

134. Jordan, *The Invention of Sodomy*, p. 176.

relationship that is also a process of subjectification. Sodomy, as an example of the will to know, produces the object of knowledge. It does not, of course, follow from this that there was not any sexual intercourse between people of the same sex before the medieval penance manuals. It is instead the case that these manuals and the practices they supported created a reasonably cohesive identity for a certain type of similar actions, which in its turn created a group of people who were identified as "sodomites." With the fact that penance produces a truth about the inner self, a mapping of the movements of the soul, it also creates, with the help of its moral categorizations, a category of people whose actions it condemns, and so a specific form of subjectivity. The instability and incoherence of the category of sodomy meant, however, that its stability was more doubtful than most other moral categories. This instability seems, however, not to have affected its use. After moral theology had lost its grip on people's sexual actions, this specific power-knowledge relationship was replaced by the classificatory ambition of modern medicine. As such, this has, as I have mentioned at the start of this chapter, been strengthened rather than weakened in the modern state.

Modern "homosexuality" thus does not have very much to do with medieval "sodomy." "Sodomy," to begin with, is instead a part of a sexual politics or subjectification process that does not have much to do with our period's "homosexuality." Homosexuality as a concept is taken from the medical science of the nineteenth century, rather than from theology. A certain continuity exists between the two, however, such as the conception of "an identity built around the genital configuration of one's sexual partners," which is a product of Christian theology.[135] The homosexuality of our period has inherited a tendency to conceive of homosexuality as an identity, as something one *is*. But perhaps there is a more productive way to speak about sexuality from a theological perspective. In a reckoning with traditional ways of looking at sexual love between people of the same sex, there can be a value in exposing this genealogy and thereby opening the possibility for not conceiving of this sexual love as a project of identity. It is likely that the Christian authors prior to the period that Jordan describes in his book did not think in terms of a specific sexual identity either. When sexual actions between people of the same sex were discussed by, for example, Paul, it was not a matter of identifying a particular *orientation* in a certain group of people, but rather of specific *actions* precisely as actions.[136]

---

135. Jordan, *The Invention of Sodomy,* p. 163.

136. Cf., for example, Boswell, *Christianity, Social Tolerance, and Homosexuality,* p. 109.

The Bodies of the Modern Period

One of the consequences of the above argument is, as Jordan points out, that as yet no possibilities exist for explaining Christian theology's condemnation of love between people of the same sex in a satisfactory way.[137] The reasons for this are several. It is not until our immediate present that theology has begun to reflect on these questions in a responsible and direct way. Nor is there an adequate theological understanding of sexuality in general. To speak of "homophobia" as an explanation for the tensions within Christian theology is no solution, but is instead given in place of an explanation. What the love between people of the same sex shows in an especially clear way is that sexual love cannot be reduced to reproductive love, and it thus evokes what the tradition experienced as a threat about a sexual sensuality without reproduction.

We can thus see the failure of the theologians in their engagement with love between people of the same sex as one part of a failure with a constructive theological conception of sensuality in general. I believe that this theological failure has in a certain sense been reinforced during the last centuries, since the person's life of desire has come to be associated by both the Christian church and the wider culture with a normative heterosexuality. For the premodern church it was obvious that the goal of desire did not exist in any human being at all, whether of the same or different biological sex, but in God.[138] Queer theologian Elizabeth Stuart writes:

> The loss of an eschatological imagination, not just in gay and lesbian theology, but across much of western Christian theology, has impoverished Christian discourse on sexuality and allowed the collapse of desire into heterosexuality and discipleship into marriage and modern constructions of the family.[139]

The loss of desire's eschatological or transcendent horizon has resulted in it being reduced to sexuality. Instead of love finding its *telos* in God, in modern Christianity it finds its *telos* in heterosexual marriage. Desire has quite

---

137. Jordan, *The Invention of Sodomy,* pp. 167–68.

138. See Michael Vasey, *Strangers and Friends: A New Exploration of Homosexuality and the Bible* (London: Hodder & Stoughton, 1995), pp. 64–66. Cf. also Fergus Kerr, *Immortal Longings: Versions of Transcending Humanity* (Notre Dame: University of Notre Dame Press, 1997).

139. Stuart, *Gay and Lesbian Theologies,* p. 110; cf. p. 3.

simply been biologized and normatively identified with reproduction, while science has come to associate human desire and the person's needs as ways to reproduce oneself.[140] Thus the heteronormativity of the Christian tradition has been reinforced in the modern period. Desire, *eros,* and sexuality were not identified with each other during the greater part of the history of the Christian church, which is clear not least in the transcending of the boundaries between male and female during the medieval period, as has been described in the previous chapter—a period that is significantly more "queer" than the contemporary Christian church has chosen to acknowledge.[141] They were aware that desire was mediated by certain images whose function was to transform the person's desire and direct it towards God. One example from the literature is where Dante Alighieri saw in Beatrice's beauty a vision of the divine glory and calling, and it is here that he finds the point in God's beauty and calling being understood as incarnated in bodies and social ideals.[142] The images that would excite, direct, and transform the person's desire in no way conformed with our contemporary Christian heterosexual ideal of beauty. Christian devotional poetry of the seventeenth century gives a sample of desire stimulating devotion by provoking human desire with images of the crucified Christ, "a nearly naked man offered up to our gazes ('Ecce homo') for worship, desire, and various kinds of identification."[143] The incarnation involved a transcending of traditional gender boundaries, both social and biological. The physical or intellectual image of the crucified Christ, penetrated, passive, and incessantly coveted, shapes the desire of the Christian in a way that prevents a simple identification between sexuality and biological reproduction. The erotic charge of the traditional Christian prayer life is such that it transcends the heteronormativity of modernity and thereby hints at another sexuality, one that differs from both the traditional and the modern Christian sexuality.

But the bodies of the modern period have lost their transcendent horizon, and so bodily desire has been reduced to a biological desire. If the problem with the dominant tradition during Antiquity and the Middle Ages was, to put it very briefly, that it separated *eros* from a legitimate sexuality, the problem of the modern Christian church is that it has reduced desire to sexuality. When the church as a social body disappears during modernity (see

140. Vasey, *Strangers and Friends,* p. 149.

141. Cf. Stuart, *Gay and Lesbian Theologies,* p. 11: "Christianity is a queer thing."

142. Vasey, *Strangers and Friends,* p. 149.

143. Richard Rambuss, *Closet Devotions* (Durham, NC/London: Duke University Press, 1998), p. 11.

the previous chapter), the person's sexuality also comes to be secularized in that her individual body is understood merely as biology, and no longer as a way to relate to God. For a contemporary theology of human sexuality it is of course neither possible nor desirable to return to the earlier tradition's understanding of sensuality, but at the same time it seems as though modern sexuality has also missed something essential. One way out of these two dead ends would perhaps be to understand sexuality against the background of *eros* without setting an equal sign between the two, which I will return to in the next section of this chapter. This has consequences for the theological understanding of same-sex relationships as well.

Beyond a Homosocial Christianity

I believe that one of the big problems with the position that the Christian tradition in general has taken with respect to sexual love between people of the same genital configuration is quite simply, though it may sound paradoxical, the theological tradition's deficient heterosexuality. The term "heterosexuality"—a linguistic compound of a Latin word with a Greek prefix—designates a sexual relationship or desire between "different" (cf. the prefix *hetero-* from the Greek term for "other" or "different"), in contrast to "homosexuality," which designates a sexual relationship or desire between "the same" (cf. Greek's *homoios,* i.e., "the same" or "similar"). If the norm is a sexual relationship between "unlike," a crucial question becomes how this difference should be understood. In this chapter (as in several of the earlier chapters) I have chosen to clarify how the Christian church had been influenced early on by its contemporary androcentric culture, and especially influenced by (culturally conditioned) biological conceptions of differences between people, which unilaterally tied the person's sexuality to the ideal of reproduction. In the majority discourse, sexual relationships between people have been viewed on the basis of the differences between their genitals, a conception that bases itself on the ideal of reproduction. The consequence is a homosociality, since the tradition reduces sexual difference to a biological difference. The question, however, is whether the thought of biological reproduction should be normative for a Christian theology of the person's sexual relationships.

Beginning in the New Testament writings, the Christian tradition has instead *relativized* the significance of biology and kinship in favor of the relationships that are established by the fellowship in the church or the congregation, and are not based on blood ties. The family was, as I touched on earlier in this chapter, not the primary institution for identification in early Christianity.[144] It instead involved a break with the person's immediate identification with her biological family. Repeated times in the New Testament's Gospels Jesus expresses the idea that a prerequisite for discipleship was to leave one's biological family.[145] For Paul as well the biological family was a secondary institution.[146] Hope no longer depended on family and children, but on God's new creation, where citizenship was based on a relationship to Jesus through the church, rather than on family ties or ethnic affiliation.

The fact that the Christian conceptions of sexuality differed from the biological, which were inherited from the earlier culture, has been noted by Jordan as well, who believes that the consequence of this ought to be that Christian sexual relationship in general should not be understood on the basis of appropriated or newly produced gender hierarchies:

> What is more interesting about human bodies in Christian teaching is not the difference that allows for bodily birth. It is the suffering and the affection that grounds evangelization and other expressions of love. Christians ought to want to know not how bodies reproduce, but what they need for wholeness. What they need is both healing and embracing.[147]

The Christian church reproduces itself, not through biology, but through conversion, which I got into above in the discussion of sexuality and sociality.[148] Relationships between Christian people ought to have their basis in conceptions of a more radical difference than the genital, especially as the Christian concept of God goes together with the doctrine of a *creatio ex nihilo* (i.e., "creation out of nothing"), which establishes a radical qualitative difference between God and world, and even goes together with the doctrine of a Trinitarian difference within the divinity itself, where God is thought to love (and so in some way to relate to Godself) already "before" creation. On the basis of such a conception of God, the differences

---

144. Countryman, *Dirt, Greed and Sex*, pp. 169–70, 199–200.

145. Cf. Matthew 3:9; 4:22; 8:21–22; 10:34–38; 12:46–50; 13:54–58; 19:10–12; 19:16–30, together with parallels in the other Gospels. See as well Mark 13:12; Luke 4:22–30; 5:11; 6:32–35; 9:61–62; 10:38–42; 11:27–28; 12:49–53; 14:12–14; 14:26–27; 18:29; and 20:34–36.

146. Cf. 1 Corinthians 7:29.

147. Jordan, *The Invention of Sodomy*, p. 174.

148. Stuart, *Gay and Lesbian Theologies*, p. 95.

between people ought to be thought of in theological terms rather than biological.

For the Christian tradition this means that biological or social sex, in the words of British theologian Gerard Loughlin, "will no longer be determinative of our freedom to give and receive love. For truly in Christ there is no male and female, only the reciprocation of bodies."[149] What is crucial is not whether two Christian people can have children, but their relationship to the other. Only by doing away with the biological conceptions of sexual difference as primary and significant for the Christian tradition can it achieve a real heterosociality that is not reductive. Sexual love between people of the same sex can in a way clarify sexual difference better than sexual love between people of different sexes, since in the former case it becomes clear that it is not a matter of a biological difference, but a *theological* difference that is founded on a mutual, ongoing giving, receiving, and reciprocation, and whose paradigmatic instance in the Christian tradition is God's relationship to human beings. This means that sexual love between people of the same genital configuration in principle runs just as little or just as big a risk of becoming a "homosexual" love, i.e., a "love of the same," as sexual love between people with different genital configurations.

For the Christian church, however, sexual love is not the primary form of love. Love for God comes first. In order to be able to bring about something more than a pragmatic reworking of discursive and practical circumstances, a theology of human sexuality—whether it deals with sexuality in general or the question of which forms of genital love are legitimate and between whom—must treat this question in light of its theological horizon in a strict sense, i.e., the relationship between God and us human beings. I will therefore attempt to tie together the discussions I have presented in this chapter by turning to the question of a theological erotics. Erotics here is not limited to sexuality, but will instead be seen as the horizon of sexuality, a horizon that also covers human relationality in general, both in its interpersonal and its divine dimensions.

Thus, according to the Christian faith, it is ultimately not sexual relationships that are determinative for a person's subjectivity, but her relationship to God. This does not mean that sexual relationships are unimportant for subjectivity, but it does mean that these sexual relationships must be seen in light of the relationship with God. What the relationship with God fosters

---

149. Gerard Loughlin, *Alien Sex: The Body and Desire in Cinema and Theology,* Challenges in Contemporary Theology (Oxford/Malden, MA: Blackwell, 2004), p. 161.

is relationships where the other cannot be reduced to my reflection—a love for the other and not for the same. This is the case regardless whether we are speaking of heterosexual or homosexual relationships; to be homosexual quite simply means to meet the other and thereby also find oneself in relation to people of the same sex.[150] In other words, homosexual love cannot be said to be a love for "the same," and so a self-centered love, to a greater degree than heterosexual love.

As I have pointed out repeated times, however, sexuality is not a phenomenon that is self-contained in relation to other human relationships. Significant for the understanding of all sorts of sexualities is the background against which they are understood. Feminist theology wants to construct a different symbolic horizon for female subjectivity than the androcentric, and queer theology strives to counter the Christian tradition's heteronormativity with a more inclusive horizon. I have also raised the question of whether sensuality, which in the modern view of sexuality should be understood against the background of biological reproduction, can possibly be thought against the background of a more theological horizon as well. A change of horizon for the understanding of sensuality also entails a change of the concrete practices that are mediated between individual and social bodies. All these questions of sensuality, gender, and desire culminate in the question of how one should formulate a theological erotics.

A Theological Erotics

If Nietzsche is right that Christianity gave *eros* poison to drink, it may not have been until the modern period that the poison cup was mixed. As I showed in chapter 7 apropos the erotic gaze, certain conceptions of *eros* coincide with Christian teaching on love, and purely historically this teaching on love has been developed within the framework of a meditation on *eros*. The fact that historical teaching on love has been a contributing reason for the partially negative understanding of sensuality, gender, and desire, which has existed and does exist within the Christian church, also means that the question of *eros* as a legitimate theological love-motif is all the more relevant in our contemporary theology. Against the background of the discussion I have presented above, I will now turn to the significance of this reread-

150. David Matzko McCarthy, "The Relationship of Bodies," in *Theology and Sexuality*, ed. Rogers Jr., pp. 212–13.

ing of the Christian tradition for theological reflection on *eros,* or perhaps instead, how theological reflection on *eros* may be thought to constitute a background for a critical rereading. My thesis is thus that theology, in order to be able to offer both a self-critical and constructive understanding of sensuality, gender, and desire for our time, needs to find a genuine theological erotics.

It was a fateful moment when desire was cut out of theological and philosophical history. The origin of this within theology is an alleged opposition between the cross of Christ and desire. People suffer, according to this way of thinking, because they follow their desires, but Christ on the cross suffered because he wanted to follow God's will. I see this as a false opposition. According to theologian Sebastian Moore, Christ instead suffered on the cross because he wanted to follow his desire, desire that was fully united with God's will.[151] What the cross ought to mean instead of the repression of desires is the liberation of desires. This does not involve a liberation *from* desires, but *of* desires. The difference lies between two different sorts of asceticism: on the one hand to deny oneself the things one wants to have, on the other hand to give up the things one does not want to have in favor of those things one actually wants to have. The first sort of asceticism builds on a moralistic cross that wants to get us to repress our desires. But such a cross is a cross without transformation, without mercy, and without resurrection. Desires are, however, not identical with egoism, but real desires instead liberate the person to be what she is actually supposed to be.

The repression of desires has led to a stunted sexual ethics within Christianity, something that it certainly shares with the rest of Western culture. Sexual desire has been understood as though it must be held in check by the will, while the actual problem undoubtedly has to do with how desire should be cultivated and kept alive. Augustine may be a theologian we can relate to in this case. Augustine certainly did not succeed, as I pointed out above, in arriving at a positive theology of human sexuality, but he at least saw that the person's real problem was not holding sexual passion in check, realizing instead that the heart of the Fall was the lust to be God.[152] It is the person's alienated will that is the real problem. It is thus not a matter of how desires should be extinguished, but how they should be cultivated. In the final section of this chapter I want to bring together the threads from those

151. Sebastian Moore, "The Crisis of an Ethic without Desire," in *Theology and Sexuality,* ed. Rogers Jr., pp. 157–69.

152. Moore, "The Crisis," p. 167.

previous by summarily discussing the significance of a theological erotics with respect to the person's desire, both her desire for God and her bodily desire, together with the relationship between the two of them. Finally, I will also mention something of the cultivation of this desire together with, very briefly, the significance of theological erotics for the understanding of the presence of God.

Theological Erotics and Human Desire

If we remain with Augustine, we may note that he represented a sort of desire-therapy in line with the Classical thinkers.[153] Augustine's *Confessions* is his own theological account of how his desire has been transformed by the encounter with God. For him it is a matter of how one shall find the proper order between finite desires for fame, sexual satisfaction, and desire for the infinite, in such a way that desire for the infinite is not confused with desires for the finite. Neither fame nor sexual satisfaction manages to bear the weight of being the object of the person's infinite desire. Thus, neither do they manage to meet (rather than sate) the person's desire for the infinite—only God manages that: "our heart is restless until it rests in you."[154] In order to describe the relationship to God Augustine takes terms from Antiquity's speculation on *eros*. A language colored by longing and tension suffuses the whole of *Confessions,* as, for example, when he speaks of hot and breathlessly returning to the fountainhead of God, or of singing love songs and uttering inexpressible sighs.[155]

Such a language, with associations with Plato's *Symposium* and neo-Platonism, which has since been linked to Christian spirituality in general and the Song of Solomon in particular, permeates not only Augustine's *Confessions,* but all of Christian Antiquity (Origen, Gregory of Nyssa) and the Middle Ages (Dionysius the Areopagite, Johannes Scotus Eriugena, Bernard of Clairvaux).[156] One may object that this *eros*-metaphor constitutes a sublimation of eroticism from the human to the divine sphere. It is important to remember that the male celibates who represent a portion of this metaphor

153. For a more thorough discussion of Augustine and desire, see the chapter "Augustinus hunger" in my book *Hungerns väg,* pp. 9–31.

154. Augustine, *Confessions,* p. 3 (1, 1).

155. Augustine, *Confessions,* pp. 250–51, 263 (12, 10; 12, 23).

156. Cf. Denys Turner, *Eros & Allegory: Medieval Exegesis of the Song of Songs* (Kalamazoo, MI: Cistercian Publications, 1995).

had both chosen their celibate status and were well aware of this transfer of sexually charged imagery.[157] Regarding the *eros* metaphor, it can therefore hardly be a question of simply an unconscious displacement of sexual needs. It is instead a matter of a language that expresses a longing for eternity. At the same time it has to do with a sublimation of bodily love to a heavenly love for many of the monks who made use of this *eros*-metaphor. The celibate life of these monks was the most genuine expression of *eros*-love, not of bodily love. But as I have shown in the previous chapter, above all apropos the medieval female mystics, it was not at all the case that during these epochs love for God was only understood in a spiritual way, if the spiritual is then understood as a contrast to all embodiment and all sexual desire. God was not understood as separate from the material world in such a way that it was incapable of expressing God's presence. On the contrary, God was intensively present in material reality, which was experienced from a theological perspective.

For both the male celibates and the female mystics an erotic language was not only possible, but in fact well suited for expressing the person's intensive relationship to God. In our time such a language has been conveyed by John of the Cross as "the faded blooms of a spiritually erotic metaphor."[158] An example on Protestant grounds is Moravianism and the "religion of the heart" as one finds it in its leader Nikolaus von Zinzendorf.[159] Swedish historian Arne Jarrick writes of the Herrnhut revival of the eighteenth century that Jesus functioned here "as recipient for a range of repressed sexual needs and as a valve for a number of guilt-ridden Oedipal, incestuous, homosexual, and polygamous fantasies."[160] As an alternative to the erotic language within Catholic and Protestant traditions, a few (for example, Aelred of Rievaulx and Thomas Aquinas) have spoken of the relationship to God as friendship, inspired in this by Aristotle.

Even if there is thus no lack of an erotic terminology, and so in a certain sense an erotic theology, in the history of the Christian church, this has seldom resulted in a non-neurotic attitude towards human sexual acts. In

157. Turner, *Eros & Allegory*, pp. 18–19.

158. Turner, *Eros & Allegory*, p. 22.

159. On Zinzendorf, see Gösta Hök, *Zinzendorfs Begriff der Religion*, Uppsala Universitets Årskrift, 1948, no. 6 (Uppsala/Leipzig: Lundequistska bokhandeln/Otto Harrassowitz, 1948); Hans Ruh, *Die christologische Begründung des ersten Artikels bei Zinzendorf* (Zürich: Evangelischer Verlag, 1967).

160. Arne Jarrick, *Den himmelske älskaren: Herrnhutisk väckelse, vantro och sekularisering i 1700-talets Sverige* (Stockholm: Ordfront, 1987), pp. 139–40.

recent times, however, attempts have been made at an erotic theology that integrates the bodily in erotic theology. One of the most notable attempts is Rowan Williams's relatively short article from 1989, "The Body's Grace," which has been described as "the best 10 pages written about sexuality in the twentieth century."[161] What Williams does in this article (which has already been discussed in chapter 7) is expound *eros*-love on the basis of the doctrine of the Trinity. This helps us understand what it means to be someone whom God desires, whether immediately or mediated through another person. Williams observes that the Christian use of the terminology of *eros*-love, as I have pointed out above, is often metaphorized instead of being used positively about concrete, human sexuality. Williams finds the key to human sexuality in the mutual desire for each other's bodies:

> For my body to be the cause of joy, the end of homecoming, for me, it must be there for someone else, must be perceived, accepted, nurtured. And that means being given over to the creation of joy in that other, because only as directed to the enjoyment, the happiness, of the other does it become unreservedly lovable. To desire my joy is to desire the joy of the one I desire: my search for enjoyment through the bodily presence of another is a longing to be enjoyed in my body.[162]

One's own body is thus without a doubt involved with the other, and not only in a mute way, but in a way that involves reciprocal communication. Bodies communicate with each other, and this communication has not only an intercorporeal, but also a symbolic dimension. I believe, with Williams, that the crucial question is how much we want our bodies to mean. Human embodiment constitutes a sort of "radical availability" that the Christian faith affirms, and sexuality is a stubborn reminder of exactly this radical availability.[163] We cannot steer our sexual desire, which challenges our belief that we can choose how and when we want to enter into contact with the environment. Even if human sexual desire can very well be

161. Eugene F. Rogers Jr., introduction to Rowan Williams, "The Body's Grace," in *Theology and Sexuality*, p. 309.

162. Rowan Williams, "The Body's Grace," p. 313. Williams draws on an argument from philosopher Thomas Nagel in his article "Sexual Perversion," in *Mortal Questions* (Cambridge/New York: Cambridge University Press, 1979), pp. 39-52.

163. The expression comes from Thomas E. Breidenthal, "Sanctifying Nearness," in *Our Selves, Our Souls & Bodies: Sexuality and the Household of God*, ed. Charles Hefling (Cambridge, MA: Cowley, 1996), pp. 46-47.

described as a biological reaction, the goal of this reaction is to go beyond one's own body in order to be together with someone else.[164] Formulated another way, it is precisely the embodiment of the person that constitutes our vulnerability. The attempt to flee from the body can thus be interpreted as an attempt to avoid this vulnerability. Rather than "hide" oneself from the world through the body, we are exposed to the world through it. Our human embodiment is always transcorporeal, or quite simply, socially mediated.

This does not mean, as Williams also points out, that *all* sexuality communicates with the other person in a proper way. "Asymmetrical" sexual situations, where one person controls the other, can be seen on the basis of such a perspective as "perverted" relationships. I take it that by this Williams means a structural asymmetry, if his model is not to go back to a simple symmetry. A perverted sexuality is a sexuality where I do not expose myself to the risk of being transformed by the other through the fact that the other perceives my body (and thereby also risks being ridiculed, misunderstood, not loved back, etc.). A perverted sexuality is a sexuality that wants to draw itself back from a common language, a common culture, and a common politics—in other words, a sexuality that refuses to remain vulnerable to the other. By objectifying one's own body or the other's body one attempts to minimize risk, but the consequence is both a pathological relationship to oneself and an oppressive relationship to the other (which has historically often been exemplified by man's oppression of woman). On the other hand, sexual fidelity must be understood, Williams says, as a way of creating a context where the partners do not flee from the other's gaze, but are exposed to this gaze over time, and can thereby strengthen both risk and trust. Conventional heterosexual marriages are, however, not the only form of sexual relations that can express such a fidelity—and neither should they be perceived as an assurance against every risk and moral ambiguity. As I argued above in the discussion of the heteronormativity of the Christian tradition, both conventional heterosexual and same-sex marriages can give rise to self-centered love as well as a love that is oriented towards the other.

What then does this view of human sexuality have to do with the divine? Concrete human sexuality as a relationship to the other is dependent on the fact that we have a language for mercy, a language that can speak of creation and salvation. Apropos of this Williams writes:

164. Quinn, *Körper—Religion—Sexualität*, p. 344.

To be formed in our humanity by the loving delight of another is an experience whose contours we can identify most clearly and hopefully if we have also learned, or are learning, about being the object of the causeless, loving delight of God, being the object of God's love for God through incorporation into the community of God's Spirit and the taking-on of the identity of God's child.[165]

In the same way that the person is transformed in sexual love in that she there experiences herself as loved by another, so the person is transformed who is loved by God. Both can be called mercy, but bodily love between people must be seen as an analogy to God's love for the person, if God's love is not to become merely a theological illustration of a general category.[166] It is with the help of the church's accounts of God's creation and salvation that the mercy of the body can in fact be identified as mercy. Then it becomes clear that the vulnerability of the body, including its vulnerability in an intimate sexual relationship, becomes a way for God to catch the person up in the mercy that embraces and transforms all of creation.

Even the celibate life can find its role within this understanding of the vulnerability of the body. Celibates are those whose identity (including their bodily and sexual identity) is created in direct relation to God outside of ordinary sexual relations. If this celibate life is not to become sterile, however, it may not be understood as an alternative to discovering the mercy of the body or living a life of desire. What is different is a different focus, a different way of approaching the question of one's own identity than the noncelibate life, rather than the celibate life being a life without reference to one's own embodiment and one's own sexual desire. The point is not to portray the celibate life as a "better" life from God's perspective, but to clarify in a particular way how the self is constituted before God as the other, who in principle cannot be reduced to the same (i.e., without God being transformed into an idol).

The contemporary cultural anxiety over sexual relations between people of the same sex is also an important question for Williams. One hypothesis he advances is that this anxiety is dependent on the fact that same-sex couples pose the question of the goal of desire more clearly than socially and religiously sanctioned heterosexual relationships. In heterosexual relationships the relationship can always (in principle, if not in practice) find its purported

---

165. Williams, "The Body's Grace," p. 317.
166. See here Eugene F. Rogers Jr., *Sexuality and the Christian Body,* pp. 239-42.

justification in reproductive procreation. In same-sex relationships it becomes clearer that desire cannot be understood instrumentally, as though it
had an aim outside of itself. Here desire seems to be found without any other
motivation than itself, other than a "nonfunctional joy."[167] At the same time
Williams points out that one of the most common uses of sexual metaphors
in the Bible, the representation of God's relationship to humanity, is itself
beyond every biological reproduction.

What I have chosen to highlight with the help of Williams is the fact
that biological reproduction cannot be the only, or even the primary biblical
metaphor for understanding the purpose of sexual desire. If the purpose of
desire is not to be sought outside of the desire itself, but in its "nonfunctional
joy," then this is not a matter of a self-centered joy, but of a joy understood
in accordance with the understanding of the body as communication and
as vulnerable. In other words, transformed desire culminates in desire for
the other, and it is primarily in this that joy also arises over the experience
of being oneself desired by someone. Same-sex relationships between two
people—or perhaps more precisely: the childless relationship—clarifies in a
particular way that biological reproduction is not the immediate motivation
for the existence of human sexuality, but that sexuality intimately concerns
the human being's sociality and is one of the ways, perhaps one of the most
important, through which her desire is cultivated, a way that also includes a
sensuality that is not instrumentalized in the service of reproduction. With
this we are on the way towards an understanding of sexuality against the
background of *eros,* without because of this reducing *eros* to a biological
sexuality that must be disciplined by theology.

Liturgy as Therapy of Desire

As I have already mentioned, in *Confessions* Augustine does not say that human desire should be extinguished, but that it should be cultivated. For most
of those within the Christian tradition the Christian life has been perceived
as a therapy of desire, and the liturgy of the church as a way to shape, or
rather, direct desires towards their true objective in God. Assuming that the
Christian tradition—and this is not only a matter of the theological tradition
in a narrow sense, but of the writing of hymns, prayer books, devotional images, liturgical instructions—has done some sort of justice to incarnational

167. Williams, "The Body's Grace," p. 318.

485

theology, it has also been aware that desire for God has been mediated via the material. So even apart from the purely figurative representation of the divine, the problem of the icon that I discussed in chapters 6 and 7 comes up. God's transcendence must be represented in an immanent way in order that it not be transformed into something totally uncomprehensible, or even uninteresting, for us human beings. God must therefore in some way have been understood as present in the material world without being identified with it (if we proceed from a conception of God that emphasizes the difference between God and God's creation). In some way the material world must place human beings in a position to seek that which is different than the material—to find the invisible in the visible. What might be said to unite such different works as Augustine's *Confessions* and Dante's *The Divine Comedy* is that both works stage just such a "way of hunger," where human desire is successfully transformed and ennobled.[168] As I have shown in the previous chapter, this is a matter of a mediation between social and individual bodies that is produced by ritual repetitions, and so includes a habituation of human desire as well, including the body's sexuality.

Central for a theologian like Augustine, presented primarily in *Confessions* and *City of God,* is the fact that the person's desire is not ahistorically stable and given by nature, but that it can be ritually transformed. For Augustine the point of *City of God* was precisely to describe how humanity lives in tension between desire's two different directions, symbolized by two cities, the heavenly and the earthly (which I discuss further in chapter 12). About these he writes the following: "Two cities, then, have been created by two loves: that is, the earthly by love of self extending even to contempt of God, and the heavenly by love of God extending to contempt of self."[169] These different cities are thus characterized by different sorts of love, love of self *(amor sui)* or love of God *(amor dei)*, which has consequences for their political governance. In the earthly city the princes rule over their subjects thanks to the lust to rule, while in the heavenly city both princes and subjects are guided by the effort to serve one another in love. For Augustine the point is not to describe two actual cities or to contrast the city of pagan people with the church, but to show how *cupiditas* is gradually defeated by *caritas* through Christ, thus, in a sense, a Christian variant of Plato's *Symposium.*

168. Cf. Martha Nussbaum, "Augustine and Dante on the Ascent of Love," in *The Augustinian Tradition,* ed. Gareth B. Matthews (Berkeley/Los Angeles/London: University of California Press, 1999), pp. 61–90.

169. Augustine, *City of God,* p. 632 (14, 28).

What I want to underline here is precisely that Augustine so clearly speaks of two *cities* that embody the different forms of human desire, which shows an awareness of the social, not to speak of ritual or liturgical, mediation of individual desires. The point is not that people in the earthly city do not cultivate their desire, but that the heavenly city stands for a *different* cultivation than the earthly. "Desire builds different cities," Graham Ward writes in a book whose title, *Cities of God,* indicates the diversity of different configurations even within the scope of the heavenly city.[170] The key to a transformed understanding of sensuality, gender, and love for the other lies, in other words, in concrete practices, which should be understood as a further development of the incarnation.

Theology (as well as philosophy) in its classical and, to an ever-greater degree, also in its contemporary sense, is a reflection on the goal and the means for the cultivation of the person's desire in different practices.[171] Inasmuch as every "city" presupposes some sort of value judgment about what is a better and what is a worse life, some sort of requirement for discrimination between desires and needs follows, or between better and worse desires, which can guide or criticize the actual configuration of desire in a given society.[172] A society's various visions of the good life (which can be relatively heterogeneous) are handed down through various media, and thereby foster the person's life of desire, inclusive of her sexuality. According to the Christian faith (before modernity) there is thus no nature-given desire, but desire is instead dependent on society's rites and discourses. The impression of ahistorical, natural constants that we find in desires is instead a sort of sedimented structure of desire that gives an appearance of stability. Through various desire structures the person comes to be directed towards different goals, and when her desires are cultivated they can also develop their full potential. Theologian T. J. Gorringe writes apropos the cultivation of desire:

> Education is the recognition that the imagination only flourishes when it is trained, pruned, disciplined, and that it requires goals. *All human*

---

170. Graham Ward, *Cities of God* (London/New York: Routledge, 2000), p. 52.

171. See T. J. Gorringe, *The Education of Desire: Towards a Theology of the Senses* (London: SCM, 2001), pp. 81–102. Cf. also Martha C. Nussbaum, *The Therapy of Desire: Theory and Practice in Hellenistic Ethics* (Princeton: Princeton University Press, 1994).

172. For a more thorough argument, see my account in *Den lyckliga filosofin: Etik och politik hos Hägerström, Tingsten, makarna Myrdal och Hedenius* (Stockholm/Stehag: Brutus Östlings Bokförlag Symposion, 2000), pp. 260–74, together with the references that are found there.

cultures rest on an education of desire in this sense. Jesus speaks of it as disci-pleship. He calls people to be disciples, which is to say to learn discipline. He is engaged in an education of desire. Plato, followed by Augustine and the whole Christian tradition, speaks of the goal of desire as 'God,' but the language of the kingdom is also about the education of desire.[173]

Thus the Christian church is a school in which one learns to cultivate one's desires, in the same way that, for example, capitalism is a school in which other sorts of desire are cultivated.[174] However, in contrast to the cultiva-tion of the Christian tradition, which is of course traditionally called ascet-icism, capitalism's cultivation is aimed at developing the refusal to accept any limitations, to put it contrastively.[175] Monotheism as such—and here monotheism may be thought to have very broad connotations—constitutes an insistence that different desires must be ranked according to some sort of norm.[176] The question of which cities we belong to is therefore critical for the cultivation of *eros,* which in its turn is critical for how we understand our embodiment.

Theological Erotics and the Presence of God

In the understanding of theological erotics that I have argued for here it is not a matter, as with all too great a part of historical theological erotics, of devaluing or even dismissing sexual desires. Instead, I want to reiterate the question of whether it is possible to establish a theologically inspired art of love on the basis of earlier traditions. The fact that desires are not given by nature also means that Christianity has the potential to develop in directions that revise and criticize even its own historical configurations, including its construction of the relationship between the biological sexes and of heteronormativity. This task is possible, in other words, with different configurations of sexuality than those we find in our liberal, late-capitalistic, or possibly postmodern society, for example, the configuration that is impli-

---

173. Gorringe, *The Education of Desire,* p. 91.

174. Cf., for example, Philip Goodchild, *Capitalism and Religion: The Price of Piety* (Lon-don: Routledge, 2002).

175. Cf. Daniel M. Bell, *Liberation Theology after the End of History: The Refusal to Cease Suffering* (London/New York: Routledge, 2001), pp. 9–41, and Michael Hardt and Antonio Negri, *Empire* (Cambridge, MA: Harvard University Press, 2000).

176. Cf. my chapter "Hur många gudar behöver vi?" in *Hungers väg,* pp. 65–79.

cated in the attempt to understand the person's sexuality in light of a theological erotics. Theological erotics thus necessarily points towards an ascetic theology (which I have discussed towards the end of the previous chapter), not in the sense of a theology that rejects sexuality or other expressions of human desire, but in the sense of a theology that cultivates sexuality and the other expressions of desire so that they may flourish in a more genuine way. Theological erotics, just like every erotics that is not simply a legitimization of the state of affairs, thus presupposes a transcendent horizon or vision on the basis of which these desires are trained, and thereby also determines the norms for what constitutes a genuine cultivation, and for the way these concrete practices should be changed.[177]

Ultimately a theology of the human being's embodiment and sexuality is a matter of how she shall understand God. One might say that erotic discourses and practices are an instrument for the understanding of God's presence, and so ultimately God's incarnation in Christ as well. For nearly two thousand years Christian theology has discussed which language may be used to speak of a God who is both transcendent and immanent. A quotation from Denys Turner well illustrates how erotic love is a useful metaphor for bringing together identity and difference:

> Within erotic love I am both more *me* and more *than* me. The search for erotic mutuality is the search for a union which does not conflict with differentiation and for a differentiation which is not set at odds with union; and so it is at least implicitly the yearning for a condition in which the very contrast between union and differentiation is itself transcended, a condition in which the affirmation of the one is not bought at the price of the denial of the other.[178]

Thus *eros* does not annul the tension between identity and difference, or between freedom and necessity. Maintaining this tension between God and human is just as theologically necessary as maintaining the difference

---

177. According to L. William Countryman, *Dirt, Greed and Sex,* p. 247, the norm for a genuine sexuality that also harmonizes with the New Testament is the following: "the degree to which it rejoices in the whole creation, in what is given to others as well as to each of us, while enabling us always to leave the final Word to God, who is the Beginning and End of all things." Even if this is correct in principle, I would like to more clearly emphasize the social dimensions of the cultivation. Cf. as well Slavoj Žižek, *For They Know Not What They Do: Enjoyment as a Political Factor,* 2nd edition (London/New York: Verso, 2002).

178. Turner, *Eros & Allegory,* p. 58.

between people. It is impossible for two people to caress each other if there are not both physical limits that make it possible to meet body to body and temporal limits that make it such that the bodies meet at the same time.[179] But the caress is also an expression of a deep intimacy between bodies. The caress is therefore a picture of both identity and difference that is not dissolved in the one or the other pole. From this there also follows a critique of the way in which Christianity has historically configured the relationship between the biological sexes. If the "erotic reciprocity" in the caress is to be genuine, it is necessary that the woman not be understood as a lower creature in relation to the man according to the same hierarchy as in Antiquity and the Middle Ages—in that case the genuine caress would really only be able to occur between men and men or women and women. Nor could the woman be understood as a contrastive complement to the man in a relationship where the man constitutes the normative and universally human, since her own subjectivity would fall short, something that in its turn would be an example of a difference that does not live up to the requirement of reciprocity. The erotic reciprocity of the interpersonal caress, if it is taken seriously, abolishes at a fundamental level the idea of an interpersonal hierarchy, and therefore contains a potential for criticizing historical configurations of the relationship between the biological sexes.

Considering the potential of erotics to bring together identity and difference in the caress, it is not surprising that the Christian tradition has made use of an erotic language to bring together God and the world, and to understand the intra-divine intimacy of the Trinity. A contemporary theological effort to achieve a more constructive and emancipatory understanding of sensuality, gender, and desire is therefore allied with the effort to develop a more consistent erotic theology, consistent in the sense that the erotics not be deprived of its concrete content through a metaphorical sublimation. At the same time the purely linguistic dimension of the erotics is naturally unavoidable for a theology that wants to bring together God and human being without denying the difference between them, since this dimension weaves the person into the linguistic and ritual community that can transform her bodily and spiritual desires, which can never be separated from each other. In order to reiterate what I pointed out earlier: if the grace of the body is to be experienced as grace, not only a sexual event is required, but also a linguistic event that gives this event its meaning. Even if the corporeal life is more than language, it is never less than language. For Christianity, even sexuality is

179. Rogers Jr., *Sexuality and the Christian Body*, p. 201.

placed within the larger horizon that is constituted by the relationship between God and human being, a relationship that receives its paradigmatic formulation in the narratives about Christ. Through theological erotics, the embodiment of the human being could be affirmed without the body being reduced because of this to an opaque immanence or a static object. The body is, according to the Christian tradition, a dynamic reality that can both be transformed and refer beyond itself. Even if the person's embodiment has been affirmed by the Christian tradition—and I have attempted to argue in this chapter for a way to theologically extend this affirmation more clearly to erotic embodiment—this does not consequently mean that her concrete body is something self-evident. In the extension of the idea of the erotic body there lies a body that opens itself, but also extends beyond itself, and thereby allows itself to be joined together with other bodies. Such a body is not a finished body, but rather, in Bakhtin's words, a grotesque body. If the erotic body in general terms clarifies aspects of reciprocity, proximity, and sociality, the grotesque body focuses instead on difference, distance, and suffering. I now turn to different aspects of the grotesque body.

11. The Grotesque Body

In everyday speech the word "grotesque" can mean ludicrous or monstrous. But the word can also be used about that which is alien, that which blends genres and exceeds everything we view as normal. The Christian tradition is full of grotesque conceptions and representations of the body in the latter meaning. In Julian of Norwich's *Revelations of Divine Love* from about 1400 she describes a vision of the dead Christ body with a highly developed sense for macabre details:

> I saw his sweet face as it were dry and bloodless, with the pallor of dying, then more dead, pale and languishing, then the pallor turning blue and then more blue, as death took more hold upon his flesh. . . . This was a grievous change to watch, this deep dying, and the nose shrivelled and dried up as I saw. The long torment seemed to me as if he had been dead for a week and had still gone on suffering pain, and it seemed to me as if the greatest and the last pain of his Passion was when his flesh dried up. . . . The blessed body was left to dry for a long time, with the wrenching of the nails and the sagging of the head and the weight of the body, with the blowing of the wind around him, which dried up his body and pained him with cold, more than my heart can think of, and with all his other pains I saw such pain that all I can describe or say is inadequate, for it cannot be described.[1]

One might perhaps object that this medieval vision is alien to a contemporary sensibility, but such a claim is contradicted by, for example, Mel Gib-

---

1. Julian of Norwich, *Showings: The Short Text,* The Classics of Western Spirituality, ed. and trans. Edmund College and James Walsh (Mahwah, NJ: Paulist Press, 1978), pp. 141–42.

son's film *The Passion of the Christ* from 2004, a depiction of Christ's suffering whose more than two-hour-long playtime is half taken up by especially detailed scenes of torture.[2] If for the time being I put aside the aesthetic and theological evaluation of these two examples of very brutal grotesques from the Christian tradition, we can instead ask ourselves what theological *function* such depictions of suffering have.

The answer is that they want to show the extent of Christ's saving work in a rhetorically convincing way. The brutal and sinful circumstances of the human being do not prevent the fact that God is present with us in Christ. Julian of Norwich's vision of and identification with Christ is, so to speak, a function of the fact that in Christ, even before the person's identification with Christ himself, God has already identified with the person. The fact that God becomes human in Christ does not, however, entail simply a general presence, but a presence even in her most alienating circumstances. In order to depict this all-encompassing solidarity with the person on God's part, the Christian church has, through all periods—but to a greater or lesser degree—made use of grotesque vehicles of expression. "God's material appearance is necessarily grotesque," argues German author Christian Morgenstern.[3] Firstly, because the Christian tradition argues that God becomes human in Christ, and thus must somehow be able to imagine that the finite is capable of housing and expressing the infinite, without because of this allowing the infinite to perish in the finite—the problem of incarnation. Secondly, because the Christian tradition argues that God manifests his presence in an especially intensive way precisely in suffering and crucifixion—the problem of the Passion. With respect to both incarnation and passion the Christian tradition breaks principally—if not always in practice—with the hierarchical order that wants to keep divine and human separate, and to set the one over the other.

One might therefore say that right from the start Christianity manifests a sort of stylistic mixture. Where the literature of classical Antiquity strictly differentiated between a high style that depicted elevated thoughts and events, often in a tragic style, and a low style that treated the everyday and common, preferably in a comic way, this stylistic principle of differentiation

2. For a more thorough discussion of *The Passion of the Christ* from a theological perspective see, for example, "Epilogue Table Talk: Reflections on Mel Gibson's *The Passion of the Christ,*" in *Cinéma Divinité: Religion, Theology and the Bible in Film,* ed. Eric S. Christianson, Peter Francis, and William R. Telford (London: SCM, 2005), pp. 311–30.

3. Christian Morgenstern, *Stufen: Eine Entwicklung in Aphorismen und Tagebuch-Notizen* (Munich: R. Piper Verlag, 1918), p. 285.

became irrelevant for the Christian church. If the classical stylistic differentiation meant that a realistic description of the everyday and the common could never be other than comic or idyllic, then the events depicted by the New Testament are, according to their authors, of globally historic significance. According to Erich Auerbach, when the Synoptic Gospels describe Peter's denial of Jesus (Matt. 26:69–75; Mark 14:66–72; Luke 22:54–62), it is a scene that breaks with the classical-antique stylistic rules: too everyday and directly depicted for tragedy, too serious for comedy, too inconsequential for history writing.[4] This stylistic mixture, or rather, indifference before the principle of stylistic differentiation, was, according to Auerbach, a direct consequence of the heart of Christian doctrine, namely, the incarnation and the passion:

> Christ had not come as a hero and king, but as a human being of the lowest social station. His first disciples were fishermen and artisans; he moved in the everyday milieu of the humble folk of Palestine; he talked with publicans and fallen women, the poor and the sick and children. Nevertheless, all that he did and said was of the highest and deepest dignity, more significant than anything else in the world.[5]

This stylistic differentiation became impossible not least as a consequence of the passion:

> That the King of Kings was treated as a low criminal, that he was mocked, spat upon, whipped, and nailed to the cross—that story no sooner comes to dominate the consciousness of the people than it completely destroys the aesthetics of the separation of styles; it engenders a new elevated style, which does not scorn everyday life and which is ready to absorb the sensorily realistic, even the ugly, the undignified, the physically base.[6]

Or one may argue the reverse as well, Auerbach says, namely that the low style, comedy, is not allowed to speak of the high, exalted, and eternal. For example, Augustine, who was at home in both classical rhetoric and Christian theology, articulates in *On Christian Doctrine* (written ca. 395–396) a

---

4. Erich Auerbach, *Mimesis: The Representation of Reality in Western Literature,* trans. W. R. Trask (Princeton: Princeton University Press, 2003), pp. 45–46.

5. Auerbach, *Mimesis,* p. 72. Cf. also pp. 41–49.

6. Auerbach, *Mimesis,* p. 72.

clear awareness of the significance of stylistic mixing and the theologically legitimated need to speak of (what were earlier perceived as) low things in a high way.[7] This did not mean that stylistic blending immediately came to dominate the Christian literature of Antiquity. This feature instead came to be clearer during the Middle Ages.[8] My point here is, however, not to point out the effective history of stylistic mixing, but rather its theological motivation. The incarnation and the passion as Christian doctrines entail a break with the aesthetic ideal of Antiquity. This stylistic break is a good reason to return to the question of embodiment from a grotesque perspective.

The stylistic break brings about a theologically motivated dialectic in the relationship between what is articulated in this chapter and what was said in the previous one. However appealing the notion of the erotic body in the Christian tradition may be, it does not get to entice us into turning our attention from what has, for good and for ill, been the center of the Christian tradition throughout virtually the whole of its history, namely, suffering, cross, and death. A unilaterally erotic theology of the body—however warranted it may be by our present and by the, in this respect, ambiguous history of the church—could be used as a means for avoiding everything that touches embodiment but is not pleasurable and exciting. The Christian conception of the body has always been more multifaceted and critical than this. The cross is the reminder that Christianity is not an unequivocal legitimation of life here and now—a reminder that is also important for the prosperous part of Christendom, which in our time might otherwise risk adapting its theology into a streamlined fetish for contemporary consumer society.[9] At the end of the previous chapter I also emphasized that the erotic body in the Christian tradition ought not be understood as an autoerotic body, but instead finds its theological legitimacy in the idea of bringing together identity and difference in the caress, not least in relation to God's presence and absence. As I pointed out in chapter 9, the Christian body is included in an existential drama of salvation, and in order to perceive the dynamic in the Christian understanding of the body, it is necessary to study this from a

7. Augustine, *De doctrina christiana,* Oxford Early Christian Texts, translated and introduced by R. P. H. Green (Oxford: Clarendon Press, 1995), pp. 241–45 (4, 18).

8. The relationship between Classical rhetoric and the Christian mixture of styles is of course a much more complex history than this. Cf., for example, Stina Hansson, *Ett språk för själen: Litterära former i den svenska andaktslitteraturen 1650–1720,* Skrifter utgivna av Litteraturvetenskapliga institutionen vid Göteborgs universitet 20 (Göteborg: Göteborgs Universitet, 1991), pp. 16–22, 232–41, 274–75, among other places.

9. Cf. Slavoj Žižek, *On Belief,* Thinking in Action (London/New York: Routledge, 2001).

perspective that more clearly focuses on how the Christian body is a body that is transformed in the direction of an eschatological horizon.

To clarify the fact that the Christian body is a body in a state of transformation in both pain and hope, I will in this chapter study embodiment from the "grotesque" perspective that I suggested in chapter 9 as well, with the help of Mikhail Bakhtin. Bakhtin undertakes a comparison between a classical body and a grotesque body, where the characteristic of the classical body is that it is individual and delimited, solid and compact, smoothed out, closed, and self-contained, while the grotesque body is instead malleable and changeable, unclosed and open, excessive and generative.[10] Bakhtin's typologizing of different forms of body canon is a good aid for an understanding of different embodiments in the Christian tradition. If the bodily drama is played out at the boundaries of the body, there is every reason to more closely study exactly those limits.

In this chapter I will argue that the Christian body should be understood as a grotesque body in several senses. Firstly, I continue to assert that the Christian grotesque body should be seen as an excessive and generative body in the modified version of Bakhtin's grotesque bodies that I presented in chapter 9. This does not mean, as I will show below, that Christianity has been unequivocally critical of classical bodies. My argument rests, however, on the fact that in significant practices and conceptions in the Christian church there implicitly or explicitly exists an understanding of embodiment that can rightly be called grotesque rather than classical, in Bakhtin's sense, and that this understanding is the most productive for a contemporary theology of embodiment. These practices and conceptions also show how theology has paid attention to the mediation between individual body and social body.

Secondly, I believe that there is a need for extending the definition of the Christian body as grotesque to include the question of the grotesque representation of the body in the Christian tradition. The goal of the Christian grotesque body is found in the resurrection body. With this the question arises, as it does already in the New Testament writings, of how this eschatological body may be represented in a way that neither reduces it to something familiar nor transforms it into something so unfamiliar that its embodiment becomes something entirely sublimated. The need for finding a middle way between these positions is also about preserving the character of grace in the Christian discourse of embodiment. The theological discourse of the

---

10. Mikhail Bakhtin, *Rabelais and His World,* trans. Helene Iswolsky (Cambridge, MA/London: MIT Press, 1968), pp. 320–21.

resurrection especially signals the demand for a terminology that transcends both the well known and the completely unknown.

In this chapter as well a running argument is that Christology has come to be received in and to influence different significant discourses and practices, and thereby has given rise to several different conceptions of the body. I will therefore discuss here the sacramental body, the body of pain, and the resurrection body, which will show how the Christian body is grotesque and how intimately connected the social and the individual bodies are even here. These three—later—sections are held together by the temporal structure of communion, which thereby also becomes the temporal structure of Christian embodiment: the sacramentally understood presence of God, the past of pain and suffering, together with the future of resurrection and hope. In the first section I will, however, more clearly illuminate the grotesque as an aesthetic and a theological category. This section on the grotesque will then function as a background for the following three sections. I hope that together these four sections will show how the Christian body is, or ought to be, a more "alien" and socially open body than has often been imagined.[11] But first I will turn to the grotesque as a more general category.

A Grotesque Embodiment?

As I now attempt to deepen our understanding of the grotesque, it is of greatest importance that we avoid misunderstandings by being exact. This is easier said than done when it comes to the definition of the grotesque, since the word commonly refers to something boundary-crossing, thus making it an unwieldy category. In everyday speech the grotesque is usually associated in a pejorative way with the absurd or the monstrous. According to the glossary of the Swedish Academy "grotesque" is synonymous with "marvelous" and "absurd." For my own theological understanding of the grotesque I want to note that our understanding of the body is always decentered, by God's alterity (communion) as well as by sin (pain) and eschatology (resurrection). The grotesque has clear associations with such categories as the abnormal and the monstrous, and none of these words is necessarily pejorative.[12] However, it

11. Cf., for example, Elisabeth Grosz, *Volatile Bodies: Towards a Corporeal Feminism* (Bloomington/Indianapolis: Indiana University Press, 1994), pp. 5–6.

12. For these closely related but not identical categories, see Michel Foucault, *Abnormal: Lectures at the Collège de France, 1974–1975,* trans. Graham Burchell (New York: Picador, 2003), primarily pp. 11–13, 35; Richard Kearney, *Strangers, Gods and Monsters: Interpreting Otherness*

would be strange to speak of the "abnormal body" or the "monstrous body," and not least because Bakhtin has already established a terminology around the grotesque body I will make use of this term. Within literary criticism and art theory the grotesque has also become a concept that has a more critical (if still elusive even here) sense, and so to begin with I will turn to several central conceptions of the grotesque as an aesthetic category. On the basis of this I will then discuss my perception of the grotesque as a theological category, and finally say something about the boundaries of the grotesque.

The Grotesque as an Aesthetic Category

As an aesthetic category, the grotesque has a history that begins at the end of the fifteenth century.[13] It was with the excavation of the subterranean baths of Titus and emperor Nero's *Domus Aurea* in Rome that ornamental painting of a hitherto unknown sort was found. Eventually this ornamentation was found in other places in Italy as well. This painting was called *la grottesca* from Italian's *grotta,* which meant subterranean cave. These artfully playful ornaments were characterized by the fact that they wove together forms taken from the realm of animals, vegetation, and humans. These forms bled into each other without any sharp boundaries. In other words, the term was minted for a previously unknown variant of Roman ornamental art. So to begin with, the word "grotesque" only meant a particular sort of painting, and it was only gradually that the term's sphere of use came to be extended. At the same time, this shows that grotesque image creation, if we limit ourselves to the original use of the term, is itself much older than the actual term. The ornamental art discovered in Rome around 1480 originated in Antiquity.

(London/New York: Routledge, 2003); Caroline Walker Bynum, *Metamorphosis and Identity* (New York: Zone Books, 2001).

13. One may read about this in most introductions to the grotesque. Besides Mikhail Bakhtin, *Rabelais,* pp. 31–32, I have made use of Geoffrey Galt Harpham, *On the Grotesque: Strategies of Contradiction in Art and Literature* (Princeton: Princeton University Press, 1982), pp. 23–47; Wolfgang Kayser, *The Grotesque in Art and Literature,* trans. Ulrich Weisstein (New York/Toronto: McGraw-Hill, 1966), pp. 19–28; Wilson Yates, "An Introduction to the Grotesque: Theoretical and Theological Considerations," in *The Grotesque in Art and Literature: Theological Reflections,* ed. James Luther Adams and Wilson Yates (Grand Rapids/Cambridge: Eerdmans, 1997), pp. 5ff. In Swedish there is a basic introduction to the grotesque in Ingemar Haag, *Det groteska: Kroppens språk och språkets kropp i svensk lyrisk modernism* (Stockholm: Aiolos, 1999), pp. 11–85.

The word grotesque would later come to designate the monstrous in the intermingling between animal and human, or more generally, the unordered or unproportional. The grotesque came to oscillate between the comically burlesque and the dreadfully monstrous. The question that was brought to the fore in literature and art history is whether the grotesque is a property of the piece of literature or work of art, or whether it is in fact an experience of the work of art that lies in the eye of the beholder. As literary scholar Wolfgang Kayser points out, someone who is not familiar with a particular culture, for example, the Inca culture, can perceive their images as grotesque, at the same time that they are involved in a clear semantic context for those who are familiar with the culture in question.[14]

The grotesque is often perceived as something controversial, since its interminglings break with classical conventions within art and the philosophy of art. The grotesque entails a break with harmonious proportions and order by playing with that which practice has kept distinct and ranked in different ways. Literary scholar Geoffrey Galt Harpham therefore wants to extend the etymology of the term itself.[15] Even if caves were not the original locations for this ornamental art, the mistake carried a truth: the Latin form of *grotta* is probably *crupta,* which may be derived from Greek *kryptē,* "vault," and this word is in its turn cognate with *kryptein,* "to hide." Even from the beginning there are thus, according to Harpham, connotations of the subterranean and the secret within the word grotesque itself.

In the modern period there is a variety of literature about the grotesque. Immanuel Kant, G. W. F. Hegel, John Ruskin, and Victor Hugo have all addressed the form and essence of the grotesque. Two of the most influential books regarding the characterization of the grotesque in the latter half of the twentieth century are the already-mentioned German literary scholar Wolfgang Kayser's work from 1957, *The Grotesque,* and the Russian scholar of language and literature Mikhail Bakhtin's work from 1965, *Rabelais and His World.* A comparison of these two can therefore serve to deepen our understanding.

Both Kayser's and Bakhtin's works are very well-informed and carefully argued accounts of the grotesque, but interestingly enough they contradict each other on the most fundamental points.[16] For Bakhtin the grotesque stands for something renewing and liberating, as in the following quotation about the function of the "carnival-grotesque form":

14. Kayser, *The Grotesque,* pp. 180–81.
15. Harpham, *On the Grotesque,* p. 27.
16. Harpham, *On the Grotesque,* pp. xvii–xviii.

to consecrate inventive freedom, to permit the combination of a variety of different elements and their rapprochement, to liberate from the prevailing point of view of the world, from conventions and established truths, from clichés, from all that is humdrum and universally accepted. This carnival spirit offers the chance to have a new outlook on the world, to realize the relative nature of all that exists, and to enter a completely new order of things.[17]

This is, according to Bakhtin, typical for the carnivalesque folk grotesque, and differs in this from the grotesque of later Romanticism, where one's own, known world was transformed into an alien world in the sense of a hostile world.[18] While the folk grotesque is a merry and joyful madness—for Bakhtin represented by Rabelais—Romanticism represents a dark and gloomy madness—which Bakhtin finds ideally represented in the Romantic author Bonaventura's work *Nachtwachen*. The Devil is transformed from a bogeyman and a trickster to a "terrifying, melancholy, and tragic" figure.[19]

For Kayser, however, who according to Bakhtin focuses on the Romantic and Modernistic grotesque, the grotesque evokes the alien as something scary.[20] According to Kayser the essential feature of the grotesque is instead the alienating, the horrible, and the inhuman, and he therefore states that "[t]he grotesque is the estranged world."[21] The alien world of the grotesque is not a different world than our own, but instead our own world that has been transformed into an inhospitable and hostile world: "It is our world which has to be transformed."[22] With this, our possibility for orienting ourselves in it disappears.

Who or what causes this transformation of the world? According to Kayser there is no real answer to the question. The transformation is inexplicable, impossible to interpret, and completely impersonal. Kayser sums up his description with that which, according to him, deepens the understanding of the grotesque world as an alien world, namely "the grotesque as the objectivation of the 'It.'"[23] This "It" is a "ghostly" It that exists as a third form of the impersonal alongside its psychological form—as in "it makes

17. Bakhtin, *Rabelais,* p. 34.
18. Bakhtin, *Rabelais,* pp. 38–39.
19. Bakhtin, *Rabelais,* p. 41.
20. Bakhtin, *Rabelais,* pp. 46–51.
21. Kayser, *The Grotesque,* p. 184. Cf. pp. 130–39.
22. Kayser, *The Grotesque,* p. 184.
23. Kayser, *The Grotesque,* p. 185.

me happy"—and its cosmic form—as in "it is raining." This impersonal, grotesque world is the absurd world, the world that it is impossible to orient oneself in since nothing is trustworthy.

Finally, Kayser offers yet another interpretation of the grotesque, namely that it is "an attempt to invoke and subdue the demonic aspects of the world."[24] If the world is mastered by an "It," this is experienced as though it were occupied by an alien power, and the invocation serves to ward off this hostile takeover. According to Kayser the grotesque is not a matter of fear of death, but of anxiety over life, and this is in line with what Kayser states about the grotesque both as a figuration of the "It" and the invocation of the same.[25] Here Kayser differs radically from Bakhtin, which Bakhtin himself attributes to the fact that Kayser views the grotesque from a modernistic perspective. In Kayser the grotesque is not at all about rebirth and liberation, but instead about captivity and paralysis.[26] There are in fact two different epochs that meet each other in Bakhtin's and Kayser's work: the grotesque of the Middle Ages and Renaissance on the one hand, and the grotesque of Romanticism and Modernity on the other. The first points to the experience of a new world, a new order, or a new understanding through the fact that the grotesque plays with conventional insights, while the second points to the experience of the demonic through the fact that the impersonal "It" causes conventions to crack. One might also see the difference between the two descriptions of the grotesque as the difference between a "socializing" grotesque in Bakhtin and an "individualizing" grotesque in Kayser.

Harpham as well, whom I mentioned above, has in the wake of Kayser and Bakhtin's work attempted to clarify what it is that characterizes the grotesque. On the basis of a consciously historical approach, Harpham states that the perspective on the grotesque changes as culture does. Despite this, there is something common to be found that makes it possible to describe the grotesque as a somewhat unified phenomenon. The grotesque is namely that which lies on the margins of our attempts to know, classify, and organize: "The word designates a condition of being just out of focus, just beyond the reach of language. It accommodates the things left over when the categories of language are exhausted; it is a defence against silence when other words have failed."[27] There are experiences that cannot be formulated in

---

24. Kayser, *The Grotesque*, p. 188.
25. Kayser, *The Grotesque*, p. 185.
26. Bakhtin, *Rabelais*, p. 51.
27. Harpham, *On the Grotesque*, pp. 3–4.

words in a satisfactory way, and it is these experiences that are indicated by the grotesque. The grotesque does not fit within those categories by which we identify the world, since it unites that which these categories presuppose is incompatible. The grotesque challenges our way of organizing the world and the hierarchies by which we do so—and here we find a feature of both Kayser and Bakhtin's understanding of the grotesque in Harpham.

Two other features, or perhaps attitudes, of the grotesque that Harpham highlights are the interval and the paradox. With regard to the interval, Harpham says that the grotesque lies between what is and what becomes. He compares the grotesque to philosopher of science Thomas Kuhn's concept of the "paradigm shift" and says that the paradigm crisis—i.e., when an old paradigm has been discredited by the anomalies it generates, but has not yet been replaced by a new one—is just such an interval as may be designated as grotesque.[28] The grotesque as interval thus hovers in the creative moment between an interpretation that has ceased to be trustworthy and an as-yet not established interpretation: "Resisting closure, the grotesque object impales us on the present moment, emptying the past and forestalling the future."[29] Like a moment of confusion, the grotesque can, as with the paradigm crises, lead to new insights and discoveries. The grotesque is therefore never something fixed or stable, but rather a process or a progression.[30]

The paradoxical in the grotesque comes, according to Harpham, out of the fact that it, like the paradox, can be a way to nevertheless express that which cannot be expressed in words: "Because it breaks the rules, paradox can penetrate to new and unexpected realms of experience discovering relationships syntax generally obscures."[31] Even here Harpham's emphasis lies on the incomplete yet anticipated interpretation: "[L]ike the grotesque, paradox is a sphinx who dies once its riddle is solved."[32] The grotesque is, at least potentially, the bearer of a deeper meaning that cannot be expressed with a conventional and contradiction-free syntax. It becomes a way to approach the holy or the sublime, Harpham says, and in this context he cites Dionysius the Areopagite (whom I come to below).[33] Here Harpham ends up very close to a conception of the grotesque as the person's response to the

28. Harpham, *On the Grotesque*, pp. 14–18. Cf. Thomas S. Kuhn, *The Structure of Scientific Revolutions*, 2nd expanded edition (Chicago: University of Chicago Press, 1970), pp. 66–91.

29. Harpham, *On the Grotesque*, p. 16.

30. Harpham, *On the Grotesque*, p. 14.

31. Harpham, *On the Grotesque*, p. 20.

32. Harpham, *On the Grotesque*, p. 20.

33. Harpham, *On the Grotesque*, p. 20.

experience of the holy, to what historian of religions and theologian Rudolf Otto calls a *mysterium tremendum et fascinans* beyond what may be manipulated and controlled by human technology and human reason. Similarly, we find a proximity to the stylistic mixing I mentioned above apropos Auerbach, and which in a sense might be called grotesque precisely because it elevates the ambivalence between high and low to a norm.[34] With this we begin to approach the theological issues that are brought forth by the grotesque as an aesthetic category.

The Grotesque as a Theological Category

A question that almost immediately comes up is whether the grotesque is or even can be a genuine theological category. Does such a thought not war with the fundamental theological presupposition of, for example, God's beauty, a thought that traditionally follows as a consequence of God's glory? Does the grotesque not carry connotations of ugliness? Karl Barth takes up this line of thought when he writes

> [i]f the beauty of Christ is sought in a glorious Christ who is not the crucified, the search will always be in vain. . . . In this self-declaration, however, God's beauty embraces death as well as life, fear as well as joy, what we might call the ugly as well as what we might call the beautiful.[35]

The point of the grotesque as a theological category is not to deny the genuine insights of the theological tradition, but rather to attempt, like Barth, to reach a more critical view of these conceptions on the basis of the cross. Perhaps it is instead the case that the hesitance in the face of connecting the religious and the grotesque is an attribute of the Christian tradition that has arisen during the twentieth century. One prefers, as John W. Cook points out, to speak of "comfort, conflict resolution, and therapeutic solutions" rather than "the reality of judgement, retribution, and pain."[36] Previously there was not such a great fear over representations that might be called grotesque. There is, in other words, reason to believe that help is to be found

34. Harpham, *On the Grotesque,* pp. 55–58, 73–76.

35. Karl Barth, *Church Dogmatics,* vol. 2: *The Doctrine of God,* part 1, trans. T. H. L. Parker, W. B. Johnston, Harold Knight, and J. L. M. Haire (Edinburgh: T. & T. Clark, 1957), p. 665.

36. John W. Cook, "Ugly Beauty in Christian Art," in *The Grotesque in Art and Literature,* ed. Adams and Yates, p. 127.

both in the theological tradition and in contemporary theology for investigating Christian embodiment as a grotesque embodiment, even if, in spite of this, it does not always go under the same name. Let me therefore additionally say something of the theological legitimacy of the grotesque as category for understanding Christian embodiment.

I believe that both Kayser's and Bakhtin's conceptions of the grotesque are valuable from a theological perspective.[37] Where the one aids investigating the reality of evil as a part of human existence, the other aids investigating the grotesque as a power that helps the person to free herself from oppressive structures, and additionally provides a new vision of her social existence. So we can then preserve the insight into the generative nature of the grotesque, which Bakhtin highlights, as well as its more traditional, demonic side. My presentation in this section does not aim to be a complete account of the theological significance of the grotesque. I want to limit myself to several aspects that I believe can be illuminating for my later discussion of communion, pain, and resurrection. I will therefore first mention something of the side of the grotesque that faces the destructive and the demonic, in order to then turn to the grotesque in relation to the representation of God and the Christian body. With this I already presume the transformative aspect of the grotesque that I discussed with the introduction of Bakhtin in chapter 9.

One aspect of the language and imagery of the grotesque is thus its symbolic character in relation to alienation, fear, evil, suffering, and death.[38] In contrast to, for example, a discursive presentation, the symbolic representation wants to involve the reader or viewer in what is presented to a higher degree than the discursive. In its demonic aspect the grotesque attempts to show how the experience of the demonic is a genuine but often repressed human experience. The rhetoric of the grotesque can thereby restore contact with chaos, evil, and death as dimensions of human experience. This does not take place through a descriptive relationship to chaos, to give one example, but through mythical excesses that allow what is fashioned to be distorted beyond its conventional proportions. With this the grotesque brings about a "paradigm crisis" through the fact that its anomalies challenge a fraudulent image of—psychic, physical, and social—reality. The person is, according to the Christian church, both created and fallen. Her fallen nature constitutes the tragic dimension of human life, both her exposed situation in the face of evil and her inclination to herself become an accomplice. The

37. See Yates, "Introduction to the Grotesque," p. 26.
38. This presentation builds on Yates, "Introduction to the Grotesque," pp. 39–68.

grotesque can give word and image to these experiences. As the American theologian and art scholar Wilson Yates writes: "The language that names and describes human evil is also the language used to describe forms of the grotesque. Grotesque images distort, exaggerate, and present to us a world that is twisted and broken."[39] Through grotesque images, such as Julian of Norwich's representation of Christ's dead body quoted above, a vision is highlighted that functions in several ways for the worshipful reader. The grotesque description of Christ's "dried up flesh" in this case exposes the reader to the fact that the human environment as it appears here and now is not in accordance with the Creator's foundational will.[40] The innocent Christ suffers in the place of the people, and thus God exposes Godself to pain and death. This ought, according to the method of the devotional literature, to lead to the person's self-awareness of her own sinfulness and to a sympathy (sometimes almost an identification) with the crucified. The crucified Christ becomes both sacrament and example, i.e., both gift and model. Christ's suffering and death (as with, for example, human and nonhuman suffering in general) inexorably exposes the illusory in all attempts to think away the destructive and demonic in existence, not least in one's own self, and therefore shares a fundamental stylistic feature with the grotesque representation. The function of the grotesque becomes both prophetic and healing in that it shows the existence of alienation and evil in the world and at the same time brings about the reunion of what has been fragmented and reestablishes contact with what has been repressed.[41]

In this context it is important to ask oneself whether grotesque rhetoric as such manages to retain the destructiveness and the demonic in Christ's

---

39. Yates, "Introduction to the Grotesque," p. 55.

40. On the representation of Christ's suffering as devotional literature in a somewhat later period, see Stina Hansson, *Ett språk för själen,* pp. 255–65. Hansson points to the proximity between the sensual expressions of devotion to Jesus and of love between people. Valborg Lindgärde, *Jesu Christi Pijnos Historia Rijmwijs betrachtad: Svenska passionsdikter under 1600- och 1700-talet,* Litteratur teater film, Nya serien 12 (Lund: Lund University Press, 1996), pp. 147, 154–61, 216–19, has pointed out the fact that in the Lutheran tradition the empathy in the reflection on the passion does not only have to do with a compassion for Christ, but primarily a compassion for one's own, sinful self. Compared to Julian of Norwich's more "objective" vision of the suffering Christ, the devotion of the passion in later times would thereby seem to emphasize the "subjective" participation in this suffering through sin. As a consequence of this, the grotesque thereby comes to be one's own "sinful soul" rather than the suffering Christ body, i.e., the grotesque is internalized.

41. Susan Corey, "The Religious Dimension of the Grotesque in Literature: Toni Morrison's *Beloved,*" in *The Grotesque in Art and Literature,* ed. Adams and Yates, p. 230.

suffering, or whether it aestheticizes this suffering, and thereby defuses the grotesque's challenging of the warpedness of existence. The healing function would then come to naught. I will return to this question, both in this section with all brevity, and further on in my discussion of the body of pain. What will be crucial here is whether the rhetoric of the grotesque manages to contribute to the process of the restoration of the creation that the Christian tradition wishes to depict. Can Kayser's demonic grotesque be overcome, so to speak, by Bakhtin's more transformative grotesque? Or does the grotesque as a theological category risk ontologizing the grotesque, and thereby relativizing the idea of God's goodness and beauty? I understand this dimension of theological discourse as a reference not to the necessary state of things, but more to the contingent fact of sin and destructiveness. To speak of the grotesque as the destructive and the demonic in existence corresponds to how our world actually appears, not how it must appear, and so it also indirectly becomes a reference to the Christian hope that evil shall be overcome—that, for God's part, the human tragedy does not constitute the final word.[42]

Another aspect of the grotesque we find by comparing the grotesque with the Christian representation of the divine. Here we can get help from the anonymous Syrian author and Christian mystic from the early sixth century who goes by the name Dionysius the Areopagite. He argued in his work *The Celestial Hierarchy* that the divine and the heavenly revealed themselves in a fitting way through the earthly symbols that are most unlike their heavenly prototypes. This is an apparently paradoxical claim, but only apparently, since Dionysius thought that "incongruities are more suitable for lifting our minds up into the domain of the spiritual than similarities are."[43] The reason for this is that images that are thought to be more alike could lull believers into the false assurance that these earthly images actually depicted the heavenly in a more adequate way. But since the difference between Creator and the created was a difference in kind, and not a difference in degree—the world was created *ex nihilo,* God was "beyond being"—*every* earthly image will fall short when it comes to similarity to the heavenly. These discordant images were thus, in their own way, more adequate, since no doubt arose there about the difference between the earthly and the heavenly, between

---

42. Cf. David Bentley Hart's treatment of the tragedy in *The Beauty of the Infinite: The Aesthetics of Christian Truth* (Grand Rapids: Eerdmans, 2003), pp. 373-94.

43. Dionysius the Areopagite, *The Celestial Hierarchy,* in *The Complete Works,* The Classics of Western Spirituality, trans. Colm Luibheid; foreword, notes, and translation collaboration by Paul Rorem (Mahwah, NJ: Paulist Press, 1987), p. 150 (141A).

the created and the Creator, as these images, at least according to Dionysius's way of understanding, *could not* be literally true. Since the Christian faith involves a discourse about that which cannot be encompassed by human thought—God—its language will always limp and stutter in relation to its subject. To the extent that this language consciously attempts to realize this insight, it will lie near the language of the grotesque. The language of the grotesque thus does not only help us catch a glimpse of what we fear, but also helps us avoid taking our descriptions of what we hope for too much for granted.

In Dionysius's conception of theological language we find both a stylistic mixing where the low expresses the high, and a proximity to Harpham's understanding of the paradoxical of the language of the grotesque. According to Harpham this paradox makes it possible for one to speak of what cannot actually be spoken about, since human language is insufficient. The language of the paradoxical and the grotesque refers both to itself and beyond itself by consciously breaking with linguistic conventions and thereby drawing attention to the insufficiency of what is said. Language thereby receives, in a theological sense, an iconic function like that of the gaze for the invisible (chapter 7). Just as the icon opens outwards and liberates the gaze from stopping at an idolatrous reflection of oneself, the language of the grotesque can open outwards in order to refer to a reality that transcends the mimetic potential of language. And just as the icon wants to establish a relationship between the one who views the icon and the one the icon refers to, theological language also wants to establish a dynamic relationship, a *kerygma,* where God's address generates the person's response.[44] This theological understanding of language does not only concern explicit discourse about God, but all theological discourse in general that concerns the relationship between God and us people. In this chapter I will primarily devote myself to two central theological conceptions that relate the human embodiment, and where theological language exhibits a grotesque structure: communion and the resurrection of the body. In both of these conceptions a linguistic, ritual, and bodily reification constantly threatens, which would thwart or seriously challenge the gift-character of the Christian faith.

---

44. For a traditional Lutheran understanding of the kerygma, see Gustaf Wingren, *Predikan* (Lund: Gleerups, 1949). For an understanding more immediately related to the theoretical foundation I work with here, see Jean-Louis Chrétien, *The Call and the Response,* trans. Anne E. Davenport (New York: Fordham University Press, 2004).

Does the nonmimetic character of theological and grotesque language mean that Christian theology does not claim to be realistic? This is a question that will be indirectly treated in the following discussion in this chapter. Preliminarily I want, however, to argue here that we, like the American Southern author Flannery O'Connor, must instead differentiate between different sorts of realism. She describes grotesque realism, which her own literary work exemplifies, as dealing with "seeing near things with their extensions of meaning and thus of seeing far things close up."[45] She speaks further of this as a "realism of distance," which is rather a matter of seeing the present state of human existence from a theological perspective, rather than from a perspective that reduces her to biology, physics, etc. The literature of the grotesque does not, according to O'Connor, abandon the concrete. No literature can do that, since fiction begins where the person's knowledge begins, namely with the senses. It is instead a matter of depicting the concrete in a more drastic way. The theologically motivated grotesque is thus a depiction of the person that is drastic in the sense that it reckons with theological conceptions of (as in O'Connor's short stories and novels) pain, sacrifice, prophetic words, the resurrection of the body, and a constant visitation by Jesus, and so thereby aims to induce dissonance rather than harmony in its reader.

O'Connor's conception of the grotesque has led theologian Carl Skrade to define the phenomenon in the following way: "[T]he grotesque is that which deviates from the conventional and the normal, that which is incongruous with that deemed real according to consensual validation."[46] According to Skrade, the grotesque points to the repression of the irrational in our culture, and by the irrational he means rather that which falls outside the instrumental domains of reason.[47] For Skrade the irrational is rather the nonrational, and thus not the antirational. In other words, it most immediately concerns affirming the experience of the holy that the above-mentioned theologian and historian of religion Rudolf Otto spoke of in his book *The Idea of the Holy* as *mysterium tremendum et fascinans* (i.e., a both terrifying and alluring mystery), beyond what can be manipulated and controlled by human technology and human reason. Instrumental reason is not only insufficient, but can also function as a protective screen in the meeting with the different.

45. Flannery O'Connor, "Some Aspects of the Grotesque in Southern Fiction," in *Mystery and Manners: Occasional Prose,* ed. Sally Fitzgerald and Robert Fitzgerald (New York: Noonday, 1995), p. 44.
46. Carl Skrade, *God and the Grotesque* (Philadelphia: Westminster Press, 1974), p. 13.
47. Skrade, *God and the Grotesque,* pp. 63–83.

The holy comes to expression, Skrade says, in grotesque forms when it is repressed by a reductive rationalism as a human response to the experience of the holy in these two dimensions. Thus the grotesque becomes a category that manages to challenge *common sense,* i.e., the reigning worldview at a particular time and in a particular culture. In other words, Skrade ends up not so far from O'Connor's "realism of distance." For Skrade the point of the grotesque as a theological category is not nonrealistic; he pleads instead for a different realism than the conventional. Everything that is real does not fit within the framework of the concepts and categories that we attempt to master the environment with. The grotesque is because of this not a descriptive category, but an expression of the fact that what exists or can exist is not always captured by "conventional" and "normal" conceptual categories.

My point in speaking about, for example, the resurrection of the body as a grotesque conception is thus not that it would "merely" be a metaphor—if by metaphor one means a noncognitive language (cf. the discussion in chapter 3). It is instead a matter of a possibility for speaking of something that it is not actually possible to speak of, since we do not possess any knowledge of what it is about. The resurrection of the body is in this sense a grotesque conception, since it breaks with *common sense* and constitutes a sort of extravagant divine action that goes beyond what we view as possible by human standards. A reasonable theology for the hope of the resurrection of the body lives by the fact that its object both invites and resists interpretation. It is in this double movement that the representation of this hope becomes grotesque and thereby also retains theological language's character of being an expression of God's promise and the person's hope, not a theologically presumptuous detailed description of eschatological realities.[48] This insight into the nature of theological language makes it such that there is something slightly comical in theology, since it continually attempts to speak of something that it does not know about, something that is in fact the source for its being able to speak at all.[49] From this perspective the grotesque becomes a protective measure against theological hubris.

48. Cf. Harpham, *On the Grotesque,* p. 178: "Art lives by resisting interpretation as well as by inviting it, and it is this double movement that is figured in both the metaphor and the grotesque."

49. Gerard Loughlin, *Alien Sex: The Body and Desire in Cinema and Theology,* Challenges in Contemporary Theology (Oxford/Malden, MA: Blackwell, 2004), p. 145.

The Boundaries of the Grotesque

Is there then no risk of the grotesque effacing every perceivable boundary between the terror inducing *(tremendum)* and the alluring *(fascinans)*, and so allowing them to run into each other? Would such a confusion not mean that it would be, so to speak, easy to mix up God and devil, since the grotesque is an attempt to represent in word or image that which cannot be represented (whether it is evil or good, high or low)? Are they perhaps two aspects of the same thing? In his book *The Idea of the Holy* Otto says that biblical monsters such as leviathan and behemoth in Job, or the dragon in Revelation, are typical manifestations of the "wholly other *[ganz Anderes]*."[50] Harpham for his part writes that "[t]he grotesque stands at that point of breakthrough, at the margin between a healthy imaginative vigor and a corrupt indulgence in the mind's unrealities."[51] If it is the case that good and evil tend to flow together in the grotesque, it is justified to explicitly attempt to differentiate between good and bad grotesque.[52]

An example of the consequences of such an ambiguity from the Christian history of theology is the ambivalent stance towards pain and suffering we find there. Is there a productive point to the pain and the suffering that Jesus experienced on the cross, or does the cross involve a focusing on pain and suffering for their own sake? If the answer is yes to the latter question— does this not in essence involve a confusion between pain and pleasure, and thereby a sadomasochistic theology? I will discuss bodily pain in the Christian history of theology below, but I want to claim here that such a discussion ought to lead to a distinction between perceptions of pain and a constructive theology of pain, and thereby avoid legitimizing pain as such, or elevating the Passion to a necessity. It is therefore essential here to attempt to differentiate between theologically productive and unproductive uses of pain—and of the grotesque—by exercising some form of hermeneutically informed theological discernment.

In his book *Strangers, Gods and Monsters* philosopher Richard Kearney seeks to find "a hermeneutic model of narrative, resolved in spite of all to say something about the unsayable, to imagine images of the unimaginable, to tell tales of the untellable, respecting all the while the border limit that defers

---

50. Rudolf Otto, *The Idea of the Holy: An Inquiry into the Non-rational Factor in the Idea of the Divine and Its Relation to the Rational,* trans. John W. Harvey (London: Humphrey Milford, 1936), pp. 25, 155 *et passim.*

51. Harpham, *On the Grotesque,* p. 131.

52. See, for example, Skrade, *God and the Grotesque,* pp. 142–44.

all Final Answers."[53] In his book Kearney devotes himself to interpreting the other—as stranger, god, or monster—rather than the grotesque, but it is in principle the same problem as in my discussion here, namely, to avoid making the different so different that it becomes completely unrecognizable for us. It would then also be impossible to aesthetically differentiate between the stranger and the oppressor. To aid himself in this, Kearney wants to make use of a "diacritical hermeneutics" that on the one hand differs from a romantic hermeneutics à la Schleiermacher, which threatens to reduce the different to the same, and from a radical hermeneutics à la John D. Caputo on the other hand, which emphasizes the sublime character of the different and claims that any sort of mediation between the self and the other is impossible.[54] Diacritical hermeneutics attempts to keep alive the tension between neither reducing the other to the same nor postulating the other as something totally different. With this the possibility is also opened for an interpretation of the other, if still provisional, that enables a critical discernment even in relation to the different, without because of this being reduced to the same: "The threat to a genuine relation to others comes in fetishizing the Other as much as it does in glorifying the Ego."[55]

As I have mentioned above, through the grotesque an experience of the demonic is mediated such that the impersonal "It" causes conventions to fragment. Without denying the existence and legitimacy of such an experience, I want to differentiate between experiences of the demonic and experiences of a new world. The divine grotesque in the Christian tradition more resembles Bakhtin's understanding of the grotesque than Kayser's.[56] For the Christian tradition it is not a matter of continually remaining in

---

53. Kearney, *Strangers, Gods and Monsters*, p. 10.

54. Kearney, *Strangers, Gods and Monsters*, pp. 17–19, 77–82, 182–90, 229–32. Cf. also pp. 33–35. Kearney is here fundamentally inspired by Paul Ricoeur. See, for example, Ricoeur's *Oneself as Another*, trans. Kathleen Blamey (Chicago: University of Chicago Press, 1994).

55. Kearney, *Strangers, Gods and Monsters*, p. 229. Kearney argues that such an interpretation is both "prudent" in Aristotle's sense *(phronesis)* and "narrative." Besides Kearney, *Strangers, Gods and Monsters*, pp. 100–103, see Kearney's book *On Stories*, Thinking in Action (London/New York: Routledge, 2002), my book *De prudentia: Om principer och personer i etiken* (Stockholm/Stehag: Brutus Östlings Bokförlag Symposion, 2001), together with my article "Varför änglar inte kan vara kloka: Om klokhet som en mänsklig dygd," *Penelopes väv: För en filosofisk och teologisk pathologi,* ed. Mats Rosengren and Ola Sigurdson (Göteborg: Glänta, 2003), pp. 101–17.

56. Cf. here, besides Kearney, *Strangers, Gods and Monsters*, pp. 83–108, John Milbank, "Evil: Darkness and Silence," in *Being Reconciled: Ontology and Pardon*, Radical Orthodoxy (London/New York: Routledge, 2003), pp. 1–25.

the "paradigm crisis," but of being able to tell the story of how the existential "paradigm crisis" was overcome (not avoided) by God through Christ.[57] As I wrote in chapter 9 apropos the difference between Bakhtin's grotesque body and the Christian body as a grotesque body, the point of the Christian account is the transformation of humanity into the image of God. The grotesque body is therefore not the end, but the means for this transformation.

One might also object that what I call grotesque can certainly appear as such on the basis of the worldview that is dominant in a certain time and a certain culture, but that on the basis of the Christian faith's own logic it is not at all an expression of anything grotesque, but rather of God's beauty, whose radiance not only shines on that which is conventional, but also on that which defies our expectations.[58] It would thus be unwise to speak of the grotesque as a theological category, since that which I suggested above might engender the suspicion that God himself might be grotesque, a *mysterium tremendum,* or perhaps a sublime darkness beyond every manifestation. However, the intention here is not to attempt to imagine how things seem from God's perspective, but rather to point out the degree of wonder, amazement, or even confusion that, according to the Christian tradition, characterizes the person's encounter with Christ.[59] From the perspective of the Christian person, conversion has to do with going from one way of perceiving existence to another (cf. chapter 7), and in the discrepancy between the two the grotesque can serve as a theological category for speaking of the Christian hope in a way that both respects its apophatic character and avoids making it speechless.

My aim here is thus to pay attention to the grotesque as an aesthetic and theological category that aids us in capturing an essential aspect of the Christian representation of the body, namely the fact that this body is dependent on other bodies and is in flux. I will therefore now switch over to discussing three central phenomena within the Christian church, where practices and discourses are intimately intertwined, namely (in turn), communion, pain, and resurrection. These will thereby also come to exemplify what I in chapter 8 called the ritual mediation between individual and social bodies. In this section I will illuminate the Christian body

57. Cf. Alasdair MacIntyre, "Epistemological Crises, Dramatic Narrative, and the Philosophy of Science," in *Why Narrative? Readings in Narrative Theology,* ed. Stanley Hauerwas and L. Gregory Jones (Grand Rapids: Eerdmans, 1989), pp. 138–57.

58. Cf. Hart, *The Beauty of the Infinite,* p. 323.

59. Cf., for example, Matthew 8:27; 9:33; 15:31; 21:20; 22:22; 27:14, etc.

in relation to God's alterity, in relation to suffering, and finally in relation to its eschatological horizon. As I mentioned by way of introduction, these aspects are held together by the temporal structure of communion, and so also the structure of Christian embodiment: the divine presence, the past of pain and suffering together with the future of resurrection and hope. The relationship to the alterity of God and the understanding of Christian embodiment is thus expressed in a paradigmatic way in the Christian tradition through communion, and I will now discuss this as an aspect of the sacramental body and the divine presence.

The Sacramental Body

Communion is viewed as a central sacrament in virtually all the Christian denominations, and also constitutes a central dimension of Christology. Both sacramental theology and Christology have to do with how God becomes present for the person in her material circumstances. It should therefore already have been clear in my discussion of Paul's theology of the body that the sacrament of communion is an example of how Christology is received in a concrete practice (and in earlier chapters that the Christian practices have given rise to its theology). In 1 Corinthians 10:16–18 and 11:23–30 Paul discusses the relationship between three sorts of bodies: the body of the communion bread, the body of the solitary Christian, and the church as the body of Christ. Without having any developed *doctrine* of real presence, it nevertheless seems as though Paul imagines that Christ is present in communion for the solitary Christian, but that this presence cannot be separated from the relationship to the church as the body of Christ. A consequence of participation in communion is the integral fellowship with Christ and the church. In chapter 9 I also recounted how the understanding of communion after the twelfth century had come to be objectified through the fact that the emphasis was shifted from the edification of the church through the presence of Christ in communion to the miracle in the transformation of the elements as an isolated phenomenon. What took place was a reification of a social relationship (to make use of a Marxist-sounding term).[60] Through the reification of communion, a fundamentally central symbol for the Christian life, the church as social body fell from view and the body of

60. On reification as a philosophical concept, see Axel Honneth, *Verdinglichung: Eine anerkennungstheoretische Studie* (Frankfurt am Main: Suhrkamp, 2005).

the solitary Christian came to be individualized, or in reality, to instead be inserted into other social bodies. In other words, the understanding of the sacraments, not least of communion, is of great significance for the Christian understanding of human embodiment. In this section I will attempt to show how the Christian body is structured as a sacramental body beyond the late medieval and modern reification of communion. A theology that is congenial to the understanding of embodiment that I present in this book would emphasize communion as a communal, bodily exercise in the encounter with the different or other, and thereby as the ever-clearer incorporation of the solitary body into the church as the body of Christ. Through communion, the body of Christ thus becomes a continually overflowing body, both in space and in time.

"Communion," or more literally, the "Last Supper," corresponds to the German *Abendmahl,* which goes back to Martin Luther's translation of the Bible. Early in Christian history one spoke of the Eucharist, *eucharistia* in Greek, which means "thanksgiving." The Eucharist is a term that has returned to use within many denominations, including the Lutheran, above all thanks to the ecumenical Liturgical Movement that has had crucial significance for both theological research and church practice when it comes to communion during the twentieth century. This Liturgical Movement, which united academic theology and religious piety, meant, to cite one of the movement's foremost figures within the Church of Sweden, theologian and later bishop Yngve Brilioth in his minor classic *Nattvarden i evangeliskt gudtjänstliv,* "a rediscovery of the Christian mystery above all others: the sacrament of communion."[61] In this book Brilioth highlights more motifs—communion as thanksgiving, fellowship, commemoration, sacrifice, and mystery—than those that have been current in traditional Lutheran theology, namely the forgiveness of sins and the presence of Christ in communion, i.e., the real presence. I will not concern myself with as rich an exposition of the doctrine of communion in this section. The focus will lie primarily on three things: how the sacrament indicates the inevitable materiality of the Christian faith, how the understanding of the real presence is affected by the temporal structure of the liturgy of communion, and how the ecclesiological dimension of communion is expressed in the breaking of the bread. The question of sacramentality and materiality will be my starting point.

---

61. Yngve Brilioth, *Nattvarden i evangeliskt gudstjänstliv,* 2nd edition (Stockholm: Svenska kyrkans diakonistyrelses bokförlag, 1951), p. 18.

Sacramentality and Materiality

In the sacrament the Christian faith is not primarily mediated through words, but through corporeally perceivable things. This does not mean that this mediation is less "spiritual" than communication with words. On the contrary, even words have a certain embodiment, since there is no language at all except in the mediation of a given, particular speech act.[62] The materiality of the sacrament is thus not an accommodation for the person's "regrettable" embodiment, but it is in fact through this concrete materiality that the person's constitutive embodiment and the inevitable materiality in all communication is made clear. The Christian faith never meets—and has never met—people as pure spirituality (if spirituality can for the moment be contrasted with embodiment) or as a pure abstraction, but in and through the entirety of their bodies. As I have attempted to show in earlier chapters, the person's physical body is never independent of, but instead contemporaneous in relation to the linguistic, social, religious bodies that constitute its practical field. The embodiment of the person is thus her fundamental way of relating to the environment. The sacraments, understood as a part of the liturgy, become an important mediation of the relationship between social body and individual body.

Against this background, it is not surprising that the French theologian Louis-Marie Chauvet speaks of the sacrament as an expression of the embodiment of faith.[63] In the sacraments the threefold body that turns the believer into a believer converges, Chauvet says. This threefold body consists of the church as the social body, whose symbolic network of values structures the believer's interpretation of history, life, and the universe. It also consists of the body of tradition, which furnishes the ritual through the references to the apostolic testimony, and finally, it also consists of the cosmic body of the universe, which the believer receives as a gift in the form of symbolic elements—water, bread, wine, oil, etc. The life of faith is not lived outside of the body, but is fundamentally embodied, which is made clear by the sacraments. The sacraments thus become a way by which God, so to speak, takes the constitutive embodiment of the human being seriously. The fact that her senses have to do with her faith is not a concern; faith and senses constitute

---

62. Cf. Jacques Derrida, *Of Grammatology,* corrected edition, trans. Gayatri Chakravorty Spivak (Baltimore/London: Johns Hopkins University Press, 1997), pp. 6–26.

63. Louis-Marie Chauvet, *Symbol and Sacrament: A Sacramental Reinterpretation of Christian Existence,* trans. Patrick Madigan and Madeleine E. Beaumont (Collegeville, MN: Liturgical Press, 1995), pp. 152–53.

the fullness with which the person's communication and communion with God take place. As with Thomas Aquinas, the materiality of the sacraments becomes something far more than a pedagogical accommodation on God's part for the person's corporeal constitution.[64]

According to Chauvet the concrete materiality of the sacraments becomes an inevitable stumbling block for every idea of an immediate and interior individual illumination from Christ. The sacraments represent an inevitable mediation of the faith, and they therefore teach us that "the faith has a body, that it adheres to our body."[65] They additionally teach us that *to become a believer is to learn to consent, without resentment, to the corporeality of faith.*[66] Thanks to the sacraments, it is impossible for the Christian theologian to cultivate any sort of nostalgia for an unmediated relationship, whether this relationship concerns God, one's fellow human being, or one's own self. An incorporeal faith is made impossible by the sacraments, according to Chauvet, and the sacraments therefore constitute the "empirical manifestation" of faith's "arch-sacramentality," which constitutes the "transcendental condition for Christian existence": "[I]t indicates that *there is no faith unless somewhere inscribed, inscribed in a body*—a body from a specific culture, a body with a concrete history, a body of desire."[67] To become Christian is to allow an institution to imprint one's body with its trademark.[68] Since the risen Christ does not allow himself to be met directly, it is through the church, its sacraments, its writings, and its ethical testimony that the risen one lets himself be corporeally encountered in mediated form.[69] The risen one is present as absent, or as radically different, and cannot be transformed into an immediate, unmediated presence, to an

64. Cf. Thomas Aquinas, *Summa theologiae* (Paris: Sumptibus P. Lethielleux, Bibliopolae Editoris, 1939), III, q 61, a 1, together with David N. Powers, *Sacrament: The Language of God's Giving* (New York: Crossroad, 1999), pp. 56–57, 121–22; and John Milbank and Catherine Pickstock, *Truth in Aquinas* (London/New York: Routledge, 2001), pp. 84–85.

65. Chauvet, *Symbol*, p. 153.

66. Chauvet, *Symbol*, p. 153. Cf. p. 376.

67. Chauvet, *Symbol*, p. 154.

68. Chauvet, *Symbol*, p. 154. Cf. my discussion of the concept of trademarks in *Världen är en främmande plats: Essäer om religionens återkomst* (Örebro, Sweden: Cordia, 2003), pp. 97–112.

69. Chauvet, *Symbol*, pp. 162–70. Cf. p. 170: "From now on, it is impossible to touch his real body; we can touch it only as *the body symbolized* through the testimony the Church gives about him, through the Scriptures reread as his own word, the sacraments performed as his own gestures, the ethical witness of the communion between brothers and sisters lived as the expression of his own 'service' *(diakonia)* for humankind."

available object.[70] The one who cannot tolerate this risks transforming Christ back into a corpse.[71] To borrow a term from the theological discussion of analogies, one might say that in every sacramental identity with Christ there is an even greater difference between church and Christ that prevents the church from becoming lord of Christ, rather than the other way around. The sacramental body is thus not a closed, classical body, but an open, generative, grotesque (in Bakhtin's sense) body that is held open by exactly this mediation of a Christ whom it can never master.

One aspect of the traditional sacramental body that appears problematic for the theology of the body that I want to formulate here is its dependence on the male gender. In the Church of Sweden the priesthood was opened to women as late as 1958, and with this a woman's body and voice could celebrate the liturgy of communion as well, which also affects the meaning of the liturgy in favor of an increased integrity for the Christian ritual.[72] But the fact that the priesthood was opened to women shows even more clearly that the sacramental body is a sexed body. Even if there are elements within the traditional liturgy that relativize traditional gender hierarchies—the celebrant is not only active in the celebration of communion but also passive, an instrument for the presence of Christ—this fact can remind us not to uncritically legitimate liturgies of communion that in most cases have exclusively been a matter for men. In her investigation of Sunday's high mass according to *Den svenska kyrkohandboken* (The Handbook of the Church of Sweden), theologian Anne-Louise Eriksson states that

> the divine in the agenda is assigned masculine gender, while humans are implicitly assigned feminine gender. Furthermore, the text tells us that as the divine is superior to human, so male/masculine is superior to female/feminine. The ritual as a bodily activity confirms the same pattern. The divine (and masculine) holds the subject position, while the human (and feminine) becomes the object. This is theology transmitted in the ritual. But also a meaning of gender is transmitted. Masculinity is compatible with the divine and subject position, and femininity with human and the object position.[73]

70. Chauvet, *Symbol,* p. 173. The typical Protestant temptation is to achieve such an unmediated presence through an infallible Bible. The typical Catholic temptation is, in contrast, an excessive sacramentalism, and the typical contemporary temptation is moralism. Cf. pp. 173–77.

71. Chauvet, *Symbol,* p. 178.

72. Powers, *Sacrament,* p. 127. Cf. as well pp. 247–53.

73. Anne-Louise Eriksson, *The Meaning of Gender in Theology: Problems and Possi-*

So even with women as priests the problem of a unisexual liturgy and ritual of communion remains. This is hardly the place for a thorough discussion of how the problem of the unisexual sacramental body will be solved. Let it therefore suffice with the suggestion of a contribution that builds on the section on the gendered body in the previous chapter, namely that the path to a multigendered sacramental body should lie in a destabilization of the prevalent contemporary gender identities by, as Eriksson argues, "refraining from using gender as a separating category" in the liturgy.[74]

This can happen by using both a masculine and a feminine rhetoric in the conceptualization of the divine and by additionally avoiding assigning the divine exclusively to the masculine and the human to the feminine. The point then should not be to invert an earlier androcentric structure to a gynocentric structure where "natural" female characteristics are ascribed to God, or to "de-sex" the sacramental body through a "neutral" metaphor (God as "being," "the rock," etc.). It is instead a matter of creating a conception of a more complex sacramental body; a multisexed rather than a unisexed sacramental body that mediates dynamic and mixed gender identities rather than static ones. Otherwise the unisexed sacramental body risks creating a classical body, a finished body with fixed boundaries, through its clear subject and object positions for masculine and feminine bodies. Since the worship service, not least the liturgy of communion, aims to incorporate people into the body of Christ through the fact that they receive Christ as a gift in the bread and wine of communion, which disrupts and challenges *every* centered subject position—every attempt to dominate the divine—a unisexed, or hierarchically sexed, sacramental body is quite simply theologically impossible. The passivity *and* activity of the human being are generated in relation to Christ, who gives himself in communion and thereby deconstructs static gender identities, as with other human identities.[75] Through the nearly grotesque language that is used in the communion liturgy, where the celebrant quotes Jesus and says of the bread that "this is my body" and of the wine that "this is my blood," every conventional identity of "bread" and "wine" is destabilized and can thereby, apart from the force of habit that obliterates any trace of the uncanny in this, also destabilize conventional

---

bilities. Acta Universitatis Upsaliensis, Uppsala Women's Studies, A, Women in Religion: 6 (Uppsala: Uppsala University, 1995), p. 85.

74. Eriksson, *The Meaning of Gender*, p. 149.

75. See Elizabeth Stuart, *Gay and Lesbian Theologies: Repetitions with Critical Difference* (Aldershot, UK: Ashgate, 2003), p. 112, together as well with my article, "En främling inför Guds ögon," *Signum* 29, no. 9 (2003): 25–33.

embodiment. Thus becoming conscious of the sacrament as an expression of and reminder of the person's embodiment must not lock those who celebrate the service into a conventional masculinity or femininity. The materiality of communion instead makes clear the need for a multisexed sacramental body.

Real Presence and Communion Liturgy

Thus I believe that the sacramental body's complex gendered constitution leads us to the question of real presence in communion, i.e., the question of Christ's actual presence in bread and wine. This is a question that the theologians of the Christian church have discussed through the entire history of the church, and where opinions have oscillated between "realism," "symbolism," and "spiritualism."[76] During the Middle Ages two important battles over communion took place: between the monks Paschasius Radbertus and Ratramnus in the ninth century, and between Berengar of Tours and Lanfranc of Canterbury in the eleventh century. The consequence was, as I have already mentioned, a reification of communion *(corpus verum)*, where the understanding of it came to be made independent of the church and the worship service *(corpus mysticum)*. The fourth Lateran council in 1215 began to use the expression transubstantiation in order to on the one hand maintain that bread and wine were in substance transformed into Jesus' flesh and blood, but on the other hand to avoid too realistic a conception of this. This did not prevent a communion praxis being realized where communion masses were perceived as an exchange between human being and God, and where realism in communion came to involve an interest in the celebration itself independent of communion.[77]

When the Reformation—and especially Luther—again emphasized the fact that the worship service is the context for the Lord's Supper and for the meaning of communion, this did not in itself mean a questioning of the real presence, but a critique of the praxis that had developed around the Supper. However, a critique of the theology that had laid the ground for this praxis indirectly followed, a critique that would eventually come to be developed

---

76. For an overview, see the article "Abendmahl: II. Kirchengeschichtlich," in *Religion in Geschichte und Gegenwart: Handwörterbuch für Theologie und Religionswissenschaft*, 4th edition, ed. Hans Dietrich Betz and Don S. Browning, vol. 1: A-B (Tübingen: J. C. B. Mohr [Paul Siebeck], 1998), col. 15–31.

77. Cf. Arnold Angenendt, *Geschichte der Religiosität im Mittelalter* (Darmstadt: Wissenschaftliche Buchgesellschaft, 1997), pp. 488–515.

in a more spiritualistic direction than with Luther himself.[78] Luther retained certain characteristic features of the medieval theology of communion and of the praxis of communion, such as the adoration of the sacrament. The theology of communion came to be discussed with Lutheranism as well, and a difference in sense could be discerned between Luther and Melanchthon. The Lutheran tradition's theology of communion, however, came to be formulated in a historically critical way in polemic with the Zwinglian "sacramentarians," in the seventh paragraph of the *Formula of Concord* (1577). Here Christ's corporeal presence in the supper is emphasized:

> We believe, teach, and confess that in the Holy Supper the body and blood of Christ are truly and essentially present, truly distributed and received with the bread and wine.[79]

The Formula of Concord also expressly rejects the doctrine of transubstantiation and the adoration of "the outward, visible elements of bread and wine" in polemic against the Roman Catholic Church. The Reformation churches came to be divided in their theology of communion. During the modern period the celebration of communion became increasingly rare in the Protestant churches up until the liturgical renewal towards the end of the nineteenth century.

There is neither reason nor space here to discuss in detail the different confessional formulations of the real presence—doctrines of transubstantiation, doctrines of trans-signification, doctrines of consubstantiation, etc. I will instead turn to a crucial controversy in the contemporary discussion of the real presence: whether the late medieval reification of communion is something past or something current. The French philosopher and theologian Jean-Luc Marion (cf. chapter 7) says that even if the classic Roman Catholic doctrine of transubstantiation may be used without subscribing to the whole Aristotelian metaphysics that it developed out of, there is a risk that it "fixes and freezes the person in an available, permanent, handy, and delimited thing."[80] God thereby threatens to become

---

78. On Martin Luther and the doctrine of communion, see Bernhard Lohse, *Martin Luther: Eine Einführung in sein Leben und sein Werk,* Second edition (Munich: Beck, 1983), pp. 78–83.

79. *Formula of Concord,* in *The Book of Concord: The Confessions of the Evangelical Lutheran Church,* ed. Robert Kolb and Timothy J. Wengert, trans. Charles Arand et al. (Minneapolis: Fortress Press, 2000), pp. 505, 510 (VII).

80. Jean-Luc Marion, *God without Being: Hors-Texte,* Religion and Postmodernism, trans. Thomas A. Carlson (Chicago: University of Chicago Press, 1991), p. 164.

a "thing" that stands at the disposal of the Christian congregation, which entails a reification of communion. It thereby comes to function as an idol in which the congregation reflects itself, rather than as a mediation of God's presence to the congregation celebrating the service. Marion writes:

> Of this 'God' made thing, one would expect precisely nothing but *real* presence: presence reduced to the dimensions of a thing, a thing that is as much disposed to 'honor by its presence' the liturgy where the community celebrates its own power, as emptied of all significance capable of contesting, in the name of God, the collective self-satisfaction.[81]

Through the doctrine of transubstantiation, and certainly in other ways through other doctrines of the real presence, theology risks making God a hostage in its system, and thereby creating an idol of communion. The reification of the body of communion can then easily entail that the body of the communion-celebrating person would be reified.

The doctrine of transubstantiation is, however, not the only or unique form of such a reification. Marion says that the contemporary critique of the doctrine of transubstantiation, which wants to locate Christ's presence in the congregation instead of in the communion elements, is threatened by this very same risk, namely that God would be made the hostage of the human being. The critical issue is namely that the presence in this attempt is not differentiated from the collective consciousness, but corresponds to it.[82] The Eucharistic presence becomes dependent on the human fellowship, dependent on the attention that this gives the Eucharist, and once more God does not become a challenge to collective complacency. The risk of idolatry has thus not been averted, but rather worsened, since it is now no longer a "thing" existing apart from the collective consciousness that mediates the presence.[83] With this the embodiment of the faith risks foundering in the dream of an unmediated presence independent of all external mediation. Thus Marion wants to finally, paradoxically enough, defend the doctrine of transubstantiation as a safeguarding of the difference between Christ and the church, and as a defense against the idolatrous and reifying tendencies of the human being: "Only distance, in maintaining a distinct separation

81. Marion, *God,* p. 164.
82. Marion, *God,* pp. 166–67.
83. Marion, *God,* pp. 168–69.

of terms (of persons), renders communication possible, and immediately mediates the relation."[84]

Distance, which in Marion ought not be understood as a spatial distance, makes impossible a presence that is exhausted by what is present. Communion thus indicates a temporal distance where memory and hope qualify the present, rather than the contrary. In the liturgy of communion—which I will come to shortly—the now becomes a gift that is received from history and future, rather than a possession. With this the possibility opens for a presence that can be reduced to neither a function of the congregation nor an available thing. The mode of presence in communion becomes that of the gift, rather than that of the static presence, and it is a gift that is not simply passively available, but that changes the one who receives it as a gift. Marion says that it is through Christ's sacramental body that the person is assimilated into his ecclesial body—compare the discussion of the liturgical body in chapter 9.[85] This does not mean that the risk of idolatry would be averted. The risk of a reification of communion remains, since the possibility of avoiding the difference always remains a possibility. But Marion seems to judge the risk of this "material idolatry" as less than its contrary, namely a "spiritual idolatry."

If Marion's argument is true, it indicates that the doctrine of transubstantiation ought not be interpreted such that it makes God a hostage, but transubstantiation could instead be imagined, in Gerard Loughlin's words, as "the name, not of an explanation, but of a rigorous recollection of the eucharistic mystery."[86] In other words, the doctrine of transubstantiation then becomes a way to attempt to preserve the mystery, i.e., to avoid reducing God to an object. In contemporary theology's attempt to theologically preserve the real presence, one might say that the common denominator is the ambition to avoid tendencies towards reification, whether these concern the elements of communion or the community of the congregation, at the same time that one does not want to reduce the mystery of communion

---

84. Marion, *God,* p. 169.

85. Marion, *God,* p. 253.

86. Gerard Loughlin, *Telling God's Story: Bible, Church and Narrative Theology* (Cambridge: Cambridge University Press, 1996), p. 229. Chauvet also points out in *Symbol,* p. 385 that the point of the doctrine of transubstantiation does not lie in its emphasis on presence, but in its rejection of every physicalism, thus the opposite of the meaning that is usually ascribed to it. According to Chauvet the problem with Thomas Aquinas's formulation of this doctrine is that he does not sufficiently take into account Christ's presence in communion in relation to the church. See *Symbol,* p. 399.

to a purely linguistic understanding of the presence in the communion elements, which would easily lead to a reification of the contemporary church as such.

The question that Marion's argument raises is whether the doctrine of transubstantiation really can be the remedy for a reification of communion. My point here is, however, not to advocate a particular doctrine of the real presence. I am a little bemused by these attempts to reconnect with the transubstantiation doctrines of scholasticism: How much do they really have to do with the classic formulation of doctrine at the fourth Lateran council and the council of Trent? In which sense is the concept of substance really current for these theologians, other than as a reactivation of a historical tradition? The reason I am bringing up these arguments in this section is rather because they help me formulate a coherent understanding of "presence," which clarifies embodiment in the Christian faith. With Marion we find a way of imagining such a presence, which cannot be reduced to something present that can thereby be controlled. Presence is instead understood in terms of memory and hope, which does not mean that it is located in a "then" and a "since" without contact with "now," but rather as an emphasis on how history and future extend towards the present. Presence is understood here "less in the way of an available permanence than as a new sort of advent."[87] What is more, it is not a possession, but a gift that one continually asks for anew: "Give us this day our daily bread" (Matt. 6:11). Even Marion's doctrine of transubstantiation thus becomes a sort of reinterpretation or transposition of the historical doctrine, from the more static ontological categories that have been used historically to more temporal categories.[88] Thus an understanding of the temporal structure of the communion liturgy is necessary in order to avoid reification.

The liturgy of communion is structured by four verbs that are taken from the account of the Last Supper in the Gospels (cf., for example, Luke 22:19), which is then repeated in the account of how two disciples eat with Jesus in Emmaus (24:30) after the crucifixion and resurrection.[89] For the Last Supper Luke recounts the following episode: "And he *took* bread, and when he had

87. Marion, *God,* p. 172.
88. Loughlin, *Telling God's Story,* p. 241.
89. As Gregory Dix points out, these four verbs—which represent four actions—are a streamlining of *seven* actions that are described in the Gospel accounts, but the liturgical tradition has consistently represented these seven actions as four. The Gospels are thus the source but not the model for the communion liturgy. See Gregory Dix, *The Shape of the Liturgy,* 2nd edition (London: Dacre Press, 1960), pp. 48–50, 78–82.

given thanks, he *broke* it and *gave* it to them, saying, 'This is my body, which is given for you. Do this in remembrance of me.'" The same formulations are central to the different communion prayers that are presented by the Church of Sweden's *Den svenska kyrkohandboken* from 1986 (which, within the Church of Sweden, is a result of the Liturgical Movement during the twentieth century) and that, according to this order of worship, are placed between the Sanctus and the Lord's prayer: "The night when he was betrayed he took bread, gave thanks, broke it and gave it to the disciples, saying: Take and eat. This is my body which has been given for you. Do this in remembrance of me."[90] The communion prayer summarizes in this way the entirety of the communion liturgy, through the fact that the bread is brought forth during the offertory *(offertorium),* through the fact that the celebrant gives thanks in the communion prayer, then breaks the bread and shares it out during communion. The communion liturgy is thus not only a remembrance in words of the last supper, but also a concrete interpretation of it.

Additionally, a short recapitulation of the salvation history is combined in the communion prayer with a prayer for the imminent arrival of the kingdom of God. In other words, the communion liturgy should not be compared to a memorial service—it is entirely oriented towards the present and the future. The remembrance here, with the Greek word *anamnēsis,* is not a memory of what once was, but rather an actualization in the present of the historical event. Through an invocation of the Holy Spirit (the epiclesis of consecration) this remembrance and this hope are woven together with a prayer that the presence of Christ in the elements of communion will give life to the entire fellowship of the church. The clearest example of this in the church handbook from 1986 is given in communion prayer D:

> Send your Spirit into our hearts so that he [sic] may ignite in us a living faith. Consecrate also through your Spirit this bread and wine, gifts of the fruit of the earth and people's work, which we bring before you. We thank you because through them we receive part of Christ's body and blood.[91]

Through remembrance and invocation that which once has happened, that is, Christ's deed in all its aspects, is made present in the celebration of com-

90. *Den svenska kyrkohandboken. Del I: Den allmänna gudstjänsten och De kyrkliga handlingarna,* Antagen för Svenska kyrkan av 1986 års kyrkomöte (Stockholm: Verbum, 1987), pp. 144–45.

91. *Den svenska kyrkohandboken,* p. 148.

munion, including the eschatological anticipation.[92] The German theologian Hans-Christoph Schmidt-Lauber formulates the dynamic character of the remembrance in the celebration of communion in the following way:

> In the Church the first communion is not just celebrated once or in an imitative way, one celebrates *with* it. The Lamb's supper is eternally not only proclaimed, it is anticipated by and bestows its glory upon the divine service in all its provisional form.[93]

The remembrance ties together the Last Supper with our time's celebration of communion and with the coming eschatological communion.[94] Past, present, and future are united by Christ through the Spirit. Through this, communion brings about a temporality that does not especially highlight a punctual now, which is significant for the understanding of the real presence. This presence should not be understood as a static being-at-hand, but rather as a dynamic arrival, an advent.

Clearly, insights of the sort that Marion offers hardly need to be limited to a strictly Roman Catholic theology of communion, or in general to a theology of communion that wants to specifically defend the doctrine of transubstantiation. Chauvet, mentioned above, who, in contrast with Marion, says that the doctrine of transubstantiation is instead an expression of the real presence that is too marked by its own time and philosophy to function in our time, can nevertheless emphasize communion in his more symbolic—which here should not be understood as nonrealistic—sacramental doctrine as a way to avoid the modern form of idolatry:

> Christ's resistance to every reduction by our "faith" finds in the Eucharist its *radical* expression. This radicalness, expressed in the formula "*body* of Christ," is represented here by both the *exteriority* and the *anteriority* of

92. For a discussion of Lutheran tradition and ecumenical theology for the initiated, which the following account has taken much inspiration and information from, see Kjell Petersson, *Åkallan och åminnelse: Nattvarden i mötet mellan luthersk tradition och ekumenisk teologi.* Bibliotheca theologiae practicae 64 (Lund: Arcus, 2000), *passim*. Petersson writes about how the epiclesis is something new in the Lutheran tradition on pp. 89–110.

93. Hans-Christoph Schmidt-Lauber, "Die Eucharistie," in Hans-Christoph Schmidt-Lauber and Karl-Heinrich Bieritz, *Handbuch der Liturgik: Liturgiewissenschaft in Theologie und Praxis der Kirche* (Leipzig/Göttingen: Evangelische Verlags-Anstalt/Vandenhoeck und Ruprecht, 1995), p. 232.

94. See Kjell Petersson, *Åkallan och åminnelse*, p. 29.

the significant manner in which the body of Christ gives itself. Here, the body of the glorified Christ is presented to us as *outside* us and *facing* us, as well as *antecedent* to its reception by us in Communion.[95]

Here we find the same paradox as in Marion, namely, that the materiality of communion is the most concrete and radical expression of the prohibition of idolatry, and at the same time the sacrament that, because of this, is most threatened by idolatrous perversions.

The emphasis on the presence of Christ in communion aims to maintain the difference between Christ and church so that Christ's presence is not turned into a function of the Christian community, and thus inverts an earlier reification that has understood the elements of communion as manipulable things in the possession of the church. The understanding of communion as a gift wants to avoid both a metaphysical, reifying view of communion and a subjectivist view of communion, in favor of the understanding of communion as a gift that transcends every human conceptualization or institutionalization.[96] The risk in such an emphasis on the "externality" of communion is, however, that communion's constitutive residence in the congregation that celebrates the divine service remains unclear. In his book *The Eucharist* the Orthodox theologian Alexander Schmemann has emphasized precisely the significance of the liturgical context for the understanding of communion, and has in strong terms criticized Western theology for the forgetfulness that has been the consequence of its reification of communion.[97] The significance of the church as the semantic context in which communion becomes at all visible can easily disappear, not least in Marion's emphasis on the externality of communion in relation to the church.[98] Without a concrete congregation that can be understood not only as passive and receptive, but also as active and involved, Marion's doctrine of transubstantiation threatens to repeat the reification of communion. The ecclesiological dimension of the real presence must be clarified in order to deepen the meaning of the doctrine of the same, and I will finally contribute to this in this section by highlighting *one* element and *one* moment in communion, namely the bread and the breaking of the bread.

95. Chauvet, *Symbol*, p. 402.

96. Powers, *Sacrament*, p. 11.

97. Alexander Schmemann, *The Eucharist: Sacrament of the Kingdom*, trans. Paul Kachur (Crestwood, NY: St. Vladimir's Seminary Press, 1988), pp. 12–14.

98. See Jayne Svenungsson, *Guds återkomst: En studie av gudsbegreppet inom postmodern filosofi*, Logos/Pathos no. 3 (Göteborg: Glänta, 2004).

Breaking of the Bread and Ecclesiology

What is the significance of the bread in communion? Why bread, exactly? To begin with, bread is one of the fundamental foods of human beings. The bread in communion connotes the "daily bread" that is mentioned in the most central Christian prayer "Our Father" (Matt. 6:11), and is best understood as the means of nourishment that is critical for the maintenance of life.[99] So what is meant is not all that is needed for a human life, but the "toil for daily bread" itself. Also a part of the essence of this bread is that it is shared with others and in this way is a "social" bread. It is shared among people at a meal and in this way creates fellowship among them. The bread can therefore not only be seen in a purely utilitarian sense as a means of nourishment that maintains biological existence, but it also mirrors the person's social community. Finally, the bread is also a symbol of the person's thankfulness towards God as the one who gives the bread and, through the bread, the person's existence. The bread in communion is, according to the previously mentioned Chauvet, not just a "thing"—here he compares it with the pitcher that Heidegger discusses in the essay "Das Ding":

> Like the "pitcher" of Heidegger, the bread never manifests its being of bread as well as in this act of religious oblation where, fruit of nature (earth and heaven) and fruit of history (the labour of people), it is recognized as a gracious gift of God, and where, sharing it as such (i.e. as a gracious gift of God), people nourish themselves from it. There is nothing more bread than this bread.[100]

The bread realizes its essence as bread in full by giving fellowship between people as well as between God and people. Bread is in general a sort of means of communication in the fact that it is a fundamental foodstuff. Christ thus has more claim to being nourishment than common bread, since Christ is the one who establishes and restores communication and communion between God and people.[101] Christ is the medium through which a genuine communion both

---

99. Ulrich Luz, *Matthew 1–7: A Commentary,* trans. Helmut Koester (Minneapolis: Fortress Press, 2007), pp. 319–22.

100. Louis-Marie Chauvet, "The Broken Bread as Theological Figure of Eucharistic Presence," in *Sacramental Presence in a Postmodern Context,* Bibliotheca ephemeridum theologicarum lovaniensium CLX, ed. Lieven Boeve and Lambert Leijssen (Leuven: Leuven University Press, 2001), p. 256.

101. This is according to Herbert McCabe, *God Matters,* Contemporary Christian Insights (London/New York: Mowbray, 2000), p. 127.

between God and people and between people takes place. This does not mean that Christ in the communion bread replaces bread as bread (its "substance" or whatever we want to call it). In the communion bread it is still bread I eat, but a bread that, thanks to its liturgical context and the action of the Spirit (epiclesis), becomes a means for Christ's presence. The idea that no bread is more bread than the communion bread does not mean that the communion bread is less bread than other bread—it instead means that the bread's character as food is *intensified* in communion to embrace a divine dimension of communication as well (cf. John 6:48: "I am the bread of life.").[102] Such an intensification should certainly not be understood as a continuous scale where bread that becomes ever-more bread suddenly exists as the body of Christ, but the discontinuity that the real presence brings about is an action with the bread where its characteristics are presented in a radically different context that leads to it receiving a different significance.[103] The communion bread experiences a paradigm shift through the fact that this context of understanding becomes, in part, different than the everyday context.

The breaking of the bread is itself meaningful for several reasons.[104] In the communion liturgy of the Swedish church—just as in several other traditions—the breaking of the bread is followed by the one leading the celebration of communion reading from 1 Corinthians 10:16–17, which in the relevant formulations in *Den svenska kyrkohandboken* is: "The bread that we break is a participation in the body of Christ. So are we, though many, a single body, for we all get to partake of one and the same bread."[105] The breaking of the bread is a prerequisite for it to be able to be shared and thereby provide fellowship with the body of Christ, such that it becomes one body. Through the breaking a "symbolic void" (Chauvet) is created, which opens a space both for the other and for the presence of Christ.[106] The bread does not come into its own as communion bread without this breaking, without this void that is able to create fellowship between human beings and God. In other words it is precisely the *broken* bread that in a particular way makes Christ present at communion. Here Christ's body becomes—both in its aspect as the risen Christ and of the church as the body of Christ—a

102. Cf. the discussion between P. J. Fitzpatrick and Herbert McCabe in Herbert McCabe, *God Matters*, pp. 130–64.

103. Cf. the discussion in Laurence Paul Hemming, "After Heidegger: Transubstantiation," in *Sacramental Presence in a Postmodern Context*, ed. Boeve and Leijssen, pp. 299–309.

104. Cf. Dix, *The Shape of the Liturgy*, pp. 80–81.

105. *Den svenska kyrkohandboken*, p. 14.

106. Chauvet, "The Broken Bread," pp. 260–61.

grotesque body in the Bakhtinian sense: generative, transcending boundaries, intertwined with other bodies. The communion bread is thus not in its essence something closed and compact (as with Bakhtin's classical body: a finished body, closed to the environment), but broken and present in order to be shared. Every part of the communion bread is the whole of Christ's body to the same degree as every other part. The breaking itself, with its associations with Christ's body that was broken apart on the cross—an aspect of embodiment that I return to in the next section—is interpreted here as something positive, since it is a prerequisite for the individual's participation in the body of Christ.

Christ's presence in communion cannot be conceived apart from the relationship to the actual and potential ecclesial fellowship, which is illustrated by the fact that the breaking of the bread is immediately followed by the Pax Domini, the Agnus Dei, and communion. The Pax Domini emphasizes the fellowship between the people in the church while communion emphasizes the fellowship with the risen Christ. These two dimensions are united in the breaking of the bread. In Chauvet's words: "[O]n the one hand, what is shared is the body itself of the risen Christ; but this eucharistic body of the Christ Head is inseparable, even if distinct, from his ecclesial body built by the sharing of the same bread."[107] To extend this point, neither can the church as the body of Christ be conceived of as a "finished," "classical" body, but as a "grotesque" body whose continually rebroken character opens it outwards. Through the breaking of the bread the crucifixion is repeated in a different way and is now spread out into the world through the church.[108] Like the bread that is broken and distributed, the congregation will be sent out into the world after the Divine Service as "bread" for the hunger of the world. The symbolic void that arises in the breaking of the bread becomes a void in the church as well, in which it opens to the other, beyond the concrete institutional form of the church. As Werner G. Jeanrond argues, communion can thereby become a space for, an occasion for, and a practice for a productive meeting with the other.[109] Through the breaking of the bread the openness for the other is manifested not only as an openness outwards, but also, and perhaps as the condition of the external openness, as an *inner* openness. The broken bread consists precisely in fragments from one and

107. Chauvet, "The Broken Bread," p. 261.

108. Graham Ward, *Cities of God* (London/New York: Routledge, 2000), p. 106. Cf. as well pp. 152–55.

109. Werner G. Jeanrond, *Guds närvaro: Teologiska reflexioner I* (Lund: Arcus, 1998), p. 174.

the same piece of bread; the void between fragments does not prevent them from still belonging together.

The fact that the church opens itself to the other and thereby exceeds its institutional form does not, however, mean that its concrete institutional form loses its meaning. Without a concrete institutional form the church risks once more losing its body. This exceeding is a matter of a particular concretion of the church again coming to an understanding of its particularity and thereby avoiding confusing itself with the whole. The real presence in communion and its exteriority in relation to the church is a presence in the living congregation that celebrates the service, which precisely in this finds a space for the difference in itself. The awareness of the exteriority of communion is kept alive by the language of the grotesque that characterizes the liturgy and attempts to express a deeper meaning in the words that are used than pure description. Like the language of the grotesque, the communion liturgy does not want to express something stable and fixed, but rather a process of the person's gradual and transformative incorporation into the Christian body as a divine action of pure grace.

In this section on the sacramental body I have discussed how the understanding of the Eucharist relates to the conception of the inevitable materiality of the Christian faith, above all in the view of the real presence and the breaking of the bread. There is, however, another aspect of the sacramental body that remains. The breaking of the bread intentionally inspires associations with Christ's suffering body on the cross. The question thus becomes to how great a degree the body that is held together by the Eucharist manages to house that pain in its body as well, without it breaking apart from internal tensions. The church has, however, traditionally been viewed as a grotesque body for which pain is no stranger, which has been thematized in Christian theology by conceptions of martyrdom in imitation of Christ. The sense in which the sacramental body is a body of pain will therefore be critical for the understanding of the Christian body.

The Body of Pain

There is a long and thorough theological reflection on pain and suffering. The passion accounts of the Gospels that culminate in the crucifixion have meant that pain and suffering have from the start been an element in the theological treatment of the relationship between God and person. The place of pain and suffering in the course of reconciliation, but also in the doctrine of God, has been treated over the centuries. It is not only theology that exhibits a treatment of the problem of pain in its most central parts. This is also the case with Christian symbolism, the central symbol of which is the cross. Jürgen Moltmann writes in his pioneering book *The Crucified God* that "Christian theology finds its identity as such in the cross of Christ. Christian life is identified as Christian in a double process of identification with the crucified"—and in principle he speaks, even if the formulations could have been different, with the whole of the Christian tradition from Paul onward.[110] The Christian life as an identification with Christ has been understood as an act of solidarity with the suffering and the poor throughout history. Through the very subject that it reflects on, Christian theology, which encompasses both theoretical reflection on the one crucified and Christians' imitation of and identification with him, has produced a range of thoughts on pain and suffering. The theological tradition's grotesque representations of Jesus' pain and suffering have served to keep the awareness of these aspects of humanity alive. In the previous section on communion I focused primarily on the aspect of God's presence, but here I will instead turn to how humanity is broken apart by pain and suffering, which is also an aspect of communion—an aspect that is, of course, all too great a part of human life in the present, but which still, through hope, belongs to the temporal aspect of the past in communion.

It would thus be possible to approach pain and suffering as themes from a range of different theological perspectives. One such would be a soteriological perspective: In which sense are pain and suffering thematized on the basis of the event of atonement?[111] Another would be theological in the strict sense: What significance does Jesus' suffering on the cross have for our understanding of God? Who must God be so that Jesus' suffering on the cross would be an occurrence that is a part of God's own life?[112] The question of pain and suffering also admits what is sometimes called the problem of evil: How can God be all powerful if God is also love, and yet there is undeserved suffering in the world?[113] These different perspectives are not independent

110. Jürgen Moltmann, *The Crucified God: The Cross of Christ as the Foundation and Criticism of Christian Theology*, trans. R. A. Wilson and John Bowden (Minneapolis: Fortress Press, 1993), p. 24.

111. Cf. Miroslav Volf, *Exclusion & Embrace: A Theological Exploration of Identity, Otherness, and Reconciliation* (Nashville: Abingdon, 1996).

112. Hans Urs von Balthasar, *Mysterium Paschale: The Mystery of Easter*, Ressourcement, trans. Aidan Nichols (Edinburgh: T. & T. Clark, 1990).

113. Cf. Kenneth Surin, *Theology and the Problem of Evil*, Signposts in Theology (Oxford: Basil Blackwell, 1986), and Douglas John Hall, *God & Human Suffering: An Exercise in the Theology of the Cross* (Minneapolis: Augsburg, 1986).

of each other, and it is therefore inevitable, even with the focus I have chosen, that we will touch on these questions. I will, however, choose a more anthropological focus, namely, how the Christian tradition has conceived of itself in the relationship between pain and suffering as physical and psychic phenomena on the one hand, and the embodiment of the person on the other. My thesis is that pain can break apart the mediation between social body and individual body that the Christian tradition presupposes, and that a legitimate theology of pain therefore ought to help restore this mediation, not legitimate pain in itself. In the following I will begin with a philosophical discussion of the phenomenology and epistemology of pain in order to then view pain as a technique of subjectification in ancient acts of the martyrs. Finally, in this section I will again pose the critical question that I mentioned at the start of this chapter: Can theology speak of pain without risking an ideological legitimation of the same?

The Phenomenology and Epistemology of Pain

What, then, is pain? A philosophical attempt to approach pain as a human phenomenon we find in the German phenomenologist Max Scheler.[114] According to him, a number of different perspectives must be included in a complete philosophical teaching on pain and all varieties of suffering. Scheler tallies up six different perspectives, and among these are included the phenomenology and physiology of pain, the psychotechnics of pain (i.e., how the subject actively relates to pain), and cultural history, such as the ethics and metaphysics of pain. Pain is thus a multidimensional phenomenon that cannot be exhaustively described from a single perspective. Even if such a phenomenological perspective differs from a more scientific view of pain as a series of nerve impulses from a part of the body to the brain, for Scheler it is a matter of achieving a genuine understanding of pain by viewing it from several perspectives. By starting with a phenomenological argument, one can differentiate between pain as a perception and pain as an experience.[115] The first is a physiological-biological reaction, and the second

114. See Max Scheler, "Zu einer philosophischen Lehre von Schmerz und Leiden," in *Gesammelte Werke*, vol. 6: *Schriften zur Soziologie und Weltanschauungslehre*, 2nd revised edition (Bern: Francke, 1963), p. 331.

115. A presentation of different ways of looking at pain may be found in Karin Johannisson, "Kroppens teater: Smärta," in *Kroppens tunna skal: Sex essäer om kropp, historia och kultur* (Stockholm: Pan/Norstedts, 1998), pp. 65–70.

is a cultural-psychological phenomenon. Pain is thus something more than an individual perception that may be more or less intense. Pain has to do with body, institution, and subjectivity.[116] Even pain has a history, which is not least demonstrated by the diminishing tolerance for pain that seems to have become an effect of the progress of medicine—previously there were few of today's remedies, and the individual was forced to meet her or his pain with much greater resignation. The cultural tolerance for pain, as well as the cultural expression of pain, has thus varied.

Scheler has also emphasized that there are different strata to the person's constitution where pain can be experienced,[117] from the level of pure sensory perceptions to the corporeal and mental conditions to the spiritual level. Even apart from a specific Schelerian anthropology, one typically differentiates between, for example, bodily pain, as if one were to receive a hammer blow to the arm, and more mental pain, as with the loss of a loved one. Pain is "a mode of embodied experience," and with theologian Graham Ward I therefore want to argue that "a theological account then of suffering must concern itself with what it means to be a soul enfleshed."[118] This means that suffering cannot be identified in a simple way as either bodily or psychic, since the person exists as an intertwining of body and consciousness—"the soul enfleshed."[119] At the same time, I believe that we ought to conceive of the experience of pain as a continuum moving from bodily to mental pain. The hammer blow that I mistakenly inflict on myself does not need to mean much more than a particular physical pain, if not yet another example for me of my extraordinary clumsiness. We can then imagine that a particular measure of mental suffering appertains to physical pain. Similarly, sorrow at the passing of a loved one can certainly be said to be a mental pain rather than a physical one, but even psychic suffering can, as we know, find expression in apparently unrelated somatic pains. My reflections below on the

116. Johannisson, "Kroppens teater," p. 70.

117. Max Scheler, "Zu einer philosophischen Lehre." Cf. as well Scheler, *Gesammelte Werke*, vol. 2: *Der Formalismus in der Ethik und die materiale Wertethik,* 4th revised edition (Bern: Francke, 1954), pp. 344–56.

118. Graham Ward, "Suffering and Incarnation," in *The Blackwell Companion to Postmodern Theology,* Blackwell Companions to Religion, ed. Graham Ward (Oxford: Blackwell, 2001), p. 193.

119. Ward, "Suffering and Incarnation," p. 194: "That which is matter already matters, is already caught up in the exchanges of signification. The soul enfleshed (where soul has much wider connotations than just the mind's cognition), the only 'body' we know, sublates any mind-body dualism."

body of pain proceed from the idea that there is such a continuum between physical and mental pain, but I will especially focus on physical pain as an aspect of the person's individual and social embodiment from a theological perspective.

We get an objection to the cultural dependence of pain, however, from Elaine Scarry in her much-discussed book *The Body in Pain,* where she says that there is an essential feature of pain that it is impossible to share with someone else through language. Even if there are many attempts to express pain in language, physical pain has no content that it can refer to, and every attempt to objectify pain in language will therefore inevitably fail. Scarry has divided those who have attempted to objectify pain through language into several different categories: people who have themselves suffered great pain, people who have not themselves suffered pain, but who speak in the place of those in pain (for example, Amnesty International), together with medical science, the law, and even art.[120] A reason for these objectifying attempts is a desire to eliminate pain. They must, however, be seen as secondary attempts: they do not express an actual pain, but attempt to thematize it in retrospect, from the outside—thereof the ambivalence of these linguistic objectifications. In other words, physical pain is a private state of consciousness, which cannot be shared with other fellow human beings, and which therefore designates a movement away from human fellowship. The epistemic difference between experiencing pain personally and hearing about pain secondhand is so great that Scarry describes it in almost Cartesian terms as a difference between "to 'have certainty'" and "to 'have doubt'": "Thus pain comes unsharably into our midst as at once that which cannot be denied and that which cannot be confirmed."[121] The one who feels pain also has an immediate certainty of her or his own pain perception; the one who does not feel pain can never be certain whether the expression of pain corresponds to a genuine perception of it.

Scarry was, however, already countered by an at least equally famous discussion of pain, namely the one we find in Ludwig Wittgenstein's *Philosophical Investigations* from 1953. Here Wittgenstein says that pain is not only a private experience, but also a public relationship.[122] Such a public dimension of pain is important for my theological formulations and I will

120. Elaine Scarry, *The Body in Pain: The Making and Unmaking of the World* (New York/Oxford: Oxford University Press, 1985), pp. 6–11.

121. Scarry, *The Body in Pain,* p. 4.

122. Ludwig Wittgenstein, *Philosophical Investigations,* 3rd edition, trans. G. E. M. Anscombe (Oxford: Blackwell, 1967), §§246, 283, 284, 293.

therefore dwell on Wittgenstein's words for a moment. It is on the basis of these words that anthropologist Talal Asad has argued that the question of the objectification of pain in language and the privatizing character of pain is not at all as unambiguous as Scarry argues. If one thinks about the possibility of being sure of another person's pain, it is important "who is expressing it to whom, how . . . and for what purpose 'certainty' is sought."[123] As an example of an area where such an objection is valid Asad mentions Scarry's discussion of torture, where Scarry argues that the pain that is expressed by the victim is denied as pain by the torturer and instead understood as power.[124] If it is impossible for the one who tortures to really know that he causes his victim pain through the torture, the repeated torture is, following Asad, difficult to understand. Scarry seems to argue that the victim's pain is denied as pain, but if this is the case, it is no longer a question of an uncertainty with regard to the victim's pain, but a sort of certainty. The problem with Scarry's account of pain is that it proceeds on the basis of a distinct difference between a pre-linguistic, "raw" experience of pain and a linguistic domain in which this pain is to be represented.[125] With this an unbridgeable "distance" is presupposed between perception and its verbalization.

If Asad is right, the question of the pain of others is not primarily a matter of judging what the claim of pain refers to, but rather of how people relate to each other and how pain affects this relationship.[126] Asad's example is a mother who suffers because of her wounded child's pain. The fact that she can suffer because of this pain is a consequence of the relationship she has to her child. This relationship namely embraces the possibility of answering the suffering of the other with one's compassion. If a person suffers thus because of someone else's pain, this does not depend on the fact that she first assesses how trustworthy signals of the other's suffering appear and then decides how to react. Her compassion is a practical consequence of the relationship she has to the child, and confronted with the child's pain, expressed through words, crying, gestures, or an unusual quiet, she also comes to act by virtue of the relationship that has already existed earlier between her and the child. Asad does not mean that it is impossible to mistake what the other feels and experiences—and this concerns not only the expression

---

123. Talal Asad, "Thinking about Agency and Pain," in *Formations of the Secular: Christianity, Islam, Modernity,* Cultural Memory in the Present (Stanford: Stanford University Press, 2003), p. 81.

124. Scarry, *The Body in Pain,* p. 28.

125. See Asad, "Thinking about Agency and Pain," p. 81 n. 27.

126. Asad, "Thinking about Agency and Pain," pp. 82–83.

of pain, but all feelings—but that such a mistake touches more the concrete relationship between people (the fact that someone dissembles and pretends to suffer or that someone suffers from a lack of ability for empathy) than her intellectual ability. Nor does Asad mean that an experience of pain cannot be experienced as impossible to share, but such experiences have more to do with a lack in communication than with an epistemologically conditioned impossibility to communicate it.

What Asad wants to come to is that pain is not necessarily private in its essence, but instead ought to be understood as "an active, practical relationship inhabiting time."[127] The physical and the more mental—including the linguistic—dimensions of pain cannot be separated other than purely analytically. Perceptions of pain are simultaneously both physically and culturally conditioned. Asad writes:

> What a subject experiences as painful, and how, are not simply mediated culturally and physically, *they are themselves modes of living a relationship.* The ability to live such relationships over time transforms pain from a passive experience into an active one, and thus defines one way of living sanely in the world.[128]

How our own pain is received by ourselves is dependent on what response we get from others who are confronted with our pain. Whether or not we are able to live in a spiritually healthy way during or after traumatic experiences of pain is dependent on if and how others share our pain. The point is therefore not that a pain can be the same in the one who suffers it and the one who only observes it in the other. There is "an irreducible excess in pain," which, however, does not mean that the pain that the individual suffers is all that pain is.[129] Even in their suffering those who suffer are social persons, and even their suffering is constituted by their relationships. Pain can therefore be constituted in a range of different ways depending on the relationship between those who suffer and their environment. Pain does not necessarily need, in other words, to be understood as a feeling that the victim of the pain passively "suffers," as though the victim were merely an object for the pain. On the contrary, Asad points out, there are historical examples of how people have seen themselves as the active subjects of pain.

127. Asad, "Thinking about Agency and Pain," p. 83.
128. Asad, "Thinking about Agency and Pain," p. 84.
129. Asad, "Thinking about Agency and Pain," p. 85.

In contrast to secular accounts of pain, these do not presume that pain is a passive state, but pain is here seen as an expression of human agency.[130] In other words, pain does not need to be only understood as a *cause* of action, but can be seen as an action in itself. One example of pain as action we find in the early Christian martyrs.

Before I get into conceptions of pain in the Christian tradition, it may yet be interesting, for the sake of comparison, to mention something of what characterizes a secular, modern perspective on suffering.[131] A part of the process of secularization is characterized by a desire to eliminate the cruelties initiated and justified by religions.[132] A secular constitution would be able to stand as guarantee against religiously motivated violence. The advocates of secularization have argued that such violence, for example, in the form of torture, is unmotivated, since it is arbitrary and meaningless. Only the suffering, which has no design in the process by which the person realizes her true humanity, is meaningless and thereby inhuman.[133] Even pain would stand in the service of progress if it had any point. This would be the case if the pain contributed to realizing the enlightened person. All other pain was seen as arbitrary. Even in today's European and American societies there is this thought of a motivated pain. In war, sports, scientific experiments, the death penalty, and sexual pleasure, physical suffering is both allowed and encouraged. As the tragic start of the twenty-first century has probably shown, not even torture is unknown in contemporary democratic states. There is a prohibition against inflicting "too much" pain, but what is too much is determined by the circumstances. This shows that pain is at present seen as something quantifiable and something whose legitimacy is determined by its effectiveness. The sum of the secularized view of pain is not that pain is something unequivocally negative, but that pain that does not match with a particular way of being human is defined as arbitrary and thereby meaningless.[134] Rather than arguing that it is characterized by unconditional relief of pain, perhaps it is more correct to argue that secularism interprets pain as cultural fact—and interprets phenomena on the basis of a different horizon than the religious traditions. This shift in horizon hangs together with the emergence of the modern state, and it thereby parallels the transition from public corporeal punishment to a more modern disciplining of bodies in

130. Asad, "Thinking about Agency and Pain," p. 79.
131. Johannisson, "Kroppens teater," p. 86.
132. Talal Asad, "Reflections on Cruelty and Torture," in *Formations of the Secular,* p. 100.
133. Asad, "Reflections on Cruelty and Torture," p. 111.
134. Asad, "Reflections on Cruelty and Torture," p. 123.

prison, in order to reach the soul of the criminal in a more effective way.[135] It was found that it was better to punish with other methods than purely corporeal punishment.

Pain as Technique of Subjectification

In different religious traditions there are different experiences of pain and the meaning of pain. One example of people who have seen themselves as the active subjects of pain are the Christian martyrs at the start of our era. Such a view of pain is presented in the letters that bear Ignatius's name. Ignatius was bishop in Antioch, probably between the years 69/70 and 107/108. He was condemned by Emperor Trajan to be thrown to the wild animals in Rome. Rather than attempting to avoid this martyrdom at any cost, Ignatius is active in his desire to embrace it. He writes a letter to his fellow believers in Rome, where he asks that they will not attempt to hinder his martyrdom by getting the emperor's verdict rescinded.[136] Through Ignatius's martyrdom the power of Christianity would be shown. He exclaims in the following wish (4:2):

> Allow me to be bread for the wild beasts; through them I am able to attain to God. I am the wheat of God and am ground by the teeth of the wild beasts, that I may be found to be the pure bread of Christ. Rather, coax the wild beasts, that they may become a tomb for me and leave no part of my body behind, that I may burden no one once I have died.

As though he were not sufficiently clear in his desire to suffer martyrdom, Ignatius continues further down in the same letter (5:2):

> May I have the full pleasure of the wild beasts prepared for me; I pray they will be found ready for me. Indeed, I will coax them to devour me quickly—not as happens with some, whom they are afraid to touch. And even if they do not wish to do so willingly, I will force them to it.

---

135. Cf. Michel Foucault, *Discipline and Punish: The Birth of the Prison,* trans. Alan Sheridan (New York: Vintage Books, 1995), pp. 3–35.

136. Ignatius, "Romans," in *The Apostolic Fathers I,* Loeb Classical Library, trans. Bart D. Ehrman (Cambridge, MA/London: Harvard University Press, 2003).

No agonies Ignatius can imagine mean anything, so long as he reaches Christ and becomes a true disciple through martyrdom. This violent martyrdom can be described by Ignatius (6:1f.) as "pains of birth" and "living" and contrasted with the death that would be the result if the Romans prevented his suffering. Only thus can Ignatius become a true Christian disciple by imitating God's suffering.

To a contemporary reader Ignatius's desire to embrace martyrdom through the wild animals in Rome can appear a bit problematic, not to say pathological. A common attitude throughout Christian history has been to accept martyrdom, but not to actively seek it, as Ignatius clearly does. But Ignatius's letters do not immediately need to be understood as an expression of a pathological disposition in the bishop. Historian of Antiquity Judith Perkins says that Ignatius's account in these letters and corresponding representations in other acts of the martyrs were a part of a conscious literary and political strategy, which boiled down to redefining what it meant to be human in the society of late Antiquity.[137] The more traditional Greco-Roman view of the person was that she consisted of body and soul, where the body was subordinate to the governance of the soul. For Christianity—but not exclusively for it—it was different. Here the person's constitution was understood as "a mind/soul joined to a body liable to pain and suffering, in need of outside attention and direction."[138] From the fact that pain and suffering, but also sickness, deformities, and poverty fell outside of the horizon of the cultural representations of the person in the Mediterranean culture of late Antiquity, the suffering body and the self as a sufferer came to be the focus of Christianity's acts of the martyrs and hagiographies, but also for contemporary medical writings (Perkins mentions the physician Galen). Through the fact that Christianity made use of this new construction of subjectivity, it could also dominate and transform classical society. Ignatius's letters to the Romans and other acts of the martyrs were thus not simply an expression of an individual pathology, but also a part of a society changing strategy. This strategy triumphed in a way that, Perkins argues, those of us who live in the wake of this Christian history cannot really imagine.

These accounts functioned as a way to represent Christians—the Christian as suffering—rather than as descriptions of real persecution. Among its cultural despisers Christianity was known for its attitude towards suffering

---

137. Judith Perkins, *The Suffering Self: Pain and Narrative Representation in the Early Christian Era* (London/New York: Routledge, 1995).

138. Perkins, *The Suffering Self,* p. 3.

and death, since it was such signals that the Christian acts of the martyrs sent. In traditional Roman narratives, marriage, according to Perkins, had represented the happy ending, but in Christian narrative this came to be replaced by death. These narratives showed a contempt for human society, just as their universal chastity showed a contempt for the prevailing social mores. The longing was not for the continuation of these mores through the birthing of children, but for a different society. The early Christian acts of the martyrs, Perkins writes, "refuse to read the martyrs' broken bodies as defeat, but reverse the reading, insisting on interpreting them as symbols of victory over society's power."[139] Thus Ignatius's pursuit of a martyr's death was not abnormal, but was instead an expression of an effort to triumph over the prevailing society. Images of death instead of marriage as the happy ending offered, through Ignatius and other written testimonies, a model for how a different subjectivity might be formed. Suffering, pain, and death were presented not as a weakness, but as power over a dying society.

In comparison to the Stoic Epictetus, this Christian construction of subjectivity entailed a new emphasis on the body. Epictetus said that that which stood outside a person's control, for example, bodily pain and bodily suffering, was not something that affected her essential humanity.[140] The main thing was to be able to control and master one's attitudes and feelings in such a way that one's equanimity was not threatened. Mastering pain thus becomes a way for the person's real self to triumph over the body.[141] What could not be controlled, for example, social and political circumstances, but also the suffering and diseases of one's own body, would not be allowed to affect the person's genuine self. If circumstances made it impossible to retain equanimity, death always remained as the ultimate solution, since death, as something outside the subject's control, was also indifferent. This aloofness from the body—even the ultimate aloofness that death entailed—became the solution to the problem of pain for the Stoics. Even if the Stoics also represent an attitude towards pain that may be characterized as an active engagement rather than a passive suffering, the consequence is that "suffering" can never be seen as a genuine attribute of the self.

In contrast with, for example, Epictetus, the suffering self and the suffering body come into focus for the Christian acts of the martyrs. Here the body is not seen as an inessential part of the person. Suffering was not primarily

139. Perkins, *The Suffering Self,* p. 117.
140. Perkins, *The Suffering Self,* pp. 77–103.
141. Johannisson, "Kroppens teater," pp. 90–91.

something that afflicted Christians from outside, but was a weapon in the fight against Roman society. By describing suffering and death as a victory, the acts of the martyrs attempted to triumph over the prevalent categories for human subjectivity. In them even women and the weak were focused on, because one could thereby show that stamina in pain is empowering even for those who are without power in the contemporary society. Nor was eternal life, which the martyrs strove to win, presented as an incorporeal life, but as the resurrection of the body. The materiality of the resurrected body and its continuity with the body that the wild animals had ripped apart in the arenas came to be emphasized all the more. The emphasis on the resurrected body thus went together with a new understanding of the person's subjectivity and of human empowerment. Perkins writes: "The Christian community's emphasis on a resurrected body suggests not only its rejection of the contemporary social order but its belief in a new social order, restructured for Christian empowerment."[142] The body received a new social meaning through Christian discourse. It became a key term for understanding what it was to be human.

For Ignatius it was primarily through suffering that the person became a real self and not only an "echo" (2:1). Suffering was thus not only something that happened to a person, but a means for constituting oneself as subject.[143] Through the writings of Ignatius and others Christianity came to reconstruct the person's self, and thereby displace interest from self-control and independence to an understanding of the person as a suffering self dependent on others. Previously "invisible" cultural categories of people, like the suffering, sick, mute, and paralytic, came through this new configuration to be visible by the individual as well as the social body. The new understanding of body, pain, and suffering was thus not only meaningful for the martyrs themselves, but also of practical significance for others. In this tradition the body is not only a passive object for pain and suffering, but, through its ability to suffer, also an active instrument for self-creation and for the battle against evil.[144]

In the Christian tradition pain has thus not involved a rejection of the body in favor of the soul. Instead, pain, at least in the premodern tradition, has involved an intensification of the experience of being a body. Caroline Walker Bynum points out that the experiences of pain that female medieval mystics describe should not be understood as either a denial of the body or a

---

142. Perkins, *The Suffering Self*, p. 121.
143. Perkins, *The Suffering Self*, p. 190.
144. Asad, "Thinking about Agency and Pain," pp. 89–92.

self-inflicted punishment. The aim was instead to use the body as an opportunity for *imitatio Christi,* in other words, as a union with Christ's suffering and thereby one's own salvation.[145] Body and pain became an active occasion for establishing a vital relationship to the savior. The experiences of pain and sensuality were often intertwined in an inextricable way. Bynum writes: "In a religiosity where wounds are the source of a mother's milk, fatal disease is a bridal chamber, pain or insanity clings to the breast like perfume, physicality is hardly rejected or transcended. Rather, it is explored and embraced."[146] It was not even the body of Christ that was saving for these medieval mystics; the body of Christ was saving in its being a broken body, and one's own bodily brokenness, or one's own bodily suffering, could therefore be seen as a participation in the body of Christ.[147] Bynum thus wants to argue that no other period set so great a positive value on embodiment itself in the humanity of Christ.[148] For the female mystics as well, whom Bynum discusses, pain established an active, practical relationship in Asad's sense, not only with Christ, but with the entirety of the Christian fellowship. Especially given how relationships between people were thought to be established through communion, which also involved a high understanding of Christ's real presence in the elements, the embodiment that came to expression here involved a particularly grotesque embodiment, in Bakhtin's sense, since it is unclosed, permeable, and excessive. The surface of the body did not constitute the delimitation of the individual towards the environment, but rather its point of contact. It was a surface that opened itself to the environment rather than closed that environment out. Pain was thus not privatizing, but the entrance to a specific intense relationship to the environment.

Pain as Sadomasochistic Pleasure?

If one turns to our contemporary Western church, it is difficult to find any signs of an understanding of pain different from the secularized pursuit of the alleviation of pain.[149] The risk in this relative silence is not that one would

---

145. Caroline Walker Bynum, *Holy Feast and Holy Fast: The Religious Significance of Food to Medieval Women* (Berkeley/Los Angeles/London: University of California Press, 1987), p. 246.

146. Bynum, *Holy Feast and Holy Fast,* pp. 249–50.

147. Bynum, *Holy Feast and Holy Fast,* p. 251.

148. Bynum, *Holy Feast and Holy Fast,* p. 252.

149. For an alternative point of view, see, for example, Stanley Hauerwas, *Naming the Silences: God, Medicine, and the Problem of Suffering* (Grand Rapids: Eerdmans, 1990).

thereby disregard the attempt to explain or legitimate suffering as a part of God's plan, which should instead be designated as a gain. It is instead a matter of theology thereby becoming a part of the present's repression of sickness and death and of the identification with a healthy, male, middle-aged body as the norm. The absence of an alternative theology of pain does not, however, mean that it would be especially advisable to now take up the historical discourse of pain from the Christian tradition. The question one must finally pose to the acts of the martyrs and to the female mystics is whether the focus on pain as an active instrument in the battle against evil does not risk making a virtue of a necessity. Have the grotesque representations of Jesus' suffering and death entailed a sort of aestheticizing of suffering in itself? Throughout Christian history there are a range of testimonies to how suffering has been exalted into an end in itself, as Ignatius was also dangerously close to doing.

Has the Christian church's historical devaluation of bodily sensuality (which I discussed in the previous chapter) in favor of bodily pain perhaps led to a confusion of the two, since bodily pain is understood as a path to the bliss of salvation?[150] The Christian tradition would thereby have carried on a more or less unspoken sadomasochism, where bodily pain and sensuality could be distinguished, but had become a part of a power play between inferiority and superiority. Sensuality without pain would then be immoral, but pain would be able to legitimate a moral sensuality.[151] This is something that survives in a hidden way even in the individualism of liberal Christianity and its view of how relationships are established between autonomous subjects. Pain and suffering thereby become—if in a more or less hidden way—something necessary for the Christian process of subjectification. In this way pain tends to become primary in the constitution of the Christian subject, and therefore meaningful in itself. Is this a necessary consequence of the Christian tradition?

---

150. Beverly Wildung Harrison and Carter Heyward, "Pain and Pleasure: Avoiding the Confusions of Christian Tradition in Feminist Theory," in *Sexuality and the Sacred: Sources for Theological Reflection,* ed. James B. Nelson and Sandra P. Longfellow (London: Mowbray, 1994), pp. 131–48. Harrison and Heyward are two of many feminist theologians who have drawn attention to and criticized this confusion. Cf. as well, for example, Rita Nakashima Brock and Rebecca Ann Parker, *Proverbs of Ashes: Violence, Redemptive Suffering and the Search for What Saves Us* (Boston: Beacon Press, 2001).

151. Harrison and Heyward, "Pain and Pleasure," p. 135. Harrison and Heyward define sadomasochism as "the embodied, sensual appropriation of absolute power, or abject powerlessness, in relation to others" ("Pain and Pleasure," p. 143, italics in original).

A constructive theology of pain would probably need to distinguish between what I want to call a productive suffering and a destructive suffering—and consequently between productive grotesques and destructive grotesques. One must, in other words, theologically discriminate the suffering that nullifies the consequences of sin, and therefore becomes a means for returning creation to that which is the divine intention of creation, and the suffering that is a consequence of sin and nullifies the divine intention of creation.[152] Such a distinction does not, however, have to do with finding a particular quality in suffering itself, with the help of which one can determine whether suffering is destructive or productive. If pain, in Asad's definition, is an "active, practical relationship inhabiting time," and thus not necessarily an individual experience, the quality of pain is dependent on which relationships the pain configures.

A prime example of destructive suffering is torture. According to Scarry, intense pain is destructive for the person's world, language, and self; torture makes the person private or alone in a unique way.[153] The immediacy of pain, the attention it imposes on the victim of the torture, makes it such that the victim loses much of her language, and the world is limited to the boundaries of the body itself. Even if I concur with the objections to Scarry's argument, when it comes to torture she has achieved an important insight. This insight is seized on by theologian William T. Cavanaugh, who describes in his book *Torture and the Eucharist* how torture was used in a systematic way in Fascist Chile. He thus makes an analysis of the torture as a phenomenon in close proximity to a description of a concrete history, and summarizes Scarry's description in the following way: "One way to think about this destruction of the victim's world is to say that the effect of torture is the creation of individuals. Pain, as we have seen, is the great isolator, that which cuts us off in a radical way from one another."[154] The content in the world as well as in language is dissolved, and thereby the basis for bodily and linguistic communication and fellowship. The body is transformed into an instrument of pain, and by pain individuals are created who have broken loose from human fellowship.

Even if pain in itself does not need to be "the great isolator"—as I have shown, there exist many different modulations of pain in human relation-

---

152. Cf. Ward, "Suffering and Incarnation," pp. 197-98.

153. Scarry, *The Body in Pain*, pp. 27-59.

154. William T. Cavanaugh, *Torture and the Eucharist: Theology, Politics, and the Body of Christ,* Challenges in Contemporary Theology (Oxford/Malden, MA: Blackwell, 1998), p. 38.

ships—I believe that this is an appropriate observation when it comes to torture. Torture breaks down both the individual and the social body. Torture afflicts not only the purely physical body, but the whole of the phenomenal body in Merleau-Ponty's sense, and therefore also the person's embodiment in the social sense. Through torture the victim becomes isolated from her or his social fellowship. The point of modern torture—if one draws the distinction fine—is not, as with medieval torture, to look for some sort of truth by getting the victim to talk, but rather to manifest institutional power over the victim of the torture.[155] Cavanaugh has compared torture to a sort of "anti-liturgy," since it is a kind of rite by which the body of the torture victim is made to display the power of the state in a dramatic form.[156] In the eyes of the state, the victim of the torture becomes the voice of putrefaction itself, the place where the power of the state triumphs precisely in that the bodies of the victims are transformed into nothing, into the antithesis of the state. The victim's world is crumpled into a nothing, while for the victim the world of the torturing regime swells to immense proportions. Torture becomes yet more individualizing through the fact that it is actually another person who subjects the victim to torture. Thus the very idea of human relationships is abased. "Modern torture as [it was] practiced in Chile," Cavanaugh concludes, "is not simply a contest over the visible, physical body; it is better understood as a contest over the social *imagination,* in which bodies are the battleground."[157] Thus torture does not only break down a subjectivity, but aims to create a new subject, not only through pain, but also through the fact that the threat of torture creates fear and opposes human fellowship.

Cavanaugh also makes a distinction between victims and martyrs that recalls the distinction between destructive and productive suffering.[158] There is no absolute difference between them, but it is instead a matter of the practical context in which they are placed—which is their horizon of

155. On torture in the service of truth in the Middle Ages, see Talal Asad, "Pain and Truth in Medieval Christian Ritual," in *Genealogies of Religion: Discipline and Reasons of Power in Christianity and Islam* (Baltimore/London: Johns Hopkins University Press, 1993), pp. 83–124. Foucault discusses torture in the Classical period in *Discipline and Punish,* pp. 3–69.

156. Cavanaugh, *Torture and the Eucharist,* p. 30. Cf. Michel de Certeau, "The Institution of Rot," in *Heterologies: Discourse on the Other,* Theory and History of Literature vol. 17, trans. Brian Massumi (Minneapolis: University of Minnesota Press, 1987), pp. 40–41: "The goal of torture, in effect, is to produce acceptance of a State discourse, through the confession of putrescence."

157. Cavanaugh, *Torture and the Eucharist,* p. 57.

158. Cavanaugh, *Torture and the Eucharist,* pp. 58–71.

interpretation. The point of torture is, seen from the perspective of the regime, to at all costs avoid creating a martyr and instead produce a victim. The fact that torture takes place in secret belongs to this strategy, as does the fact that the regime lets the bodies of the tortured victims disappear. Visible and public torture, whether it concerns still-living or dead bodies, would have been easier to interpret into a different liturgy besides the state's "anti-liturgy." In the bodies of the tortured the Latin American church would namely have been able to see Christ's crucified body, Cavanaugh says.[159] It is not so much a matter of the victim's intentions—what she or he died for, or any heroism in the one tortured—but more of which interpretive model the dead body inspires in those who see it. "The body of the martyr is thus the battleground for a larger contest of rival imaginations, that of the state and that of the church."[160] The difference between these different social imaginations does not lie between the social fantasies of two rival states, but has more to do with the different eschatological horizons of the state and the church. Is the dead body a sign of the power of the state, or of the advent of the kingdom of God? A triumph of the state over the vanished victim, or a visible triumph of the martyr over the state? For the early Christians, as I have discussed above, the martyrs were a way for God's power to make itself effective on the earth, and additionally in a way that had become paradigmatic for the Christian tradition through Christ's death on the cross, namely as a power that triumphs through weakness.[161] Cavanaugh therefore sets the anti-liturgy of torture against the communion liturgy of the church, two rites that use different means and have different goals:

> Where torture is an anti-liturgy for the realization of the state's power on the bodies of others, Eucharist is the liturgical realization of Christ's suffering and redemptive body in the body of His followers. Torture creates fearful and isolated bodies, bodies docile to the purposes of the regime; the Eucharist effects the body of Christ, a body marked by resistance to worldly power. Torture creates victims; Eucharist creates witnesses, *martyrs*. Isolation is overcome in the Eucharist by the building of a communal body which resists the state's attempts to disappear it.[162]

159. Cavanaugh, *Torture and the Eucharist*, p. 64.

160. Cavanaugh, *Torture and the Eucharist*, p. 65.

161. In *Mysterium Paschale*, pp. 164–65, Hans Urs von Balthasar discusses a solidarity in Jesus with the dead that does not deny the relationlessness of death, but becomes a "being solitary like, and with, the others."

162. Cavanaugh, *Torture and the Eucharist*, p. 206. Cf. pp. 278–81.

The martyrs therefore should not, seen theologically, be understood as heroes who triumph over physical pain, but their theological significance is instead found in their triumph over an unjust political power. We see in the quotation from Cavanaugh both that pain has a social dimension from a theological perspective and how communion becomes a way to re-create self, world, and language—in short: human relationships—that torture has broken apart. To avoid misunderstanding, it may be important to emphasize that Cavanaugh neither believes that this is a simple process nor attempts to idealize the concretely existing church in Chile (or anywhere else). Even Cavanaugh's church is sinful and imperfect. The point lies, as in all good theology, in the attempt to reform the Christian church by reminding it of its true errand.

The example of torture ought to make it clear that the point of Christian theology of martyrdom is not to imagine all sorts of pain and suffering as in themselves a necessary part of the Christian process of subjectification. It instead has to do with accepting suffering as something that *de facto* characterizes the existence that all people inhabit throughout history—even during less extreme conditions than the period in Chile that Cavanaugh discusses. What must crucially be discussed is the horizon from which pain and suffering should be interpreted.[163] Pain and suffering are historically contingent features of reality, which therefore do not necessarily need to characterize human reality in itself, and which additionally are not impossible to change or annul. Pain is thus something real, but not the last word about the condition of the human being. On the basis of the inner logic of Christian theology (in opposition to the concrete history of the Christian tradition[164]), pain is not an end in itself, but meaningful only to the degree that the sufferer becomes participatory in the suffering of Christ (cf. Rom. 8:22; Col. 1:24).[165] The point of theologically legitimate suffering is to thwart the consequences of sin, just as communion becomes a way to re-create broken relationships. Productive pain is a suffering that does not culminate in passive resignation, but in an active empowerment of those who are often marginalized. Liberation theologian Daniel M. Bell writes, in accordance with such a perspective as I have outlined here, that:

163. See Hall, *God & Human Suffering*, pp. 31–48.
164. See Harrison and Heyward, "Pain and Pleasure," pp. 133–40.
165. See Ward, "Suffering and Incarnation," as well as Ward, "Theology and Cultural Sadomasochism," *Svensk Teologisk Kvartalskrift* 78, no. 1 (2002): 2–10.

This crucified love does not seek out suffering; rather, it seeks the suffering in order to restore communion. Desire that has been liberated does not seek to be wounded; rather, it reaches out to those who wound in the hopes of joining them in the circle of charity that is the divine life.[166]

It is in this sense that pain, according to the Christian tradition, can be an active, productive relationship, which strives to restore the relationship between individual bodies and thereby between the individual body and the social body. It is this pain that the Christian church can harbor within its grotesque body. The grotesque representation of the body of pain also finds its limit here, namely in the distinction between—to put it schematically—the grotesque that leads to despair and the grotesque that leads to hope. The grotesque rhetorical mode in Christian iconography must therefore respect a delicate balance between recalling Jesus' sufferings and elevating them to an end in themselves.[167] The point of such a recalling ought to be to restore human relationships as a reaction against the pain that breaks them apart.

From the perspective of the Christian tradition pain ought to be understood as a contingent rather than a necessary feature of reality in order to not theologically legitimate its existence.[168] If pain and suffering belong to the Christian experience of the body, they thus also go together with another modulation of the body. Hope also belongs to the reality of pain, which has traditionally been expressed through the Creed's conception of a "resurrection from the dead." This is a hope that all of a person's relationships—to God, to other people, to nature, and even to oneself—will be restored. Communion is a symbol that can be said to be mediator between the broken body of pain (the social as well as the individual) and the hope of a re-creation of the body and of bodily relationships. The hope that is expressed in communion is a hope that pain and suffering will at last be overcome and de facto be relegated to the past. "The resurrection of the dead" has traditionally been thought of as a bodily resurrection. The body of

---

166. Daniel M. Bell, *Liberation Theology after the End of History: The Refusal to Cease Suffering* (London/New York: Routledge, 2001), p. 193. Cf. pp. 190–95.

167. This should also have certain consequences for the doctrine of atonement, although I will not discuss this here.

168. The question, however, is whether this concerns all sorts of pain. Is the pain of birth a contingent feature of reality? For me this seems to me in large part to be a productive form of pain. The question cannot be decided here. Let me therefore pursue a more nuanced work on the phenomenology and theology of pain.

pain thus goes intimately together with the body of resurrection, and with this I have reason to reflect in conclusion on an eschatological dimension of human embodiment.

The Body of Resurrection

Athenagoras, a Christian apologete in Athens in the second century, argued in his text *De resurrectione* that even if a person's dead body has been fragmented and her body parts spread out in many directions, God has the power to reunite these bodily fragments to her resurrection body at the resurrection.[169] Even if animals had devoured her body parts, and even if these animals in their turn have been consumed or decomposed, God can still find this person's body parts in order to put them together at the resurrection. It does not even constitute a problem for God if a person has eaten another person, since human flesh, according to Athenagoras, cannot possibly absorb other human flesh. The flesh of two people can quite simply not be mixed. Athenagoras is an example of how literally certain periods have understood the material continuity between the perishable earthly body and the imperishable resurrection body.

The theme itself of this chapter concerns events where theology needs in a particular way to beware of coming with overconfident statements. Like pain, communion is a phenomenon that is to a certain degree accessible to human experience here and now, but the question of the resurrection body accentuates the eschatological dimension that is also present in the sacramental body and the body of pain, and makes the question of the grotesque representation more acute. It would therefore be impossible to avoid the resurrection body in a discussion of Christian embodiment, since conceptions about what the person will become (eschatology) cast light on what or who she is and where she comes from (doctrine of creation). Why it is theologically impossible to speak in an unproblematic way of the "resurrection of the body" without specifying what sort of embodiment one speaks of—as if we knew what "the body" was—ought to be clear from this and the previous three chapters. The task is thus to maneuver between the restraint in the question, which is theologically appropriate considering the eschatological theme, and the unavoidable topic: With what sort of body shall the dead resurrect?

---

169. Caroline Walker Bynum, *The Resurrection of the Body in Western Christianity, 200–1336* (New York: Columbia University Press, 1995), pp. 31–33.

The resurrection body is, however, not an unknown theological theme. A crucial question in an investigation both of the Christian understanding of, as it is called the apostolic creed, "the resurrection of the dead" (Greek: *anastasis tōn nekrōn,* Latin: *resurrectio mortuorum*) and of the resurrection of Jesus is what context we are dealing with. Do I pose my question within the framework of an academic context, where I inquire after the possibility and plausibility of the resurrection, or do I do it on the basis of a social or personal suffering, where resurrection becomes a matter of liberation? Or is the context, as a third possibility, the Christian liturgy? As several theologians have pointed out, the question of the resurrection is not just a historical question for academics, but also a question of hope for the oppressed and suffering, and of the aim for the liturgy of the worship service; and it would be to reduce the understanding of the resurrection if one of these contexts were allowed to dominate.[170] The difference between immersing oneself in this mystery as a scholar or allowing oneself to be permeated by it as suffering and worshiping person is a difference of degree, a difference whose boundaries are not always self-evident or clear. The question of the possible historical reference of the resurrection, namely whether the resurrection of Jesus actually took place, can therefore not be posed independently of the question of its meaning. The North American theologian Marianne Sawicki agrees with this when she writes: "The distinctive reality of the resurrection requires something more than a historical approach. What happened to Jesus is not the sort of thing that can be over, done, completed, and closed like a historical event."[171] The resurrection does not only have to do with what happened or did not happen to a certain person Jesus once upon a time, but to an equally high degree concerns, at least from the perspective of Christian theology, people's lives here and now, i.e., which way of being-in-the-world makes a doctrine of the resurrection meaningful. Theoretical content and practical strategies—catechism and liturgy—here constitute dimensions of the resurrection that can hardly be entirely distinguished.[172] Articulated

170. For example, Gerald O'Collins, *Jesus Risen: The Resurrection—What Actually Happened and What Does It Mean?* (London: Darton, Longman & Todd, 1987), pp. 1–3, and also Marianne Sawicki in the following note.

171. Marianne Sawicki, *Seeing the Lord: Resurrection and Early Christian Practices* (Minneapolis: Fortress Press, 1994), p. 1.

172. Cf. here as well Sarah Coakley, "The Resurrection and the 'Spiritual Senses': On Wittgenstein, Epistemology and the Risen Christ," in *Powers and Submissions: Spirituality, Philosophy and Gender,* Challenges in Contemporary Theology (Oxford/Malden, MA: Blackwell, 2002), pp. 130–52.

from the perspective on embodiment that I have built up in this chapter: the question of the resurrection body is not independent of understandings of the sacramental body as the presence of God or the body of pain as the breaking down of human relationships overcome in hope. The language of the grotesque will thereby again be relevant as a ward against theological hubris.

My thesis in this section is that the resurrection body cannot be understood in a theologically adequate way unless one emphasizes the affinity between individual and social body, as well as the event's character of grace. The question of continuity between the earthly body and the heavenly bodies ends up in the right light only if it is posed against the background of an understanding of the church as an excessive social body in the service of God's liberating story, not of a speculative interest in how the heavenly bodies might appear. By emphasizing the grotesque character of the language of resurrection I want to avoid the coarse and often static materialism of the Middle Ages with regard to the individual body, as well as the spiritualizing tendencies of modernity, and instead preserve the character of grace in the discourse on resurrection.

In order to find a defining focus for the discussion of the resurrection body in this section, I will concentrate on several concrete issues and exclude others. To begin with, I have not planned on discussing the contested question of how one should understand Jesus' resurrection. In the New Testament there are a number of different accounts of and references to Jesus' resurrection, or rather, to the circumstances around that which has come to be called Jesus' resurrection. Nowhere, not even in the four Gospels, is there an account of the resurrection event as such. Instead the New Testament presents references to the empty tomb on the one hand, and references to meetings with the risen Jesus on the other. These are primarily presented in the New Testament with the language of sight, which I partially touched on in chapter 5. These visual impressions implied a certain preparation and cooperation on the part of the disciples, and they were thus not passive observers. There is also a remarkable "normality" in these meetings, without a trace of any "heavenly glory." Jesus eats with his disciples on repeated occasions (Luke 24:28–32, 41–43; John 21:12–14; Acts 1:4), his hands show traces from the nails that fastened him to the cross (Luke 24:39f.; John 20:20), the women at his grave touch him (Matt. 28:9, though not Mary Magdalene according to John 20:17), and the disciple Thomas (John 20:24–29) sticks his fingers in the hole that one of the soldiers had made in his side at the crucifixion. At the same time these accounts claim that the risen Christ is no longer limited by a common, physical embodiment (John 20:19). Jesus appears where and for whom he wants, and disappears when he wants (John 21:1).

Instead of directly discussing Jesus' resurrection and resurrection body, I want to approach the understanding of the resurrection body by looking at how one has understood the body with which the Christian is thought to resurrect. The theological tradition has in principle always emphasized the connection between Christ's resurrection and the general resurrection. Christ is the basis for the resurrection from the dead that the creed mentions. My discussion will thus not revolve around the question of the historicity of Jesus' resurrection or of Jesus' embodiment in more than an indirect way. I will instead focus on the understanding of the resurrection body in general in Paul, in order to then transition to how it has been understood in the later theological tradition. I will finally also bring a constructive discussion of a contemporary understanding of the resurrection body that attempts to respect, in a grotesque way, both the topic's relative inaccessibility and its necessity. This does not mean that the question of Jesus' embodiment is uninteresting from my perspective, only that this question will not be the focus.

An important problem for a contemporary theology that wants to take into account the eschatological dimensions of embodiment will therefore be to investigate the relationship between the earthly body and the resurrection body. Against this background it is crucial whether the emphasis lies on continuity or discontinuity—a question that will run through this section like a red thread. It is also a question that Paul is intensively occupied with in one of his letters.

Heavenly Bodies in Paul

In Paul's first letter to the Corinthians the apostle takes up the question of the resurrection body: "But someone will ask, 'How are the dead raised? With what kind of body [poiō de sōmati] do they come?'" (15:35).[173] Paul goes on to claim that this is a "foolish" question (v. 36). Wherein lies the foolish-

---

173. Cf. Wolfgang Schrage, *Der Erste Brief an die Korinther: 1 Kor 15,1–16,24*, 4th volume, Evangelisch-Katholischer Kommentar zum Neuen Testament vol. VII/4, ed. Norbert Brox, Joachim Gnilka, et al. (Zürich/Düsseldorf/Neukirchen-Vluyn: Benziger Verlag/Neukirchener Verlag, 2001), pp. 266–359.

ness? For Paul it lies in the fact that the implied addressee does not grasp the breadth of God's power. It is thus instead a matter of a spiritual rather than an intellectual lack. In order to answer the question he has posed, in the following passage (vv. 36–41) Paul takes two parables from creation that ought to make it evident even for the foolish what God is capable of doing. The first of these is taken from the plant kingdom, and is probably the most important image of the resurrection in the text that has historically been the most influential, namely the parable of the seed:[174]

> What you sow does not come to life unless it dies. And what you sow is not the body that is to be *[to sōma to genēsomenon speireis],* but a bare kernel, perhaps of wheat or of some other grain. But God gives it a body *[sōma]* as he has chosen, and to each kind of seed its own body *[idiom sōma]* (vv. 36–38).

For Paul this image is not a matter of a potentiality in the seed to become a plant, or, in other words, a continuity between seed and plant, but on the contrary of a discontinuity between seed and plant: that which is sown must die in order to receive life. The emphasis thus lies not on the seed's innate power of growth, but on God's action. In other words, this means that the resurrection body cannot be seen as something that potentially arises from the earthly body. Even if there indeed remains some sort of continuity between seed and plant, as between the earthly body and the resurrection body, it is a matter of a discontinuity, marked by the death of the seed, that only God's power can bridge. Karl Barth comments on the relationship between continuity and discontinuity in Paul's parable with the following words: "[F]or something does not come out of nothing here, but, equally strange, out of Something comes something different."[175] The point of the parable is to show that the God who can give "each kind of seed" its "own body" also has the ability to give new form to people's perishable bodies. But Paul has thereby hardly answered the question he takes up at the start of the text I discuss here: what sort of body the resurrection body is.

In the second parable Paul takes his interpretive horizon from both the animal kingdom and from an ancient cosmology:

174. Bynum, *The Resurrection of the Body,* p. 3.

175. Karl Barth, *The Resurrection of the Dead,* trans. H. J. Stenning (New York: Fleming H. Revell, 1933), p. 188.

> For not all flesh is the same *[ou pasa sarx hē autē sarx]*, but there is one kind for humans, another for animals *[sarx ktēnōn]*, another for birds *[sarx ptēnōn]*, and another for fish. There are heavenly bodies *[sōmata epourania]* and earthly bodies *[sōmata epigeia]*, but the glory of the heavenly is of one kind, and the glory of the earthly is of another. There is one glory of the sun, and another glory of the moon, and another glory of the stars; for star differs from star in glory. (vv. 39–41)

Earthly and cosmic bodies have different sorts of bodies and different sorts of "glory" *(doxa)*. Creation offers a variety rather than a homogeneity, and it is therefore not unimaginable that God is able to create an embodiment for the resurrected as well. Thus the parable yet again reinforces the differentiation and thereby the discontinuity between different sorts of bodies, for example between the person's earthly body and her resurrection body. Nor is Paul's point here to say something about what sort of body the resurrection body is. It is instead a matter of an emphasis on the difference between different sorts of bodies and God's power to shape them.

It is not until verses 42–44 that Paul brings together his parables through an explicit comparison: "So it is with the resurrection of the dead." The God who in the world of creation is able to create such different bodies will also be able to create resurrection bodies that differ from the earthly, perishable bodies:

> What is sown is perishable; what is raised is imperishable. It is sown in dishonor; it is raised in glory. It is sown in weakness; it is raised in power. It is sown a natural body *[sōma psychikon]*; it is raised a spiritual body *[sōma pneumatikon]*. If there is a natural body *[sōma psychikon]*, there is also a spiritual body.

Here Paul enumerates a series of contrasts between perishability and imperishability, dishonor and glory, weakness and power together as well as *sōma psychikon* and *sōma pneumatikon*. The emphasis thus lies on the discontinuity between the earlier and the later term in the comparison. The new resurrection body is not some sort of extension of the old earthly, perishable body. If I pursue the interpretation of Paul's view of the body that I presented in chapter 9, these two contrastive bodies should not be understood on the basis of some sort of metaphysical dualism. It is instead a matter of the person's embodiment embedded in the salvation history that God is in the process of realizing through Jesus Christ. Nor should the final, summary pair *sōma psychikon* and *sōma pneumatikon* be perceived as two substances, a "mental" and a "spiritual," of which the last would be understood as the higher. It is again a matter of a contrast between the old, perishable creation and the new, imperishable creation; about what will determine the person's embodiment, her *sōma,* the perishable epoch or the imperishable. Now, however, the emphasis lies on the discontinuity, which means that *sōma* is here hardly understood as an underlying structural continuity. It is instead the case, as exegete Wolfgang Schrage argues, that "Paul cannot conceive of the human as an abstract person even in the pneumatic mode of existence that characterizes her resurrection, but only as a newly created *sōma.*"[176] The person cannot be a person "in general" but must be a concrete person who is characterized by embodiment. This embodiment is understood as determined either by the physical or by the spiritual.

So can we understand Paul here as thinking of a nonphysical body which is not because of this identical with a purely spiritual substance? Paul hardly thought of the person—even after she had given up her perishable body—as a monad, but as a being with the ability to relate and communicate. It was in this that the essential embodiment of the person consisted. But does this mean that we must imagine a nonmaterial embodiment? We get some additional guidance regarding what Paul thinks of the resurrection body from the following verses, where he wants to show how what he has said so far also has support in the scriptures:

> Thus it is written, 'The first *man* Adam became a living being'; the last Adam *became a life-giving spirit.* But it is not the spiritual that is first but the natural, and then the spiritual. The first man was from the earth, a man of dust; the second man is from heaven. As was the man of dust, so also are those who are of the dust, and as is the man of heaven, so also are those who are of heaven. Just as we have borne the image of the man of dust, we shall also bear the image of the man of heaven. (vv. 45–49)

Here Paul makes use of a typological description of Adam vis-à-vis Christ that he had already made use of earlier in the fifteenth chapter of 1 Corinthians: "For as in Adam all die, so also in Christ shall all be made alive" (v. 22). The first Adam was an earthly, physical person, while the last Adam was a heavenly, spiritual person—again an emphasis on the contrast between the old (the first Adam) person and the new (the last Adam). Ac-

---

176. Schrage, *Der Erste Brief an die Korinther,* p. 300.

cording to Genesis 2:7 the old person was formed of "dust from the ground" and became alive because God "breathed into his nostrils the breath of life," and as such the person is a perishable creature according to the anthropology of the Hebrew Bible (cf. Gen. 3:19; Job 34:15; Ps. 90:3; 103:14). In this respect she differs from that which will be her heritage through the new person, which Paul emphasizes in the following verses in the text I discuss here: "flesh [sarx] and blood cannot inherit the kingdom of God, nor does the perishable inherit the imperishable" (v. 50). "Flesh and blood" are the constitution of the old person. She is created by God and as such not sinful, but is on the other hand perishable, and her perishability makes her vulnerable to sin. However, the perishability of the embodiment of the old person corresponds contrastively to the new person's heavenly embodiment, which is characterized by imperishability that is not latent in her earlier, earthly body, but which constitutes a new beginning, a new act of creation by God. The fact that according to Paul the "physical" comes before the "spiritual" does not mean that the "physical" constitutes a condition of possibility for the "spiritual." The order here should be seen as strictly temporal. The person's purpose after the resurrection is anthropologically to be a *"sōma pneumatikon"* (v. 44), Christologically an "image of the man of heaven" (v. 49).

In these verses Paul is thus particularly concerned with emphasizing the discontinuity between the old person's embodiment and the new, resurrected person's embodiment, as well as with emphasizing the fact that the initiative for this new embodiment comes from God, and not from an innate potentiality in the person or her embodiment, which the parable of the seed in particular might lead a modern reader, at least, to believe. The power that creates new life exists in God, not in the person or in an independently existing power in nature. Throughout the text's nearly two-thousand-year history of effect, one of the central points of discussion has concerned precisely how one ought to imagine continuity and discontinuity. Even if Paul's emphasis lies, as said, on the discontinuity, it would be a mistake to imagine a total discontinuity, since the question would then arise whether God in some sense can be said to save, liberate, or transform the person through the resurrection instead of quite simply letting her begin anew somewhere else. If there was no continuity between Jesus' earthly body and Jesus' resurrection body, in which sense would it then be relevant to identify Jesus as Jesus after the resurrection? Similarly one may ask whether there would be any direction for the Christian life at all, if there were no continuity between the earthly bodily life and the future bodily life.[177] The questions I want to focus on here primarily concern how the relationship between death and the new resurrection life has been imagined within Christian theology, and then, once more, which sort of continuity in contrast to discontinuity has been imagined between the earthly, perishable body and the heavenly resurrection body. How has this relationship been viewed in the history of theology?

The Resurrection of the Body—a Historical Sketch

The emphasis that the resurrection is bodily, however we may understand that, is something that unites Christian theologians, mystics, and poets throughout time, at least up until the modern period. Early Christianity is often accused of being hostile towards the body (in contrast with our time, which is often presented as body affirming). But even if there were strong forces that attempted to spiritualize Christianity during this period (Antiquity to the Middle Ages), this is a seriously misleading image. One can, for example, point to the pervasive significance assigned to the resurrection of the body. Caroline Walker Bynum writes in her study of classical and medieval conceptions of the resurrection of the body that:

> Christians clung to a very literal notion of resurrection despite repeated attempts by theologians and philosophers to spiritualize the idea. So important indeed was literal, material body that by the fourteenth century not only were spiritualized interpretations firmly rejected; soul itself was depicted as embodied.[178]

The medieval understanding of the person's subjectivity was fundamentally psychosomatic, and medieval Christians' understanding of the resurrection emphasized, in contrast with Paul, the continuity rather than the discontinuity between the earthly body and the resurrection body.[179] Above all they devoted themselves to the significance of the identity—both material and formal—between the old and the new body. Material identity was seen as so important that people gladly speculated about how this continuity would be

---

177. N. T. Wright, *The Resurrection of the Son of God,* Christian Origins and the Question of God vol. 3 (London: SPCK, 2003), p. 359.

178. Bynum, *The Resurrection of the Body,* p. xviii.

179. Bynum, *The Resurrection of the Body,* p. 8.

preserved even with regard to body parts and even smaller particles of the body. In certain ways, such as in its speculations around material continuity at the resurrection and in the ancillary passion for relics, the Middle Ages were thus crudely materialistic in a way that our time probably has difficulty imagining. I will here very briefly give a survey of the ways Christianity perceived the embodiment of the resurrection in Antiquity and the Middle Ages, in order to thus clarify the different forms of materialism that have historically been represented by the Christian tradition.

Before I turn to the task of describing how theologians in the history of the church have imagined the embodiment of the resurrection, there is reason to note an interpretation of Jesus' resurrection that nearly all other theologians have guarded against, namely that Jesus' resurrection would have meant that he became alive in exactly the same way that he was alive before. Jesus' resurrection would then only entail a return to life under the same material, physical conditions in time and space as earlier, and death would thereby not be averted once and for all. To take an example from the history of theology, Thomas Aquinas argues thus in *Summa theologiae* for the idea that a resurrection in which one is only saved from one actual death, not from death in general, is only a shadow of the genuine resurrection.[180] Jesus was, however, the first to experience genuine resurrection, in contrast with the resurrection that is, for example, discussed in Hebrews 11:35 (the author is here thinking of narratives from the Old Testament about how "[w]omen received back their dead by resurrection"), and the resurrection he experienced, Thomas says, was therefore of a different quality than other resurrections, since he rose to immortal life. According to the accounts that exist about Jesus' resurrection in the New Testament this resurrection, whatever else it may be, is a transformation of Jesus' existence, an exaltation and a glorification of Jesus' life, either understood as in Acts (1:9–11) as a second step after the resurrection through the ascension, or as in the other New Testament witnesses, an exaltation in the resurrection itself. Jesus' resurrection thus has qualities, according to the New Testament witnesses, that make it something more, and different from an extension of the life that Jesus lived before he died on the cross. In the efforts to show the continuity between the earthly body and the resurrection body there was thus a risk that theologians in general attempted to avoid, namely, such a great emphasis on the continuity that the difference between the earthly body and the resurrection body would become unclear or disappear entirely. But there were reasons

180. Thomas Aquinas, *Summa theologiae*, III, q 53, a 3.

that it was the continuity that would come to dominate the first centuries of our era.

Towards the end of the second century the question of the resurrection of the body was brought to a head. Where previously Christian theologians could speak more generally of the resurrection of "the dead" or "the body" *(sōma* or *corpus)*, one now began to emphasize that it was "the flesh" *(sarx* or *caro)* that resurrected. The term *sarx* was now understood not as in Paul, namely the person in her earthly sphere with her inclination to sin, but the person in her earthly, bodily shape in contrast to the divine, immortal Spirit *(pneuma)*. When the Christian church responded to interpretations of the Christian message from Docetism (that Christ's body was not a real, physical body) and Gnosticism (that salvation consisted in salvation from the body), one emphasized that the resurrection body—both the one Christ resurrected with and the one whose resurrection his disciples look forward to—was a physical body and not a semblance of a body. One thereby wanted to defend not only the salvation of the body, but the salvation of the whole created world, as well as the conviction that the individual finds her salvation together with others.[181]

Martyrdom also resulted in an emphasis on the physical resurrection body and its continuity with the earthly body, a train of thought I touched on above.[182] If the physical body resurrected, it could be thought that something of the imperishable body's attributes was conveyed to the highly perishable bodies of the martyrs as well, and made it possible to suffer through martyrdom. But above all the resurrection of the body meant that the fragmentation of the martyred body would be annulled in the resurrection. The bodily fragmentation that was often the consequence of martyrdom was a threat to personal identity. The resurrection was understood in relation to martyrdom not as a sort of justice in light of their unjust execution, but as a warding off of the threat that fragmentation meant for Christians of the time: to not be able to be properly buried.

The creeds that were formulated around the year 200, of which a later one came to be developed into the Apostles' Creed, professed precisely *resurrectio carnis,* i.e., "the resurrection of the flesh," and not *mortuorum* or

---

181. Gisbert Greshake, "Theologiegeschichtliche und systematische Untersuchungen zum Verständnis der leiblichen Auferstehung," in *Resurrectio mortuorum: Zum theologischen Verständnis der leiblichen Auferstehung,* ed. Gisbert Greshake and Jacob Kremer (Darmstadt: Wissenschaftliche Buchgesellschaft, 1986), p. 193.

182. Cf. Bynum, *The Resurrection of the Body,* p. 27.

corporum.[183] Even during the third century metaphors were used that dealt with seed and plant, but in contrast with those in Paul, these metaphors came to be used here in order to emphasize the continuity rather than the discontinuity between the earthly, perishable body and the imperishable resurrection body—"a rather crude material continuity" according to Bynum.[184] This deep "materialistic" impulse was found in the apologist Athenagoras, who was mentioned in the introduction to this section, but also in more well-known theologians from the second century like Irenaeus of Lyons and Tertullian, even if with them there are also accents on the discontinuity between earthly body and resurrection body.[185] In *Against Heresies* Irenaeus emphasizes that salvation is for the whole person, "that is, of the soul *[animae]* and body *[corporis]*," and argues that the one who receives the Lord's flesh *(corpus)* and blood in communion, but denies the resurrection of the flesh, has not understood God's power.[186] We become that which we eat, and since we can consume the Lord's flesh without the Lord dissolving in us, so can the corporeality of the resurrection also be preserved even if our earthly body decays or is dissolved. Tertullian also argues in *On the Resurrection of the Flesh* that "our flesh *[caro]* shall remain even after the resurrection."[187] It will still be able to suffer, since it is the same flesh as in the earthly body, but will at the same time be liberated from suffering by the Lord.

More than many "materialistic" Christians, Origen emphasized that transformation was something that characterized the resurrection body, and for that matter, the person's being as such.[188] It is the form *(eidos)* of the body, not the material continuity between earthly body and resurrection body, that is preserved. The body's form preserves its identity and its characteristic features, but its realization does not occur via identical matter. There is therefore no need for the same physical particles to be returned to the res-

183. J. N. D. Kelly, *Early Christian Creeds,* 3rd edition (Harlow, UK: Longman, 1986), pp. 163–66.

184. Bynum, *The Resurrection of the Body,* p. 27.

185. Bynum, *The Resurrection of the Body,* pp. 34–43; Greshake, "Untersuchungen," pp. 183–202.

186. Irenaeus, *Against Heresies,* in *Ante-Nicene Fathers,* vol. 1: *The Apostolic Fathers, Justin Martyr, Irenaeus,* ed. Alexander Roberts and James Donaldson, revised by A. Cleveland Coxe (Grand Rapids: Eerdmans, 1979), p. 548 (V, xx, 1).

187. Tertullian, *On the Resurrection of the Flesh,* in *Ante-Nicene Fathers,* vol. 3: *Its Founder, Tertullian,* ed. Alexander Roberts and James Donaldson, revised by A. Cleveland Coxe (Grand Rapids: Eerdmans, 1978), p. 590 (chapter 57).

188. Bynum, *The Resurrection of the Body,* pp. 63–68; Greshake, "Untersuchungen," pp. 202–8.

urrection body, as with Athenagoras. Just as it is in some sense one and the same body that is transformed from birth to old age, so one can imagine that the form of the body is also preserved between the perishable, earthly life and the imperishable, heavenly life without some continuity (which guarantees personal identity) being lost. There is a continuity between the seed that is sown and the plant that is the result, even if the discontinuity between the seed and the plant is striking. Origen therefore fights on two fronts: in part against those who say that the resurrection has nothing at all to do with the person's earthly body, in part against those who identify the earthly body with the resurrection body in a naïve way and thereby risk understanding the resurrection as the awakening of a cadaver.

For Western Christianity, however, the emphasis on material continuity was predominant. It was feared that Origen's perspective involved a Gnostic compromise. The German theologian Gisbert Greshake says that this had critical—and negative—consequences for the continued understanding of the resurrection, since the "quite simply physical—and unbiblical!—concept of the flesh that Origen wants to avoid precisely through his understanding of the resurrection now becomes the criterion for the orthodox doctrine of the resurrection."[189] With Augustine we find a clear (and in Antiquity common) suspicion of transformation, and he thus wanted to avoid giving the impression that the body was changeable.[190] The imperishable resurrection body was a body whose earlier fragmented pieces had been collected together by the power of God. In *Enchiridion* Augustine says that the matter of the body never perishes, but will return at the resurrection to the body it has been separated from.[191] Here Augustine compares the person's body to a statue—an especially static metaphor—which, even if it can be melted down or destroyed, can still be restored so long as all the matter that it originally consisted of has been preserved. Even if the body's matter never perishes, it may be arranged differently at the resurrection of the body. The differences and inequalities between the resurrection bodies that correspond to the earthly bodies will be preserved, but not as objectionable or disproportionate differences. Even when Augustine takes up the question of cannibalism in *City of God* he avers that the original physical body will be re-created: "The flesh of the man who is eaten, therefore, will be restored to him in whom it

189. Greshake, "Untersuchungen," p. 208.

190. Bynum, *The Resurrection of the Body*, pp. 94–104; Greshake, "Untersuchungen," pp. 208–15.

191. Augustine, *The Augustine Catechism: The Enchiridion on Faith, Hope and Charity*, The Augustine Series, trans. Bruce Harbert (Hyde Park, NY: New City Press, 1999), chapters 88, 89.

first began to be human flesh."[192] Nothing, not even cannibals, could threaten the material continuity between the earthly body and the resurrection body.

The emphasis of Augustine and Western Christianity on the material continuity between earthly body and resurrection body and on the ideal of unchangeability came to dominate Western theology well into the Middle Ages as well, and during its "Renaissance" in the twelfth century.[193] One of the most influential theologians of the twelfth century, Peter Lombard, made it clear (with words that he borrowed from Augustine's *Enchiridion*) that the person would be reintegrated at the resurrection as a statue is restored. Materially as well as formally the resurrection body is continuous with the earthly body. With Bynum I therefore want to state that:

> The overriding impression left by twelfth-century eschatological discussion . . . is one of materialism and literalism. It was Jonah vomited up whole by the whale or the bones of saints reassembled at the trumpet's blast that provided the fundamental image of bodily resurrection.[194]

The resurrected body is compared to a crystal: hard, perfect, static, without pain. The cult of relics was therefore a consequence of or a condition for this continuity; the bodily relic from a saint could be thought to have already achieved its imperishable state, and so the relic indicated the presence of the resurrection body.[195]

This resurrection materialism would be retained during the thirteenth century as well, even if it included different accents, such as the emphasis on the person's continuity and psychosomatic whole, rather than the exact material particles that her earthly body had consisted of.[196] Thomas Aquinas said that the soul could be understood as the form of the body (but then the significance of the soul had been displaced and had come to take over some of the attributes of the body), and thus identity between the earthly body

---

192. Augustine, *The City of God against the Pagans,* Cambridge Texts in the History of Political Thought, trans. R. W. Dyson (Cambridge: Cambridge University Press, 1998), p. 1151 (22, 20).

193. In an intentionally exaggerated contrast, Greshake characterizes the difference between the early and the medieval church thus ("Untersuchungen," p. 217): "War in der frühen Kirche die Anthropologie eine Funktion der Eschatologie, so wird jetzt die Eschatologie eine Funktion der Anthropologie."

194. Bynum, *The Resurrection of the Body,* pp. 156–57.

195. Bynum, *The Resurrection of the Body,* pp. 200–225.

196. Bynum, *The Resurrection of the Body,* pp. 229–43.

and the resurrection body could be guaranteed without a strict material identity being necessary.[197] This does not mean that the soul alone was the human self, any more than the body alone; the "self" is the whole person. Thomas himself, however, did not take the last step away from the particulate identity of the earthly body with the heavenly body. Probably inspired by the statements of his theological predecessors, he himself argued a material identity, but in spite of this the possibility of imagining an identity that was not dependent on the resurrection body's particulate identity with the earthly body was in principle evident. Here Thomas's conception of a soul that in itself bore all the body's attributes is not especially far from Foucault's conception of "the soul is the prison of the body" and other conceptions of the discursive dimension of the body. "In such a theory . . . body became an expression of soul."[198]

The body was thus quite crucial for the understanding of personal integrity during the Middle Ages. The prevailing theology was anything but substance dualism, whether in the classical or the modern sense. Here, above all in the late Middle Ages, an erotic language flourished (in mysticism as well as courtly love) that described the desire of God as a bodily—or rather psychosomatic—desire, not least in Mechthild of Magdeburg and in Dante's *Divine Comedy.* Here the static understanding of the resurrection begins to be more dynamic, as at the end of Dante's *Paradiso,* where the dynamic movement of love becomes the motor that drives all of existence forward. The view of the body here is different than the static body that Augustine and others imagined.

The hyper-materialistic emphasis on continuity that we find in theologians during Antiquity and the Middle Ages is also accompanied by an accentuation of social and religious differences.[199] In Bakhtin's terms, it is a classical body that most classical and medieval theologians in the West defend, a body whose social and religious characteristics are preserved intact from the earthly body to the resurrection body. In our evaluation of this period we must, however, take into account the fact that it concerned a reaction against what was perceived as the dissolution of body and personal identity in, for example, martyrdom. Here we meet—expressed very generally—in a certain sense a paradoxical embodiment: ecclesiologically,

197. Greshake, "Untersuchungen," pp. 223–36.

198. Caroline Walker Bynum, "Why All the Fuss about the Body? A Medievalist's Perspective," *Critical Inquiry* 22 (1995): 32. See also p. 22 n. 70. The comparison should, however, not be taken for granted; see the warning on p. 29.

199. Bynum, *The Resurrection of the Body,* p. 150.

sacramentally, and martyrologically the Christian body was understood as an open, generative body, while physically or biologically the ideal for the person's embodiment was static and closed. This paradoxical embodiment can be explained as a sublimation of *eros* to a spiritual plane (cf. the previous chapter). Such a sublimation tends to hide the possibility for a dynamic understanding of the individual body and its relationality that has existed and exists in large portions of the Christian tradition.

In summary I want to argue that a large part of the Christian patristic and medieval church's emphasis on the continuity between the earthly body and the resurrection body becomes grotesque in the pejorative sense, i.e., "monstrous" and "absurd," precisely through the absence of respect for the unspeakable in the grotesque rhetorical mode of the resurrection body. The discontinuity, the emphasis on the different in the resurrection body that one finds, for example, in Paul, is obscured by the continuity between the two bodies and thus the conceptions of the resurrected bodies exude a certain theological hubris. A greater emphasis on the grotesque in the rhetorical mode would be able to preserve the concreteness in the Christian conceptions of the body without confusing this concreteness with literalism. The resources for such an understanding existed, both in the erotic metaphor and in the understanding of God's alterity.[200] In the, despite everything, predominant lack of such attempts to understand the resurrection body as other than a static, crystalline, even classical body in the Bakhtinian sense, it is not especially surprising that the understanding of the resurrection body in the modern period would be further transformed, in the direction of a more dynamic, but often spiritualizing and abstract understanding.

The Eschatological Body

Even if there is on the whole no clear theological understanding of the resurrection's embodiment in our contemporary period, it is still possible to argue that spiritualizing interpretations are more common than before. The

---

200. On the inexpressibility of God, see, for example, Gregory of Nyssa, *Life of Moses*, Classics of Western Spirituality, trans. Abraham J. Malherbe and Everett Ferguson (New York: Paulist Press, 1978); Gregory of Nazianzus, *Five Theological Orations*, in *On God and Christ: Five Theological Orations and Two Letters to Cledonius*, Popular Patristics Series, trans. Frederick Williams and Lionel Wickman (Crestwood, NY: St. Vladimir's Seminary Press, 2002); John Chrysostom, *On the Incomprehensible Nature of God*, Fathers of the Church Series, trans. Paul W. Harkins (Washington, DC: Catholic University of America Press, 1984).

resurrection of the body has been hit by the same critique as all other "supernatural" elements in Christian doctrine, and the question has been raised whether "resurrection" really must be understood—historically as well as in our time—as a literal, historical event, and not in another way, for example as a myth or a metaphor.[201] The question I will take up here is not whether the resurrection should be understood as a historical event or not, but what the resurrection means from a contemporary perspective. In other words, I want to investigate how the bodily dimension of the Christian hope should be understood today. Above all we will find an emphasis on the social dimension of the resurrection, which means that it cannot be understood as a solitary event for the individual body. One can possibly see this interest as a displacement of the theological agenda when even modern Enlightenment reason has been challenged.

German exegete and theologian Rudolf Bultmann has argued in a famous presentation that Jesus is resurrected in the kerygma: "Christ meets us in the preaching as one crucified and risen. He meets us in the word of preaching and nowhere else."[202] By this he wants to argue the significance of the resurrection is not a historical event that it is possible to objectify through human knowing. The resurrection is instead a matter of God's merciful inspiration of faith in the person. To "understand" the resurrection is therefore not to relate to a certain event far back in time, but to God who liberates the person from an inauthentic existence here and now. Bultmann's theology has been criticized for being too individualistic or spiritualistic, but his discussion has, whatever the case may be, in many places brought to the fore a deepened discussion of what is meant by the resurrection. Is it a naked

---

201. Peter Carnley gives a typology of contemporary interpretations of the resurrection by differentiating between the resurrection as a historical event, the resurrection as an eschatological event, and the resurrection as a nonevent. See Peter Carnley, *The Structure of Resurrection Belief* (Oxford: Clarendon Press, 1993; 1987), pp. 29–182. A comparison between Wolfhart Pannenberg's "historical" understanding of the resurrection and Rudolf Bultmann's "eschatological" understanding may be found in Magnus Abrahamsson, *Jesu uppståndelse som historiskt problem: En studie av Rudolf Bultmanns och Wolfhart Pannenbergs tolkningar* (Skellefteå, Sweden: Norma, 2001). Within contemporary exegetics A. J. M. Wedderburn, for example, argues in *Beyond Resurrection* (London: SCM Press, 1999) that there is no unequivocal argument for an understanding of the resurrection as a historical, bodily event, while N. T. Wright in *The Resurrection of the Son of God* argues for the opposite viewpoint.

202. Rudolf Bultmann, *New Testament and Mythology,* in *Kerygma and Myth: A Theological Debate,* with contributions by Rudolf Bultmann, Ernst Lohmeyer, Julius Schniewind, Friedrich Schumann, Helmut Thielecke, and Austin Farrer, ed. Hans-Werner Bartsch, trans. Reginald H. Fuller (London: SPCK, 1953), p. 41.

fact to take a position on, or are there other dimensions of the resurrection that concern the person's embodiment here and now? Most theologians in our time emphasize that the point of the resurrection is greater than a solitary historical fact (however significant this "fact" may be eschatologically). The understanding of the resurrection has consequences for, generally speaking, all anthropological questions of human embodiment, sociality, gender, etc. The resurrection is, according to this way of understanding it, a multidimensional phenomenon. Questions of sociality hang together with questions of the embodiment of the resurrection, questions of gender touch questions of eschatology, and so on.

One example of such a multidimensional understanding of the resurrection we find with Rowan Williams, who in his book *Resurrection* discusses whether Jesus' resurrection can be thought of as a resurrection not only *in* but also *as* the Christian congregation.[203] He affirms such an understanding in one sense: the church may be thought of as the "body" of Christ's presence. It is in the church as bodily and historical that grace and redemption take concrete form, and it is also there that one meets the risen Christ. But at the same time Williams emphasizes that Christ is in a certain sense always a stranger even for the church: "We need to be cautious about any tendency to see the church as a simple 'undialectical' extension of Christ. . . . Christ is with the believer and beyond the believer at the same time: we are in Christ and yet face to face with him."[204] The church can therefore never—and this agrees with the argument I presented in chapter 9—absorb Christ. That the church is the body of Christ does not mean that Christ is identical with the church. Seen from the perspective of the resurrection, one might say that the church does not inhabit its true embodiment, but receives the glorified body from the risen Christ. The empty grave, Williams says, is not proof of the resurrection of Christ, but it is an indication of how this resurrection came to be perceived, namely as bodily. If the grave is empty, the meeting with the risen Christ that the apostles experienced was a meeting with a "bodily other."

With the help of Williams, we can understand how the embodiment of Christ is the condition for us to be able to experience his actions as grace. Not primarily in the sense that embodiment itself might be called grace,

203. Rowan Williams, *Resurrection: Interpreting the Easter Gospel* (Harrisburg, PA: Morehouse, 1994), pp. 100–123.

204. Williams, *Resurrection*, p. 84. Cf. pp. 76–99, where Williams discusses different senses of Jesus as "stranger" as a counterweight against using Jesus as an ideological legitimizing of one's own positions, political or theological.

but because embodiment makes possible his concrete actions of mercy and redemption. In the supper that Jesus shared with the disciples before the crucifixion this grace was embodied in a concrete sharing of bread and wine, and through the repetition of this action the concretization of the grace is also repeated. The fact that this concretization can take place in other places and times and in other circumstances than the original supper also gives us a key to understanding the resurrection of Christ, namely as the concrete, material mediation of his redemption even to circumstances that are far away in time and space from his biological, historical body.[205] Grace and redemption are in a sense not "spiritual" phenomena—if we want to set spiritual in opposition to physical, bodily, or material—but processes that are mediated "materially" through the concrete persons and institutions that surround us. Jesus' embodiment after the resurrection is not limited to what was previously his biological, earthly body. In communion, and in the actions that more concretely materialize Christ's love in the world, the material world is transformed from a possession to a gift. The presence of the risen Christ can thus be understood as a transformation of the material conditions we people live in, both socially and politically, and at least one aspect of the embodiment of this presence consists precisely in what this presence does with these concrete, material circumstances. To a certain extent it is a matter of discovering what the material creation was intended for right from the start, namely a mutual gift-giving, rather than a possession. The resurrection does not thereby become a reinforcement of the *status quo,* but a critical interrogation of the prevalent circumstances.

The experience of the resurrection does not, in other words, present itself in any way whatsoever, but presupposes a "gaze" for Christ's presence in these material circumstances. Here I want to turn to Marianne Sawicki, who argues that the resurrection "is at once a textual and bodily event. The body of Jesus is heavily inscribed. In its fragility, it continues to offer itself for reinterpretation."[206] The tradition of knowledge that is designated by the Greek term *theōria* is not sufficient for understanding the resurrection. *Praxis* and *poiēsis* are also forms of knowledge that are crucial for understanding it; *praxis* as the ability to repeat an event time after time, *poiēsis* as the ability to make something new with established genres and themes. All three forms of knowledge were used by the early church when one wanted to explain one's gospel in theology, diakonia, and liturgy. To be able to "behold

---

205. Williams, *Resurrection,* p. 111.
206. Sawicki, *Seeing the Lord,* p. 9. Cf. pp. 1–23.

Jesus" was therefore not only a question of "seeing" in a simple way an object placed right in front of one or of "hearing" the right message: "To get at the real Jesus, you need to do the right kind of seeing. To train for the practice of proper seeing, you need the right kind of teaching."[207] To "behold Jesus" thus entails being involved in a process that creates a certain competence in the person in question, a competence that I spoke of in chapter 7 as "the eyes of faith" and a "generous gaze," and cannot be separated from practices that relate to hunger and justice, at the same time that they are textual discourses (the Bible) and ritual practices (liturgy).[208]

But is this the only aspect of the embodiment of the resurrection, a transformed and glorified perception? Sawicki argues in one passage that the resurrection is not something that happens "*to* persons; it happens *between and among* them."[209] On the question of what happened to Jesus' body, she answers that "[i]t became the textual site of the rupture of material impediments to the transhistorical availability of the human person who was Jesus of Nazareth."[210] This may naturally be said in principle about all dead bodies, even if the interest in such a transhistorical accessibility is significantly less for other people than for Jesus. Sawicki does not mean that it is possible to reduce a body to text; there is a resistance against too thorough a textualization of the body, even if it is continually inscribed in a textual field: "Text is made for the body, not the body for the text."[211] Applied to Jesus' body, this means that the resurrection can be seen as a textual event that is generated by his body, and in its turn generates bodily practices that are exemplified by Matthew 25:35–36: to give food to the hungry, to give drink to the thirsty, and to take care of the homeless, the naked, the sick, and the imprisoned. But however worthy and biblically anchored these practices may be, one may ask oneself whether there is any defense against an ideological appropriation of Jesus' body, or whether the resurrection may be said to be fulfilled through the *praxis* of the church. His body is left in the hands of strangers, Sawicki points out quite correctly, and cannot be made accessible in any other way.[212] The references for the narratives of the Gospels are thus not a dead body in the past, but the discovery of the risen Lord here and now in diakonia, liturgy, and theology.[213] But does this not

207. Sawicki, *Seeing the Lord*, p. 66.
208. Sawicki, *Seeing the Lord*, pp. 92, 302.
209. Sawicki, *Seeing the Lord*, p. 79.
210. Sawicki, *Seeing the Lord*, p. 181.
211. Sawicki, *Seeing the Lord*, p. 229.
212. Sawicki, *Seeing the Lord*, p. 284.
213. Sawicki, *Seeing the Lord*, p. 334.

exclude the idea that Jesus can also be a stranger to his own church? Sawicki concludes her book with the finding that she does not have especially much to say about any personal aspect of the resurrection, and with the synoptics wants to avoid speculating about it. Instead she writes that "[r]esurrection is the aesthetic consequence of our divinely designed, *bodily* imaging of God."[214] Her conclusion should not be seen as a denial of the weight of the question. It is instead a consequence of the fact that she wants to avoid an "objectification" of Jesus' resurrection into something past, as well as avoid understanding Christ's presence among his disciples in history or the present as a "subjective" interpretation.

I am inclined to hold more to Williams's interpretation of the Gospels' depiction of the empty grave and the meetings with the risen Jesus as relatively "objectivist." Such an interpretation boils down to the idea that God actually has intervened in history by raising Christ from the dead, despite the fact that, with Williams, this can be characterized as "extremely baffling," and it can be difficult to see what would be a satisfactory theological or philosophical explanation for this. The reason for such an interpretation is instead that it seems to be the least difficult of several possible interpretations of the New Testament witnesses. At the same time it is important to remember that even in such an objectivist interpretation the resurrection cannot be understood isolated from the processes through which humanity is redeemed and renewed. This means that the question of potential historical reference of the resurrection is not independent of the question of its meaning. To speak of the resurrection is then, with Williams, to speak of one's own humanity as healed, renewed, and restored. The discourse of the resurrection is therefore an involving one: "Jesus' risenness and our risenness are visible only obliquely, in relation to each other."[215] The resurrection can thus not be reduced to something that eventually happens to the person after death; it must be understood as something that is significant for the understanding of human life already here and now.

In a critique of arguments of the above sort the British New Testament exegete N. T. Wright says that they confuse meaning and referent.[216] The social and political implications of the resurrection are not strengthened,

214. Sawicki, *Seeing the Lord,* p. 336.

215. Williams, *Resurrection,* p. 120.

216. N. T. Wright, *The Resurrection of the Son of God,* Christian Origins and the Question of God vol. 3 (London: SPCK, 2003), p. 730, as well as n. 26 on the same page.

Wright seems to say, by arguing that nothing special happened on the third day after Jesus' death on the cross. If the original referent (which Wright understands as Jesus' bodily resurrection) disappears, that which it implies cannot take its place. This is a simplified critique of the arguments I gave an account of (and myself agreed with) above, even if it has a particular point. The point does not lie so much in Wright's hope that it is possible to differentiate in a clear way between meaning and referent in the question of Jesus' resurrection, but rather in the risk of reducing the alien, the discontinuity, in the understanding of the resurrection. In several of the New Testament's depictions of the resurrection there is a moment of wonder, or even terror in the meeting with the resurrected (cf. Matt. 28:1–8; Luke 24:1–12; John 20:11–18). However one understands the resurrection, these narratives indicate that the meeting with the resurrected was a meeting with something that was able to challenge their understanding of themselves. Even here there is a difference between Christ and the church that protects the person from her personal idolatrous and reifying tendencies. But does the resurrection from the dead really have to be understood as bodily because of this? It is naturally not possible to give a definitive answer to such a difficult question, but let me give a few concluding points of view on the significance of embodiment for the question of the resurrection. Above all it is the soteriological and the eschatological dimensions of human embodiment that are of the greatest weight here.

The embodiment of the person is a constitutive part of Christian anthropology. The body does not only make up the person's biological constitution, but is also the condition for her to be able to relate to the world and to God. It is precisely in the person's way of being-in-the-world that her relationship to God is realized as well. As I have argued multiple times, there are several aspects to the person's embodiment: her biological versus her phenomenal body, her individual and her social body. The body is thus a medium for the person's relationality, a medium that is, however, not independent of the person's subjectivity, but a medium that constitutes the person's subjectivity, so a sort of quasi-transcendental condition for the person's relationality. To imagine "the resurrection of the dead" as a disembodied state would therefore be to imagine a whole other anthropology than what has traditionally been maintained by the Christian church. Salvation in the sense of the perfection of the person cannot be thought apart from her embodiment, if we are not imagining a whole other person. If Jesus really is to be the person's savior—the whole person, not only a part of her—then the resurrection must also be understood physically, according to the patristic maxim that "that which He has not assumed He has not healed."[217]

However, the historical excurses above have shown that the understanding of the embodiment of the body and the continuity in contrast to the discontinuity between earthly body and resurrection body has changed over the centuries. What it is that constitutes the person's embodiment according to the Christian tradition thus has no straightforward theological answer. One attempt at a contemporary understanding of the resurrection of the body we find with the German theologian Gisbert Greshake who—inspired primarily by Origen and Thomas—has offered several proposals in systematic theology about how the resurrection from the dead might be understood in a corporeal way without the classical and medieval understanding of material identity between the earthly body and the resurrection body being reproduced.[218] Greshake is interesting because he wants to find a path between, on the one hand, the history of theology's exaggerated faith in the continuity between earthly body and resurrection body, and, on the other hand, the risk of, as with some parts of theological modernity, entirely losing sight of the body.

The thought of a bodily resurrection preserves the insight that the person's embodiment and relationality belong to her constitution, and it is thus the whole person that resurrects, not a part of the person that lives on. When the person dies, her body—and thereby her sociality and relationality—is not left behind. Instead the person's embodiment achieves its final destination in death. With death and the encounter with God that occurs there, the person is precisely that which she has become in her embodiment, i.e., in her relationship to history and the world. The person's sociality is preserved as well in that the resurrection cannot be thought to be complete until all have resurrected, and Greshake writes:

> The *resurrectio* of the individual occurs . . . through the fact that she is taken up and added into Christ's resurrection body, which itself remains incomplete so long as the last human brother and the last human sister have not been incorporated into him.[219]

---

217. Gregory of Nazianzus, "Epistle 101," in *Nicene and Post-Nicene Fathers,* ser. 2, vol. 7: *S. Cyril of Jerusalem, S. Gregory Nazianzen* (Grand Rapids: Eerdmans, 1978), p. 440.

218. Greshake, "Untersuchungen," pp. 264–76. Cf. pp. 318–22.

219. Greshake, "Untersuchungen," p. 266.

This does not mean that this resurrection must be understood as the revival of a dead body and a material identity between earthly body and resurrection body. With support from Paul, Greshake wants to assert the discontinuity between the earthly body and the resurrection body, at the same time that he asserts a continuity in embodiment itself as such. Phenomenologically all people already have the experience now of a different materiality than that of objectifying, strictly physically understood materiality. Thus bodily resurrection must not be understood as a third act after birth and death, and Greshake wants to emphasize that the resurrection is neither an individual nor an entirely future phenomenon. With regard to the last, Greshake, in analogy to Clement of Alexandria, imagines the resurrection as a progressive event: from baptism through death to the universal consummation. This also means that the person's relationality, as a significant feature of her embodiment, does not diminish after death, but on the contrary, grows.

Greshake speaks of his understanding of the resurrection from the dead as a "resurrection in death," and says that the condition for this understanding to be imaginable is that one accepts that some principle of identity must bind the earthly body to the resurrection body.[220] If this principle were not to exist, it would not be a matter of a resurrection, but rather of a "second new creation." In Western thought this principle has been called the "soul," and Greshake's understanding of the soul approaches that of Thomas Aquinas. This soul, which is the form of the body, thus carries bodily characteristics and is not the autonomously existing monad that "soul" has often represented in the Western, modern tradition. Greshake writes in one passage that "soul" should primarily be understood as the person's relationship to God, not as the opposite of the body. It is this relationship that remains when the earthly body dies.

Even if Greshake has an important message in his emphasis on a different materiality than the strictly physical and in his emphasis on the sociality of the resurrection, his understanding of the soul may raise the critical question whether a philosophical anthropology of this sort is necessary for a contemporary theological understanding of the resurrection body. Is this not a speculative exposition that believes itself to know all too much of the nature of the resurrection body? In other words: Does he take the discontinuity between earthly body and resurrection body seriously enough? Does he not miss the grotesque in the very idea of the resurrection of the body? Whether these objections really do touch Greshake's theology of the res-

---

220. Greshake, "Untersuchungen," pp. 269–70, 302–4.

urrection body I will not get to the bottom of here. In my own theology I want to attempt to preserve the theological point of the discontinuity between earthly body and resurrection body even more clearly, or, perhaps instead, again attempt to understand how the continuity and the discontinuity should be related to each other. The concluding question in this section will therefore be the eschatological horizon of embodiment, and at the same time an attempt at a grotesque presentation of the resurrection body.

In her comparison between Judith Butler and Gregory of Nyssa, which I mentioned back in chapter 9 in the discussion of the transformed body, Sarah Coakley says that Gregory offers a vision of the risen body that gives the human body an eschatological significance.[221] Gregory imagines that the resurrection body is transformed after the resurrection as well—in which he resembles Origen rather than Augustine. The essentialism and dualism of later periods are also missing with Gregory. This means that the social aspect of the body's gender as well as its desire continues to be transformed beyond a binary conception of gender even after the resurrection. What Coakley finds congenial in Butler's conception of a performative body is not so much that the corporeality of the body is dissolved in discourse, but rather the opposite, that there is, despite her pessimism with regard to social change for the better, an implicit eschatological desire in her approach. This eschatological desire finds expression in her conception of the possibility of denaturalizing conventional conceptions of gender, a theme that Butler shares with the Christian ascetic tradition. Change namely does not come into being through thought exercises, but through changed practices that in the long term transform the body from its sedimented habits. Butler has, however, no explicit conception of any (eschatological) *telos* for the transformation of embodiment, which makes her argument vulnerable to the objection that resistance against the ruling heteronormativity becomes impossible, since there is no given conception about what the liberation of the body would entail. Without a transcendent horizon of some sort—divine or worldly—the transformations of the body risk becoming meaningless, and thereby can only reinforce rather than challenge the dominant corporeal order.[222] It is primarily through the eschatological horizon that the restless postmodern body can find some sort of rest, without because of this becoming something all too familiar, and so being captured by the ideological

221. Sarah Coakley, "The Eschatological Body: Gender, Transformation and God," in *Powers and Submissions: Spirituality, Philosophy and Gender,* Challenges in Contemporary Theology (Oxford/Malden, MA: Blackwell, 2002), p. 166.
222. Cf., for example, Bynum, "Why All the Fuss," pp. 27–30.

573

constructions of the body (cf. the discussion of the boundaries of the grotesque at the start of this chapter).[223] With this the hope of a liberation from the fragmenting consequences of pain and suffering can have a theological anchor.

In other words, the question is whether there is any continuity between a person's various performative bodies, which makes it such that they in some sense may be said to be the "same" body. Bynum has argued that the visible body relates to space like narrative to time. Without narrative, no shape, and without shape, no self: "For my self is my story, known only in my shape, in the marks and visible behaviors I manifest—whether generic or personal. I am my skin and my scars, my gender and pigment, my height and bearing, all forever changing."[224] Here the continuity of the changeable body lies in the narrative; it is the narrative that conditions the possibility of recognizing the body from one time to another. At the same time the narrative form of identity means that it becomes possible to also imagine change and discontinuity. Bynum's idea recalls the insight guided by the diacritical hermeneutic according to the argument earlier in this chapter. Here the possibility can be opened for speaking of the resurrection body in a concrete way without presupposing an understanding of the correspondence of these concretions with that in the afterlife.

In accordance with this, I want to argue with the German-American theologian Hans Frei that the New Testament texts testify to the continuity between the earthly Jesus and the risen Jesus.[225] Their testimony is not at all some speculation over the constitution of the physics of the resurrection body, but they instead merely want to affirm *some* sort of continuity by testifying to it. The texts give us no historically correct *description* of what had happened, but only an adequate *testimony* of a real event: "Something does indeed take place in the resurrection, but it is not described and doubtless cannot be described."[226]

223. On the need for an eschatological horizon for ideology criticism, see Graham Ward, "Introduction: 'Where We Stand,'" in *The Blackwell Companion to Postmodern Theology,* Blackwell Companions to Religion, ed. Graham Ward (Oxford/Malden, MA: Blackwell, 2001), pp. xii-xvii.

224. Caroline Walker Bynum, *Metamorphosis and Identity* (New York: Zone Books, 2001), p. 181.

225. See Hans Frei, "Theological Reflections on the Accounts of Jesus' Death and Resurrection," together with "Of the Resurrection of Christ," in *Theology & Narrative: Selected Essays,* ed. George Hunsinger and William C. Placher (New York/Oxford: Oxford University Press, 1993), pp. 45–93 and 200–206. Cf. as well Gerard Loughlin, "Living in Christ: Story, Resurrection and Salvation," in *Resurrection Reconsidered,* ed. Gavin D'Costa (Oxford: Oneworld, 1996), pp. 118–34.

226. Frei, "Theological Reflections," p. 75.

To be content with the fact that the New Testament texts emphasize that such a continuity exists, but not speculate about how that can or should be understood, respects the grotesque in the language of the resurrection, that it has to do with something that one, in a certain sense, cannot say anything about. The task of the text is quite simply to preserve the continuity between the earthly and the risen Jesus, to establish in this way that it is Jesus who saves the church, not the church that saves itself. But this continuity is a promise that demands trust rather than a possibility of ascertaining in a specific way the nature of the resurrection body. This way of understanding the continuity contains a large dose of agnosticism with regard to the nature of the continuity.

Such a restrained attitude regarding the possibilities for saying something of the nature of the resurrection body does not need to be understood as an attempt to avoid difficult philosophical problems, but can instead be seen as a way to respect the discontinuity between the earthly body and the resurrection that Paul emphasizes in 1 Corinthians 15, and thereby preserve a contemporary project, namely, avoiding reducing the body to one or the other contemporary ideological construction of the same.[227] It would be best for historical and theological research to avoid too great an emphasis on continuity. Otherwise the risk is that the resurrection body would be reduced to something familiar, and that its grotesque character would be denied. Properly understood, the resurrection body is a critical challenge to the present, which means that it is neither a denial of embodiment as such nor a legitimation of a certain understanding of embodiment. There can very well be a theological reason that the New Testament witness is not more clear-cut than it actually is. Attempting to bring them back to a common denominator, whatever that may be, would thus be a theological reduction. According to Williams "the resurrection narratives themselves insist that the risen Jesus is not grasped, owned, or perfectly obeyed by his friends."[228] Here we come close to an understanding of the language of the resurrection body as a grotesque language, which approaches the unknown with the help of the known and at the same time draws attention to the inevitable difference between what is referred to and the way in which it is referred to. We can perhaps even speak of a grotesque "realism of distance"—"seeing

227. N. T. Wright speaks in *Resurrection*, vol. 3, pp. 477-78, 606, 612, 678-79, of *"transphysicality"* as a designation for the physical nature of the resurrection body, but this designation becomes just a designation for the difficulty of describing the new physicality.

228. Rowan Williams, "Between the Cherubim: The Empty Tomb and the Empty Throne," in *On Christian Theology*, Challenges in Contemporary Theology (Oxford/Malden, MA: Blackwell, 2000), p. 188.

575

far things close up"—where the continuity between the unknown and the known is not allowed to overshadow the discontinuity. With the language of the grotesque, as applied to the understanding of the resurrection body, we are able to avoid taking our descriptions of what we even now hope for as all too given, and so can preserve the character of grace in eschatology.

What the stories of the resurrection say, among other things, is that Jesus is still present with his church in a way that does not turn him into a function of the church. The story is not done yet, and how the person's glorified body should be understood, as with Jesus' resurrection body, is still a mystery. What can be said is that the human being in the entirety of her person is related to the body of Christ through an eschatological desire; her body is not something finished, closed, but something open, generative, boundary exceeding, intertwined with other bodies. Her body is, also in Bakhtin's sense, a grotesque body that shares the hope of a new world order for all of existence. To speak of the resurrection body without in the same breath speaking of the mediation between individual and social body would be a theological abstraction. To speak of the resurrection body without at the same time emphasizing the grotesque character of the theological language would be to reduce the body to something all too familiar and to lose sight of the character of grace in the resurrection body.

In this chapter and in the previous one I have investigated theological doctrines and practices in an attempt to allow historical and contemporary perspectives to meet, and through this to bring about a systematic-theological discussion of the person's embodiment according to the tradition of the Christian church. I have argued that Christian embodiment can be described as grotesque in the sense of excessive and generative, but also in the sense that it cannot be reduced to something all too familiar. The temporal structure of communion is also that of the body, and I have therefore accounted for the body as a medium for pain (past), the presence of God (present), and hope (future). I have also shown for all three of these temporalities, and in accordance with my thesis in chapter 9, how individual and social body are intimately intertwined through a ritual mediation. What remains to be done in the final chapter is to bring together the threads from the chapters on the erotic and the grotesque bodies, as well as the other chapters on the incarnation, gaze, and embodiment. But the task also remains to once more return to the question of the eschatological and social horizon of the Christian body. With this I will finish in a conclusion concerning Christianity and embodiment, and the anthropological implications of the doctrine of the incarnation for the person's way of being-in-the-world.

12. Of Heavenly Bodies and Divine Cities

On Body and Theology

This study of incarnation, the gaze, and embodiment is my contribution to the interpretation of several of the anthropological implications of the doctrine of the incarnation for the human being's way of being-in-the-world. I have concentrated on three questions, which I formulated thus by way of introduction in chapter 1: whether the theological conception of the incarnation has allowed the humanity of the human being to come into its own; how one would imagine a gaze that preserves the human being's relationship to the presence of God in a way that acknowledges both God's presence and our human relationship to this presence; and how the embodiment of the human being should be understood in light of God's incarnation in Jesus Christ. This book is thus a study in the Christian problem of incarnation. My focus has, however, not been the traditional one, that which has been prevalent in Christological studies of the last centuries. I have instead chosen to focus on the embodiment of the person and have started from Nietzsche's assertion that Christianity is nihilistic and body-denying.[1]

Was Nietzsche right or wrong? The perhaps not especially surprising result of my study is that the question is more complex than the simple division into right and wrong is able to clarify. As so often, Nietzsche's provocations become a reason to take up various issues in a new way and force oneself to think differently. Nonetheless, I have argued here via various historical excurses that the Christian tradition's view of embodiment is not unequivocally

---

1. To my surprise, this choice of perspective was also taken by Pope Benedict XVI's first encyclical *Deus est caritas* (The Vatican, 2006). See here primarily §3–8 on love and embodiment, §12–15 on incarnation, and §16–18 on the gaze.

negative. There are instead resources here for a constructive contemporary somatology that, perhaps like the theologies of the body of other periods, can contribute to a productive renegotiation of the conception of the body on the basis of the challenges of the present. Just as embodiment itself is ambiguous, so also is the representation of the body, and I have therefore attempted to avoid a stereotypical division of different types of embodiment into good and bad conceptions running like common threads throughout history. If Christian ascetic practice can be one way to deny the person's embodiment in *one* situation, it can on the other hand be a way of protecting the integrity of the body in *another*. What is critical for concretely differentiating between different somatologies is not simply, or even primarily, what they explicitly say about the body, but the particular context that provides the rules for how one should speak about and conceive of the body in a specific way. The concreteness of the body is ultimately a practical question. For a theology of the body it has thus been extremely pressing to not only discuss different conceptions of the body, but also concrete practices where these conceptions become flesh. What remains to be done in this final chapter is to bring together several of the threads from the investigation in the chapters on incarnation, the gaze, and embodiment, and see where they lead.

I want to begin by stating that there seem to be certain historical displacements within the Christian tradition that go together. When the ecclesial body changes meaning from *corpus verum* to *corpus mysticum* (a development I described in chapter 9) this simultaneously involves a reification of the understanding of communion and a dilution of the understanding of Christianity's social body. From having been understood within the framework of a social and historical course of events, the church as well as communion and the body were reified and transformed into objects—so communion, for example, becomes a "spectacle" rather than a liturgical event. In the early church's polemic against Docetism and Gnosticism the ideal for the resurrection body came to be a body whose materiality was emphasized together with its unchangeability, which modern theology reacted to by emphasizing the dynamic character of the body, an emphasis that often went hand in hand with a spiritualizing of the understanding of the resurrection.

Through a series of displacements the Christian tradition has in the modern period come to adopt a spiritualized and individualized character, where the ghostliness of its form has been reinforced by a Cartesian dualism between body and consciousness. This should hardly be interpreted as a direct contempt for the body in modern theology, but rather as an effect of the fact that one quite simply loses sight of the body—the individual as well as the social—and materiality. The Christian faith has thereby come to embrace a subjectivist, atomistic vocabulary. The embodiment of the person and the rest of the material world to a large extent came to be compared to a machine, and the relationship to God came to refer to the person's interior in a way that reinforced certain tendencies in the understanding of earlier epochs, and obscured others (cf. chapters 4 and 6). Sexuality came to be secularized through the fact that it lost its eschatological horizon in the desire for God (chapter 10). In the fact that concrete, social practices thereby come to have less significance for the intellectual understanding of Christianity, the relationship between Christ's divinity and humanity also becomes a problem in a different way than it had been earlier (chapters 2 and 3). The divine becomes a contrast to the human, a potential competitor; and the circumstances, i.e., the social context, for the understanding of the ancient doctrines become different. The dogmas have come to be "dogmatized" (chapter 1), i.e., changed from more or less doxological and apophatic statements, whose context was the liturgy and life orientation of the worshiping congregation, to become predicative propositions of divine facts. The sum of these displacements is that the environment for a productive theological understanding of the body has in part (historical events are seldom unequivocal) become less favorable in the modern period. Since history goes ever onward, any return to a premodern theological conception of embodiment is neither possible nor desirable. What I have attempted to do in this study is to instead use historical theology as a resource, both for discovering hidden presuppositions in contemporary conceptions of embodiment and for contributing to a constructive theology of the body for our time.

How will such a constructive theology of the body become possible? One of the conclusions of this study is that the embodiment of the solitary human being cannot be understood without reference to the social body, and thus our eventual appraisal of one embodiment or the other must attend to the social circumstances. For this reason I have attempted to avoid a particular mistake, which the American theologian Nicholas M. Healy describes apropos a tendency within ecclesiology to want to present a template for a normative ecclesiology by working out a detailed and systematic account of the implications of biblical texts and the theological tradition for our understanding of the church.[2] Modern theological thought about the

---

2. Nicholas M. Healy, *Church, World and the Christian Life: Practical-Prophetic Ecclesiology,* Cambridge Studies in Christian Doctrine (Cambridge: Cambridge University Press, 2000), pp. 25-51.

church has often presented a comprehensive model or metaphor for how the church should be understood, Healy says, and this model or metaphor is imagined to organize other models and metaphors, as well as the concrete reality that the church constitutes. The problem with such a model is that it becomes all too clear-cut. It is not an especially big step to change focus from church to body. The risk in presenting a template for what the body, theologically understood, is or should be, is that the body is once more reduced to something conceptualizable, and so becomes familiar and manageable.

There is in modern systematic theology a fondness for unequivocal explanations, as though the body could be captured in a single concept, a single metaphor, or a single model.[3] But to create a theological synthesis of its insights would be to risk domesticating the unknown and intangible of human embodiment, not least in terms of its eschatological horizon. The three keywords that stand as rubrics in the previous chapters—the liturgical body, the erotic body, and the grotesque body—aim to emphasize several comprehensive aspects of a contemporary theological somatology, but cannot and should not be understood as unequivocal conceptions on the basis of which it would be possible to deduce an unequivocal theology of the body. So some Christian ideal body, in the sense of a theological template on the basis of which concrete Christian embodiment can be understood and assessed, has not been presented here. It is instead, when it comes to theology, a matter of using its heuristic discernment in the presentation of a constructive theology of the body, conscious of and explicitly guided by insights taken from the tradition, critically interpreted, and set in relationship to the way the contemporary embodiment is configured and articulated. My interpretation of Christian embodiment has, in accordance with the methodological conditions I drew up in chapter 1, related not only to formulated doctrines and theologies, but also to concrete practices, and continuation of the theological work thus also builds on the insight that our understanding of embodiment is of a practical nature; since we are embodied beings, all our arguments are always embedded in a theoretical and practical context that constitutes its concrete horizon.

But is there not, in spite of this qualification, still in some sense just such a comprehensive metaphor in the theological somatology I have presented in the previous chapters? Is the Christian body primarily a liturgi-

---

3. Cf. William C. Placher, *The Domestication of Transcendence: How Modern Thinking about God Went Wrong* (Louisville: Westminster/John Knox Press, 1996), p. 1.

cal body that expresses in rituals its hymn of existence as such and thereby becomes a social body? Or is it perhaps an ascetic body, not as a way to deny the body, but as an empowering practice that can, at least potentially, become an instrument of social critique? Perhaps it is an erotic body that in its practical bodily actions expresses its longing for God, other people, and salvation? Or perhaps even a grotesque body, where the fragile, sin-inclined, and fragmented character of human existence becomes clear? I have in fact mentioned one of the reasons that I have not chosen any of these as a comprehensive metaphor, namely the risk of reducing the ambiguity in a metaphor to the putative clarity of a concept, and by extension of reducing the ambiguity of several metaphors to the relative clarity of a single one. The Christian body is all this and more.

The fact that I highlight in this final chapter an eschatological aspect of Christian embodiment under the rubric "heavenly bodies," which in part attempts to sum up several of the insights I have made in previous chapters, should not be interpreted as an attempt to, in spite of the above-named objections, exchange ambiguity for univocity. Here it is instead a matter of an eschatological aspect that both wants to avoid an *extreme* ambiguity, where the very affinity between the different ways of speaking of the body is threatened, and a monotonous univocity, which believes itself to have defined the body and determined its conceptual nature. The term heavenly body may be said to be a paraphrase of Paul's *sōma pneumatikon* and the Apostle's reference to Christ as a "heavenly person," whose image the human being will become (1 Cor. 15:44, 49). Embodiment is consequently viewed from an eschatological perspective. The expression "heavenly bodies" thus does not intend to refer to a sort of spectral or spiritualized body, or a body determined from above, but a body determined by the life of the Spirit, and so by the fellowship of the Trinity. An eschatological perspective on the body should not be played off against a creation theology perspective, since in Christian doctrine eschatology has to do with the perfection of creation. That the body is created by God is a given in Christian theology, but without asking *what* it is created *for,* creation theology is incomplete. A creation theology that ignores eschatology would involve reducing creation to a static state, created by the God of the deists, who, after his work, has withdrawn from his creation like a retired industrialist who, after retirement, is satisfied with living on the interest from what his earlier work has brought in. The understanding of the resurrection body thus affects the understanding of the Christian body here and now.

The creation entails, according to Christian doctrine *(creatio ex nihilo)*, no reworking of already-existing material (the Creator is not a demiurge), nor any thought of an eternally existing divine spark that is given a corporeal shell. *Psychē* as well as *sōma* are thus to an equally high degree created, and therefore equally unlike God and equally near God. Even Origen, who spoke of two creations, one spiritual and one corporeal, said that both were in fact created. God's transcendence is thus not a threat to the integrity of the human body, but rather the contrary. A radical doctrine of creation, i.e., a doctrine of creation out of nothing, deconstructs the hierarchization of body and soul, since both are equally contingent in relation to God. Nor is difference thereby equal to sin. The basis for difference instead lies in the original divine differentiation between that which is God himself and that which is not God (creation). The act of creation (which is still an act of creation here and now, not only *in principio*) is not an "alien work" for God, since it has its basis in God's self-differentiation (the Trinity), which implies a self-giving love of God already "before" the act of creation. The differentiation that God causes through the act of creation is thus without sin. Sin instead consists in a person reducing the world to perceivable, mute entities that thereby become possible to conquer and manipulate—the human project of conquering the world, people, and God, rather than loving them with an erotic love that gives and only takes back in the hope of getting to give itself anew. Salvation involves not only the restoration of creation to its original intention, but also its perfection. The person is thus not something that statically exists and onto which salvation is added as a bonus. Through his or her eschatological completion the person comes to be in accordance with the original intent of creation.[4]

Nor is the body a fixed and finished object, seen from the perspective of Christian theology. The body cannot be reduced to a three-dimensional, material artifact, but is a complex intertwining of materiality, experiences, and linguistic concepts. This means that the body takes on more of a social character here, since the body, as it is represented in the communion ritual (cf. chapter 11), is primarily an act of communication (or an act of communication as communion): "Take and eat. This is my body, which is given for you." Through communion Christ gives himself bodily to those who celebrate the supper and thereby communicate with God. Christ's body becomes a medium that establishes relationships not only between God and person but in the same act also between people, in that it is manifested in

4. Cf. Gustaf Wingren, *Människan och inkarnationen enligt Irenaeus* (Lund: Gleerups, 1947), pp. 200–211.

sacraments and in liturgies, in writing and in practices.[5] With this the world is highlighted in a vicarious way as a gift in the bread and wine of the supper, a ritual that becomes a thanksgiving (i.e., *eucharistia*) for the very existence of the world. The body, in the Christian tradition, is thus not an autonomous, delimited entity, but something that is unfinished, permeable, and excessive, which exists in the very act of giving oneself to and becoming participatory in other bodies. This is what I spoke of in chapter 8 as the body's intercorporeality and transcorporeality.

Through communion and other liturgical actions, in particular baptism, the individual body is incorporated into the body of Christ, and Christ thereby achieves a contemporary concretion. One of the conclusions in the chapters on the incarnation (2 and 3) was that Christology remains abstract so long as the concrete reception of Christ in different practices is not thematized. The incarnation is constituted, so to speak, not only by the fact that God becomes human in Jesus Christ, but also by the fact that this incarnation continues in people's concrete reception of Christ, which always achieves a specific form in different historical, cultural, and social circumstances. Part of modern Christology's constantly returning problem with Christ's humanity—from Schleiermacher, to Barth, to the theologians involved in *The Myth of God Incarnate*—has to do with precisely the distinction between Christ as such and people's concrete reception of Christ.[6] In other words, the anthropological implications of the doctrine of the incarnation for the person's way of being-in-the-world ought to be a part of Christology rather than a consequence of it. One does not comprehend who Christ is other than in relation to other people, and one does not comprehend what the body is other than in relation to the body of Christ. Paradoxically enough—given its critique of Chalcedon—it is especially within contemporary feminist Christology that this premodern theological insight is recovered.

I will now, as I have already announced, proceed by returning to the question of the eschatological horizon of the body in a section on heavenly bodies. Then in a section on divine cities I turn to the question of the sociality of the body and to the risk that such a study of a theological somatology would, in spite of everything, conclude with an idealized body. Finally I conclude with some concrete reflections on Christ, the church, the body, and love as relations to the invisible.

---

5. Cf. Graham Ward, *Cities of God,* Radical Orthodoxy (London/New York: Routledge, 2000), pp. 87–96.

6. Ward, *Cities of God,* pp. 114–16.

On Heavenly Bodies

A theology of the body must, in the terms that Hans Urs von Balthasar borrows from Hegel, be dramatic rather than epic in order to avoid reducing its subject to a distinct object. Human existence as we know it is an existence that is characterized by "complications, tensions, catastrophes and reconciliations."[7] An epic theology would, according to von Balthasar's definition, be a theology that attempted to observe the human drama from a standpoint outside of this drama.[8] In the pursuit of formal rigor, theology has grasped for an epic standpoint outside of the drama by expressing itself in static and essentialist ways. But such a standpoint does not exist, von Balthasar says. Whether or not we want it, there is no human observer who can judge the human drama from the outside. Even God has allowed Godself to become participatory in the human drama through the incarnation.

The theology of the body that I have attempted to sketch out by interpreting different Christian texts, doctrines, and practices could be called dramatic rather than epic in the above sense. As philosopher Donn Welton points out (see chapter 9), the biblical texts place the body at the intersection between good and evil, life and death, and many other texts and practices as well have testified to the same thing. The body is an arena where the conflict between good and evil is played out, and as such is not neutral territory. A theology of the body can therefore not content itself with describing the transcendental structure of human embodiment, but must also clarify the fact that the body is embedded in an existential drama of salvation. A static definition of the body also becomes impossible for this reason. The body will be transformed from a perishable earthly body to an imperishable heavenly body (see chapter 11) at the resurrection, but just as Paul emphasized the discontinuity between the earthly body and the resurrection body, a theology of the body does best to refrain from overly confident claims about what the body will become. Here I can also support myself with the authority of Augustine in *City of God,* when he speaks of the spiritual body that will

---

7. Hans Urs von Balthasar, *Theo-drama: Theological Dramatic Theory, 1. Prolegomena,* trans. Graham Harrison (San Francisco: Ignatius Press, 1988), p. 17.

8. Hans Urs von Balthasar, *Theo-Drama: Theological Dramatic Theory, 2: Dramatis Personae: Man in God,* trans. Graham Harrison (San Francisco: Ignatius Press, 1990), pp. 54–62. However, Ben Quash criticizes von Balthasar because his theo-drama does not live up to his dramatic category, but remains epic in character. See J. B. Quash, "'Between the brutely given, and the brutally, banally free': Von Balthasar's Theology of Drama in Dialogue with Hegel," *Modern Theology* 13, no. 3 (1997): 293–318.

be clothed in imperishability and immortality: "But no experience that we have yet had enables us to know what the nature of that spiritual body and the extent of its grace will be; and so it would, I fear, be rash to offer any description of it."[9] The heavenly body is something unknown that we really cannot speak of without faltering.

But even if both Paul and Augustine emphasized the discontinuity of the heavenly body with regard to the earthly body, they retained the entire time the tension in the possibility of a continuity between heavenly and earthly body. Probably even more in our time than for Paul and Augustine the very thought of a resurrection body can seem curious, and so the idea of a continuity between an earthly body and a resurrection body threatens to dissolve. If the continuity is not also emphasized in some way, the heavenly body threatens to be dissolved by becoming either completely unknown or something meaningless; thus the dramatic character of theology also threatens to come to naught. What was it, then, that made it such that Augustine, for example, did not refrain from certain references that make it possible to speak of continuities and not only discontinuities between earthly body and resurrection body? Despite his well-motivated fear of saying something hasty on the topic, he did not refrain from writing a good deal on the heavenly body.

The resurrection of the body is, writes medieval historian Caroline Walker Bynum in her work on the view of the resurrection of the body in Western Christendom, "a concept of sublime courage and optimism" that touches human hope and longing in the midst of a world characterized by death and disappointment.[10] It is just such a hope that Augustine paints a picture of in *City of God,* namely, to be liberated from the desire to rule in favor of the possibility of a love that is capable of loving without owning. A central example of this is when Augustine paints a vision of a time "when we shall enjoy *[perfruamur]* each other's beauty *[pulchritudine]* without any lust *[libidine],*" and thereby gives an image of a love purified from its lust to possess the other and liberated to love beauty for its own sake.[11] The physical beauty of the human being is obvious for Augustine, and it is based on balance and proportion between her different parts, a balance that will

9. Augustine, *The City of God against the Pagans,* Cambridge Texts in the History of Political Thought, trans. R. W. Dyson (Cambridge: Cambridge University Press, 1998), p. 1153 (22, 21).

10. Caroline Walker Bynum, *The Resurrection of the Body in Western Christianity 200–1336* (New York: Columbia University Press, 1995), p. 343.

11. Augustine, *The City of God,* p. 1164 (22, 24).

become even clearer in the heavenly body.[12] But the person will not be able to enjoy this beauty without lust until eternity. In other words, Augustine speaks of a desire purified from all avarice, which manages to enjoy human beauty without desiring to own it, i.e., to see with a so-called erotic gaze. For Augustine this is not only an eschatological possibility, but to a certain degree possible already here and now, for example, at the sight of the beauty of creation.[13] This purified desire allows itself to be both satisfied and deepened by the sight of beauty.[14] Now if the enjoyment of beauty is already possible in the earthly life, Augustine points out in an argument proceeding from the lower to the higher, how much greater then would the enjoyment not be in eternity? Augustine is thus not resistant to the possibility of a continuity between the earthly body here and now and the resurrection body, and this continuity can be said to consist in our ability to imagine and experience a pleasure purified from all lust. There already exist certain bodily indications of such a non-instrumental beauty, Augustine says, for example "the nipples on a man's chest and the beard on his face."[15] Augustine's example may not translate so directly for our time, considering our insight into physiognomic evolution and the cultural dependence of ideals of beauty, but the thought of hope and of pleasure purified from lust probably achieves even greater resonance.

An additional way to speak of the continuity between the earthly body and the heavenly body would be, on the basis of Paul's discourse on the imperishability of the resurrection body (in, for example, 1 Cor. 15:42), to speak of it as, in a certain sense, an indication of the inviolability of the body. Against the objection that "imperishability" *(aphtharsia)* is not an "ethical" term, but rather a "biological" term, and that a transposition from imperishability to inviolability would thereby entail a "moralizing" of the Christian church, I want to highlight two things: Firstly, that Paul hardly made a distinction between "ethics" and "biology," but situated the transformation from earthly to heavenly body within salvation history. Secondly, it is a matter of finding a meaningful analogy, not replacing the conception of the imperishability of the body with its inviolability. To speak of the heavenly body as inviolable would thus be a way to show how the Christian tradition stands against the contemporary tendency to reduce the body to an entirely

12. Augustine, *The City of God*, 11, 22. If one may shave off an eyebrow, Augustine writes, the body as such loses almost nothing, but its beauty loses a lot. Cf. as well book 22, chapter 20.

13. Cf. Augustine, *The City of God*, 22, 24.

14. Cf. Ward, *Cities of God*, pp. 172–73.

15. Augustine, *The City of God*, p. 1164 (22, 24).

immanent "naked life"—what the Italian philosopher Giorgio Agamben calls *homo sacer*—as is administrated by the totalitarian states.[16] This is not to deny the existence of this "bio-politics." On the contrary, the eschatological body provides an understanding of why such a reduction is theologically impossible: it would be a denial of the fact that the person is created in the image of God and that she was thus never meant to be instrumentalized. Even in the most extreme forms of torture the perpetrators do not possess the power to expunge the person's quality of being made in God's image, which is an imperishable feature of her embodiment; the side of the body that faces the invisible. Opposition to bio-politics finds a transcendent anchor here—the person as citizen in *civitas Dei*. Theological somatology becomes a protest against the reification and disciplining of the body; its embodiment is not a matter of a docile body, but of a suffering body.

If there then also exist continuities to other aspects of the heavenly body, and it is therefore possible to speak of it in a meaningful, if not yet complete, way, the question also becomes what the concept of the heavenly body means for a contemporary theology. What I have wanted to argue in this study of embodiment can also be illustrated by my pointing out what I have avoided. The first thing I have attempted to avoid is what in patristic Christological terminology might be called a somatological Nestorianism (cf. the discussion of Nestorius in chapter 2), i.e., a theology of the body that tends to secularize and thereby radically differentiate between human embodiment and the experience of the divine. As I have shown in chapter 10, the modern period has entailed a secularization of sexuality in comparison with the more apparent erotic horizon of earlier theologies. Thus a bodily experience that was, especially around the most recent turn of the century, considered to be central for the humanity of the person, sexuality, comes to lose its theological horizon. What remains is just a more or less realistic sexual ethics. But the very theological reduction of sexuality to something that should be judged by an "ethics" testifies to the fact that something has been lost in the modern theological self-understanding. This reduction has gone hand in hand with the evaporation or the decorporealizing of the Christian faith that I described in chapter 9 with the help of de Lubac, Bakhtin, and de Certeau. As a counterweight to this almost Nestorian somatological ten-

---

16. See Giorgio Agamben, *Homo Sacer: Sovereign Power and Bare Life,* Meridian Crossing Aesthetics, trans. Daniel Heller-Roazen (Stanford: Stanford University Press, 1998). Cf. Maria Johansen, *Offentlig skrift om det hemliga: Raison d'état, SOU och varulven,* Logos/Pathos 4 (Göteborg: Glänta, 2005), pp. 168–89.

dency within modern theology, by highlighting the erotic body I have shown the possibility of a theology that also takes the person's sexual and erotic experiences seriously. One might say that the erotic body as a theological theme epitomizes and expresses the body as the experience of a presence that goes beyond every attempt to conceptualize embodiment, including beyond the desire that is directed towards it. The ecstasy of this presence means that the body is always more than what we know of it and manage to perceive of it. In relation to desire, the erotic body of the other is so near mine that my desire is made mute by its presence, and precisely through this experiences a desire that can never be filled by the body of the other, but is in fact endless.

The second thing I have attempted to avoid can with the same patristic Christological terminology be called a somatological monophysitism (see chapter 2 here as well), i.e., a theology of the body that tends to confuse human embodiment with the experience of the divine, as though the experience of sensual pleasure could be identical with the experience of God. Here one might imagine either an erotic theology that does not clarify the difference between the interpersonal erotic encounter and the experience of God, the gaping lack in our desire that is its constant shadow and hostage, or also the theology that quite simply avoids or trivializes the person's sin as well as her finiteness and perishability. A counterweight to this somatological monophysitism is presented in the chapter on the grotesque body (chapter 11). Here I attempt to draw attention to experiences of bodily absence through experiences of pain, but also to experiences of how fundamental material conditions for our lives are given to us through circumstances wholly or partially outside our own conscious control (communion as the breaking of bread) and the fact that we are therefore communal beings, impossible to reduce to solitary creatures, not even in our own bodily constitution. The eschatological experience of the body as unknown belongs to the Christian tradition as well, this quite simply not knowing what embodiment entails, since our analogies and metaphors are not sufficient for knowing exactly what we speak of when we speak of the resurrection body. If the erotic body thematizes the ecstasy of embodiment, the chapter on the grotesque body has to do with the experience of absence in the midst of our embodiment, how we must always say and perceive more than we know and control. The body draws back from objectification, both as ecstasy and as absence, and its transcendence is more immanent and its immanence more transcendent than what a theology proceeding from objectifying premises is able to manage. This means that its boundaries are not obvious in any direction.

The body can never be conceptualized in an exhaustive way; this may be both its tragedy and its hope. Its tragedy because, despite the endless, multifaceted, and intensive discourse about it that goes perpetually on, it can itself never be heard in this discourse. The body as a lived and ever-changing reality does not let itself be captured by conceptual language, but always remains incommensurably evasive in relation to this language that, so to speak, always comes too late. Even if it is an abstraction to speak of a pre-linguistic body, it is clear that the body is pre-theoretical and does not allow itself to be captured—or perhaps rather annihilated?—by an objectifying discourse. At the same time this theoretical estrangement—the body can never understand itself—also constitutes a basis for hope, namely a hope for the body's transcendence (with regard to all claims for apodictic evidence) or its alterity, and thereby also a hope for its eventual transformation. The body is not identical with the corpse, the zombie, or the automaton, but is instead sensible, temporal, desiring, and thereby constantly underway. The body remains a mystery even in the moment that it manifests itself before our gazes, since it cannot be reduced to a static presence, but always exists in relation to its past associations and its future potential. The body, theologically understood, is ultimately not a docile body, such as Foucault speaks of (cf. chapter 8), and such as, for example, the practice of torture attempts to reduce it to. A theological somatology is therefore a continual deconstruction of representations of the body, but not of its presentation.

The Christian hope, which ultimately cannot be anything other than an embodied hope, thus latches onto the fact that the body is always in a sense something alien that escapes every attempt to exploit or objectify it. Thus the hope is also opened of a glorified or transfigured body, whose visible embodiment faces the invisible (like an icon), and which already here and now allows itself to be poetically transfigured in word as well as movement. The estrangement of the body is thus overcome without dissolving it. Since the person is created in the image of God (Gen. 1:27) and God himself is invisible, the bodily existence of the person is also an image of something invisible. This does not entail any reduction of the concreteness of the body, but is instead a reminder that concreteness may not be confused with univocity or comprehensibility. Or is it perhaps clearer to argue that the body's apparently incurable homelessness is cured without its transcendence or alterity being dissolved? It remains a body, but illuminated by God's erotic gaze. The person's soul should not be understood here in Cartesian terms as a substance that exists parallel to or apart from a mechanically understood body, but rather as an enigmatic density in the body, its vertiginous, invisible depth that makes it such that the person never completely coincides with the exterior that the body presents (cf. the account of the invisible flesh according to Merleau-Ponty in chapter 8).

The erotic gaze is able to bridge the distance between the observer and the observed—i.e., between myself and the other—without annulling or denying the distance as such. Thus the other is not reduced to an object for the erotic gaze. Nor should the observer be understood as a closed, finished subject, but rather as open, offering herself for the gaze of the other through her embodiment. The erotic gaze is an incarnated gaze that establishes a relationship to the other without reducing the other either to something familiar or to something completely unknown. It is thus a part of the person's embodiment that involves both distance—my body situates me in a way that radically distinguishes this bodily situation from another body's situation—and presence or radical accessibility—"here I am!"—at one and the same time. Just as my skin both unites me with the environment (presence) and separates me from it (distance) at one and the same time, the erotic caress involves both the union of bodies and their separation. Embodiment is thus in a way the very condition for sociality, since embodiment is just such a situation of the person that makes her accessible for the other, i.e., possible to localize. Without distance, no presence. Through the body we are exposed for the other, through the body we expose ourselves to the other.

This is also one reason that I have emphasized gender differences in this study. The point, as emerged in chapter 10, is not to deny the presence of a pervasive androcentrism and heteronormativity in the Christian church and tradition throughout history. On the contrary, I have attempted to show why there exist latent possibilities in Christian theology for a more genuine emphasis on gender differences and sexual differences than that which is presented on the basis of an essentially narcissistic male, heterosexual perspective. The risk in reducing everything to the same in a critique of gender differences in favor of some sort of gender neutrality would be that one thereby ignores the fact that it is difference that drives desire. I have therefore argued for a difference that is not motivated by a person's set of chromosomes, but is essentially a theological difference. Gender difference should thus not be seen as symmetrical and thereby as complementary, but as instead indicating the trace of a more fundamental difference that cannot be reduced to something familiar.

The body is thus also a medium of communication for God's presence. Perhaps it is true that it is the sense of touch, which Aristotle said was the most fundamental sense, that shows most clearly how the body is able to be open for the other. Touch is, as Jean-Louis Chrétien writes, through its very finiteness "already open to a presence without image or representation, to an intimate proximity that never turns into possession, to a naked exposure to the ungraspable."[17] It is therefore not surprising that several theologians and mystics have made use of precisely the sense of touch as a way to describe the relationship between God and creation. God's movement towards the person occurs through the fact that her entire being is touched, setting her body afire. John of the Cross, who is described by Chrétien as the great mystic of the sense of touch, writes in *The Living Flame of Love* from 1591 (using a division between soul and body typical for the time) about how God touches the soul and how this touching flows "into the body and all the sensory substance, all the members and bones and marrow rejoice."[18] Both the soul and the body are thereby given a taste of eternal life by being caught up in God's own movement. In a certain sense, says philosopher Jean-Luc Nancy, Christianity is "the invention of the religion of touch, of the sensible, of presence that is immediate to the body and to the heart."[19] In the Christian tradition embodiment goes together with the person's relationality, and so also her communication and communion with God. To deny the significance of embodiment for the Christian faith, and to deny the heavenly embodiment, however impossible it may be for us to imagine, would therefore be to deny the social character of Christianity, whether we speak of human relationship or the relationship to God (or relationships to the nonhuman parts of creation). The individual body as a medium for the person's sociality is thus also dependent on the social body. It is therefore also important to say something in conclusion about the sociality of the body.

On Divine Cities

It is often said that the Bible begins in a paradisal Eden in the creation account of Genesis, but ends in a city, the heavenly Jerusalem that is described

17. Jean-Louis Chrétien, *The Call and the Response,* trans. Anne A. Davenport (New York: Fordham University Press, 2004), p. 129.

18. St. John of the Cross, *The Living Flame of Love,* from *The Collected Works of St. John of the Cross,* trans. Kieran Kavanaugh and Otilio Rodriguez (Washington, DC: ICS Publications, 1979), p. 603 (stanza 2, 22).

19. Jean-Luc Nancy, *Noli Me Tangere: On the Raising of the Body,* Perspectives in Continental Philosophy, trans. Sarah Clift, Pascale-Anne Brault, and Michael Naas (New York: Fordham University Press, 2008), p. 14.

in John's Revelation. Highlighting the hope of eternity as a city is a recurring theme within the tradition, not only for the author of the book of Revelation. In his epochal work *City of God,* Augustine implements this theme in dialogue with his contemporary Roman understanding of the person as a social being. Augustine's work on cities is also in large part a reflection on the person's embodiment and her desire. Another appropriate question to bring up apropos Augustine's *City of God* is whether the risk with the understandings of the Christian gaze and body that I have given in this study is not that they seem, in spite of everything, to be abstract fictions, far distant from the more diffuse, ambiguous, and unstable bodies that we meet and ourselves are in our daily lives. In this next, final section of the chapter and the book I want to take up the question of divine cities in order to again bring up certain themes that I especially want to highlight from earlier chapters.

I want to begin by turning to the question of the gaze of faith. A possible objection to the account in chapter 7 is that even if the erotic gaze is not a panoptic gaze that hovers like a security camera above the person's embodiment, one can wonder just how concretely incarnated the erotic gaze really is. As art historian James Elkins has pointed out, human seeing is "irrational, inconsistent, and undependable. It is immensely troubled, cousin to blindness and sexuality, and caught up in the threads of the unconscious."[20] The same thing could apply to human embodiment: irrational, inconsistent, and undependable. And that is of course the case. There is no unambiguous Christian gaze, embodiment, or culture in the material world. Christian practices are hybrids, i.e., the progeny of both the tradition of the Christian church and contemporary culture. Christian "identity" (to the degree that one can speak of identity in this case) is relational and is established from the start through borrowed material. Even where Christian social practices oppose themselves to the society they find themselves in, they simultaneously borrow from it, and Christian identity can therefore not exclude overlapping activities and membership. On the contrary, it is an approach that is both necessary and productive for a social group that in most societies does not belong to the majority culture. What is crucial is therefore not simply *which* cultural and social material the Christian church uses when it forms its identity, but also *how* it uses it.[21] Put another way: even if there are boundaries

---

20. James Elkins, *The Object Stares Back: On the Nature of Seeing,* A Harvest Book (San Diego/New York/London: Harcourt, 1997), p. 11.

21. Kathryn Tanner, *Theories of Culture: A New Agenda for Theology,* Guides to Theological Inquiry (Minneapolis: Fortress Press, 1997), p. 112.

between the Christian church as a social body and other social bodies, its boundaries are fluid and permeable. The Christian body is a grotesque body in the Bakhtinian sense that I dealt with in chapters 9 and 11.

The understanding of the Christian church's mixed character is expressed in a way that has become normative in Augustine, in particular in his *City of God*. I have already touched on this theme in chapter 10, but will complement it here with some additional points. Throughout his work Augustine paints an allegory of two cities, the city of God and the earthly city, which may be distinguished by the sort of love that characterizes them, love for God *(amor dei)* or love for self *(amor sui)*, which also expresses itself in the desire to rule *(dominandi libido)*.[22] So in one city love for God rules, in the other city love for the self.[23] But God's city cannot be identified with the Christian church that exists here and now, according to Augustine; rather, this concrete church is instead a mixed body *(corpus permixtum)* that consists of both the city of God and the earthly city.[24] It is only possible to distinguish between the cities eschatologically, and the church's journey through history is therefore a pilgrimage until it reaches the peace of the heavenly city at the end of the ages.[25] The individual body cannot be imagined apart from the relationship to the social body, the church, which is the body of Christ. What makes theological somatology different from other somatologies is therefore the fact that the *telos* (what Augustine in Latin calls its *finis*) that defines and constitutes the social body, the church, differs from the *telos* that defines and constitutes its other social bodies and that comes to concrete (if still not unambiguous) expression in their respective practices.[26] Expressed differently: the Christian body should be understood against the background of a different eschatology than that which constitutes the horizon for other bodies.[27]

22. Augustine, *The City of God*, 1, *praefatio*, and 14, 28. On cities as allegories, cf. 15, 1.

23. Augustine, *The City of God*, 14, 13.

24. Augustine, *The City of God*, 1, 35.

25. Augustine, *The City of God*, 18, 49; 16, 25; 19, 13.

26. Augustine, *The City of God*, book 19, chapters 1, 4, 11.

27. Here I intentionally do not differentiate between teleology and eschatology. A larger investigation than this would naturally be desired, but cannot be carried out here. However, I believe generally that teleology and eschatology should not be understood as each other's opposites, as though teleology were a way to "calculate the future" while eschatology would be understood as the future as a gift. Such a binary opposition is deconstructed in the Christian tradition by the conception of the incarnation. For Christian theology God's incarnation in Jesus Christ means that the future is in a certain sense anticipated here and now, at the same time that it also remains open. An eschatology without teleology, on the other hand, risks

Such a *telos,* or such an eschatological horizon, Augustine presents in the last books of *City of God.* It is thus the conception of time governing their action that distinguishes the two cities, not competition over a particular territory. The different eschatological horizons condition different ways of being-in-the-world.

With regard to the gaze and embodiment it is also important to remind oneself that these do not exist in some "pure," i.e., unalloyed, form in people's concrete gazes and bodies. Through certain aspects of the grotesque body I have attempted to emphasize how the concrete, social-body church cannot be understood as a body that is smooth and well defined towards the environment, but that it is instead a body in the making (see chapters 9 and 11). The same thing applies, of course, to the gaze. The very point in presenting the gaze in pure form in particular is precisely to allow it to more clearly be seen how I imagine that the gaze of faith is constituted. Even if Augustine said that the city of God and the earthly city were mixed together in their concrete existence, there was still the possibility of distinguishing them through their orientation. The two different sorts of love that Augustine describes as distinctive for the two cities does not separate them, as one may easily understand it, merely through different sorts of objects, as though one and the same love were legitimate if it were directed towards God and illegitimate if it were directed towards the world. It is just as much a matter of a difference in attitude within the love itself, or even of "a different faith, a different hope, a different love."[28] One can indicate this difference through the keywords that I introduced in chapters 5 and 7, generosity and greed. This tension-filled mixing in the concrete church does not mean that generosity and greed cannot be distinguished in some sense, but rather that their historical and social embodiment will never be unambiguous. What I have attempted to describe in this study is for the most part the possibility of generosity, not how widespread its concrete existence is.

---

remaining an abstract possibility that in principle can never be incarnated in the concrete life-world. Cf. Anselm Kyongsuk Min's discussion of Jacques Derrida's conception of an absolute messianicity in contrast to a concrete Messiah, "The Other without History and Society: A Dialogue with Derrida," in *The Solidarity of Others in a Divided World: A Postmodern Theology after Postmodernism* (New York/London: T. & T. Clark, 2004), pp. 30–46—even if I believe that more may be found to say about Derrida. Cf. as well Paul S. Fiddes, *The Promised End: Eschatology in Theology and Literature,* Challenges in Contemporary Theology (Oxford/Malden, MA: Blackwell, 2000).

28. Augustine, *The City of God,* p. 908 (18, 54). Cf. as well 14, 7.

The differences that I have illustrated above with the help of Augustine's two cities could lead to several misunderstandings. One of these would consist in a contrasting of the earthly love we know with the heavenly love, as though they were each other's opposites. But this can hardly be done without the argument becoming incoherent. We are dependent on the concrete acts of love and generosity that we know here and know in order to be able to say something about the possibility of a completely generous love. As Gerard Loughlin writes: "We can only think paradise from our knowledge of earthly gardens."[29] The very thought of such a heavenly love can therefore not be posed as a simple contrast to the concrete, earthly love, since it is from the latter that we are given the very possibility of imagining the heavenly love. In the attempt to concretely imagine this heavenly love we must therefore proceed from the love we know and attempt to show the way in which it transcends itself on the way to the generous love. As I have described in chapter 10, throughout history various theologians have been unable to avoid an erotic language for describing the relationship between God and person, and even if it was for them a question of a sublimated eroticism, the interplay between the sublimated and the more fleshly or bodily eroticism is never entirely avoided or rejected. The distinction between sacramentality and sexuality—between divine and interpersonal presence—has never been especially stable. The heavenly love, just like the heavenly embodiment, must therefore be understood partially as a critique of the earthly love, but partially also as an intensifying of the same.

A second misunderstanding would be if one understood Augustine's— and by extension also my—argument as a way to lament the fact that the church cannot exist in any pure form, as though the possibility of generosity would thereby have found an unambiguous and concrete incarnation in history. The fact that the church is not a smooth and bounded body, resistant to influences from contemporary culture, is not a problem. God's city is indeed present in the church, but not identical with it. The intermixture is more far-reaching than this; the possibility of generosity as well as the immediacy of greed exists within as well as outside of the concretely existing church, and there is therefore no reason to categorize all human thoughts, activities, and practices that occur outside of the church's auspices under the desire to rule. One can instead argue that the city of God exists as an immanent potential in all earthly cities. Without any justice at all the kingdoms of humanity would

---

29. Gerard Loughlin, *Alien Sex: The Body and Desire in Cinema and Theology*, Challenges in Contemporary Theology (Malden, MA/Oxford: Blackwell, 2004), p. 281.

be nothing but dens of thieves. Justice finds its perfection in God, even if it can be realized more or less incompletely in human kingdoms.[30] As I have pointed out above, it is not the boundaries that constitute the identity of the Christian church and its practices, even if such boundaries must always exist, but its conception of time or its orientation, its *telos*. The orientation of Christian practices and Christian doctrine, their *telos,* consists precisely in the fact that they will, if yet in an incomplete and anticipatory way, be participatory in the transformation of human desire that Augustine speaks of in *City of God*. Christian doctrine and Christian practices together make up a therapy of desire whose purpose is not to extinguish human desire, but to transform a greedy *libido dominandi* into a generous love.[31] The aim of this therapy, "the heavenly city," is a life in harmony with God and with neighbors.[32] One aspect of the resurrection body is thus the hope of a love purified from the lust to rule, a love that according to one of the Augustine quotations above "enjoy[s]" our human beauty "without any lust." In *this* sense the ideal of virginity that exists in the classical theologians (see the discussion in chapter 9) can also achieve a positive sense: not from necessity as sexual abstinence, but primarily as a giving up of possessive relationships, i.e., the desire to devour and so consume the other.[33]

It may also be important to finally point out that Augustine, in his vision of eternity, does not reduce eschatological beholding to merely a beholding of God, and thereby abandon the person's sociality. On the contrary, it is also a distinctive feature of Augustine's anthropology that the person is social by nature.[34] The person's eternal life, he imagines, is also a life in community, and a more genuine one since the cause of human conflicts is gone. The lust to rule is in other words a contingent, not a necessary, human feature. The beholding of God therefore becomes a question of the fact that "we shall see Him by the spirit in ourselves, in one another, in Himself, in the new heavens and the new earth, and in every created thing which shall then exist." But Augustine does not describe this beholding as a purely spiritual beholding, but instead "by the body we shall see Him in every body to which the keen

30. Augustine, *The City of God*, 2, 21; 4, 4; 5, 19. Augustine's judgment of the Roman Empire in *City of God* is, however, relatively pessimistic.

31. Cf. the chapter "Augustinus Hunger" in my book *Hungerns väg: Om Gud, kyrka och mångfald* (Lund: Arcus, 2000), primarily pp. 10–11.

32. Augustine, *The City of God,* 19, 13.

33. Such an ideal of virginity we find, Loughlin says (*Alien Sex,* p. 276), in Gregory of Nyssa, for example.

34. Augustine, *The City of God,* 12, 28.

vision of the eye of the spiritual body shall extend."[35] The other—the other person, as well as God and ourselves—we reach here not within ourselves, but only between bodies. To cite the above-mentioned Nancy once more: "*An other is a body* because only *a body is an other.*"[36] Similarly, Augustine's vision of the city of God is both individually and socially a bodily vision and a vision of the body. The Christian ambition is therefore, yet again, not an ambition to be liberated from body and desire, but rather a longing for a heavenly body and a paradisal desire.

The Lips of God: Difference and Nearness

In the end it happens that this investigation of the person's embodiment in the Christian tradition has come to have a lot to do with Christ, church, and love. The body, from a theological perspective, is not only about biology, but above all about the iconic character of the body and its relationality and sociality. The body is, according to what I have argued in this study, fundamental not only for people's relationships to each other, but also for our relationships to God. If the incarnation is about how God's otherness should be understood in a way that makes it compatible with God's presence in our world, the converse question for a theological somatology becomes how the body should be understood in a way that makes the idea of God's presence for us compatible with the idea of God's otherness. To be body has to do with presence and invisibility, with nearness and difference. To be body has to do with relationships, and so also with gazes.

One part of our gaze is a sort of longing, not only a longing to touch and be touched by other people, but to behold the invisible, to brush up against the transcendent. As the French literary scholar and philosopher Hélène Cixous writes in an autobiographical account of how her sight was restored after a lifelong and very grave nearsightedness:

> But at this dawn without subterfuge she had seen the world with her own eyes, without intermediary, without the non-contact lenses. The continuity of her flesh and the world's flesh, touch then, was love, and that was

---

35. Augustine, *The City of God*, pp. 1177–78 (22, 29). Cf. as well Loughlin, *Alien Sex*, pp. 124–26.

36. Jean-Luc Nancy, *Corpus*, Perspectives in Continental Philosophy, trans. Richard A. Rand (New York: Fordham University Press, 2008), p. 31.

the miracle, giving. Ah! She hadn't realized the day before that eyes are miraculous hands, had never enjoyed the delicate tact of the cornea, the eyelashes, the most powerful hands, these hands that touch imponderably near and far-off heres. She had not realized that eyes are lips on the lips of God.[37]

The strict distinction between the sense of touch and the sense of sight is itself dissolved in the ecstasy of the gaze. The caress of the sense of sight after her eye operation was experienced as a gift, which demands a theological terminology. Where the lips of the eyes meet the lips of God difference and nearness coincide, in that the boundary that separates also becomes the boundary that unites. Without difference no nearness. The inherent distance between Creator and the created is transcended by the gift of sight (objective genitive) and the desire of sight (subjective genitive). And this is by extension an incarnational terminology: Christ is the person, the Christian church says, in whom transcendence and immanence, difference and presence, meet and coincide. Christ is, as Loughlin writes, "the difference that unites; the cut that connects."[38] So the Christian church's pursuit of the Christ who also continually gives the church as a gift is, finally, a bodily pursuit.

The church seeks Christ, not primarily by directing the gaze towards the clouds, but by directing the gaze towards the other. As in one of the quotations from Loughlin cited above, we can thus only imagine paradise by analogy to earthly gardens, just as we can only seek Christ in the caress of the other, the stranger. It is through other people, who are "strangers" for us in the sense that they can never be reduced to wholly familiar people possessing no additional depth, that the way to God himself is shown, God as stranger in an eminent sense, who can never be reduced to something familiar. The physical, the bodily, is not erased, but it is instead *through* the iconic character of the bodily that we can even behold that which is beyond the bodily. The body is, strictly speaking, not self-defined. What the body is we know only by examining in which social and historical context it is inscribed. In the Christian church the individual body is inscribed, or rather incorporated, into the body of Christ, a body that opens itself but also reaches outside of itself and so allows itself to be joined together with other bodies.

37. Hélène Cixous, "Savoir," in *Veils*, ed. Hélène Cixous and Jacques Derrida, trans. Geoffrey Bennington (Stanford: Stanford University Press, 2001), p. 9.
38. Loughlin, *Alien Sex*, p. xx.

This bodily sociality is expressed already here and now through various rituals and liturgies. As I pointed out in chapter 9 and developed in chapter 11, the ritual of communion entails that individual bodies are choreographed and thereby woven together with—and to—a larger social body, namely the ecclesial body. Both the individual and the social body thereby become to the highest degree a medium for communicating with God. Communication with God is not only a matter of words, but to a large degree also of images and bodily actions, which also means that what Christians mean by "God" is not only articulated by doctrines and theologies, but also by concrete practices like baptism, communion, prayer, and worship.

Thus it is ultimately a matter of which sort of embodiment our conceptions construct for us. If I were to try to capture in one sentence what I have attempted to accomplish in this final chapter, as in the book as a whole, I would argue that the emphasis lies instead on attempting to make the known less known through the unknown, rather than the unknown more known through the known.[39] For us human beings the body is not necessarily the fixed point we often imagine, but rather a dimension of ourselves whose mystery continually turns toward the invisible.

---

39. Cf. Viktor Shklovsky, "Art as Device," in *Theory of Prose,* trans. Benjamin Sher (Elmwood Park, IL: Dalkey Archive Press, 1998), pp. 1–14.

Bibliography

A. Biblical Editions, Dictionaries, and Encyclopedias

Biblia hebraica stuttgartensia. 3rd edition. Edited by K. Elliger and W. Rudolph. Stuttgart: Deutsche Bibelgesellschaft, 1987.

The Book of Concord: The Confessions of the Evangelical Lutheran Church. Edited by Robert Kolb and Timothy J. Wengert. Translated by Charles Arand et al. Minneapolis: Fortress Press, 2000.

Decrees of the Ecumenical Councils. Volume One: *Nicaea I to Lateran V.* Edited by Norman P. Tanner. London/Washington, DC: Sheed & Ward/Georgetown University Press, 1990.

Enchiridion symbolorum definitionum et declarationum de rebus fidei et morum. Edited by Heinrich Denzinger. Improved and expanded edition with German translation. Published by Peter Hünermann in cooperation with Helmut Hoping. 37th edition. Freiburg im Breisgau/Basel/Rome/Vienna: Herder, 1991.

The Encyclopedia of Religion. Edited by Mircea Eliade. New York: Macmillan, 1987.

The English Standard Version Bible: Containing the Old and New Testaments with Apocrypha. Oxford: Oxford University Press, 2009.

A Greek-English Lexicon. Edited by Henry George Liddell and Robert Scott. 9th edition. Revised and expanded by Roderick McKenzie et al. Oxford: Clarendon Press, 1976.

A Greek-English Lexicon of the New Testament and Other Early Christian Literature: A translation and adaptation of the fourth revised and augmented edition of Walter Bauer's Griechisch-Deutsches Wörterbuch zu den Schriften des Neuen Testaments und der übrigen urchristlichen Literatur. 2nd edition. William F. Arndt and F. Wilbur Gingrich. Revised and expanded by F. Wilbur Gingrich and Frederick W. Danker from Walter Bauer's 5th edition, 1958. Chicago/London: University of Chicago Press, 1979.

Nationalencyklopedin. Höganäs, Sweden: Bra Böcker, 1994.

Novum testamentum graece. 26th edition. Post Eberhard Nestle et Erwin Nestle. Stuttgart: Deutsche Bibelgesellschaft, 1988.

Religion in Geschichte und Gegenwart: Handwörterbuch für Theologie und Religionswis-

senschaft. 4th edition. Edited by Hans Dieter Betz, Don S. Browning, et al. Tübingen: Mohr Siebeck, 1998–.

Septuaginta. Edited by Alfred Rahlfs. Stuttgart: Deutsche Bibelgesellschaft, 1979.

Svenska akademiens ordlista över svenska språket. 12th edition. Stockholm: Norstedts ordbok, 1998.

Den svenska kyrkohandboken. Del I: Den allmänna gudstjänsten och De kyrkliga handlingarna. Antagen för Svenska kyrkan av 1986 års kyrkomöte. Stockholm: Verbum, 1987.

Theological Dictionary of the New Testament. Ten volumes. Edited by Gerhard Kittel and Gerhard Friedrich. Translated and edited by Geoffrey W. Bromiley. Grand Rapids: Eerdmans, 1964–1976.

Theological Dictionary of the Old Testament. Fifteen volumes. Edited by G. Johannes Botterweck and Helmer Ringgren. Translated by John T. Willis. Grand Rapids: Eerdmans, 1974–.

Theologische Realenzyklopädie. Berlin/New York: Walter de Gruyter, 1976–.

Wörterbuch der phänomenologischen Begriffe. Philosophische Bibliothek vol. 555. Edited by Helmuth Vetter. Hamburg: Felix Meiner Verlag, 2004.

B. Additional Literature

Aagaard, Anna Marie. *Identifikation af kirken.* Frederiksberg, Denmark: Anis, 1991.

Abel, Ulf. *Ikonen – bilden av det heliga.* Hedemora, Sweden: Gidlunds Bokförlag, 1989.

Abrahamsson, Magnus. *Jesu uppståndelse som historiskt problem: En studie av Rudolf Bultmanns och Wolfhart Pannenbergs tolkningar.* Skellefteå, Sweden: Norma, 2001.

Adams, James Luther, and Wilson Yates, eds. *The Grotesque in Art and Literature: Theological Reflections.* Grand Rapids/Cambridge: Eerdmans, 1997.

Agamben, Giorgio. *Homo Sacer: Sovereign Power and Bare Life.* Meridian Crossing Aesthetics. Translated by Daniel Heller-Roazen. Stanford: Stanford University Press, 1998.

Ahearne, Jeremy. "The Shattering of Christianity and the Articulation of Belief," *New Blackfriars* 77 (November 1997): 493–504.

Alanen, Lilli. *Descartes's Concept of Mind.* Cambridge, MA/London: Harvard University Press, 2003.

Alberti, Leon Battista. *On Painting: A New Translation and a Critical Edition.* Edited and translated by Rocco Sinisgalli. Cambridge: Cambridge University Press, 2013.

Alcoff, Linda Martín. "Merleau-Ponty and Feminist Theory on Experience." In *Chiasms: Merleau-Ponty's Notion of Flesh.* SUNY Series in Contemporary Continental Philosophy. Edited by Fred Evans and Leonard Lawlor. Albany: State University of New York Press, 2000, pp. 251–71.

Alexander, Paul J. *The Patriarch Nicephorus of Constantinople: Ecclesiastical Policy and Image Worship in the Byzantine Empire.* Oxford: Clarendon Press, 1958.

Allen, Jeffner, and Iris Marion Young, eds. *The Thinking Muse: Feminism and Modern French Philosophy.* Bloomington/Indianapolis: Indiana University Press, 1989.

Ammicht Quinn, Regina. *Körper—Religion—Sexualität: Theologische Reflexionen zur Ethik der Geschlechter.* Mainz: Matthias-Grünewald-Verlag, 1999.

Angenendt, Arnold. *Geschichte der Religiosität im Mittelalter*. Darmstadt: Wissenschaftliche Buchgesellschaft, 1997.

Aristotle. *The Complete Works of Aristotle*. The Revised Oxford Translation. Vols. 1 & 2. Edited by Jonathan Barnes. Princeton: Princeton University Press, 1984.

Aristotle. *Nicomachean Ethics*. Loeb Classical Library. Translated by H. Rackham. Cambridge, MA/London: Harvard University Press, 1934.

Arvidsson, Bengt. *Bildstrid Bildbruk Bildlära: En idéhistorisk undersökning av bildfrågan inom den begynnande lutherska traditionen under 1500-talet*. Studia Theologica Lundensia No. 41. Lund, Sweden: Lund University Press, 1987.

Asad, Talal. *Formations of the Secular: Christianity, Islam, Modernity*. Cultural Memory in the Present. Stanford: Stanford University Press, 2003.

Asad, Talal. *Genealogies of Religion: Discipline and Reasons of Power in Christianity and Islam*. Baltimore/London: Johns Hopkins University Press, 1993.

Asad, Talal. "Remarks on the Anthropology of the Body." In *Religion and the Body*. Edited by Sarah Coakley. Cambridge: Cambridge University Press, 2000, pp. 42–52.

Athanasius of Alexandria. *Against the Arians*. In *Nicene and Post-Nicene Fathers*, ser. 2, vol. 4: *Athanasius: Select Works and Letters*. Edited by Philip Schaff and Henry Wace. Grand Rapids: Eerdmans, 1957.

Athanasius of Alexandria. *Against the Arians*, together with *Contra gentes/De incarnatione*. Oxford Early Christian Texts. Translated by Robert W. Thomason. Oxford: Clarendon Press, 1971.

Athanasius of Alexandria. *Orationes adversus Arianos*. Patrologiae Cursus Completus, Series Graeca. Vol. 26. Edited by J. P. Migne. Paris, 1887.

Auerbach, Erich. *Mimesis: The Representation of Reality in Western Literature*. Translated by W. R. Trask. Princeton: Princeton University Press, 2003.

Augustine. *The Augustine Catechism: The Enchiridion on Faith, Hope and Charity*. The Augustine Series. Translated by Bruce Harbert. Hyde Park, NY: New City Press, 1999.

Augustine. *The City of God against the Pagans*. Cambridge Texts in the History of Political Thought. Translated by R. W. Dyson. Cambridge: Cambridge University Press, 1998.

Augustine. *Confessions*. Translated by Henry Chadwick. Oxford/New York: Oxford World Classics, 2008.

Augustine. *De civitate dei contra paganos*. Patrologiae Cursus Completus, Series Latina, vol. 41. Edited by J. P. Migne. Paris, 1845.

Augustine. *De doctrina christiana*. Oxford Early Christian Texts. Translated and introduced by R. P. H. Green. Oxford: Clarendon Press, 1995.

Augustine. *Enchiridion ad Laurentium de fide, spe et caritate*. Patrologiae Cursus Completus, Series Latina, vol. 40. Edited by J. P. Migne. Paris, 1845.

Aurelius, Carl Axel. *Hjärtpunkten: Evangeliets bruk som nyckel till Augsburgska bekännelsen*. Skellefteå, Sweden: Artos, 1995.

Austin, J. L. *How to Do Things with Words: The William James lectures delivered at Harvard University in 1955*. Edited by J. O. Urmson and Marina Sbisà. Oxford: Oxford University Press, 1976.

Axelson, Tomas, and Ola Sigurdson. "Om frälsaren, filmstjärnan och samtidsmänniskan: Jesus på vita duken." In *Film och religion: Livstolkning på vita duken*. Edited by Tomas Axelson and Ola Sigurdson. Örebro, Sweden: Cordia, 2005, pp. 119–49.

Bakhtin, Mikhail. *Rabelais and His World*. Translated by Helene Iswolsky. Cambridge, MA/London: MIT Press, 1968.

Balthasar, Hans Urs von. *Cosmic Liturgy: The Universe according to Maximus the Confessor*. Communio Books. Translated by Brian E. Daley. San Francisco: Ignatius Press, 2003.

Balthasar, Hans Urs von. *The Glory of the Lord: A Theological Aesthetics*. Vol. 1: *Seeing the Form*. Translated by Leiva-Merikakis Erasmo. Edinburgh: T. & T. Clark, 1982.

Balthasar, Hans Urs von. *Mysterium Paschale: The Mystery of Easter*. Ressourcement. Translated by Aidan Nichols. Edinburgh: T. & T. Clark, 1990.

Balthasar, Hans Urs von. *Theo-Drama: Theological Dramatic Theory*, 1: *Prolegomena*. Translated by Graham Harrison. San Francisco: Ignatius Press, 1988.

Balthasar, Hans Urs von. *Theo-Drama: Theological Dramatic Theory*, 2: *Dramatis Personae: Man in God*. Translated by Graham Harrison. San Francisco: Ignatius Press, 1990.

Balthasar, Hans Urs von. *The Theology of Karl Barth: Exposition and Interpretation*. Communio Books. Translated by Edward T. Oakes. San Francisco: Ignatius Press, 1992.

Balthasar, Hans Urs von. *Two Sisters in the Spirit: Therese of Lisieux and Elizabeth of the Trinity*. Translated by Donald Nichols, Anne Englund Nash, and Dennis Martin. San Francisco: Ignatius Press, 1992.

Barth, Karl. *Church Dogmatics*, vol. 1: *The Doctrine of the Word of God*, part 1. 2nd edition. Translated by G. W. Bromiley. Edinburgh: T. & T. Clark, 1975.

Barth, Karl. *Church Dogmatics*, vol. 1: *The Doctrine of the Word of God*, part 2. Translated by G. T. Thomson and Harold Knight. Edinburgh: T. & T. Clark, 1956.

Barth, Karl. *Church Dogmatics*, vol. 2: *The Doctrine of God*, part 1. Translated by T. H. L. Parker, W. B. Johnston, Harold Knight, and J. L. M. Haire. Edinburgh: T. & T. Clark, 1957.

Barth, Karl. *Church Dogmatics*, vol. 2: *The Doctrine of God*, part 2. Translated by G. W. Bromiley, J. C. Campbell, Iain Wilson, J. Strathern McNab, Harold Knight, and R. A. Stewart. Edinburgh: T. & T. Clark, 1957.

Barth, Karl. *Church Dogmatics*, vol. 3: *The Doctrine of Creation*, part 1. Translated by J. W. Edwards, O. Bussey, and Harold Knight. Edinburgh: T. & T. Clark, 1958.

Barth, Karl. *Church Dogmatics*, vol. 3: *The Doctrine of Creation*, part 2. Translated by Harold Knight, G. W. Bromiley, J. K. S. Reid, and R. H. Fuller. Edinburgh: T. & T. Clark, 1960.

Barth, Karl. *Church Dogmatics*, vol. 3: *The Doctrine of Creation*, part 4. 2nd edition. Translated by A. T. Mackay et al. Edinburgh: T. & T. Clark, 1961.

Barth, Karl. *Church Dogmatics*, vol. 4: *The Doctrine of Reconciliation*, part 1. Translated by G. W. Bromiley and T. F. Torrance. Edinburgh: T. & T. Clark, 1956.

Barth, Karl. *Church Dogmatics*, vol. 4: *The Doctrine of Reconciliation*, part 2. Translated by G. W. Bromiley. Edinburgh: T. & T. Clark, 1958.

Barth, Karl. *The Resurrection of the Dead*. Translated by H. J. Stenning. New York: Fleming H. Revell, 1933.

Barth, Karl. "The Strange New World within the Bible." In *The Word of God and the*

Word of Man. Translated by Douglas Horton. Gloucester, MA: Peter Smith, 1978, pp. 28–50.

Barth, Markus. *Ephesians: Introduction, Translation, and Commentary on Chapters 1–3.* The Anchor Bible vol. 34. New York/London: Doubleday, 1974.

Barthes, Roland. *Camera Lucida: Reflections on Photography.* Translated by Richard Howard. New York: Hill & Wang, 1981.

Barthes, Roland. "Le message photographique," *Communications* 1 (1961): 127–38.

Basil of Caesarea [Basil the Great]. *On the Spirit.* In *Nicene and Post-Nicene Fathers,* ser. 2, vol. 8: *Letters and Select Works.* Edited by Philip Schaff. Grand Rapids: Eerdmans, 1996.

Baudrillard, Jean. *Simulacra and Simulation.* Translated by Sheila Faria Glaser. Ann Arbor: University of Michigan Press, 1994.

Bauerschmidt, Frederick Christian. "The Abrahamic Voyage: Michel de Certeau and Theology," *Modern Theology* 12, no. 1 (1996): 1–26.

Bauerschmidt, Frederick Christian. *Julian of Norwich and the Mystical Body Politic of Christ.* Notre Dame/London: University of Notre Dame Press, 1999.

Bauerschmidt, Frederick Christian. "Walking in the Pilgrim City," *New Blackfriars* 77 (November 1996): 504–58.

Beattie, Tina. "Carnal Love and Spiritual Imagination: Can Luce Irigaray and John Paul II Come Together?" In *Sex These Days.* Studies in Theology and Sexuality 1. Edited by Jon Davies and Gerard Loughlin. Sheffield: Sheffield Academic Press, 1997, pp. 177–81.

Beattie, Tina. *God's Mother, Eve's Advocate: A Marian Narrative of Women's Salvation.* London/New York: Continuum, 2002.

Beattie, Tina. *Woman.* New Century Theology. London/New York: Continuum, 2003.

Beauvoir, Simone de. *The Second Sex.* Translated by H. M. Parsley. London: Jonathan Cape, 1956.

Beckwith, Sarah. *Christ's Body: Identity, Culture and Society in Late Medieval Writings.* London/New York: Routledge, 1993.

Bell, Catherine. *Ritual: Perspectives and Dimensions.* New York/Oxford: Oxford University Press, 1997.

Bell, Catherine. *Ritual Theory, Ritual Practice.* New York/Oxford: Oxford University Press, 1992.

Bell, Daniel M. *Liberation Theology after the End of History: The Refusal to Cease Suffering.* London/New York: Routledge, 2001.

Belting, Hans. *Das echte Bild: Bildfragen als Glaubensfragen.* Munich: C. H. Beck, 2005.

Belting, Hans. *Likeness and Presence: A History of the Image before the Era of Art.* Translated by Edmund Jephcott. Chicago/London: University of Chicago Press, 1994.

Benedictus XVI. *Deus est caritas.* Encyclical. Vatican, 2006.

Benjamin, Walter. "Little History of Photography." In *Selected Writings,* vol. 2: *1927–1934,* translated by Rodney Livingstone and others. Cambridge, MA/London: Harvard University Press, 1999, pp. 507–30.

Benjamin, Walter. "The Work of Art in the Age of Its Technological Reproducibility: Third Version." In *Selected Writings,* vol. 4: *1938–1940.* Translated by Edmund Jephcott and others. Cambridge, MA/London: Belknap Press, 2006, pp. 251–83.

Benson, Bruce Ellis. *Graven Ideologies: Nietzsche, Derrida & Marion on Modern Idolatry.* Downers Grove, IL: InterVarsity Press, 2002.

Bentham, Jeremy. *The Panopticon Writings. Wo es war.* Edited and introduced by Miran Božovič. London: Verso, 1995.

Berger, John. *Ways of Seeing.* London: British Broadcasting Corporation and Penguin Books, 1972.

Berger, Teresa. "A Female Christ Child in the Manger and a Woman on the Cross, Or: The Historicity of the Jesus Event and the Inculturation of the Gospel," *Feminist Theology* 11 (January 1996): 32–45.

Bergmann, Sigurd. *I begynnelsen är bilden: En befriande bild-konst-kultur-teologi.* Stockholm: Proprius, 2003.

Berkouwer, G. C. *The Triumph of Grace in the Theology of Karl Barth: An Introduction and Critical Appraisal.* Translated by Harry R. Boer. Grand Rapids: Eerdmans, 1956.

Bernard, Bruce, ed. *Century: One Hundred Years of Human Progress, Regression, Suffering and Hope.* London: Phaidon Press, 1999.

Bernasconi, Robert, and Simon Critchley, eds. *Re-Reading Levinas.* Bloomington/Indianapolis: Indiana University Press, 1991.

Bette, Karl-Heinrich. "Wo ist der Körper?" In *Theorie als Passion: Niklas Luhmann zum 60 Geburtstag.* Edited by Dirk Baecker, Jürgen Markowitz, Rudolf Stichweh, Hartmann Tyrell, and Helmut Wilke. Frankfurt am Main: Suhrkamp, 1987, pp. 600–28.

Bexell, Peter. *Kyrkan som sakrament: Henri de Lubacs fundamentalecklesiologi.* Stockholm/Stehag: Brutus Östlings Bokförlag Symposion, 1997.

Bigwood, Carol. "Renaturalizing the Body (with the Help of Merleau-Ponty)." In *Body and Flesh.* Edited by Donn Welton. Malden, MA/Oxford: Blackwell, 1998, pp. 99–114.

Bjerg, Svend. *Synets teologi.* Frederiksberg, Denmark: Anis, 1999.

Blond, Phillip. "Introduction." In *Post-Secular Philosophy: Between Philosophy and Theology.* Edited by Phillip Blond. London/New York: Routledge, 1998, pp. 1–66.

Blondel, Éric. *Nietzsche, the Body and Culture: Philosophy as Philological Genealogy.* Translated by Séan Hand. Stanford: Stanford University Press, 1991.

Blumenberg, Hans. *The Legitimacy of the Modern Age.* Translated by Robert M. Wallace. Cambridge, MA: MIT Press, 1983.

Boeve, Lieven, and Lambert Leijssen, eds. *Sacramental Presence in a Postmodern Context.* Bibliotheca ephemeridum theologicarum lovaniensium CLX. Leuven: Leuven University Press, 2001.

Bordo, Susan. "Bringing Body to Theory." In *Body and Flesh: A Philosophical Reader.* Edited by Donn Welton. Malden, MA/Oxford: Blackwell, 1998, pp. 84–97.

Bordo, Susan. *The Male Body: A New Look at Men in Public and in Private.* New York: Farrar, Straus & Giroux, 1999.

Bordo, Susan. *Unbearable Weight: Feminism, Western Culture, and the Body.* Berkeley/Los Angeles/London: University of California Press, 1993.

Boswell, John. *Christianity, Social Tolerance, and Homosexuality: Gay People in Western Europe from the Beginning of the Christian Era to the Fourteenth Century.* Chicago/London: University of Chicago Press, 1980.

Boswell, John. *Same-Sex Unions in Premodern Europe.* New York: Villard Books, 1994.

Bourdieu, Pierre. *Esquisse d'une théorie de la pratique: Précédé de trois études d'ethnologie kabyle.* Travaux de droit, d'économie, de sociologie et de sciences politiques, no. 92. Geneva: Librairie Droz, 1972.

Bourdieu, Pierre. *Homo Academicus.* Translated by Peter Collier. Cambridge: Polity, 1988.

Bourdieu, Pierre. *On Television.* Translated by Priscilla Parkhurst Ferguson. New York: New Press, 1996.

Bourdieu, Pierre. *Outline of a Theory of Practice.* Translated by Richard Nice. Cambridge: Cambridge University Press, 1977.

Bouyer, Louis. *Liturgical Piety.* Notre Dame: University of Notre Dame Press, 1955.

Bovon, François. *Luke 1: A Commentary on the Gospel of Luke 1:1–9:50.* Translated by Christine M. Thomas. Minneapolis: Fortress Press, 2002.

Boyarin, Daniel. *Carnal Israel: Reading Sex in Talmudic Culture.* Berkeley/Los Angeles/ Oxford: University of California Press, 1993.

Boyarin, Daniel. *A Radical Jew: Paul and the Politics of Identity.* Berkeley: University of California Press, 1994.

Bramly, Serge, and Bettina Rheims. *INRI.* Munich: Gina Kehayoff Verlag, 1998.

Breidenthal, Thomas E. "Sanctifying Nearness." In *Our Selves, Our Souls & Bodies: Sexuality and the Household of God.* Edited by Charles Hefling. Cambridge, MA: Cowley, 1996, pp. 45–57.

Brilioth, Yngve. *Nattvarden i evangeliskt gudstjänstliv.* 2nd edition. Stockholm: Svenska kyrkans diakonistyrelses bokförlag, 1951.

Broady, Donald. *Sociologi och epistemologi: Om Pierre Bourdieus författarskap och den historiska epistemologin.* Skeptronserien. Stockholm: HLS förlag, 1990.

Brock, Rita Nakashima, and Rebecca Ann Parker. *Proverbs of Ashes: Violence, Redemptive Suffering and the Search for What Saves Us.* Boston: Beacon Press, 2001.

Brown, Peter. *The Body and Society: Men, Women and Sexual Renunciation in Early Christianity.* London: Faber & Faber, 1989.

Brown, Raymond E. *The Gospel according to John: I–XII.* Vol. 1. London: Geoffrey Chapman, 1971.

Bruns, Gerald L. "Midrash and Allegory." In *The Literary Guide to the Bible.* Edited by Robert Alter and Frank Kermode. Cambridge, MA: Belknap Press, 1987, pp. 625–46.

Bultmann, Rudolf. *New Testament and Mythology.* In *Kerygma and Myth: A Theological Debate.* With contributions by Rudolf Bultmann, Ernst Lohmeyer, Julius Schniewind, Friedrich Schumann, Helmut Thielecke, and Austin Farrer. Edited by Hans-Werner Bartsch. Translated by Reginald H. Fuller. London: SPCK, 1953.

Bultmann, Rudolf. *Theology of the New Testament,* vol. 1. Translated by Kendrick Grobel. London: SCM, 1988.

Bultmann, Rudolf. *Theology of the New Testament,* vol. 2. Translated by Kendrick Grobel. London: SCM, 1983.

Bultmann, Rudolf. *Das Urchristentum im Rahmen der antiken Religionen.* 2nd edition. Zürich: Artemis-Verlag, 1954.

Busch, Eberhard. *Unter dem Bogen des einen Bundes: Karl Barth und die Juden, 1933–1945.* Neukirchen-Vluyn: Neukirchener Verlag, 1996.

Butler, Judith. *Bodies That Matter: On the Discursive Limits of "Sex."* 2nd edition. New York/London: Routledge, 1993.

Butler, Judith. *Gender Trouble: Feminism and the Subversion of Identity.* New York/London: Routledge, 1999.

Butler, Judith. "Sexual Ideology and Phenomenological Description: A Feminist Critique of Merleau-Ponty's *Phenomenology of Perception.*" In *The Thinking Muse: Feminism and Modern French Philosophy.* Edited by Jeffner Allen and Iris Marion Young. Bloomington/Indianapolis: Indiana University Press, 1989, pp. 85–100.

Bynum, Caroline Walker. *Fragmentation and Redemption: Essays on Gender and the Human Body in Medieval Religion.* New York: Zone Books, 1992.

Bynum, Caroline Walker. *Holy Feast and Holy Fast: The Religious Significance of Food to Medieval Women.* Berkeley/Los Angeles/London: University of California Press, 1987.

Bynum, Caroline Walker. *Jesus as Mother: Studies in the Spirituality of the High Middle Ages.* Berkeley/Los Angeles/London: University of California Press, 1982.

Bynum, Caroline Walker. *Metamorphosis and Identity.* New York: Zone Books, 2001.

Bynum, Caroline Walker. *The Resurrection of the Body in Western Christianity, 200–1336.* New York: Columbia University Press, 1995.

Bynum, Caroline. "Why All the Fuss about the Body? A Medievalist's Perspective," *Critical Inquiry* 22 (1995): 1–33.

Byrskog, Samuel. *Story as History – History as Story: The Gospel Tradition in the Context of Ancient Oral History.* Wissenschaftliche Untersuchungen zum Neuen Testament 123. Tübingen: J. C. B. Mohr (Paul Siebeck), 2000.

Calcagno, Antonio. "The Incarnation, Michel Henry, and the Possibility of an Husserlian-Inspired Transcendental Life," *Heythrop Journal* 45, no. 3 (2004): 290–304.

Carlson, Thomas A. *Indiscretion: Finitude and the Naming of God.* Chicago: University of Chicago Press, 1999.

Carnley, Peter. *The Structure of Resurrection Belief.* Oxford: Clarendon Press, 1993.

Carrette, Jeremy R. *Foucault and Religion: Spiritual Corporality and Political Spirituality.* London: Routledge, 2000.

Casey, Edward. "The Ghost of Embodiment: On Bodily Habitudes and Schemata." In *Body and Flesh: A Philosophical Reader.* Edited by Donn Welton. Malden, MA/Oxford: Blackwell, 1998, pp. 207–25.

Castoriadis, Cornelius. *The Imaginary Institution of Society.* Translated by Kathleen Blamey. Cambridge: Polity Press, 1987.

Cataldi, Suzanne Laba. "Embodying Perceptions of Death: Emotional Apprehension and Reversibilities of Flesh." In *Chiasms: Merleau-Ponty's Notion of Flesh.* SUNY Series in Contemporary Continental Philosophy. Edited by Fred Evans and Leonard Lawlor. Albany: State University of New York Press, 2000, pp. 189–201.

Cavanaugh, William T. *Torture and Eucharist: Theology, Politics, and the Body of Christ.* Challenges in Contemporary Theology. Oxford/Malden, MA: Blackwell, 1998.

Caygill, Howard. *The Art of Judgement.* Oxford: Basil Blackwell, 1989.

Certeau, Michel de. *La faiblesse de croire.* Edited by Luce Giard. Paris: Éditions du Seuil, 1987.

Certeau, Michel de. *Heterologies: Discourse on the Other.* Theory and History of Literature, vol. 17. Translated by Brian Massumi. Minneapolis: University of Minnesota Press, 1987.

Certeau, Michel de. "How Is Christianity Thinkable Today?" In *The Postmodern God: A Theological Reader.* Edited by Graham Ward. Oxford/Malden, MA: Blackwell, 1997, pp. 142–55.

Certeau, Michel de. *The Mystic Fable: The Sixteenth and Seventeenth Centuries.* Translated by Michael B. Smith. Chicago: University of Chicago Press, 1995.

Certeau, Michel de. *The Practice of Everyday Life.* Translated by Steven Rendall. Berkeley/Los Angeles//London: University of California Press, 1988.

Certeau, Michel de. "The Weakness of Believing: From the Body to Writing, a Christian Transit." In *The Certeau Reader.* Edited by Graham Ward. Oxford/Malden, MA: Blackwell, 2000, pp. 214–43.

Chalier, Catherine. "Ethics and the Feminine." In *Re-Reading Levinas.* Edited by Robert Bernasconi and Simon Critchley. Bloomington/Indianapolis: Indiana University Press, 1991, pp. 119–29.

Chanter, Tina. *Ethics of Eros: Irigaray's Rewriting of the Philosophers.* New York/London: Routledge, 1995.

Chanter, Tina. "Wild Meaning: Luce Irigaray's Reading of Merleau-Ponty." In *Chiasms: Merleau-Ponty's Notion of Flesh.* SUNY Series in Contemporary Continental Philosophy. Edited by Fred Evans and Leonard Lawlor. Albany: State University of New York Press, 2000, pp. 219–36.

Chauvet, Louis-Marie. "The Broken Bread as Theological Figure of Eucharistic Presence." In *Sacramental Presence in a Postmodern Context.* Bibliotheca ephemeridum theologicarum lovaniensium CLX. Edited by Lieven Boeve and Lambert Leijssen. Leuven: Leuven University Press, 2001, pp. 236–62.

Chauvet, Louis-Marie. *Symbol and Sacrament: A Sacramental Reinterpretation of Christian Existence.* Translated by Patrick Madigan and Madeleine E. Beaumont. Collegeville, MN: Liturgical Press, 1995.

Chenu, M.-D. *Nature, Man, and Society in the Twelfth Century: Essays on New Theological Perspectives in the Latin West.* New edition. Selected, edited, and translated by Jerome Taylor and Lester K. Little. Chicago: University of Chicago Press, 1979.

Chrétien, Jean-Louis. *The Call and the Response.* Translated by Anne E. Davenport. New York: Fordham University Press, 2004.

Chrétien, Jean-Louis. *Hand to Hand: Listening to the Work of Art.* Translated by Stephen E. Lewis. Fordham: Fordham University Press, 2003.

Christianson, Eric S., Peter Francis, and William R. Telford, eds. *Cinéma Divinité: Religion, Theology and the Bible in Film.* London: SCM, 2005.

Cixous, Hélène. "Savoir." In *Veils.* Edited by Hélène Cixous and Jacques Derrida, translated by Geoffrey Bennington. Stanford: Stanford University Press, 2001, pp. 1–16.

Clark, Stephen R. L. "Plotinus: Body and Soul." In *The Cambridge Companion to Plotinus.* Edited by Lloyd P. Gerson. Cambridge: Cambridge University Press, 1999, pp. 275–91.

Clarke, Graham. *The Photograph.* Oxford History of Art. Oxford/New York: Oxford University Press, 1997.

Coakley, Sarah. *Christ without Absolutes: A Study of the Christology of Ernst Troeltsch.* Oxford: Clarendon Press, 1988.

Coakley, Sarah. *Powers and Submissions: Spirituality, Philosophy and Gender.* Challenges in Contemporary Theology. Oxford/Malden, MA: Blackwell, 2002.

Coakley, Sarah. "What Does Chalcedon Solve and What Does It Not? Some Reflections on the Status and Meaning of the Chalcedonian 'Definition.'" In *The Incarnation: An Interdisciplinary Symposium on the Incarnation of the Son of God.* Edited by Stephen T. Davis, Daniel Kendall, and Gerald O'Collins. New York: Oxford University Press, 2002.

Cook, John W. "Ugly Beauty in Christian Art." In *The Grotesque in Art and Literature: Theological Reflections.* Edited by James Luther Adams and Wilson Yates. Grand Rapids/Cambridge: Eerdmans, 1997, pp. 125–42.

Connerton, Paul. *How Societies Remember.* Cambridge: Cambridge University Press, 1989.

Corey, Susan. "The Religious Dimension of the Grotesque in Literature: Toni Morrison's *Beloved.*" In *The Grotesque in Art and Literature: Theological Reflections.* Edited by James Luther Adams and Wilson Yates. Grand Rapids/Cambridge: Eerdmans, 1997, pp. 227–42.

Countryman, L. William. *Dirt, Greed and Sex: Sexual Ethics in the New Testament and Their Implications for Today.* London: SCM Press, 2001.

Cranfield, C. E. B. *The Epistle to the Romans: An Exegetical and Critical Commentary.* Vol. 1: *I–VIII.* The International Critical Commentary. Edited by J. A. Emerton and C. E. B. Cranfield. Edinburgh: T. & T. Clark, 1975.

Crary, Jonathan. *Suspensions of Perception: Attention, Spectacle, and Modern Culture.* Cambridge, MA/London: MIT Press, 1999.

Crary, Jonathan. *Techniques of the Observer: On Vision and Modernity in the Nineteenth Century.* Cambridge, MA/London: MIT Press, 1990.

Crites, Stephen. "The Narrative Quality of Experience." In *Why Narrative? Readings in Narrative Theology.* Edited by Stanley Hauerwas and L. Gregory Jones. Grand Rapids: Eerdmans, 1989, pp. 65–88.

Cullmann, Oscar. *The Christology of the New Testament.* Translated by Shirley C. Guthrie and Charles A. M. Hall. London: SCM, 1963.

Dahlberg, Helena. *Vad är kött? Kroppen och människan i Merleau-Pontys filosofi.* Göteborg, Sweden: Glänta, 2013.

Dalferth, Ingolf U. *Der auferweckte Gekreuzigte: Zur Grammatik der Christologie.* Tübingen: J. C. B. Mohr (Paul Siebeck), 1994.

Dalferth, Ingolf U. *Jenseits von Mythos und Logos: Die christologische Transformation der Theologie.* Quaestiones Disputatae 142. Freiburg/Basel/Vienna: Herder, 1993.

Dalferth, Ingolf U. *Theology and Philosophy.* Signposts in Theology. Oxford: Basil Blackwell, 1988.

Daly, Mary. *Beyond God the Father: Toward a Philosophy of Women's Liberation.* New edition. London: Women's Press, 1986.

Davies, Jon, and Gerard Loughlin, eds. *Sex These Days: Essays on Theology, Sexuality and Society.* Studies in Theology and Sexuality 1. Sheffield: Sheffield Academic Press, 1997.

D'Costa, Gavin. *Sexing the Trinity: Gender, Culture and the Divine.* London: SCM, 2000.

D'Costa, Gavin. *Theology and Religious Pluralism: The Challenge of Other Religions.* Oxford: Basil Blackwell, 1986.

D'Costa, Gavin, ed. *Christian Uniqueness Reconsidered: The Myth of a Pluralistic Theology of Religions.* Maryknoll, NY: Orbis, 1990.

Debord, Guy. *The Society of the Spectacle.* Translated by Donald Nicholson-Smith. New York: Zone Books, 1995.

Deleuze, Gilles, and Félix Guattari. *What Is Philosophy?* Translated by Hugh Tomlinson and Graham Burchell. New York: Columbia University Press, 1994.

Derrida, Jacques. "Faith and Knowledge: The Two Sources of 'Religion' at the Limits of Reason Alone." In *Religion.* Edited by Jacques Derrida and Gianni Vattimo, translated by Samuel Weber. Cambridge: Polity Press, 1998, pp. 1–78.

Derrida, Jacques. "Foi et savoir: Les deux sources de la 'religion' aux limites de la simple raison." In *La religion.* Edited by Jacques Derrida and Gianni Vattimo. Paris: Éditions du Seuil, 1996, pp. 9–86.

Derrida, Jacques. *The Gift of Death.* Religion and Postmodernism. Translated by David Wills. Chicago: University of Chicago Press, 1995.

Derrida, Jacques. *Margins of Philosophy.* Translated by Alan Bass. Brighton, UK: Harvester Press, 1982.

Derrida, Jacques. *Memoirs of the Blind: The Self-Portrait and Other Ruins.* Translated by Pascale-Anne Brault and Michael Naas. Chicago: University of Chicago Press, 1993.

Derrida, Jacques. *Of Grammatology.* Corrected edition. Translated by Gayatri Chakravorty Spivak. Baltimore/London: Johns Hopkins University Press, 1997.

Derrida, Jacques. "On the Gift: A Discussion between Jacques Derrida and Jean-Luc Marion." In *God, the Gift and Postmodernism.* Edited by John D. Caputo and Michael J. Scanlon. Bloomington/Indianapolis: Indiana University Press, 1999, pp. 54–78.

Derrida, Jacques. *On Touching: Jean-Luc Nancy.* Meridian: Crossing Aesthetics. Translated by Christine Irizarry. Stanford: Stanford University Press, 2005.

Derrida, Jacques. "Plato's Pharmacy." In *Dissemination.* Translated by Barbara Johnson. London: Athlone Press, 1981, pp. 61–172.

Derrida, Jacques. *Voice and Phenomenon: Introduction to the Problem of the Sign in Husserl's Phenomenology.* Northwestern University Studies in Phenomenology & Existential Philosophy. Translated by Leonard Lawlor. Evanston, IL: Northwestern University Press, 2011.

Descartes, René. *Discours de la méthode/Discourse on the Method.* A Bilingual Edition with an Interpretative Essay. Translated and introduced by George Heffernan. Notre Dame/London: University of Notre Dame Press, 1994.

Descartes, René. *Meditationes de prima philosophia/Meditations on First Philosophy.* A Bilingual Edition. Translated and introduced by George Heffernan. Notre Dame/London: University of Notre Dame Press, 1990.

Descartes, René. "Optics." In *The Visual Culture Reader.* Edited by Nicholas Mirzoeff. London/New York: Routledge, 1998, pp. 60–65.

Descartes, René. *The Passions of the Soul.* Translated by Stephen Voss. Indianapolis/Cambridge: Hackett, 1989.

Dinzelbacher, Peter. *Bernhard von Clairvaux: Leben und Werk des berühmten Zister-*

ziensers. Gestalten des Mittelalters und der Renaissance. Edited by Peter Herde. Darmstadt: Wissenschaftliche Buchgesellschaft, 1998.

Dionysius the Areopagite. *The Complete Works*. The Classics of Western Spirituality. Translated by Colm Luibheid. Foreword, notes, and translation collaboration by Paul Rorem. Mahwah, NJ: Paulist Press, 1987.

Dix, Gregory. *The Shape of the Liturgy*. 2nd edition. London: Dacre Press, 1960.

Donfried, Karl P. "Introduction: The Nature and Scope of the Romans Debate." In *The Romans Debate*. Edited by Karl P. Donfried. Minneapolis: Augsburg, 1977, pp. ix-xvii.

Dostoevsky, Fyodor. *The Idiot*. Translated by Richard Pevear and Larissa Volokhonsky. New York: Vintage Classics, 2003.

Douglas, Mary. *Purity and Danger: An Analysis of Concepts of Pollution and Taboo*. London/New York: Routledge, 2002.

Dreyfus, Hubert L. *On the Internet*. London/New York: Routledge, 2001.

Dumeige, Gervais. *Nicée II*. Histoire des conciles oecuméniques vol. 4. Edited by Gervais Dumeige. Paris: Éditions de l'Orante, 1978.

Dunn, James D. G. *Christology in the Making: An Inquiry into the Origins of the Doctrine of the Incarnation*. 2nd edition. London: SCM, 1989.

Dunn, James D. G. *Romans 1–8*. Word Biblical Commentary. Vol. 38A. Edited by David A. Hubbard, Glenn W. Barker, et al. Dallas: Word Books, 1988.

Dunn, James D. G. *Unity and Diversity in the New Testament: An Inquiry into the Character of Earliest Christianity*. London: SCM, 1977.

Dupré, Louis. *Passage to Modernity: An Essay on the Hermeneutics of Nature and Culture*. New Haven/London: Yale University Press, 1993.

Dyke, Doris. "Crucified Woman: Art and the Experience of Faith," *Toronto Journal of Theology* 5, no. 2 (1989): 161–69.

Eiesland, Nancy L. *The Disabled God: Toward a Liberatory Theology of Disability*. Nashville: Abingdon Press, 1994.

Elkins, James. *The Object Stares Back: On the Nature of Seeing*. A Harvest Book. San Diego/New York/London: Harcourt, 1997.

Elshtain, Jean Bethke. *Public Man, Private Woman: Women in Social and Political Thought*. 2nd edition. Princeton: Princeton University Press, 1993.

Eriksson, Anne-Louise. *Kvinnor talar om Jesus: En bok om feministisk kristologisk praxis*. Nora, Sweden: Nya Doxa, 1999.

Eriksson, Anne-Louise. *The Meaning of Gender in Theology: Problems and Possibilities*. Acta Universitatis Upsaliensis. Uppsala Women's Studies. A. Women in Religion: 6. Uppsala: Uppsala University, 1995.

Eriksson, Anne-Louise, ed. *Tolkning för livet: Åtta teologer om bibelns auktoritet*. Stockholm: Verbum, 2004.

Eusebius of Caesarea. *Church History*. In *The Nicene and Post-Nicene Fathers*, ser. 2, vol. 2: *Eusebius*. Edited by Philip Schaff and Henry Wace. Grand Rapids: Eerdmans, 1952.

Evans, Fred, and Leonard Lawlor, ed. *Chiasms: Merleau-Ponty's Notion of Flesh*. SUNY Series in Contemporary Continental Philosophy. Albany: State University of New York Press, 2000.

Evdokimov, Paul. *The Art of the Icon: A Theology of Beauty.* Translated by Steven Bigham. Redondo Beach, CA: Oakwood, 1990.

Everson, Stephen. "Psychology." In *The Cambridge Companion to Aristotle.* Edited by Jonathan Barnes. Cambridge: University of Cambridge, 1995, pp. 168–94.

Fabian, Johannes. *Time and the Other: How Anthropology Makes Its Object.* New edition. New York: Columbia University Press, 2002.

Feher, Michel. "Introduction." In *Fragments for a History of the Human Body.* Part One. Edited by Michel Feher together with Ramona Naddaff and Nadia Tazi. New York: Zone Books, 1989, pp. 11–17.

Ferry, Luc. *Homo Aestheticus: The Invention of Taste in the Democratic Age.* Translated by Robert de Loaiza. Chicago: University of Chicago Press, 1993.

Fiddes, Paul S. *The Creative Suffering of God.* Oxford: Clarendon Press, 1988.

Fiddes, Paul S. *The Promised End: Eschatology in Theology and Literature.* Challenges in Contemporary Theology. Oxford: Blackwell, 2000.

Fiddes, Paul S. "The Status of Woman in the Thought of Karl Barth." In *After Eve: Women, Theology and the Christian Tradition.* Edited by Janet Martin Soskice. London: Marshall Pickering, 1990, pp. 138–55.

Finaldi, Gabriele, et al. *The Image of Christ: The catalogue of the exhibition* Seeing Salvation. Introduction by Neil MacGregor. London: National Gallery, 2000.

Flood, Gavin. *Beyond Phenomenology: Rethinking the Study of Religion.* London: Cassell, 1999.

Flusser, Vilém. *Towards a Philosophy of Photography.* Translated by Anthony Mathews. London: Reaktion Books, 2000.

Ford, David F. *Barth and God's Story: Biblical Narrative and the Theological Method of Karl Barth in the 'Church Dogmatics.'* 2nd edition. Frankfurt am Main/Bern/New York: Peter Lang, 1985.

Ford, David F. *Self and Salvation: Being Transformed.* Cambridge Studies in Christian Doctrine. Cambridge: Cambridge University Press, 1999.

Foucault, Michel. *Abnormal: Lectures at the Collège de France, 1974–1975.* Translated by Graham Burchell. New York: Picador, 2003.

Foucault, Michel. *Discipline and Punish: The Birth of the Prison.* Translated by Alan Sheridan. New York: Vintage Books, 1977.

Foucault, Michel. *History of Sexuality,* vol. 1: *An Introduction.* Translated by Robert Hurley. New York: Pantheon Books, 1978.

Foucault, Michel. *History of Sexuality,* vol. 2: *The Use of Pleasure.* Translated by Robert Hurley. New York: Vintage Books, 1990.

Foucault, Michel. *History of Sexuality,* vol. 3: *The Care of Self.* Translated by Robert Hurley. New York: Pantheon Books, 1986.

Foucault, Michel. *The Order of Things: An Archaeology of the Human Sciences.* Translated from the French. London: Routledge, 1986.

Foucault, Michel. *Religion and Culture.* Manchester Studies in Religion, Culture and Gender. Edited by Jeremy R. Carrette. Manchester: Manchester University Press, 1999.

Fowl, Stephen. Review of Daniel Boyarin, *A Radical Jew.* In *Modern Theology* 12, no. 1 (1996): 131–33.

Fredlund, Anna Petronella. "När tanken tar kropp—om Merleau-Pontys filosofi." In

Lovtal till filosofin: Essäer I urval. Maurice Merleau-Ponty. Translated into Swedish by Anna Petronella Fredlund. Stockholm/Stehag: Brutus Östlings Bokförlag Symposion, 2004, pp. 7–40.

Frei, Hans W. *The Eclipse of Biblical Narrative: A Study in Eighteenth and Nineteenth Century Hermeneutics.* New Haven/London: Yale University Press, 1974.

Frei, Hans W. *The Identity of Jesus Christ: The Hermeneutical Bases of Dogmatic Theology.* Philadelphia: Fortress Press, 1975.

Frei, Hans W. *Theology & Narrative: Selected Essays.* Edited by George Hunsinger and William C. Placher. New York/Oxford: Oxford University Press, 1993.

Frymer-Kensky, Tikva, David Novak, Peter Ochs, et al., eds. *Christianity in Jewish Terms.* Boulder, CO/Oxford: Westview Press, 2000.

Funkenstein, Amos. *Theology and the Scientific Imagination from the Middle Ages to the Seventeenth Century.* Princeton: Princeton University Press, 1986.

Furnish, Victor Paul. *II Corinthians.* Translation with introduction, notes, and commentary. The Anchor Bible vol. 32A. New York/London: Doubleday, 1974.

Gadamer, Hans-Georg. *Neuere Philosophie: I. Hegel, Husserl, Heidegger.* Gesammelte Werke vol. 3. Tübingen: J. C. B. Mohr (Paul Siebeck), 1987.

Gadamer, Hans-Georg. *Truth and Method.* 2nd, revised edition. Translation revised by Joel Weinsheimer and Donald G. Marshall. London/New York: Continuum, 2004.

Geertz, Clifford. *The Interpretation of Cultures: Selected Essays.* New York: Basic Books, 1973.

Gerhardsson, Birger. *The Origins of the Gospel Traditions.* London: SCM, 1979.

Giakalis, Ambrosios. *Images of the Divine: The Theology of the Icons at the Seventh Ecumenical Council.* Studies in the History of Christian Thought vol. 54. Leiden/New York/Cologne: E. J. Brill, 1994.

Gnilka, Joachim. *Das Evangelium nach Markus: Mk 1–8,26.* First volume. Evangelisch-Katholischer Kommentar zum Neuen Testament vol. II/1. Edited by Josef Blank, Rudolf Schnackenburg, et al. 3rd revised edition. Zürich/Braunschweig/Neukirchen-Vluyn: Benziger Verlag/Neukirchener Verlag, 1989.

Gnilka, Joachim. *Das Evangelium nach Markus: Mk 8,27–16,20.* 2nd volume. Evangelisch-Katholischer Kommentar zum Neuen Testament vol. II/2. Edited by Josef Blank, Rudolf Schnackenburg, et al. 3rd revised edition. Zürich/Einsiedeln/Neukirchen-Vluyn: Benziger Verlag/Neukirchener Verlag, 1989.

Golding, Martin. "Photography, Memory and Survival," *Literature and Theology* 14, no. 1 (2000): 52–67.

Goodchild, Philip. *Capitalism and Religion: The Price of Piety.* London: Routledge, 2002.

Goodman, Nelson. *Languages of Art: An Approach to a Theory of Symbols.* 2nd edition. Indianapolis/Cambridge: Hackett, 1976.

Goppelt, Leonhard. *Theology of the New Testament,* vol. 2: *The Variety and Unity of the Apostolic Witness to Christ.* Translated by John Alsup. Grand Rapids: Eerdmans, 1982.

Gorringe, T. J. *The Education of Desire: Towards a Theology of the Senses.* London: SCM, 2001.

Graham, Elaine L. *The Representation of the Posthuman.* Manchester: Manchester University Press, 2002.

Grässer, Erich. *An die Hebräer: Hebr. 1–6.* Part 1. Evangelisch-Katholischer Kommentar zum Neuen Testament vol. XVII/1. Edited by Norbert Brox, Rudolf Schnackenburg, et al. Braunschweig/Neukirchen-Vluyn: Benziger Verlag/Neukirchener Verlag, 1990.

Gray, Janette. "Celibacy These Days." In *Sex These Days.* Studies in Theology and Sexuality 1. Edited by Jon Davies and Gerard Loughlin. Sheffield: Sheffield Academic Press, 1997, pp. 153–56.

Green, Michael, ed. *The Truth of God Incarnate.* London: Hodder & Stoughton, 1977.

Gregory of Nazianzus. "Epistle 101." In *Nicene and Post-Nicene Fathers,* ser. 2, vol. 7: *S. Cyril of Jerusalem, S. Gregory Nazianzen.* Edited by Philip Schaff. Grand Rapids: Eerdmans, 1977.

Gregory of Nazianzus. *Five Theological Orations.* In *On God and Christ: Five Theological Orations and Two Letters to Cledonius.* Popular Patristics Series, translated by Frederick Williams and Lionel Wickman. Crestwood, NY: St. Vladimir's Seminary Press, 2002.

Gregory of Nyssa. *Life of Moses.* Classics of Western Spirituality. Translated by Abraham J. Malherbe and Everett Ferguson. New York: Paulist Press, 1978.

Grenholm, Cristina. *Barmhärtig och sårbar. En bok om Kristen tro på Jesus.* Stockholm: Verbum, 1999.

Grenholm, Cristina. *Moderskap och kärlek: Schabloner och tankeutrymme i feministteologisk livsåskådningsreflektion.* Nora, Sweden: Nya Doxa, 2005.

Greshake, Gisberth. "Theologiegeschichtliche und systematische Untersuchungen zum Verständnis der Auferstehung." In *Resurrectio mortuorum: Zum theologischen Verständnis der leiblichen Auferstehung.* Edited by Gisbert Greshake and Jacob Kremer. Darmstadt: Wissenschaftliche Buchgesellschaft, 1986, pp. 163–371.

Grillmeier, Aloys. *Jesus der Christus im Glauben der Kirche,* vol. I: *Von der apostolischen Zeit bis zum Konzil von Chalcedon (451).* 3rd improved and expanded edition. Freiburg: Herder, 1990.

Grimwood, Steven. "Iconography and Postmodernity," *Literature and Theology* 17, no. 1 (2003): 76–97.

Grosz, Elisabeth. *Volatile Bodies: Towards a Corporeal Feminism.* Bloomington/Indianapolis: Indiana University Press, 1994.

Gustafsson, Johanna. *Kyrka och kön – om könskonstruktioner i Svenska kyrkan 1945–1985.* Stockholm/Stehag: Brutus Östlings Bokförlag Symposion, 2001.

Haag, Ingemar. *Det groteska: Kroppens språk och språkets kropp i svensk lyrisk modernism.* Stockholm: Aiolos, 1999.

Habermas, Jürgen. "Der Universalitätsanspruch der Hermeneutik." In *Hermeneutik und Ideologikritik.* Edited by Karl-Otto Apel. Frankfurt am Main: Suhrkamp, 1971, pp. 120–59.

Hadot, Pierre. *Philosophy as a Way of Life: Spiritual Exercises from Socrates to Foucault.* Translated by Michael Chase. Oxford/Malden, MA: Blackwell, 1995.

Hafstad, Kjetil. *Wort und Geschichte: Das Geschichtsverständnis Karl Barths.* Beiträge zur evangelischen Theologie. Munich: Chr. Kaiser, 1985.

Haight, Roger. *Jesus Symbol of God.* Maryknoll, NY: Orbis, 1999.

Hall, Douglas John. *God & Human Suffering: An Exercise in the Theology of the Cross.* Minneapolis: Augsburg, 1986.

Hallonsten, Gösta. "Är Jesus frälsare? Skiftande frälsningsuppfattningar och Jesus som konstant i teologin," *Svensk Teologisk Kvartalskrift* 77 (2001): 107–17.

Hallonsten, Gösta. "Harnack, helleniseringen och frågan om trons inkulturation—några synpunkter." In *Med hjärtats öga: Studier och essayer tillägnade Lars Cavallin på sextioårsdagen 15 augusti 2000.* Edited by Ann Blückert and Kjell Blückert. Vejbystrand, Sweden: Catholica, 2000, pp. 239–52.

Hallonsten, Gösta. "Sexualiteten och traditionen: Svar till Ola Sigurdson," *Svensk Teologisk Kvartalskrift* 80, no. 3 (2004): 120–23.

Hanson, R. P. C. *The Search for the Christian Doctrine of God: The Arian Controversy 318–381.* Edinburgh: T. & T. Clark, 1988.

Hansson, Stina. *Ett språk för själen: Litterära former i den svenska andaktslitteraturen 1650–1720.* Skrifter utgivna av Litteraturvetenskapliga institutionen vid Göteborgs universitet 20. Göteborg, Sweden, 1991.

Haraway, Donna J. *Simians, Cyborgs, and Women: The Reinvention of Nature.* London: Free Association Books, 1991.

Hardt, Michael, and Antonio Negri. *Empire.* Cambridge, MA: Harvard University Press, 2000.

Harnack, Adolf von. *History of Dogma,* vol. I. Translated by Neil Buchanan. New York: Dover Publications, 1961.

Harnack, Adolf von. *History of Dogma,* vols. IV and V. Translated by Neil Buchanan. New York: Dover Publications, 1961.

Harpham, Geoffrey Galt. *The Ascetical Imperative in Culture and Criticism.* Chicago: University of Chicago Press, 1987.

Harpham, Geoffrey Galt. *On the Grotesque: Strategies of Contradiction in Art and Literature.* Princeton: Princeton University Press, 1982.

Harries, Karsten. *Infinity and Perspective.* Cambridge, MA/London: MIT Press, 2001.

Harrison, Beverly Wildung, and Carter Heyward. "Pain and Pleasure: Avoiding the Confusions of Christian Tradition in Feminist Theory." In *Sexuality and the Sacred: Sources for Theological Reflection.* Edited by James B. Nelson and Sandra P. Longfellow. London: Mowbray, 1994, pp. 131–48.

Harrison, Verna E. F. "The Breast of the Father." In *Feminism & Theology.* Oxford Readings in Feminism. Edited by Janet Martin Soskice and Diana Lipton. Oxford/New York: Oxford University Press, 2003, pp. 327–32.

Hart, David Bentley. *The Beauty of the Infinite: The Aesthetics of Christian Truth.* Grand Rapids: Eerdmans, 2003.

Harvey, Susan A. "Embodiment in Time and Eternity: A Syriac Perspective." In *Theology and Sexuality: Classic and Contemporary Readings.* Blackwell Readings in Modern Theology. Edited by Eugene F. Rogers Jr.. Malden, MA/Oxford: Blackwell, 2002, pp. 3–22.

Hauerwas, Stanley. *Naming the Silences: God, Medicine, and the Problem of Suffering.* Grand Rapids: Eerdmans, 1990.

Hays, Richard B. *Echoes of Scripture in the Letters of Paul.* New Haven/London: Yale University Press, 1989.

Healy, Nicholas M. *Church, World and the Christian Life: Practical-Prophetic Ecclesiology.* Cambridge Studies in Christian Doctrine. Cambridge: Cambridge University Press, 2000.

Healy, Nicholas M. "The Logic of Karl Barth's Ecclesiology: Analysis, Assessment and Proposed Modifications," *Modern Theology* 10, no. 3 (1994): 253–70.

Heelas, Paul, and Linda Woodhead, eds. *The Spiritual Revolution: Why Religion Is Giving Way to Spirituality.* Religion and Spirituality in the Modern World. Malden, MA/Oxford/Victoria: Blackwell, 2005.

Hefling, Charles, ed. *Our Selves, Our Souls & Bodies: Sexuality and the Household of God.* Cambridge, MA: Cowley, 1996.

Hegel, Georg Wilhelm Friedrich. *Enzyklopädie der philosophischen Wissenschaften im Grundrisse: Zweiter Teil: Die Naturphilosophie,* Werke 9. Frankfurt am Main: Suhrkamp, 1986.

Hegel, Georg Wilhelm Friedrich. *Phenomenology of Spirit.* Translated by A. V. Miller. Oxford: Oxford University Press, 1977.

Hegel, Georg Wilhelm Friedrich. *Vorlesungen über die Philosophie der Religion I.* Werke 16. Frankfurt am Main: Suhrkamp, 1990.

Heidegger, Martin. *Being and Time.* Translated by John Macquarrie and Edward Robinson. Oxford/Malden, MA: Blackwell, 1962.

Heidegger, Martin. *Identity and Difference.* Translated by Joan Stambaugh. New York: Harper & Row, 1969.

Heidegger, Martin. *Off the Beaten Track.* Edited and translated by Julian Young and Kenneth Haynes. Cambridge: Cambridge University Press, 2002.

Heidegger, Martin. *On Time and Being.* Translated by Joan Stambaugh. New York: Harper & Row, 1972.

Heidegger, Martin. *Pathmarks.* Translated by James G. Hart and John C. Maraldo. Cambridge: Cambridge University Press, 1998.

Heidegger, Martin. *Poetry, Language, Thought.* Translated by Albert Hofstadter. New York: Harper & Row, 1971.

Hekman, Susan. "Material Bodies." In *Body and Flesh: A Philosophical Reader.* Edited by Donn Welton. Malden, MA/Oxford: Blackwell, 1998, pp. 60–70.

Hemming, Laurence Paul. "After Heidegger: Transubstantiation." In *Sacramental Presence in a Postmodern Context.* Bibliotheca ephemeridum theologicarum lovaniensium CLX. Edited by Lieven Boeve and Lambert Leijssen. Leuven: Leuven University Press, 2001, pp. 299–309.

Henry, Michel. *Incarnation: Une philosophie de la chair.* Paris: Éditions de Seuil, 2000.

Heraclitus. *The Art and Thought of Heraclitus: An Edition of the Fragments with Translation and Commentary,* by Charles H. Kahn. Cambridge: Cambridge University Press, 1979.

Heschel, Abraham J. *The Prophets: An Introduction,* vol. 1. New York/Cambridge: Harper Torchbooks, 1969.

Hick, John. *The Metaphor of God Incarnate: Christology in a Pluralistic Age.* Louisville: Westminster/John Knox Press, 1993.

Hick, John, ed. *The Myth of God Incarnate.* London: SCM, 1977.

Hök, Gösta. *Zinzendorfs Begriff der Religion.* Uppsala Universitets Årsskrift, 1948:6. Uppsala/Leipzig: Lundequistska bokhandeln/Otto Harrassowitz, 1948.

Hollywood, Amy. *Sensible Ecstasy: Mysticism, Sexual Difference, and the Demands of History.* Religion and Postmodernism. Chicago: University of Chicago Press, 2002.

Holmberg, Bengt. "Den historiske Jesus—nutida diskussionsläge och bedömning."

In *Jesustolkningar i dag: Tio teologer om kristologi.* Stockholm: Verbum, 1995, pp. 23–54.

Honneth, Axel. *Verdinglichung: Eine anerkennungstheoretische Studie.* Frankfurt am Main: Suhrkamp, 2005.

Horner, Robyn. *Rethinking God as Gift: Marion, Derrida and the Limits of Phenomenology.* New York: Fordham University Press, 2001.

Hughes, Graham. *Worship as Meaning: A Liturgical Theology for Late Modernity.* Cambridge Studies in Christian Doctrine. Cambridge: Cambridge University Press, 2003.

Hull, John M. *In the Beginning There Was Darkness: A Blind Person's Conversations with the Bible.* London: SCM Press, 2001.

Hunsinger, George. *How to Read Karl Barth: The Shape of His Theology.* New York/Oxford: Oxford University Press, 1991.

Husserl, Edmund. *Cartesian Meditations: An Introduction to Phenomenology.* Translated by Dorion Cairns. The Hague/Dordrecht: Nijhoff/Kluwer, 1973.

Husserl, Edmund. *The Crisis of European Sciences and Transcendental Phenomenology: An Introduction to Phenomenology.* Translated by David Carr. Evanston, IL: Northwestern University Press, 1970.

Husserl, Edmund. *The Idea of Phenomenology.* Collected Works vol. 8. Translated by Lee Hardy. Dordrecht/Boston/London: Kluwer Academic Publishers, 1999.

Husserl, Edmund. *Ideas Pertaining to a Pure Phenomenology and to a Phenomenological Philosophy: First Book: Introduction to a Pure Phenomenology.* Edmund Husserl Collected Works vol. 2. Translated by F. Kersten. The Hague/Boston/Lancaster: Martinus Nijhoff, 1983.

Husserl, Edmund. *Ideas Pertaining to a Pure Phenomenology and to a Phenomenological Philosophy: Second Book: Studies in the Phenomenology of Constitution.* Edmund Husserl Collected Works, vol. 3. Translated by Richard Rojcewicz and André Schuwer. Dordrecht/Boston/London: Kluwer Academic Publishers, 1989.

Husserl, Edmund. *Die Idee der Phänomenologie: Fünf Vorlesungen.* Philosophische Bibliothek vol. 392. Edited by Paul Janssen. Hamburg: Felix Meiner Verlag, 1986.

Hütter, Reinhard. *Theologie als kirchliche Praktik: Zur Verhältnisbestimmung von Kirche, Lehre und Theologie.* Beiträge zur evangelischen Theologie vol. 117. Gütersloh: Chr. Kaiser/Gütersloher Verlagshaus, 1997.

Ignatius. "Romans." In *The Apostolic Fathers I.* Loeb Classical Library. Translated by Bart D. Ehrman. Cambridge, MA/London: Harvard University Press, 2003.

Ihde, Don. "Bodies, Virtual Bodies and Technology." In *Body and Flesh: A Philosophical Reader.* Edited by Donn Welton. Malden, MA/Oxford: Blackwell, 1998, pp. 349–57.

Irenaeus. *Against Heresies.* In *Ante-Nicene Fathers,* vol. 1: *The Apostolic Fathers, Justin Martyr, Irenaeus.* Edited by Alexander Roberts and James Donaldson. Revised by A. Cleveland Coxe. Grand Rapids: Eerdmans, 1979.

Irigaray, Luce. "Equal to Whom?" Translated by Robert L. Mazzola. In *The Postmodern God: A Theological Reader.* Edited by Graham Ward. Oxford: Blackwell, 1997, pp. 198–213.

Irigaray, Luce. *An Ethics of Sexual Difference.* Translated by Carolyn Burke and Gillian C. Gill. Ithaca, NY: Cornell University Press, 1993.

Irigaray, Luce. "Fécondité de la caresse: Lecture de Lévinas *Totalité et infini,* section IV, B, 'Phénoménologie de l'éros.'" In *Éthique de la difference sexuelle.* Collection "critique." Paris: Les Éditions de Minuit, 1984, pp. 173–99.

Irigaray, Luce. *je, tu, nous: Toward a Culture of Difference.* Translated by Alison Martin. New York: Routledge, 1993.

Irigaray, Luce. "The Language of Man." Translated by Erin G. Carlston. In *Cultural Critique* 13 (1989): 191–202.

Irigaray, Luce. *Marine Lover of Friedrich Nietzsche.* Translated by Gillian C. Gill. New York: Columbia University Press, 1991.

Irigaray, Luce. "Questions to Emmanuel Levinas: On the Divinity of Love." Translated by Margaret Whitford. In *Re-Reading Levinas.* Edited by Robert Bernasconi and Simon Critchley. Bloomington/Indianapolis: Indiana University Press, 1991, pp. 109–18.

Irigaray, Luce. *Sexes and Genealogies.* Translated by Gillian C. Gill. New York: Columbia University Press, 1993.

Irigaray, Luce. *This Sex Which Is Not One.* Translated by Catherine Porter with Carolyn Burke. Ithaca, NY: Cornell University Press, 1985.

Isherwood, Lisa, and Elizabeth Stuart. *Introducing Body Theology.* Introductions in Feminist Theology 2. Sheffield: Sheffield Academic Press, 1998.

Jacob, Louis. "The Body in Jewish Worship: Three Rituals Examined." In *Religion and the Body.* Edited by Sarah Coakley. Cambridge: Cambridge University Press, 2000, pp. 71–89.

Janicaud, Dominique. *The Theological Turn of French Phenomenology.* In *Phenomenology and the "Theological Turn": The French Debate.* Dominique Janicaud et al. New York: Fordham University Press, 2000.

Jarrick, Arne. *Den himmelske älskaren: Herrnhutisk väckelse, vantro och sekularisering i 1700-talets Sverige.* Stockholm: Ordfront, 1987.

Jarrick, Arne. "Har könen blivit fler med tiden? En kritik av Thomas Laqueur." In *Seklernas sex: Bidrag till sexualitetens historia.* Edited by Åsa Bergenheim and Lena Lennerhed. Stockholm: Carlsson, 1997, pp. 22–38.

Jay, Martin. *Downcast Eyes: The Denigration of Vision in Twentieth-Century French Thought.* Berkeley/Los Angeles/London: University of California Press, 1993.

Jay, Martin. "Scopic Regimes of Modernity." In *The Visual Culture Reader.* Edited by Nicholas Mirzoeff. London/New York: Routledge, 1998, pp. 66–69.

Jeanrond, Werner G. "Att reflektera över Gud idag," *Svensk Teologisk Kvartalskrift* 71, no. 4 (1995): 171–76.

Jeanrond, Werner G. *Guds närvaro: Teologiska reflexioner I.* Lund: Arcus, 1998.

Jeanrond, Werner G. "Teologen som tolk." In *Penelopes väv: För en filosofisk och teologisk pathologi.* Edited by Mats Rosengren and Ola Sigurdson. Logos/Pathos 1. Göteborg, Sweden: Glänta, 2003, pp. 59–82.

Jeanrond, Werner G. *Text and Interpretation as Categories of Theological Thinking.* Translated by Thomas J. Wilson. New York: Crossroad, 1988.

Jeanrond, Werner G. *Theological Hermeneutics: Development and Significance.* New York: Crossroad, 1991.

Joas, Hans. "On the Articulation of Experience." In *Do We Need Religion? On the Ex-*

perience of Self-Transcendence. The Yale Cultural Sociology Series. Translated by Alex Skinner. Boulder, CO: Paradigm Publishers, 2008, pp. 37–48.

Joest, Wilfried. *Ontologie der Person bei Luther.* Göttingen: Vandenhoeck & Ruprecht, 1967.

Johannisson, Karin. *Kroppens tunna skal: Sex essäer om kropp, historia och kultur.* Stockholm: Bokförlaget Pan, 1998.

Johansen, Maria. *Offentlig skrift om det hemliga: Raison d'état, SOU och varulven.* Logos/Pathos 4. Göteborg: Glänta, 2005.

John Chrysostom. *On the Incomprehensible Nature of God.* Fathers of the Church Series. Translated by Paul W. Harkins. Washington, DC: Catholic University of America Press, 1984.

John of Damascus. *On the Divine Images.* Translated by David Anderson. Crestwood, NY: St. Vladimir's Seminary Press, 2000.

John of the Cross. *The Living Flame of Love.* In *The Collected Works of St. John of the Cross.* Translated by Kieran Kavanaugh and Otilio Rodriguez. Washington, DC: ICS Publications, 1979.

Johnson, Elizabeth A. "Wisdom Was Made Flesh and Pitched Her Tent among Us." In *Reconstructing the Christ Symbol.* Edited by Maryanne Stevens. Mahwah, NJ: Paulist Press, 1993, pp. 95–117.

Jonas, Hans. *Das Prinzip Leben: Ansätze zu einer philosophischen Biologie.* Frankfurt am Main: Suhrkamp, 1997.

Jones, Serene. *Feminist Theory and Christian Theology: Cartographies of Grace.* Guides to Theological Inquiry. Minneapolis: Augsburg Fortress, 2000.

Jones, Serene. "This God Which Is Not One: Irigaray and Barth on the Divine." In *Transfiguration: Theology & the French Feminists.* Edited by C. W. Maggie Kim, Susan M. St. Ville, and Susan M. Simonaitis. Minneapolis: Fortress Press, 1993, pp. 109–41.

Jordan, Mark D. *Blessing Same-Sex Unions: The Perils of Queer Romance and the Confusions of Christian Marriage.* Chicago/London: University of Chicago Press, 2005.

Jordan, Mark D. *The Ethics of Sex.* New Dimensions to Religious Ethics. Oxford/Malden, MA: Blackwell, 2002.

Jordan, Mark D. *The Invention of Sodomy in Christian Theology.* Chicago/London: University of Chicago Press, 1997.

Judovitz, Dalia. *The Culture of the Body: Genealogies of Modernity.* Ann Arbor: University of Michigan Press, 2001.

Julian of Norwich. *Showings: The Short Text.* The Classics of Western Spirituality. Edited and translated by Edmund College and James Walsh. Mahwah, NJ: Paulist Press, 1978.

Jüngel, Eberhard. *God as the Mystery of the World: On the Foundation of the Theology of the Crucified One in the Dispute between Theism and Atheism.* Translated by Darrell L. Guder. Edinburgh: T. & T. Clark, 1983.

Kant, Immanuel. *Critique of the Power of Judgment.* The Cambridge Edition of the Works of Immanuel Kant. Translated by Paul Guyer and Eric Matthews. Cambridge: Cambridge University Press, 2000.

Kant, Immanuel. *Groundwork of the Metaphysics of Morals.* Cambridge Texts in the

History of Philosophy. Edited and translated by Mary Gregor. Cambridge: Cambridge University Press, 1998.

Kantorowicz, Ernst H. *The King's Two Bodies: A Study in Mediaeval Political Theology.* With a new preface by William Chester Jordan. Princeton: Princeton University Press, 1997.

Käsemann, Ernst. *An die Römer.* 4th edition. Handbuch zum Neuen Testament, 8a. Edited by Günther Bornkamm. Tübingen: J. C. B. Mohr (Paul Siebeck), 1980.

Kasper, Walter. *Jesus the Christ.* New edition. London/New York: T. & T. Clark, 2011.

Kavanagh, Aidan. *On Liturgical Theology.* Collegeville, MN: Liturgical Press, 1992.

Kayser, Wolfgang. *The Grotesque in Art and Literature.* Translated by Ulrich Weisstein. New York/Toronto: McGraw-Hill, 1966.

Kearney, Richard. *The God Who May Be: A Hermeneutics of Religion.* Bloomington: Indiana University Press, 2001.

Kearney, Richard. *On Stories.* Thinking in Action. London/New York: Routledge, 2002.

Kearney, Richard. *Strangers, Gods and Monsters: Interpreting Otherness.* London/New York: Routledge, 2003.

Kelly, J. N. D. *Early Christian Creeds.* 3rd edition. Harlow, UK: Longman, 1972.

Kemp, Peter. *Lévinas: En introduktion.* Translated by Rikard Hedenblad. Göteborg, Sweden: Daidalos, 1992.

Kerr, Fergus. *Immortal Longings: Versions of Transcending Humanity.* Notre Dame: University of Notre Dame Press, 1997.

Kieffer, René. "Den mångfacetterade kristologin i Nya testamentet." In *Jesustolkningar i dag: Tio teologer om kristologi.* Stockholm: Verbum, 1995, pp. 55–87.

Klauck, Hans-Josef. *Der erste Johannesbrief.* Evangelisch-Katholischer Kommentar zum Neuen Testament vol. XXIII/1. Edited by Norbert Brox, Rudolf Schnackenburg, et al. Zürich/Braunschweig/Neukirchen-Vluyn: Benziger Verlag/Neukirchener Verlag, 1991.

Kort, Wesley A. *Bound to Differ: The Dynamics of Theological Discourses.* University Park: Pennsylvania State University Press, 1992.

Kristensson Uggla, Bengt. *Kommunikation på bristningsgränsen: En studie i Paul Ricoeurs projekt.* Stockholm/Stehag: Brutus Östlings Bokförlag Symposion, 1994.

Kristeva, Julia. "Holbein's Dead Christ." In *Black Sun: Depression and Melancholia.* Translated by Leon S. Roches. New York: Columbia University Press, 1980, pp. 105–38.

Kuhn, Thomas S. *The Structure of Scientific Revolutions.* 2nd, expanded edition. Chicago: University of Chicago Press, 1970.

Kümmel, Werner G. *The New Testament: The History of the Investigations of Its Problems.* Translated by S. McLean Gilmour and Howard C. Kee. London: SCM Press, 1973.

Kuschel, Karl-Josef. *Born before All Time? The Dispute over Christ's Origin.* Translated by John Bowden. London: SCM, 1992.

Lacoste, Jean-Yves. *Experience and the Absolute: Disputed Questions on the Humanity of Man.* Perspectives in Continental Philosophy. Translated by Mark Raftery-Skehan. New York: Fordham University Press, 2004.

Lange, Günter. *Bild und Wort: Die katechetischen Funktionen des Bildes in der griechischen Theologie des sechsten bis neunten Jahrhunderts.* Schriften zur Religionspädagogik und Kerygmatik vol. VI. Edited by Theoderich Kampmann. Würzburg: Echter-Verlag, 1969.

Laqueur, Thomas. *Making Sex: Body and Gender from the Greeks to Freud.* Cambridge, MA/London: Harvard University Press, 1990.

Laqueur, Thomas. *Solitary Sex: A Cultural History of Masturbation.* New York: Zone Books, 2003.

Larsson, Edvin. "Jesu uppståndelse och kristologins framväxt." In *Jesustolkningar i dag: Tio teologer om kristologi.* Stockholm: Verbum, 1995, pp. 88–118.

Lash, Nicholas. *Change in Focus: A Study of Doctrinal Change and Continuity.* London: Sheed & Ward, 1981.

Lash, Nicholas. *Easter in Ordinary: Reflections on Human Experience and the Knowledge of God.* London: SCM, 1988.

Lash, Nicholas. "Up and Down in Christology." In *New Studies in Theology I.* Edited by Stephen Sykes and Derek Holms. London, 1980, pp. 30–46.

Leder, Drew. *The Absent Body.* Chicago/London: University of Chicago Press, 1990.

Leder, Drew. "A Tale of Two Bodies: The Cartesian Corpse and the Lived Body." In *Body and Flesh: A Philosophical Reader.* Edited by Donn Welton. Malden, MA/Oxford, 1998, pp. 117–30.

Levinas, Emmanuel. *Entre Nous: Thinking-of-the-Other.* Translated by Michael B. Smith and Barbara Harshav. New York: Columbia University Press, 1998.

Levinas, Emmanuel. "Language and Proximity." In *Collected Philosophical Papers.* Translated by Alphonso Lingis. Dordrecht/Boston/Lancaster: Martinus Nijhoff Publishers, 1987, pp. 109–26.

Levinas, Emmanuel. *Time and the Other.* Translated by Richard A. Cohen. Pittsburgh: Duquesne University Press, 1987.

Levinas, Emmanuel. *Totality and Infinity: An Essay on Exteriority.* Translated by Alphonso Lingis. Pittsburgh: Duquesne University Press, 1969.

Liepe, Lena. *Den medeltida kroppen: Kroppens och könets ikonografi i nordisk medeltid.* Lund: Nordic Academic Press, 2003.

Lindbeck, George A. *The Nature of Doctrine: Religion and Theology in a Postliberal Age.* Philadelphia: Westminster Press, 1984.

Lindgärde, Valborg. *Jesu Christi Pijnos Historia Rijmwijs betrachtad: Svenska passionsdikter under 1600- och 1700-talet.* Litteratur teater film, Nya serien 12. Lund: Lund University Press, 1996.

Lingis, Alphonso. "Translator's Preface." In *The Visible and the Invisible: Followed by Working Notes.* Maurice Merleau-Ponty. Evanston, IL: Northwestern University Press, 1968.

Lloyd, Genevieve. *The Man of Reason: 'Male' & 'Female' in Western Philosophy.* 2nd edition. London: Routledge, 1993.

Lohse, Bernhard. *Martin Luther: Eine Einführung in sein Leben und sein Werk.* 2nd edition. Munich: Beck, 1983.

Lossky, Vladimir. *The Mystical Theology of the Eastern Church.* Cambridge: James Clarke, 1957.

Loughlin, Gerard. *Alien Sex: The Body and Desire in Cinema and Theology.* Challenges in Contemporary Theology. Malden, MA/Oxford: Blackwell, 2004.

621

Loughlin, Gerard. "Living in Christ: Story, Resurrection and Salvation." In *Resurrection Reconsidered*. Edited by Gavin D'Costa. Oxford: Oneworld, 1996, pp. 118–34.

Loughlin, Gerard. *Telling God's Story: Bible, Church and Narrative Theology*. Cambridge: Cambridge University Press, 1996.

Louth, Andrew. "The Body in Western Catholic Christianity." In *Religion and the Body*. Edited by Sarah Coakley, pp. 111–30. Cambridge: Cambridge University Press, 2000.

Louth, Andrew. *St John Damascene: Tradition and Originality in Byzantine Theology*. Oxford Early Christian Studies. New York: Oxford University Press, 2002.

Lowe, Walter. "Second Thoughts about Transcendence." In *The Religious*. Edited by John D. Caputo. Malden, MA/Oxford: Blackwell, 2001, pp. 241–51.

Lubac, Henri de. *Catholicism: Christ and the Common Destiny of Man*. Translated by Lancelot C. Sheppard and Elizabeth Englund. San Francisco: Ignatius Press, 1988.

Lubac, Henri de. *Corpus Mysticum: The Eucharist and the Church in the Middle Ages*. Faith in Reason. Translated by Gemma Simmonds et al. Notre Dame: University of Notre Dame Press, 2007.

Lundgren-Gothlin, Eva. *Sex and Existence: Simone de Beauvoir's* The Second Sex. Translated by Linda Schenk. London: Athlone, 1996.

Luther, Martin. *On the Councils and the Church*. In *Luther's Works*, vol. 41: *Church and Ministry III*. Edited by Eric W. Gritsch. Philadelphia: Fortress Press, 1966.

Luz, Ulrich. *Matthew 1–7: A Commentary*. Translated by Wilhelm C. Linss. Minneapolis: Augsburg, 1989.

Luz, Ulrich. *Matthew 1–7: A Commentary*. Hermeneia. Translated by Helmut Koester. Minneapolis: Fortress Press, 2007.

Luz, Ulrich. *Matthew 8–20: A Commentary*. Hermeneia. Translated by James E. Crouch. Minneapolis: Fortress Press, 2001.

Luz, Ulrich. *Matthew 21–28: A Commentary*. Hermeneia. Translated by Helmut Koester. Minneapolis: Fortress Press, 2005.

MacCannell, Juliet Flower, and Laura Zakarin, eds. *Thinking Bodies*. Stanford: Stanford University Press, 1994.

MacCulloch, Diarmaid. *Reformation: Europe's House Divided 1490–1700*. London: Allen Lane, 2003.

MacGregor, Neil, with Erika Langmuir. *Seeing Salvation: Images of Christ in Art*. London: BBC, 2000.

MacIntyre, Alasdair. *After Virtue: A Study in Moral Theory*. 2nd edition. London: Duckworth, 1985.

MacIntyre, Alasdair. "Epistemological Crises, Dramatic Narrative, and the Philosophy of Science." In *Why Narrative? Readings in Narrative Theology*. Edited by Stanley Hauerwas and L. Gregory Jones. Grand Rapids: Eerdmans, 1989, pp. 138–57.

Mackinlay, Shane. "Eyes Wide Shut: A Response to Jean-Luc Marion's Account of the Journey to Emmaus," *Modern Theology* 20, no. 3 (2004): 447–56.

MacKinnon, Donald M. "'Substance' in Christology—a Cross-Bench View." In *Christ, Faith and History*, Cambridge Studies in Christology. Edited by Stephen W. Sykes and John P. Clayton. Cambridge: Cambridge University Press, 1972, pp. 279–300.

Macquarrie, John. *Jesus Christ in Modern Thought*. London/Philadelphia: SCM/Trinity Press International, 1990.

McCabe, Herbert. *God Matters.* Contemporary Christian Insights. London/New York: Mowbray, 2000.

McCabe, Herbert. *God Still Matters.* Edited by Brian Davies. London/New York: Continuum, 2002.

McCarthy, David Matzko. "Homosexuality and the Practices of Marriage," *Modern Theology* 13, no. 3 (1997): 371–97.

McCarthy, David Matzko. "The Relationships of Bodies: A Nuptial Hermeneutics of Same-Sex Unions." In *Theology and Sexuality: Classic and Contemporary Readings.* Blackwell Readings in Modern Theology. Edited by Eugene F. Rogers Jr. Malden, MA/Oxford: Blackwell, 2002, pp. 200–216.

McCarthy, David Matzko. *Sex and Love in the Home: A Theology of the Household.* London: SCM, 2001.

McClintock Fulkerson, Mary. *Changing the Subject: Women's Discourses and Feminist Theology.* Minneapolis: Fortress Press, 1994.

McFague, Sallie. *Models of God: Theology for an Ecological, Nuclear Age.* London: SCM Press, 1987.

McGinn, Bernard. *The Foundations of Mysticism: Origins to the Fifth Century.* The Presence of God: A History of Western Christian Mysticism. New York: Crossroad, 1991.

McIntosh, Mark A. *Mystical Theology: The Integrity of Spirituality and Theology.* Challenges in Contemporary Theology. Oxford: Blackwell, 1998.

McLaughlin, Eleanor. "Feminist Christologies: Re-Dressing the Tradition." In *Reconstructing the Christ Symbol.* Edited by Maryanne Stevens. Mahwah, NJ: Paulist Press, 1993, pp. 118–49.

Malm, Mats. *Det liderliga språket: Poetisk ambivalens i svensk 'barock.'* Stockholm/Stehag: Brutus Östlings Bokförlag Symposion, 2004.

Marcel, Gabriel. *Journal métaphysique.* Paris: Gallimard, 1927.

Marien, Mary Warner. *Photography: A Cultural History.* London: Laurence King, 2002.

Marion, Jean-Luc. *Being Given: Toward a Phenomenology of Givenness.* Cultural Memory in the Present. Translated by Jeffrey L. Kosky. Stanford: Stanford University Press, 2002.

Marion, Jean-Luc. *The Crossing of the Visible.* Translated by James K. A. Smith. Stanford: Stanford University Press, 2004.

Marion, Jean-Luc. "The Final Appeal of the Subject." In *The Religious.* Blackwell Readings in Continental Philosophy. Edited by John D. Caputo. Malden, MA/Oxford: Blackwell, 2002, pp. 131–44.

Marion, Jean-Luc. *God without Being: Hors-Texte.* Religion and Postmodernism. Translated by Thomas A. Carlson. Chicago/London: University of Chicago Press, 1991.

Marion, Jean-Luc. *The Idol and Distance: Five Studies.* Perspectives in Continental Philosophy. Translated by Thomas A. Carlson. New York: Fordham University Press, 2001.

Marion, Jean-Luc. *In Excess: Studies of Saturated Phenomena.* Perspectives in Continental Philosophy. Translated by Robyn Horner and Vincent Beraud. New York: Fordham University Press, 2002.

Marion, Jean-Luc. *Reduction and Givenness: Investigations of Husserl, Heidegger, and Phenomenology.* Northwestern University Studies in Phenomenology & Existential Philosophy. Translated by Thomas A. Carlson. Evanston, IL: Northwestern University Press, 1998.

Marion, Jean-Luc. "The Saturated Phenomenon." In *Phenomenology and the "Theological Turn": The French Debate*. Dominique Janicaud et al. New York: Fordham University Press, 2000, pp. 176–216.

Marion, Jean-Luc. "They Recognized Him; and He Became Invisible to Them." Translated by Stephen E. Lewis. In *Modern Theology* 18, no. 2 (2002): 145–52.

Markus, R. A. *The End of Ancient Christianity*. Canto. Cambridge: Cambridge University Press, 1998.

Marquardt, Friedrich-Wilhelm. *Was dürfen wir hoffen, wenn wir hoffen dürften? Eine Eschatologie*, vol. 1. Gütersloh: Chr. Kaiser/Gütersloher Verlagshaus, 1993.

Marshall, Bruce. *Christology in Conflict: The Identity of a Saviour in Rahner and Barth*. Oxford: Basil Blackwell, 1987.

Marshall, I. Howard. *The Origins of New Testament Christology*. Downers Grove, IL: InterVarsity Press, 1976.

Martin, Dale B. *The Corinthian Body*. New Haven/London: Yale University Press, 1995.

Mauss, Marcel. *The Gift: The Form and Reason for Exchange in Archaic Societies*. Translated by W. D. Halls. London/New York: Routledge Classics, 2002.

Mauss, Marcel. "Techniques of the Body," *Economy and Society* 2, no. 1 (1973): 70–88.

May, Gerhard. *Schöpfung aus dem Nichts: Die Entstehung der Lehre von der creatio ex nihilo*. Berlin/New York: Walter de Gruyter, 1978.

Meijering, E. P. *Von den Kirchenvätern zu Karl Barth: Das altkirchliche Dogma in der 'Kirchlichen Dogmatik.'* Amsterdam: Verlag J. C. Gieben, 1993.

Melanchthon, Philipp. *Commonplaces/Loci communes 1521*. Translated with introduction and notes by Christian Preus. Saint Louis: Concordia, 2014.

Merleau-Ponty, Maurice. "Eye and Mind." In *The Primacy of Perception: And Other Essays on Phenomenological Psychology, the Philosophy of Art, History and Politics*. Northwestern University Studies in Phenomenology & Existential Philosophy. Translated by Carleton Dallery. Evanston, IL: Northwestern University Press, 1964, pp. 159–90.

Merleau-Ponty, Maurice. *Phénoménologie de la perception*. Paris: Gallimard, 1945.

Merleau-Ponty, Maurice. *Phenomenology of Perception*. Translated by Colin Smith. London: Routledge, 1992.

Merleau-Ponty, Maurice. *Sense and Non-Sense*. Translated by Hubert L. Dreyfus and Patricia Allen Dreyfus. Evanston, IL: Northwestern University Press, 1971.

Merleau-Ponty, Maurice. *The Visible and the Invisible: Followed by Working Notes*. Translated by Alphonso Lingis. Evanston, IL: Northwestern University Press, 1968.

Mettinger, Tryggve N. D. *Namnet och närvaron: Gudsnamn och gudsbild i böckernas bok*. Örebro, Sweden: Libris, 1987.

Milbank, John. *Being Reconciled: Ontology and Pardon*. Radical Orthodoxy. London/New York: Routledge, 2003.

Milbank, John. "Can a Gift Be Given? Prolegomena to a Future Trinitarian Metaphysics," *Modern Theology* 11, no. 1 (1995): 119–61.

Milbank, John. "Postmodern Critical Augustinianism: A Short *Summa* in Forty-two Responses to Unasked Questions." In *The Postmodern God: A Theological Reader*.

Blackwell Readings in Modern Theology. Edited by Graham Ward. Oxford: Blackwell, 1997, pp. 265–78.

Milbank, John. *Theology and Social Theory: Beyond Secular Reason.* Oxford: Blackwell, 1990.

Milbank, John. *The Word Made Strange: Theology, Language, Culture.* Oxford/Malden, MA: Blackwell, 1997.

Milbank, John, and Catherine Pickstock. *Truth in Aquinas.* Oxford: Blackwell, 2001.

Miles, Margaret R. *Image as Insight: Visual Understanding in Western Christianity and Secular Culture.* Boston: Beacon Press, 1985.

Miles, Margaret R. *Plotinus on Body and Beauty: Society, Philosophy, and Religion in Third-Century Rome.* Oxford: Blackwell, 1999.

Min, Anselm Kyongsuk. "The Other without History and Society: A Dialogue with Derrida." In *The Solidarity of Others in a Divided World: A Postmodern Theology after Postmodernism.* New York/London: T. & T. Clark, 2004, pp. 30–46.

Mirzoeff, Nicholas. *An Introduction to Visual Culture.* London/New York: Routledge, 1999.

Mirzoeff, Nicholas, ed. *The Visual Culture Reader.* London/New York: Routledge, 1998.

Mitchell, William. *Iconology: Image, Text, Ideology.* Chicago/London: University of Chicago Press, 1986.

Mitchell, William. *The Reconfigured Eye: Visual Truth in the Post-Photographic Era.* Cambridge, MA/London: MIT Press, 1992.

Moi, Toril. *Simone de Beauvoir: The Making of an Intellectual Woman.* Oxford: Blackwell, 1994.

Moltmann, Jürgen. *The Crucified God: The Cross of Christ as the Foundation and Criticism of Christian Theology.* Translated by R. A. Wilson and John Bowden. Minneapolis: Fortress Press, 1993.

Moore, Sebastian. "The Crisis of an Ethic without Desire." In *Theology and Sexuality: Classic and Contemporary Readings.* Blackwell Readings in Modern Theology. Edited by Eugene F. Rogers Jr. Malden, MA/Oxford: Blackwell, 2002, pp. 157–69.

Moran, Dermot. *Introduction to Phenomenology.* London/New York: Routledge, 2000.

Morgenstern, Christian. *Stufen: Eine Entwicklung in Aphorismen und Tagebuch-Notizen.* Munich: R. Piper Verlag, 1918.

Mulvey, Laura. "Visual Pleasure and Narrative Cinema." In *Feminism and Film.* Oxford Readings in Feminism. Edited by E. Ann Kaplan. Oxford/New York: Oxford University Press, 2000, pp. 34–47.

Mussner, Franz. *Die johanneische Sehweise und die Frage nach dem historischen Jesus.* Quaestiones Disputatae 28. Freiburg/Basel/Vienna: Herder, 1965.

Nagel, Thomas. "Sexual Perversion." In *Mortal Questions.* Cambridge/New York: Cambridge University Press, 1979, pp. 39–52.

Nagel, Thomas. *The View from Nowhere.* New York: Oxford University Press, 1986.

Nancy, Jean-Luc. *Au ciel et sur la terre: Petite conférence sur Dieu.* Paris: Bayard, 2004.

Nancy, Jean-Luc. *Corpus.* Perspectives in Continental Philosophy. Translated by Richard A. Rand. New York: Fordham University Press, 2008.

Nancy, Jean-Luc. "Corpus." Translated by Claudette Sartiliot. In *Thinking Bodies.* Edited by Juliet Flower MacCannell and Laura Zakarin. Stanford: Stanford University Press, 1994, pp. 17–31.

Nancy, Jean-Luc. "Des lieux divins." In *Que'est-ce que dieu? Philosophie/Théologie. Hommage à l'abbé Daniel Coppieters de Gibson (1929–1983)*. Brussels: Publications des Facultés Universitaires Saint-Louis, 1985, pp. 539–87.

Nancy, Jean-Luc. *Noli Me Tangere: On the Raising of the Body*. Perspectives in Continental Philosophy. Translated by Sarah Clift, Pascale-Anne Brault, and Michael Naas. New York: Fordham University Press, 2008.

Nelson, James B. *Body Theology*. Louisville: Westminster/John Knox Press, 1992.

Niebuhr, Richard R. *Christ and Culture*. Challenges in Contemporary Theology. Malden, MA/Oxford: Blackwell, 2005.

Niebuhr, Richard R. *Schleiermacher on Christ and Religion: A New Introduction*. New York: Charles Scribner's Sons, 1964.

Nielsen, Bent Flemming. *Genopførelser: Ritual, kommunikation og kirke*. Copenhagen: Anis, 2004.

Nielsen, Bent Flemming. *Die Rationalität der Offenbarungstheologie: Die Struktur des Theologieverständnisses von Karl Barth*. Århus: Aarhus University Press, 1988.

Nietzsche, Friedrich. *The Anti-Christ, Ecce Homo, Twilight of the Idols*. Cambridge Texts in the History of Philosophy. Translated by Judith Norman. Cambridge: Cambridge University Press, 2005.

Nietzsche, Friedrich. *Beyond Good and Evil*. Cambridge Texts in the History of Philosophy. Edited by Rolf-Peter Horstmann and Judith Norman. Translated by Judith Norman. Cambridge: Cambridge University Press, 2002.

Nietzsche, Friedrich. *On the Genealogy of Morals*. Oxford World's Classics. Translated by Douglas Smith. Oxford: Oxford University Press, 1998.

Nikephoros of Constantinople. *Antirrhetici tres adversus Constantinum Copronymum*. Patrologiae Cursus Completus, Series Graeca, vol. 100. Edited by J. P. Migne. Paris, 1865.

Nordgren, Kenneth. *God as a Problem and Possibility: A Critical Study of Gordon Kaufman's Thought toward a Spacious Theology*. Uppsala: Acta Universitatis Upsaliensis, 2003.

Nussbaum, Martha C. "Augustine and Dante on the Ascent of Love." In *The Augustinian Tradition*. Edited by Gareth B. Matthews. Berkeley/Los Angeles/London: University of California Press, 1999, pp. 61–90.

Nussbaum, Martha C. *The Therapy of Desire: Theory and Practice in Hellenistic Ethics*. Princeton: Princeton University Press, 1994.

Nygren, Anders. *Agape and Eros: The Christian Ideal of Love*. Translated by Philip S. Watson. Chicago: University of Chicago Press, 1982.

O'Collins, Gerald. *Incarnation*. New Century Theology. London/New York: Continuum, 2002.

O'Collins, Gerald. *Jesus Risen: The Resurrection – What Actually Happened and What Does It Mean?* London: Darton, Longman & Todd, 1987.

O'Connor, Flannery. "Some Aspects of the Grotesque in Southern Fiction." In *Mystery and Manners: Occasional Prose*. Edited by Sally Fitzgerald and Robert Fitzgerald. New York: Noonday, 1995, pp. 36–50.

O'Donovan, Oliver. *The Desire of the Nations: Rediscovering the Roots of Political Theology*. Cambridge: Cambridge University Press, 1996.

Ohlson, Elisabeth. *Ecce homo.* Photographs by Elisabeth Ohlson 1996–1998. Stockholm: Ecce homo, 1998.

O'Malley, John W. "Postscript." In *The Sexuality of Christ in Renaissance Art and in Modern Oblivion.* Leo Steinberg. 2nd revised and expanded edition. Chicago/London: University of Chicago Press, 1996, pp. 213–16.

Origen. *Against Celsus.* In *The Ante-Nicene Fathers,* vol. 4: *Tertullian, Part Fourth; Minucius Felix; Commodian; Origen, Parts First and Second.* Edited by Alexander Roberts and James Donaldson. Revised by A. Cleveland Coxe. Grand Rapids: Eerdmans, 1956.

Otto, Rudolf. *The Idea of the Holy: An Inquiry into the Non-rational Factor in the Idea of the Divine and Its Relation to the Rational.* Translated by John W. Harvey. London: Humphrey Milford, 1936.

Ouspensky, Leonid. *Theology of the Icon,* vol. 1. Translated by Anthony Gythiel and Elizabeth Meyendorff. Crestwood, NY: St. Vladimir's Seminary Press, 1978.

Ouspensky, Leonid. *Theology of the Icon,* vol. 2. Translated by Anthony Gythiel and Elizabeth Meyendorff. Crestwood, NY: St. Vladimir's Seminary Press, 1992.

Pannenberg, Wolfhart. *Jesus – God and Man.* 2nd edition. Translated by Lewis L. Wilkins and Duane A. Priebe. Philadelphia: Westminster Press, 1977.

Parry, Kenneth. *Depicting the Word: Byzantine Iconophile Thought of the Eighth and Ninth Centuries.* The Medieval Mediterranean Peoples, Economies and Cultures, 400–1453. Vol. 12. Leiden/New York/Cologne: E. J. Brill, 1996.

Parsons, Susan Frank. *The Ethics of Gender.* New Dimensions to Religious Ethics. Oxford/Malden, MA: Blackwell, 2002.

Pelikan, Jaroslav. *The Christian Tradition,* vol. 1: *The Emergence of the Catholic Tradition (100–600).* Chicago/London: University of Chicago Press, 1971.

Pelikan, Jaroslav. *Christianity and Classical Culture: The Metamorphosis of Natural Theology in the Christian Encounter with Hellenism.* New Haven/London: Yale University Press, 1993.

Pelikan, Jaroslav. *The Illustrated Jesus through the Centuries.* New Haven/London: Yale University Press, 1997.

Pelikan, Jaroslav. *Imago Dei: The Byzantine Apologia for Icons.* The A. W. Mellon Lectures in the Fine Arts, 1987. The National Gallery of Art. Washington, DC. Bollingen Series XXXV:36. Princeton: Princeton University Press, 1990.

Pelikan, Jaroslav. *Jesus through the Centuries: His Place in the History of Culture.* New York: Perennial Library, 1987.

Perez, Nissan N. *Revelation: Representations of Christ in Photography.* London: Merrell, 2003.

Perkins, Judith. *The Suffering Self: Pain and Narrative Representation in the Early Christian Era.* London/New York: Routledge, 1995.

Persson, Per-Erik. *Sacra Doctrina: Reason and Revelation in Aquinas.* Translated by Ross Mackenzie. Oxford: Blackwell, 1970.

Petersson, Kjell. *Åkallan och åminnelse: Nattvarden i mötet mellan luthersk tradition och ekumenisk teologi.* Bibliotheca theologiae practicae 64. Lund: Arcus, 2000.

Pettersen, Alvyn. *Athanasius.* Outstanding Christian Thinkers. London: Geoffrey Chapman, 1995.

Pickstock, Catherine. *After Writing: On the Liturgical Consummation of Philosophy.* Oxford: Blackwell, 1998.

Pickstock, Catherine. "Justice and Prudence: Principles of Order in the Platonic City." In *The Blackwell Companion to Postmodern Theology.* Edited by Graham Ward. Oxford: Blackwell, 2001, pp. 162–76.

Pietri, Charles, and Christoph Markschies. "Theologische Diskussionen zur Zeit Konstantins: Arius, der 'arianische Streit' und das Konzil von Nizäa, die nachnizänischen Auseinandersetzungen bis 337." In *Die Geschichte des Christentums: Religion—Politik—Kultur,* vol. 2: *Das Entstehen der einen Christenheit (250–430).* Edited by Charles and Luce Piétre. Freiburg/Basel/Vienna: Herder, 1996, pp. 271–344.

Placher, William C. *The Domestication of Transcendence: How Modern Thinking about God Went Wrong.* Louisville: Westminster/John Knox Press, 1996.

Plato. *Gorgias.* In *Plato in Twelve Volumes, 3: Lysias, Symposium, Gorgias.* Loeb Classical Library. Translated by W. R. M. Lamb. Cambridge, MA/London: Harvard University Press, 1925.

Plato. *Phaedo.* In *Plato in Twelve Volumes, 1: Euthyphro, Apology, Crito, Phaedo, Phaedrus.* Loeb Classical Library. Translated by Harold North Fowler. Cambridge, MA/London: Harvard University Press, 1914.

Plato. *Phaedrus.* In *Plato in Twelve Volumes, 1: Euthyphro, Apology, Crito, Phaedo, Phaedrus.* Loeb Classical Library. Translated by Harold North Fowler. Cambridge, MA/London: Harvard University Press, 1914.

Plato. *Republic.* Books VI–X. Loeb Classical Library; Plato VI. Translated by Paul Shorey. Cambridge, MA/London: Harvard University Press, 1994.

Plato. *Symposium.* In *Plato in Twelve Volumes, 3: Lysias, Symposium, Gorgias.* Loeb Classical Library. Translated by W. R. M. Lamb. Cambridge, MA/London: Harvard University Press, 1925.

Plato. *Timaeus.* In *Timaeus, Critias, Cleitophon, Menexenus, Epistles.* Loeb Classical Library. Translated by R. G. Bury. Cambridge, MA/London: Harvard University Press, 1929.

Powers, David N. *Sacrament: The Language of God's Giving.* New York: Crossroad, 1999.

Prokes, Mary Timothy. *Toward a Theology of the Body.* Edinburgh: T. & T. Clark, 1996.

Proust, Marcel. *In Search of Lost Time,* vol. 1: *Swann's Way.* Translated by C. K. Scott Moncrieff and Terence Kilmartin. Revised by D. J. Enright. New York: The Modern Library, 1992.

Quash, J. B. "'Between the brutely given, and the brutally, banally free': Von Balthasar's Theology of Drama in Dialogue with Hegel," *Modern Theology* 13, no. 3 (1997): 293–318.

Quenot, Michel. *The Icon: Window on the Kingdom.* Translated by a Carthusian monk. Crestwood, NY: St. Vladimir's Seminary Press, 1991.

Rahner, Karl. "Current Problems in Christology." In *Theological Investigations,* vol. 1: *God, Christ, Mary and Grace.* Translated by Cornelius Ernst. New York: Crossroad, 1982, pp. 149–200.

Rambuss, Richard. *Closet Devotions.* Durham, NC/London: Duke University Press, 1998.

Raschkover, Randi. "The Christian Doctrine of the Incarnation." In *Christianity in*

Jewish Terms. Edited by Tikva Frymer-Kensky, David Novak, Peter Ochs, et al. Boulder, CO/Oxford: Westview Press, 2000, pp. 254–61.

Rasmusson, Arne. "En gång fanns inte det sekulära – Social teologi från Ernst Troeltsch till John Milbank." In *På spaning efter framtidens kyrka.* Edited by Sune Fahlgren. Örebro, Sweden: Libris, 1998, pp. 105–30.

Ricoeur, Paul. *The Conflict of Interpretations: Essays in Hermeneutics.* Edited by Don Ihde. Translated by Kathleen McLaughlin. London: Continuum, 2004.

Ricoeur, Paul. "Experience and Language in Religious Discourse." In *Phenomenology and the "Theological Turn": The French Debate.* Dominique Janicaud et al. New York: Fordham University Press, 2000, pp. 127–46.

Ricoeur, Paul. *From Text to Action: Essays in Hermeneutics II.* Translated by Kathleen Blamey and John B. Thompson. Evanston, IL: Northwestern University Press, 1991.

Ricoeur, Paul. *Interpretation Theory: Discourse and the Surplus of Meaning.* Fort Worth: Texas Christian University Press, 1976.

Ricoeur, Paul. "Manifestation and Proclamation." In *Figuring the Sacred: Religion, Narrative, and Imagination.* Translated by David Pellauer. Minneapolis: Fortress Press, 1995, pp. 48–67.

Ricoeur, Paul. *Oneself as Another.* Translated by Kathleen Blamey. Chicago: University of Chicago Press, 1994.

Riesner, Rainer. *Jesus als Lehrer: Eine Untersuchung zum Ursprung der Evangelienüberlieferung.* 3rd expanded edition. J. C. B. Mohr (Paul Siebeck), 1988.

Ritter, Adolf Martin. "Dogma und Lehre in der alten Kirche." In *Handbuch der Dogmen- und Theologiegeschichte,* vol. 1: *Die Lehrentwicklung im Rahmen der Katholizität.* Edited by Carl Andresen. Ungekürzte Studienausg. UTB Grosse Reihe. Göttingen: Vandenhoeck and Ruprecht, 1989, pp. 99–283.

Rogers, Eugene F., Jr. Introduction to Rowan D. Williams, "The Body's Grace." In *Theology and Sexuality: Classic and Contemporary Readings.* Edited by Eugene F. Rogers Jr. Blackwell Readings in Modern Theology. Malden, MA/Oxford: Blackwell, 2002, p. 309.

Rogers, Eugene F., Jr. *Sexuality and the Christian Body: Their Way into the Triune God.* Challenges in Contemporary Theology. Oxford/Malden, MA: Blackwell, 1999.

Rogers, Eugene F., Jr., ed. *Theology and Sexuality: Classic and Contemporary Readings.* Blackwell Readings in Modern Theology. Malden, MA/Oxford: Blackwell, 2002.

Rogoff, Irit. "Studying Visual Culture." In *The Visual Culture Reader.* Edited by Nicholas Mirzoeff. London/New York: Routledge, 1998, pp. 14–26.

Rorty, Richard. *Philosophy as the Mirror of Nature.* Oxford: Basil Blackwell, 1980.

Rosengren, Mats. *Doxologi: En essä om kunskap.* Åstorp, Sweden: Rhetor förlag, 2002.

Rosengren, Mats. "Den ohörda tanken, den slumpartade formuleringen och den nytänkta idén: Skäl att bry sig om filosofins historia." In *Penelopes väv: För en filosofisk och teologisk pathologi.* Logos/Pathos 1. Edited by Mats Rosengren and Ola Sigurdson. Göteborg: Glänta, 2003, pp. 11–26.

Ross, Susan A. "Embodiment and Incarnation: A Response to Elliot Wolfson." In *Christianity in Jewish Terms.* Edited by Tikva Frymer-Kensky, David Novak, Peter Ochs, et al. Boulder, CO/Oxford: Westview Press, 2000, pp. 262–68.

Rubin, Miri. *Corpus Christi: The Eucharist in Late Medieval Culture.* Cambridge: Cambridge University Press, 1991.

Rudolph, Kurt. *Gnosis: The Nature and History of Gnosticism.* Translated by Robert McLachlan Wilson. San Francisco: Harper, 1987.

Ruether, Rosemary Radford. "Can Christology Be Liberated from Patriarchy?" In *Reconstructing the Christ Symbol.* Edited by Maryanne Stevens. Mahwah, NJ: Paulist Press, 1993, pp. 7–29.

Ruether, Rosemary Radford. *Sexism and God-Talk: Towards a Feminist Theology.* London: SCM, 1983.

Ruh, Hans. *Die christologische Begründung des ersten Artikels bei Zinzendorf.* Zürich: Evangelischer Verlag, 1967.

Sawicki, Jana. *Disciplining Foucault: Feminism, Power, and the Body.* New York/London: Routledge, 1991.

Sawicki, Marianne. *Seeing the Lord: Resurrection and Early Christian Practices.* Minneapolis: Fortress Press, 1994.

Scarry, Elaine. *The Body in Pain: The Making and Unmaking of the World.* New York/Oxford: Oxford University Press, 1985.

Scheler, Max. *Gesammelte Werke. Der Formalismus in der Ethik und die materiale Wertethik*, vol. 2: *Der Formalismus in der Ethik und die materiale Wertethik.* 4th revised edition. Bern: Francke, 1954.

Scheler, Max. *Schriften zur Soziologie und Weltanschauungslehre*, vol. 6: *Schriften zur Soziologie und Weltanschauungslehre.* 2nd revised edition. Bern: Francke, 1963.

Schillebeeckx, Edward. *Christ: The Christian Experience in the Modern World.* Translated by John Bowden. London: SCM, 1980.

Schleiermacher, Friedrich D. E. *The Christian Faith.* Edited by H. R. Mackintosh and J. S. Stewart. London/New York: T. & T. Clark, 1999.

Schleiermacher, Friedrich D. E. *On Religion: Speeches to Its Cultured Despisers.* Translated by John Oman. London: K. Paul, Trench, Trubner & Co, 1893.

Schmemann, Alexander. *The Eucharist: Sacrament of the Kingdom.* Translated by Paul Kachur. Crestwood, NY: St. Vladimir's Seminary Press, 1988.

Schmidt-Lauber, Hans-Christoph. "Die Eucharistie." In Hans-Christoph Schmidt-Lauber and Karl-Heinrich Bieritz, *Handbuch der Liturgik: Liturgiewissenschaft in Theologie und Praxis der Kirche.* Leipzig/Göttingen: Evangelische Verlags-Anstalt/Vandenhoeck and Ruprecht, 1995, pp. 209–47.

Schönborn, Christoph. *God's Human Face: The Christ-Icon.* Translated by Lothar Kraut. San Francisco: Ignatius Press, 1994.

Schrage, Wolfgang. *Der erste Brief an die Korinther: 1 Kor 6,12–11,16.* Part 2. Evangelisch-Katholischer Kommentar zum Neuen Testament vol. VII/2. Edited by Norbert Brox, Joseph Gnilka, et al. Solothurn/Düsseldorf/Neukirchen-Vluyn: Benziger Verlag/Neukirchener Verlag, 1995.

Schrage, Wolfgang. *Der erste Brief an die Korinther: 1 Kor 11,17–14,40.* Part 3. Evangelisch-Katholischer Kommentar zum Neuen Testament vol. VII/3. Edited by Norbert Brox, Joseph Gnilka, et al. Zürich/Düsseldorf/Neukirchen-Vluyn: Benziger Verlag/Neukirchener Verlag, 1999.

Schrage, Wolfgang. *Der Erste Brief an die Korinther: 1 Kor 15,1–16,24.* Part 4. Evangelisch-Katholischer Kommentar zum Neuen Testament vol. VII/4. Edited by Norbert

Brox, Joachim Gnilka, et al. Zürich/Düsseldorf/Neukirchen-Vluyn: Benziger Verlag/Neukirchener Verlag, 2001.

Schuback, Marcia Sá Cavalcante. "Philosophy and Religion," *Svensk Teologisk Kvartalskrift* 78, no 3 (2002): 98–106.

Schulz, Hans-Joachim. *Bekenntnis statt Dogma: Kriterien der Verbindlichkeit kirchlicher Lehre.* Quaestiones Disputatae 163. Freiburg/Basel/Vienna: Herder, 1996.

Schüssler Fiorenza, Elisabeth. *In Memory of Her: A Feminist Theological Reconstruction of Christian Origins.* London: SCM, 1993.

Schüssler Fiorenza, Elisabeth. *Jesus: Miriam's Child, Sophia's Prophet: Critical Issues in Feminist Christology.* New York: Continuum, 1994.

Schütz, Alfred. *The Phenomenology of the Social World.* Northwestern University Studies in Phenomenology & Existential Philosophy. Translated by George Walsh and Frederick Lehnert. Evanston, IL: Northwestern University Press, 1967.

Schweizer, Eduard. *Der Brief an die Kolosser.* Evangelisch-Katholischer Kommentar zum Neuen Testament vol. XII. Edited by Josef Blank, Rudolf Schnackenburg, et al. 3rd revised edition. Zürich/Braunschweig/Neukirchen-Vluyn: Benziger Verlag/Neukirchener Verlag, 1989.

Schweizer, Eduard. *Der Briefe an die Kolosser und an Philemon.* Kritisch-Exegetischer Kommentar über das Neue Testament vol. IX/2. 2nd edition. Göttingen: Vandenhoeck & Ruprecht, 1977.

Schweizer, Eduard. *Jesus Christus im vielfältigen Zeugnis des Neuen Testaments.* Munich/Hamburg: Siebenstern Taschenbuch Verlag, 1968.

Senn, Frank C. *Christian Liturgy: Catholic and Evangelical.* Minneapolis: Fortress Press, 1997.

Sennett, Richard. *Flesh and Stone: The Body and City in Western Civilisation.* London/Boston: Faber & Faber, 1994.

Shapiro, Gary. "Jean-Luc Nancy and the Corpus of Philosophy." In *Thinking Bodies.* Edited by Juliet Flower MacCannell and Laura Zakarin. Stanford: Stanford University Press, 1994, pp. 52–62.

Shklovsky, Viktor. "Art as Device." In *Theory of Prose.* Translated by Benjamin Sher. Elmwood Park, IL: Dalkey Archive Press, 1998, pp. 1–14.

Shohat, Ella, and Robert Stam. "Narrativizing Visual Culture: Towards a Polycentric Aesthetics." In *The Visual Culture Reader.* Edited by Nicholas Mirzoeff. London/New York: Routledge, 1998, pp. 27–49.

Sigurdson, Ola. "Bibeln som Skrift: Om bibelns anspråk på aktualitet och auktoritet i den kristna kyrkan." In *Tolkning för livet: Åtta teologer om bibelns auktoritet.* Edited by Anne-Louise Eriksson. Stockholm: Verbum, 2004, pp. 215–38, 271–73.

Sigurdson, Ola. *Den lyckliga filosofin: Etik och politik hos Hägerström, Tingsten, makarna Myrdal och Hedenius.* Stockholm/Stehag: Brutus Östlings Bokförlag Symposion, 2000.

Sigurdson, Ola. *De prudentia: Om principer och personer i etiken.* Stockholm/Stehag: Brutus Östlings Bokförlag Symposion, 2001.

Sigurdson, Ola. "En främling inför Guds ögon," *Signum* 29, no. 9 (2003): 25–33.

Sigurdson, Ola. "Från intratextualitet till intertextualitet: Bortom Lindbecks postliberala teologi," *Svensk Teologisk Kvartalskrift* 72, no. 3 (1996): 126–35.

Sigurdson, Ola. "Herdemakten och biktens hemlighet," *Res Publica: Hemligheter* 59 (2003): 56–65.

Sigurdson, Ola. *Hungerns väg: Om Gud, kyrka och mångfald*. Lund: Arcus, 2000.

Sigurdson, Ola. *Karl Barth som den andre: En studie av den svenska teologins Barth-reception*. Stockholm/Stehag: Brutus Östlings Bokförlag Symposion, 1996.

Sigurdson, Ola. *Kärlekens skillnad: Att gestalta kristen tro i vår tid*. Stockholm: Verbum, 1998.

Sigurdson, Ola. "Kristus och människan: Om inkarnationen och kärleksbegreppet," *Svensk Teologisk Kvartalskrift* 77, no. 2 (2001): 66–76.

Sigurdson, Ola. "Kyrkan som de heligas samfund: På väg mot en evangelisk *communio*-ecklesiologi." In *På spaning efter framtidens kyrka*. Edited by Sune Fahlgren. Örebro, Sweden: Libris, 1998, pp. 49–72.

Sigurdson, Ola. "On Ghosts and Bodies: A Response to Marcia Sá Cavalcante Schuback," *Svensk Teologisk Kvartalskrift* 78, no. 3 (2002): 107–9.

Sigurdson, Ola. "Varför änglar inte kan vara kloka: Om klokhet som en mänsklig dygd." In *Penelopes väv: För en filosofisk och teologisk pathologi*. Edited by Mats Rosengren and Ola Sigurdson. Logos/Pathos no. 1. Göteborg: Glänta, 2003, pp. 101–17.

Sigurdson, Ola. *Världen är en främmande plats: Essäer om religionens återkomst*. Örebro, Sweden: Cordia, 2003.

Sigurdson, Ola. "Vems tradition? Vilken sexualitet? Svar till Gösta Hallonsten," *Svensk Teologisk Kvartalskrift* 80, no. 3 (2004): 124–26.

Sigurdson, Ola, et al. *Ljus av ljus: Läsning av en kristen bekännelse*. Stockholm: Verbum, 1998.

Sigurdson, Ola, and Jayne Svenungsson, eds. *Postmodern teologi: En introduktion*. Stockholm: Verbum, 2006.

Sigusch, Volkmar. *Kritik der disziplinierten Sexualität: Aufsätze 1986–1989*. Frankfurt/New York: Campus, 1989.

Skrade, Carl. *God and the Grotesque*. Philadelphia: Westminster Press, 1974.

Smith, James K. A. *Speech and Theology: Language and the Logic of Incarnation*. Radical Orthodoxy. London/New York: Routledge, 2002.

Söderbergh Widding, Astrid. "Att gestalta det osynliga i det synligas medium." In *Film och religion: Livstolkning på vita duken*. Edited by Tomas Axelson and Ola Sigurdson. Örebro, Sweden: Cordia, 2005, pp. 77–95.

Söderbergh Widding, Astrid. *Blick och blindhet*. Bonnier Alba Essä. Stockholm: Bonnier Alba, 1997.

Sokolowski, Robert. *Introduction to Phenomenology*. Cambridge: Cambridge University Press, 2000.

Sontag, Susan. *On Photography*. London: Penguin Books, 1979.

Soskice, Janet Martin. *Metaphor and Religious Language*. Oxford: Clarendon Press, 1985.

Soskice, Janet Martin. "Sight and Vision in Medieval Christian Thought." In *Vision in Context: Historical and Contemporary Perspectives on Sight*. Edited by Teresa Brennan and Martin Jay. New York/London: Routledge, 1996, pp. 29–43.

Spivak, Gayatri Chakravorty. "French Feminism in an International Frame." In *In Other Worlds: Essays in Cultural Politics*. New York/London: Methuen, 1987, pp. 134–53.

Spivak, Gayatri Chakravorty. "Response to Jean-Luc Nancy." In *Thinking Bodies*. Edited by Juliet Flower MacCannell and Laura Zakarin. Stanford: Stanford University Press, 1994, pp. 32–51.

Steinberg, Leo. *The Sexuality of Christ in Renaissance Art and in Modern Oblivion*. 2nd revised and expanded edition. Chicago/London: University of Chicago Press, 1996.

Stendahl, Krister. *Paul among Jews and Gentiles and Other Essays*. Philadelphia: Fortress Press, 1976.

Steppa, Jan-Eric. *John Rufus and the World Vision of Anti-Chalcedonian Culture*. Diss. Lund, 2001.

Stevens, Maryanne, ed. *Reconstructing the Christ Symbol*. Mahwah, NJ: Paulist Press, 1993.

Stock, Alex. *Poetische Dogmatik: Christologie: 2. Schrift und Gesicht*. Paderborn/Munich/Vienna/Zürich: Schöningh, 1996.

Stock, Alex. *Poetische Dogmatik: Christologie: 3. Leib und Leben*. Paderborn/Munich/Vienna/Zürich: Schöningh, 1998.

Stock, Alex. *Zwischen Tempel und Museum: Theologische Kunstkritik – Positionen der Moderne*. Paderborn/Munich/Vienna/Zürich: Schöningh, 1991.

Stuart, Elizabeth. *Gay and Lesbian Theologies: Repetitions with Critical Difference*. Aldershot, UK: Ashgate, 2003.

Studer, Basil. *Gott und unsere Erlösung im Glauben der alten Kirche*. Düsseldorf: Patmos Verlag, 1985.

Studer, Basil. *Schola Christiana: Die Theologie zwischen Nizäa und Chalcedon*. Paderborn/Munich/Vienna/Zürich: Schöningh, 1998.

Sturken, Marita, and Lisa Cartwright. *Practices of Looking: An Introduction to Visual Culture*. Oxford/New York: Oxford University Press, 2001.

Surin, Kenneth. "Some Aspects of the 'Grammar' of 'Incarnation' and 'Kenosis': Reflections prompted by the writings of Donald MacKinnon." In *Christ, Ethics and Tragedy: Essays in Honor of Donald MacKinnon*. Edited by Kenneth Surin. Cambridge: Cambridge University Press, 1989, pp. 93–116.

Surin, Kenneth. *Theology and the Problem of Evil*. Signposts in Theology. Oxford: Basil Blackwell, 1986.

Svartvik, Jesper. "Teologi på andra sidan Hippos stadsmurar," *Svensk exegetisk årsbok* 69 (2004): 51–70.

Svartvik, Jesper. "Vem vaktar väktarna? En undersökning av bibelbruket i debatten om homosexualitet." In *Tolkning för livet: Åtta teologer om bibelns auktoritet*. Edited by Anne-Louise Eriksson. Stockholm: Verbum, 2004, pp. 168–92, 260–67.

Svenbro, Jesper. *Myrstigar: Figurer för skrift och läsning i antikens Grekland*. Stockholm: Bonnier, 1999.

Svenbro, Jesper. "Voir en voyant: La perception visuelle chez Empédocle." In *Métis: Anthropologie des mondes grecs anciens*. Paris/Athens: Daedalus 2 (2004), pp. 47–70.

Svenungsson, Jayne. *Guds återkomst: En studie av gudsbegreppet inom postmodern filosofi*. Logos/Pathos 3. Göteborg: Glänta, 2004.

Syreeni, Kari. "Den sublimerade kroppen: Jesu kroppslighet som symbol i Johannesevangeliet," *Svensk exegetisk årsbok* 63 (1998): 201–15.

Tanner, Kathryn. *God and Creation in Christian Theology: Tyranny or Empowerment?* Oxford: Basil Blackwell, 1988.

Tanner, Kathryn. *Theories of Culture: A New Agenda for Theology.* Guides to Theological Inquiry. Minneapolis: Fortress Press, 1997.

Taylor, Charles. *Philosophical Arguments.* Cambridge, MA/London: Harvard University Press, 1995.

Taylor, Charles. *Sources of the Self: The Making of Modern Identity.* Cambridge: Cambridge University Press, 1989.

Tertullian. *Against Praxeas.* In *Ante-Nicene Fathers*, vol. 3: *Latin Christianity: Its Founder, Tertullian.* Edited by Alexander Roberts and James Donaldson. Revised by A. Cleveland Coxe. Grand Rapids: Eerdmans, 1957.

Tertullian. *On the Resurrection of the Flesh.* In *Ante-Nicene Fathers*, vol. 3: *Latin Christianity: Its Founder, Tertullian.* Edited by Alexander Roberts and James Donaldson. Revised by A. Cleveland Coxe. Grand Rapids: Eerdmans, 1978.

Theodore the Studite. *Antirrhetici tres adversus Iconomachos.* Patrologiae Cursus Completus, Series Graeca, vol. 99. Edited by J. P. Migne. Paris, 1860.

Theodore the Studite. *On the Holy Icons.* Translated by Catharine P. Roth. Crestwood, NY: St. Vladimir's Seminary Press, 1981.

Thomas Aquinas. *Summa theologiae.* Paris: Sumptibus P. Lethielleux, Bibliopolae Editoris, 1939.

Thon, Nikolaus. *Ikone und Liturgie.* Sophie; Quellen östlicher Theologie vol. 19. Edited by Julius Tyciak and Wilhelm Nyssen. Trier: Paulinus-Verlag, 1979.

Thunberg, Lars. *Man and the Cosmos: The Vision of St. Maximus the Confessor.* Crestwood, NY: St. Vladimir's Seminary Press, 1985.

Tillich, Paul. *Systematic Theology,* vol. 1: *Reason and Revelation: Being and God.* Chicago: University of Chicago Press, 1951.

Todes, Samuel. *Body and World.* Introduced by Hubert L. Dreyfus and Piotr Hoffman. Cambridge, MA: MIT Press, 2001.

Tracy, David. *The Analogical Imagination: Christian Theology and the Culture of Pluralism.* London: SCM Press, 1981.

Tracy, David. *On Naming the Present: Reflections on God, Hermeneutics, and Church.* Maryknoll, NY/London: Orbis/SCM, 1994.

Tripp, David. "The Image of the Body in the Formative Phases of the Protestant Reformation." In *Religion and the Body.* Edited by Sarah Coakley. Cambridge: Cambridge University Press, 2000, pp. 131–52.

Turner, Denys. *The Darkness of God: Negativity in Christian Mysticism.* Cambridge: Cambridge University Press, 1998.

Turner, Denys. *Eros & Allegory: Medieval Exegesis of the Song of Songs.* Kalamazoo, MI: Cistercian Publications, 1995.

Vasey, Michael. *Strangers and Friends: A New Exploration of Homosexuality and the Bible.* London: Hodder & Stoughton, 1995.

Virilio, Paul. *The Aesthetics of Disappearance.* Translated by Philip Beitchman. New York: Semiotext[e], 1991.

Virilio, Paul. *The Art of the Motor.* Translated by Julie Rose. Minneapolis: University of Minnesota Press, 1995.

Virilio, Paul. *The Vision Machine.* Translated by Julie Rose. Bloomington/Indianapolis: Indiana University Press, 1994.

Volf, Miroslav. *Exclusion & Embrace: A Theological Exploration of Identity, Otherness, and Reconciliation.* Nashville: Abingdon, 1996.

Waldrop, Charles T. *Karl Barth's Christology: Its Basic Alexandrian Character.* Religion and Reason 21. Edited by Jacques Waardenburg. Berlin/New York/Amsterdam: Mouton Publishers, 1984.

Ward, Graham. "The Beauty of God." In *Theological Perspectives on God and Beauty.* Edited by John Milbank, Graham Ward, and Edith Wyschogrod. Rockwell Lecture Series. Harrisburg, PA/London/New York: Trinity Press International, 2003, pp. 35–65.

Ward, Graham. *Christ and Culture.* Challenges in Contemporary Theology. Malden, MA/Oxford: Blackwell, 2005.

Ward, Graham. *Cities of God.* Radical Orthodoxy. London/New York: Routledge, 2000.

Ward, Graham. *Cultural Transformation and Religious Practice.* Cambridge: Cambridge University Press, 2005.

Ward, Graham. "Divinity and Sexuality: Luce Irigaray and Christology," *Modern Theology* 12, no. 2 (1996): 221–37.

Ward, Graham. "Introduction: 'Where We Stand.'" In *The Blackwell Companion to Postmodern Theology.* Blackwell Companions to Religion. Edited by Graham Ward. Malden, MA/Oxford: Blackwell, 2001, pp. xii–xxvii.

Ward, Graham. "Suffering and Incarnation." In *The Blackwell Companion to Postmodern Theology.* Edited by Graham Ward, pp. 192–208. Malden, MA/Oxford: Blackwell, 2001.

Ward, Graham. "The Theological Project of Jean-Luc Marion." In *Post-Secular Philosophy: Between Philosophy and Theology.* Edited by Phillip Blond. London/New York: Routledge, 1998, pp. 229–39.

Ward, Graham. *Theology and Critical Theory.* 2nd edition. Basingstoke, UK: Macmillan, 2000.

Ward, Graham. "Theology and Cultural Sadomasochism," *Svensk Teologisk Kvartalskrift* 78, no. 1 (2002): 2–10.

Ward, Graham. *True Religion.* Blackwell Manifestos. Malden, MA/Oxford: Blackwell, 2003.

Ware, Kallistos. "'My Helper and My Enemy': The Body in Greek Christianity." In *Religion and the Body.* Edited by Sarah Coakley. Cambridge: Cambridge University Press, 2000, pp. 90–110.

Weber, Max. "'Objectivity' in Social Science and Social Policy." In *The Methodology of the Social Sciences.* Translated by Edward A. Shils and Henry A. Finch. Glencoe, IL: Free Press, 1949, pp. 49–112.

Weber, Max. "Science as a Vocation." In *The Vocation Lectures.* Translated by Rodney Livingstone. Indianapolis/Cambridge: Hackett, 2004, pp. 1–31.

Wedderburn, A. J. M. *Beyond Resurrection.* London: SCM Press, 1999.

Weder, Hans. *Die Gleichnisse Jesu als Metaphern: Traditions- und redaktionsgeschichtliche Analysen und Interpretationen.* 3rd, revised edition. Göttingen: Vandenhoeck & Ruprecht, 1984.

Weder, Hans. *Neutestamentliche Hermeneutik.* 2nd revised edition. Zürich: Theologischer Verlag, 1986.

Weeks, Jeffrey. *Sexuality.* 2nd edition. London/New York: Routledge, 2003.

Weiss, Gail. *Body Images: Embodiment and Intercorporeality.* New York/London: Routledge, 1999.

Welton, Donn. "Affectivity, Eros and the Body." In *Body and Flesh: A Philosophical Reader.* Edited by Donn Welton. Malden, MA/Oxford: Blackwell, 1998, pp. 181–206.

Welton, Donn. "Biblical Bodies." In *Body and Flesh: A Philosophical Reader.* Edited by Donn Welton. Malden, MA/Oxford: Blackwell, 1998, pp. 229–58.

Welton, Donn, ed. *Body and Flesh: A Philosophical Reader.* Malden, MA/Oxford: Blackwell, 1998.

Westerholm, Stephen. *Israel's Law and the Church's Faith: Paul and His Recent Interpreters.* Grand Rapids: Eerdmans, 1988.

Whelan, Richard. "Robert Capa's Falling Soldier: A Detective Story," *Aperture* 166 (Spring 2002): 48–55.

Wiles, Maurice. "Christianity without Incarnation?" In *The Myth of God Incarnate.* Edited by John Hick. London: SCM, 1977, pp. 1–10.

Wiles, Maurice. "Myth in Theology." In *The Myth of God Incarnate.* Edited by John Hick. London: SCM, 1977, pp. 148–66.

Wiles, Maurice. *The Remaking of Christian Doctrine.* London: SCM, 1974.

Wilkens, Ulrich. *Der Brief an die Römer: Röm. 6–11.* 2nd volume, Evangelisch-Katholischer Kommentar zum Neuen Testament vol. VI/2. Edited by Joseph Blank, Rudolf Schnackenburg, et al. 2nd revised edition. Zürich/Einsiedeln/Cologne/Neukirchen-Vluyn: Benziger Verlag/Neukirchener Verlag, 1987.

Williams, Rowan. *Arius: Heresy and Tradition.* 2nd edition. London: SCM Press, 2001.

Williams, Rowan. "The Body's Grace." In *Our Selves, Our Souls & Bodies: Sexuality and the Household of God.* Edited by Charles Hefling. Cambridge, MA: Cowley, 1996, pp. 58–68.

Williams, Rowan. "Doctrinal Criticism: Some Questions." In *The Making and Remaking of Christian Doctrine.* Edited by Sarah Coakley and David A. Pailin. Oxford: Clarendon Press, 1993, pp. 239–64.

Williams, Rowan. *Lost Icons: Reflections on Cultural Bereavement.* Edinburgh: T. & T. Clark, 2000.

Williams, Rowan. "The Nicene Heritage." In *The Christian Understanding of God Today.* Edited by James Byrne. Dublin: Columba Press, 1993, pp. 45–48.

Williams, Rowan. *On Christian Theology.* Challenges in Contemporary Theology. Oxford/Malden, MA: Blackwell, 2000.

Williams, Rowan. "Postscript (Theological)." In *Arius: Heresy and Tradition.* 2nd edition. London: SCM Press, 2001, pp. 233–45.

Williams, Rowan. *Resurrection: Interpreting the Easter Gospel.* Harrisburg, PA: Morehouse, 1994.

Williams, Rowan. *Teresa of Avila.* Outstanding Christian Thinkers. London: Geoffrey Chapman, 1991.

Wingren, Gustaf. *Människan och inkarnationen enligt Irenaeus.* Lund: Gleerups, 1947.

Wingren, Gustaf. *Predikan.* Lund: Gleerups, 1949.

Wingren, Gustaf. *Teologiens metodfråga*. Lund: Gleerups, 1954.

Wittgenstein, Ludwig. *Philosophical Investigations*. 3rd edition. Translated by G. E. M. Anscombe. Oxford: Blackwell, 1967.

Wolfson, Elliot R. "Judaism and Incarnation: The Imaginal Body of God." In *Christianity in Jewish Terms*. Edited by Tikva Frymer-Kensky, David Novak, Peter Ochs, et al. Boulder, CO/Oxford: Westview Press, 2000, pp. 239–54.

Woodhead, Linda. "Sex in a Wider Context." In *Sex These Days: Essays on Theology, Sexuality and Society*. Studies in Theology and Sexuality 1. Edited by Jon Davies and Gerard Loughlin. Sheffield: Sheffield Academic Press, 1997, pp. 98–120.

Wright, N. T. *The Resurrection of the Son of God*. Christian Origins and the Question of God vol. 3. London: SPCK, 2003.

Wyschogrod, Edith. "Doing before Hearing: On the Primacy of Touch." In *Textes pour Emmanuel Lévinas*. Edited by François Laruelle. Paris: Jean-Michel Place Éditeur, 1980, pp. 179–203.

Yates, Wilson. "An Introduction to the Grotesque: Theoretical and Theological Considerations." In *The Grotesque in Art and Literature: Theological Reflections*. Edited by James Luther Adams and Wilson Yates. Grand Rapids/Cambridge: Eerdmans, 1997, pp. 1–68.

Young, Frances M. "A Cloud of Witnesses." In *The Myth of God Incarnate*. Edited by John Hick. London: SCM, 1977, pp. 13–47.

Young, Frances M. *From Nicaea to Chalcedon: A Guide to the Literature and Its Background*. London: SCM, 1988.

Young, Frances M. "*Paideia* and the Myth of Static Dogma." In *The Making and Remaking of Christian Doctrine: Essays in Honour of Maurice Wiles*. Edited by Sarah Coakley and David A. Pailin. Oxford: Clarendon Press, 1993, pp. 265–83.

Young, Frances M. "Two Roots or a Tangled Mass?" In *The Myth of God Incarnate*. Edited by John Hick. London: SCM, 1977, pp. 87–121.

Young, Iris Marion. "Pregnant Embodiment." In *Body and Flesh: A Philosophical Reader*. Edited by Donn Welton. Malden, MA/Oxford: Blackwell, 1998, pp. 274–85.

Young, Iris Marion. "Throwing like a Girl: A Phenomenology of Feminine Body Comportment, Motility, and Spatiality." In *The Thinking Muse: Feminism and Modern French Philosophy*. Edited by Jeffner Allen and Iris Marion Young. Bloomington/Indianapolis: Indiana University Press, 1989, pp. 51–70.

Young, Iris Marion. "'Throwing like a Girl': Twenty Years Later." In *Body and Flesh: A Philosophical Reader*. Edited by Donn Welton. Malden, MA/Oxford: Blackwell, 1998, pp. 286–90.

Zahavi, Dan. *Fænomenologi*. Frederiksberg, Denmark: Roskilde Universitetsforlag, 2003.

Zahavi, Dan. *Husserl's Phenomenology*. Cultural Memory in the Present. Stanford: Stanford University Press, 2003.

Žižek, Slavoj. *For They Know Not What They Do: Enjoyment as a Political Factor*. 2nd edition. London/New York: Verso, 2002.

Žižek, Slavoj. *On Belief*. Thinking in Action. London/New York: Routledge, 2001.

Name Index

Subject Index

Note: Page spans in italics denote general discussions of concepts across an entire section or chapter.

Scripture Index